For behold, the time cometh,
and is not far distant, that with power the Lord Omnipotent
who reigneth, who was, and is from all eternity
to all eternity, shall come down from heaven among
the children of men, and shall dwell
in a tabernacle of clay, and shall go forth
amongst men, working mighty miracles, such as healing
the sick, raising the dead, causing the lame to walk,
the blind to receive their sight, and the deaf to hear,
and curing all manner of diseases.
And he shall cast out devils, or the evil spirits which
dwell in the hearts of the children of men.
And lo, he shall suffer temptations,
and pain of body, hunger, thirst, and fatigue,
even more than man can suffer,
except it be unto death; for behold, blood cometh
from every pore, so great shall be his anguish
for the wickedness and the abominations of his people.
And he shall be called Jesus Christ,
the Son of God, the Father of heaven and earth,
the Creator of all things from the beginning;
and his mother shall be called Mary.
And lo, he cometh unto his own, that salvation
might come unto the children of men
even through faith on his name; and even after all this
they shall consider him a man, and say that he
hath a devil, and shall scourge him, and shall crucify him.
And he shall rise the third day
from the dead; and behold, he standeth
to judge the world; and behold, all these things are done
that a righteous judgment might
come upon the children of men.
—Mosiah 3:5-10

The. Promised Messiah

The first coming of Christ

Bruce R. McConkie

Deseret Book Company
Salt Lake City, Utah

Library of Congress Cataloging-in-Publication Data

McConkie, Bruce R.
    The promised Messiah.

    Includes index.
    1. Jesus Christ—Mormon interpretations.
2. Messiah—Prophecies.   3. Mormons and
Mormonism—Doctrinal and controversial works.
I. Title.
BX8643.J4M32   232'.12   78-3478
ISBN 0-87747-702-7

Printed in the United States of America

10   9   8

CONTENTS

v

CHAPTER 4

MESSIAH DWELT WITH GOD 46

CHAPTER 5

PROPHETS REVEAL THE COMING OF CHRIST . . . 66

CHAPTER 6

MESSIAH REVEALED IN ALL THE WORLD 84

ix

CHAPTER 21

ALL THINGS BEAR RECORD OF CHRIST 374

CHAPTER 22

LAW OF MOSES BEARS WITNESS OF CHRIST . . . 404

CHAPTER 23

MOSAIC FEASTS AND SACRIFICES TESTIFY
OF CHRIST 426

CHAPTER 24

PROPHETIC TYPES OF CHRIST 438

CHAPTER 25

JEHOVAH BECOMES THE MORTAL MESSIAH . . . 454

CHAPTER 26

MESSIAH MINISTERS AS A MORTAL 474

ABBREVIATIONS

Scriptural references are abbreviated in a standard and self-identifying way. Other books are cited by author and title except the following: *Mormon Doctrine* (Bruce R. McConkie, *Mormon Doctrine*, Bookcraft, 2nd ed.) and *Teachings* (Joseph Fielding Smith, comp., *Teachings of the Prophet Joseph Smith*, Deseret Book).

PREFACE

Since the Lord laid his hands upon me, on October 12, 1972, by the hands of his servant, President Harold B. Lee, and ordained me to the holy apostleship, I have had but one desire—to testify of our Lord's divine Sonship and to teach, in purity and perfection, the truths of his everlasting gospel.

I was born with a testimony, and from my earliest days have known with absolute certainty of the truth and divinity of his great latter-day work. Doubt and uncertainty have been as foreign to me as the gibberish of alien tongues. But even so, a gracious God has now given me a new heart and a renewed and increased determination to bear witness of spiritual things and to proclaim, insofar as I am able, the truths of salvation, in all their glory, beauty, and perfection.

And so now, with holy zeal—having no private views to expound, no personal doctrines to set forth, no ideas that originate with me alone—I desire to present those things which will cause men of good will everywhere to believe in Him by whom salvation comes.

This work is sent forth to persuade men to believe in Christ, to accept him as their Lawgiver, Savior, and King, and to guide them in that course of obedience and devotion which will prepare them to enjoy his companionship forever in eternal glory. It deals with revealed truth as such is found in the Holy Scriptures. My objective is to interpret those scriptures by the power of that same Spirit which inspired the apostles and prophets who first recorded the eternal truths which in them are. And it is devoutly to be hoped that all who read and study the teachings here declared will ponder their deep import and seek wisdom from the one Source from which spiritual things can be known with perfect surety.

Our Lord came once, in time's meridian, to reveal his Father, to teach his truths, and to work out the infinite and eternal atonement. All of the holy prophets, during the four long millenniums from Adam to the son of Zacharias, looked forward to that coming; all knew that the Promised Messiah would dwell as a mortal on earth; all taught that portion of his saving truth which their hearers were prepared to receive; and their message was that salvation, and all that appertains to it, is in Christ who was to come.

Our Lord shall come again, in the fulness of times, in all the glory of his Father's kingdom, to complete the salvation of men and to reign in glory on this earth after it has been renewed and has received again its paradisiacal glory. And no subject is of greater concern to men today than his return in power and glory to divide the sheep from the goats and to say to those who believe in him: "Come, ye blessed of my Father, inherit the kingdom prepared for you from the foundation of the world." (Matt. 25:34.)

At his First Coming he performed the most transcendent work ever wrought by man or God from creation's morn to eternity's endless duration. Standing as the Resurrection and the Life, at his Father's behest, he brought to pass the immortality and eternal life of man and ransomed all creation from its fallen doom.

While he dwelt on earth he lived a life like no other mortal who ever came forth from a mother's womb. His words and deeds, his teachings and miracles, his triumph over the tomb—all that he did and said—all things appertaining to him have neither equal nor parallel among all the billions of souls who have breathed or shall breathe the breath of life on planet earth.

At his Second Coming he shall reap the harvest, sown in Gethsemane, as all those who have washed their garments in his blood come forth to live and reign with him on earth a thousand years.

What wonders of redeeming grace were manifest when he dwelt among men as Mary's Son and took upon himself the sins of the world on conditions of repentance!

And what miracles of glory, triumph, and victory shall attend his return as God's Almighty Son to take vengeance on the wicked and usher in the year of his redeemed!

This work—*The Promised Messiah: The First Coming of Christ*—is my attempt to distill in one volume the teachings of the ancient prophets about his First Coming. And be it remembered that what is here considered was the heart and core of the teachings of all the preachers of righteousness who lived before he dwelt among men, which is to say that herein we shall view the gospel as it is seen through the eyes of Enoch and Elijah, Moses and Melchizedek, Abraham and Moriancumer, and all those whom God favored with a sure knowledge of his divine truth.

It is my desire and intent—the Lord willing, and building upon the foundation herein laid—to publish, hereafter, *The Mortal Messiah*, which will deal with the life he lived among men.

Then finally, to complete this triad, this trilogy, this trinity—again the Lord willing, and building upon the two preceding works—it is my desire and intent to set forth in summary form those things which we know about his near advent, under the title *The Millennial Messiah*.

As with my other published works, I am deeply indebted to a most efficient and able secretary, Velma Harvey, for her thoughtful suggestions and careful handling of the many details involved.

Chapter 1

MESSIAH BRINGETH SALVATION TWICE

God Ministers Among Men Twice

Salvation is in Christ—now and forever!

He came once—born in a stable, cradled in a manger—to redeem his people; to restore his everlasting gospel; to work out the infinite and eternal atonement; *to bring salvation.*

He shall come again—with ten thousands of his saints, in all the glory of his Father's kingdom—to slay the wicked by the breath of his lips; to cleanse the vineyard of corruption; to ransom those who love his appearing; *to bring salvation.*

He is the Lord Omnipotent by whom all things are and through whose atoning blood redemption cometh.

He is the Father and the Son, the Lord Jehovah, the Almighty God.

He is our King.

He is our Lawgiver.

He is our Judge.

It is in his holy name, his name only, that we may gain eternal life.

It is he who has given a law unto all things, and no man cometh unto the Father but by him and by his law.

Without him there would be no creation; no mortal probation; no redemption from death, hell, the devil, and endless torment.

1

Without him there would be no life after death; no eternal life for those who believe and obey; no eternal felicity for all created things.

And the most transcendent event in his entire eternal existence, the most glorious single happening from creation's dawn to eternity's endless continuance, the crowning work of his infinite goodness—such took place in a garden called Gethsemane, outside a city called Jerusalem, when he, tabernacled in the flesh, bore the weight of the sins of all those who believe in his name and obey his gospel.

He came into the world in time's meridian to put into full operation all the terms and conditions of his Father's plan; to bring to pass immortality and to make eternal life available to man; to abolish death and bring life and immortality to light through his gospel.

And he shall come again—perhaps while some of us on earth yet live as mortals—first, to dwell and reign on earth a thousand years, and then, after a short season, to transform this earth into his own celestial home, where he shall dwell, from time to time, among exalted beings.

These are the most glorious events in the whole history of planet earth. From Adam to John, called the Baptist, all the prophets looked forward to both of these comings; and from Peter to the last apostle who shall rise up in this dispensation, all have and shall testify of his destined return in power, attended by the hosts of heaven, to bring surcease from all care and sorrow to those who have been valiant in the cause of truth and righteousness.

How to Read the Signs of the Times

Those who lived when he was born of Mary in Bethlehem of Judea needed the spirit of inspiration to discern the signs of the times, to know which of the prophetic utterances described his First Coming, which his Second. Theirs was the responsibility to search the scriptures and seek the Spirit so they could know and believe the truths

revealed by him in their dispensation.

And those of us who now live as mortals—and more particularly those who are members of his latter-day kingdom—need and seek the spirit of revelation to read the signs of the times, to know when he will come again, to know which parts of the revealed word have reference to the millennial cleansing of the earth, and which have reference to the earth in its final celestial state.

We have the advantage of hindsight in pondering the Messianic prophecies and seeing their fulfillment in the mortal ministry of the Son of God among men. Their meanings are clear, and the understanding of them is certain, because the events forecast have transpired; because their application to these events has been confirmed by latter-day revelation; because of the spirit of interpretation shed forth upon the saints by the Holy Spirit of God.

Accordingly, as we rejoice in the efficacy and virtue of the infinite and eternal atonement, wrought by God himself in a dispensation past, we also search, ponder, and pray to know how to interpret and apply Holy Writ in the dispensation present. We desire to know how to read the signs of our times, as they read the signs of theirs.

We desire to know of our Lord's promised return to dwell among us; and next to the spirit of revelation and prophecy itself, there is probably no better guide than to know and understand those Messianic utterances whose fulfillment is now a matter of assured reality. To know how Deity has dealt with men is to forecast how he will continue to do so, for he is the same yesterday, today, and forever; his course is one eternal round; and as he offered goodness and grace to the ancients, so will he to us, if we walk as they did. The fact is, no one can comprehend the future Second Coming without first gaining a knowledge of the First Coming.

In this work we shall consider the testimony and teachings of the prophets of old relative to the Promised Messiah: the First Coming of Christ. This knowledge will lay the foundation for an understanding of the life that he lived

among mortals and of his future return to reign among them during the Millennium.

Come unto Christ and Learn of Him

We shall, by the doctrine taught and the testimony borne in this work, invite men to come unto Christ, believe his word, live his law, and gain salvation in his Father's kingdom.

We know—with absolute certainty—that the teachings given and testimonies borne by the ancient prophets, concerning Him who is their Lord and our Lord, are true. And we shall attempt to interpret these Messianic utterances by the power of the same Spirit that rested upon those of old who taught that "salvation was, and is, and is to come, in and through the atoning blood of Christ, the Lord Omnipotent." (Mosiah 3:18.)

Our purpose, as we launch forth on the great ocean of truth relative to the Lord Jesus Christ and his eternal ministry, is to persuade men to believe that he is the Son of God by whom salvation comes.

We know that men are saved no faster than they gain a knowledge of God, of Christ, and of the laws which they have ordained. We cannot be saved in ignorance of the One who made salvation possible, nor of the everlasting gospel which bears his name.

We know that it is life eternal to know the Father, who is God above all, and the Son, who is in the image of the Father and through whom are transacted all the dealings of Deity with mortals.

We also know that the Father is revealed by the Son; that no man cometh unto the Father but through the Son; and that to know One is to know the Other.

We know that the plan of salvation is always and everlastingly the same; that obedience to the same laws always brings the same reward; that the gospel laws have not changed from the day of Adam to the present; and that al-

ways and everlastingly all things pertaining to salvation center in Christ.

We shall, therefore, learn of Christ and his laws as such knowledge is set forth in the Messianic preachings and prophecies of old, and we shall know that these same laws and doctrines will guide us, as they guided the saints of old, to that eternal life which we and they so devoutly desire.

We shall—reverently, with awe and adoration, in the true spirit of worship—turn our attention to the Lord Jesus Christ. We shall seek to learn who he is, what he has done for us, and what we must do to pay the debt.

The Messiah and "the Mystery of Godliness"

Our revelations speak of "the mystery of godliness" and say, "How great is it!" Then they explain that eternal punishment does not last forever, that endless punishment has an end, and that the scriptures which speak of them have an express and unique meaning that is not conveyed by a mere knowledge of the usual definition of terms. (D&C 19:10-13.)

We shall attempt in this work to uncover the *mystery of the Messiah,* as it were, so that he and his mission will be revealed clearly before us. All gospel mysteries become plain and simple and easy to understand once the light of heaven sheds its darkness-dispelling rays into the hearts and souls of sincere seekers of truth.

It is almost superfluous to suggest that those who seek the truth and desire understanding will, by instinct, reserve judgment on issues they may not understand (as, for instance, that Christ is both the Father and the Son; or that the Father, Son, and Holy Ghost are one God in a sense far greater than merely being one in purpose) until the mystery of godliness, on whatever point is involved, has been set forth in full. After full investigation and an analysis of all the scriptures involved, we are confident that all gospel students whose hearts are open will come with us to a unity of the

5

faith with reference to the great concepts we are now to consider.

We shall study many things about the Son of the Highest, some of them plain and easy and simple; others, deep, hidden, and mysterious. We shall ponder, pray, and seek wisdom from on high as we weigh and evaluate the various Messianic utterances, for we know "that no prophecy of the scripture is of any private interpretation." Revealed truth came when "holy men of God spake as they were moved by the Holy Ghost." (2 Pet. 1:20-21.) That same Holy Spirit will interpret the sayings of the seers of old, and there is no other sure and certain means of receiving spiritual truth.

The Holy Scriptures—all of them, both ancient and modern—speak of many things that are hard to understand without an over-all knowledge of the plan of salvation and without the enlightening power of the Holy Ghost. For instance:

The Book of Mormon teaches that "Christ the Son, and God the Father, and the Holy Spirit . . . is one Eternal God." (Alma 11:44.) Is there one God or are there three Gods; and if there are three, how and in what manner are they one?

Abinadi says "that God himself shall come down among the children of men, and shall redeem his people. And because he dwelleth in flesh he shall be called the Son of God, and having subjected the flesh to the will of the Father, being the Father and the Son—The Father, because he was conceived by the power of God; and the Son, because of the flesh; thus becoming the Father and Son—And they are one God, yea, the very Eternal Father of heaven and of earth. And thus the flesh becoming subject to the Spirit, or the Son to the Father, being one God, suffereth temptation, and yieldeth not to the temptation, but suffereth himself to be mocked, and scourged, and cast out, and disowned by his people." (Mosiah 15:1-5.) What is Abinadi's message? He tells us that God comes down and is called the Son; he is the Father, and as the Son, he is subject to the Father. So it is recorded in the Book of Mormon; the translation is correct and the doctrine is true. Ought we not to understand these things and to come to a knowledge of what is meant by the inspired author? Are we not obligated to know the true meaning of all that is in the Book of Mormon and in all the scriptures?

Christ said to the brother of Jared, "I am Jesus Christ. I am the Father and the Son." (Ether 3:14.) If the Father and the Son are two Personages—as we know from their appearance to Joseph Smith in the Sacred Grove—why does Christ here say he is the Father and the Son?

He also said, "Man have I created after the body of my spirit." (Ether 3:16.) Why does Christ say he created man, when other scriptures affirm that the Father is our Creator?

Isaiah calls Christ "The mighty God, The everlasting Father." (Isa. 9:6.) Again, why this emphasis on Christ as the Father?

John says of Christ, "The worlds were made by him; men were made by him; all things were made by him, and through him, and of him." (D&C 93:10.) Isaiah says he is man's "Maker." (Isa. 17:7.) Again we are faced with our Lord's role in the creation of man. Shall we not seek to learn what these things mean and why they are so recorded in Holy Writ?

Paul tells the faithful saints that "Jesus Christ is in you." (2 Cor. 13:5.) Is God a spirit essence or is there some other meaning?

John says the saints have "power to become the sons of God" (John 1:12); King Benjamin says the true saints are "the children of Christ, his sons, and his daughters" (Mosiah 5:7); and when we are baptized and again when we partake of the sacrament, we take upon ourselves the name of Christ. What doctrine is this and why is it taught with such emphasis?

Isaiah prophesies that the Messiah, who is Christ, "shall see his seed." (Isa. 53:10.) Who are the seed of the Promised Messiah?

7

Many scriptures recite the laws relative to the infinite and eternal atonement; to a temporal and spiritual redemption; to a resurrection of life and of damnation; to reconciliation, intercession, advocacy, mediation, justification, sanctification, and salvation by grace. What doctrines are these, and how do they affect us?

Others tell how God is omnipotent, omnipresent, and omniscient—terms that are seldom mentioned in the Church but find common usage among sectarian theologians. Again, shall we not seek to learn the truth and to put each scriptural passage in its proper relationship to all else found in the Holy Word?

That scriptures dealing with all these and a host of other Messianic matters might easily be misconstrued, as they have been by the learned in an apostate Christendom, is perfectly clear. Our problem is to come to a proper understanding of their meaning. We cannot brush them aside as though they were an unnecessary part of revealed writ. The mere fact that the Lord has preserved them for us in the scriptures is a sufficient witness that he expects us to ponder their deep and hidden meanings so that we shall be as fully informed about his eternal laws as were the saints of old.

The mystery of godliness! How great it is! With the help of the Lord we shall turn the light of understanding upon many of the mysteries, glories, and wonders of his kingdom as we now pursue our study of the Messianic prophecies and doctrines.

Chapter 2

MESSIAH'S FATHER IS GOD

Who Is the Father?

Before we can comprehend either of our Lord's ministries on earth, we must come to know his Father and the infinite and eternal plan of salvation which he ordained for the glory, honor, and exaltation of Christ and of all his spirit children.

That there never was a son without a father, nor a father without a son, is self-evident; and in the very nature of things both sire and son partake of the same nature and are members of the same house and lineage.

In the exalted family of the Gods, the Father and the Son are one. They have the same character, perfections, and attributes. They think the same thoughts, speak the same words, perform the same acts, have the same desires, and do the same works. They possess the same power, have the same mind, know the same truths, live in the same light and glory. To know one is to know the other; to see one is to see the other; to hear the voice of one is to hear the voice of the other. Their unity is perfect. The Son is in the express image of his Father's person; each has a body of flesh and bones as tangible as man's; and both reign in power, might, and dominion over all the creations of their hands.

Who, then, is the Father, by whom the Son came? Who is the Almighty God, by whom all things are? How can he (and

9

his Son) be known by mortal man? Can man comprehend God? Can the finite envision the infinite, the worm comprehend the universe, and the dust of the earth conceive of the grandeur of the galaxies of heaven?

Two great truths chart our course as we seek to know God and to conform to his image:

1. He is a glorified and perfect Being, a Holy Man, an exalted Person, a Personage of tabernacle, who has a resurrected body of flesh and bones and who lives in the family unit.

2. He is "the one supreme and absolute Being; the ultimate source of the universe; the all-powerful, all-knowing, all-good Creator, Ruler, and Preserver of all things." (*Mormon Doctrine,* 2nd ed., p. 317.)

As to his personal nature, the revealed word says that "in the language of Adam, Man of Holiness is his name" (Moses 6:57); that he "has a body of flesh and bones as tangible as man's" (D&C 130:22); that he created man "in the image of his own body" (Moses 6:9); and that we are his offspring, his spirit children (Heb. 12:9; Moses 6:36; D&C 93:21-23).

As to his glory, might, and omnipotence, our revelations say simply: "There is a God in heaven, who is infinite and eternal, from everlasting to everlasting the same unchangeable God, the framer of heaven and earth, and all things which are in them," and that he "gave his Only Begotten Son" to redeem the world. (D&C 20:17, 21.)

Where Gods Began to Be

We do not now know, nor can the mortal mind discern, how all things came to be. We have the divine promise that if we are faithful in all things, the day will come when we shall know "all things" (D&C 93:28) and "comprehend even God" (D&C 88:49). But for the present our finite limitations shut out the view of the infinite. How element, matter, life, organized intelligence, and God himself first came into being, we can no more comprehend than we can suppose that

10

life, the earth, and the universe shall vanish away. And so we
sing:

> If you could hie to Kolob
> In the twinkling of an eye,
> And then continue onward
> With that same speed to fly,
> D'ye think that you could ever,
> Through all eternity,
> Find out the generation
> Where Gods began to be?
>
> Or see the grand beginning,
> Where space did not extend?
> Or view the last creation,
> Where Gods and matter end?
> Methinks the Spirit whispers,
> "No man has found 'pure space'."
> Nor seen the outside curtains,
> Where nothing has a place.
>
> The works of God continue,
> And worlds and lives abound;
> Improvement and progression
> Have one eternal round.
> There is no end to matter;
> There is no end to space;
> There is no end to spirit;
> There is no end to race.
> —*Hymns*, no. 257

And yet these things we do know:

1. Life, matter, and time (continuance) have existed and
do and shall exist, everlastingly and without end, as
eternities roll.

2. There is a Supreme Organized Intelligence who
governs, controls, organizes, and reorganizes in all things
both temporal and spiritual.

11

3. This Supreme Intelligence—the Lord our God—has, from our perspective, existed from eternity; yet, in the language of the Prophet Joseph Smith, "God himself was once as we are now, and is an exalted man, and sits enthroned in yonder heavens! . . . I am going to tell you how God came to be God. We have imagined and supposed that God was God from all eternity. I will refute that idea, and take away the veil, so that you may see. . . . It is the first principle of the Gospel to know for a certainty the Character of God, and to know that we may converse with him as one man converses with another, and that he was once a man like us; yea, that God himself, the Father of us all, dwelt on an earth, the same as Jesus Christ himself did; and I will show it from the Bible. . . .

"Here, then, is eternal life—to know the only wise and true God; and you have got to learn how to be Gods yourselves, and to be kings and priests to God, the same as all Gods have done before you, namely, by going from one small degree to another, and from a small capacity to a great one; from grace to grace, from exaltation to exaltation, until you attain to the resurrection of the dead, and are able to dwell in everlasting burnings, and to sit in glory, as do those who sit enthroned in everlasting power. . . . [Such persons are] heirs of God and joint heirs with Jesus Christ. What is it? To inherit the same power, the same glory and the same exaltation, until you arrive at the station of a God, and ascend the throne of eternal power, the same as those who have gone before." (*Teachings,* pp. 345-47.)

Who Is the Lord Our God?

Having before us, then, these eternal verities: that there are Gods many and Lords many; that God himself was once as we are now and is an exalted Man; that we may become as he is in the same way he gained his exaltation; and that, in fact, as Joseph Smith said, "Every man who reigns in ce-

12

lestial glory is a God to his dominions" (*Teachings,* p. 374)—with this perspective and background before us, let us turn to those Gods with whom we have to do, to that Eternal Godhead which created and rules our universe, each member of which has all power, all might, and all dominion.

From Joseph Smith we learn: "Everlasting covenant was made between three personages before the organization of this earth, and relates to their dispensation of things to men on the earth; these personages, according to Abraham's record, are called God the first, the Creator; God the second, the Redeemer; and God the third, the witness or Testator." (*Teachings,* p. 190.)

From the pen of Paul we read: "There is none other God but one. For though there be . . . gods many, and lords many, . . . to us there is but one God, the Father, of whom are all things, and we in him; and one Lord Jesus Christ, by whom are all things, and we by him." (1 Cor. 8:4-6.)

And from God himself comes this word to his people: "Before me there was no God formed, neither shall there be after me. I, even I, am the Lord; and beside me there is no saviour." (Isa. 43:10-11.) "I am the Lord, and there is none else, there is no God beside me." (Isa. 45:5; 46:9.) "The Lord is God, and beside him there is no Savior." (D&C 76:1.)

Our Godhead consists of the Father, Son, and Holy Ghost. They are supreme over all, and though they administer their kingdoms through a hierarchy of appointed angels who also are exalted, one of whom is Adam or Michael, in the ultimate sense these members of the Eternal Godhead are the only Gods with whom we have to do. We worship the Father, in the name of the Son, by the power of the Holy Ghost. We follow the Son as he follows his Father. We labor and strive to be like the Son as he is like the Father, and the Father and Son and Holy Ghost are one. For these holy Beings we have unbounded love, reverence, and worship.

13

How to Find and Know God

How can man find and know his God?

However much philosophers may reason and reach this or that conclusion as to what God must be, or whence he came, or why things are as they are; however much scientists may assert that there must be an intelligent, directing force in this well-ordered universe; however much pagan or Christian man by instinct may choose to worship wood or stone, the sun, moon, or stars, or the forces and powers of nature; however much any mortal man by finite means seeks to find and know the Infinite, yet he has failed and shall fail for this one reason: God is known only by revelation. God stands revealed or he remains forever unknown.

The truth seeker asks, "Canst thou by searching find out God? canst thou find out the Almighty unto perfection?" (Job 11:7.)

The answer: Yes and no. Yes, if the search is in the realm of the Spirit so that the laws are learned and lived whereby revelation comes; no, if the search is in the laboratory, in the philosopher's classroom, or through the scientist's telescope. Yes, if the spiritual laws by which he may be found are obeyed; no, in all other circumstances. Truly did the Holy Ghost say, by the mouth of Paul: "For after that in the wisdom of God the world by wisdom knew not God, it pleased God by the foolishness of preaching to save them that believe." (1 Cor. 1:21.)

And so thanks be to God, revelation has come to many and is available to all, and the Eternal Father may be found and known by any or all of the following means:

1. *By personal appearance, or by the opening of the heavens so that he is seen in vision.*

Before the fall, the Father was with Adam in Eden's garden. In the spring of 1820, accompanied by his Beloved Son, he appeared to Joseph Smith to usher in this dispensation; and nearly sixteen years later, on January 21, 1836, that same prophet "beheld the celestial kingdom of God" and

14

ness of both the Father and the Son. In recording the most transcendent theophany of which we have record, he said: "I saw two Personages, whose brightness and glory defy all description, standing above me in the air. One of them spake unto me, calling me by name and said, pointing to the other—This is My Beloved Son. Hear Him!" (JS-H 17.)

Then with reference to the "prejudice," "reviling," and "bitter persecution" heaped upon him by "professors of religion" and their followers, he said that his position was like Paul before Agrippa. Opposition and ridicule could not change the reality of his experience. "I had actually seen a light, and in the midst of that light I saw two Personages, and they did in reality speak to me," he testified, "and though I was hated and persecuted for saying that I had seen a vision, yet it was true; and while they were persecuting me, reviling me, and speaking all manner of evil against me falsely for so saying, I was led to say in my heart: Why persecute me for telling the truth? I have actually seen a vision; and who am I that I can withstand God, or why does the world think to make me deny what I have actually seen? For I had seen a vision; I knew it, and I knew that God knew it, and I could not deny it, neither dared I do it." (JS-H 17-25.)

And so it is with the faithful elders of latter-day Israel, to all of whom Deity says: "Ye are my witnesses, saith the Lord, that I am God." (Isa. 43:12.) Accordingly, this disciple, as one among many, adds his testimony that he has found the Father; that he knows by personal revelation, given by the power of the Holy Ghost, that God himself is an exalted and perfected Being, possessed of infinite power, wisdom, and goodness; that he is a Holy Man in whose image we are; and that if we are faithful in all things we shall dwell with him in immortal glory and be as he is.

4. *By accepting Christ as the Son of God.*

God was and is in Christ manifesting himself to the world. Christ came to reveal his Father to mankind. There is no better way to envision who and what the Father is than to

17

come to know his Son. The Son is in all respects as the Father. They look alike; each is in the express image of the person of the other. Their thoughts are the same; they speak forth the same eternal truths; and every deed done by one is the same thing the other would do under the same circumstances. In their great doctrinal exposition on the Father and the Son, the First Presidency and the Twelve say: "In all his dealings with the human family Jesus the Son has represented and yet represents Elohim His Father in power and authority . . . so far as power, authority, and Godship are concerned His words and acts were and are those of the Father." (Cited in James E. Talmage, *Articles of Faith,* pp. 470-71.) Truly the Father and the Son are one in all things.

Jesus said: "He that believeth on me, believeth not on me, but on him that sent me. And he that seeth me seeth him that sent me." (John 12:44-45.)

Also: "No man cometh unto the Father, but by me. If ye had known me, ye should have known my Father also: and from henceforth ye know him, and have seen him. . . . He that hath seen me hath seen the Father." And as to how all this could be, he explained that he was in the Father and the Father in him, even as his disciples should be in him and he in them. (John 14:6-20.)

5. *By keeping the commandments of God.*

In the final and all-comprehensive sense, the sole and only way to find and know God is to keep his commandments. As a result of such a course, knowledge and revelation will come in one way or another until man knows his Maker. The more obedient a person is, the clearer his views become, the nearer he approaches his God, and the more he comes to know those holy Beings whom to know is eternal life. (John 17:3.)

"And hereby we do know that we know him, if we keep his commandments. He that saith, I know him, and keepeth not his commandments, is a liar, and the truth is not in him. But whoso keepeth his word, in him verily is the love of God perfected: hereby know we that we are in him." (1 Jn. 2:3-5.)

Those who keep the whole law of the whole gospel finally, in celestial exaltation, know God in full. They then think as he thinks, say what he says, do what he does, and experience what he experiences. They are Gods and they have eternal life, which is the name of the kind of life he lives.

God Is Omnipotent, Omnipresent, and Omniscient

Joseph Smith taught these seven things about God our Eternal Father:

1. He is "the only supreme governor and independent Being in whom all fulness and perfection dwell."

2. He is "omnipotent, omnipresent, and omniscient."

3. He is "without beginning of days or end of life."

4. "In him every good gift and every good principle dwell."

5. "He is the Father of lights."

6. "In him the principle of faith dwells independently."

7. "He is the object in whom the faith of all other rational and accountable beings center for life and salvation." (*Lectures on Faith*, p. 9, cited in *Mormon Doctrine*, 2nd ed., pp. 317-18.)

These are simple, basic, scriptural truths. The Prophet here summarizes them by the spirit of inspiration, and his statements are the doctrines of the Church; they are the mind and will of the Lord relative to himself and the powers he possesses. Unfortunately some have supposed that the Almighty is not almighty, that he has not attained the high ultimates of perfection and power here named, and that somehow he is still learning new truths and progressing in knowledge and wisdom. Such a view comes from a total misconception of what eternal progress really is. The simple, unadorned fact is that God is omnipotent and supreme. He has all power, all knowledge, all truth, and all wisdom, and is everywhere present by the power of his Spirit. In him every good and wholesome attribute dwells independently

19

and in its eternal fulness and perfection. There is no charity, no love, no honesty, no integrity, no justice, mercy, or judgment, that he does not possess in the absolute and total and complete sense of the word. If there were some truth he did not know, some power that was denied him, some attribute of perfection still to be obtained, he would not be God; and if progression lay ahead for him where his character, perfections, or attributes are concerned, then retrogression would also be a possibility; and by falsely so assuming, we would soon find ourselves mired in such a morass of philosophical absurdities that we would be as far removed from saving truth as are the pagans and heathens.

Our mission is not to belittle but to exalt that Being "who is infinite and eternal" (D&C 20:17); who "made the world and all things therein," and is in fact "Lord of heaven and earth" (Acts 17:24); who is indeed the Creator of "worlds without number," and whose plan of redemption, salvation, and eternal life applies to all the creatures of his creating on all the creations of his hands (Moses 1:33-39).

How, then, can we envision the greatness and status of such a Being? As Isaiah asked relative to the Son-Jehovah, "To whom then will ye liken God? or what likeness will ye compare unto him?" (Isa. 40:18.) We know of no better way to show God's incomparable position than to point to the works of his hands and the results of his labors—to the earth, the universe, all living beings of whom man is chief, and to the assurance of immortality and the glory of eternal life. And so Isaiah himself, seeking to set forth the supreme station of Deity, asked: "Who hath measured the waters in the hollow of his hand, and meted out heaven with the span, and comprehended the dust of the earth in a measure, and weighed the mountains in scales, and the hills in a balance? Who hath directed the Spirit of the Lord, or being his counseller hath taught him? With whom took he counsel, and who instructed him, and taught him in the path of judgment, and taught him knowledge, and shewed to him the way of understanding?" (Isa. 40:12-14.)

Let us consider man and all forms of life; let us look upon the earth and all the laws which govern it; let us view the universe and the ordered expanse of unnumbered worlds; let us think of preexistence, of mortality, of an eternal resurrection for all things—and then let us ask why and how all these things are, and how anyone but an exalted Being who knows all things and has all power could have brought them into being.

Truly, "The heavens declare the glory of God; and the firmament sheweth his handywork." (Ps. 19:1.) And truly, as he said of all the orbs that move in the sidereal heavens, "any man who hath seen any or the least of these hath seen God moving in his majesty and power." (D&C 88:47.)

Chapter 3

MESSIANIC PROPHECIES: THEIR NATURE AND USE

Who Is the Messiah?

No questions have greater impact—not alone for the Jews and for the rest of us who are of Israel (and whose Deliverer he is), but for all mankind—than these: Who is the Messiah? Who is the Anointed One who cometh to save his people from their sins? Who is the promised Christ?

"We have found the Messias, which is, being interpreted, the Christ." (John 1:41.) So spake Andrew to his brother Simon Peter, whose destiny was to become the chief witness of Him whom the Baptist had but recently immersed in Jordan to fulfill all righteousness.

"I know that Messias cometh, which is called Christ," said the Samaritan woman at Jacob's well.

"I that speak unto thee am he" (John 4:25-26) was the simple response of Him to whom Nathanael but shortly before had testified: "Thou art the Son of God; thou art the King of Israel." (John 1:49.)

To the spiritually benighted Jews of his day, the Messiah was deemed to be a temporal Deliverer, one who would free them from the yoke of Roman bondage and restore again the glory of David's throne. But to those who then did or yet would come to a true knowledge of the prophetic utterances concerning his coming and mission, he was the One who would ransom all mankind from the temporal and spiritual death brought upon them by the fall of Adam; he was the One by whom salvation comes.

And of this there is no doubt: The Lord Jesus—begotten by the Supreme God, conceived by Mary, born in Bethlehem, crucified on Calvary—the Lord Jesus, who is called Christ, is the Messiah. He is the Redeemer and Deliverer, the King of Israel, the Son of God, the Savior of the world.

What Is a Prophet?

To many of the spiritually illiterate in modern Christendom, prophets are strange, perhaps even freakish, characters from bygone ages to whom the Lord somehow revealed future events. In fact prophets are simply members of the true Church who have testimonies of the truth and divinity of the work. They are the saints of God who have learned by the power of the Holy Ghost that Jesus is the Christ, the Son of the living God.

A heavenly visitant, upon whom the Lord had placed his name, told the Beloved Revelator: "The testimony of Jesus is the spirit of prophecy." (Rev. 19:10.) That is, every person who receives revelation so that he knows, independent of any other source, of the divine Sonship of the Savior, has, by definition and in the very nature of things, the spirit of prophecy and is a prophet. Thus Moses exclaimed, "Would God that all the Lord's people were prophets, and that the Lord would put his spirit upon them!" (Num. 11:29.) And thus Paul counseled all the saints, "Covet to prophesy," and promised the faithful among them, "Ye may all prophesy." (1 Cor. 14:31-39.)

A testimony comes by revelation from the Holy Ghost, whose mission it is to bear "record of the Father and the Son." (Moses 1:24.) Of Christ, Moroni says: "Ye may know that he is, by the power of the Holy Ghost." (Moro. 10:7.) Prophecy comes from the same source and by the same power. In Peter's language, "Prophecy came not in old time

23

by the will of man: but holy men of God spake as they were moved by the Holy Ghost." (2 Pet. 1:21.)

When a person abides the law which enables him to gain a revealed knowledge of the divine Sonship of our Lord, he thereby abides the law which empowers him, as occasion may require, to prophesy. In Nephite history we find an account of a people who gained testimonies and as a consequence had also the gift of prophecy. After expounding the plan of salvation, as such operates through the atoning blood of Christ, King Benjamin desired "to know of his people if they believed the words which he had spoken unto them." Their answer: "We believe all the words which thou hast spoken unto us; and also, we know of their surety and truth, because of the Spirit of the Lord Omnipotent." That is, they had gained testimonies. Then they said, "We, ourselves, also, through the infinite goodness of God, and the manifestations of his Spirit, have great views of that which is to come; and were it expedient, we could prophesy of all things." (Mosiah 5:1-3.) That is, the testimony of Jesus is the spirit of prophecy; both testimony and prophecy come by the power of the Holy Ghost; and any person who receives the revelation that Jesus is the Lord is a prophet and can, as occasion requires and when guided by the Spirit, "prophesy of all things."

What Is Scripture?

Prophetic utterances, both oral and written, are scripture. "To some it is given by the Holy Ghost to know that Jesus Christ is the Son of God, and that he was crucified for the sins of the world." (D&C 46:13.) Testimonies borne by such persons, when moved upon by the Spirit, are scripture. In fact, all the elders of the Church, by virtue of their ordination, are called "to proclaim the everlasting gospel, by the Spirit of the living God," with this promise: "Whatsoever they shall speak when moved upon by the Holy Ghost shall be scripture, shall be the will of the Lord, shall be the mind of the Lord, shall be the word of the Lord, shall be the voice of the Lord, and the power of God unto salvation." (D&C 68:1, 4.) And as it is with the elders on earth, so it is with their fellow servants beyond the veil. The words of the angels of God in heaven are scripture, for, "Angels speak by the power of the Holy Ghost; wherefore, they speak the words of Christ." (2 Ne. 32:3.)

Manifestly, all prophets are not equal, and all scripture is not of identical worth. Most persons with the spirit of testimony, of inspiration, and of prophecy are prophets to themselves only, or to their families. Some are called to preside over and give inspired guidance to one organization or another. In our day the First Presidency and the Twelve are sustained as prophets, seers, and revelators to the whole Church, with the revealed provision that the President of the Church, who is the senior apostle of God on earth at any given time, shall "preside over the whole church" and "be like unto Moses," being "a seer, a revelator, a translator, and a prophet, having all the gifts of God which he bestows upon the head of the church." (D&C 107:91-92.) To the Church, the Lord says: "Thou shalt give heed unto all his words and commandments which he shall give unto you as he receiveth them, walking in all holiness before me; For his word ye shall receive, as if from mine own mouth, in all patience and faith." (D&C 21:4-5.)

Such scripture as is canonized—meaning, at the present moment, the Bible, the Book of Mormon, the Doctrine and Covenants, and the Pearl of Great Price—comes from prophets who held positions of leadership and trust in the Lord's earthly kingdom. It is binding upon the Church and the world and is the standard by which all men shall be judged when they shall stand before the pleasing bar of the great Jehovah to receive according to their works.

What Are Messianic Prophecies?

Prophets reveal Christ to the world. "To him give all the

25

prophets witness, that through his name whosoever believeth in him shall receive remission of sins." (Acts 10:43.) All those who spake before his coming were looking forward to a future event, and their utterances were *Messianic prophecies.* Those who have spoken since he ministered in mortality have looked back to that time, and their utterances are *Messianic testimonies,* though they may, of course, also prophesy of the future.

Salvation is in Christ—eternally. It matters not what age of the earth is involved. Adam and all his seed, down to the last person who shall dwell upon the earth, all are subject to the same law. Every accountable person must live the same law to gain a celestial inheritance. There is no exception. All who gain eternal life must believe in Christ, accept his everlasting gospel, live in harmony with its laws, and devote their whole souls to the Cause of Righteousness. As Abinadi said: "There could not any man be saved except it were through the redemption of God." (Mosiah 13:32.)

When the Father speaks of Christ, when our Lord speaks of himself, when the Holy Ghost bears record of the Son, when angels testify of salvation, and when prophets, as struggling, persecuted mortals, bear their witness of eternal truth, all have one concordant testimony: Salvation is in Christ.

Thus, whenever there have been prophets, they have spoken of Christ; whenever the Lord has sent teachers, they have taught of Christ; whenever legal administrators have ministered among men, they have performed the ordinances of salvation which are ordained by Christ; whenever the Lord has performed signs and wonders, either by his own voice or by the voice of his servants, such have been witnesses of the goodness and greatness of Christ.

Moses prophesied "concerning the coming of the Messiah, and that God should redeem his people." And Abinadi asked: "Even all the prophets, who have prophesied ever since the world began—have they not spoken more or less concerning these things? Have they not said that God

26

himself should come down among the children of men, and take upon him the form of man, and go forth in mighty power upon the face of the earth? Yea, and have they not said also that he should bring to pass the resurrection of the dead, and that he, himself, should be oppressed and afflicted?" (Mosiah 13:33-35.) And Peter, speaking of that salvation which is in Christ, said that the ancient prophets, to say nothing of "the angels" themselves, "inquired and searched diligently, . . . Searching what, or what manner of time the Spirit of Christ which was in them did signify, when it testified beforehand the sufferings of Christ, and the glory that should follow." (1 Pet. 1:10-12.)

How many Messianic prophecies have there been? In the real and true perspective of things, ten thousand times ten thousand is not a beginning to their number. They are in multitude like the sand upon the seashore. Obviously, all the prophetic utterances about Christ and the plan of salvation were Messianic in nature. But such teachings merely introduce the subject. For instance:

Every proper and perfect prayer uttered by a righteous man, woman, or child, from the day Adam stepped through Eden's portals into his lone and dreary habitation, to the day the angelic hosts acclaimed the birth of God's own Son, was in fact a Messianic prophecy. The mere saying, with sincerity and understanding, of the words of the prayer itself constituted a Messianic affirmation. Why? Because all the prophets, saints, and righteous hosts prayed to the Father in the name of Christ, thus witnessing that they knew that salvation came through him and his atoning blood. Similarly, every true prayer today is a reaffirmation that Jesus is the Lord and that through his blood the believing saints are redeemed.

Every shout of praise and exultation to the Lord Jehovah was Messianic in nature, for those who so acclaimed worshiped the Father in the name of Jehovah-Messiah who would come to redeem his people.

And so with every baptism, every priesthood ordination,

every patriarchal blessing, every act of administering to the sick, every divine ordinance or performance ordained of God, every sacrifice, symbolism, and similitude; all that God ever gave to his people—all was ordained and established in such a way as to testify of his Son and center the faith of believing people in him and in the redemption he was foreordained to make.

Why Have Messianic Prophecies?

In the economy of God there is a reason for all things, and the greater the event, the more important the reason. For four millenniums nothing ever said by men or angels was as important as their Messianic prophecies. From that day in Eden when the Lord said that Eve's Seed should crush the serpent's head, to a glorious night four thousand years later in the Judean hills, when angelic hosts sang praise to the Seed of Eve and Mary, the most important utterances made on earth were the Messianic prophecies. And from Messiah's birth as long as time endures, the most glorious language that has been or can be spoken contains the Messianic testimonies borne by the power of the Spirit for the edification, blessing, and salvation of the receptive part of earth's inhabitants.

There are three reasons why Messianic prophecies began with Adam and continued among all the righteous people on earth until the coming of the Son of God among men. These are:

1. *Messianic prophecies enabled those who lived from the beginning down to the time of his coming to have faith in Christ and thereby gain salvation.*

Salvation is administered on the same terms and conditions to all men in all ages. Whether it be in Adam's day or in ours it is the same. In every dispensation obedience to the same laws confers the same blessings. Everlastingly and always salvation is in Christ; his atoning sacrifice brings life and immortality to light through the same gospel in every

28

era of the history of the earth. All men from the beginning to the end must have faith in him; repent of all their sins; be baptized for their remission in his holy name; receive the gift of the Holy Ghost, which the Father sends because of him; and then press forward in steadfastness and obedience to his laws, if they are to gain eternal life with him in his Father's kingdom. And so it is written, "That as many as would believe and be baptized in his holy name, and endure in faith to the end, should be saved—Not only those who believed after he came in the meridian of time, in the flesh, but all those from the beginning, even as many as were before he came, who believed in the words of the holy prophets, who spake as they were inspired by the gift of the Holy Ghost, who truly testified of him in all things, should have eternal life, As well as those who should come after, who should believe in the gifts and callings of God by the Holy Ghost, which beareth record of the Father and of the Son." (D&C 20:25-27.)

In this day we believe on the Lord Jesus Christ and gain salvation, and the prophets and apostles of our day reveal him to the world and serve as the legal administrators to perform the ordinances of salvation in his name so that such ordinances will be binding on earth and sealed everlastingly in the heavens. So likewise was it in days of old. Salvation was in Christ then as it is now, and the prophets of those days taught the same doctrines we teach today.

At the very beginning of his ministry, the prophet Nephi recorded his purpose and summarized his divine commission by saying, "For the fulness of mine intent is that I may persuade men to come unto the God of Abraham, and the God of Isaac, and the God of Jacob, and be saved." (1 Ne. 6:4.) King Benjamin (reciting the words spoken to him by an angel) affirmed and expanded the same concept in these words: "Salvation cometh . . . through repentance and faith on the Lord Jesus Christ. And the Lord God hath sent his holy prophets among all the children of men, to declare these things to every kindred, nation, and tongue, that

29

thereby whosoever should believe that Christ should come, the same might receive remission of their sins, and rejoice with exceeding great joy, even as though he had already come among them." (Mosiah 3:12-13.)

Alma's son Corianton, rebellious and carnally inclined, was unable to understand "concerning the coming of Christ." His father said to him, "I will ease your mind somewhat on this subject. Behold, you marvel why these things should be known so long beforehand." And this was Alma's reasoning:

"Is not a soul at this time as precious unto God as a soul will be at the time of his coming?"

"Is it not as necessary that the plan of redemption should be made known unto this people as well as unto their children?"

"Is it not as easy at this time for the Lord to send his angel to declare these glad tidings unto us as unto our children, or as after the time of his coming?" (Alma 39:15-19.)

2. *Messianic prophecies enable those who lived at the time of and after the coming of Christ to believe that it was he of whom the prophets had spoken so that they too might be saved.*

"These glad tidings"—that salvation was in Christ and came by obedience to his holy gospel—were declared unto those in the so-called pre-Christian era so "that salvation might come unto them," and also "that they may prepare the minds of their children to hear the word at the time of his coming." (Alma 39:16.)

That relatively few who lived when he came, or who have thereafter dwelt on this benighted globe, were in fact prepared to receive him as Savior, Lord, and King is the saddest commentary found in all the history of his dealings with men. However, many of the prophecies (together with much of the doctrine interwoven as an essential part thereof) are still extant, and, the Lord guiding, many sincere souls will yet be brought to a knowledge of the truth through a Spirit-led study of them.

3. *Messianic prophecies reveal the manner and system of prophetic utterance and fulfillment so that the prophecies relative to the Second Coming may be understood, thus enabling men to prepare for that great day and the salvation that attends it.*

Prophetic utterances foretell the future. That God who knows the end from the beginning, before whose face all things are present, and who views the future as men recall the past, speaks to his prophets, and they, in his name, announce what is to be. Such proclamations are prophecies.

For the first four thousand years of this earth's temporal continuance, the Lord's prophets, though concerned with all things relative to their Master's hand dealings with men, yet knew of and sought foreknowledge about the two most glorious events destined to occur on earth. These were:

1. Our Lord's First Coming, his birth as God's Son, having life in himself so he could work out the infinite and eternal atoning sacrifice whereby immortality and eternal life come; and

2. His return in glory and might to cleanse his vineyard from corruption, to gather the remainder of his elect from the four quarters of the earth, and to reign in their midst for a thousand years of peace and perfection.

For the past two thousand years of our planet's existence, those with seeric vision, already knowing of the fulfillment of the Messianic utterances, have desired above all else to tell what shall precede, accompany, and prevail after our Lord's return in all the glory of his Father's kingdom.

Knowing that the God they worship is a being in whom there is no variableness, neither shadow of turning from that course which he has and shall pursue everlastingly, it is no surprise to spiritually literate souls to learn that the prophecies of the First Coming are but types and shadows of similar revelations relative to the Second Coming.

If the prophetic system embraced some plain and some hidden prophecies relative to our Lord's meridian ministry—so that all men, because of the plainness, would be left without excuse, while the more obedient souls, having as a consequence greater spiritual insight, would thereby know more about his coming—so we may expect it to be relative to his imminent millennial ministry.

If some of the ancient prophecies about his birth, death, and resurrection were hidden in historical recitations of little-known events, so may we anticipate it will be with some things concerning his future appearance.

If his ministers used similitudes and types and shadows to tell of one coming, such also will be their approach to his later appearing.

If it took the spirit of prophecy and revelation to know and understand what was said and written about his mortal ministry, so shall it be with reference to his immortal reign on earth.

And all of this means that a knowledge of what was foretold and fulfilled in his first ministry becomes the basis of comprehending what shall be before, at, and after his imminent ministry again among men, albeit this time he shall minister only among the righteous who abide the day of his coming.

Why Prophets Are Persecuted

Look and behold the righteous ones, the prophets of God:

Abel—slain because he worshiped the Lord, slain by the hand of one who gloried in wickedness, who loved Satan more than God (Moses 5:16-41);

Three virgins, daughters of Onitah—sacrificed on Potiphar's Hill because they "would not bow down to worship gods of wood or stone" (Abr. 1:5-11);

Abraham—taken by violence, bound upon an Egyptian altar, appointed unto death in the name of Pharaoh's god (Abr. 1:12-20);

Moses—rejoicing in "the reproach of Christ" and "choosing rather to suffer affliction with the people of God, than to enjoy the pleasures of sin for a season" (Heb. 11:25-26);

And others without number: Daniel, in a den of lions (Dan. 6); Shadrach, Meshach, and Abednego, walking unharmed in the fiery furnace (Dan. 3); Isaiah, sawn asunder, as we suppose (Heb. 11:37); Jeremiah, in a dungeon and a prison (Jer. 38:6; 1 Ne. 7:14); Zenos, slain (Hel. 8:19); Zenock, stoned (Alma 33:17); Nephi, smitten (1 Ne. 3:28-29); Alma and Amulek, delivered from cords and prison (Alma 14); Joseph and Hyrum, martyred in Carthage jail (D&C 135), and their people, the saints of the Most High, driven by godless fiends from Ohio to Missouri, from Missouri to Illinois, and from Illinois to the deserts of western America; and, finally, Christ our Lord—mocked, smitten, scourged, derided—now hanging in agony on a cross (Matt. 27:31-38; Mark 15:20-28; Luke 23:26-38; John 19:16-22).

As the horror of the vision spreads before us, we wonder: Why? Why should the best blood of earth be shed? Why are prophets smitten, spit upon, and stoned? Why are they cursed, criticized, crucified? Why does the world reject the very ones who light the path to the kingdom of heaven? In revealed writ we find these answers:

1. *Prophets are persecuted because they testify of Christ.*

"Which of the prophets have not your fathers persecuted?" was the stinging rebuke of Stephen to those who stoned him. "They have slain them which shewed before of the coming of the Just One," he said, "of whom ye have been now the betrayers and murderers." (Acts 7:52.) One of those killed because of the witness he bore of the promised Messiah was Zenock. Because he "testified of the Son of God," Alma said, "they stoned him to death." (Alma 33:17.)

The reason worldly and ungodly people so react to the witness of the truth is clear. Salvation is in Christ, and prophets preach Christ and his saving truths to the world. Where there are prophets, salvation is available; and where there are no prophets, there is no hope of salvation. It is no wonder that Lucifer hates prophets and seeks their destruction.

2. *Prophets are persecuted because there are false churches.*

Nephi saw in vision "a church which is most abominable above all other churches, which slayeth the saints of God, yea, and tortureth them and bindeth them down, and yoketh them with a yoke of iron, and bringeth them down into captivity." (1 Ne. 13:5.) From this vision we learn two of the saddest truths of all history: (1) prophets are persecuted by religiously inclined people, and (2) the fact that there are false churches is itself the very reason why the Lord's saints suffer at the hands of evil and ungodly men.

There are different churches because there are different doctrines. No two churches espouse and expound the same plan of salvation. If all men believed the same doctrines, all would belong to the same church. The mere existence of a false church of itself requires the support of false doctrines, false ordinances, false teachers, false prophets. In the very nature of things, a false church, in an attempt to survive, must oppose the truth as it is found in the true Church, and this includes opposition to true doctrine, true ordinances, true teachers, and true prophets. Accordingly, we find the Prophet Joseph Smith teaching that there always has been and always will be "opposition in the hearts of unbelievers and those that know not God, against the pure and unadulterated religion of heaven," and that such adherents to false systems of worship "will persecute, to the uttermost, all that worship God according to his revelations, receive the truth in the love of it, and submit themselves to be guided and directed by his will." (*Lectures on Faith,* p. 57.)

Thus it is that persecution comes from religious zealots. Those who are lukewarm or neutral in the realm of religion, those who have no interest in spiritual things, could not care less whether prophets succeed or fail. It is those who have strong religious convictions who rise up to oppose the truth and fight its exponents.

There have been no more zealous religionists on earth than the inhabitants of Jerusalem, nor has there been another locale where more of the blood of the prophets has flowed. Truly, there is more than irony and sorrow in our Lord's pronouncement: "It cannot be that a prophet perish out of Jerusalem. O Jerusalem, Jerusalem, which killest the prophets, and stonest them that are sent unto thee." (Luke 13:33-34.)

When the hosts of Israel forsook the Lord and his law, when they "transgressed very much after all the abominations of the heathen," when they "polluted the house of the Lord which he had hallowed in Jersualem," yet he in his mercy—"because he had compassion on his people, and on his dwelling place"—sent messengers to call them to repentance, to plead with them to return to the Lord their God and his law. The issue was thus squarely set. Those in Israel must either repent and forsake their evils or—to justify their apostate course—they must fight the prophets. And as worldly people are wont to do, "They mocked the messengers of God, and despised his words, and misused his prophets." (2 Chr. 36:14-16; 1 Kgs. 19:10-14; Rom. 11:1-3.)

When Paul preached with power in Ephesus and all Asia that salvation was in Christ and not their graven images, and when converts forsook the worship of Diana and no longer patronized the silversmiths who made the silver shrines in the worship of this pagan deity, what choice had the religionists of the day but to receive the truth or persecute Paul? And what better rallying cry for fighting against God than to exclaim, "Our craft is in danger"? (See Acts 19:21-41.)

When Joseph Smith "saw two Personages, whose brightness and glory defy all description," standing above him in the air; when the Beloved Son of Almighty God commanded him to join none of the churches then on earth, saying plainly that "they were all wrong; . . . that all their creeds were an abomination in his sight" and "that those professors were all corrupt"—what choice did these modern religionists have but to accept the newly revealed light from heaven or heap their opprobrium on its purveyor? "It seems as though the adversary was aware, at a very early period of my life," the Prophet said, "that I was destined to prove a disturber and an annoyer of his kingdom; else why should the powers of darkness combine against me? Why the opposition and persecution that arose against me, almost in my infancy?" (JS-H 17-20.)

Persecution is the child of Satan; it proceeds forth from perdition; it is used because no weapon that is formed can destroy truth. Persecution comes by and from false churches. If there were no religionists whose crafts were endangered by the onrush of truth, the Lord's prophets would be free to preach and guide men without let or hindrance.

3. *Prophets are persecuted as a form of false worship.*

"The time cometh," our Lord said to his ancient disciples, "that whosoever killeth you will think that he doeth God service." (John 16:2.) Serve God by killing his prophets! The very thought seems unbelievable, but such is the fact. In our dispensation most of the persecution poured out upon the Lord's people has been and is planned and led by ministers of other churches who, we may assume, were and are sincere in their belief that by destroying Mormonism they will free men from what they esteem to be its snares and delusions.

Like the Jews who rejected their Messiah when he ministered among them, such religious zealots suppose they believe in the ancient prophets and that they are only fighting against false prophets. But of them the Lord Jesus said: "Ye build the tombs of the prophets, and garnish the sepulchres of the righteous, And say, If we had been in the days of our fathers, we would not have been partakers with them in the blood of the prophets. Wherefore ye be witnesses unto yourselves, that ye are the children of them which killed the prophets. Fill ye up then the measure of your fathers. Ye serpents, ye generation of vipers, how can ye escape the damnation of hell?" (Matt. 23:29-33.)

Samuel the Lamanite raised the same cry against the Nephites of his day. "Ye do cast out the prophets," he said, "and do mock them, and cast stones at them, and do slay them, and do all manner of iniquity unto them, even as they did of old time. And now when ye talk, ye say: If our days had been in the days of our fathers of old, we would not have slain the prophets; we would not have stoned them, and cast them out. Behold ye are worse than they; for as the Lord liveth, if a prophet come among you and declareth unto you the word of the Lord, which testifieth of your sins and iniquities, ye are angry with him, and cast him out and seek all manner of ways to destroy him; yea, you will say that he is a false prophet, and that he is a sinner, and of the devil, because he testifieth that your deeds are evil." (Hel. 13:24-26.)

In the very nature of things, persecution of true prophets includes the acceptance of false prophets. It is a philosophical impossibility to reject truth without accepting error, to depart from true teachers without cleaving to false ones, to reject the Lord's ministers without giving allegiance to those who follow the other Master. How aptly these further words of Samuel, spoken of those of old, describe the popular teachers both of Christendom and pagandom: "If a man shall come among you and shall say: Do this, and there is no iniquity; do that and ye shall not suffer; yea, he will say: Walk after the pride of your own hearts; yea, walk after the pride of your eyes, and do whatsoever your heart desireth— and if a man shall come among you and say this, ye will receive him, and say that he is a prophet. Yea, ye will lift him up, and ye will give unto him of your substance; ye will give unto him of your gold, and of your silver, and ye will clothe him with costly apparel; and because he speaketh flattering words unto you, and he saith that all is well, then ye will not find fault with him." (Hel. 13:27-28.)

37

4. *Prophets are persecuted because they reveal the wickedness and abominations of the people.*

It is just as simple as that. Implicit in the proclamation that Christ comes to save sinners is the fact that men must repent and forsake their evil ways or they will lose their souls. "He that believeth not shall be damned." (Mark 16:16.) Tell a man he is a liar, a thief, a murderer who is destined to dwell in an endless hell, and he will hate and persecute you. Tell him he has forsaken the truth, that his beliefs are false, his practices carnal, and he will fight back with the only weapon at his command—persecution.

Lehi delivered the Lord's message to the Jews, and they "did mock him because of the things which he testified of them; for he truly testified of their wickedness and their abominations; and he testified that the things which he saw and heard, and also the things which he read in the book, manifested plainly of the coming of a Messiah, and also the redemption of the world. And when the Jews heard these things they were angry with him; yea, even as with the prophets of old, whom they had cast out, and stoned, and slain; and they also sought his life, that they might take it away." (1 Ne. 1:19-20.)

5. *Prophets are persecuted and slain as a witness against the wicked and ungodly.*

In a revelation to Brigham Young, the Lord said: "Thy brethren have rejected you and your testimony, even the nation that has driven you out; And now cometh the day of their calamity, even the days of sorrow, like a woman that is taken in travail; and their sorrow shall be great unless they speedily repent, yea, very speedily. For they killed the prophets, and them that were sent unto them; and they have shed innocent blood, which crieth from the ground against them." (D&C 136:34-36.)

That same Lord, in even more severe language, said to the Jews whose hearts were set on killing him and his ancient apostles: "I send unto you prophets, and wise men, and scribes: and some of them ye shall kill and crucify; and some

38

of them shall ye scourge in your synagogues, and persecute them from city to city: That upon you may come all the righteous blood shed upon the earth, from the blood of righteous Abel unto the blood of Zacharias son of Barachias, whom ye slew between the temple and the altar." (Matt. 23:34-35.)

That is, the condemnation prepared for those who reject God and his ministers is justified because of the magnitude of their rebellion against him. Having shed the best blood in this fallen and benighted world, the judgments of a just God rest righteously upon them in time and eternity. These are they who are cast out with "the fearful, and unbelieving, and the abominable, and murderers, and whoremongers, and sorcerers, and idolaters, and all liars," and who "shall have their part in the lake which burneth with fire and brimstone: which is the second death." (Rev. 21:8.)

6. *Prophets are persecuted to test their integrity, to make sure of their allegiance to that Lord whose they are.*

Life never was intended to be easy, and when persecution is poured out upon the Lord's people, it is but part of the testing, probationary experiences which prepare them for celestial crowns. "I will try you and prove you," the Lord says to his saints. "And whoso layeth down his life in my cause, for my name's sake, shall find it again, even life eternal. . . . I will prove you in all things, whether you will abide in my covenant, even unto death, that you may be found worthy." (D&C 98:12-14.)

When Joseph Smith pled with the Lord for surcease from the wrongs and oppressions heaped upon him and his fellows, the answer that came was: "My son, peace be unto thy soul; thine adversity and thine afflictions shall be but a small moment; And then, if thou endure it well, God shall exalt thee on high; thou shalt triumph over all thy foes." (D&C 121:7-8.)

After this same prophet (together with his brother Hyrum) had met a martyr's death, the Lord said: "Many have marveled because of his death; but it was needful that ne should seal his testimony with his blood, that he might be honored and the wicked might be condemned." (D&C 136:39.) "And their innocent blood on the floor of Carthage jail is a broad seal affixed to 'Mormonism' that cannot be rejected by any court on earth, and their innocent blood on the escutcheon of the State of Illinois, with the broken faith of the State as pledged by the governor, is a witness to the truth of the everlasting gospel that all the world cannot impeach; and their innocent blood on the banner of liberty, and on the magna charta of the United States, is an ambassador for the religion of Jesus Christ, that will touch the hearts of honest men among all nations; and their innocent blood, with the innocent blood of all the martyrs under the altar that John saw, will cry unto the Lord of Hosts till he avenges that blood on the earth." (D&C 135:7.)

How Prophets Are Rewarded

But look again! Let your vision extend without limit! This time behold beyond the bounds of mortality! View now within the veil! What do you see relative to the righteous ones now? In this brief life the prophets are persecuted. In this moment of mortality the apostles "are made a spectacle unto the world," are esteemed "as the filth of the world," and are deemed to be "the offscouring of all things." (1 Cor. 4:9, 13.) But what of the eternal days ahead?

One who viewed within the veil and saw the end of those who had overcome the world was the Beloved John. As he beheld, an angelic ministrant asked: "What are these which are arrayed in white robes? and whence came they?" Answering his own question, the heavenly being proclaimed: "These are they which came out of great tribulation, and have washed their robes, and made them white in the blood of the Lamb. Therefore are they before the throne of God, and serve him day and night in his temple: and he that sitteth on the throne shall dwell among them." (Rev. 7:13-15.)

These are they who have been faithful and true in this mortal probation. These are they who have eternal life. These are they of whom the Lord Jesus said: "And blessed are all they who are persecuted for my name's sake, for theirs is the kingdom of heaven. And blessed are ye when men shall revile you and persecute, and shall say all manner of evil against you falsely, for my sake; For ye shall have great joy and be exceeding glad, for great shall be your reward in heaven; for so persecuted they the prophets who were before you." (3 Ne. 12:10-12.)

Let us, then—and let all men who desire righteousness—accept the Lord and his prophets, hearken to their teachings, and strive to be like them, for it is written: "He that receiveth a prophet in the name of a prophet shall receive a prophet's reward." (Matt. 10:41.) And a prophet's reward is eternal life in the kingdom of God.

How Messianic Prophecies Came

There is one way and one way only in which Messianic prophecies came (or by which Messianic testimonies can be borne), and that is by the power of the Holy Ghost. "No man can say"—or know, as Joseph Smith says (*Teachings* p. 223), or reveal, or testify—"that Jesus is the Lord, but by the Holy Ghost." (1 Cor. 12:3.)

True, the prophecy itself may have been spoken by the Eternal Father, as when he said in Eden that the Seed of Eve should bruise the serpent's head (Gen. 3:15); or it may have been uttered by Jehovah himself, as when he said to Enoch, "I am Messiah, the King of Zion, the Rock of Heaven," who shall be "lifted up on the cross" (Moses 7:53, 55); or it may have come from the lips of an angel, as when such a heavenly ministrant said to King Benjamin: "The Lord Omnipotent . . . shall come down from heaven among the children of men, and shall dwell in a tabernacle of clay" (Mosiah 3:5). But always and without exception the Holy Spirit of God is present and rests upon the recipient so that

41

the spoken words carry their Messianic meaning into the recipient's heart. The words themselves, without an accompanying and interpreting spirit, would be jangling jargon, without meaning, without sense, nothing more than the ravings of a deranged mind.

Most Messianic prophecies, however, were uttered by mortal men as they were moved upon by the power of the Holy Ghost. In some instances the Holy Spirit dictated the very words to be spoken, as when the Holy Ghost, "which beareth record of the Father and the Son," "fell upon Adam, . . . saying: I am the Only Begotten of the Father from the beginning, henceforth and forever, that as thou hast fallen thou mayest be redeemed, and all mankind, even as many as will." (Moses 5:9.) But in most cases, without question, the Holy Spirit simply planted the thought in the mind of that man who had, as it were, attuned his receiving set to the wave band upon which the Lord's eternal Revelator, who is the Holy Ghost, was broadcasting eternal truth; and that man was then left to phrase the thought in his own words, to speak revealed truth, "after the manner" of his language. (D&C 1:24.)

How to Understand Messianic Prophecies

There are numerous keys that open the door to a partial understanding of the Messianic prophecies, but there is only one way in which their full meaning can sink into a human heart with converting power.

It is helpful—indeed, almost imperative—that those of us who seek to know the deep and hidden things about Christ and his coming first gain an overall knowledge of the plan of salvation. Unless we believe in an Eternal Father who is God, we cannot conceive of a Son of God who is Christ. Unless we know that God created us in his own image, that he is our Father, that he ordained the laws whereby we may advance and progress and become like him, and that those laws are made operative through an infinite and eternal atonement; unless we believe and accept the eternal truths relative to the great plan of redemption, we are in no position to envision the meaning of the prophetic utterances concerning the birth, ministry, death, and resurrection of Christ.

It is also helpful—extremely so—to know that revelations and prophetic utterances given during and since our Lord's mortal ministry hark back to what was foretold about him anciently, and announce, plainly, that the former prophetic utterances about him are fulfilled. The Book of Mormon is by all odds the best source of this knowledge, as witness his own declaration to the Nephites: "Behold, I am Jesus Christ, whom the prophets testified shall come into the world." (3 Ne. 11:10.) "And the scriptures concerning my coming are fulfilled." (3 Ne. 9:16.) The New Testament also abounds in passages that quote or allude to the Messianic prophecies and then testify that these are fulfilled in the coming and ministry of Mary's Son. Revealed truths about his birth and ministry, with particular reference to those which tell of his atoning sacrifice and the salvation which comes by him, as these are found in the Doctrine and Covenants and other latter-day inspired writings, have this same effect. They affirm the verity and interpret the hidden meanings of those things which were foreknown, foreseen, and foreannounced by those who knew the mind and will of the Great Jehovah in olden times.

Help and understanding also comes—and this is a matter of no small moment—to those who acquaint themselves with "the manner of prophesying" among those who ministered in the name of Christ before he manifested himself among men. (2 Ne. 25:1-8.) Isaiah's prophecy of the virgin birth, for instance, is dropped into the midst of a recitation of local historical occurrences so that to the spiritually untutored it could be interpreted as some ancient and, to us, unknown happening that had no relationship to the mortal birth of the Lord Jehovah some seven hundred years later. (Isa. 7.)

Many of the prophets used types and shadows, figures and similitudes, their purpose ofttimes being, as it were, to hide that which is "holy" from the "dogs" and "swine" of their day (Matt. 7:6), while at the same time revealing it to those whose hearts were prepared for that light and knowledge which leads to salvation. Nephi, on the other hand, because of both the isolation and the spiritual development of his people, chose in the main to couch his prophetic utterances in plain and simple declarations. And so it is that, with propriety, we consider the context, the people involved, their social, cultural, and spiritual state, and the degree of understanding they already had of Messianic things.

But in the final analysis, there is no way—absolutely none (and this cannot be stated too strongly!)—to understand any Messianic prophecy, or any other scripture, except to have the same spirit of prophecy that rested upon the one who uttered the truth in its original form. Scripture comes from God by the power of the Holy Ghost. It does not originate with man. It means only what the Holy Ghost thinks it means. To interpret it, we must be enlightened by the power of the Holy Spirit. As Peter said, "No prophecy of the scripture is of any private interpretation. For the prophecy came not in old time by the will of man: but holy men of God spake as they were moved by the Holy Ghost." (2 Pet. 1:20-21.) Truly, it takes a prophet to understand a prophet, and every faithful member of the Church should have "the testimony of Jesus" which "is the spirit of prophecy." (Rev. 19:10.) Thus, as Nephi says, "The words of Isaiah"—and the principle applies to all scripture, all inspired writing, all Messianic prophecies—"are plain unto all those that are filled with the spirit of prophecy." (2 Ne. 25:4.) This is the sum and substance of the whole matter and an end to all controversy where discovering the mind and will of the Lord is concerned.

Seek Knowledge of Christ

It is now our purpose, prayerfully and perceptively, to

pore over the ponderous works of the prophets of the past, to find the Messianic prophecies proclaimed by our predecessors, and then to show their fulfillment in the birth, ministry, death, resurrection, and ascension into heaven of Him who is the source of saving truth, the Savior of those who believe in him and keep his word.

It is now our desire to know what the voice of God has spoken by the mouths of his servants the prophets in all ages concerning Jesus Christ our Lord, so that believing (and obeying!) we may become his friends and associates in the kingdom of his Father. We approach our most pleasant task with the realization that there are no unneeded scriptures, no prophecies without a purpose, no Messianic utterances devoid of worth, and that we—and all who read and ponder the recitations herein written—need above all the guidance and enlightenment which the Almighty sheds forth by the power of his Spirit. If we do not find and analyze to the full all that is now extant that tells of Christ and his coming, at least we shall build such a mountain of knowledge and truth on the various points involved that none who truly seek truth will be left without excuse or be unaware of the wealth of revealed truth about the Messiah that is available.

Can we do better than to guide our seeking steps with these words of Moroni: "Seek this Jesus of whom the prophets and apostles have written, that the grace of God the Father, and also the Lord Jesus Christ, and the Holy Ghost, which beareth record of them, may be and abide in you forever." (Ether 12:41.) And then, can we do better than to add to them these words of promise, written by that same Nephite prophet: "And by the power of the Holy Ghost ye may know the truth of all things." (Moro. 10:5.)

Chapter 4

MESSIAH DWELT WITH GOD

Christ Is the Firstborn

The Lord Jesus, who is called Christ, was in the beginning with God. He was the "Only Begotten Son, who was in the bosom of the Father, even from the beginning." (D&C 76:13.) He was "prepared from before the foundation of the world." (Moses 5:57; 3 Ne. 26:5.) And his solemn prayer, uttered near the climax of his mortal ministry, was: "O Father, glorify thou me with thine own self with the glory which I had with thee before the world was." (John 17:5.)

Though he has now attained unto that exalted state in which he is described as being "from everlasting to everlasting" (D&C 61:1) and "from all eternity to all eternity" (D&C 39:1)—as will eventually be the description and state of all those who gain exaltation (D&C 132:20)—yet, as a conscious identity, he had a beginning. He was born, as were all the spirit children of the Father. God was his Father, as he is of all the rest. For him, as for all men—and he is the Prototype—the eternal spirit element that has neither beginning nor end, and is self-existent by nature, was organized into a spirit body. He was one of "the intelligences that were organized before the world was." (Abr. 3:22.) He was and is the Firstborn of the Father.

In a Messianic vein, in the midst of a number of prophecies about his coming, the Psalmist records the mind of the

Father in these words: "I will make him my firstborn, higher than the kings of the earth" (Ps. 89:27), and nearly three millenniums later our Lord said to Joseph Smith, "I was in the beginning with the Father, and am the Firstborn" (D&C 93:21). His servant Paul spoke of him as "the firstborn among many brethren" (Rom. 8:29) and as "the firstborn of every creature" (Col. 1:15). And as *The Church of Jesus Christ* is his earthly church, so *The Church of the Firstborn* is his heavenly church, albeit its members are limited to exalted beings, for whom the family unit continues and who gain an inheritance in the highest heaven of the celestial world. (Heb. 12:22-23; D&C 93:22.)

Messiah Was a Spirit Man

Spirits are eternal beings, men and women created in the image of the Eternal Father, whose offspring they are. Their bodies are made of a more pure and refined substance than that which composes the mortal body. "All spirit is matter," the Prophet said, "but it is more fine or pure, and can only be discerned by purer eyes." (D&C 131:7.)

And this was the nature and kind of body possessed by the Firstborn before it was clothed upon with clay through the mortal birth processes. Nowhere is this truth preserved to us as perfectly as in the extract we have of the writings of Moriancumer, the greatest of the Jaredite prophets. Some twenty-two hundred or more years before our Lord took upon himself flesh and blood, he permitted the brother of Jared to see his spirit finger and then his whole spirit body, withdrawing more completely the veil between him and mortals than had ever been done before. "This body, which ye now behold, is the body of my spirit," he said, "and even as I appear unto thee to be in the spirit will I appear unto my people in the flesh." (Ether 3:16.)

Moroni, who preserved for us this Jareditish vision, appended to it this comment: "Jesus showed himself unto this man in the spirit, even after the manner and in the likeness

47

of the same body even as he showed himself unto the Nephites." (Ether 3:17.) In this connection, the ancient apostles, assembled in the upper room, recognized the Risen Lord as the same Being with whom they had been on familiar terms as a mortal (Luke 24:36-49), all of which taken together is as though the Eternal Messiah had said:

'As a Spirit Man, I had hands and feet and all the parts of a normal body, all patterned after my Father's glorified body of flesh and bones. In mortality I appeared as I appeared in the spirit. And then I came forth from Joseph's tomb, glorified and exalted, with a body of flesh and bones, which in appearance is like both my Spirit Body and my Mortal Body; and as it is with me, so shall it be with all men. I am the Prototype.'

Elohim Presents His Plan

God the Eternal Father, the Father of the Firstborn and of all the spirit hosts, as an exalted and glorified Being, having all power and dominion, possessing all knowledge and all truth, personifying and being the embodiment of all godly attributes, did, of his own will, ordain and establish the plan of salvation whereby Christ and all his other spirit children might have power to advance and progress and become like him.

God ordained the plan. He established it. It is his plan. It was not adopted by the Father following one suggestion coming from Christ and another originating with Lucifer. The Father is the author of the plan of salvation, a plan that he created so that Christ, his Firstborn, plus all the rest of his spirit children might be saved. As Joseph Smith expressed it: "God himself, finding he was in the midst of spirits and glory, because he was more intelligent, saw proper to institute laws whereby the rest could have a privilege to advance like himself." (*Teachings,* p. 354.)

The Father's plan, known first as the gospel of God, was taught to Christ, to Lucifer, and to all our Father's spirit children. Each person, endowed with the divine power of

48

agency, was free to believe or disbelieve, to obey or disobey, to follow Elohim or reject his goodness and grace. The plan itself included the creation and peopling of an earth. God's children were to have the privilege of gaining mortal bodies and of being tried and tested in a probationary estate to see if they would keep their Father's commandments at all hazards. The plan called for one of Deity's spirit sons to be born into mortality as the Only Begotten in the flesh, who would thus inherit from the Father the power of immortality; it called for this Chosen One to work out an infinite and eternal atonement whereby fallen men would be raised in immortality, while those who believed and obeyed would also gain eternal life.

After this plan had been taught to all the hosts of heaven; after it was known and understood by all; after all its facets had been debated and evaluated—then the Father asked for a volunteer to put the full terms and all of the conditions of his plan into force. Then it was, after all else was in readiness, that the call went forth in the Grand Council, "Whom shall I send" to be the Savior and Redeemer? (Abr. 3:27.) That is: Who will work out the infinite and eternal atoning sacrifice? Who will champion my cause? Who will go forth and do my will? Who will put all the terms and conditions of my plan in operation? Who will be my Son? Who will be the Messiah?

And thus the scene was set; thus the appointed time had come; thus the choosing and foreordination of the Messiah was at hand!

Christ Adopts the Father's Plan

Two spirits of renown, two men of power and influence, two whose voices had been heard by all the hosts of heaven, stepped forth to answer the Father's call, "Whom shall I send?" (Abr. 3:27.) One was Christ, the other Lucifer.

Our Lord said: "Father, thy will be done, and the glory be thine forever." (Moses 4:2.) That is: 'Father, I accept all

49

of the terms and conditions of thy plan. I will do thy will. I will go down as thy Son, the Only Begotten in the flesh. With thy help I will atone for the sins of the world, and will ascribe the honor and the glory unto thee in all things.'

Lucifer said: "Behold, here am I, send me, I will be thy son, and I will redeem all mankind, that one soul shall not be lost, and surely I will do it; wherefore give me thine honor." (Moses 4:1.) That is: 'I reject thy plan. I am willing to be thy Son and atone for the sins of the world, but in return let me take thy place and sit upon thy throne. Yea, "I will ascend into heaven, I will exalt my throne above the stars of God; . . . I will be like the most High." ' (Isa. 14:13-14.)

It was of the dramatic and transcendent events of that day that Elder Orson F. Whitney has written these words:

> A stature mingling strength with grace
> Of meek though Godlike mien,
> The glory of whose countenance
> Outshone the noonday sheen.
> Whiter his hair than ocean spray,
> Or frost of alpine hill.
> He spake:—attention grew more grave,
> The stillness e'en more still.
>
> "Father!"—the voice like music fell,
> Clear as the murmuring flow
> Of mountain streamlet trickling down
> From heights of virgin snow.
> "Father," it said, "since one must die,
> Thy children to redeem,
> Whilst earth, as yet unformed and void,
> With pulsing life shall teem;
>
> "And mighty Michael foremost fall,
> That mortal man may be,
> And chosen Savior Thou must send,
> Lo, here am I—send me!

I ask, I seek no recompense,
Save that which then were mine;
Mine be the willing sacrifice,
The endless glory Thine."

—In Joseph Fielding Smith, *Way to Perfection,* p. 52

Then came the decree. The issue was settled, except for the rebellion and war that was to follow. The voice of the Almighty said: "I will send the first." (Abr. 3:27.) The God of heaven said: "My Beloved Son, which was my Beloved and Chosen from the beginning," shall be the Savior and Redeemer, the Deliverer and Messiah. (Moses 4:2.)

Lucifer rebelled. He and one-third of the hosts of heaven, all being of one mind and one spirit, were cast down to earth, denied mortal bodies, and forever damned, damned to suffer the fulness of the wrath of Him whose plan they rejected. (Moses 4:3-4; Abr. 3:28; Rev. 12:7-9.)

From the beginning the destined Deliverer had adopted, advocated, and sponsored the Father's plan. Now with the decree issued that he should redeem and save mankind, that his atonement would enable men to become like their Father and God, and that the purposes of the Eternal Elohim should be brought to pass in full—now that all this was assured, two things transpired:

1. Messiah "verily was foreordained" (1 Pet. 1:20), and became "the Lamb slain from the foundation of the world" (Rev. 13:8).

2. The gospel of God became the gospel of Jesus Christ; or, as Paul was later to write, "The gospel of God, . . . Concerning his Son Jesus Christ our Lord." (Rom. 1:1, 3.) And so the very plan of salvation itself—to signify that salvation comes through Christ—was named after the One who was "Beloved and Chosen from the beginning." (Moses 4:2.) He thus, as Paul expressed it, "became the author," or as the better translation states, "the cause," "of eternal salvation unto all them that obey him." (Heb. 5:9.) He became "the

51

captain," meaning leader, of the salvation of the faithful. (Heb. 2:10.)

What Is the Gospel?

"The gospel of Jesus Christ is the plan of salvation. It embraces all of the laws, principles, doctrines, rites, ordinances, acts, powers, authorities, and keys necessary to save and exalt men in the highest heaven hereafter. It is the covenant of salvation which the Lord makes with men on earth." (*Mormon Doctrine,* 2nd ed., p. 331.)

From the perspective of the Eternal Elohim, the gospel is all that he has arranged and ordained to save his children. It is the laws given them in preexistence; it is the creation of the earth; it is the choosing of a Redeemer; it is this second estate wherein they are exposed to the lusts of the flesh; and it is the hope of everlasting life with him and his saints forever.

From the perspective of him who is our Redeemer, the gospel is the atoning sacrifice which puts into full operation and makes binding and efficacious all that the Father has prepared for them that love him. It is our Lord's birth in Bethlehem, his childhood in Nazareth, his ministry in Judea and Perea. It is the miracles he wrought, the works he did, the laws he made known. It is the Garden of Gethsemane and the hill of Calvary. It is great drops of blood dripping from every pore, as he took upon himself the sins of the world. It is a Roman spear piercing a sinless side. It is an open tomb outside a city wall. It is all power given him in heaven and on earth. It is immortality as a free gift for all and eternal life for the faithful.

From the perspective of man, the gospel is a better way of life. It is light bursting forth in a wilderness of darkness. It is faith, repentance, baptism, and the gift of the Holy Ghost. It is signs and gifts and miracles. It is the eyes of the blind being opened, the ears of the deaf unstopped, and the dead rising from their funeral biers. It is persecution and suffering and trials. It is learning to live as becometh a saint. It is overcoming the world until, eventually, in glorious immortality, the true saints dwell with Him who is their Friend and into whose image they have been molded.

The gospel is all this and ten thousand times ten thousand things more. But all that it is, all that it has ever been, all that it shall ever be, all that appertains to it centers in Him of whom the prophets testify and of which this work speaks. How can we say too often that salvation is in Christ and comes to the contrite souls who live his law!

Christ Became Like God

Abraham saw in vision all the spirit hosts of heaven. Among them were "the noble and great ones" who participated in the creation of this earth and who were foreordained to serve the Almighty in special capacities while they dwelt in mortality. Christ was there, the foremost spirit of the innumerable host. Of him the account says: "There stood one among them that was like unto God, and he said unto those who were with him: We will go down, for there is space there, and we will take of these materials, and we will make an earth whereon these may dwell." (Abr. 3:24.)

"Like unto God!" Like the Exalted Elohim who, in the ultimate sense, is the Creator, Upholder, and Preserver of the universe! Like unto God—how and in what way? Like him in length of days or the possession of progeny or the exalted nature of his tangible body? No, for the Son of the Father had yet to pass through a mortal probation, to overcome the world, to attain a resurrection, and to come back to his Father with his own glorious and tangible body. But like him in intelligence, in knowledge and understanding, in the possession of truth, in conformity to divine law, and therefore in power. Like him in plan and purpose, in desires for righteousness, in a willingness to serve his brethren, in all things that lead to that fulness of the glory of the Father which none can receive until they live in the eternal family

53

unit as he does. Like him as a guide and a light to all others. Like him as a Creator of worlds and planets innumerable.

But mighty and glorious as the Spirit-Messiah then was—and the title "The Lord Omnipotent" (Mosiah 3:5) is descriptive of his already attained Eternal Godhood—he yet had to gain a mortal and then an immortal body before he could enter into the fulness of the glory of his Father and his God. He had to work out his own salvation by doing on earth the will of the Father in all things. "Though he were a Son," Paul says, "yet learned he obedience by the things which he suffered" (Heb. 5:8), meaning that "The Lord Omnipotent" himself had to overcome the world and stand against all opposition before he could (and again it is Paul's language) be "made perfect" (Heb. 5:9) in the ultimate and absolute sense of the term; that is, "perfect, even as your Father which is in heaven is perfect" (Matt. 5:48). After his resurrection, when he had so obtained, this Sermon-on-the-Mount statement, as given to the Nephites, was properly expanded to say: "Perfect even as I, or your Father who is in heaven is perfect." (3 Ne. 12:48.)

It was John, whom men call the Baptist, who saw the heavens open, the Holy Ghost descend, and heard the Father's voice proclaim, "This is my Beloved Son"—it was this John who left us the most perfect account known of the mortal progression and achievements of Him who was God before the world was. "And I, John," he wrote, "saw that he received not of the fulness at the first, but received grace for grace; And he received not of the fulness at first, but continued from grace to grace, until he received a fulness; And thus he was called the Son of God, because he received not of the fulness at the first." Then this ancient witness told of the baptism itself, and continued: "And I, John, bear record that he received a fulness of the glory of the Father; And he received all power, both in heaven and on earth, and the glory of the Father was with him, for he dwelt in him" (D&C 93:12-17)—which accords with our Lord's own pronouncement, made after his resurrection, to his ancient

54

apostles: "All power is given unto me in heaven and in earth" (Matt. 28:18).

Christ Is the Creator

"We will go down, for there is space there, and we will take of these materials, and we will make an earth whereon these may dwell." So spake the One who was "like unto God." (Abr. 3:24.) And so they did—Christ, Michael, and all that great host of "noble and great ones," all laboring in their assigned spheres, all aiding the Great Creator who is Christ, and he and they all subject to the Father of them all, in whom all fulness and perfection dwells.

But where Christ himself was concerned, this small planet was but one speck of dust in a storm swirling over the Sahara. There is not one earth, but many; not one planet inhabited by our Father's children, but an infinite number. Moses, by the power of God, "beheld many lands; and each land was called earth, and there were inhabitants on the face thereof," and the Almighty said to him: "For mine own purpose have I made these things. . . . And by the word of my power, have I created them, which is mine Only Begotten Son, who is full of grace and truth. And worlds without number have I created; . . . and by the Son I created them, which is mine Only Begotten. . . . For behold, there are many worlds that have passed away by the word of my power. And there are many that now stand, and innumerable are they unto man; but all things are numbered unto me, for they are mine and I know them." (Moses 1:29-35.)

Worlds without number! Innumerable unto man! There is no finite way to envision the extent of the worlds created by Christ at the behest of his Father. Count the grains of sand on all the seashores and Saharas of the world, add the stars in the firmament for good measure, multiply the total by like sums from other worlds, and what do we have? Scarcely a dot in the broad expanse of an infinite universe— all created by Christ. Enoch, as guided by the Spirit, in conversation with the Lord expressed it this way: "Were it possible that man could number the particles of the earth, yea, millions of earths like this, it would not be a beginning to the number of thy creations; and thy curtains are stretched out still." (Moses 7:30.)

And Christ is the Creator of them all, a fact which, though not quite as dramatically expressed as by Enoch, has been known in all ages when spiritual enlightenment rested upon the people. Does not our revelation say, "By him, and through him, and of him, the worlds are and were created"? (D&C 76:24.) Did not John record, "All things were made by him; and without him was not anything made that was made"? (John 1:3.) And Paul, did he not say of the Father, "God . . . hath . . . spoken unto us by his Son, whom he hath appointed heir of all things, by whom also he made the worlds"? (Heb. 1:1-2.) And yet again, are not these his words concerning Christ: "There is but . . . one Lord Jesus Christ, by whom are all things, and we by him"? (1 Cor. 8:6.) And again, speaking of God's "dear Son," "By him were all things created, that are in heaven, and that are in earth, visible and invisible, whether they be thrones, or dominions, or principalities, or powers: all things were created by him, and for him: And he is before all things, and by him all things consist." (Col. 1:13-17.) Is it any wonder then that he was foreknown as "The Lord Omnipotent who reigneth, who was, and is from all eternity to all eternity, . . . the Father of heaven and earth, the Creator of all things from the beginning"? (Mosiah 3:5, 8.)

Messiah: Father of Heaven and Earth

"Thus saith the Lord your God, even Jesus Christ, . . . I am the same which spake, and the world was made, and all things came by me." (D&C 38:1, 3.) So spake the Great Creator, "the very Eternal Father of heaven and of earth" (Mosiah 15:4), to his servant and seer, Joseph the Prophet. "I am Jesus Christ the Son of God. I created the heavens and the earth, and all things that in them are. I was with the Father from the beginning." (3 Ne. 9:15.) So he spake to the preserved remnant of the Nephites when he descended from heaven to minister personally among them. And some four hundred years later, to Moroni, the last of the Nephite prophets, he identified himself as "Jesus Christ, the Son of God, the Father of the heavens and of the earth, and all things that in them are." (Ether 4:7.)

Accordingly, there neither is nor can be any question as to who created the earth and all things that are therein. And so we read in the Ten Commandments: "In six days the Lord made heaven and earth, the seas, and all that in them is" (Ex. 20:11), and ask: Who is speaking? Who is the Great Creator? Who made the heavens and the earth? The answer thunders back: The Great Jehovah who is the Lord Jesus Christ. And we thereby learn that all of the statements, of all of the prophets, of all of the ages, which speak of God the Creator are Messianic in nature. They are speaking of that Being who came in time's meridian to do the only work equal to that of creation, to do the work of redemption.

Our ancient scriptures are speaking of Christ when they say, "Our help is in the name of the Lord, who made heaven and earth." (Ps. 124:8.) "The Lord that made heaven and earth bless thee out of Zion." (Ps. 134:3.) "Happy is he that hath the God of Jacob for his help, whose hope is in the Lord his God: Which made heaven, and earth, the sea, and all that therein is." (Ps. 146:5-6.) "The Lord thy maker, . . . hath stretched forth the heavens, and laid the foundations of the earth." (Isa. 51:13.) After saying that Christ "made the worlds," Paul quotes this Old Testament scripture to prove it: "Thou, Lord, in the beginning hast laid the foundation of the earth; and the heavens are the works of thine hands: They shall perish; but thou remainest; and they all shall wax old as doth a garment; And as a vesture shalt thou fold them up, and they shall be changed: but thou art the same, and thy years shall not fail." (Heb. 1:2, 10-12; Ps. 102:25-27.) And it also follows that all the rest of the Old Testament scriptures which speak of this same Lord, though explicit words are not used identifying him as the Creator, are also Messianic in nature.

But it is to the Book of Mormon that we turn for the most perfect illustrations of Messianic prophecies that identify the Creator as the promised Deliverer. We find there that the Father of heaven and earth has ministered or will minister in the following ways:

1. *He is the God of Abraham and the prophets.*

He, "the Father of heaven," is the one, Nephi says, who covenanted "unto Abraham, saying: In thy seed shall all the kindreds of the earth be blessed," and these covenants shall be made known again in the last days. (1 Ne. 22:9.) We have already noted, in this connection, that the Psalmist called him "the God of Jacob." (Ps. 146:5.)

2. *He is the Only Begotten of the Father.*

"The day cometh," prophesied Nephi, "that the Only Begotten of the Father, yea, even the Father of heaven and of earth, shall manifest himself unto them in the flesh." (2 Ne. 25:12.)

3. *He shall dwell in Jerusalem and die for the sins of men.*

"In the body he shall show himself unto those at Jerusalem, . . . for it behooveth the great Creator that he suffereth himself to become subject unto man in the flesh, and die for all men, that all men might become subject unto him." (2 Ne. 9:5.)

4. *He shall atone for the sins of the world and bring to pass the resurrection.*

"For as death hath passed upon all men, to fulfil the merciful plan of the great Creator, there must needs be a power of resurrection. . . . It must needs be an infinite atonement—save it should be an infinite atonement this corruption could not put on incorruption." (2 Ne. 9:6-7.) "O have mercy, and apply the atoning blood of Christ that we may receive forgiveness of our sins, and our hearts may be purified; for we believe in Jesus Christ, the Son of God, who created heaven and earth, and all things; who shall come down among the children of men." (Mosiah 4:2.)

5. *He is the Lord Omnipotent.*

"I would that ye should be steadfast and immovable," King Benjamin exhorted his people, "always abounding in good works, that Christ, the Lord God Omnipotent, may seal you his, that you may be brought to heaven, that ye may have everlasting salvation and eternal life, through the wisdom, and power, and justice, and mercy of him who created all things, in heaven and in earth, who is God above all." (Mosiah 5:15.)

6. *He shall take upon him flesh and blood.*

Speaking of the death of Abinadi at the hands of King Noah and his wicked followers, Limhi said to his people: "A prophet of the Lord have they slain, . . . because he said unto them that Christ was the God, the Father of all things, and said that he should take upon him the image of man, and it should be the image after which man was created in the beginning; or in other words, he said that man was created after the image of God, and that God should come down among the children of men, and take upon him flesh and blood, and go forth upon the face of the earth—And now, because he said this, they did put him to death." (Mosiah 7:26-28.)

7. *He offers salvation through baptism and personal righteousness.*

"This is my church," he said to Alma, and "whosoever is baptized shall be baptized unto repentance. And whomsoever ye receive shall believe in my name; and him will I freely forgive. For it is I that taketh upon me the sins of the world; for it is I that hath created them; and it is I that granteth unto him that believeth unto the end a place at my right hand. For behold, in my name are they called; and if they know me they shall come forth, and shall have a place eternally at my right hand." (Mosiah 26:22-24.)

8. *He is the Redeemer.*

At the time of his conversion, Alma the younger confessed his past rebellion by saying: "I rejected my

Redeemer, and denied that which had been spoken of by our fathers; but now that they may foresee that he will come, and that he remembereth every creature of his creating, he will make himself manifest unto all." (Mosiah 27:30.)

9. *He is the Son of God who shall redeem his people.*

Zeezrom asked: "Is the Son of God the very Eternal Father?" Amulek replied: "Yea, he is the very Eternal Father of heaven and of earth, and all things which in them are; he is the beginning and the end, the first and the last; And he shall come into the world to redeem his people." (Alma 11:38-40.) Samuel the Lamanite prophesied of "the coming of Jesus Christ, the Son of God, the Father of heaven and of earth, the Creator of all things from the beginning." (Hel. 14:12.)

Did Christ Create Man?

We have now seen that Christ created all things—this earth and all that on it is. "By him were all things created, that are in heaven, and that are in earth." (Col. 1:16.) We have seen that he is "the very Eternal Father of heaven and of earth, and all things which in them are" (Alma 11:39)—that is, that he created all forms of life on the face of the earth. Are we to understand that this means he created man? So it might be reasoned from the blanket assertions made in these and other revelations, and as a matter of fact there are some scriptures which we shall now note which, according to the plain usage of words, some might interpret to mean that mortal man was in fact created not by the Father, but by the Son.

In a deep and difficult passage revealed to Joseph Smith, Christ says: "The Father and I are one—The Father because he gave me of his fulness, and the Son because I was in the world and made flesh my tabernacle, and dwelt among the sons of men. I was in the world and received of my Father, and the works of him were plainly manifest." Then this revelation quotes from an ancient record written first by

John the Baptist but paraphrased and preserved in part by
John the Revelator in his gospel, which speaks of Christ in
his creative capacity and includes these words: "The worlds
were made by him; men were made by him; all things were
made by him, and through him, and of him." Then the account explains that "he was called the Son of God, because
he received not of the fulness at the first," but that in due
course, after the resurrection, "he received a fulness of the
glory of the Father." (D&C 93:3-16.) Now, bear in mind that
this passage, among other things, is treating Christ in his capacity as both the Father and the Son. It is much the same
thought as that expressed by Abinadi when he said of
Christ: "Because he dwelleth in the flesh he shall be called
the Son of God, and having subjected the flesh to the will of
the Father, being the Father and the Son—The Father, because he was conceived by the power of God; and the Son,
because of the flesh; thus becoming the Father and Son—
And they are one God, yea, the very Eternal Father of
heaven and of earth." (Mosiah 15:2-4.)

In the most complete revelation of himself ever given up
to that time, our Lord said to the brother of Jared: "I am
Jesus Christ. I am the Father and the Son. . . . Seest thou that
ye are created after mine own image? Yea, even all men
were created in the beginning after mine own image. Behold,
this body, which ye now behold, is the body of my spirit."
(Ether 3:14-16.) Bear in mind once more that this passage
also is treating Christ in his capacity as both the Father and
the Son.

In a passage already quoted by us in another connection,
Limhi rehearses the teaching of Abinadi "that Christ was the
God, the Father of all things, and said that he should take
upon him the image of man, and it should be the image after
which man was created in the beginning; or in other words,
he said that man was created after the image of God, and
that God should come down among the children of men,
and take upon him flesh and blood, and go forth upon the
face of the earth." (Mosiah 7:27.) Note that this passage is

61

affirming in large measure the same truth relative to the creation of man which the Lord Jesus had afore given to the brother of Jared, and that therefore Christ's status as the Father and the Son is necessarily involved.

In a passage of great doctrinal worth and of surpassing literary beauty, Isaiah speaks of the Lord Jehovah, "the Holy One of Israel," who is Christ, as man's "Maker." "I have made the earth, and created man upon it," says he who is the Son of God. "I, even my hands, have stretched out the heavens, and all their host have I commanded." (Isa. 45:9-12.) And once again we have the creation of man ascribed, seemingly, to the Son of God.

However, from other sacred sources we know that Jehovah-Christ, assisted by "many of the noble and great ones" (Abr. 3:22), of whom Michael is but the illustration, did in fact create the earth and all forms of plant and animal life on the face thereof. But when it came to placing man on earth, there was a change in Creators. That is, the Father himself became personally involved. All things were created by the Son, using the power delegated by the Father, except man. In the spirit and again in the flesh, man was created by the Father. There was no delegation of authority where the crowning creature of creation was concerned.

"I am the Beginning and the End, the Almighty God," says the great Elohim. "By mine Only Begotten I created these things; yea, in the beginning I created the heaven, and the earth." (Moses 2:1.) That is, God did all these things by and through his Son. Then of the planned and proposed creation of mortal man, the inspired record says: "And I, God, said unto mine Only Begotten, which was with me from the beginning: Let us make man in our image, after our likeness; and it was so." (Moses 2:26.) But when the plan becomes a reality and the proposal an accomplished fact, then the record personalizes the occurrence and centers it in the Supreme Head. "And I, God, created man in mine own image, in the image of mine Only Begotten created I him; male and female created I them." (Moses 2:27.) That is, God himself, personally, created man, although he continued to honor the Son in that the creature of his creating came forth in the image of both the Father and the Son, as necessarily must have been the case because they were in the image of each other.

In this connection, we find it worthy of note that Joseph Smith said: "Everlasting covenant was made between three personages before the organization of this earth, and relates to their dispensation of things to men on the earth; these personages, according to Abraham's record, are called God the first, the Creator; God the second, the Redeemer; and God the third, the witness or Testator." (*Teachings*, p. 190.) From this we learn that the work of the Father is creation (though he uses the Son and others in the creation of all things except man); the work of the Son is redemption (though he performs this infinite work by the power of the Father); and the work of the Holy Ghost is to bear witness of the Father and the Son, whose minister he is.

In 1916, the duly constituted heads of the earthly Church, who have the ultimate responsibility, under Deity, to interpret and promulgate the mind and will of the Lord to mortals, issued a document entitled *The Father and The Son: A Doctrinal Exposition by The First Presidency and The Twelve.* Therein are set forth, among other things, three distinct senses in which Christ is also known as the Father. These are:

1. He is the Father as Creator, the Father of the heavens and the earth.

2. He is the Father of those who abide in his gospel, the Father of all those who take upon themselves his name and are adopted into his family.

3. He is the Father by divine investiture of authority, meaning that the Father-Elohim has placed his name upon the Son, has given him his own power and authority, and has authorized him to speak in the first person as though he were the original or primal Father.

"In all his dealings with the human family," the Brethren

set forth in their official exposition, "Jesus the Son has represented and yet represents Elohim his Father in power and authority. This is true of Christ in his pre-existent, antemortal, or unembodied state, in the which he was known as Jehovah; also during his embodiment in the flesh; and during his labors as a disembodied spirit in the realm of the dead; and since that period in his resurrected state. . . . The Father placed his name upon the Son; and Jesus Christ spoke and ministered in and through the Father's name; and so far as power, authority, and Godship are concerned his words and acts were and are those of the Father." (*The Father and The Son: A Doctrinal Exposition by The First Presidency and The Twelve,* cited in James E. Talmage, *Articles of Faith,* pp. 465-73.)

"His words and acts were and are those of the Father!"

He speaks in the first person as though he were the Father. They are so perfectly united in all things that, in like circumstances, they think the same thoughts, speak the same words, and do the same acts.

The Son may speak to man in his own name, and then, to dramatize and teach more effectively and powerfully whatever is involved, he may begin to speak in his Father's name, without so much as a break in thought presentation. He begins section 29 in the Doctrine and Covenants by saying, "Listen to the voice of Jesus Christ, your Redeemer, the Great I Am, whose arm of mercy hath atoned for your sins," and without hesitation or explanation he soon assumes the voice of the Father, saying, "I the Lord God" shall "send forth angels to declare unto them repentance and redemption, through faith on the name of mine Only Begotten Son." (D&C 29:1, 42-43.) In such a context the meaning is clear; Christ is choosing to speak in the first person as though he were the Father.

And so we read the various passages in which he says he created man, and although the meanings are not as plainly and clearly set forth as is his declaration in section 29, the principle is the same. He is once again teaching what the

Father did, although to the spiritually untutored it seems as though he is saying that he did it. His words are those of the Father. And upon us the obligation rests, in Paul's language, of "rightly dividing the word of truth" (2 Tim. 2:15)—which we have here done, as should be clear to all.

Chapter 5

PROPHETS REVEAL THE COMING OF CHRIST

Man Comes to Dwell on Earth

From our premortal life as spirit beings, to this mortal vale of sorrow and tears, is one simple, easy step. Life on a celestial sphere, in the Eternal Presence, is but a breath removed from life on this fallen orb. The one step is birth, and the breath of difference that divides spirit men from mortal men is the breath of life. Our home here is but a temporary abiding place, one where we are separated, for the moment, from the home eternal.

And so, in his infinite wisdom, for his own purposes and for our advancement and progression, God our Father placed us here on earth. "God created man, in the likeness of God made he him; In the image of his own body, male and female, created he them, and blessed them, and called their name Adam, in the day when they were created and became living souls in the land upon the footstool of God." (Moses 6:8-9.) God is our Father, and "Adam . . . was the son of God, with whom God, himself, conversed." (Moses 6:22.)

After he had taken the step from preexistence to this newly created earth, after the breath of life filled his being, Adam our father, "the first man of all men" (Moses 1:34), chose to fall from his paradisiacal state to one in which the full woes of mortality would weigh upon him. His fall brought temporal and spiritual death into the world. In his mortal and fallen state the procreative powers promised in the Garden of Eden became his natural inheritance, and patterning his course after that of his Eternal Father, he begat sons and daughters "in his own likeness, after his own image." (Moses 6:10.) His posterity, in their fallen and lost state, became "carnal, sensual, and devilish, by nature." (Alma 42:10.)

What Is Messiah's Mission?

To save mankind from eternal temporal death (which is the grave) and from eternal spiritual death (which is everlasting banishment from the presence of God), a gracious Father provided a Savior, his Son, a promised Deliverer or Messiah. Deliverance was to come through his atoning sacrifice, coupled—in the case of salvation from spiritual death—with obedience on the part of man to the laws and ordinances of His everlasting gospel. In the wisdom of God, this infinite and eternal atonement would cause all men to come forth from the grave (thus ransoming them from temporal death) and would bring the believing and obedient saints back into the presence of God, which is eternal life (thus ransoming them from spiritual death). Immortality, which is resurrection, is a free gift for all men; eternal life, which is the kind of life God lives, is reserved for those who are true and faithful in all things. Thus the probationary nature of man's mortal estate is established.

The promised Messiah must thus be the Son of God, who inherits from his Father the power of immortality whereby he can bring to pass, through his redeeming death, the immortality and eternal life of man. He must be the resurrection and the life.

The Messiah thus becomes the One through whom salvation comes. The gospel of God, which is the plan of salvation, becomes his gospel.

The Messiah thus stands as the Mediator between God

and man, as man's Advocate with the Father, as the One who pleads the cause of his brethren in the courts above.

The Messiah thus steps forward as the God of his people, their Savior and Redeemer, the God of Israel, the Revealer of eternal truth, the Lord of Hosts.

The Messiah is Christ.

How far removed from these saving truths are the billions of non-Christians who dwell on earth! They know neither the Father nor the Son, and are without the knowledge leading to that pure and perfect worship which cleanses and sanctifies the souls of men.

How far removed from these saving truths are millions of professing Christians! They have yet to envision that Jesus who is called Christ is in fact the Lord Jehovah of old; that his truths of salvation have been shed forth in one gospel dispensation after another from the days of Adam to the present; and that an unchangeable God has prophets again on earth who minister in his name with binding and sealing power.

How far afield the once chosen race has gone from the knowledge of their Messiah is seen in this statement summarizing their concept of deliverance:

"The Messiah whom we expect is not to be a god, nor a part of the godhead, nor a Son of God in any sense of the word; but simply a man eminently endowed, like Moses and the prophets in the days of the Bible, to work out the will of God on earth in all that the prophets have predicted of him.

"His coming, we believe, will be the signal for universal peace, universal freedom, universal knowledge, universal worship of the One Eternal; objects all of high import, and well worthy to be attested by the visible display of the divine glory before the eyes of all flesh, just as was the presence of the Lord manifested at Sinai, when the Israelites stood assembled to receive the law which was surrendered to their keeping. In the days of this august ruler, the law, which was at first given as 'an inheritance of the congregation of Jacob,' will become the only standard of righteousness, of salvation, for all mankind, when will be fulfilled to its fullest extent the blessings conferred upon Abraham, Isaac, and Jacob, that 'in their seed all the families of the earth should be blessed.'

"We believe, further, that the time of this great event is hidden from our knowledge, and is only known to the Creator, who in his own good time will regenerate the earth, remove the worship of idols, banish all erroneous beliefs, and establish his kingdom firmly and immovably over the hearts of all the sons of man, when all will invoke Him in truth, and call him God, King, Redeemer, the One who was, is, and will be, for ever and ever.

"We believe that the time may be distant, thousands of years removed; but we confidently look forward to its coming, in the full confidence that He who has so miraculously preserved his people among so many trials and dangers, is able and willing to fulfil all he has promised, and that his power will surely accomplish what his goodness has foretold; and that he will not rest in the fulfilment of his word, till all the world shall acknowledge his power, and ceaseless incense ascend to his holy name from the rising of the sun even unto his setting; when the altars of falsehood shall crumble, and the dominion of unbelief be swept from the face of the earth." (Isaac Lesser, *History of the Jews and Their Religion*, p. 7.)

God Giveth His Gospel to Man

Christ is the promised Messiah by whom salvation comes, and so an angel of the Lord commanded Adam: "Thou shalt do all that thou doest in the name of the Son, and thou shalt repent and call upon God in the name of the Son forevermore." (Moses 5:8.) Then, by the power of the Holy Ghost, Adam, in his lost and fallen state, heard the voice of the Son, saying: "I am the Only Begotten of the Father from the beginning, henceforth and forever, that as

69

thou hast fallen thou mayest be redeemed, and all mankind, even as many as will." (Moses 5:9.) And Eve, knowing what was being taught, acclaimed the blessings given them through the fall and redemption, saying: "Were it not for our transgression we never should have had seed, and never should have known good and evil, and the joy of our redemption, and the eternal life which God giveth unto all the obedient." (Moses 5:11.)

Beginning in this early day, that God who is no respecter of persons, and in whose sight the souls of those in all ages are equally precious, began to reveal the plan of salvation to his mortal children. The knowledge of a Deliverer was made known unto them. They were promised salvation by obedience to the laws and ordinances of Messiah's gospel, and the decree went forth: "Believe on his Only Begotten Son, even him whom he declared should come in the meridian of time, who was prepared from before the foundation of the world." Then the record says: "And thus the Gospel began to be preached, from the beginning, being declared by holy angels sent forth from the presence of God, and by his own voice, and by the gift of the Holy Ghost. And thus all things were confirmed unto Adam, by an holy ordinance, and the Gospel preached, and a decree sent forth, that it should be in the world, until the end thereof; and thus it was." (Moses 5:57-59.)

This same gospel was revealed to Enoch, Noah, and Abraham; to Melchizedek, Moses, and Moriancumer; to the Jaredites and the Nephites, and insofar as they would receive it, to the prophets and apostles of all ages and on all continents. It was restored from time to time in new and glorious dispensations, especially and particularly in time's meridian by the Son of God himself. The final dispensation of grace is that in which we now live—the dispensation of Joseph Smith, the dispensation which will prepare a people for the Second Coming of the Messiah.

In all these dispensations the plan of redemption and salvation has been the same, namely, that salvation comes through the atoning blood of Him whom Almighty God sent to atone for the sins of the world.

In all these dispensations the faithful have received the same gospel, known the same truths, rejoiced in the same knowledge, enjoyed the same gifts of the Spirit, and had the same hope of eternal life.

In all these dispensations, following the pattern set in Adam's day, those who have received the everlasting gospel have heard the voice of God, received the ministering of angels, and possessed the gift of the Holy Ghost.

In all of these dispensations salvation has been in Christ; those who have received the gospel have received him; and by faith they have gained peace in this life and a guarantee of eternal life in the mansions that are prepared.

Messiah Revealed to Men

Our sources of knowledge concerning King Messiah all stem back to God who is our Father. Every true and authorized witness borne of Christ has come by the power of the Holy Ghost; it has been planted and sealed in the hearts of men by the Holy Spirit. However, for convenience in study, we may properly classify Messianic utterances in the following categories:

1. Those spoken by the mouth of God, meaning by either the Father or the Son.

2. Revelations given by the Holy Ghost to all those who prepare themselves to receive the promptings of this divine Revelator.

3. Angelic proclamations delivered to righteous men, women, and children.

4. Utterances of prophets, men whose mission it is to reveal and bear record of their Messiah.

5. Testimonies of living witnesses, meaning all the saints, all of the members of the Church, all who hold the holy priesthood, all who have the testimony of Jesus. Properly speaking, all of these are prophets—prophets to themselves

71

and their families, as distinguished from those who wear the prophetic mantle which obligates them to proclaim and send the witness of truth to all the world.

6. That which is recorded in the Holy Scriptures and is thus preserved for all men to study and ponder.

Messianic Prophecies Borne by Gods and Angels

The greatest witness of the Son is the Father. "I bear witness of myself," the Lord Jesus said to the Jews. (JST, John 5:31.) Then of his Father—concerning whom he was later to say, "My Father is greater than I" (John 14:28)—our Lord said: "The Father himself, which hath sent me, hath borne witness of me. Ye have neither heard his voice at any time, nor seen his shape." (John 5:37.)

But other men in other days had both heard his voice and seen his shape. His voice had been the voice of One testifying of the divine Sonship of the promised Messiah, and his shape had been the express image of that of the Son. (Heb. 1:3.) Indeed, the Lord's eternal law is: "No man hath seen God at any time, except he hath borne record of the Son." (JST, John 1:19.) Nephi is one who heard the voice, and the record it bore to him was: "The words of my Beloved are true and faithful." (2 Ne. 31:15.) Six centuries later, hosts of his descendants were to hear the same voice acclaim: "Behold my Beloved Son, in whom I am well pleased, in whom I have glorified my name—hear ye him." (3 Ne. 11:7.)

Of Enoch's Zion, the record says: "The Lord came and dwelt with his people, and they dwelt in righteousness." (Moses 7:16.) That he bore testimony among them of his own divine status and redeeming power is self-evident. Then, after "Zion, in process of time, was taken up into heaven . . . Enoch beheld angels descending out of heaven, bearing testimony of the Father and Son; and the Holy Ghost fell on many, and they were caught up by the powers of heaven into Zion." (Moses 7:21, 27.) Then it was that the same Lord who had dwelt among them said to Enoch: "I am Messiah, the King of Zion, the Rock of Heaven, which is broad as eternity; whoso cometh in at the gate and climbeth up by me shall never fall." (Moses 7:53.)

As the time of Christ's coming drew near—the year was about 82 B.C.—the great prophet Alma said to his Nephite brethren: "Now is the time to repent, for the day of salvation draweth nigh." Then follows this profound and comprehensive explanation of how angels were foretelling the coming of Christ and how they would announce the fulfillment of their prophecies to other men in due course: "Yea, and the voice of the Lord, by the mouth of angels," Alma continues, "doth declare it unto all nations; yea, doth declare it, that they may have glad tidings of great joy; . . . For behold, angels are declaring it unto many at this time in our land; and this is for the purpose of preparing the hearts of the children of men to receive his word at the time of his coming in his glory. And now we only wait to hear the joyful news declared unto us by the mouth of angels, of his coming; for the time cometh, we know not how soon. . . . And it shall be made known unto just and holy men, by the mouth of angels, at the time of his coming, that the words of our fathers may be fulfilled, according to that which they have spoken concerning him, which was according to the spirit of prophecy which was in them." (Alma 13:21-26.) And the impartiality of God is shown from the fact these "glad tidings" and this "joyful news" were being imparted "by angels unto men, . . . women [and] . . . little children." (Alma 32:23.) Probably the most glorious angelic pronouncements about Christ, his coming and his atoning sacrifice, were made by the heavenly ministrant who visited King Benjamin, as is recorded in the third chapter of Mosiah. That chapter contains a sermon preached by an angel on the most important of all gospel subjects, the atonement of the Lord Jesus Christ.

But probably the best summary we have of how and why God spoke by his own voice and sent angels to confirm his word is given by Mormon in these words: "God knowing all things, being from everlasting to everlasting, behold, he sent angels to minister unto the children of men, to make manifest concerning the coming of Christ; and in Christ there should come every good thing. And God also declared unto prophets, by his own mouth, that Christ should come. And behold, there were divers ways that he did manifest things unto the children of men, which were good; and all things which are good cometh of Christ; otherwise men were fallen, and there could no good thing come unto them. Wherefore, by the ministering of angels, and by every word which proceeded forth out of the mouth of God, men began to exercise faith in Christ; and thus by faith, they did lay hold upon every good thing; and thus it was until the coming of Christ." (Moro. 7:22-25.)

Messianic Prophecies Borne by the Holy Ghost

As already set forth in that portion of Chapter 3 entitled "How Messianic Prophecies Came," all such prophecies have come by the power of the Holy Ghost, even though they were spoken by Gods, angels, or men. Let us here bring into focus how and under what circumstances this third member of the Godhead bears record of Christ, so that believing men may abide the law involved and gain for themselves the personal witness that Jesus is the Messiah.

In this connection, be it noted: "No man can receive the Holy Ghost without receiving revelations. The Holy Ghost is a Revelator." (*Teachings*, p. 328.) The question, then, is how to gain revelation from the Lord's Revelator, and the answer is easily found: Obey the law upon which the receipt of that revelation is predicated. That law is:

1. The Holy Ghost will not dwell in an unclean tabernacle. "The Lord hath said he dwelleth not in unholy temples, but in the hearts of the righteous doth he dwell." (Alma 34:36.)

2. Sins are remitted through faith, repentance, and bap-

tism. Thereby, and thereby only, is the contrite soul made clean so as to become a fit recipient of revelation from the Revelator.

An honest and sincere truth-seeker may receive a flash of revelation from the Holy Ghost telling him that Jesus is the Christ; that Joseph Smith is a prophet of God; that the Lord has restored the fulness of his everlasting gospel in this day; that the Book of Mormon is the mind and will and voice of God to the world today. That blaze of newly encountered light will be as lightning in a night storm; it will show the path leading to the pure light of day; but unless the one receiving the light walks therein, unless he follows the path, he will remain in darkness and lose the new knowledge he was once ready to receive.

In the full and complete sense required to receive enduring revelations of the divine Sonship of our Lord, the Comforter, "whom the world cannot receive" (John 14:17) and whose companionship is reserved for the saints of God, comes only to Church members. It is the faithful only who receive the gift of the Holy Ghost. This gift is the right to the constant companionship of that member of the Godhead. It is received by the laying on of hands following faith and repentance. It is only then that those who love the Lord receive a fulfillment of the promise: "By the power of the Holy Ghost ye may know the truth of all things." (Moro. 10:5.)

To prepare men to receive revelation from the Holy Ghost, the Lord sends forth his Spirit—meaning the Light of Christ, the omnipresent Spirit that quickens the mind and enlightens the intellect, that leads and guides into paths of righteousness, and that entices men to come to the covenant of baptism and receive the gift of the Holy Ghost. (D&C 84:45-58.) Thus the record says of the Nephites in about 78 B.C.: "The Lord did pour out his Spirit on all the face of the land to prepare the minds of the children of men, or to prepare their hearts to receive the word which should be taught among them at the time of his coming—That they might not be hardened against the word, that they might not be unbelieving, and go on to destruction, but that they might receive the word with joy, and as a branch be grafted into the true vine, that they might enter into the rest of the Lord their God." (Alma 16:16-17.) Those who followed the promptings of this Spirit received the gospel, were baptized, gained the gift of the Holy Ghost, and became the recipients of personal revelation concerning Christ and his coming.

When the servants of the Lord preach the gospel by the power of the Holy Ghost to those who have hearkened to the Light of Christ, the persons thus mellowed and prepared receive the truth, repent of their sins, and gain for themselves the gift of the Holy Ghost. When the scripture says, "The Lord God called upon men by the Holy Ghost everywhere and commanded them that they should repent" (Moses 5:14), it means that the Lord called upon them by the mouths of his servants who were inspired and guided by the Holy Ghost, not that unclean persons received the promptings of that Holy Being.

And thus it is that men come to know of "the Messiah who is the Lamb of God, of whom the Holy Ghost beareth record, from the beginning of the world until this time, and from this time henceforth and forever." (1 Ne. 12:18.)

All the Prophets Prophesied of Christ

Man is fallen; man is lost. There is no hope for Adam's seed. Death prevails and darkness reigns. God alone can loose the bands; he alone can break the chains. There must be a Deliverer, a Savior of the world. "How great the importance to make these things known unto the inhabitants of the earth, that they may know that there is no flesh that can dwell in the presence of God, save it be through the merits, and mercy, and grace of the Holy Messiah." (2 Ne. 2:8.) His coming and ministry, the atonement he was to make, the redemption provided through his blood, the resurrection that would pass upon all men because of him, eternal life with the Gods of heaven for all the faithful—these are the things that were the burden of the messages and ministries of all the holy prophets since the world began, even as they are of the prophets and apostles who have come since he ministered among mortal men.

Such sectarian scholars as happen to believe in Messianic prophecies suppose that these divine statements are few in number and came from a comparatively few seeric souls. The fact is, these prophecies are in number as the sands upon the seashore, and those who spoke them are sufficient in number to people cities, populate nations, and cover continents. All of the prophets, all of the ancient preachers of righteousness, all of the citizens of Zion, all of the saints of old, all of those from Adam to John who had the gift of the Holy Ghost—all of these bore testimonies in Messianic terms. They all had a Spirit-borne hope in Christ who was to come, and fortunately some few of them were called to be prophets to the people and have had portions of their words preserved for us.

Nephi speaks of the visions and prophecies of his father, Lehi, who taught that "a prophet would the Lord God raise up among the Jews—even a Messiah, or, in other words, a Savior of the world. And he also spake concerning the prophets, how great a number had testified of these things, concerning this Messiah, of whom he had spoken, or this Redeemer of the world." (1 Ne. 10:4-5.)

Nephi's brother Jacob says of the Nephite people: "We also had many revelations, and the spirit of much prophecy; wherefore, we knew of Christ and his kingdom, which should come." (Jacob 1:6.) "We knew of Christ, and we had a hope of his glory many hundred years before his coming; and not only we ourselves had a hope of his glory, but also all the holy prophets which were before us." (Jacob 4:4.) Then Jacob recites the great and eternal truths pertaining to the atonement, and says: "We are not witnesses alone in these things; for God also spake them unto prophets of old." (Jacob 4:13.) In his contention with the anti-Christ, Sherem, Jacob testified: "None of the prophets have written, nor prophesied, save they have spoken concerning this Christ." (Jacob 7:11.)

As part of one of the greatest sermons ever delivered on the atonement, the angelic preacher said to King Benjamin: "And the Lord God hath sent his holy prophets among all the children of men, to declare these things to every kindred, nation, and tongue, that thereby whosoever should believe that Christ should come, the same might receive remission of their sins, and rejoice with exceeding great joy, even as though he had already come among them." (Mosiah 3:13.)

Abinadi, who had a talent for speaking plainly and bluntly and leaving a testimony that could not be refuted, asked: "Did not Moses prophesy unto them concerning the coming of the Messiah, and that God should redeem his people? Yea, and even all the prophets who have prophesied ever since the world began—have they not spoken more or less concerning these things? Have they not said that God himself should come down among the children of men, and take upon him the form of man, and go forth in mighty power upon the face of the earth? Yea, and have they not said also that he should bring to pass the resurrection of the dead, and that he, himself, should be oppressed and afflicted?" (Mosiah 13:33-35.) "All the holy prophets," he said, "have prophesied concerning the coming of the Lord." (Mosiah 15:11.)

Nephi the son of Helaman comments on the extent of the prophetic witness of our Lord by citing the testimony of Moses and then saying: "Moses did not only testify of these things, but also all the holy prophets, from his days even to the days of Abraham. Yea, and behold, Abraham saw of his coming, and was filled with gladness and did rejoice. Yea, and behold I say unto you, that Abraham not only knew of these things, but there were many before the days of Abraham who were called by the order of God; yea, even after the order of his Son; and this that it should be shown unto the people, a great many thousand years before his coming, that even redemption should come unto them. And now I would that ye should know, that even since the days of Abraham there have been many prophets that have testified these things." He then names Zenos, Zenock, Ezias, Isaiah, and Jeremiah as among the group, and looking back on nearly six hundred years of Nephite history he says further: "Nephi also testified of these things, and also almost all of our fathers, even down to this time; yea, they have testified of the coming of Christ, and have looked forward, and have rejoiced in his day which is to come." (Hel. 8:16-22.)

Peter, our Lord's chief apostle of the last previous dispensation, quoted a Messianic utterance of Moses and then affirmed: "Yea, and all the prophets from Samuel and those that follow after, as many as have spoken, have likewise foretold of these days." (Acts 3:22-24.) On a later occasion, Peter said of his Lord: "To him give all the prophets witness." (Acts 10:43.) And Stephen, with biting irony, said to the murderous mob who made him a martyr: "Which of the prophets have not your fathers persecuted? and they have slain them which shewed before of the coming of the Just One; of whom ye have been now the betrayers and murderers." (Acts 7:52.)

King Messiah Shall Come

We shall now present, prophet by prophet, doctrine by doctrine, and testimony by testimony, a summary of the knowledge revealed to them of old about Him who was to come and redeem his people. By way of introduction, let us name a few of the inspired men of ancient days who knew of the coming of a Messiah and of the salvation that would come because of him. Other prophets will be named and their teachings and testimonies analyzed, as the whole Messianic message is set forth, line upon line and precept upon precept, in succeeding chapters.

Messianic truths were revealed to the first man, and he taught them to his children and wrote them in a Book of Remembrance. His righteous posterity read them in the

79

recorded revelations and prevailed upon God to give them personal prophetic insight. After naming Adam, Seth, Enos, Cainan, Mahalaleel, Jared, and Enoch, the line of prophets through whom priesthood powers and gospel truths descended, the inspired historian Moses concludes: "And they were preachers of righteousness, and spake and prophesied, and called upon all men, everywhere, to repent; and faith was taught unto the children of men." (Moses 6:23.)

Then came the prophets Methuselah, Lamech, and Noah, each in turn, with the scripture saying that "Noah prophesied, and taught the things of God, even as it was in the beginning." (Moses 8:16.) From Noah the prophetic powers passed to Shem and his descendants, including Melchizedek. Up to this point the perfect patriarchal system had prevailed and the prophetic powers and patriarchal priesthood had passed from father to son. Melchizedek conferred the priesthood upon Abraham, and soon it was spread out among peoples and nations of whom we have no knowledge, spread out without apparent reference to the perfect system of patriarchal descent. By way of lineage, it went from Abraham to Isaac, Jacob, Joseph, Ephraim and Manasseh, and to the increasing hosts of Israel. But from Esaias, who lived in the days of Abraham and of whom we know nothing else, it went successively to Gad, Jeremy, Elihu, Caleb, and Jethro, who was the father-in-law of Moses and the one who conferred the priesthood upon Israel's greatest prophet. (D&C 84:5-16.)

All of these, and all of the prophets in Israel, sang the same song, the song of redeeming grace as found in God's own Son. Isaiah, known as the Messianic prophet because of the multitude of his inspired sayings concerning the coming and mission of Israel's God, gave of him, among a host of others, such declarations as these: "I will wait upon the Lord, . . . and I will look for him," he said, after prophesying that some among the Jews would accept him, while to others he would be a stumbling block. (Isa. 8:13-17.) "The Lord cometh," he proclaimed as part of a resurrection passage.

(Isa. 26:19-21.) "Your God will come. . . . He will come and save you," was his reassurance to disconsolate Israel. (Isa. 35:1-10.) "Prepare ye the way of the Lord," for "the Lord God will come with strong hand," was part of his oft-repeated message. (Isa. 40:1-11.) "I the Lord have called thee in righteousness," Isaiah quoted the Father as saying of Christ, "and will hold thine hand, and will keep thee, and give thee for a covenant of the people, for a light of the Gentiles." (Isa. 42:6.) As part of one of his longest and most wondrous prophecies, he affirmed: "Thy God Reigneth! . . . The Lord shall bring again Zion. . . . [He] shall deal prudently, he shall be exalted and extolled, and be very high." (Isa. 52 and 53.)

Other prophets also spoke of his coming. For instance, Haggai said, "The desire of all nations shall come." (Hag. 2:7.) And scattered through the Psalms are great numbers of Spirit-inspired statements such as these: "Blessed be he that cometh in the name of the Lord" (Ps. 118:26), and "Then said I, Lo, I come: in the volume of the book it is written of me, I delight to do thy will, O my God: yea, thy law is within my heart" (Ps. 40:7-8). And it was of this great body of prophetic utterances that he himself spoke when, after his resurrection, he said to his apostles: "All things must be fulfilled, which were written in the law of Moses, and in the prophets, and in the psalms concerning me." (Luke 24:44.)

But all of these Biblical passages are either hidden in difficult contexts, have other matters interwoven with them which open the door to uncertainty as to their real meaning, or have a dual application; that is, they apply both to our Lord's First Coming, when he was subject to mortal men, and to his Second Coming, his glorious appearing, when all men shall be subject unto him. That they might be understood following his mortal ministry among them, the scripture says of his ancient disciples: "Then opened he their understanding, that they might understand the scriptures." (Luke 24:45.)

Nephite Prophets Reveal Christ

It is to our Nephite brethren that we turn for our plain and perfect prophetic utterances about "the Apostle and High Priest of our profession, Christ Jesus." (Heb. 3:1.) By way of illustration only, let us note:

Lehi saw in vision the coming of Christ and the Twelve who ministered with him. He was given a book by a heavenly ministrant, and "the things which he read in the book, manifested plainly of the coming of a Messiah, and also the redemption of the world." (1 Ne. 1:19.)

Nephi had many visions and revelations, and from the knowledge thus gained, he was able to say authoritatively: "The Messiah cometh; . . . and according to the words of the prophets, and also the word of the angel of God, his name shall be Jesus Christ, the Son of God." (2 Ne. 25:19.)

"The great question," as Amulek termed it—and there neither is nor can be a more important one—"is whether the word be in the Son of God, or whether there shall be no Christ." His answer: "The word is in Christ unto salvation." His personal testimony: "These things are true. . . . I do know that Christ shall come among the children of men, to take upon him the transgressions of his people, and that he shall atone for the sins of the world; for the Lord God hath spoken it." (Alma 34:5-8.)

"Believest thou in Jesus Christ, who shall come?" (Alma 45:4.) Such was the question put by Alma to his son Helaman, less than a century before our Lord's birth. As he had borne it to Korihor, Alma's own testimony was: "I know there is a God, and also that Christ shall come." (Alma 30:39.) His similar testimony to his son Corianton was: "I say unto you, that it is he that surely shall come to take away the sins of the world; yea, he cometh to declare glad tidings of salvation unto his people." (Alma 39:15.)

Teaching that salvation was in Christ, and then bearing testimony that such teachings were true, was the perfect missionary approach then as it is now. When Ammon stood before King Lamoni, for instance, "he began at the creation of the world, and also the creation of Adam, and told him all things concerning the fall of man. . . . But this is not all; for he expounded unto them the plan of redemption, which was prepared from the foundation of the world; and he also made known unto them concerning the coming of Christ." (Alma 18:36, 39.) Similarly, when Aaron was doing missionary work among the Lamanites, he asked: "Believest thou that the Son of God shall come to redeem mankind from their sins?" After receiving a negative reply, he "began to open the scriptures unto them concerning the coming of Christ, and also concerning the resurrection of the dead, and that there could be no redemption for mankind save it were through the death and sufferings of Christ, and the atonement of his blood." (Alma 21:7-9.)

When prophets and missionaries bear record of Christ and his gospel, such has the effect of dividing the people. They either believe and obey, or disbelieve and disobey. This is true in and out of the Church. In Alma's day, many who belonged to the Church itself had a spirit of disbelief and rebellion, "and the wickedness of the church was a great stumbling-block to those who did not belong to the church; and thus the church began to fail in its progress." This spirit of iniquity encouraged nonmembers of the Church in courses of evil, until the whole Nephite nation was full of corruption. "Now this was a great cause for lamentations among the people, while others were abasing themselves, succoring those who stood in need of their succor, such as imparting their substance to the poor and the needy, feeding the hungry, and suffering all manner of afflictions, for Christ's sake, who should come according to the spirit of prophecy; Looking forward to that day, thus retaining a remission of their sins; being filled with great joy because of the resurrection of the dead, according to the will and power and deliverance of Jesus Christ from the bands of death." (Alma 4:10-14.) What an effect the preaching of the word has upon the righteous! And the unrighteous!

Chapter 6

MESSIAH REVEALED IN ALL THE WORLD

Witnesses Testify of Christ

In this mortal probation it is the design and purpose of the Lord to test us: to see if we will believe in him and obey his laws now that we no longer dwell in his presence, hear his voice, and see his face. He already knows how we respond—what we believe and how we act—when we walk by sight. Now he is testing our devotion to him when we walk by faith: when his presence is veiled, his voice is afar off, and his face is seen by few men only.

Accordingly, he has ordained the law of witnesses, the law whereby he reveals himself to prophets and righteous men and sends them forth to teach his laws and bear testimony of their truth and divinity. "In the mouth of two or three witnesses shall every word be established." (2 Cor. 13:1.) "Whether by mine own voice or by the voice of my servants, it is the same." (D&C 1:38.)

This law of witnesses is described by Isaiah in a glorious prophecy about the gathering of Israel and the spread of truth in the last days. In so applying the law he is simply projecting to a future dispensation the principles that were in full operation in his own day, and for that matter had been binding upon his forebears back to the first man. "I am the Lord thy God, the Holy One of Israel, thy Saviour," was the voice of Israel's God to Isaiah. Then came the prophecy: "I will bring thy seed from the east, and gather thee from the west." I will "bring my sons from far, and my daughters from the ends of the earth; Even every one that is called by my name." That is, in the last days Israel shall be gathered again, and those who come to a knowledge of their true Messiah shall take upon them his name and become members of his family. To them, as Isaiah records it, comes this promise and directive: "Ye are my witnesses, saith the Lord, . . . ye may know and believe me, and understand that I am he. . . . I, even I, am the Lord; and beside me there is no saviour. . . . Ye are my witnesses, saith the Lord, that I am God." (Isa. 43:3-12.)

Christ and his laws are known to and taught by witnesses. Salvation was made available before his coming by those who testified that they knew he would come to redeem his people. Salvation has been made available since his coming by those who now testify that he has come and shed his blood in an infinite and eternal atoning sacrifice. The Israelites of old carried with them in the wilderness a portable tabernacle, the tabernacle of the congregation, a place of worship. To signify its use and purpose, it was named "the tent of testimony" (Num. 9:15), or "the tabernacle of witness" (Num. 17:7). Therein testimony was borne of the coming of the Messiah.

Those of us today in whose veins the blood of Father Jacob flows, who are of the blood lineage of those who moved with Moses from Egypt toward their promised land, have built our synagogues, as it were, our houses of worship, wherein we teach and testify of him who has now come and whose redeeming blood has been shed for all those who have faith in him. Our houses of worship are the tents of testimony and the tabernacle of witness of the last days. And our missionaries, who are witnesses, bear—on the streets, in the homes, at whatever place people are found—the same testimony of the divine Sonship that was borne by their counterparts of old.

Scriptures Testify of Christ

There is no way to overstate the importance of a written language and of having scriptural accounts that preserve the knowledge that God has revealed to prophets both past and present. Civilization could not exist without a written language. By the simple process of erasing all writing and of ceasing to teach people to write, civilization would end in one generation. All of earth's inhabitants would sink into that social and cultural limbo possessed by the pygmies in the African jungles.

As society is now constituted, and under the circumstances in which men now dwell on earth, salvation could not be made available without written scripture. If men could neither read nor write—and as a consequence God's holy word was not available to guide them—the hope of salvation would cease except to those prophets to whom God and angels appear, plus such as could personally hear their voices and be baptized by them. For all practical purposes the spread of saving truth would cease and Satan would come off triumphant in the warfare for the souls of men.

And so, from the beginning, the Lord provided a language and gave men the power to read and write. "It was given unto as many as called upon God to write by the spirit of inspiration. And by them their children were taught to read and write, having a language which was pure and undefiled." (Moses 6:5-6.) The thing which they first wrote, and which of all their writings was of the most worth unto them, was a Book of Remembrance, a book in which they recorded what the Lord had revealed about himself, about his coming, and about the plan of salvation, which plan would have force and validity because of his atonement. This was the beginning of the Holy Scriptures, than which inspired writing there is nothing that is more important.

"The law of the Lord is perfect, converting the soul: the testimony of the Lord is sure, making wise the simple. The statutes of the Lord are right, rejoicing the heart: the commandment of the Lord is pure, enlightening the eyes. The fear of the Lord is clean, enduring for ever: the judgments of the Lord are true and righteous altogether. More to be desired are they than gold, yea, than much fine gold: sweeter also than honey and the honeycomb. Moreover by them is thy servant warned: and in keeping of them there is great reward." (Ps. 19:7-11.)

Jesus said: "Search the scriptures; for . . . they are they which testify of me." (John 5:39.) What better use can language be put than to use it as a vehicle to gain a knowledge of Christ? Of certain devout and honest truth seekers of Paul's day, it is written: "They received the word with all readiness of mind, and searched the scriptures daily." (Acts 17:11.) Should our search for salvation be any less intensive than theirs?

After quoting extensively from Isaiah, Jesus also said: "Ye ought to search these things. Yea, a commandment I give unto you that ye search these things diligently; for great are the words of Isaiah." Then he said: "Write the things which I have told you; and according to the time and the will of the Father they shall go forth unto the Gentiles." At this point he expanded his counsel that his people should be gospel scholars: "Search the prophets, for many there be that testify of these things." And finally, making himself the Perfect Pattern, he "expounded all the scriptures unto them which they had received" and commanded them to write "other scriptures" which had not previously been preserved according to his mind and purpose.

"And now it came to pass that when Jesus had said these words he said unto them again, after he had expounded all the scriptures unto them which they had received, he said unto them: Behold, other scriptures I would that ye should write, that ye have not. And it came to pass that he said unto Nephi: Bring forth the record which ye have kept. And when Nephi had brought forth the records, and laid them before him, he cast his eyes upon them and said: Verily I say unto you, I commanded my servant Samuel, the Lamanite, that

87

he should testify unto this people, that at the day that the Father should glorify his name in me that there were many saints who should arise from the dead, and should appear unto many, and should minister unto them. And he said unto them: Was it not so? And his disciples answered him and said: Yea, Lord, Samuel did prophesy according to thy words, and they were all fulfilled. And Jesus said unto them: How be it that ye have not written this thing, that many saints did arise and appear unto many and did minister unto them? And it came to pass that Nephi remembered that this thing had not been written. And it came to pass that Jesus commanded that it should be written; therefore it was written according as he commanded. And now it came to pass that when Jesus had expounded all the scriptures in one, which they had written, he commanded them that they should teach the things which he had expounded unto them." (3 Ne. 23:1-14.)

A perfect illustration of the blessings that flow to a nation and people who have the scriptures and search them is seen in the account of the Nephites, an account that tells of their problems, sorrows, triumphs, and final destruction. When Nephi and his brethren went back to Jerusalem to get the brass plates from Laban, Nephi said: "It is wisdom in God that we should obtain these records, that we may preserve unto our children the language of our fathers; And also that we may preserve unto them the words which have been spoken by the mouth of all the holy prophets, which have been delivered unto them by the Spirit and power of God, since the world began, even down unto this present time." (1 Ne. 3:19-20.)

Without question the revealed accounts on these plates of brass—and "they did contain the five books of Moses, which gave an account of the creation of the world, and also of Adam and Eve, who were our first parents; And also a record of the Jews from the beginning, even down to the commencement of the reign of Zedekiah, king of Judah; And also the prophecies of the holy prophets, from the beginning, even down to the commencement of the reign of Zedekiah; and also many prophecies which have been spoken by the mouth of Jeremiah," including a genealogy of Lehi's fathers (1 Ne. 5:10-14)—without question these accounts contained that guidance which led generation after generation of people to walk in paths of truth and righteousness. A part of their use and value was summarized by Alma as he spoke to his son Helaman: "It has hitherto been wisdom in God that these things should be preserved; for behold, they have enlarged the memory of this people, yea, and convinced many of the error of their ways, and brought them to the knowledge of their God unto the salvation of their souls. Yea, I say unto you, were it not for these things that these records do contain, which are on these plates, Ammon and his brethren could not have convinced so many thousands of the Lamanites of the incorrect tradition of their fathers; yea, these records and their words brought them unto repentance; that is, they brought them to the knowledge of the Lord their God, and to rejoice in Jesus Christ their Redeemer." (Alma 37:8-9).

Similarly, for nearly four hundred years the King James Version of the Bible has been one of the most stabilizing forces in all Christendom. It has been one of the chief means of preserving the English language as such; but more than this, it has kept right principles before millions of people who have been and are without personal contact with the prophets and witnesses who teach personally the Lord's message of salvation to his earthly children.

In contrast, the Lamanites and the Mulekites dwindled in unbelief and apostasy because they did not have the holy scriptures to guide them. King Benjamin, speaking of the brass plates, said to his sons: "Were it not for these plates, which contain these records and these commandments, we must have suffered in ignorance, even at this present time, not knowing the mysteries of God. For it were not possible that our father, Lehi, could have remembered all these things, to have taught them to his children, except it were for the help of these plates; for he having been taught in the language of the Egyptians therefore he could read these engravings, and teach them to his children, that thereby they could teach them to their children, and so fulfilling the commandments of God, even down to this present time. I say unto you, my sons, were it not for these things, which have been kept and preserved by the hand of God, that we might read and understand of his mysteries, and have his commandments always before our eyes, that even our fathers would have dwindled in unbelief, and we should have been like unto our brethren, the Lamanites, who know nothing concerning these things, or even do not believe them when they are taught them, because of the traditions of their fathers, which are not correct." (Mosiah 1:3-5.)

As to the Mulekites, they followed Mulek the son of King Zedekiah from Jerusalem to the Western Hemisphere; and when they were discovered by Mosiah and his people, "their language had become corrupted; and they had brought no records with them; and they denied the being of their Creator." (Omni 17.) What a contrast this is with the Nephite peoples whose forebears said: "We talk of Christ, we rejoice in Christ, we preach of Christ, we prophesy of Christ, and we write according to our prophecies, that our children may know to what source they may look for a remission of their sins." (2 Ne. 25:26.)

The Book of Mormon Testifies of Christ

For the first four thousand years of earth's temporal continuance the prophetic writings, of which the Old Testament is a fragmentary part, contained Deity's doctrine about the Messiah and the plan of salvation. During this period the Jaredite scriptures and much of the Nephite record were composed and used; also, many prophets kept sacred accounts of what the Lord revealed to them, of which accounts we have little or no knowledge.

During and after our Lord's ministry on earth the New

Testament record came into being, along with that portion of the Book of Mormon starting with Third Nephi. The Book of Mormon, however, does not contain "even a hundredth part of the things which Jesus did truly teach unto the people." (3 Ne. 26:6.) And the Beloved John gives us to understand that the New Testament preserves for us only a drop of the great ocean of our Lord's Old World teachings. (John 20:30-31; 21:25.)

Each part of the prophetic writings has come forth for the guidance of those then living and those who thereafter should be privileged to study and ponder its contents. But the amount of Holy Writ that the Lord makes available in any given day depends upon the spiritual status of the people then living. As Alma said: "It is given unto many to know the mysteries of God; nevertheless they are laid under a strict command that they shall not impart only according to the portion of his word which he doth grant unto the children of men, according to the heed and diligence which they give unto him. And therefore, he that will harden his heart, the same receiveth the lesser portion of the word; and he that will not harden his heart, to him is given the greater portion of the word, until it is given unto him to know the mysteries of God until he know them in full. And they that will harden their hearts, to them is given the lesser portion of the word until they know nothing concerning his mysteries; and then they are taken captive by the devil, and led by his will down to destruction." (Alma 12:9-11.)

Thus, for instance, we have that knowledge about the three degrees of glory which is written in section 76, but we do not have a full understanding of those kingdoms of eternal glory, "which surpass all understanding in glory, and in might, and in dominion." Such added knowledge was received by the Prophet and Sidney Rigdon, but they were forbidden to write it, and it is "not lawful for man to utter." (D&C 76:114-19.)

Although we do not have a fraction of the teachings of the Resurrected Lord to the Nephites, "the plates of Nephi do contain the more part of the things which he taught the people." (3 Ne. 26:7.) If and when we ever receive these added truths depends upon us. In making his abridgment of the ancient records, Mormon said of those living in our day: "When they shall have received this, which is expedient that they should have first, to try their faith, and if it shall so be that they shall believe these things then shall the greater things be made manifest unto them. And if it so be that they will not believe these things, then shall the greater things be withheld from them, unto their condemnation. Behold, I was about to write them, all which were engraven upon the plates of Nephi, but the Lord forbade it, saying: I will try the faith of my people." (3 Ne. 26:9-11.)

On this same basis the Lord withheld from the Nephites who lived before his birth the Messianic knowledge he had given the Jaredites. "Thou shalt not suffer these things which ye have seen and heard to go forth unto the world," he told the brother of Jared, "until the time cometh that I shall glorify my name in the flesh." (Ether 3:21.) When Moroni made his abridgment of the book of Ether, he kept these same things back so that they are not known unto us. "They shall not go forth unto the Gentiles," he wrote, "until the day that they shall repent of their iniquity, and become clean before the Lord. And in that day that they shall exercise faith in me, saith the Lord, even as the brother of Jared did, that they may become sanctified in me, then will I manifest unto them the things which the brother of Jared saw, even to the unfolding unto them all my revelations, saith Jesus Christ, the Son of God, the Father of the heavens and of the earth, and all things that in them are." (Ether 4:6-7.)

Now, these comments about the canon of scripture of the past and of the present bring us to this point of understanding, namely, that the Book of Mormon is that portion of the Lord's word which he has preserved for our day to introduce and establish his work. As a source for testimony about Christ, and as a source for an understanding of the plain and simple doctrines of salvation, the Book of Mormon surpasses any scripture now available to men. We have already seen, and shall yet hereafter see more fully, the purity, perfection, and beauty of the Messianic message found in these writings of Nephite origin.

As early as the day of Enoch, the Lord made this promise: "Righteousness will I send down out of heaven; and truth will I send forth out of the earth, to bear testimony of mine Only Begotten; his resurrection from the dead; yea, and also the resurrection of all men." (Moses 7:62.) The same thought, written by the Psalmist, with reference to the Book of Mormon, came forth as: "Truth shall spring out of the earth; and righteousness shall look down from heaven." (Ps. 85:11.) And on the title page of the book itself, in language coined by Moroni, the announcement is made that it shall come forth "to the convincing of the Jew and Gentile that Jesus is the Christ, the Eternal God, manifesting himself unto all nations."

Our course, then, is clear. It is incumbent upon us to believe the Book of Mormon, to rivet its truths in our souls, to accept them without reservation, to ponder their deep and hidden meanings, and to live in harmony with them. Then, and then only, shall we receive the added words spoken by Jesus to the Nephites, and the added teachings had by the Jaredites.

Messianic Knowledge Revealed in All Nations

Most Christians assume, falsely, that such slivers of Messianic knowledge as they suppose were known of old were reserved for and had by a few patriarchs, a few prophets, and a limited number of the so-called chosen race. But such is not the Lord's manner and way of dealing with the races of men. All men are precious in his sight; and in the providences of the Father of us all, and on his own timetable, salvation is made available to every living soul from the first to the last man. There is a destined day, either in this life or the next, either in mortality or in the world of spirits while awaiting a resurrection, when all men shall have borne to them the witness of the living Lord. "The voice of the Lord is unto all men, and there is none to escape; and there is no eye that shall not see, neither ear that shall not hear, neither heart that shall not be penetrated." (D&C 1:2.) "And he inviteth them all to come unto him and partake of his goodness; and he denieth none that come unto him, black and white, bond and free, male and female, and he remembereth the heathen; and all are alike unto God, both Jew and Gentile." (2 Ne. 26:33.)

Here and now, while in the flesh, the word of revealed truth is destined to go, in one form or another, to far more of our Father's children than some may have supposed. "The voice of warning shall be unto all people," the Lord says, "by the mouths of my disciples, whom I have chosen in these last days." (D&C 1:4.)

Moroni wrote on the title page of the Book of Mormon, "Jesus is the Christ, the Eternal God, manifesting himself unto all nations." That is, Christ manifests himself unto all nations, both unto the Jews and unto the Gentiles. Speaking of the fact that the Jews would reject and crucify the Messiah and would then be scattered by other nations, Nephi says: "And after they have been scattered, and the Lord God hath scourged them by other nations for the space of many generations, yea, even down from generation to generation until they shall be persuaded to believe in Christ, the Son of God, and the atonement, which is infinite for all mankind—and when that day shall come that they shall believe in Christ, and worship the Father in his name, with pure hearts and clean hands, and look not forward any more for another Messiah, then, at that time, the day will come that it must needs be expedient that they should believe these things." (2 Ne. 25:16.) As to the revelation of the knowledge of Christ to the Gentiles, Nephi says: "As I spake concerning the convincing of the Jews, that Jesus is the very Christ, it must needs be that the Gentiles be convinced also that Jesus is the Christ, the Eternal God; And that he manifesteth himself unto all those who believe in him, by the power of the Holy Ghost; yea, unto every nation, kindred, tongue, and people, working mighty miracles, signs, and wonders, among the children of men according to their faith." (2 Ne. 26:12-13.)

By revelation to Nephi, the Lord proclaimed the same truth. "I speak the same words unto one nation like unto another," he said. "For behold, I shall speak unto the Jews and they shall write it; and I shall also speak unto the Nephites and they shall write it; and I shall also speak unto the other tribes of the house of Israel, which I have led away, and they shall write it; and I shall also speak unto all nations of the earth and they shall write it." (2 Ne. 29:8-12.) Certainly the United States of America is a nation to which God hath spoken in our day through Joseph Smith, Jr., his prophet and seer. And certainly, for that matter, that same prophet has spoken to all the nations of the earth, inviting their inhabitants to repent and believe the restored gospel and thus become heirs of salvation in the kingdom of heaven.

As the day of our Lord's mortal birth drew nigh, and as it was requisite that men should repent and gain salvation, Alma was caused by the Spirit to say: "The voice of the Lord, by the mouth of angels, doth declare it unto all nations; yea, doth declare it, that they may have glad tidings of great joy; yea, and he doth sound these glad tidings among all his people, yea, even to them that are scattered abroad upon the face of the earth; wherefore they have come unto us. And they are made known unto us in plain terms, that we may understand, that we cannot err; and this because of our being wanderers in a strange land; therefore, we are thus highly favored, for we have these glad tidings declared unto us in all parts of our vineyard." (Alma 13:22-23.)

The issue is not whether the Lord manifests himself unto all nations, but how and to what extent he does so. It is clear that angels minister to the faithful, that the Holy Ghost is poured out upon all those who believe and obey, and that

95

the visions of eternity are opened to those who abide the laws entitling them so to receive. But there are also some preparatory works done among and for those who are not yet prepared to receive the full message of salvation. Alma, whose desire was to cry repentance in plain language to every soul, came to know that some other things had to precede his pure testimony. "The Lord doth grant unto all nations," Alma said, "of their own nation and tongue, to teach his word, yea, in wisdom, all that he seeth fit that they should have; therefore we see that the Lord doth counsel in wisdom, according to that which is just and true." (Alma 29:8.)

For our day it seems clear that one of the ways in which the Lord sends his word forth in all nations is to make the Bible available to them. Of itself this volume of ancient scripture bears witness of Christ, teaches his doctrines, and leads good people everywhere to live by higher standards. But what is equally, perhaps even more, important in the long run is that the Bible prepares men for the Book of Mormon and therefore for belief in living prophets who have power both to teach the truth and to administer the ordinances of salvation. Truly we are coming nearer and nearer to that day spoken of by the angel to King Benjamin, "when the knowledge of the Savior shall spread throughout every nation, kindred, tongue, and people." (Mosiah 3:20.)

Messianic Prophecies Fulfilled in Christ

From what has already been set forth, from our overall knowledge of the plan of salvation, and from the expressions set forth in the Messianic prophecies themselves, it is self-evident that they all found fulfillment in our Lord's coming. Perhaps these plain statements of the Resurrected Lord to the Nephites will show the seal of divine approval that accompanies Messianic utterances:

"I came unto mine own, and my own received me not. And the scriptures concerning my coming are fulfilled. . . .

96

By me redemption cometh, and in me is the law of Moses fulfilled." (3 Ne. 9:16-17.)

"They saw a Man descending out of heaven; and he was clothed in a white robe; and he came down and stood in the midst of them; and the eyes of the whole multitude were turned upon him, and they durst not open their mouths, even one to another, and wist not what it meant, for they thought it was an angel that had appeared unto them. And it came to pass that he stretched forth his hand and spake unto the people, saying: Behold, I am Jesus Christ, whom the prophets testified shall come into the world." (3 Ne. 11:8-10.)

"Behold, I have given unto you the commandments; therefore keep my commandments. And this is the law and the prophets, for they truly testified of me." (3 Ne. 15:10.)

"I am he of whom Moses spake. . . . Yea, and all the prophets from Samuel and those that follow after, as many as have spoken, have testified of me." (3 Ne. 20:23-24.)

And so it is that all the prophets testify of Christ; and so it is that all their prophecies were fulfilled in Jesus of Nazareth; and so it is that "by denying him ye also deny the prophets and the law." (2 Ne. 25:28.)

Chapter 7

MESSIAH IS GOD

Christ Is the Lord God Omnipotent

Christ-Messiah is God!

Such is the plain and pure pronouncement of all the prophets of all the ages. In our desire to avoid the false and absurd conclusions contained in the creeds of Christendom, we are wont to shy away from this pure and unadorned verity; we go to great lengths to use language that shows there is both a Father and a Son, that they are separate Persons and are not somehow mystically intertwined as an essence or spirit that is everywhere present. Such an approach is perhaps essential in reasoning with the Gentiles of sectarianism; it helps to overthrow the fallacies formulated in their creeds.

But having so done, if we are to envision our Lord's true status and glory, we must come back to the pronouncement of pronouncements, the doctrine of doctrines, the message of messages, which is that Christ is God. And if it were not so, he could not save us. Let all men, both in heaven and on earth, hear the proclamation and rejoice in its eternal verity: "The Lord is God, and beside him there is no Savior." (D&C 76:1.)

Without the need to explain away the vagaries found in the writings of uninspired men, those who knew by personal revelation what the fact is have left us such statements as these:

Both Nephi and Moroni testified: "Jesus is the Christ, the Eternal God." (2 Ne. 26:12; Title Page, Book of Mormon.)

Nephi also said: "There is a God, and he is Christ, and he cometh in the fulness of his own time." (2 Ne. 11:7.) "The Jews," he said, "shall crucify him—for thus it behooveth our God, and there is none other nation on earth that would crucify their God." (2 Ne. 10:3.) For truly, Nephi explains, "The Lord God . . . layeth down his own life that he may draw all men unto him." (2 Ne. 26:23-24.)

The angelic ministrant who taught King Benjamin the doctrine of the atonement called Christ "The Lord Omnipotent who reigneth, who was, and is from all eternity to all eternity" (Mosiah 3:5), and King Benjamin spoke of him as "Christ, the Lord God Omnipotent" (Mosiah 5:15).

Moses taught "concerning the coming of the Messiah, and that God should redeem his people," and Abinadi said that "God himself should come down among the children of men, and take upon him the form of man." (Mosiah 13:33-34.) Yea, "God himself shall come down among the children of men," Abinadi prophesied, "and shall redeem his people" (Mosiah 15:1; 17:8), and Nephi said this deliverance should be made by "the Mighty God" (2 Ne 6:17), which title was also used by Isaiah in prophesying of his birth into mortality (Isa. 9:6).

"God will redeem my soul from the power of the grave," said David. (Ps. 49:15.) "God himself atoneth for the sins of the world" is the inspired word given by Alma. (Alma 42:15.) Nephi the son of Helaman, just a score of years before the birth of Christ, said of the Nephite prophets who preceded him: They "have testified of the coming of Christ, and have looked forward, and have rejoiced in his day which is to come. And behold, he is God." (Hel. 8:22-23.) And when the Risen Lord did minister among the Nephites, he called himself "The Lord their God, who hath redeemed them." (3 Ne. 20:13.)

"Prepare ye the way of the Lord," proclaimed Isaiah. "Say unto the cities of Judah, Behold your God! Behold, the

Lord God will come with strong hand. . . . He shall feed his flock like a shepherd." (Isa. 40:3-11.)

And after his coming the prophets and seers were still acclaiming, "Alleluia: for the Lord God omnipotent reigneth." (Rev. 19:6.)

Truly, Christ is God. Thus it is written, and thus it is.

Christ Is the Lord Jehovah

Christ is Jehovah!

Among those whose source of religious knowledge is the intellect and not the spirit of revelation, it is falsely supposed that the designations *Father, Son*, and *Holy Ghost* are three terms identifying the same incomprehensible spirit essence, which is everywhere and nowhere in particular present, and which they assume is God. This is untrue. The fact is, and Holy Writ so avers, that the three members of the Godhead are separate and distinct Persons; that they have their own bodies, occupy identifiable space, and are in one place only at a given time.

Being thus aware of how far astray the religious intellectualists have gone in defining their three-in-one God, it comes as no surprise to learn that they thrash around in the same darkness in trying to identify Elohim and Jehovah and to show their relationship to the promised Messiah. Some sectarians even believe that Jehovah is the Supreme Deity whose Son came into mortality as the Only Begotten. As with their concept that God is a Spirit, this misinformation about the Gods of Heaven is untrue. The fact is, and it too is attested by Holy Writ, that Elohim is the Father, and that Jehovah is the Son who was born into mortality as the Lord Jesus Christ, the promised Messiah.

As Paul said of those in his day, that "in the wisdom of God the world by wisdom knew not God" (1 Cor. 1:21), so say we of all those in our day who seek God by study and research alone. He is not to be discovered by an archaeologist's pick, a translator's interpretation of an ancient text, nor a theologian's imagination about how he was named and known by them of old. God is and can be known only by revelation; the wisdom of the wise does not make him manifest, and all the conjecture and debate as to how this or that ancient name-title should be translated is as naught compared to one plain inspired utterance. These utterances we have, and because of them we know what was meant by the ancient prophets when they spoke of him under his name Jehovah. The Almighty has such names as he has, and these are known to man only when he reveals them. We shall now, by way of illustration only and without any attempt at comprehensive coverage, note some of the revealed truths showing that Jehovah and Christ are one and the same person, the Eternal Son of the Eternal Father.

Jehovah Sits on the Right Hand of God

Of whom spake David when his tongue was touched by the Holy Spirit and he testified, "The Lord said unto my Lord, Sit thou at my right hand, until I make thine enemies thy footstool"? (Ps. 110:1.) Two Lords are here involved: one is speaking to the other; one is greater than the other; one is making provision for the triumph and glory of the other. Who are they and what message is contained in this Messianic prophecy?

"What think ye of Christ?" our Lord asked certain of his detractors toward the end of his mortal ministry. "Whose son is he?" Is Christ the Son of God or of someone else? Is he to be born of a divine Parent or will he be as other men—a mortal son of a mortal father? That he was to be a descendant of David was a matter of great pride to all the Jews. And so they answered, "The Son of David."

David's son? Truly he was. But he was more, much more. And so our Lord, with irrefutable logic and to their complete discomfiture, asked, "How then doth David in spirit call him Lord, saying, The Lord said unto my Lord, Sit thou on my right hand, till I make thine enemies thy footstool? If David then call him Lord, how is he his son?" That is, if he is only the Son of David, how is it that the great King, acting under inspiration, calls him Lord and worships him as such? And we might add: Who is the other Lord, the one who spake unto David's Lord? Can there be any question as to how Jesus is interpreting the words of the Psalm? He is saying that it means: 'The Father said unto the Son, Elohim said unto Jehovah, sit thou on my right hand, until after your mortal ministry; then I will raise you up to eternal glory and exaltation with me, where you will continue to sit on my right hand forever.' Is it any wonder that the inspired account concludes the matter by saying, "And no man was able to answer him a word, neither durst any man from that day forth ask him any more questions." (Matt. 22:41-46.)

Peter gave precisely this same inspired interpretation of David's declaration. As to the Lord Jehovah being the Son of David, Peter said: "God had sworn with an oath to him, that of the fruit of his loins, according to the flesh, he would raise up Christ to sit on his throne." But as to this same Lord Jesus' status as the Son of God, Peter testified that Jesus had come forth from the tomb and that he had then been exalted "by the right hand of God," even as David had prophesied in the Psalm, which prophecy Peter then quoted, concluding with his own testimony: "Therefore let all the house of Israel know assuredly, that God hath made that same Jesus, whom ye have crucified, both Lord and Christ." (Acts 2:22-36.)

That this same Jesus, "when he had by himself purged our sins," did in fact sit "down on the right hand of the Majesty on high" (Heb. 1:3) is abundantly testified to by many prophets. Paul says he is the one of whom David spoke who should sit on the Lord's right hand. (Heb. 1:13; 8:1; 12:2.) Stephen, "being full of the Holy Ghost, looked up stedfastly into heaven, and saw the glory of God, and Jesus standing on the right hand of God." And then, dying a martyr's death, he passed to his reward with this testimony on his lips: "Behold, I see the heavens opened, and the Son of man standing on the right hand of God." (Acts 7:55-56.)

And that the same witness might be had in our day, Joseph Smith wrote by way of prophecy and revelation: "He was crucified, died, and rose again the third day; And ascended into heaven, to sit down on the right hand of the Father, to reign with almighty power according to the will of the Father." (D&C 20:23-24.)

Jehovah Is the Great I Am

Out of the bush that burned and was not consumed, God spoke unto Moses, identifying himself as "the God of thy father, the God of Abraham, the God of Isaac, and the God of Jacob," and commanded him to deliver Israel from her Egyptian bondage. "When I come unto the children of Israel," Moses said, "and shall say unto them, The God of your fathers hath sent me unto you; and they shall say to me, What is his name? what shall I say unto them?" Then the Eternal One, the Great Jehovah, he who has neither beginning of days nor end of years, replied: I AM THAT I AM. . . . Thus shalt thou say unto the children of Israel, I AM hath sent me unto you." Lest there be any misunderstanding, and to reassure Israel that the Everlasting God, whose course is one eternal round, who is "from everlasting to everlasting" (Ps. 90:2), was in fact the same God who had appeared to Abraham their father, he also said: "Thus shalt thou say unto the children of Israel, The Lord God of your fathers, the God of Abraham, the God of Isaac, and the God of Jacob, hath sent me unto you: this is my name for ever, and this is my memorial unto all generations." (Ex. 3:2-15.)

In his mortal ministry, our Lord announced to the Jews that he was the Great I AM. When they refused to countenance this claim, as we shall set forth more fully under the heading "Jehovah's Birth, Death, and Resurrection Revealed to Abraham," he responded, "Before Abraham was, I am." (John 8:57-58.) That is: 'Before Abraham, was I AM; before Abraham, was I Jehovah; before Abraham, was I the Eternal One, for I am the Everlasting God.' And in our day,

103

his prophet, the same unchanging Being said:
nd listen to the voice of him who is from all
all eternity, the Great I AM, even Jesus
~~~~~. (D&C 39:1.)

Jehovah Appeared to Abraham and the Prophets

When Satan's minions, in the guise of priests of Pharaoh, sought to sacrifice Abraham to their false gods, the Father of the Faithful pleaded with his God for deliverance. "I lifted up my voice unto the Lord my God," Abraham said, "and the Lord hearkened and heard, and he filled me with the vision of the Almighty. . . . And his voice was unto me: Abraham, Abraham, behold, my name is Jehovah, and I have heard thee, and have come down to deliver thee. . . . I will lead thee by my hand, and I will take thee, to put upon thee my name, even the Priesthood of thy father, and my power shall be over thee. As it was with Noah so shall it be with thee; but through thy ministry my name shall be known in the earth forever, for I am thy God." (Abr. 1:15-19.)

Referring back to this and other appearances to the ancient patriarchs, it is written: "And God spake unto Moses, and said unto him, I am the Lord; And I appeared unto Abraham, unto Isaac, and unto Jacob. I am the Lord God Almighty; the Lord JEHOVAH. And was not my name known unto them?" (JST, Ex. 6:2-3.)

Appearances of Jehovah to prophets and righteous men have been many. Three of them deserve special note because they contain descriptive detail of his person, and they tie together the fact that the spirit Jehovah who is Christ, and the resurrected Jehovah who is Christ, are one and the same person.

One account says: "Moses, and Aaron, Nadab, and Abihu, and seventy of the elders of Israel" went up into the mount. "And they saw the God of Israel: and there was under his feet as it were a paved work of a sapphire stone, and as it were the body of heaven in his clearness." (Ex. 24:9-10.)

The next account tells us what happened on Patmos, a bare island in the Aegean Sea, where the Beloved Revelator had been banished "for the word of God, and for the testimony of Jesus Christ." Being "in the Spirit on the Lord's day," John saw "one like unto the Son of man. . . . His head and his hairs were white like wool, as white as snow, and his eyes were as a flame of fire; And his feet like unto fine brass, as if they burned in a furnace; and his voice as the sound of many waters. . . . His countenance was as the sun shineth in his strength." Of this vision John says: "When I saw him, I fell at his feet as dead. And he laid his right hand upon me, saying unto me, Fear not; I am the first and the last: I am he that liveth, and was dead; and, behold, I am alive for evermore." (Rev. 1:9-18.)

And the final account, for us the most glorious of all, was vouchsafed to Joseph Smith and Oliver Cowdery in the Kirtland Temple on April 3, 1836. "The veil was taken from our minds, and the eyes of our understanding were opened," the scriptural record recites. "We saw the Lord standing upon the breastwork of the pulpit, before us; and under his feet was a paved work of pure gold, in color like amber. His eyes were as a flame of fire; the hair of his head was white like the pure snow; his countenance shone above the brightness of the sun; and his voice was as the sound of the rushing of great waters, even the voice of Jehovah, saying: I am the first and the last; I am he who liveth, I am he who was slain; I am your advocate with the Father." (D&C 110:1-4.)

Jehovah Gave His Gospel to Abraham

We speak of the gospel of the Lord Jesus Christ. We teach that it is the great plan of salvation which is made operative through the atoning sacrifice of the Son of God, and that salvation is in Christ.

We might with equal propriety speak of the gospel of the Lord Jehovah. We might appropriately teach, as they did anciently, that this very plan of salvation, this everlasting and unchanging gospel, centers in the atonement of the Son of Elohim, and that salvation is in Jehovah.

Abraham—and for that matter all the prophets and patriarchs from Adam to Moses, plus many thereafter—had the gospel. What gospel? The gospel of the Lord Jehovah who is Christ and in whose name alone salvation comes. "The Lord appeared unto me," Abraham records. "I am the Lord thy God," he said. "I dwell in heaven; the earth is my footstool; I stretch my hand over the sea, and it obeys my voice; I cause the wind and the fire to be my chariot; I say to the mountains—Depart hence—and behold, they are taken away by a whirlwind, in an instant, suddenly. My name is Jehovah, and I know the end from the beginning; therefore my hand shall be over thee."

Then came the promises that the Lord would make of Abraham a great nation, that in him and in his seed all generations would be blessed, and that his seed "shall bear this ministry and Priesthood unto all nations." Included in this Abrahamic covenant was the Lord's promise: "As many as receive this Gospel shall be called after thy name, and shall be accounted thy seed, and shall rise up and bless thee, as their father," and that through his seed "shall all the families of the earth be blessed, even with the blessings of the Gospel, which are the blessings of salvation, even of life eternal." (Abr. 2:6-11.)

Knowing of these promises given of old by the Lord Jehovah to Abraham, Paul, a special witness of the Lord Jesus Christ, said, "They which are of faith, the same are the children of Abraham," and "God . . . preached before the gospel unto Abraham. . . . They which be of faith are blessed with faithful Abraham." Paul's conclusion: "If ye be Christ's, then are ye Abraham's seed, and heirs according to the promise." (Gal. 3:7-29.)

Jehovah Gave His Gospel to Moses

As those who are spiritually literate well know, the plan of salvation, which is the gospel, has been revealed to man in successive ages or dispensations beginning with Adam and going down through Enoch, Noah, Abraham, Moses, and many others. We shall, under the next heading, "Jehovah Led Israel," quote Paul's Spirit-given declaration that it was Christ who went before Israel in a cloud by day and a pillar of fire by night. (1 Cor. 10:1-4.) But let us now, for the record, point to his Bible-located statement in which he taught that the saints of Moses' day had the same plan of salvation offered to them that Christ and the apostles had given to the saints in the meridian of time. "For unto us was the gospel preached, as well as unto them: but the word preached did not profit them, not being mixed with faith in them that heard it." (Heb. 4:2.) Let us also record his explanation that the I AM THAT I AM, the Great Jehovah who appeared to Moses in the burning bush, was named Christ. "Moses," he said, "when he was come of years," chose "rather to suffer affliction with the people of God, than to enjoy the pleasures of sin for a season; Esteeming the reproach of Christ greater riches than the treasures in Egypt: for he had respect unto the recompence of the reward." (Heb. 11:24-26.) Then Paul explains that it was by faith in this same Christ, whom they worshiped as Jehovah, that all of the prophets had that faith which worked miracles, wrought righteousness, raised the dead, and sealed men up unto eternal life. (Heb. 11.)

Jehovah Led Israel

Who delivered Israel from Egyptian bondage by the hand of Moses his servant? Who parted the Red Sea so that the waters congealed, forming a wall of water on the right hand and a wall of water on the left? Who revealed unto

107

them his law amid the thunders and smoking of Sinai? Who gave them manna for forty years as they wandered in a desert wilderness, preparing themselves spiritually to enter their promised land? Who drove out before them the Hittites and the Amorites, the Canaanites and the Perizzites, the Hivites and the Jebusites, so that Israel ate of vineyards they did not plant and drank from wells they had not digged? Who was the Lord their God?

The Old Testament says it was Jehovah. The New Testament and the Book of Mormon reaffirm this, but call him by the name-title of Christ.

In Moses' account it is written: "And the Lord went before them by day in a pillar of a cloud, to lead them the way; and by night in a pillar of fire, to give them light; to go by day and night: He took not away the pillar of the cloud by day, nor the pillar of fire by night, from before the people." (Ex. 13:21-22.) The Psalmist wrote: "He spread a cloud for a covering; and fire to give light in the night." (Ps. 105:39.) That none in the Church should be confused as to what God did these mighty works, Paul wrote: "Brethren, I would not that ye should be ignorant, how that all our fathers were under the cloud, and all passed through the sea; And were all baptized unto Moses in the cloud and in the sea; And did all eat the same spiritual meat; And did all drink the same spiritual drink: for they drank of that spiritual Rock that followed them: and that Rock was Christ." (1 Cor. 10:1-4.) And in the Book of Mormon account, we read these words spoken by the Risen Lord to the Nephites: "I am the God of Israel, and the God of the whole earth, and have been slain for the sins of the world." (3 Ne. 11:14.)

Jehovah to Be Resurrected

Isaiah says plainly that Jehovah shall be resurrected, or rather, Jehovah says it through the mouth of Isaiah. First we read, "He will swallow up death in victory" (Isa. 25:8), and are counseled: "Trust ye in the Lord for ever: for in the Lord JEHOVAH is everlasting strength." Then comes the promise of the greatest triumph ever wrought by his "everlasting strength": "Thy dead men shall live, together with my dead body shall they arise. Awake and sing, ye that dwell in dust: . . . and the earth shall cast out the dead." (Isa. 26:4-21.)

How plainly it is stated! Jehovah comes forth from the tomb. Jehovah breaks the bands of death. Jehovah takes captivity captive. Jehovah is resurrected. And therefore Jehovah was born: "The mighty God" (Isa. 9:6) becomes mortal. And therefore Jehovah died: "he hath poured out his soul unto death," "he was cut off out of the land of the living, . . . he made his grave with the wicked, and with the rich in his death." (Isa. 53:8-12.) All this transpired that he and all men might be resurrected. And who is it other than Christ who hath done all these things?

Jehovah's Birth, Death, and Resurrection Revealed to Abraham

To believe in Abraham is to believe in Christ. No one can claim true kinship to that ancient patriarch without believing what he believed and accepting the testimony he bore. Jesus once said to the unbelieving Jews: "Had ye believed Moses, ye would have believed me: for he wrote of me. But if ye believe not his writings, how shall ye believe my words?" (John 5:46-47.) And so it is with Abraham. Had the Jews believed in their great patriarch—who of old worshiped Jehovah and looked forward to his mortal birth and atoning sacrifice—they would have accepted that same Jehovah when he ministered among them.

"Your father Abraham rejoiced to see my day," Jesus said to them, "and he saw it, and was glad." Refusing to give credence to the claim that Jesus was Jehovah by so much as responding to this bold assertion, our Lord's enemies replied with a complete *non sequitur;* they twisted Jesus' words so as to respond, with a question, to a statement he had not made.

109

"Thou art not yet fifty years old," they said, "and hast thou seen Abraham?" True it was that Jesus had in fact seen Abraham and in turn been seen by him; and so our Lord responded, "Before Abraham was, I am." That is, 'Before Abraham, was I AM; before Abraham, was I Jehovah.' That the Jews understood perfectly the claim of divinity which thus fell from the lips of the lowly Nazarene is evident from what followed. "Then took they up stones to cast at him," the record says—an almost instinctive reaction on their part to an utterance that they esteemed as blasphemy. (John 8:56-59.)

The specific scriptural account to which Jesus referred in this great proclamation of his own divine Sonship, which account in all probability was had among the Jews, was the ancient Patriarch's discussion with the Lord as to how he and his seed could inherit their promised Palestine. "Lord God, how wilt thou give me this land for an everlasting inheritance?" Abraham asked. "And the Lord said, Though thou wast dead, yet am I not able to give it thee? And if thou shalt die, yet thou shalt possess it, for the day cometh, that the Son of Man shall live; but how can he live if he be not dead? he must first be quickened." Having been so instructed relative to the birth and death and resurrection of the Son of Man, and of his own resurrection and that of his seed, Abraham then saw in vision the very thing our Lord had named. "And it came to pass, that Abram [his name had not yet been changed] looked forth and saw the days of the Son of Man, and was glad, and his soul found rest, and he believed in the Lord; and the Lord counted it unto him for righteousness." (JST, Gen. 15:9-12.)

Jehovah to Judge All Men

After all the testimonies borne by him and his Hebrew brethren, Moroni concludes his Nephite record with this crowning certification: "I soon go to rest in the paradise of God, until my spirit and body shall again reunite, and I am brought forth triumphant through the air, to meet you before the pleasing bar of the great Jehovah, the Eternal Judge of both quick and dead." (Moro. 10:34.)

Among the many testimonies which Jesus bore of himself, we find this forthright proclamation: "The Father judgeth no man, but hath committed all judgment unto the Son: That all men should honour the Son, even as they honour the Father." (John 5:22-23.)

The issue is thus squarely put. Jehovah is the Eternal Judge of all men. None are judged by the Father, for he is Elohim, not Jehovah. Christ only is appointed to sit in judgment on all men. Thus Jehovah is Christ, and Christ is Jehovah; they are one and the same person.

Praise Jehovah, Who Is Christ

One of the most interesting of all the prophetic pronouncements revealing that Jehovah and Christ are one and the same in person and identity is the great liturgical call of praise given to each of them by inspired authors. Let us note with particularity the words used and their meaning both in the original Hebrew and in the tongues into which they have been transliterated.

Yahweh is the name of the God of the Hebrews. The Anglicized or English rendition of this name is *Jehovah.* The shortened form of *Yahweh* is *Yah,* and the contracted form of *Jehovah* (*Jahveh* or *Yahweh*) is *Jah.* Thus David writes: "Sing unto God, sing praises to his name: extol him that rideth upon the heavens by his name JAH, and rejoice before him." (Ps. 68:4.) Most Old Testament passages containing the name *Jah* (for *Jehovah*) have been translated *Lord.*

Halleluyah is the Hebrew term meaning "Praise ye Yah," or as we would say, "praise ye the Lord." The transliterated form of *Halleluyah* is *Hallelujah* (*Hallelu-Jah*). It is thus clear how ancient Israel sang praises to her God who was the Lord Jehovah.

Alleluia is the New Testament rendition of *Hallelujah;* it

111

is derived from the Greek form of *Halleluyah.* In other words, *Alleluia* means "Praise ye Jah," or "praise ye Jehovah," or "praise ye the Lord."

And so when the apostles of New Testament times desired to sing praises to Jehovah who had been born and resurrected, and whom they worshiped as the Lord Jesus Christ, they cried, "Alleluia." And when their fellow servants beyond the veil joined in the chorus of praise to Christ, the words of the eternal choir were: "Alleluia; Salvation, and glory, and honour, and power, unto the Lord our God: For true and righteous are his judgments. . . . Alleluia: for the Lord God omnipotent reigneth. . . . And his name is called The Word of God. . . . And he hath on his vesture and on his thigh a name written, KING OF KINGS, AND LORD OF LORDS." (Rev. 19:1-16.)

And should we not sing praises to his holy name forever? Hath he not redeemed us from death, hell, the devil, and endless torment? Are we not begotten sons and daughters unto God through his atoning sacrifice? Hath he not made us joint-heirs with him of all the glory of his Father's kingdom? Alleluia, for the Lord God Omnipotent reigneth, and through his atoning blood we shall have salvation and glory and honor forever!

Chapter 8

THERE IS ONE GOD

Are There Three Gods or One?

It is written that there is one God—not two Gods, not three Gods, not many Gods. And so it is: There is but one God, beside whom there are no others.

It is also written that there are two Gods, and three Gods, and many Gods—not one God only. And so also is it: We worship two Gods who are personages of tabernacle; there are three Gods in the Godhead; and there are Lords many and Gods many, all of whom are exalted beings having eternal dominion.

To those devoid of spiritual understanding, it is as though the inspired authors had set out, deliberately and with earnest intent, to sow the seeds of darkness and misunderstanding as to the God or Gods who live and abide and are. And again, in a manner of speaking, so it is, for "without controversy great is the mystery of godliness." (1 Tim. 3:16.) At least to the spiritually sick and to the spiritually dead, who seek God through reason and the intellect alone, the scriptures appear to be a compilation of confusion and contradiction. And it was not intended to be otherwise, for salvation is of the Spirit and comes only to those who are spiritually alive and well, those who come to know God, not by reason and the intellect alone, but through the spirit of prophecy and revelation.

God is revealed by preachers who speak by the power of the Holy Ghost, who "speak the wisdom of God in a mystery" (1 Cor. 2:7), who have the same Spirit resting upon them that inspired the prophets of old who wrote of the Lord and his ways. It is, as Paul says, "After that in the wisdom of God the world by wisdom knew not God, it pleased God by the foolishness of preaching to save them that believe." (1 Cor. 1:21.)

"The Lord Our God Is One Lord"

The Father and the Son are personages of tabernacle; they have bodies of flesh and bones and are in fact resurrected, glorified, and holy Men. The Holy Ghost is a personage of spirit, a spirit person, a spirit entity. These three individuals, each of whom is separate from the other, comprise the Godhead; each is God in his own right. They are three Gods as distinct from each other as are the man Peter, the man John, and the man James, who together comprised the First Presidency of the Church in time's meridian.

And yet, let there be no misunderstanding, the revelations teach that there is one God. In one of the most profound proclamations ever to fall from his lips, Moses proclaimed: "Hear, O Israel: The Lord our God is one Lord." (Deut. 6:4.) Paul picked up the same theme and said simply: "God is one" (Gal. 3:20), and "There is none other God but one" (1 Cor. 8:4). Jesus quoted Moses' teaching with approval (Mark 12:29), and Zechariah, speaking of the millennial day, confirmed the same eternal truth in these words: "The Lord shall be king over all the earth: in that day shall there be one Lord, and his name one" (Zech. 14:9). So speaks the Bible on the oneness of God.

The Book of Mormon is even more express and even more expansive. After setting forth the terms and conditions of the plan of salvation, Nephi says: "This is the doctrine of Christ, and the only and true doctrine of the Father, and of the Son, and of the Holy Ghost, which is one God, without end." (2 Ne. 31:21.) Amulek speaks plainly of salvation in the kingdom of heaven, of being raised from death to life through the atonement of Christ, of the wicked retaining a bright recollection of their guilt, and of the eternal judgment that awaits them, when they "shall be brought and be arraigned before the bar of Christ the Son, and God the Father, and the Holy Spirit, which is one Eternal God, to be judged according to their works, whether they be good or whether they be evil." (Alma 11:44.) Mormon records that the righteous shall be found guiltless in that great day and shall "dwell in the presence of God in his kingdom, to sing ceaseless praises with the choirs above, unto the Father, and unto the Son, and unto the Holy Ghost, which are one God, in a state of happiness which hath no end." (Morm. 7:7.)

Truly, there is one God, and one God only!

Men Make Their Own Gods

This one-God concept is preserved in the creeds of Christendom in such a way as to subvert and alter, completely and totally, the truth about those Holy Beings whom it is life eternal to know. These creeds are confessions of faith brought forth in councils of confusion and contention. They preserve the names of each member of the Godhead and attempt to show how these three are one.

These creedal confessions of faith are numerous. For instance, the first Article of Religion of the Church of England, entitled "Of Faith in the Holy Trinity," sets forth this view: "There is but one living and true God, everlasting, without body, parts, or passions; of infinite power, wisdom, and goodness; the Maker, and Preserver of all things both visible and invisible. And in unity of this Godhead there be three Persons, of one substance, power, and eternity; the Father, the Son, and the Holy Ghost." (*Book of Common Prayer.*)

But of all the creeds ever composed, the one named for Athanasius spreads more darkness and preserves more contradictions than any other. The portion of the

Athanasian creed dealing with the Godhead contributes this mass of confusion to what men call Christianity: " 'Whosoever will be saved, before all things it is necessary that he hold the Catholic Faith. Which Faith except everyone do keep whole and undefiled, without doubt he shall perish everlastingly. And the Catholic Faith is this, that we worship one God in Trinity and Trinity in Unity. Neither confounding the Persons, nor dividing the Substance. For there is one Person of the Father, another of the Son, and another of the Holy Ghost. But the Godhead of the Father, of the Son and of the Holy Ghost is all One, the Glory Equal, the Majesty Co-Eternal. Such as the Father is, such is the Son, and such is the Holy Ghost. The Father Uncreate, the Son Uncreate, the Holy Ghost Uncreate. The Father Incomprehensible, the Son Incomprehensible, and the Holy Ghost Incomprehensible. The Father Eternal, the Son Eternal, and the Holy Ghost Eternal and yet they are not Three Eternals but One Eternal. As also there are not Three Uncreated, nor Three Incomprehensibles, but One Uncreated, and One Incomprehensible. So likewise the Father is Almighty, the Son Almighty, and the Holy Ghost Almighty. And yet they are not Three Almighties but One Almighty.

" 'So the Father is God, the Son is God, and the Holy Ghost is God. And yet they are not Three Gods, but One God. So likewise the Father is Lord, the Son Lord, and the Holy Ghost Lord. And yet not Three Lords but One Lord. For, like as we are compelled by the Christian verity to acknowledge every Person by Himself to be God and Lord, so are we forbidden by the Catholic Religion to say, there be Three Gods or Three Lords. The Father is made of none, neither created, nor begotten. The Son is of the Father alone; not made, nor created, but begotten. The Holy Ghost is of the Father, and of the Son; neither made, nor created, nor begotten, but proceeding.

" 'So there is One Father, not Three Fathers; one Son, not Three Sons; One Holy Ghost, not Three Holy Ghosts.

116

And in this Trinity none is afore or after Other, None is greater or less than Another, but the whole Three Persons are Co-eternal together, and Co-equal. So that in all things, as is aforesaid, the Unity in Trinity, and the Trinity in Unity is to be worshipped. He therefore that will be saved, must thus think of the Trinity.' " (*Catholic Encyclopedia* 2:33-34.)

These creedal certifications, along with all the others devised during the long night of apostate darkness, came from uninspired men who had lost communion with those in the celestial realm who alone have power to reveal the truth about the Godhead. That such would be the case was foreknown and forerevealed by the prophets of old. It was Jeremiah, for one, who told how scattered Israel, in her dispersed state, would "serve other gods" than the Lord, but that in the day of restoration and gathering she would once more come to the knowledge of the Lord Jehovah. Of his gathered house, the Lord would then say: "I will this once cause them to know"—and the new knowledge commenced to come in the spring of 1820 with the appearance of the Father and the Son to Joseph Smith—"I will cause them to know mine hand and my might; and they shall know that my name is The Lord."

Of the false and apostate concepts theretofore had, gathered Israel, as Jeremiah expressed it, would come together from the ends of the earth and say: "Surely our fathers have inherited lies, vanity, and things wherein there is no profit. Shall a man make gods unto himself, and they are no gods?" (Jer. 16:10-21.)

Is it any wonder that the Lord of heaven, as he stood by his Father's side on that glorious day in 1820, speaking of all the churches in all Christendom, told young Joseph "that all their creeds were an abomination in his sight." (JS-H 19.)

How the Father and the Son Are One

To those who are bound to defend the mass of confusion in the creeds of Christendom, the concept that the Father,

Son, and Holy Ghost are one God is totally incomprehensible. They are baffled by their beliefs, confused by their creeds, unconverted by the incomprehensible. Their only recourse is to glory in the mystery of godliness and to suppose there is something wonderful in worshiping a spirit nothingness that is neither here nor there any more than he exists now or then. The total inability to know God becomes the most basic tenet of their religion and closes the door to that progress which leads to exaltation and Godhood.

To those who are free from creedal chains and who can and do turn to the teachings of the prophets and apostles to whom God revealed himself, there is no problem, no confusion, no uncertainty. To them the oneness of the Godhead is neither unknown nor mysterious. They know that God is their Father and that a father is a parent whose offspring bear the image, bodily and spiritually, of the progenitor. They know that Christ is the Son in the literal and full sense of the word, that he is in the express image of his Father's person, and that having come forth in the resurrection, he now has a glorified body of flesh and bones like that of the Father whose Child he is. Their ability to comprehend even God—as in due course they shall!—becomes the most important doctrine of their religion and opens the door to that eternal progress which enables them to become like him.

For reasons that we shall delineate hereafter—in language as plain, as simple, and as persuasive as in our power lies—Jesus taught, repetitiously, both while a mortal man and after being raised in glorious immortality, that he and his Father are one. And implicit in all of his utterances to this effect is found the nature of their oneness, the manner in which, though separate personages, they are one in a way of tremendous import to the children of men.

While a mortal he said to his Jewish brethren: "I and my Father are one," which they understood to mean that he "being a man" was making himself "God." (John 10:30-33.) Speaking of his Twelve Disciples he prayed: "Holy Father, keep through thine own name those whom thou hast given

118

me, that they may be one, as we are." Then because every blessing bestowed upon or offered to those who hold the holy apostleship is also available for and offered to all of the faithful, he also said to his Father: "Neither pray I for these alone, but for them also which shall believe on me through their word; That they all may be one; as thou, Father, art in me, and I in thee, that they also may be one in us: that the world may believe that thou hast sent me." At this point in his great Intercessory Prayer, his petitions again centered on the Twelve, though in principle all that he said does or shall apply to all the saints. "And the glory which thou gavest me I have given them," he said, "that they may be one, even as we are one: I in them, and thou in me, that they may be made perfect in one. . . . And I have declared unto them thy name, and will declare it: that the love wherewith thou hast loved me may be in them, and I in them." (John 17:11-26.)

After the inseparable union of his body and spirit in immortal glory, he said to his Nephite brethren: "I am in the Father, and the Father in me; and in me hath the Father glorified his name." (3 Ne. 9:15.) Also: "Verily I say unto you, that the Father, and the Son, and the Holy Ghost are one; and I am in the Father, and the Father in me, and the Father and I are one. . . . I bear record of the Father and the Father beareth record of me, and the Holy Ghost beareth record of the Father and me; . . . Whoso believeth in me believeth in the Father also; and unto him will the Father bear record of me, for he will visit him with fire and with the Holy Ghost. And thus will the Father bear record of me, and the Holy Ghost will bear record unto him of the Father and me; for the Father, and I, and the Holy Ghost are one." (3 Ne. 11:27-36.)

Later, of the whole body of Nephite believers, in a prayer reminiscent of and greater than his mortal Intercessory Prayer, our Lord said: "And now Father, I pray unto thee for them, and also for all those who shall believe on their words, that they may believe in me, that I may be in them as thou, Father, art in me, that we may be one. . . . Father, I pray not for the world, but for those whom thou hast given me out of the world, because of their faith, that they may be purified in me, that I may be in them as thou, Father, art in me, that we may be one, that I may be glorified in them." (3 Ne. 19:23, 29.)

From these and related teachings found in revealed writ, and all such are declarations which cannot be gainsayed, we learn these truths relative to the Gods we worship:

1. They are three in number, three separate persons: the first is the Father; the second, the Son; and the third, the Holy Ghost. They are three individuals who meet together, counsel in concert, and as occasion requires travel separately through all immensity. They are three holy men, two having bodies of flesh and bones, the third being a personage of spirit.

2. They are one and dwell in each other, meaning: They have the same mind one with another; they think the same thoughts, speak the same words, and perform the same acts—so much so that any thought, word, or act of one is the thought, word, or act of the other.

3. They possess the same character, enjoy the same perfections, and manifest the same attributes, each one possessing all of these in their eternal and godly fulness.

4. Their unity in all things, their perfect oneness in mind, power, and perfections, marks the course and charts the way for faithful mortals, whose chief goal in life is to unite together and become one with them, thereby gaining eternal life for themselves.

5. Our Lord is the manifestation of the Father, meaning: God is in Christ revealing himself to men so that those who believe in the Son believe also in the Father, and unto such the Father gives the Holy Ghost, and they being thus purified in Christ are fit to dwell with him and his Father forever.

That this glorious unity of which these and other revelations speak is attainable for mortals is shown by the righteous works of certain ancient saints, of whom the record says: "The Lord came and dwelt with his people, and they dwelt in righteousness. . . . And the Lord called his people ZION, because they were of one heart and one mind, and dwelt in righteousness." These were they who dwelt in "the City of Holiness, even ZION," which "in process of time, was taken up into heaven," because they had made themselves one with their Lord. (Moses 7:16-21.)

That other faithful saints—being otherwise assigned to labor in the Lord's vineyard, and not being translated as were Enoch's people—have yet attained similar unity with each other and with him whose they are, is attested by Paul's pronouncement relative to certain ones in his day: "We have the mind of Christ." (1 Cor. 2:16.) That is, by obedience and righteousness there were those in his day who, guided by the power of the Holy Spirit, thought and spoke and acted as the Lord would have them do. To the extent that they were so inspired, they were one with their God.

Jehovah Speaks the Words of Elohim

In discussing how and in what sense Christ created man, we have already noted in Chapter 4 that "the Father placed his name upon the Son; and [that] so far as power, authority, and Godship are concerned his words and acts were and are those of the Father." (*The Father and the Son: A Doctrinal Exposition by the First Presidency and the Twelve,* cited in James E. Talmage, *Articles of Faith,* pp. 465-73.) As we now set forth the basic thesis that the Father and the Son are one, we come to the most extensive, perhaps the greatest illustration of how this unity of thought and word operates.

Our illustrations will show, not alone how the Father and the Son operate as one, but why uninspired scriptural exegetes have so much difficulty in seeking to learn spiritual truths by the power of the intellect alone. When Jesus (the Son) quotes Jehovah (the Son), in teaching the Nephites, he attributes the pronouncements so made to Elohim (the Father). Why? Because the words so revealed by Jehovah to

121

the prophets of old are and were those of both the Father and the Son.

We shall hereafter set forth in some detail the fact that Jehovah-Christ is the God of Israel. For our present purposes we shall note only that when he, as a resurrected person, invited the Nephites to feel the prints of the nails in his hands and in his feet, he did it so that they may know that he was the God of Israel, and the God of the whole earth, and had been "slain for the sins of the world." (3 Ne. 11:14.) As Israel's God, it is clear that he and not the Father spoke to all the ancient prophets—to Moses, Isaiah, Malachi, to all who were called as guides and lights to the Lord's ancient peoples. He it was who gave the Law of Moses, and in him it was fulfilled. (3 Ne. 15:1-10.) In fact, the whole Old Testament is most explicit that the Deity in whose name the ancient prophets spoke was Jehovah, not Elohim. Of this there is no question.

But in the Book of Mormon, in one sentence he says he is the One who covenanted with the house of Israel and in another he attributes the ancient hand dealings of Deity to the Father. When the resurrected Lord quoted what he himself as the spirit Jehovah had told Micah, Isaiah, and Malachi, he attributed the words to the Father. (3 Ne. 20-22, 24-25; Isa. 52, 54; Mal. 3-4; Micah 4.) His quotations, standing alone and taken out of context, leave the impression that it was Elohim and not Jehovah who spoke to the ancient prophets when in fact it was Jehovah relaying the word of Elohim, for the Father and the Son, as one, both speak the same words.

Peter did precisely the same thing in principle. He applied one of Christ's chief titles to the Father: "The God of Abraham, and of Isaac, and of Jacob, the God of our fathers," who is in fact the Lord Jehovah, "hath glorified his Son Jesus," Peter says, thus applying the name of the Son to the Father. (Acts 3:13.)

How truly they are one! The name of the one is the name of the other. The words of the one are the words of the other.

The thoughts, acts, purposes, and perfections of the one are identical to those of the other.

He that hath seen one hath seen the other. He that hath heard the voice of one hath heard the voice of the other. He that hath felt the spirit of one has felt the spirit of the other. He that hath lived the laws of the one has lived the laws of the other.

"I and my Father are one." (John 10:30.)

Christ Dwelleth in His Saints

As we have seen, Paul taught that faithful saints "have the mind of Christ." (1 Cor. 2:16.) That is: They think what he thinks; they say what he says; they do what he does; and their souls are attuned to his—all because they live the way he lives and have acquired the same attributes and perfections that he possesses.

As we have also seen, our Lord prayed that he might be in his saints in the same sense that the Father was in him, so that Christ and his people would ever be one. (3 Ne. 19:23.) And this brings us to one of the most glorious of all gospel doctrines—that Jesus Christ dwelleth in his saints.

This wondrous concept is one about which the apostles of old had much to say. "I am crucified with Christ" (Gal. 2:20), Paul said, meaning that he had "crucified" the "old man, . . . the body of sin," that henceforth he "should not serve sin" (Rom. 6:6). As a result—that is, because he had forsaken the world to "walk in newness of life" (Rom. 6:4), and had "put on Christ" (Gal. 3:27)—he was able to say: "Christ liveth in me: and the life which I now live in the flesh I live by the faith of the Son of God" (Gal. 2:20).

As taught by the inspired men of old, this doctrine is that the true saints turn from all evil and cleave unto all good "until Christ be formed" in them. (Gal. 4:19.) They are then able to say: We shall triumph over all the trials of mortality because we go forth, "Always bearing about in the body the dying of the Lord Jesus, that the life also of Jesus might be made manifest in our body." Their pledge then is: We shall so live "that the life also of Jesus might be made manifest in our mortal flesh." (2 Cor. 4:10-11.)

Paul said to his Ephesian brethren: I pray to the Father that you shall "be strengthened with might by his Spirit in the inner man; That Christ may dwell in your hearts by faith," until through knowledge, obedience, and righteousness "ye might be filled with all the fulness of God." (Eph. 3:14-19.)

"The fulness of God"! What is it? It is to be one with the Father. Jesus spoke of gaining "all power . . . in heaven and in earth." (Matt. 28:18.) Such is the reward for all those who "pass by the angels, and the gods, . . . to their exaltation and glory in all things, . . . which glory shall be a fulness. . . . Then shall they be gods." (D&C 132:19-20.)

This doctrine that man crucifies his old, sinful self so that Christ can dwell in him, and that man as a consequence has power, through faith, to inherit all things, is truly a mystery to spiritually untutored souls. And Paul so designates it. If the saints "continue in the faith grounded and settled, and be not moved from the hope of the gospel," he says, they shall through this doctrine become "holy and unblameable and unreproveable" in the Lord's sight. They shall then understand this great mystery, "even the mystery which hath been hid from ages and from generations, but now is made manifest to his saints; To whom God would make known what is the riches of the glory of this mystery among the Gentiles; which is Christ in you, the hope of glory." (Col. 1:21-27.)

What is the mystery? It is that Christ dwells in the hearts of those who have crucified the old man of sin, and that as a consequence they have a hope of eternal glory! Such is what the Lord requires of his children in working out their "own salvation with fear and trembling" before him. (Phil. 2:12.) And it is in this connection that Paul says, somewhat caustically, "But if our gospel be hid, it is hid to them that are lost." (2 Cor. 4:3.)

Hidden from the world, but revealed in the hearts of those who are enlightened by the Spirit, this doctrine becomes the measuring rod by which the saints determine whether they are faithful and true. "Examine yourselves, whether ye be in the faith; prove your own selves," Paul directs. His standard for such self-judgment is: "Know ye not your own selves, how that Jesus Christ is in you, except ye be reprobates?" (2 Cor. 13:5.)

How to Cause Christ to Dwell in Us

Now let us set forth the New Testament formula whereby the Lord's saints can measure whether and to what extent Christ dwells in them. It is:

1. *Know the true God.*

It is life eternal to know the Father and the Son. It is the first principle of revealed religion to know the nature and kind of being that God is. There is no real progress in spiritual things until we know who God is and what his character, perfections, and attributes are. "We know that the Son of God is come, and hath given us an understanding," John says. Why? His answer: "That we may know him that is true." There is no substitute for a true knowledge of God, which truth having been taught, the beloved apostle drives home this point: "And we are in him that is true, even in his Son Jesus Christ." Then speaking of the Father and the Son as the one God that they are, he concludes: "This is the true God, and eternal life." (1 Jn. 5:20.) Thus those who know the Father and the Son, and are thereby inheritors of eternal life, so obtain because they are in God and he is in them and they twain are one.

2. *Believe in Christ.*

Believe in him in the literal and true sense of the word, not in some figurative and mystical way; believe that God was his Father, "after the manner of the flesh" (1 Ne. 11:18), as the angelic ministrant affirmed to Nephi; believe that the Father-Son relationship is as real and personal as that which

125

exists between parent and child among us mortals—all of which presupposes that his Father is an immortal Man of Holiness. Believe that because of this holy relationship the Offspring had power to work out the infinite and eternal atonement.

"We have seen and do testify that the Father sent the Son to be the Saviour of the world," John certifies. Of all who have this same knowledge, he then proclaims: "Whosoever shall confess that Jesus is the Son of God, God dwelleth in him, and he in God." (1 John 4:14-15.)

3. *Keep the commandments; live righteously.*

Obedience is the first law of heaven. All progression, all perfection, all salvation, all godliness, all that is right and just and true, all good things come to those who live the laws of Him who is Eternal. There is nothing in all eternity more important than to keep the commandments of God.

Christ himself set the example. "I and my Father are one" because I keep the commandments and do "the works of my Father," and thereby you "may know, and believe, that the Father is in me, and I in him," was his teaching. (John 10:30-38.)

"Believest thou not that I am in the Father, and the Father in me?" he asked. To explain how this was and why it came to pass, he continued, "The words that I speak unto you I speak not of myself: but the Father that dwelleth in me, he doeth the works. Believe me that I am in the Father, and the Father in me." (John 14:10-11.)

If Christ was in the Father because he did the works of the Father (and the Father was thereby in him), it follows that if we do the works of Christ, we will be in him (and he in turn will dwell in us). And so it is, for the scripture saith: "He that keepeth his commandments dwelleth in him, and he in him." (1 Jn. 3:24.) And further: "He that saith he abideth in him ought himself also so to walk, even as he walked." Why? Because "whoso keepeth his word, in him is the love of God perfected: [and] hereby know we that we are in him." (1 Jn. 2:5-6.)

4. *Obtain the gift of the Holy Ghost.*

It is well known among the saints that our bodies are "the temple of the Holy Ghost," which is in us, "which we have of God." (1 Cor. 6:19.) Of us the scripture asks: "Know ye not that ye are the temple of God, and that the Spirit of God dwelleth in you?" (1 Cor. 3:16.)

When we are confirmed members of the only true and living church, we receive the gift of the Holy Ghost. This gives us the right to the constant companionship of that member of the Godhead based on faithfulness. The world cannot receive this priceless gift. It is to the faithful saints only that the promise is made: "He dwelleth with you, and shall be in you." (John 14:17.)

What did Paul mean when he said of the saints: "Ye are not in the flesh, but in the Spirit, if so be that the Spirit of God dwell in you. Now if any man have not the Spirit of Christ, he is none of his. And if Christ be in you, the body is dead because of sin; but the Spirit is life because of righteousness. But if the Spirit of him that raised up Jesus from the dead dwell in you, he that raised up Christ from the dead shall also quicken your mortal bodies by his Spirit that dwelleth in you." (Rom. 8:9-11.)

And what did John mean when he said, "And hereby we know that he abideth in us, by the Spirit which he hath given us"? (1 Jn. 3:24.) And also: "Hereby know we that we dwell in him, and he in us, because he hath given us of his Spirit"? (1 Jn. 4:13.)

Truly, Christ dwells in those who enjoy the gift of the Holy Ghost, and they in turn are in their Lord!

5. *Partake worthily of the sacrament.*

In his church we partake often of the sacrament, to renew our baptismal covenant, to assert anew that we will "always remember him and keep his commandments," and to plead that we "may have his Spirit" to be with us. (D&C 20:77.) When this is done in righteousness, by those who are just and true, the Spirit of the Lord comes to dwell in their hearts; and as we have seen, Christ himself thereby dwells in

127

them and they in him. Thus we find our Lord teaching: "He that eateth my flesh, and drinketh my blood, dwelleth in me, and I in him." (John 6:56.)

6. *Acquire the attributes of godliness.*

The Father and the Son possess, in their fulness and perfection, all godly graces and all ennobling attributes. They have all charity, all love, and all mercy; they are the possessors of the fulness of judgment, the fulness of justice, and the fulness of truth; and so it is through every good thing. They are thus one, for if the Father has all charity and the Son likewise, they are thus alike where that attribute is concerned, and so it is with them where all uplifting and edifying attributes are concerned. And to the extent that we acquire charity or love or any godly attribute, we also dwell in God and he in us.

"God is love," John writes, "and he that dwelleth in love dwelleth in God, and God in him." (1 Jn. 4:16.) Also: "If we love one another, God dwelleth in us, and his love is perfected in us." (1 Jn. 4:12.) Similarly, God is charity (meaning he is the personification and embodiment of this attribute), and he that dwelleth in charity (that is, possesses it) dwelleth in God, and he in him; and if we have charity one for another, then God dwelleth in us, and his charity is perfected in us. The same reasoning applies to all of the attributes of his nature.

7. *Reward of those who dwell in God and he in them.*

Of Christ our Prototype it is written: "In him dwelleth all the fulness of the Godhead bodily." (Col. 2:9.) In other words, in Christ is found every godly attribute in its perfection, which means that the Father dwells in him and he in the Father. It follows that when men so attain, they become like God, or, as Joseph Smith expressed it:

"Those who keep his commandments shall grow up from grace to grace, and become heirs of the heavenly kingdom, and joint-heirs with Jesus Christ; possessing the same mind, being transformed into the same image or likeness, even the express image of him who fills all in all; being filled with the fulness of his glory, and become one in him, even as the Father, Son and Holy Spirit are one." (*Lectures on Faith,* cited in *Mormon Doctrine,* 2nd ed., pp. 320-21.)

What Is Salvation?

As a necessary prelude to a full comprehension of why the Lord and his prophets put such repeated and strong emphasis on the one-God concept, we must know what is meant by salvation in the true and ultimate sense of the word.

We are ofttimes prone to create artificial distinctions, to say that salvation means one thing and exaltation another, to suppose that salvation means to be resurrected, but that exaltation or eternal life is something in addition thereto. It is true that there are some passages of scripture that use salvation in a special and limited sense in order to give an overall perspective of the plan of salvation that we would not otherwise have. (2 Ne. 9:1-27; D&C 76:40-49; 132:15-17.) These passages show the difference between general or universal salvation that consists of coming forth from the grave in immortality, and specific or individual salvation that consists of an inheritance in the celestial kingdom. All men will be resurrected and all men (except the sons of perdition) will thus be saved from death, hell, the devil, and endless torment. But only those who keep the commandments will "be raised [both] in immortality [and] unto eternal life." (D&C 29:43.)

Since it is the prophetic purpose to lead men to full salvation in the highest heaven of the celestial world, when they speak and write about salvation, almost without exception, they mean eternal life or exaltation. They use the terms *salvation, exaltation,* and *eternal life* as synonyms, as words that mean exactly the same thing without any difference, distinction, or variance whatever. Thus Amulek says that "no unclean thing can inherit the kingdom of heaven," and then asks: "How can ye be saved, except ye inherit the kingdom of heaven?" He teaches that men "cannot be saved" in their sins; that Christ will come to "take upon him the transgression of those who believe on his name"; and that "these are they that shall have eternal life, and salvation cometh to none else." Having thus spoken of the salvation which the saints seek, he also says: "The wicked remain as though there had been no redemption made, except it be the loosing of the bands of death," meaning they shall come forth in immortality. (Alma 11:37-41.) Thus all men—except the sons of perdition who are cast out into an eternal hell—are saved, in that they become immortal and go to a telestial or terrestrial inheritance, but only those who believe and obey become inheritors of that celestial rest which the whole body of revealed writ speaks of as salvation.

Eternal life is the name of the kind of life which God lives and is therefore "the greatest of all the gifts of God" (D&C 14:7); and because those who gain it become like God, they are one with him.

Exaltation consists of an inheritance in the highest heaven of the celestial world, where alone the family unit continues and where each recipient gains for himself an eternal family unit, patterned after the family of God our Heavenly Father, so that every exalted person lives the kind of life which God lives and is therefore one with him.

Salvation consists in gaining—and this is Joseph Smith's language—"the glory, authority, majesty, power and dominion which Jehovah possesses and in nothing else; and no being can possess it but himself or one like him" (Lectures on Faith, cited in Mormon Doctrine, 2nd ed., p. 258), and since he is one with his Father, so also are all saved beings. Truly, "There is no gift greater than the gift of salvation." (D&C 6:13.)

Thus, to be saved, to gain exaltation, to inherit eternal life, all mean to be one with God, to live as he lives, to think as he thinks, to act as he acts, to possess the same glory, the same power, the same might and dominion that he possesses.

Thus also, the Father is the great Prototype of all saved beings, and he and his Son, who also has become a saved being, are the ones into whose "likeness" Joseph Smith said we should be "assimilated." (*Lectures on Faith,* cited in *Mormon Doctrine,* 2nd ed., p. 258.) And thus, all those who overcome by faith, who become joint-heirs with Christ, who become one in him, as he is one in the Father, become themselves saved beings.

Why the Gods Proclaim Themselves as One

Now let us turn to the immeasurably great and important reason why three Gods proclaim themselves to be One God. We find it in this concept:

The greatest teaching device ever devised by Deity, whether in heaven or on earth, whether in time or in eternity, is embraced within the simple statement: "Hear, O Israel: The Lord our God is one Lord," followed as it then is by the divine decree: "And thou shalt love the Lord thy God with all thine heart, and with all thy soul, and with all thy might." (Deut. 6:4-5.)

Why is this so, and wherein is this such a transcendent teaching device? Rightly understood, these seven words— "The Lord our God is one Lord"—point the way and mark the course to eternal life in our Father's kingdom. Every true believer, every person who worships the Father in spirit and in truth, knows because of this one-God concept that if he himself is to be saved, he must be one with his fellow saints and with the Gods of heaven, as they are one with each other.

Would it be amiss now to reason together on this matter, to reason together as to why men must know the nature and kind of being God is, if they are ever to become like him and go where he is?

Since salvation comes by worshiping the true God; since to be saved is to be one with Christ as he is one with the Father; since salvation and eternal life consist of living the

131

kind of life that Deity lives—and the fact that man can be as God is, is the greatest concept that can enter the heart of man—it follows that any teaching, any doctrine, any dramatization that can keep the mind of man riveted on his goal and what he must do to gain it, any such device is the greatest of all teaching devices.

And so it is that now and always—past, present, and future—for all those who have accepted the Lord as their God, the rallying cry, the slogan of slogans, the divine statement which crystallizes in the minds of men what they must do to be saved is the great Mosaic proclamation: "The Lord our God is one Lord." (Deut. 6:4.)

The Lord speaks with one voice. He is the creator of one plan of salvation. There is only one way to become like him. That way is to come to a knowledge of him and to obey the laws which lead men to a like status of glory and exaltation. No one can pursue such a course until he knows of its existence. No one will ever make the sacrifice necessary to gain eternal life until he believes in his heart that the reward is worth the price. There can never be any true and saving worship without a knowledge of the nature and kind of being God is. Immortality is a free gift; eternal life is reserved for those who believe and obey, who keep the commandments, who are faithful and true in all things, who become one with their Lord.

Satan speaks with many voices and sponsors many plans of salvation. He says: There is no God; atheism and pure reason—these are all that count. Or: God is a spirit—an essence, force, or power—that fills immensity and is everywhere and nowhere in particular present. Or: He is the laws of nature, some great First Cause, some impersonal power in the universe—as all scientists and thinking men must agree! Or: He is made of wood or stone, is carved by man's device, and sits as Diana in her Parthenon atop her Athenian acropolis. Or: The Godhead is the Father, Son, and Holy Ghost, but this Holy Trinity compose one spirit nothingness that is really not three Gods but one God, which means they are not really one God but three Gods—incomprehensible, unknowable, incorporeal, and uncreated. Or: Whatever the mind of man can imagine or the machinations of devils devise, it matters not. As long as men believe in false Gods they are damned. What else need Lucifer do than to spawn and sponsor systems of false worship? There is no salvation in anything except truth—pure, diamond truth, the truth about God and his laws.

"As God Now Is, Man May Be"

No doctrine is more basic, no doctrine embraces a greater incentive to personal righteousness, and no doctrine so completely embraces the whole realm of revealed religion as does the wondrous concept that man can be as his Maker. It was revealed first to Adam, to whom—after his baptism, after he had received the holy priesthood, after he had walked in paths of righteousness—the Lord said: "Thou art one in me, a son of God; and thus may all become my sons." (Moses 6:68.) Thereafter, in all ages, whenever the Lord has had a people on earth, the same hope and the same promise have been renewed.

After this doctrine had been revealed to Enoch, in a declaration of wonder and exultation, he exclaimed to the Lord: "Thou hast made me, and given unto me a right to thy throne." (Moses 7:59.) In ancient Israel the repeated proclamation of their God was: "Ye shall be holy: for I the Lord your God am holy." (Lev. 19:2.) The Risen Lord, being holy and desiring that all his spirit brethren attain a like state of holiness and oneness with him, uttered these words: "To him that overcometh will I grant to sit with me in my throne, even as I also overcame, and am set down with my Father in his throne." (Rev. 3:21.) And to certain faithful disciples among the Nephites who had so qualified he said: "Ye shall sit down in the kingdom of my Father; yea, your joy shall be full, even as the Father hath given me fulness of joy; and ye shall be even as I am, and I am even as the Father; and the Father and I are one." (3 Ne. 28:10.)

"Let this mind be in you," writes our theological friend Paul, "which was also in Christ Jesus: Who, being in the form of God, thought it not robbery to be equal with God" (Phil. 2:5-6), thus showing how Christ, our Prototype, has attained oneness with his Father. Paul's associate apostle John takes the next step and applies the same principle to all who by faith become the sons of God. "Now are we the sons of God," he wrote, meaning that here and now while in mortality we have been adopted into the family of Deity and have become joint-heirs with his natural Son. "And it doth not yet appear what we shall be," he continues, meaning that no mortal man can conceive of the glory and dominion which shall be heaped upon those who reign on thrones in the exalted realms. "But we know that, when he shall appear [the Second Coming of our Lord], we shall be like him; for we shall see him as he is." As a natural conclusion to such a doctrine, John draws this obvious conclusion: "And every man that hath this hope in him purifieth himself, even as he is pure." (1 John 3:2-3.)

Pondering these words of the two ancient apostles, Paul and John, President Lorenzo Snow, a modern apostle—who also is the author of the couplet: "As man now is, God once was; As God now is, man may be"—addressed these poetically phrased truths to Paul:

Dear Brother:

Hast thou not been unwisely bold,
Man's destiny to thus unfold?
To raise, promote such high desire,
Such vast ambition thus inspire?

Still, 'tis no phantom that we trace
Man's ultimatum in life's race;

This royal path has long been trod
By righteous men, each now a God:

As Abra'm, Isaac, Jacob, too,
First babes, then men—to gods they grew.
As man now is, our God once was;
As now God is, so man may be,—
Which doth unfold man's destiny.

For John declares: When Christ we see
Like unto him we'll truly be.
And he who has this hope within,
Will purify himself from sin.

Who keep this object grand in view,
To folly, sin, will bid adieu,
Nor wallow in the mire anew;

Nor ever seek to carve his name
High on the shaft of worldly fame;
But here his ultimatum trace:
The head of all his spirit-race.

Ah, well: that taught by you, dear Paul,
'Though much amazed, we see it all;
Our Father God, has ope'd our eyes,
We cannot view it otherwise.

The boy, like to his father grown,
Has but attained unto his own;
To grow to sire from state of son,
Is not 'gainst Nature's course to run.

A son of God, like God to be,
Would not be robbing Deity;
And he who has this hope within,
Will purify himself from sin.

135

You're right, St. John, supremely right:
Whoe'er essays to climb this height,
Will cleanse himself of sin entire—
Or else 'twere needless to aspire.
　　　　　—Cited in *Commentary* 2:532-33

In the light of all that in our revelations is written, is it any wonder that the same God who has offered salvation to his brethren in all dispensations should say, "*Be one; and if ye are not one ye are not mine.*" (D&C 38:27. Italics added.)

Chapter 9

MESSIAH IS THE SON OF GOD

Son of God Chosen in Preexistence

As set forth in Chapter 4, the Father ordained and established the plan of salvation to enable his spirit children (Christ included) to advance and progress and become like him. According to the terms and conditions of this plan, the Father chose one of his spirit sons to be born among mortal men as the Son of God. This Chosen One was destined to inherit from his Father the power of immortality so that—in a way incomprehensible to us, but known to God—he could work out the infinite and eternal atonement. As a result of this atoning sacrifice all mortal men were destined to be raised in immortality while those who believed and obeyed the fulness of gospel law would also inherit eternal life.

The Firstborn of the Father, who was the Spirit-Jehovah, was the One, beloved and chosen of the Father, to be born among men as his Son. Salvation was to be made available to all men in and through the atonement of this promised Messiah, this Son of God who would be born in the meridian of time. To return to the presence of the Father, men would be required to believe in their Deliverer, to accept him as their Savior, and to live in harmony with the laws ordained by him and his Father.

It follows that whenever the Lord has had a people on earth, whenever the saving truths of his plan of salvation have been revealed to men, whenever there has been a dispensation of the gospel, the faithful saints have known that their Messiah and Deliverer would be the Son of God.

Son of God Revealed to Adam

As part of the first unfoldment of the plan of salvation to mortal man, Father Adam was told that redemption from the fall came through "the Only Begotten of the Father" and was available to him "and all mankind, even as many as will." An angel from the Eternal Presence relayed to him this command of Deity: "Thou shalt do all that thou doest in the name of the Son, and thou shalt repent and call upon God in the name of the Son forevermore." (Moses 5:8.) In that early day, "the Lord God called upon men by the Holy Ghost everywhere and commanded them that they should repent; And as many as believed in the Son, and repented of their sins, should be saved; and as many as believed not and repented not, should be damned." (Moses 5:14-15.) Thus, from the beginning, the great and eternal decree was: "Believe on his Only Begotten Son, even him whom he declared should come in the meridian of time, who was prepared from before the foundation of the world." As a result of this proclamation, the record says: "Thus the Gospel began to be preached, from the beginning." (Moses 5:57-58.)

This gospel, as revealed to Adam, was, "If thou wilt turn unto me, and hearken unto my voice, and believe, and repent of all thy transgressions, and be baptized, even in water, in the name of mine Only Begotten Son, who is full of grace and truth, which is Jesus Christ, the only name which shall be given under heaven, whereby salvation shall come unto the children of men, ye shall receive the gift of the Holy Ghost, asking all things in his name, and whatsoever ye shall ask, it shall be given you." (Moses 6:52.)

This gospel was, "That the Son of God hath atoned for original guilt." This gospel was "the plan of salvation unto all men." This gospel was "the record of the Father, and the

Son, from henceforth and forever." (Moses 6:54, 62, 66.)

Thus, beginning with Adam, "the first man of all men" (Moses 1:34), and with Eve, "the mother of all living" (Moses 4:26), and continuing to the day of the Lord's birth on earth, every man, woman, and child having prophetic insight knew that the Messiah would be the Son of God.

Christ Is the Son of Man

Our Lord assumed the prerogative, during his mortal ministry, of identifying himself as the Son of Man. For instance, to justify himself and his disciples in violating the restrictive Jewish rules relative to Sabbath observance he said, "The Son of man is Lord also of the Sabbath." (Mark 2:23-28.) And to Peter and the other apostles he put the incisive question, "Whom do men say that I the Son of man am?" and received the Spirit-revealed answer: "Thou art the Christ, the Son of the living God." (Matt. 16:13-17.) There are in fact some seventy New Testament passages in which he identifies himself as the Son of Man and speaks of such things as having power on earth to forgive sins; of his betrayal, crucifixion, death, and resurrection; of confessing fellowship with the righteous before his Father; and of returning in great power and glory, attended by the angelic hosts.

Why this designation? Did he have in mind the sectarian notion that he was the offspring of a mortal woman and that therefore he was born of man? Obviously the title could be so applied if we simply looked at the words used and had no spirit of scriptural interpretation and understanding. But the fact is that this exalted name-title has a deep and glorious connotation and is in many respects one of the most meaningful and self-identifying appellations applying to the divine Son. Its greatest significance lies in the fact that it identifies and reveals who the Father is.

In the early dispensations, the Father revealed many of his names. "Behold, I am God; Man of Holiness is my name; Man of Counsel is my name; and Endless and Eternal is my name, also," he said to Enoch. (Moses 7:35.) As we shall see shortly, another of his names is "Righteousness," or, perhaps better, "Man of Righteousness." In other words, to signify that he is the personification and embodiment of those godly attributes which men must obtain if they are to be one with him, he takes these attributes as his names. Thus we read that it was said to the first man: "In the language of Adam, Man of Holiness is his name, and the name of his Only Begotten is the Son of Man, even Jesus Christ, a righteous Judge, who shall come in the meridian of time." (Moses 6:57.)

That is, the Father is a Holy Man. Man of Holiness is his name, and the name of his Only Begotten is the Son of Man of Holiness, or in its abbreviated form, the Son of Man.

Joseph Smith received a revelation in which the question was put, "What is the name of God in the pure language," and the answer came, "Ahman." A second question was, "What is the name of the Son of God," and the answer came, "Son Ahman." (*Mormon Doctrine,* 2nd ed., p. 29.) In two of the revelations in the Doctrine and Covenants the Lord calls himself "Son Ahman." (D&C 78:20; 95:17.) As nearly as we can tell, Man of Holiness is the English rendition of Ahman, and Son of Man of Holiness, of Son Ahman.

Enoch received extensive visions in which the Only Begotten Son—then still a spirit being in the presence of God—was identified as the Son of Man. This ancient seer "was high and lifted up, even in the bosom of the Father, and of the Son of Man." One of the questions he asked was, "When the Son of Man cometh in the flesh, shall the earth rest?" By way of answer, "he looked and beheld the Son of Man lifted up on the cross, after the manner of men; And he heard a loud voice; and the heavens were veiled; and all the creations of God mourned; and the earth groaned; and the rocks were rent; and the saints arose, and were crowned at the right hand of the Son of Man, with crowns of glory." Enoch also "beheld the Son of Man ascend up unto the

Father" after his meridian ministry and learned that he would come again. "And it came to pass that Enoch saw the day of the coming of the Son of Man, in the last days, to dwell on the earth in righteousness for the space of a thousand years." (Moses 7:24, 54-56, 59, 65.)

Abraham saw in vision the Great Council in which the Son of Man volunteered to be born as the Son of God and work out the infinite and eternal atonement. (Abr. 3:23.) He also "saw the days of the Son of Man, and was glad, and his soul found rest, and he believed in the Lord; and the Lord counted it unto him for righteousness." He saw further that the Son of Man should die and be resurrected. (JST, Gen. 15:9-12.) It was of this vision of our Lord's mortal ministry that Jesus spoke when he said, "Abraham rejoiced to see my day: and he saw it, and was glad," and when he made the great proclamation, "Before Abraham was, I am." (John 8:56-58.)

While dying as a martyr, Stephen saw "the heavens opened, and the Son of man standing on the right hand of God." (Acts 7:56.) There are numerous revelations in the Doctrine and Covenants, mainly those dealing with his Second Coming, in which the Lord identifies himself in this same exalted way.

In the same sense that the Father's name is Man of Holiness and the Son's name is the Son of Man, so the Father's name is Righteousness and the Son's is the Son of Righteousness.

Our King James Version of the Bible records a prophecy of Malachi about the Second Coming of the Son of Man that specifies that "all the proud, yea, and all that do wickedly, shall be stubble" in that day. "But unto you that fear my name," the prophetic utterance continues, "shall the Sun of righteousness arise with healing in his wings." (Mal. 4:1-2.) That this is a prophecy relative to the Second Coming is clear from the context, and it was confirmed by Moroni as such when he appeared to Joseph Smith. (JS-H 36-39.) So that the account would be had among the Nephites, the

141

resurrected Jesus quoted it to them in A.D. 34, but what he said was that "the Son of Righteousness" shall "arise with healing in his wings." (3 Ne. 25:2.) The book of Ether tells us that Emer, a righteous ruler among the Jaredites, "saw the Son of Righteousness, and did rejoice and glory in his day." (Ether 9:21-22.) Nephi the son of Lehi used the same thoughts expressed by Malachi, but applied them to the first coming of the Messiah. Speaking of the righteous Nephite people at the time of our Lord's resurrected ministry among them, he said: "But the Son of Righteousness shall appear unto them; and he shall heal them, and they shall have peace with him, until three generations shall have passed away, and many of the fourth generation shall have passed away in righteousness." (2 Ne. 26:9.)

Old Testament Prophets Speak of the Son of God

Statements by the seers of Old Testament times, which have been preserved for us, that God should have a Son are few and far between. There are a great many prophetic utterances that speak of his birth, ministry, death, and resurrection—in all of which it is implicit in the very nature of things that God was to be his Father—but there are only a few places where he is spoken of as a Son in so many words. This, however, is not overly strange. There is also very little in the Old Testament about baptism for the remission of sins or the laying on of hands for the receipt of the Holy Ghost. And yet these ordinances began with Adam and were performed ever thereafter among the faithful. Providentially, a knowledge of them and of our Lord's divine Sonship have been restored in that portion of the Old Testament now published in the Pearl of Great Price. It is apparent that these plain and precious truths are among those deleted from Holy Writ by evil and conspiring men, along the line indicated by Nephi. (1 Ne. 13.) But perhaps also that Old Testament had among the ancient Jews contained as much of the truth in as great plainness as that rebellious and spiritually benighted people were entitled to possess. The Lord gives only that portion of his word to any people which they are prepared spiritually to receive. (Alma 12:9-11.)

But we do have some utterances which, though not all that might be desired, are somewhat helpful. In the midst of a passage that is clearly Messianic, the Lord says of the Seed of David: "I will be his father, and he shall be my son." (2 Sam. 7:14.) In the second Psalm, the whole of which is also clearly Messianic, occurs this statement: "Thou art my Son; this day have I begotten thee." (Ps. 2:7.) Paul quotes both of these statements in Hebrews 1:5 and says they are prophecies that Christ would come as the Son of God. This second Psalm contains the instruction, "Kiss [or better, receive instruction from] the Son. . . . Blessed are all they that put their trust in him" (Ps. 2:12), which manifestly is a Messianic message.

Paul also quotes from Psalm 45, which again is Messianic in its entirety, these words: "Thy throne, O God, is for ever and ever: the sceptre of thy kingdom is a right sceptre. Thou lovest righteousness, and hatest wickedness: therefore God, thy God, hath anointed thee with the oil of gladness above thy fellows." (Ps. 45:6-7.) He says in Hebrews 1:8 that they were said "unto the Son," meaning that when words speak of one God who himself has a God, they are speaking of a Son who has a Father. A prophecy about the coming of the Son that is not found in our version of the Old Testament reads: "And let all the angels of God worship him." This Paul says finds fulfillment in the bringing of "the firstbegotten into the world." (Heb. 1:6.) The only Old Testament reference in which the plain words "the Son of God" are used is in the case of Shadrach, Meshach, and Abednego being cast into the fiery furnace. What Nebuchadnezzar sees is not three, but "four men loose, walking in the midst of the fire, and they have no hurt; and the form of the fourth is like the Son of God." (Dan. 3:25.)

Actually the Book of Mormon tells us more about the usage of the name *the Son of God* by Old Testament

143

prophets than does that volume of Holy Writ itself. Nephi the son of Helaman, as he sought diligently to prepare his people for the coming of their Messiah, told them that both Moses and Abraham bore record "that the Son of God should come"; that "many before the days of Abraham" so certified; that "all the holy prophets" from Abraham to Moses did likewise; and that "since the days of Abraham there have been many prophets that have testified of these things," including Zenos, Zenock, Ezias, Isaiah, and Jeremiah, all of whom labored among Old Testament peoples. The same witness, he said, had been born by "almost all of our fathers" among the Nephites. (Hel. 8:13-23.)

Alma, with the brass plates of Laban as his source, quoted these words from a prayer of Zenos: "And thou didst hear me. And again, O God, when I did turn to my house thou didst hear me in my prayer. And when I did turn unto my closet, O Lord, and prayed unto thee, thou didst hear me. Yea, thou art merciful unto thy children when they cry unto thee, to be heard of thee and not of men, and thou wilt hear them. Yea, O God, thou hast been merciful unto me, and heard my cries in the midst of thy congregations. Yea, and thou hast also heard me when I have been cast out and have been despised by mine enemies; yea, thou didst hear my cries, and wast angry with mine enemies, and thou didst visit them in thine anger with speedy destruction. And thou didst hear me because of mine afflictions and my sincerity; and it is because of thy Son that thou hast been thus merciful unto me, therefore I will cry unto thee in all mine afflictions, for in thee is my joy; for thou hast turned thy judgments away from me, because of thy Son." Also: "Thou hast turned away thy judgments because of thy Son." And these expressions of Zenock: "Thou art angry, O Lord, with this people, because they will not understand thy mercies which thou hast bestowed upon them because of thy Son." (Alma 33:3-16.)

Fragmentary as our records are, it is nonetheless clear

that all of the prophets of Old Testament times knew and taught that the promised Messiah would be the Son of God.

The Book of Mormon Testifies of the Son of God

It is the will and purpose of the Lord to reveal to his children on earth as much about Christ and salvation as they are prepared to receive. Some, like the brother of Jared, gain a perfect knowledge of these things (Ether 3:6-26); others are taught in dark similitudes only, as was often the case with Israel from the time of Moses to our Lord's coming; and yet others, including portions at least of the Nephite nation, were taught the truth in relative perfection and fulness.

Nephi says that the limitations placed upon the Jews, whence he and his father came, were because "their works were works of darkness, and their doings were doings of abominations," but that his purpose was to prophesy in "plainness" unto his people. (2 Ne. 25:1-10.) Subsequent Book of Mormon prophets followed Nephi's pattern so that we now have in that volume of divine truth a great treasure house of light and knowledge about Him who came as God's Son to redeem his people. If ever there was a compilation of inspired writings that stand as a witness of the divine Sonship of the Lord Jesus Christ, that work is the Book of Mormon!

Of it, and the great restoration of eternal truth of which it is a part, the inspired Psalmist wrote: "I will hear what God the Lord will speak: for he will speak peace unto his people, and to his saints: but let them not turn again to folly. Surely his salvation is nigh them that fear him; that glory may dwell in our land. Mercy and truth are met together; righteousness and peace have kissed each other. Truth shall spring out of the earth; and righteousness shall look down from heaven." (Ps. 85:8-11.)

Of it, as he revealed his latter-day purposes to Enoch, that Lord who comprehended the end from the beginning said: "Righteousness will I send down out of heaven; and truth will I sent forth out of the earth, to bear testimony of mine Only Begotten; his resurrection from the dead; yea, and also the resurrection of all men." (Moses 7:62.)

Through it, as Isaiah so prophetically foresaw, "the eyes of the blind shall see out of obscurity, and out of darkness. The meek also shall increase their joy in the Lord, and the poor among men shall rejoice in the Holy One of Israel"; "They also that erred in spirit shall come to understanding, and they that murmured shall learn doctrine." (Isa. 29.)

Because it came forth, as the seeric insight of Ezekiel has so plainly set forth, latter-day Israel would be gathered, her people would become clean before the Lord, he would make with them again his everlasting gospel covenant, and his tabernacle and temple would be in their midst forevermore. (Ezek. 37:15-28.)

And to it we now turn to take samples only of that pure prophecy, of that plain and perfect utterance, which reveals the commission of the Holy Messiah to come to earth as the Son of God. Since the whole purpose of the Book of Mormon, a companion volume to the Bible, written as it was "by the spirit of prophecy and of revelation," is to convince "the Jew and Gentile that Jesus is the Christ, the Eternal God" (title page), it comes as no surprise to find the record abounding in such plain statements as these:

"The great question," Amulek taught, "is whether the word be in the Son of God, or whether there shall be no Christ." His testimony was: "The word is in Christ unto salvation." (Alma 34:5-6.)

In presenting the message of salvation to nonmembers of the Church, Aaron asked: "Believest thou that the Son of God shall come to redeem mankind from their sins?" He then testified: "There could be no redemption for mankind save it were through the death and sufferings of Christ, and the atonement of his blood." (Alma 21:7, 9.)

And the testimony of all the prophets of this branch of the house of Israel was: "The gate of heaven is open unto all, even to those who will believe on the name of Jesus Christ, who is the Son of God." (Hel. 3:28.)

Nephi, on whose shoulders so much of the future of his people rested, spoke of the faith of his father, Lehi, in the Son of God, and then said: "The Son of God was the Messiah who should come." (1 Ne. 10:17.) Nephi also identified this Savior as "the Son of the most high God" (1 Ne. 11:6), "the Son of the Eternal Father" (1 Ne. 11:21), and "the Son of the everlasting God" (1 Ne. 11:32). "The Messiah," Nephi said, "shall be Jesus Christ, the Son of God" (2 Ne. 25:19), and he is "the Holy One of Israel" (2 Ne. 30:2). The 31st chapter of Second Nephi contains several plain statements about the Father and the Son, as does also the 15th chapter of Mosiah.

The angel who taught the doctrine of the atonement to King Benjamin called our Lord "Jesus Christ, the Son of God, the Father of heaven and earth." (Mosiah 3:8.) Alma said: "Jesus Christ shall come, yea, the Son, the Only Begotten of the Father, full of grace, and mercy, and truth." Also: "The Son of God cometh in his glory, in his might, majesty, power, and dominion." (Alma 5:48, 50.) And so, in plainness, using language that cannot be misunderstood, one after another of the Nephite prophets testified of Him through whom salvation comes. Similar passages, all interwoven into the same general theme, are quoted by the score in other parts of this heaven-sent work.

Our Lord's Disciples Testify of Him

We have seen how the prophets who were before him bore record of the coming birth and ministry of their Messiah as the Son of God. For four thousand years all those with prophetic insight looked forward to his redemptive sacrifice and the salvation resulting therefrom. But those four millenniums of prophecy were but the beginning of what is to be. After he came, the same witness of his divine Sonship fell from the lips of his mortal disciples, and it continues now on the tongues of all who are like-minded with the ancients and who are endowed with the same power from on high which they possessed. A prophet is a prophet whether he lived before Christ came, during his mortal ministry, or since his ascension to sit on the right hand of the Majesty on high—and all prophets everlastingly are witnesses of their Lord.

Among those who saw him while he dwelt as a mortal on earth and to whom the Spirit bore record that he was the Lord's Christ we note the following:

Mary, his mother. She it was to whom Gabriel came with the message, "Thou shalt conceive in thy womb, and bring forth a son, and shalt call his name JESUS. He shall be great, and shall be called the Son of the Highest." (Luke 1:31-32.) She it was to whom the angel said: "The Holy Ghost shall come upon thee, and the power of the Highest shall overshadow thee: therefore also that holy thing which shall be born of thee shall be called the Son of God." (Luke 1:35.) She it was who "was carried away in the Spirit" and became "the mother of the Son of God, after the manner of the flesh." (1 Ne. 11:18-19.) Mary knew that the fruit of her womb was the Eternal One.

Joseph, the carpenter. It was to this quiet, self-effacing man that the angelic ministrant said: "Fear not to take unto thee Mary thy wife: for that which is conceived in her is of the Holy Ghost. And she shall bring forth a son, and thou shalt call his name JESUS: for he shall save his people from their sins." (Matt. 1:20-21.) It was to him that an angel of the Lord came, declaring: "Arise, and take the young child and his mother, and flee into Egypt, and be thou there until I bring thee word: for Herod will seek the young child to destroy him." (Matt. 2:13.) It was to him that Mary confided what great things had been done to her. Joseph knew who Jesus was.

Elisabeth, the mother of John. Dwelling in an unnamed city of Judah, her womb housing the unborn Baptist, she it was to whom Mary fled for consolation and comfort after

148

Gabriel gave forth his grave pronouncement. And she, Elisabeth, seeing Mary, "was filled with the Holy Ghost," and it was revealed to her that Mary was to be the "mother of my Lord." (Luke 1:36-45.)

John the Baptist. This is he who stands alone among all earth's inhabitants of whom we have knowledge. He was "filled with the Holy Ghost from his mother's womb." (D&C 84:27.) While still encased therein, Elisabeth his mother being in "the sixth month" of her pregnancy, the unborn John was filled with the Holy Ghost and "leaped in her womb," as he received the witness that the mother of his Lord was present. (Luke 1:36-45.) This is he who baptized Jesus, saw the heavens open and the Holy Ghost descend in calm serenity, and heard the voice of the Father say, "This is my beloved Son, in whom I am well pleased." (Matt. 3:13-17; Luke 3:21-22.) This is he whose enduring witness for all ages is: "Behold the Lamb of God, which taketh away the sin of the world." (John 1:29.)

Peter, the chief apostle. Speaking for all of the Twelve, he gave this witness: "Thou art the Christ, the Son of the living God." (Matt. 16:16.) And: "We believe and are sure that thou art that Christ, the Son of the living God." (John 6:69.)

Martha of Bethany. "I believe that thou art the Christ, the Son of God, which should come into the world." (John 11:27.)

John the apostle. "Jesus is the Christ, the Son of God." (John 20:31.)

Andrew, Simon Peter's brother. "We have found the Messias, which is, being interpreted, the Christ." (John 1:41.)

Philip of Bethsaida. "We have found him, of whom Moses in the law, and the prophets, did write, Jesus of Nazareth." (John 1:45.)

Nathaneal. "Rabbi, thou art the Son of God; thou art the King of Israel." (John 1:49.)

Simeon, a just and devout man. "It was revealed unto him by the Holy Ghost" that Jesus was "the Lord's Christ." (Luke 2:25-35.)

149

Anna, a prophetess. As with Simeon, she too knew of our Lord's divinity by the power of the Spirit, "and spake of him to all them that looked for redemption in Jerusalem." (Luke 2:36-38.)

Unnamed and Unnumbered Others. The ancient scriptures do not pretend to record all the testimonies of all the witnesses who knew by revelation from on high that Jesus was the Lord, any more than our modern scriptures attempt to name and record the witness of all who believe and know in our day. Did not Mary of Bethany believe with the same fervor found in the heart of her sister Martha? Were not Peter's words simply a sample of what all the apostles felt and knew in their souls? Surely Lazarus, whose spirit had spent four days in paradise and who was called back to mortal life by the voice of Him to whom all things are subject, surely he knew Jesus was Lord of all. And what of the man blind from birth who came seeing at Jesus' word; and the shepherds who saw the angelic ministrant and heard the heavenly choir; and the wise men who came from the east; and the many who believed because Lazarus arose and because of the other miracles; and what of all those who were converted by the Master's teachings and by the ministry of the apostles and seventies; and so we might go on and on. Truly, the testimony of Jesus was had by and borne among his fellow mortals. The record is not silent in letting it be known that faithful men, women, and children knew and testified that he was God's Holy Son.

Disciples Testify of the Resurrected Lord

Testimonies borne by inspired mortals gained a new dimension after our Lord rose from the dead. Now his witnesses could point to the fact of his resurrection as the conclusive proof that God was his Father. That our Lord appeared as a resurrected being many times to hosts of people is well known to the saints. Pages 839 to 876 of volume one of my *Doctrinal New Testament Commentary* contain a discussion of his various appearances in the Old World. Chapters 11 through 30 of Third Nephi in the Book of Mormon tell of his resurrected ministry among the Nephites, so that thousands of that noble race would become living witnesses of his status as the Savior and Redeemer of men. For our purposes here, let us but sample the post-resurrection witness borne by saints who knew whereof they spoke.

After Jesus rose from the dead, Peter and the congregation (probably composed of male and female believers) who saw him in the upper room were able to say: 'We felt the nail marks in his hands and in his feet; we thrust our hands into his wounded side; we felt the flesh and bones of which his body is composed; he ate before us; we heard his voice; we recognized him as the same Jesus with whom we walked and talked and lived for three and a half years; and we know he is the Son of God.' (See Luke 24.)

After he rose from the dead, Thomas knelt before him and exclaimed in worshipful awe: "My Lord and my God." (John 20:28.)

After he rose from the dead, he appeared to Paul on the Damascus road, and that newly found witness, being converted, straightway "preached Christ in the synagogues, that he is the Son of God." (Acts 9:20.)

After he rose from the dead, he stood before his beloved John, then banished on Patmos, placed his right hand upon that holy apostle, and said: "Fear not; I am the first and the last: I am he that liveth, and was dead; and, behold, I am alive for evermore, Amen; and have the keys of hell and of death." (Rev. 1:17-18.)

After he rose from the dead, he was introduced by his Father to the Nephites in these words: "Behold my Beloved Son, in whom I am well pleased, in whom I have glorified my name—hear ye him." (3 Ne. 11:7.) He thereupon ministered personally among that remnant of the house of Israel, set up his kingdom as he had done in Jerusalem, called Twelve to whom he gave apostolic keys and power, and prepared the way for other chosen vessels to bear record

151

of his holy name. Such of their witness as we now have is in the Book of Mormon, of which record one of them, Mormon, says: It was written that men "may be persuaded that Jesus is the Christ, the Son of the living God." (Morm. 5:14.) This same Mormon, writing to his brethren the Lamanites, bore this testimony: "Know ye that ye must come to the knowledge of your fathers, and repent of all your sins and iniquities, and believe in Jesus Christ, that he is the Son of God, and that he was slain by the Jews, and by the power of the Father he hath risen again, whereby he hath gained the victory over the grave." (Morm. 7:5.)

But as pertaining to us, and to all who live in our day, the crowning and most important testimony of the risen Lord is that given by those called and sent so to testify at this time. Of these Joseph Smith is the chief. "I saw two Personages," he says of the great theophany which ushered in this dispensation, "whose brightness and glory defy all description, standing above me in the air. One of them spake unto me, calling me by name and said, pointing to the other—*This is My Beloved Son. Hear Him!*" (JS-H 17.) Later, he and Oliver Cowdery gave us this testimony: "We saw the Lord," whom they then described, and he said unto them: "I am the first and the last; I am he who liveth, I am he who was slain; I am your advocate with the Father." (D&C 110:1-4.) And it was Joseph Smith and Sidney Rigdon who left us this fervent witness: "And now, after the many testimonies which have been given of him, this is the testimony, last of all, which we give of him: That he lives! For we saw him, even on the right hand of God; and we heard the voice bearing record that he is the Only Begotten of the Father." (D&C 76:22-23.)

Who can doubt that believing disciples have seen Him whose Father is God and whose atoning sacrifice has given efficacy, virtue, and force to the Father's plans and purposes?

Our Lord Bears Testimony of Himself

If the Man Jesus, a Jewish Rabbi, who was born of Mary in Bethlehem of Judea, who grew to manhood in Nazareth of Galilee, who ministered among men for three and a half years in Palestine, and who was crucified outside Jerusalem's wall at a place called Golgotha; if this Man was the Son of God, if he came to fulfill all that was spoken from the beginning by all the holy prophets, we would expect him to know it and to say so. And that is precisely what happened. He knew God was his Father, and he so testified again and again and again, day in and day out, early and late, to every receptive person who would give heed to his voice. The four Gospels contain one continuous proclamation of his divine Sonship, with our Lord himself doing nearly all of the teaching. His personal testimony is everywhere to be found. For our purposes, although some of his testimonies fall into more categories than one, let us note six ways and means used by him to teach his divine Sonship:

1. *Pure testimony: that is, plain, categorical statements that he was the Messiah, the Son of God.*

The first of these, in point of time and of which we have record, is his famous reply to Mary and Joseph when he was but twelve years of age: "Wist ye not that I must be about my Father's business?" It is clear that he, even then, considered his teaching in the temple as the work of Him whose Son he was. (Luke 2:42-52.) How much more teaching and how many more testimonies he bore between then and the commencement of his formal ministry when he was about thirty years of age we can only guess.

During his formal ministry he found opportunity to say: "I and my Father are one," which his hearers considered blasphemy, at which point in their colloquy he said plainly, "I am the Son of God." (John 10:30-36.)

At Jacob's well, the Samaritan woman said, "I know that

Messias cometh, which is called Christ: when he is come, he will tell us all things." With that simplicity and plainness by which the greatest of all truths are conveyed, Jesus replied: "I that speak unto thee am he." (John 4:25-26.)

Because the Jews persecuted him for healing a man on the Sabbath, he said, "My Father worketh hitherto, and I work. Therefore the Jews sought the more to kill him, because he not only had broken the sabbath, but said also that God was his Father, making himself equal with God." Thereupon Jesus made an elaborate statement amplifying and explaining his relationship with his Father, including an announcement of these eternal verities about the Son: He worked by the power of the Father; he would bring to pass the resurrection; he was to be honored along with the Father; he would judge all men; he would preach to the spirits in prison and open the graves of earth's departed ones; he had life in himself, even as did the Father—all this and much, much more, ending with this stinging rebuke: "Do not think that I will accuse you to the Father: there is one that accuseth you, even Moses, in whom ye trust. For had ye believed Moses, ye would have believed me: for he wrote of me. But if ye believe not his writings, how shall ye believe my words?" (John 5:1-47.)

When Jesus made no response to the false witnesses who testified against him during the nighttime trial before Caiaphas, the high priest, that conspiring functionary said: "I adjure thee by the living God, that thou tell us whether thou be the Christ, the Son of God. Jesus saith unto him, Thou hast said: nevertheless I say unto you, Hereafter shall ye see the Son of man sitting on the right hand of power, and coming in the clouds of heaven." (Matt. 26:63-64.) Mark's account of this same blasphemously spoken query and its divinely inspired answer is: "Art thou the Christ, the Son of the Blessed? And Jesus said, I am: and ye shall see the Son of man sitting on the right hand of power, and coming in the clouds of heaven." (Mark 14:61-62.)

Then, when it was morning and he came formally before the Sanhedrin, he was asked: "Art thou the Christ? tell us. And he said unto them, If I tell you, ye will not believe: And if I also ask you, ye will not answer me, nor let me go. Hereafter shall the Son of man sit on the right hand of the power of God. Then said they all, Art thou then the Son of God? And he said unto them, Ye say that I am." (Luke 22:67-70.) The statement "Ye say that I am" is an idiomatic expression meaning 'You asked the question, and the answer is Yes,' and it was so understood by all who heard it.

Later, before Pilate, the Roman governor asked: "Art thou the King of the Jews? Jesus answered him, Sayest thou this thing of thyself, or did others tell it thee of me? Pilate answered, Am I a Jew? Thine own nation and the chief priests have delivered thee unto me: what hast thou done? Jesus answered, My kingdom is not of this world: if my kingdom were of this world, then would my servants fight, that I should not be delivered to the Jews: but now is my kingdom not from hence. Pilate therefore said unto him, Art thou a king then? Jesus answered, Thou sayest that I am a king. To this end was I born, and for this cause came I into the world, that I should bear witness unto the truth." (John 18:33-37.) And truly the greatest truths of which he bore record were that God was his Father and that he was the promised Son.

2. *Figurative statements understood by all who were acquainted with Jewish theology to mean that he was the Christ.*

These were numerous and for all practical purposes were as clearly understood by his hearers as any of his claims to divinity. To the extent we have learned the Jewish system of similitudes and imagery they are also envisioned by us. For instance:

Jesus said, "I am the good shepherd" (John 10:14), which was tantamount to saying, 'I am the Lord Jehovah,' because his Jewish hearers revered the Davidic declaration: "Jehovah is my shepherd; I shall not want," and so on through the 23rd Psalm. Our anglicized reading is "The Lord is my shepherd," but in the Hebrew the title *Lord* is the name *Jehovah.*

Speaking in a parable, Jesus said, "I am the door of the sheep. . . . I am the door: by me if any man enter in, he shall be saved, and shall go in and out, and find pasture." (John 10:7-9.) That is, 'I am the Messianic Deliverer who is to come. I am he of whom Isaiah wrote: "He shall feed his flock like a shepherd: he shall gather the lambs with his arm, and carry them in his bosom, and shall gently lead those that are with young." ' (Isa. 40:11.)

Jesus said: "I am the bread of life. . . . I am living bread which came down from heaven." (John 6:35, 51.) Their fathers had lived for forty years on manna, doing so, in the language of Moses, to certify that "man doth not live by bread only, but by every word that proceedeth out of the mouth of the Lord doth man live." (Deut. 8:3.) To those with this background and understanding, our Lord's declaration that he was the living bread meant that he was the Lord in whose memory their fathers had eaten manna in the wilderness and that he had now come down from heaven to give them that living bread.

Other of our Lord's statements—such as, "I am the way, the truth, and the life: no man cometh unto the Father, but by me" (John 14:6); "I am the light of the world" (John 8:12); "I am the true vine, and my Father is the husbandman" (John 15:1)—all had similar meanings and bore record that salvation was in him and that therefore he was the Messiah. His declaration "Before Abraham was, I am" (John 8:58) meant to his hearers: 'Before Abraham was I, the Great I AM,' or 'Before Abraham was I, Jehovah.' And his practice of quoting known and recognized Messianic prophecies and then saying, "This day is this scripture fulfilled in your ears" (Luke 4:16-21), had no effect except to identify the speaker as the One of whom the ancient prophet spoke.

3. *Doctrinal teachings which, spoken by Jesus and*

156

weighed in context, presuppose that the Speaker is more than a mortal.

These are interwoven in nearly all his preachments and are illustrated by the following:

"Not every one that saith unto me, Lord, Lord, shall enter into the kingdom of heaven; but he that doeth the will of my Father which is in heaven. Many will say to me in that day, Lord, Lord, have we not prophesied in thy name? and in thy name have cast out devils? and in thy name done many wonderful works? And then will I profess unto them, I never knew you: depart from me, ye that work iniquity." (Matt. 7:21-23.)

"All things are delivered unto me of my Father: and no man knoweth the Son, but the Father; neither knoweth any man the Father, save the Son, and he to whomsoever the Son will reveal him. Come unto me, all ye that labour and are heavy laden, and I will give you rest." (Matt. 11:27-28.)

"I will give unto thee the keys of the kingdom of heaven: and whatsoever thou shalt bind on earth shall be bound in heaven: and whatsoever thou shalt loose on earth shall be loosed in heaven." (Matt. 16:19.)

"He that heareth my word, and believeth on him that sent me, hath everlasting life, and shall not come into condemnation; but is passed from death unto life. Verily, verily, I say unto you, The hour is coming, and now is, when the dead shall hear the voice of the Son of God: and they that hear shall live. For as the Father hath life in himself; so hath he given to the Son to have life in himself." (John 5:24-26.)

"He that believeth on me hath everlasting life. . . . Whoso eateth my flesh, and drinketh my blood, hath eternal life; and I will raise him up at the last day." (John 6:47, 54.)

"If ye believe not that I am he, ye shall die in your sins." (John 8:24.)

"He that hath seen me hath seen the Father." (John 14:9.)

"All things that the Father hath are mine." (John 16:15.)

"And this is life eternal, that they might know thee the

only true God, and Jesus Christ, whom thou hast sent. I have glorified thee on the earth: I have finished the work which thou gavest me to do. And now, O Father, glorify thou me with thine own self with the glory which I had with thee before the world was." (John 17:3-5.)

Implicit in these and hundreds of other passages is the simple truth that he is the Son of God. Truly, never man spake as this man spake.

4. *Our Lord's repeated Son of Man pronouncements.*

These are so numerous, so persuasive, and yet so little understood in their status as testimony of his divine Sonship that, although they might be classified merely as testimony by him about himself, they deserve special consideration. Whenever he used the designation Son of Man, it was as though he said Son of God, for the Man to whom he referred was Man of Holiness, his Father.

"The Son of man came not to be ministered unto, but to minister," he said, "and to give his life a ransom for many." (Matt. 20:28.) In the day when that ransoming sacrifice is made, "The Son of man shall be betrayed into the hands of men: And they shall kill him, and the third day he shall be raised again." (Matt. 17:22-23.) "Ye know that after two days is the feast of the passover, and the Son of man is betrayed to be crucified." (Matt. 26:2.) "When ye have lifted up the Son of man, then shall ye know that I am he, and that I do nothing of myself; but as my Father hath taught me, I speak these things. And he that sent me is with me: the Father hath not left me alone; for I do always those things that please him." (John 8:28-29.) "Whosoever therefore shall be ashamed of me and of my words in his adulterous and sinful generation; of him also shall the Son of man be ashamed, when he cometh in the glory of his Father with the holy angels." (Mark 8:38.)

5. *The works he performed bear record of his divinity.*

It is not in word only that true testimony is borne. False ministers and the devils themselves can claim to represent the true Master and to present the true gospel. Satan himself came personally to Moses and commanded: "I am the Only Begotten, worship me." (Moses 1:19.) Good works must always accompany the testimony of true ministers. When true words are spoken by the power of the Spirit, all who hear are obligated to believe that which is said and to make it a part of their lives. Jesus' spoken testimony, standing alone, is binding. But it is also proper to view his works along with his words.

When his Jewish detractors doubted his testimony, the Man Jesus said: "The works which the Father hath given me to finish, the same works that I do, bear witness of me, that the Father hath sent me." (John 5:36.) Also: "If I do not the works of my Father, believe me not. But if I do, though ye believe not me, believe the works: that ye may know, and believe, that the Father is in me, and I in him." (John 10:37-38.)

It was this test of eternal verity that he used when two men came and said: "John Baptist hath sent us unto thee, saying, Art thou he that should come? or look we for another?" The scripture records no immediate answer to this interrogatory. Instead it says:"And in that same hour he cured many of their infirmities and plagues, and of evil spirits; and unto many that were blind he gave sight." After the miracles were wrought, "Then Jesus answering said unto them, Go your way, and tell John what things ye have seen and heard; how that the blind see, the lame walk, the lepers are cleansed, the deaf hear, the dead are raised, to the poor the gospel is preached. And blessed is he, whosoever shall not be offended in me." (Luke 7:20-23.)

6. *His works, coupled with the spoken word, combine to bear witness that he is God's Son.*

Such are the most irrefutable of all testimonies. The spoken word is there. Those who hear it are aware of the issue involved. A miracle, which cannot be denied or gainsaid, is performed. None but God or one approved by him could do the miracle. Sinners do not raise the dead. Blind eyes are not opened by impostors. "There was not any

159

man who could do a miracle in the name of Jesus save he were cleansed every whit from his iniquity." (3 Ne. 8:1.) And so when Jesus both performed miracles and said he was the Son of God, who could deny the fact? Three illustrations will suffice for our purpose:

First, he forgave sins (which none but God can do), and then to prove he had the power so to act, he healed the same person from his palsy. "Son, be of good cheer; thy sins be forgiven thee," he said. (Matt. 9:2.) Those who heard this reasoned: "Why doth this man thus speak blasphemies? who can forgive sins but God only?" (Mark 2:7.) Thereupon Jesus said: "Wherefore think ye evil in your hearts? For whether is easier, to say, Thy sins be forgiven thee; or to say, Arise, and walk? But that ye may know that the Son of man hath power on earth to forgive sins, (then saith he to the sick of the palsy,) Arise, take up thy bed, and go unto thine house. And he arose, and departed to his house." (Matt. 9:4-7.)

Second, he sought out and opened the eyes of a man born blind. He let the word of the miracle spread throughout the city. There was a division among the people, some saying he was a sinner, others that he was of God. To the one whose eyes had been opened, Jesus said: "Dost thou believe on the Son of God? He answered and said, Who is he, Lord, that I might believe on him? And Jesus said unto him, Thou hast both seen him, and it is he that talketh with thee. And he said, Lord, I believe. And he worshipped him." (John 9:35-38.) Then to the multitude who had assembled because the fact of the miracle had been noised about, he preached his great sermon on the good shepherd, announcing himself as the Lord Jehovah and as the Son of God. "There was a division therefore again among the Jews for these sayings. And many of them said, He hath a devil, and is mad; why hear ye him? Other said, These are not the words of him that hath a devil. Can a devil open the eyes of the blind?" (John 10:1-41.) Thus, the issue was clearly put. He said he was the Son of God and he did what no one could do without God's approval. Truly his testimony is irrefutable.

Third, he received word of Lazarus' death, deliberately waited four days before arriving at the tomb, heard the importuning pleas of Martha, told her, "Thy brother shall rise again," and then said, "I am the resurrection, and the life: he that believeth in me, though he were dead, yet shall he live: And whosoever liveth and believeth in me shall never die." (John 11:25-26.) That is: 'Immortality and eternal life come by me. As thou hast said, I am the Son of God, and if ye believe in me, ye shall have eternal life.' She replied: "I believe that thou art the Christ, the Son of God, which should come into the world." (John 11:27.) Then it was that the Lord of Life called, "Lazarus, come forth," and he who had been dead four days, whose body stank, whose flesh and bones had started to decay and to return to mother earth, then it was that the dead and decomposing body came forth to live again. If he who does such things says he is the Son of God, surely it is so.

Was the Man Jesus the Promised Son of God?

Who can doubt that the Great Jehovah was chosen before the world was to be the Son of God? Who will question that he was revealed to Adam? That all of the prophets of all the ages—inspired men on both continents—foretold his birth and ministry? That he was to be the promised Messiah, the Great Deliverer, our Savior and Redeemer? So it is written, and so it is!

And similarly may we inquire: Was the Man Jesus the promised Son of God? Was he who dwelt on earth in time's meridian the One prepared from all eternity to work out the infinite and eternal atonment? He testified that he was, and the Jews understood his witness. Before Pilate, as calls of "Crucify him, crucify him" filled the air, they testified: "By our law he ought to die, because he made himself the Son of

God." (John 19:6-7.) While he hung in agony upon the cross these same voices mocked: "He saved others; himself he cannot save. If he be the King of Israel, let him now come down from the cross, and we will believe him. He trusted in God; let him deliver him now, if he will have him: for he said, I am the Son of God." (Matt. 27:42-43.)

There is no question that the mortal testimony of the Son of Man was known for what it was by those who heard it. Nor is there any question that he spoke the truth. The Son of Man came to be a ransom for many—to save all men from that everlasting prison, the grave, and to save those who believe and obey from that everlasting darkness which is spiritual death.

He is God's Son. This we know. And the Spirit beareth witness.

Chapter 10

CHRIST IS THE GOD OF ISRAEL

Who Is the God of Our Fathers?

This is the word of the Lord to all Israel: "Hearken unto me, ye that follow after righteousness. Look unto the rock from whence ye are hewn, and to the hole of the pit from whence ye are digged. Look unto Abraham, your father, and unto Sarah, she that bare you." (2 Ne. 8:1-2.)

Why? What purpose is there in looking to Abraham, our father, and to Sarah, our mother? The answer is not hard to find. Abraham, as also Isaac and Jacob, worshiped the Father in spirit and in truth and thereby gained an inheritance in the kingdom of heaven; if we who are Israel can look to them and do the works they did, we can have a like inheritance of glory and honor with them. "Go ye, therefore, and do the works of Abraham" is the Lord's decree; "enter ye into my law and ye shall be saved." (D&C 132:32.)

Salvation comes only by worshiping the true God. Abraham and "all the holy prophets . . . believed in Christ and worshiped the Father in his name." (Jacob 4:4-5.) They have now entered into their exaltation and sit upon their thrones. (D&C 132:29-37.) To rivet our minds forever on the eternal truth that we must worship and live as they did, that Lord who saves us chose to call attention to their true form of worship by naming himself after Abraham, Isaac, and Jacob.

Abraham saw the Lord. "I am the Almighty God; walk before me, and be thou perfect," was the message given him. (Gen. 17:1.) Also: "I am the Lord thy God," came the word; "I dwell in heaven; the earth is my footstool. . . . My name is Jehovah, and I know the end from the beginning; therefore my hand shall be over thee. And I will make of thee a great nation." (Abr. 2:7-9.) Isaac and Jacob, each in turn, received similar visions and promises. (Gen. 26:1-5; 28:10-15.)

When this same God appeared to Moses in the burning bush, he announced himself as "The Lord God of your fathers, the God of Abraham, the God of Isaac, and the God of Jacob," and then proclaimed: "This is my name for ever, and this is my memorial unto all generations." (Ex. 3:15.)

Who, then, is the God of our Fathers, the God of Abraham, of Isaac, and of Jacob? He is the one who "yieldeth himself, . . . as a man, into the hands of wicked men, to be lifted up, . . . to be crucified, . . . and to be buried in a sepulchre" (1 Ne. 19:10), and to rise again in glory and triumph. He is Christ. It was Christ who appeared to Abraham. It was Christ who covenanted with him and then with Isaac and with Jacob. It was Christ of whom Nephi spoke when he said: "The fulness of mine intent is that I may persuade men to come unto the God of Abraham, and the God of Isaac, and the God of Jacob, and be saved." (1 Ne. 6:4.)

Who Is the God of Israel?

Before weighing and interpreting the numerous and expressive designations of Deity used by the prophets in Israel, we should have securely lodged in our hearts the everlasting verity that Christ is the God of Israel. Whatever the world may imagine, whatever any of the cultist sects of Christendom may attempt to expound relative to Jehovah, whatever the wisdom of men may suppose, the plain, unalterable fact is that the Lord Jehovah was the promised Savior, Redeemer, Deliverer, and Messiah, and that he is

Christ. This truth is recorded in the Old Testament so that all who will believe may do so. But it is set forth so specifically and plainly in the Book of Mormon that one either believes and accepts the witness or he rejects the book itself.

One of Nephi's great Messianic prophecies proclaimed that when "the very God of Israel" dwelt among men, they would "set him at naught, and hearken not to the voice of his counsels," and would themselves "be scourged by all people, because they crucify the God of Israel." (1 Ne. 19:7-14.) The most perfect witness that Israel's God and Mary's Son were one and the same person was borne by the resurrected Jesus to the Nephites in these words: "I am Jesus Christ. . . . Come forth unto me, that ye may thrust your hands into my side, and also that ye may feel the prints of the nails in my hands and in my feet, that ye may know that I am the God of Israel, and the God of the whole earth, and have been slain for the sins of the world." (3 Ne. 11:10-14.)

With this reality firmly established, we are now ready to analyze and interpret many of the Messianic utterances which are interwoven in the ancient scriptures.

Israel's God Is the Eternal One

Our Lord, who is the Firstborn spirit child of the Eternal Elohim, is himself also the Eternal One. Implicit in his spirit birth as the Firstborn is the fact that, as with all the spirit children of the Father, he had a beginning; there was a day when he came into being as a conscious identity, as a spirit entity, as an organized intelligence. How then is he the Eternal One? It might be said that he is eternal, as all men are, meaning that spirit element—the intelligence which was organized into intelligences—has always existed and is therefore eternal. But the full and complete meaning of the designation is that he has become eternal as an individual; he has joined the ranks of eternal beings; and he is thus described as being from eternity to eternity.

Eternity is the name of that infinite duration of existence when we lived as the spirit children of the Eternal Father. It contrasts with time, which is our temporal or mortal existence. Eternity is also that existence gained by exalted beings who gain eternal families of their own that are patterned after the family of God the Father. When our revelations say of Christ, "From eternity to eternity he is the same, and his years never fail" (D&C 76:4), they mean that from one preexistence to the next he does not vary, his course is one eternal round. They mean, for instance, that from our premortal or preexistent state to the day when the exalted among us provide a preexistence for our spirit children, he is the same.

Those who enter the order of celestial marriage have the potential of being "from everlasting to everlasting" (D&C 132:20), which means from one preexistence to the next. Theirs also is the state of exaltation, because they are married for time and *all* eternity, the designation *all eternity* being one which would be redundant were it not for the scriptural use of the word *eternity* as applying to the successive and recurring expanses of the creative periods.

Israel's prophets made it clear to that ancient people that their God was the Eternal One; our Lord's meridian ministers asserted the same verity in describing him in their day; and those of us in the sheepfold that is latter-day Israel have received the revealed word reasserting the same truth for our day.

"The eternal God is thy refuge," said Moses to those whom he led. (Deut. 33:27.) "I am the first, and I am the last," he himself said to Isaiah. (Isa. 44:6.) "Art thou not from everlasting, O Lord my God, mine Holy One?" intoned Habakkuk. (Hab. 1:12.) From Psalms resounds the answer: "Thou art from everlasting" (Ps. 93:2), "even from everlasting to everlasting, thou art God" (Ps. 90:2). "Thy years are throughout all generations." (Ps. 102:24.) "He is the beginning and the end, the first and the last" is Alma's testimony.

(Alma 11:39.) All these things were said of Israel's God anciently.

After his mortal probation, Paul said of him: "Jesus Christ the same yesterday, and to day, and for ever." (Heb. 13:8.)

As a resurrected being, he said to John: "I am Alpha and Omega, the first and the last. . . . Fear not; I am the first and the last: I am he that liveth, and was dead; and, behold, I am alive for evermore." (Rev. 1:11, 17-18.) This accords with his declaration to Joseph Smith and Oliver Cowdery, "I am the first and the last; I am he who liveth, I am he who was slain." (D&C 110:4.) "I am Alpha and Omega, the beginning and the end," was his affirmation to the Nephites. (3 Ne. 9:18.) It is clear that he—"the Holy One, who is without beginning of days or end of life" (D&C 78:16), who is "Alphus" and "Omegus; even Jesus Christ" (D&C 95:17)— wants a record kept, in all scripture both ancient and modern, that he is an everlasting and eternal being in whom all fulness and perfection dwell.

Christ Is the Holy One of Israel

The prophets and peoples of olden times paid homage to Jehovah under his names Holy (Isa. 57:15), Holy One (Hab. 1:12), Holy One of Jacob (Isa. 29:23), and Holy One of Israel (Isa. 45:11), thereby being constantly aware that he being holy, so should they be. (Lev. 11:45.)

Our Lord's friends and enemies acclaimed him as the Holy One when he dwelt on earth. Peter so designated him in speaking to his Jewish brethren of the great day of restoration that was to be. (Acts 3:14-21.) The better translation of one of Peter's earlier testimonies is: "We believe and are sure that thou art that Christ, the Holy One of God." (John 6:69.) Both Peter and John praised the Lord for sending his "holy child Jesus" to earth (Acts 4:23-30), and John designated him as the Holy One in his major epistle (1 Jn.

2:20). Even an unclean spirit, being cast from his ill-gotten human habitation by the Savior, cried out: "I know thee who thou art, the Holy One of God." (Mark 1:24; Luke 4:34.) And the resurrected Lord described himself to John as "He that is holy." (Rev. 3:7.)

Our Nephite brethren, both before and after our Lord's mortal sojourn, used these same terms with reference to him. Lehi called him the Holy Messiah and the Holy One. (2 Ne. 2:8-10.) Nephi (1 Ne. 22:5), Jacob (2 Ne. 9:11-51), and Amaleki (Omni 1:25-26) designated him as the Holy One of Israel. Alma (Alma 5:52) and Nephi the son of Helaman (Hel. 12:2) said simply the Holy One, as did Moroni after the bands of death had been broken (Morm. 9:14). In latter-day revelation he is called the Holy One and the Holy One of Zion. (D&C 78:15-16.)

Can anyone suppose other than that Israel's God, the mortal Master, and the risen Lord are one and the same, and that he is the Eternal Christ? So it is; and it comes, accordingly, as no surprise to find the plain-speaking Nephite prophets saying: "Christ is the Holy One of Israel" (2 Ne. 25:29), and of their setting forth the terms and conditions of the whole plan of salvation in terms of the Holy One of Israel working out the infinite and eternal atonement and of men having faith in his name to gain salvation (2 Ne. 9).

With the knowledge thus before us that the Holy One of Israel is Christ, the door is open to us to gain a new insight into the deeper and hidden meanings of many passages.

Isaiah expounds about the glory and praise to be heaped upon the Holy One of Israel in the day of restoration and of millennial peace. "In that day," he says—meaning when Israel is gathered the second time and millennial peace is settling over all the earth—Israel will be comforted and will say: "Behold, God is my salvation; I will trust, and not be afraid; for the Lord JEHOVAH is my strength and my song." In that day, Jehovah's atoning sacrifice being a thing of the past, they will say: "He also has become my salvation." To men in that day the promise is: "Therefore, with joy shall ye draw water out of the wells of salvation." In that day believing Israel shall say: "Praise the Lord, call upon his name, declare his doings among the people, make mention that his name is exalted." They shall "sing unto the Lord; for he hath done excellent things; this is known in all the earth." And then shall the righteous say: "Cry out and shout, thou inhabitant of Zion; for great is the Holy One of Israel in the midst of thee." (2 Ne. 22:1-5.)

The Holy One of Israel in the midst of thee! The Lord reigns personally upon the earth! He who came once has come again, and he is Christ the Holy One!

Christ Is the Rock of Heaven

"I am Messiah, the King of Zion, the Rock of Heaven, which is broad as eternity." (Moses 7:53.) So spake the Lord to Enoch. "I will publish the name of the Lord: ascribe ye greatness unto our God. He is the Rock, his work is perfect: for all his ways are judgment: a God of truth and without iniquity, just and right is he." (Deut. 32:3-4.) So proclaimed Moses the great lawgiver. "O thou Rock of our Salvation,/Jesus, Savior of the world" (*Hymns,* no. 130) and "Rock of Ages, cleft for me,/Let me hide myself in thee" (*Hymns,* no. 382)—so sing the modern saints. And all of this is to teach that the great Redeemer, who is Christ the Lord, is the secure foundation, a foundation "broad as eternity," upon which all men must build if they are to inherit, receive, and possess the full blessings of the infinite and eternal atonement.

Christ is the foundation upon which the house of salvation is built, and "other foundation can no man lay than that is laid, which is Jesus Christ." (1 Cor. 3:11.) He is the Rock; by him salvation comes; without him there would be neither immortality nor eternal life; and all those who build upon him, when the rains descend and the floods come and the winds blow, their houses shall stand, for they are founded upon the Rock.

"Fear not, little flock," is the voice of the Lord to his Latter-day Saints, "do good; let earth and hell combine against you, for if ye are built upon my rock, they cannot prevail." (D&C 6:34.) "Build upon my rock, which is my gospel," is his decree. (D&C 11:24.) In commanding his little flock to preach faith, repentance, baptism, and the receipt of the Holy Ghost, he says: "This is my gospel." Then of those to whom it is preached comes this word: "They shall have faith in me or they can in nowise be saved; And upon this rock I will build my church; yea, upon this rock ye are built, and if ye continue, the gates of hell shall not prevail against you." (D&C 33:12-13.) To his Nephite saints he taught that all who repent and are baptized, who remember him and keep his commandments, who partake worthily of the sacrament and have the companionship of the Holy Spirit, "are built upon my rock. But whoso among you shall do more or less than these are not built upon my rock, but are built upon a sandy foundation; and when the rain descends, and the floods come, and the winds blow, and beat upon them, they shall fall, and the gates of hell are ready open to receive them." (3 Ne. 18:12-13.)

Knowing all these things—and they have also been known by the faithful people in all ages—it comes as no surprise to find prophets in all ages speaking of the Lord as their Rock. Knowing all these things, we can also discern the inspired Messianic meanings of the many passages which extol the Rock.

David, exulting over the goodness of God, sang these words: "The Lord is my rock, and my fortress, and my deliverer; The God of my rock; in him will I trust: he is my shield, and the horn of my salvation, my high tower, and my refuge, my saviour." (2 Sam. 22:2-3.) The Psalms abound in such statements as: "Thou art my rock and my fortress." (Ps. 71:3.) "Thou art my father, my God, and the rock of my salvation." (Ps. 89:26.) "Let us make a joyful noise to the rock of our salvation." (Ps. 95:1.)

"Of the Rock that begat thee thou art unmindful," Moses

170

said in upbraiding rebellious Israel, "and hast forgotten God that formed thee." (Deut. 32:18.) Isaiah spoke of the desolation that should come upon them "because thou hast forgotten the God of thy salvation, and hast not been mindful of the rock of thy strength." (Isa. 17:10.)

Expounding the same truths—albeit more plainly, as it was their wont to do—Nephite prophets said such things as: "It is upon the rock of our Redeemer, who is Christ, the Son of God, that ye must build your foundation; that when the devil shall send forth his mighty winds, yea, his shafts in the whirlwind, yea, when all his hail and his mighty storm shall beat upon you, it shall have no power over you to drag you down to the gulf of misery and endless wo, because of the rock upon which ye are built, which is a sure foundation, a foundation whereon if men build they cannot fall." (Hel. 5:12.) Also: "Come unto that God who is the rock of your salvation." (2 Ne. 9:45.)

Paul, with a plainness rivaling in this instance that of his Nephite compatriots, endorsed the whole body of Old Testament terminology in which Israel's God is called the Rock. Theologian and scriptorian that he was, Paul referred to the ancient hand-dealings of Deity with Moses and those who followed him and the fact that "the Lord went before them by day in a pillar of a cloud, to lead them the way; and by night in a pillar of fire, to give them light." (Ex. 13:21.) He noted that being thus guided, the hosts of Israel passed through the Red Sea (Ex. 14), at which time they "did all eat the same spiritual meat; And did all drink the same spiritual drink: for they drank of that spiritual Rock that followed them: and that Rock was Christ." (1 Cor. 10:1-4.) This is one of the plainest and bluntest New Testament declarations that the God of Israel and Jesus who is called Christ are one and the same person.

The language of the Old Testament prophets describes God as their Rock, their fortress, their buckler and shield and the like. Our Christian Era hymn, written by Martin Luther, acclaims: "A mighty fortress is our God,/A tower of strength ne'er failing." (*Hymns,* no. 3.) In keeping with this view relative to the strength and power of Deity, we have the expressive declaration of Samuel: "The Strength of Israel will not lie nor repent: for he is not a man, that he should repent." (1 Sam. 15:29.) This name, the Strength of Israel, might also be translated the Victory of Israel or the Glory of Israel—all of which are designations appropriate for the Lord of Hosts, who is "a man of war" (Ex. 15:3), a God of Battles, who at his Second Coming shall "go forth, and fight against those nations [who oppose him], as when he fought in the day of battle." (Zech. 14:3.)

Christ Is the Stone of Israel

"The mighty God of Jacob . . . is the shepherd, the stone of Israel." (Gen. 49:24.) His role as a Shepherd we shall discuss shortly. His status as the Stone of Israel is akin to that of the Rock of Heaven; that is, he is the stone or foundation upon which all men must build to gain salvation in his Father's kingdom. "I am the good shepherd, the stone of Israel. He that buildeth upon this rock shall never fall" is his declaration in our day. (D&C 50:44.)

There are three great Messianic prophecies that deal with the blessings and curses to fall upon men through their acceptance or rejection of the Stone of Israel. These three prophetic utterances were generally accepted by the people of Jesus' day as being Messianic, though their full meaning and application were matters of extended study and debate.

In one of them, Isaiah's record says: "Thus said the Lord God, Behold, I lay in Zion for a foundation a stone, a tried stone, a precious corner stone, a sure foundation: he that believeth shall not make haste." (Isa. 28:16.) The emphasis here is clearly upon the blessings which shall flow from building a house of faith and salvation upon the only sure foundation, which is Christ.

In another of them, the Lord says by the mouth of Isaiah: "Sanctify the Lord of hosts himself; and let him be your fear, and let him be your dread." (Isa. 8:13.) Now, note it well, the prophecy is speaking of the God of Israel, of the Lord Jehovah. He is the one they are to fear. The dread of him is to rest upon the disobedient.

"And he shall be for a sanctuary; but for a stone of stumbling and for a rock of offence to both the houses of Israel." (Isa. 8:14.) Israel's God shall be—the tense is future—a blessing or a cursing to the whole house of Israel, to both the kingdom of Ephraim and the kingdom of Judah, and for that matter to the whole of mankind. Those who believe and obey shall find peace and rest and security in his arms; he is their sanctuary. Those who stumble at his doctrine, who are offended by his claims of divinity, shall be cast out and rejected for their disbelief.

"And he shall be . . . for a gin and for a snare to the inhabitants of Jerusalem." (Isa. 8:14.) Here the prophecy deals specifically with those among whom he ministers in mortality—"the inhabitants of Jerusalem." They lose their souls because they reject their Messiah. They are caught in the traps and snares of the adversary. "And many among them shall stumble, and fall, and be broken, and be snared, and be taken." (Isa. 8:15.)

"Bind up the testimony, seal the law among my disciples." (Isa. 8:16.) This refers to the fate of men who reject the Lord and his law. As set forth in latter-day revelation, the "disciples," those who are the Lord's servants, "go forth" with power given them "to seal both on earth and in heaven, the unbelieving and rebellious; Yea, verily, to seal them up unto the day when the wrath of God shall be poured out upon the wicked without measure." (D&C 1:8-9.) Of these wicked and unbelieving ones the revealed word says: "Behold, and lo, there are none to deliver you; for ye obeyed not my voice when I called to you out of the heavens; ye believed not my servants, and when they were sent unto you ye received them not. Wherefore, they sealed up the testimony and bound up the law, and ye were delivered over unto darkness. These shall go away into outer darkness,

173

where there is weeping, and wailing, and gnashing of teeth." (D&C 133:71-73.)

The gospel brings blessings or curses. Both are administered to men by the Lord's agents. Those whom they bless are blessed, and those whom they curse are cursed. (D&C 124:93.) The Lord's servants go forth "to bind up the law and seal up the testimony, and to prepare the saints for the hour of judgment which is to come." (D&C 88:84.) The crowning blessing bestowed is: "And of as many as the Father shall bear record, to you shall be given power to seal them up unto eternal life." (D&C 68:12.)

As we ponder the deep and wondrous meaning of these Messianic words given through Isaiah, there comes to mind the kindred expression of another, one John Baptist, than whom there was no greater prophet. He said: "He that believeth on the Son hath everlasting life: and he that believeth not the Son shall not see life; but the wrath of God abideth on him." (John 3:36.)

In the third of these Old Testament utterances, which are all in effect linked together as one, we read: "The stone which the builders refused is become the head stone of the corner. This is the Lord's doing; it is marvellous in our eyes." (Ps. 118:22-23.) The meaning here is clear. The Jews reject their Messiah, but he nonetheless becomes and remains the Stone which holds the whole structure of salvation together, a thing that is marvelous in all eyes.

At this point we might well insert these words of Nephi's brother Jacob: "I perceive by the workings of the Spirit which is in me," he said, "that by the stumbling of the Jews they will reject the stone upon which they might build and have safe foundation." So he speaks of the rejection by the Jews of their King. "But behold, according to the scriptures," he says—speaking of a yet future day when the Jews, at the Second Coming, will be converted—"this stone shall become the great, and the last, and the only sure foundation, upon which the Jews can build." (Jacob 4:15-16.)

How were these prophecies about the Stone of Israel

used and interpreted by Jesus and his disciples in New Testament times? As it happens our Lord took special occasion to endorse and approve the concept that he was the Stone of Israel, and Peter and Paul, the two chief theologians among the ancient apostles, used the prophetic utterances to testify of Christ and to teach doctrines of deep import.

In the parable of the wicked husbandmen, Jesus taught that a householder (who is God) planted and prepared a vineyard; that he let it out to husbandmen; that he sent his servants (his prophets) to receive the fruit; and that one after another they were beaten, stoned, and killed. Finally he sent his son (Christ), who also was cast out of the vineyard and slain. With this recitation before them, the Jews admitted that the householder would destroy the wicked men and let out his vineyard to others who would render fruit in due season. (*Doctrinal New Testament Commentary,* 1:590-95.)

Then the record says: "Jesus saith unto them, Did ye never read in the scriptures, The stone which the builders rejected, the same is become the head of the corner: this is the Lord's doing, and it is marvellous in our eyes? Therefore say I unto you, The kingdom of God shall be taken from you, and given to a nation bringing forth the fruits thereof. And whosoever shall fall on this stone shall be broken: but on whomsoever it shall fall, it will grind him to powder. And when the chief priests and Pharisees had heard his parables, they perceived that he spake of them." (Matt. 21:42-45.)

Resentful that Jesus so spake of them, "They said among themselves, Shall the man think that he alone can spoil this great kingdom? And they were angry." And at this point in the account, the Prophet Joseph Smith, acting by the spirit of revelation, inserted the following:

"And now his disciples came to him, and Jesus said unto them, Marvel ye at the words of the parable which I spake unto them? Verily, I say unto you, I am the stone, and those wicked ones reject me. I am the head of the corner. These Jews shall fall upon me, and shall be broken. And the kingdom of God shall be taken from them, and shall be given to a nation bringing forth the fruits thereof; (meaning the Gentiles.) Wherefore, on whomsoever this stone shall fall, it shall grind him to powder. And when the Lord therefore of the vineyard cometh, he will destroy those miserable, wicked men, and will let again his vineyard unto other husbandmen, even in the last days, who shall render him the fruits in their seasons. And then understood they the parable which he spake unto them, that the Gentiles should be destroyed also, when the Lord should descend out of heaven to reign in his vineyard, which is the earth and the inhabitants thereof." (JST, Matt. 21:48-56.)

Paul's usage of the Stone of Israel prophecies is part of a long doctrinal presentation showing that the gospel was to go to the Gentiles, who through faith in Christ and personal righteousness would gain its blessings. "But Israel, which followed after the law of righteousness, hath not attained to the law of righteousness." That is, Israel sought righteousness and salvation through their system of worship, but had not in fact obtained it. "Wherefore? Because they sought it not by faith, but as it were by the works of the law"—meaning that they sought righteousness and salvation through the works of the Mosaic law alone rather than by faith in Christ. "For they stumbled at that stumblingstone; As it is written, Behold, I lay in Sion a stumblingstone and rock of offence: and whosoever believeth on him shall not be ashamed." (Rom. 9:31-33.)

To those, both Jew and Gentile, who did accept the saving truths of the gospel, Paul wrote: "Ye are no more strangers and foreigners, but fellowcitizens with the saints, and of the household of God; And are built upon the foundation of the apostles and prophets, Jesus Christ himself being the chief corner stone; In whom all the building fitly framed together groweth unto an holy temple in the Lord: In whom ye also are builded together for an habitation of God through the Spirit." (Eph. 2:19-22.)

Peter's usage of the prophecies is similar. When he and John were examined by the Jews as to the power and name used by them in healing the man lame from his mother's womb, Peter said with boldness: "Be it known unto you all, and to all the people of Israel, that by the name of Jesus Christ of Nazareth, whom ye crucified, whom God raised from the dead, even by him doth this man stand here before you whole. This is the stone which was set at nought of you builders, which is become the head of the corner. Neither is there salvation in any other; for there is none other name under heaven given among men, whereby we must be saved." (Acts 4:10-12.)

Later, Peter wrote that Christ was "a living stone, disallowed indeed of men, but chosen of God, and precious. . . . Wherefore also it is contained in the scripture, Behold, I lay in Sion a chief corner stone, elect, precious: and he that believeth on him shall not be confounded. Unto you therefore which believe he is precious: but unto them which be disobedient, the stone which the builders disallowed, the same is made the head of the corner, And a stone of stumbling, and a rock of offence, even to them which stumble at the word, being disobedient: whereunto also they were appointed."

Interwoven with this testimony about and these teachings concerning our Lord, Peter exhorts those who have accepted the "living stone" to be themselves "lively stones," to build up that "spiritual house" which is the Church, and to honor and use the "holy priesthood" which they possess. (1 Pet. 2:4-9.)

Christ Is the Good Shepherd

One of the sweetest and most tender terms by which the Lord was known anciently was that of the Shepherd of Israel. To a pastoral people who loved their sheep, who cared for them with tender solicitude, and whose very lives depended upon keeping them safe, this designation taught great truths about the relationship of the Lord to his people.

Father Jacob called him "the shepherd . . . of Israel"

177

(Gen. 49:24), and ever thereafter he was so identified by Israel's hosts. "He is our God; and we are the people of his
pasture, and the sheep of his hand." (Ps. 95:7; 100:3.) "Give
ear, O Shepherd of Israel, thou that leadest Joseph like a
flock. . . . Come and save us. Turn us again, O God, and
cause thy face to shine; and we shall be saved." (Ps. 80:1-3.)
So sang the people in their Psalms.

Of his future ministry among mortals, Isaiah said: "The
Lord God will come. . . . He shall feed his flock like a
shepherd: he shall gather the lambs with his arm, and carry
them in his bosom, and shall gently lead those that are with
young." (Isa. 40:10-11.)

And his Nephite counterparts spoke the same truth, using words having a familiar spirit. "There is one God and
one Shepherd over all the earth," Nephi said. "And the time
cometh that he shall manifest himself unto all nations, both
unto the Jews and also unto the Gentiles"—meaning that
when he is born as a mortal on earth, his gospel will be
offered first to his Jewish kin and later will go to the nations
of the Gentiles.

"And after he has manifested himself unto the Jews and
also unto the Gentiles, then he shall manifest himself unto
the Gentiles and also unto the Jews, and the last shall be
first, and the first shall be last" (1 Ne. 13:41-42)—meaning
that in the last days his everlasting gospel will be revealed to
the non-Jews (who are here called Gentiles) and from them
will go in due course to his Jewish kinsmen. It is of this
latter-day work that Nephi says: "The Holy One of Israel
must reign in dominion, and might, and power, and great
glory. And he gathereth his children from the four quarters
of the earth; and he numbereth his sheep, and they know
him; and there shall be one fold and one shepherd; and he
shall feed his sheep, and in him they shall find pasture." (1
Ne. 22:24-25.)

Speaking as the Shepherd of Israel, the Lord said to
Alma the elder, "He that will hear my voice shall be my
sheep; and him shall ye receive into the church, and him will

178

I also receive." (Mosiah 26:21.) After his conversion Alma the younger taught, "The good shepherd doth call you; yea, and in his own name he doth call you, which is the name of Christ. . . . The good shepherd doth call after you; and if you will hearken unto his voice he will bring you into his fold, and ye are his sheep." (Alma 5:38, 60.) Describing the degenerate and apostate state of his people, Mormon wrote: "They are without Christ and God in the world. . . . They were once a delightsome people, and they had Christ for their shepherd." (Morm. 5:16-17.)

In Palestine sheep are led, not driven. The American practice is for sheepherders to drive sheep; the Palestinian custom is for the shepherds to go before their sheep, to call them by name, and to lead them to green pastures and beside still waters. At night the flocks of several shepherds are sheltered and protected together in one sheepfold. In the morning each shepherd calls his own sheep by name, out of the larger intermingled flock, and they follow him into the places of food and water.

Jesus reminded the Jews of this practice, equated himself with the porter who guarded the sheep during the night, and said: "I am the door of the sheep. . . . I am the door: by me if any man enter in, he shall be saved, and shall go in and out, and find pasture." In other words: 'Even as sheep are pastured and preserved by their shepherds, so are men, the people of the Lord's pasture, led and saved by me.' "I am come that they might have life, and that they might have it more abundantly," Jesus continued. "I am the good shepherd: the good shepherd giveth his life for the sheep. . . . I am the good shepherd, and know my sheep, and am known of mine. As the Father knoweth me, even so know I the Father: and I lay down my life for the sheep."

To all who heard his declaration "I am the good shepherd," with its accompanying assertions about his Father, the meaning was clear. To a people who studied the scriptures and knew the imagery and meaning of what the prophets had said, who themselves exulted in the Psalm,

179

"The Lord is my shepherd" (Psalm 23), Jesus' spoken words meant: 'I am the Lord Jehovah, and I shall work out the infinite and eternal atonement by laying down my life for the sheep.'

However, captious and conniving as they were, they still propounded to him the question: "If thou be the Christ, tell us plainly." In other words: 'We know you are claiming to be the Lord Jehovah in figurative language, but we hesitate to stone you for blasphemy until you say plainly that such is the case.' Jesus answered by saying, "I told you, and ye believed not." And truly he had. "But ye believe not," he continued, "because ye are not of my sheep, as I said unto you. My sheep hear my voice, and I know them, and they follow me." (John 10:1-28.)

It was during this discourse that the Master spoke of other sheep which were not of the Jewish fold, a group whom he subsequently identified by saying to the Nephites, "Ye are they of whom I said: Other sheep I have which are not of this fold; them also I must bring, and they shall hear my voice; and there shall be one fold, and one shepherd." (3 Ne. 15:21.)

Jesus' statements to Peter, "Feed my lambs" and "Feed my sheep," spoken after his resurrection, are a reaffirmation of his standing as the Shepherd of Israel. (John 21:15-17.) It was this same presiding apostle who wrote that our Lord was "the Shepherd and Bishop" of our souls (1 Pet. 2:25) and also the "chief Shepherd" who shall come again in glory in due course. (1 Pet. 5:4.) Paul, in testifying that the good Shepherd and Christ are one and the same, uttered this prayer: "Now the God of peace, that brought again from the dead our Lord Jesus, that great shepherd of the sheep, through the blood of the everlasting covenant, Make you perfect in every good work to do his will." (Heb. 13:20-21.)

Christ Is Known by Many Names

Our Lord is and has been known by many names. Some

have been revealed in one dispensation, some in another; some have been used in a single age, some in many; and no doubt there are many names yet to be revealed. To collect and analyze all those by which he is known to us would be a work of major proportions and constitute a large volume by itself. Our purpose in this work is to note the more important instances in which he was known both before and after his coming by the same names, thus showing that the mortal Christ and the promised Messiah are one and the same. In addition to the designations so far noted, and to those not scheduled for more elaborate consideration later in this work, we here note the following:

1. *He is the Servant of the Lord.*

Jesus came to do the will of his Father because his Father sent him. (3 Ne. 27:13-14.) He was the Servant, not the master, in his relationship with his Father. "I am among you as he that serveth," he said. (Luke 22:27.) Also: "The Son can do nothing of himself, but what he seeth the Father do: for what things soever he doeth, these also doeth the Son likewise." (John 5:19.) Submissive, willing, obedient, walking only in the path charted for him by his Father—such was the course pursued by the Son.

How natural it is to find Christ serving both the Father and his fellowmen, for so it had been predicted. The introductory sentence of the longest single Messianic prophecy in the Old Testament (and one of the greatest and most comprehensive of them all) says: "Behold, my servant shall deal prudently, he shall be exalted and extolled, and be very high." (Isa. 52:13.) Another of Isaiah's long and plain predictions about the coming of the Messiah begins: "Behold my servant, whom I uphold; mine elect, in whom my soul delighteth; I have put my spirit upon him: he shall bring forth judgment to the Gentiles." (Isa. 42:1.) "I will bring forth my servant" (Zech. 3:8) is the scriptural promise, as also: "O Lord, truly I am thy servant: I am thy servant, and the son of thine handmaid: thou hast loosed my bonds. I will offer to thee the sacrifice of thanksgiving, and will call upon the name of the Lord. I will pay my vows unto the Lord now in the presence of all his people, in the courts of the Lord's house, in the midst of thee, O Jerusalem." (Ps. 116:16-19.)

And so, truly, did our Lord act during his mortal ministry! Truly, this is he of whom it is written: "He shall stand and feed in the strength of the Lord, in the majesty of the name of the LORD his God; . . . for now shall he be great unto the ends of the earth." (Mic. 5:4.)

2. *He is the Star out of Jacob.*

Of him Balaam prophesied: "I shall see him, but not now: I shall behold him, but not nigh: there shall come a Star out of Jacob, and a Sceptre shall rise out of Israel. . . . Out of Jacob shall come he that shall have dominion." (Num. 24:17-19.) "In figurative language, the spirit hosts in pre-existence are referred to as the stars of heaven." (*Mormon Doctrine,* 2nd ed., pp. 765-66.) The morning stars who joined with all the sons of God when the foundations of the earth were laid were the noble and preeminent spirits. As the Star who came out of Jacob, Christ is thus the most outstanding one of all the hosts of that unnumbered house. And so he testified of himself: "I am . . . the bright and morning star." (Rev. 22:16.)

3. *He is the Beloved and Chosen One.*

Before, during, and after his mortal ministry he was and is known as the Beloved and Chosen One, terms that carry a connotation of election and selection, of choosing and fore-ordination. He is "My Beloved and Chosen from the beginning" (Moses 4:2); "My Chosen" (Moses 7:39); "My Beloved" (2 Ne. 31:15); "My Well Beloved" (Hel. 5:47); "His most Beloved" (Morm. 5:14); and "My Beloved Son" (3 Ne. 11:7; Matt. 3:17; JS-H 17).

4. *He is the Anointed One.*

A number of Messianic passages speak of "the Lord, and . . . his anointed" (Ps. 2:2), signifying that the Chosen One was consecrated and set apart for the ministry and mission that was his. Jesus applied these passages to himself by quoting Isaiah's prophecy, "The Lord hath anointed me to preach good tidings unto the meek" (Isa. 61:1), and then saying: "This day is this scripture fulfilled in your ears" (Luke 4:21). Peter made the same application by speaking of "thy holy child Jesus, whom thou hast anointed" (Acts 4:27), and by telling "how God anointed Jesus of Nazareth with the Holy Ghost and with power" (Acts 10:38). In a revealed prayer, given in our day, we find this petition: "Wilt thou turn away thy wrath when thou lookest upon the face of thine Anointed." (D&C 109:53.)

5. *He is the Bridegroom.*

"Thy Maker is thine husband; the Lord of hosts is his name; and thy Redeemer the Holy One of Israel; The God of the whole earth shall he be called. For the Lord hath called thee as a woman forsaken and grieved in spirit, and [as] a wife of youth." (Isa. 54:5-6.) "And as the bridegroom rejoiceth over the bride, so shall thy God rejoice over thee." (Isa. 62:5.) So spake the Eternal One to his chosen Israel. Speaking of his Second Coming, this same Jesus called himself the Bridegroom (Matt. 25:1-13), and the same terminology has been preserved in latter-day revelation (D&C 133:10, 19).

Paul makes quite a point of this concept. "The husband is the head of the wife," he says, "even as Christ is the head of the church." That is, it is as though Christ were married to the Church. "Therefore as the church is subject unto Christ, so let the wives be to their own husbands in every thing. Husbands, love your wives, even as Christ also loved the church, and gave himself for it." Then because of the figurative nature of the language used, he says: "This is a great mystery: but I speak concerning Christ and the church." (Eph. 5:23-32.)

6. *He is the Hope of Israel.*

In and through and by and because of him we and all men have a hope of peace in this life and eternal glory in the world to come. He is our Hope. Without him we would have no hope of immortality, no hope of eternal life, no hope of the continuation of the family unit, no hope of eternal progress, no hope of exaltation, no hope of any good thing. All the hopes of all the righteous of all the ages center in him. "O Lord, the hope of Israel, all that forsake thee shall be ashamed, and they that depart from me shall be written in the earth, because they have forsaken the Lord, the fountain of living waters." (Jer. 17:13; 14:8; 50:7.)

"We are saved by hope" (Rom. 8:24), and the "Lord Jesus Christ . . . is our hope," said Paul (1 Tim. 1:1). The lives of the righteous are spent "looking for that blessed hope," he also said, which hope is for "the glorious appearing of the great God and our Saviour Jesus Christ." (Titus 2:13.)

7. *He is the Nazarene.*

In a prophecy no longer found in any scripture now had among us, it is written: "He shall be called a Nazarene," which was fulfilled, Matthew tells us, because he dwelt "in a city called Nazareth." (Matt. 2:23.) Subsequent developments confirmed that he was to bear that designation during and after his mortal probation. While he yet dwelt in mortality, he was called Jesus of Nazareth by his disciples (John 1:45), and after he rose from the dead, he himself said to Paul, "I am Jesus of Nazareth whom thou persecutest" (Acts 22:8). Peter spoke of him similarly (Acts 2:22), although when he healed the lame man, he used the more formal words, "In the name of Jesus Christ of Nazareth rise up and walk" (Acts 3:6).

Chapter 11

"THE LORD IS OUR KING"

Who Is Our Eternal King?

From the earliest days of the earth's existence righteous men have known that the Lord our God is its King. In one form or another this truth has been taught and preached among the saints of all dispensations. They envisioned him as being a King while he yet dwelt as a Spirit Son in his Father's court; while he lived on earth among mortals; and after he came forth from the grave to reign forever in glorious immortality. We shall now touch briefly upon some of the ways in which he was known to be and announced as King.

"I am Messiah, the King of Zion." (Moses 7:53.) So spoke the Son of Man to that Enoch who founded the City of Zion. Millenniums later, David, exulting that Mount Zion was "the joy of the whole earth," acclaimed it also as "the city of the great King, . . . the city of the Lord of hosts, . . . the city of our God." (Ps. 48:1-8.)

Speaking of the Lord Jehovah, the record says such things as: "God is my King." (Ps. 74:12.) "The Lord is a great God, and a great King above all gods." (Ps. 95:3.) "Let the children of Zion be joyful in their King." (Ps. 149:2.) That there are hosts of similar Psalmic declarations is well known.

He is also called "the King of glory" (Ps. 24), "the King

of Jacob" (Isa. 41:21), "the King of Israel, and his redeemer the Lord of hosts" (Isa. 44:6), "your Holy One, the creator of Israel, your King" (Isa. 43:15), and "the Holy One of Israel" (Ps. 89:18). Jeremiah said, "The Lord is the true God, he is the living God, and an everlasting king" (Jer. 10:10), and Isaiah testified: "Mine eyes have seen the King, the Lord of hosts" (Isa. 6:5). Declarations of this sort abound in Holy Writ. None can doubt that the God of ancients, the God of Israel, the great Jehovah of old was universally acclaimed as Lord and King.

Christ Is Our Eternal King

Interwoven with the repeated assertions that Jehovah was Lord and King are the declarations that this same King-Messiah shall come to save and redeem his people. Speaking Messianically, Isaiah said, "Behold, a king shall reign in righteousness" (Isa. 32:1), which no king could do, in the full sense of the word, except the Holy One. In prophesying that "the Son of God cometh in his glory, in his might, majesty, power, and dominion," Alma said: "Behold the glory of the King of all the earth; and also the King of heaven shall very soon shine forth among all the children of men." (Alma 5:50.) And Zechariah even spelled out in detail one of the events in the mortal life of the King of Zion. "Rejoice greatly, O daughter of Zion," he proclaimed; "shout, O daughter of Jerusalem: behold, thy King cometh unto thee: he is just, and having salvation; lowly, and riding upon an ass, and upon a colt the foal of an ass." (Zech. 9:9.)

That many people recognized Jesus as the promised King is clear from the New Testament account. Following his birth in Bethlehem, "there came wise men from the east to Jerusalem, Saying, Where is he that is born King of the Jews?" (Matt. 2:1-2.) Before Pilate, Jesus himself answered "Thou sayest," meaning "I am," when asked, "Art thou the King of the Jews?" and that Roman governor, over the objection of the Jews, placed this writing over the cross: "THIS

IS JESUS THE KING OF THE JEWS." (Matt. 27:11-37.)

And as to Zechariah's prophecy, it was fulfilled in detail. "Go into the village over against you," Jesus said to two of his disciples, when the time had arrived for his triumphal entry into Jerusalem, "and straightway ye shall find an ass tied, and a colt with her: loose them, and bring them unto me. And if any man say ought unto you, ye shall say, The Lord hath need of them; and straightway he will send them."

"All this was done," Matthew recites, "that it might be fulfilled which was spoken by the prophet, saying, Tell ye the daughter of Sion, Behold, thy King cometh unto thee, meek, and sitting upon an ass, and a colt the foal of an ass. And the disciples went, and did as Jesus commanded them, And brought the ass, and the colt, and put on them their clothes, and they set him thereon. And a very great multitude spread their garments in the way; others cut down branches from the trees, and strawed them in the way. And the multitudes that went before, and that followed, cried, saying, Hosanna to the Son of David: Blessed is he that cometh in the name of the Lord; Hosanna in the highest." (Matt. 21:1-9.) That the multitude spoke with the deliberate intent of testifying that our Lord was their promised King is seen from the fact that they mingled with their shouts of Hosanna and praise the Messianic prophecy taken from the Psalms, "Blessed be he that cometh in the name of the Lord." (Ps. 118:26.)

After Jesus rose from the dead he continued to bear his kingly title. Paul wrote of him that he "is the blessed and only Potentate, the King of kings, and the Lord of lords, to whom be honor and power everlasting." (JST, 1 Tim. 6:15.) John called him "the prince of the kings of the earth" (Rev. 1:5), the "King of saints" (Rev. 15:3), and the "Lord of lords, and King of kings" (Rev. 17:14; 19:16).

In due course this same Almighty King shall come again to reign on earth and to fulfill in their entirety all of the Messianic prophecies. "And the Lord shall be king over all the earth," Zechariah says, and "in that day shall there be one Lord, and his name one." This will be the day when men "shall even go up [to Jerusalem] from year to year to worship the King, the Lord of hosts, and to keep the feast of tabernacles." (Zech. 14:9, 16.)

Why David Is a Symbol of the Messiah

No single concept was more firmly lodged in the minds of the Jews in Jesus' day than the universal belief that their Messiah would be the Son of David. They expected him to come and reign on David's throne. They looked for a temporal deliverer who would throw off the yoke of Roman bondage and make Israel free again. They sought a ruler who would restore that glory and worldwide influence and prestige which was enjoyed when the Son of Jesse sat on Israel's throne. The true concepts of deliverance from spiritual darkness, of being freed from the bondage of sin, of a kingdom which is not of this world—all made possible through an infinite and eternal atonement—all this was lost and unknown doctrine to them.

It comes as no surprise, then, when Jesus asks, "What think ye of Christ? whose son is he?" to have them respond, "The son of David." (Matt. 22:42.) That their answer was true is of no particular moment. Of course Christ was the Son of David; who had any doubt about that? What really counted was that God was his Father, and hence that he had power to ransom and redeem. Their acceptance of him as David's Son—nothing more—still left them without salvation. It is as though we should ask today: "What think ye of Christ? Is he the Savior of the world?" and receive the response, "He is the greatest moral teacher that ever lived." True. But salvation comes to us not because we accept him as the greatest teacher of the ages, which he was, but because he is known to us to be the Son of God.

With these distinctions before us, we shall now consider our Lord's status as the Son of David, see why he was so designated, and learn from the Davidic-Messianic prophecies those truths which the prophetic mind intended to convey by using David, the great king, as a type and shadow of his infinitely greater Son.

First we must note David's place and stature in Israel and the high esteem in which he was held by all. Born in Bethlehem in 1085 B.C., the youngest of the eight sons of Jesse, he grew up as a shepherd; endowed with great physical strength and courage, he slew Goliath and became a national hero; anointed king by Samuel, he reigned over part of the people for seven years and over all of them for another thirty-three. His military conquests were legendary, his court comparable to those of the great Oriental sovereigns, and his influence in world affairs like that of the greatest kings and warriors in history.

· He was a poet, a musician and sweet singer, a man of deep religious bent. Indeed he was a man after the Lord's own heart (1 Sam. 13:13-14), until the day he forsook the path of righteousness and lost his soul through sin. He "served his own generation by the will of God" (Acts 13:36), and there were none before and none after whose privilege it was to hold temporal rule in Israel, who so caught the imagination of the people and so dramatized the greatness that comes by following inspiring leadership.

As he was the destined ancestor of the Messiah, it was the most natural thing in the world for the prophets in Israel to use him and his kingly glory to crystallize in the minds of men the kingly state and everlasting dominion that would rest in due course upon the promised Seed of David.

Christ Is the Son of David

David himself was the first to receive the prophetic word that the Seed of Israel's temporal king would be her Eternal King. "I will set up thy seed after thee," was the Lord's word given by Nathan the prophet, "and I will establish his kingdom. . . . And I will stablish the throne of his kingdom for ever." In substance and thought content Gabriel reaffirmed this same truth to Mary when he said in Luke 1:33, "And he shall reign over the house of Jacob for ever; and of his kingdom there shall be no end."

"I will be his father, and he shall be my son," the word continued to David, thus formulating the Messianic statement which Paul used in Hebrews 1:5 to show that Christ was the Son of God. Then, by way of Nathan, came this assured promise: "And thine house and thy kingdom shall be established for ever before thee: thy throne shall be established for ever." (2 Sam. 7:12-16.)

Later we find David receiving direct and personal revelation relative to the perpetuity of his throne and the divinity of the Seed who should sit thereon. "The Lord hath sworn in truth unto David; he will not turn from it," came the word, that "of the fruit of thy body will I set upon thy throne. . . . I will make the horn of David to bud," and surely "shall his crown flourish." (Ps. 132:11-18.) And also: "I have made a covenant with my chosen, I have sworn unto David my servant, Thy seed will I establish for ever, and build up thy throne to all generations. . . . His seed shall endure for ever, and his throne as the sun before me." (Ps. 89:3-36.) Needless to say the inspired references are to the eternal throne of him who is Eternal and not to the temporal throne which tottered and swayed and fell, never to rise again after its original pattern.

In Hebrews 1:8-9, Paul applied these Davidic words about the eternal throne to the eternal Christ: "Thy throne, O God, is for ever and ever: the sceptre of thy kingdom is a right sceptre. Thou lovest righteousness, and hatest wickedness: therefore God, thy God, hath anointed thee with the oil of gladness above thy fellows." (Ps. 45:6-7.) And the same application should be made of these Psalmic syllables, said of "the glorious majesty of his kingdom": "Thy kingdom is an everlasting kingdom, and thy dominion endureth throughout all generations." (Ps. 145:12-13.)

Isaiah said of his future Savior: "The government shall

be upon his shoulder. . . . Of the increase of his government and peace there shall be no end, upon the throne of David, and upon his kingdom, to order it, and to establish it with judgment and with justice from henceforth even for ever." (Isa. 9:6-7.) Further: "And in mercy shall the throne be established: and he shall sit upon it in truth in the tabernacle of David, judging, and seeking judgment, and hasting righteousness." (Isa. 16:5.) Zechariah prophesied: "He shall speak peace unto the heathen: and his dominion shall be from sea even to sea, and from the river even to the ends of the earth." (Zech. 9:10.) And even Balaam, of questionable fame, proclaimed by the inspiration of the Almighty: "A Sceptre shall rise out of Israel. . . . Out of Jacob shall come he that shall have dominion." (Num. 24:17-19.)

As all the Jews knew and all the prophets from David's day onward have testified, the promised Messiah was to be the Son of David who should reign on the throne of Israel's greatest king. When Jesus performed miracles and testified of himself, an instinctive reaction among the common people was, "Is not this the son of David?" (Matt. 12:23.) Blind men sought sight at his hands with the plea: "Thou son of David, have mercy on us." (Matt. 9:27.) Even the non-Israelitish woman of Canaan claimed his attention with the cry: "O Lord, thou son of David; my daughter is grievously vexed with a devil." (Matt. 15:22.) Indeed, people on every hand so identified him and so addressed him, in all of which was the implicit realization that they were speaking to the mighty Messiah.

Truly, "Of this man's seed," the man called David, "hath God according to his promise raised unto Israel a Saviour, Jesus." (Acts 13:23.)

Christ Reigns on David's Throne

When shall the Son of David, within the full meaning of the Messianic messages, reign in power and might upon the throne of David his father?

It is true that as a mortal man he exercised justice and judgment and went forth in power and majesty among his fellowmen. But such was only a sample and a foretaste of what is to be at his Second Coming. Nearly all that is written of his power and dominion will find complete fulfillment only when he comes to dwell among men during the millennial era. Such, for instance, shall be the day when "he shall have dominion also from sea to sea, and from the river unto the ends of the earth," and when "all nations shall call him blessed." (Ps. 72:8, 17.)

Since it takes a first and a second coming to fulfill many Messianic prophecies, we of necessity must consider them here, and in the case of the Davidic-Messianic utterances show also how they apply to our Lord's Second Coming. Christ is the Son of David, the Seed of David, the inheritor, through Mary his mother, of the blood of the great king. He is also called the Stem of Jesse and the Branch, meaning Branch of David. Messianic prophecies under these headings deal with the power and dominion he shall wield as he sits on David's throne, and have reference almost exclusively to his second sojourn on planet earth.

Jesse was the father of David. Isaiah speaks of the Stem of Jesse, whom he also designates as a branch growing out of the root of that ancient worthy. He recites how the Spirit of the Lord shall rest upon him; how he shall be mighty in judgment; how he shall smite the earth and slay the wicked; and how the lamb and the lion shall lie down together in that day—all of which has reference to the Second Coming and the millennial era thereby ushered in. (Isa. 11.) As to the identity of the Stem of Jesse, the revealed word says: "Verily thus saith the Lord: It is Christ." (D&C 113:1-2.) This also means that the Branch is Christ, as we shall now see from other related scriptures.

By the mouth of Jeremiah, the Lord foretells the ancient scattering and the latter-day gathering of his chosen Israel. After they have been gathered "out of all countries whither I have driven them," after the kingdom has been restored to

Israel as desired by the ancient apostles in Acts 1:6, then this eventuality, yet future and millennial in nature, shall be fulfilled: "Behold, the days come, saith the Lord, that I will raise unto David a righteous Branch, and a King shall reign and prosper, and shall execute judgment and justice in the earth. In his days Judah shall be saved, and Israel shall dwell safely: and this is his name whereby he shall be called, THE LORD OUR RIGHTEOUSNESS." (Jer. 23:3-6.) That is to say, the King who shall reign personally upon the earth during the Millennium shall be the Branch who grew out of the house of David. He shall execute judgment and justice in all the earth because he is the Lord Jehovah, even him whom we call Christ.

Through Zechariah the Lord spoke similarly: "Thus saith the Lord of hosts: . . . I will bring forth my servant the BRANCH. . . . I will remove the iniquity of the land in one day [meaning that the wicked shall be destroyed and the millennial era of peace and righteousness commence]. In that day, saith the Lord of hosts, shall ye call every man his neighbour under the vine and under the fig tree." (Zech. 3:7-10.) Of that glorious millennial day the Lord says also: "Behold the man whose name is The BRANCH; and he shall grow up out of his place, and he shall build the temple of the Lord: Even he shall build the temple of the Lord; and he shall bear the glory, and shall sit and rule upon his throne." (Zech. 6:12-13.)

That the Branch of David is Christ is perfectly clear. We shall now see that he is also called David, that he is a new David, an Eternal David, who shall reign forever on the throne of his ancient ancestor. "It shall come to pass in that day, saith the Lord of hosts," that is, in the great millennial day of gathering, that "they shall serve the Lord their God, and David their king, whom I will raise up unto them." (Jer. 30:8-9.)

"In those days, and at that time, will I cause the Branch of righteousness to grow up unto David; and he shall execute judgment and righteousness in the land. In those days shall Judah be saved, and Jerusalem shall dwell safely: and this is the name wherewith she shall be called, The Lord our righteousness," which is to say that because the Great King himself reigns in her midst, even the city shall be called after him. "For thus saith the Lord; David shall never want a man to sit upon the throne of the house of Israel. . . . If ye can break my covenant of the day, and my covenant of the night, and that there should not be day and night in their season; Then may also my covenant be broken with David my servant, that he should not have a son to reign upon his throne." (Jer. 33:15-21.) David's temporal throne fell long centuries before our Lord was born, and that portion of Israel which had not been scattered to the ends of the earth was in bondage to the iron yoke of Rome. But the promises remain. The eternal throne shall be restored in due course with a new David sitting thereon, and he shall reign forever and ever.

In one of his great Messianic prophecies Nephi acclaimed: "There is one God and one Shepherd over all the earth." Of the Lord's First Coming and his Second Coming, this Hebrew prophet then said: "And the time cometh that he shall manifest himself unto all nations, both unto the Jews and also unto the Gentiles; and after he has manifested himself unto the Jews and also unto the Gentiles, then he shall manifest himself unto the Gentiles and also unto the Jews, and the last shall be first, and the first shall be last." (1 Ne. 13:41-42.)

Through Ezekiel, the Lord speaks of this One Shepherd in this way: "I will save my flock. . . . And I will set up one shepherd over them, and he shall feed them, even my servant David; he shall feed them, and he shall be their shepherd. And I the Lord will be their God, and my servant David a prince among them." When that day comes, "I will make with them a covenant of peace," the Lord says, meaning they shall have again the fulness of the everlasting gospel. Then "there shall be showers of blessing"; all Israel

194

shall dwell safely and know that the Lord is their God. (Ezek. 34:22-31.)

Through Ezekiel, the Lord also tells of the coming forth of the Book of Mormon, which becomes the instrument in his hands to bring to pass the gathering of Israel. Of that day of gathering he says, "I will make them one nation in the land upon the mountains of Israel; and one king shall be king to them all." In that day he promises to "cleanse them," by baptism, "so shall they be my people, and I will be their God. And David my servant shall be king over them; and they all shall have one shepherd: they shall also walk in my judgments, and observe my statutes, and do them. And they shall dwell in the land that I have given unto Jacob my servant, wherein your fathers have dwelt; and they shall dwell therein, even they, and their children, and their children's children for ever: and my servant David shall be their prince for ever."

Then the Lord restates that his gathered people shall have his everlasting gospel with all its blessings; that he will set his sanctuary, meaning his temple, in their midst forevermore (as Zechariah recorded); and all Israel shall know that the Lord is their God. (Ezek. 37:15-28.)

How glorious shall be the coming day when the second David, who is Christ, reigns on the throne of the first David; when all men shall dwell safely; when the earth shall be dotted with temples; and when the gospel covenant shall have full force and validity in all the earth!

Christ the Lord Reigneth

"The Lord reigneth, he is clothed with majesty." (Ps. 93:1.) "The Lord is our King." (Isa. 33:22.) "He is a great King over all the earth." (Ps. 47:2.) He is that David whose throne shall be established forever. His "kingdom is an everlasting kingdom," and his "dominion endureth throughout all generations." (Ps. 145:13.)

195

He is "the Root of David" (Rev. 5:5), for David came by him. "I am the root and the offspring of David" (Rev. 22:16), he said, for David was his father. It was of him that the Lord said through Isaiah: "And I will clothe him with thy robe, and strengthen him with thy girdle, and I will commit thy government into his hand: and he shall be a father to the inhabitants of Jerusalem, and to the house of Judah. And the key of the house of David will I lay upon his shoulder; so he shall open, and none shall shut; and he shall shut, and none shall open. . . . And he shall be for a glorious throne to his father's house. And they shall hang upon him all the glory of his father's house." (Isa. 22:20-24.) And it was he himself who said: "These things saith he that is holy, he that is true, he that hath the key of David, he that openeth, and no man shutteth; and shutteth, and no man openeth." (Rev. 3:7.)

And the day soon cometh when that which is written shall be fulfilled: "The kingdoms of this world are become the kingdoms of our Lord, and of his Christ; and he shall reign for ever and ever." (Rev. 11:15.)

"Alleluia: for the Lord God omnipotent reigneth." (Rev. 19:6.)

Chapter 12

MESSIAH IS THE PERFECT ONE

Messiah Is Always the Same

"From eternity to eternity he is the same." (D&C 76:4.) So it is written of that Lord who is both Jehovah and Jesus. And so it is. As the *Unembodied One,* while he dwelt in preexistence as the Firstborn spirit Son of the Eternal Elohim; as the *Embodied One,* while he dwelt among us, with his spirit shackled in a tabernacle of clay, a tabernacle created in the womb of Mary whose Son he was; as the *Disembodied One,* while he ministered for a moment among the spirits of the righteous dead; and finally as the *Reembodied One,* which he became when he rose from the dead, clothed with glory, immortality, and eternal life—in all of these states he was and is the same. He does not vary. His course is one eternal round. In every state of existence he was and is the possessor and personification of every godly attribute and characteristic in its fulness and perfection.

Among the *attributes* of God are knowledge, faith or power, justice, judgment, mercy, and truth. As the Supreme Being, as the Source of Righteousness, all such things dwell in him independently.

His *character* fits a like pattern. He was the same God before the earth was created that he now is. From everlasting to everlasting, he is merciful and gracious, slow to anger, and abundant in goodness. With him there is no variableness; he changes not; neither doth he walk in crooked paths; and his course is one eternal round. He is a God of truth; he cannot lie; his word endureth to all generations. He is no respecter of persons, and that man only is blessed who keeps his commandments. And he is love.

As to his *perfections,* they are the perfections which belong to all of the attributes of his nature, which is to say that he has all knowledge, all power, all truth, and the fulness of all good things. These statements about his character, perfections, and attributes are simply a digest and a paraphrase of the teachings of the Prophet Joseph Smith. (*Mormon Doctrine,* 2nd ed., pp. 262-63.)

And as with the Father, so with the Son. The attributes of one are the attributes of the other; the character of each is the same; and both are possessors of the same perfections in their eternal fulness. The Messiah is truly "like unto God." (Abr. 3:24.) He was such in preexistence; he is such now as he sits on the right hand of the Majesty on high; and what is of special concern to us in our Messianic studies, he was the possessor of the same character, perfections, and attributes while he dwelt as a mortal among men. Indeed, the very fact that Jesus of Nazareth enjoyed these godly graces and manifested them in the acts of his life—as he taught truth, as he wrought miracles, as he lived without sin, and as he atoned for the sins of others—the very fact that he pursued such a course is one of the great evidences that he was all that he claimed to be: the Son of God. It is to this portion of the Messianic message that we now turn our attention.

Christ Is the Word of God

Messiah is the Word of God. He speaks for the Father. His voice is the voice of the Father. He is the mouthpiece of and spokesman for the Most High. The message he delivers is one of glory and honor, of immortality and eternal life. He is thus the Messenger of Salvation.

These truths have been known and taught in all dispensations. To dramatize this high status of the Son, this peculiar prerogative he alone possessed, he bears the name-title "the Word of God." Generally this designation is associated with the creative enterprises of the Father as these are accomplished by the Son, the unique designation thus bearing witness that the Father used the Son to perform the creative acts.

Thus, in revealing to Moses the creation of "worlds without number," Deity says: "By the Son I created them, which is mine Only Begotten." Worlds come and worlds go, he said, "by the word of my power." (Moses 1:33, 35.) With reference to various creative steps taken in the organizing of this earth from existent matter, Deity said to Moses: "And this I did by the word of my power" (Moses 2:5, 16; 3:7), meaning "by the power of mine Only Begotten" (Moses 4:3). The Book of Mormon prophets also speak of "the power of his word" and point to the creation of the earth as the great manifestation of this omnipotence. (Jacob 4:9; Morm. 9:17.) Our modern revelations pick up the same theme. "All things," the Lord says, "I have created by the word of my power, which is the power of my Spirit. For by the power of my Spirit created I them." (D&C 29:30-31.)

John the Beloved began his gospel account by speaking of the then risen Lord in the same way. "In the beginning was the Word," he said, "and the Word was with God, and the Word was God. The same was in the beginning with God. All things were made by him; and without him was not anything made that was made. . . . And the Word was made flesh, and dwelt among us, (and we beheld his glory, the glory as of the only begotten of the Father,) full of grace and truth." (John 1:1-3, 14.) A more perfect rendition of John's writing was revealed to Joseph Smith in these words: "I saw his glory, that he was in the beginning, before the world was; Therefore, in the beginning the Word was, for he was the Word, even the messenger of salvation—The light and the Redeemer of the world; the Spirit of truth, who came into the world, because the world was made by him, and in him was the life of men and the light of men. The worlds were made by him; men were made by him; all things were made by him, and through him, and of him. And I, John, bear record that I beheld his glory, as the glory of the Only Begotten of the Father, full of grace and truth, even the Spirit of truth, which came and dwelt in the flesh, and dwelt among us." (D&C 93:6-11.) In this connection we should also note that his coming was announced by calling him "the messenger of the covenant." (Mal. 3:1.)

John it was also who saw the resurrected Christ in glory and was taught: "His name is called The Word of God" (Rev. 19:13), and who wrote of him as "the Word of life" (1 Jn. 1:1).

Closely associated with this concept that the Lord Jesus is the Word of God is the kindred verity that he is the Truth. "Thy word," O God, "is truth." (John 17:17.) "The word of the Lord is truth." (D&C 84:45.) Jehovah, says Isaiah, is "the God of truth" (Isa. 65:16), and when he dwells in mortality, "he shall bring forth judgment unto truth" (Isa. 42:3). That the living Word, dwelling among men as the Truth, should bring forth that truth which saves is implicit in many prophetic utterances, such as: "Thy law is the truth. . . . Thy word is true from the beginning." (Ps. 119:142, 160.) "The Lord, . . . Which made heaven, and earth, the sea, and all that therein is . . . keepeth truth for ever." (Ps. 146:5-6.) How aptly and conclusively the Lord Jesus tied all these pronouncements into himself when he said: "I am the way, the truth, and the life." (John 14:6.)

Messiah Is the Sinless One

Sin entered the world with Adam. Through his transgression man became mortal and was cast out from the presence of God. Temporal and spiritual death thus entered the world. And every accountable mortal who has lived on earth, from that day onward, has committed sin. This is inherent in the very nature of existence. It is part of the

200

divine plan; it is a necessary requisite for all who undergo the probationary experiences of mortality.

Sin and death are absolutely universal among us mortals. There are no exceptions. "As by one man sin entered into the world, and death by sin; and so death passed upon all men, for that all have sinned." (Rom. 5:12.) "All have sinned, and come short of the glory of God." (Rom. 3:23.)

Knowing, then, that death and sin are the established, unvarying order of existence, suppose, among the teeming billions of earth's inhabitants, we found one person who did no sin and upon whom death had no power. What would we think of such a one? Truly might we exclaim: "He is God, the Son of God, the promised Messiah."

We shall speak hereafter of his power over death, noting for the present that it goes hand in hand with his sinless state. Reason alone should tell us that if there was or is or shall be one alone among all men who is sinless, he is more than a mortal and must be the One of whom the prophets spoke. Our analysis on this point might well follow this line:

First, God himself is holy and without sin. He is just and true and perfect. His ways are righteous and there is no iniquity in any of his doings.

Second, he shall come as the Mighty Messiah to save his people. When he comes he shall be without sin. No guile shall be found in his mouth. His judgments shall be just, for he is both God and God's Son.

And third, among all who have dwelt on earth, the Carpenter of Nazareth of Galilee, he only, has been without sin. He alone walked in perfect uprightness before the Father, and therefore he is the sole claimant to Messiahship. He alone is the sinless Son of God.

Having so reasoned, let us see if the revelations accord with our views.

Of the great Jehovah, they say: "He is the Rock, his work is perfect: for all his ways are judgment: a God of truth and without iniquity, just and right is he." (Deut. 32:4.) "There is no iniquity with the Lord our God, nor respect of persons,

201

nor taking of gifts." (2 Chr. 19:7.) "Doth God pervert judgment? or doth the Almighty pervert justice?" (Job 8:3.) "Far be it from God, that he should do wickedness; and from the Almighty, that he should commit iniquity." (Job 34:10.) "The Lord our God is holy." (Ps. 99:9.) He is "the high and lofty One that inhabiteth eternity, whose name is Holy." (Isa. 57:15.) These are but samples from Holy Writ. There neither is nor can be any question whatever as to the righteousness and perfection of God.

Knowing that he is the same eternally, we would expect him to manifest the same character, perfections, and attributes as a mortal that possessed his being before his spirit entered its earthly tenement. The Messianic utterances say he will do so: "Enoch saw the day of the coming of the Son of Man, even in the flesh; and his soul rejoiced, saying: The Righteous is lifted up, and the Lamb is slain from the foundation of the world." (Moses 7:47.) The Righteous, seen by Enoch, said through Isaiah: "My righteousness shall not be abolished," and "My righteousness shall be for ever" (Isa. 51:6, 8), which of necessity means that even as he was righteous in preexistence, so shall that attribute attend him in mortality. And so Isaiah, speaking of the day of his mortal death, prophesied: "He had done no violence, neither was any deceit in his mouth." (Isa. 53:9.) Of him also the record says: "With righteousness shall he judge the poor, and reprove with equity for the meek of the earth. . . . And righteousness shall be the girdle of his loins, and faithfulness the girdle of his reins." (Isa. 11:4-5.) Also: "I the Lord have called thee in righteousness." (Isa. 42:6.) And there is, of course, much more.

Now as to his mortal life, what say the scriptures? He himself drove the point home with unerring accuracy when he asked: "Which of you convinceth me of sin?" (John 8:46), echoing, as it were, the ancient query: "Who can say," of God, "Thou hast wrought iniquity?" (Job 36:23.) Peter says, "Christ . . . did no sin, neither was guile found in his mouth." (1 Pet. 2:21-22.) Paul says, "He knew no sin" (2 Cor. 5:21);

that he "was in all points tempted like as we are, yet without sin" (Heb. 4:15); that he was "holy, harmless, undefiled, separate from sinners" (Heb. 7:26); and that he shall "appear the second time without sin unto salvation" (Heb. 9:28). John says his very name is "Faithful and True" and that "in righteousness he doth judge and make war." (Rev. 19:11.)

Truly he was and is righteous, sinless, and perfect forever, which course of conduct while in mortality identifies him beyond peradventure as the Messiah.

"The Lord Is Our Lawgiver"

Jehovah is our Lawgiver! Few eternal verities are more obvious, more axiomatic than this. The Lord God is the source of truth and light and law. He it is that ordains the way and says to men, 'Walk ye in it.' "I will give thee tables of stone, and a law, and commandments which I have written; that thou mayest teach them," he said to Moses. (Ex. 24:12.) "A law shall proceed from me" (Isa. 51:4), is his voice to Israel, and Isaiah echoes the call by proclaiming Messianically, "the isles shall wait for his law" (Isa. 42:4), and "the Lord is our lawgiver" (Isa. 33:22).

Unto what then can we liken his law, and with it what can compare? "O how love I thy law! it is my meditation all the day" (Ps. 119:97), for, "The law of the Lord is perfect" (Ps. 19:7). So sang the Psalmist. To us the Lord says: "I am the Lord thy God; and I give unto you this commandment— that no man shall come unto the Father but by me or by my word, which is my law, saith the Lord." (D&C 132:12.) And of him it is written: "He hath given a law unto all things, by which they move in their times and their seasons." (D&C 88:42.) And also: "Ye shall have no laws but my laws when I come, for I am your lawgiver, and what can stay my hand?" (D&C 38:22.) Is it any wonder that he said to the Nephites, "I am the law, and the light." (3 Ne. 15:9.)

Clearly our concern is not alone one of extolling his law,

203

or of identifying him as the Lawgiver, or of knowing that to him and his word all· things must bow in submissive reverence. Our concern is to crystallize in the minds of men that the great Lawgiver walked among men and that his name was Jesus. "Judah is my lawgiver" (Ps. 108:8) is the Messianic proclamation that he who held the Scepter would come in that lineage. And when he came, it was still his prerogative to give the law. The prophets who went before had said: 'Thus saith the Lord: These are the words of my law; walk ye in them and live.' Our Lord followed no such pattern. Instead he assumed, as was his right, the stance of the Lawgiver himself. He altered, amended, and revoked the word of God as given by the prophets of old. "Ye have heard that it hath been said," relative to such and such, "but I say unto you," do thus and so instead. (Matt. 5.)

Truly, "There is one lawgiver, who is able to save and to destroy" (James 4:12), and he is Christ!

Messiah Giveth Living Water

Without water man dies—temporally and spiritually. Bread and breath and water, these three, they are the essentials of existence. If any one of them is withdrawn, life ceases—temporally and spiritually.

Our concern at this point is with water, with the strivings men undergo to gain it, and with the agony that engulfs the mortal soul when it is taken away. Even the Son of God— pierced, bleeding, in pain beyond recording, hanging at death's door on the cross of Calvary—had but one plea pertaining to his physical suffering, and that was the agonizing cry, "I thirst." (John 19:28.) How vital it is that men have water. A dearth of drink deals death to those so deprived. Those who dwell in deserts and pitch their tents on arid plains, as ancient Israel often did, have the need and desire for drink ever before them.

How natural it was, then, for the Lord and his prophets to use the search for water as a pattern for the search for sal-

204

vation. Just as a man is spared temporally by drinking the life-giving liquids of mortality, so he is saved eternally by downing great draughts of living water. Moses at Meribah smote the rock and a great flood of water gushed forth to give drink to all Israel and their cattle, thus teaching them that if they would look to Jehovah, by whose power the miracle was wrought, they might drink forever from streams of living water. (Num. 20:1-13.) Jeremiah proclaimed that "the Lord" was "the fountain of living waters." (Jer. 17:13.) And the Lord himself, complaining about the rebellious nature of his people, said: "For my people have committed two evils; they have forsaken me the fountain of living waters, and hewed them out cisterns, broken cisterns, that can hold no water." (Jer. 2:13.) After his resurrection this same Jehovah, identifying himself as the Lord Jesus Christ, spoke similarly to Moroni in these words: "Faith, hope and charity bringeth unto me—the fountain of all righteousness." (Ether 12:28.)

Under the circumstances we might well expect to find Messianic prophecies saying that King-Messiah, during his mortal ministry, would be the source of living waters. And so it is. One of the greatest of these is Isaiah's proclamation that "a king shall reign in righteousness," and that among other things, he shall be "as rivers of water in a dry place." (Isa. 32:1-4.) Most of the Messianic utterances of this nature, however, were destined to have only partial fulfillment in the meridian of time and were to come to a glorious consummation in the dispensation of restoration when the promised King would reign personally upon the earth.

Speaking of the latter-day gathering of Israel, Jehovah's promise is: "I will open rivers in high places, and fountains in the midst of the valleys: I will make the wilderness a pool of water, and the dry land springs of water." (Isa. 41:18.) That this has reference to more than climatic changes which bring forth literal streams is shown by the latter-day revelation which speaks of the barren deserts bringing forth "pools of living water" (D&C 133:29), meaning among other things

205

that when the desert blossoms as a rose in the literal sense of the word, it will be but a similitude of the living waters then being poured out upon the Lord's people.

Another great Messianic utterance says: "I will pour water upon him that is thirsty, and floods upon the dry ground: I will pour my spirit upon thy seed, and my blessing upon thine offspring." (Isa. 44:3.) Similar truths are found in Isaiah 41:10-20; 48:20-21; and 49:9-12. Isaiah 12 tells of a millennial day when men shall "draw water out of the wells of salvation"; and Zechariah, speaking of that same day of peace and righteousness, tells how "living waters shall go out from Jerusalem" (Zech. 14:8).

From all this it is perfectly clear that men must drink living water to be saved. As Moroni expressed it: "Come unto the fountain of all righteousness and be saved." (Ether 8:26.) And the same truths flow from the same fountain yesterday, today, and forever.

Before his mortal birth our Lord's call was: "Ho, every one that thirsteth, come ye to the waters, . . . and I will make an everlasting covenant with you." (Isa. 55:1-3; 2 Ne. 9:50.) To the Nephites he said: "Come unto me and ye shall partake of the fruit of the tree of life; yea, ye shall eat and drink of the bread and the waters of life freely." (Alma 5:34.) And Alma echoed his words by saying: "Whosoever will come may come and partake of the waters of life freely." (Alma 42:27.)

During his mortal sojourn it was the same. On the eighth day of the Feast of Tabernacles, while the priest poured water upon the altar and the words of Isaiah were sung, "With joy shall ye draw water out of the wells of salvation" (Isa. 12:3), our Lord stepped forth and proclaimed: "If any man thirst, let him come unto me, and drink." (John 7:37.) Earlier, at Jacob's Well, he had said to the woman of Samaria, "If thou knewest the gift of God, and who it is that saith to thee, Give me to drink; thou wouldest have asked of him, and he would have given thee living water. . . . Whosoever drinketh the water that I shall give him shall never thirst; but the water that I shall give him shall be in him a well of water springing up into everlasting life." (John 4:7-14.)

After his resurrection, the same proclamation was continued. The risen Lord still feeds his flock, still leads them "unto living fountains of waters" (Rev. 7:17), for, he says, "I will give unto him that is athirst of the fountain of the water of life freely" (Rev. 21:6). The message to all is: "Come. And let him that is athirst come. And whosoever will, let him take the water of life freely." (Rev. 22:17.) And the same promise has been renewed by revelation in our day. (D&C 10:66.)

Those who do come to quench their thirst, and who are true and faithful, shall drink forever from the pure fountain. As Isaiah expressed it, their "waters shall be sure" (Isa. 33:16), meaning they shall be as their Lord, enjoying and possessing the same eternal life which he lives. As he said in our day: "Unto him that keepeth my commandments I will give the mysteries of my kingdom, and the same shall be in him a well of living water, springing up unto everlasting life." (D&C 63:23.)

"I Am the Light and the Life of the World"

If there is a self-evident truth—one that needs no proof, one that must be accepted automatically by all men everywhere—it is that life and being and existence come from God. He is the Source of existence, the Creator of all things, the Originator and Organizer of the universe, the Father of Spirits. Without him there would be nothing; life comes by him; because of him all things are. He is the Life.

That this Supreme Being, who is the Author of Life, has appointed his Well-Beloved Son to stand in his place and stead, in administering salvation and giving life and light to the children of men, is the burden of the scriptures. The Lord Jesus, at his Father's behest, has become and is the Life of the World. Under the Father he is the Creator of all

207

things. It is the Light of Christ, which "proceedeth forth from the presence of God to fill the immensity of space," that "giveth life to all things." (D&C 88:12-13.) And through him eternal life comes, so that in every sense he is the Life of the World.

Speaking Messianically, both Abinadi and Alma said, "He is the light and the life of the world." (Mosiah 16:9; Alma 38:9.) One of his meridian witnesses recorded: "In him was life; and the life was the light of men" (John 1:4); or, as translated so as to reveal how he is the life of men: "In him was the gospel, and the gospel was the life, and the life was the light of men" (JST, John 1:4). During his mortal ministry Jesus said: "As the Father hath life in himself; so hath he given to the Son to have life in himself." (John 5:26.) After his resurrection, he has continued to proclaim to the Nephites, to Moroni, and to Joseph Smith: "I am the light and the life of the world." (3 Ne. 9:18; 11:11; Ether 4:12; D&C 10:70.)

There are at least three ways, each intertwined with the others, in which our Lord is the Light of the World. These are:

1. Through the Light of Christ he governs and controls the universe and gives life to all that therein is.

2. By this same immensity-filling light—and also, to certain faithful ones, by the power of the Holy Ghost!—he enlightens the mind and quickens the understanding.

3. By his own upright, sinless, and perfect course, in preexistence, in mortality, and in resurrected glory, he sets a perfect example and is able to say to all men: "Follow thou me." (2 Ne. 31:10.)

Our understanding of the Light of Christ is limited. Finite powers and capacities cannot comprehend that which is infinite. But we do know certain basic principles, among which are these:

1. That it is the light which proceeds forth from the presence and person of Deity to fill immensity, and that it is therefore everywhere present;

2. That it is the agency of God's power, the law by which all things are governed;

3. That it is the divine power which gives life to all things, and that if it were completely withdrawn life would cease;

4. That it enlightens the mind and quickens the understanding of every person born into the world (all have a conscience!);

5. That it strives with all men (the Holy Ghost testifies but does not strive) unless and until they rebel against light and truth, at which time the striving ceases, and in that sense the Spirit is withdrawn;

6. That those who hearken to its voice come unto Christ, receive his gospel, are baptized, and gain the gift of the Holy Ghost. (Moro. 7:12-18; D&C 84:43-53; 88:7-13.)

In the light of all this, we find the ancient prophets ascribing to the Lord Jehovah all things connected with the Light of Christ, and we find the Lord Jesus and his apostles ascribing those same things to him who was Mary's Son.

Of Jehovah the scriptures say: "Thou wilt light my candle: the Lord my God will enlighten my darkness." (Ps. 18:28.) "The Lord is my light and my salvation." (Ps. 27:1.) "O send out thy light and thy truth: let them lead me." (Ps. 43:3.) "God is the Lord, which hath shewed us light." (Ps. 118:27.) "Thy word is a lamp unto my feet, and a light unto my path." (Ps. 119:105.) And much, much more.

As a means of applying all of this—and much, much more—to himself, Jesus said: "I am the light of the world." (John 9:5.)

Isaiah foretold that Israel's Messiah would come as "a light to the Gentiles" (Isa. 49:6) and that the light would pierce the darkness of error and unbelief (Isa. 60:1-3). Concerning those dwelling in "the land of Zebulun and the land of Naphtali," Israel's Messianic seer said: "The people that walked in darkness have seen a great light: they that dwell in the land of the shadow of death, upon them hath the light shined." (Isa. 9:1-2.) Matthew quoted this prophecy and

209

pronounced its fulfillment on the occasion that Jesus, "leaving Nazareth, . . . came and dwelt in Capernaum, which is upon the sea coast, in the borders of Zabulon and Nephthalim." (Matt. 4:13-16.)

The spirit Jehovah, destined to be the mortal Jesus and the resurrected Christ, is the great Exemplar, our guide and leader, the one who everlastingly marked the way and charted the course for all of his brethren. "Be holy, for I am holy" (Lev. 11:45), was Jehovah's counsel to Israel. Peter applied these words to Christ and counseled the saints of his day that "as he which hath called you is holy, so be ye holy." (1 Pet. 1:13-16.)

When he came in resurrected glory to the Nephites he said: "Behold, I am the law, and the light. Look unto me." (3 Ne. 15:9.) Also: "Behold I am the light; I have set an example for you. . . . Therefore, hold up your light that it may shine unto the world. Behold I am the light which ye shall hold up—that which ye have seen me do." (3 Ne. 18:16, 24.)

In all dispensations the saints "rejoice" because of his "judgments. . . . For this God"—be he called Jehovah, or Jesus, or Christ—"is our God for ever and ever: he will be our guide." (Ps. 48:11-14.)

Truly, as he said to Moriancumer two thousand years before his mortal birth: "In me shall all mankind have light, and that eternally, even they who shall believe on my name." (Ether 3:14.)

Messiah Offereth Peace to All

If the scriptures teach that peace comes from the Lord Jehovah, that he is the source, author, and founder of this greatly to be desired state of mind and being, and that such a blessing and feeling comes from no other source; and if these same holy writings acclaim with equal fervor and finality that peace comes from the Lord Jesus, that he is the author and source thereof, and that none can so obtain except in and through him and by obedience to the laws of his everlasting gospel—if such are the pronouncements of all the prophets who have ever spoken on these matters, it is thereby irrefutably established that the Lord Jehovah and the Lord Jesus are one and the same. And none but those who willfully choose to reject the Spirit-borne witness, falling from the lips of Spirit-led teachers, can reach any other conclusion.

What, then, say the scriptures as to peace—whose it is, whence it comes, and how struggling, feeble, wayward man may gain it?

1. They say: *Peace comes from Jehovah.*

"Jehovah," or, as it has been Anglicized in the translation process, "the Lord," says the Psalmist, "will bless his people with peace." (Ps. 29:11.) "He will speak peace unto his people, and to his saints." (Ps. 85:8.) The great blessing, revealed through Moses and pronounced upon all Israel, contained the promise: "The Lord lift up his countenance upon thee, and give thee peace." (Num. 6:26.) And it was Jehovah himself who said, "If ye walk in my statutes, and keep my commandments, and do them, . . . I will give peace in the land." (Lev. 26:3-6.) He it is who promises to make, with the righteous of all ages, his "covenant of peace," which is the gospel covenant. (Ezek. 37:26; Isa. 54:10.)

2. They say: *The Messiah shall bring peace.*

Much that is Messianic centers around the theme of peace. As Isaiah set forth the sufferings of our Lord, when he was "wounded for our transgressions," he used this poetic and prophetic phrase: "The chastisement of our peace was upon him," meaning that through his atonement our Lord bore the chastisement for sins that, save for our faith and repentance, would justly rest upon us. (Isa. 53:5.) This same Messianic prophet, in exulting strains of joy, called our Lord "The Prince of Peace" and said, "Of the increase of his government and peace there shall be no end." (Isa. 9:6-7.)

Micah's seeric pronouncement that the Messiah would be born in "Bethlehem Ephratah" contains this graphic expression: "And this man shall be the peace," thus setting forth that the bringing forth of peace by the Messiah is so vital a part of his ministry that he is the very personification of that godly attribute. (Micah 5:2-5.) Zechariah's vision of the Man Jesus' triumphal entry into Jerusalem includes this promise: "He shall speak peace unto the heathen." (Zech. 9:9-10.) And Haggai's inspired declaration, that "the desire of all nations shall come" in the latter days to reign among restored Israel, includes this divine assurance: "In this place will I give peace, saith the Lord of hosts." (Hag. 2:5-9.)

When our Messianic friend Isaiah wrote, "How beautiful upon the mountains are the feet of him that bringeth good tidings, that publisheth peace; that bringeth good tidings of good, that publisheth salvation: that saith unto Zion, Thy God reigneth!" (Isa. 52:7), he afforded Paul the chance to identify the "good tidings" as "the gospel of peace" (Rom. 10:15), and he provided a text for Abinadi, whose sermon contained this Messianic doctrine: "O how beautiful upon the mountains are the feet of him that bringeth good tidings, that is the founder of peace, yea, even the Lord, who has redeemed his people; yea, him who has granted salvation unto his people" (Mosiah 15:18).

3. They say: *The Lord Jesus brought peace.*

It is clear that the Lord Jehovah is the source of peace for his people. It is also clear that the promised Messiah would bring peace to those same people. Fully aware of these verities, the Lord Jesus—whose very birth had been heralded by angelic choirs singing "Glory to God in the highest, and on earth peace, good will toward men" (Luke 2:14)—this same Jesus near the climax of his ministry said: "Peace I leave with you, my peace I give unto you" (John 14:27), and "in me ye might have peace" (John 16:33). That is to say: 'I am the Lord Jehovah who is the source of peace; I am the Messiah who is the founder of peace; look unto me and gain peace unto your souls.'

4. They say: *Peace comes through the gospel of him who is our Lord.*

Because he "established righteousness" among his people, Melchizedek (who is one of the prototypes of Christ) was called "the King of peace." (JST, Gen. 14:36.) Similarly, the Prince of Peace, through his gospel, establishes peace in the hearts of those who believe and obey. Peace in this life and eternal life in the world to come are the greatest of all blessings, and they are the reward reserved for those who do the works of righteousness. (D&C 59:23.)

This doctrine that the Founder of Peace brings to the faithful is interwoven through and implicit in all of the revelations. Peter counsels, "Eschew evil, . . . do good, . . . seek peace" (1 Pet. 3:11), and says that the very message of salvation which God sends to men is one of "preaching peace by Jesus Chirst" (Acts 10:36). Paul calls this same Jesus "the Lord of peace" (2 Thess. 3:16), speaks of that peace which "passeth all understanding" (Phil. 4:7), and says that "the kingdom of God" itself is "righteousness, and peace, and joy in the Holy Ghost" (Rom. 14:17). And so it goes throughout revealed writ. Peace is reserved for the faithful saints, for the meek and the upright (Ps. 37:11, 37), and for those who love the Lord's law (Ps. 119:165). On the other hand, "The wicked are like the troubled sea, when it cannot rest, whose waters cast up mire and dirt. There is no peace, saith my God, to the wicked." (Isa. 57:20-21.)

"The Lord Is Our Judge"

"Shall not the Judge of all the earth do right?" (Gen. 18:25.) So asked Abraham as he conversed with the Almighty—which raises the question: Who is the great Judge? Is it Elohim or Jehovah? Is it the Father, Son, and Holy Spirit, acting in unison as one Godhead? And what of delegated power to judge, as the ancient Twelve who shall sit with their Lord upon thrones judging certain specified ones?

By way of answer, we turn to these words of Jesus: "The Father judgeth no man, but hath committed all judgment unto the Son: That all men should honour the Son, even as

213

they honour the Father." (John 5:22-23.) The Lord Jesus Christ is the Judge of all!

And so once again we discover that both reason and revelation testify that the Lord Jesus is the Lord Jehovah. Since the Old Testament word is that Jehovah only is the sole judge of both quick and dead, and Jesus proclaims that this power is his, it follows that Israel's Jehovah must be and is the Son of God.

To catch the vision of the Messianic message involved, let us note a few of the great prophetic utterances. Moroni speaks of the day when his spirit and body shall come forth in the resurrection and he shall come forth triumphant to meet us "before the pleasing bar of the great Jehovah, the Eternal Judge of both quick and dead." (Moro. 10:34.)

Speaking of Jehovah, various of the Old Testament prophets made such assertions as: "The Lord shall judge the people." (Ps. 7:8.) "He shall judge the world in righteousness." (Ps. 9:8.) "The Lord reigneth; . . . he shall judge the people righteously." (Ps. 96:10.) "The Lord is our judge." (Isa. 33:22.) And there are a great many more.

And speaking of Jehovah-Messiah, we find ancient prophecies of this sort: "He cometh to judge the earth: he shall judge the world with righteousness, and the people with his truth." (Ps. 96:13.) "He shall not judge after the sight of his eyes, neither reprove after the hearing of his ears: But with righteousness shall he judge the poor, and reprove with equity for the meek of the earth." (Isa. 11:3-4.) "In mercy shall the throne be established: and he shall sit upon it in truth in the tabernacle of David, judging, and seeking judgment, and hasting righteousness." (Isa. 16:5.) And again there are many more.

To Adam the Lord revealed that "the name of his Only Begotten is the Son of Man, even Jesus Christ, a righteous Judge, who shall come in the meridian of time." (Moses 6:57.) Peter, in his day, testified that "God anointed Jesus of Nazareth with the Holy Ghost and with power," that after his crucifixion the Father raised him up in glorious immortality, and that the ancient apostles were commanded to testify that "it is he which was ordained of God to be the Judge of quick and dead." (Acts 10:38-42.)

But as is not uncommon in our Messianic questing, it is to the Book of Mormon that we turn for the plainest and most perfect preannouncements of the eternal truth that judgment is the Lord's and that the Lord's name is Christ. Lehi said that all men shall stand in the presence of "the Holy Messiah, . . . to be judged of him according to the truth and holiness which is in him." (2 Ne. 2:8-10.) Jacob taught that after all men are resurrected, "they must appear before the judgment-seat of the Holy One of Israel; and then cometh the judgment," and that "he suffereth the pains of all men" and bringeth to pass the resurrection of all, so "that all might stand before him at the great and judgment day." (2 Ne. 9:15-22.) Alma was bold to say that to the Redeemer, "every knee shall bow, and every tongue confess, . . . even at the last day, when all men shall stand to be judged of him, [and] then shall they confess that he is God." (Mosiah 27:30-31.) And so the teachings go, prophet after prophet, throughout the whole history of the Nephite peoples, with the crowning statement of them all being the words of the risen Christ as he ministered personally among that favored remnant of Israel: "My Father sent me that I might be lifted up upon the cross; and after that I had been lifted up upon the cross, that I might draw all men unto me, that as I have been lifted up by men even so should men be lifted up by the Father, to stand before me, to be judged of their works, whether they be good or whether they be evil." (3 Ne. 27:14.)

The scriptural assertion that all men "shall be brought and be arraigned before the bar of Christ the Son, and God the Father, and the Holy Spirit, which is one Eternal God, to be judged according to their works, whether they be good or whether they be evil" (Alma 11:44) means simply that Christ's judicial decisions are those of the other two members of the Godhead because all three are perfectly

215

united as one. The ancient Twelve and the Nephite Twelve, and no doubt others similarly empowered, will sit in judgment, under Christ, on selected portions of the house of Israel; but their decrees will be limited to those who love the Lord and have kept his commandments, "and none else." (D&C 29:12; 3 Ne. 27:27; Matt. 19:28.)

Chapter 13

MESSIAH REDEEMS MANKIND

Fall and Atonement Foreordained

In Chapter 4 we set forth that Christ our Lord is the Firstborn of the Father; that the great Elohim ordained and established a gospel plan whereby the Firstborn and all his spirit kindred might advance and progress and become like their Eternal Father; that this same preeminent Spirit Son adopted the Father's plan and was chosen and foreordained to be the Savior and Redeemer therein; and that the Gospel of God thus became the gospel of Jesus Christ and was and is the plan of salvation for all men.

In Chapter 5 we saw man come to dwell on earth; we beheld the fall of Adam, which brought temporal and spiritual death into the world; and we learned thereby of the need for a Redeemer to ransom Adam and all men from the effects of the planned and foreordained fall. We saw that this mortal life became a probationary estate, and that a gracious God gave his gospel to men so they might believe on his Only Begotten and be raised, not alone in immortality, but unto eternal life; and that this gospel plan (destined to be on earth in a series of gospel dispensations) consisted of believing in Christ, accepting his atoning sacrifice, and living in harmony with his revealed laws.

Now we shall turn our attention to that infinite and eternal atonement, that redemption wrought for all man-

217

kind, which is the very heart and core and center of the gospel of our Lord. This atoning sacrifice; this redemption of the world; this most transcendent of all events from creation's dawn to the endless ages of eternity; this shedding of the blood of a God, which was to occur in Gethsemane and on Calvary; this ransom paid for man, for all forms of life, and for the very earth itself—all this rests on two foundations. Either these foundations are secure or there is no atonement of Christ, no plan of salvation, no immortality, no eternal life, and no purpose in creation. These foundations, whose importance cannot be overemphasized, are:

1. The fall of Adam whereby that greatest of all mortal men (save Jesus only) became mortal and began the process of providing bodies for those of our Father's children who kept their first estate; and

2. The divine Sonship of Him who gained power from the Father to ransom himself and all his fellow mortals from their fallen state.

We shall here show the relationship of the fall and the atonement; the matter of the divine Sonship will be developed in Chapter 25 when we consider our Lord's birth into mortality.

Lucifer Rebels and Falls

"It must needs be"—that is, it is inherent in the very nature of life and being, it is something without which there could be neither life nor being—"that there is an opposition in all things." So say the scriptures. Then they set forth that if there were no opposites—righteousness and wickedness; good and bad; life and death; corruption and incorruption; happiness and misery; sense and insensibility—there would be nothing, and "all things must have vanished away." (2 Ne. 2:10-13.) All this is self-evident. Unless there is light there can be no darkness; unless there is vice there can be no virtue; without love there is no hate; without damnation, no salvation, for all these are opposites; they are in opposition to each other.

As it happens, and we need not reason on the whys and wherefores, but simply accept the realities as they are, Lucifer (and his followers) are in opposition to the Lord and his eternal purposes. Agency means freedom of choice. With God and his goodness pulling in one direction and Satan and his evil forces pulling in the other, man is in a position to choose. Thus it is written: "Men are free according to the flesh; and all things are given them which are expedient unto man. And they are free to choose liberty and eternal life, through the great Mediator of all men, or to choose captivity and death, according to the captivity and power of the devil; for he seeketh that all men might be miserable like unto himself." (2 Ne. 2:27.)

Our revelations recite that Lucifer and his fellow rebels are, like us, the spirit children of the Father. Lucifer himself is a son of the morning. He and his like-minded associates comprised one-third of the hosts of heaven, and because of their open rebellion against light and truth, because they defied God and his government, knowing perfectly what the will of the Father was, they were cast out of heaven onto this earth. Their punishment: eternal damnation. Progression ceased for them. No mortal bodies would ever house their spirit forms. For them there was to be no second estate, no probationary experiences, no resurrection, no eternal life—nothing but darkness and defiance; nothing but wickedness and rebellion; nothing but hatred and evil to all eternity, because they came out in open rebellion and with a perfect knowledge of the course they then pursued and of the consequences that attended it; they fought against God. It is an awful thing to defy the Lord, to make open warfare against the Supreme Being.

"I beheld Satan as lightning fall from heaven," Jesus said. (Luke 10:18.) "And I, Lehi, according to the things which I have read, must needs suppose that an angel of God,

219

according to that which is written, had fallen from heaven; wherefore, he became a devil, having sought that which was evil before God." (2 Ne. 2:17.) Certainly one of the scriptures Lehi had read, with spiritual insight and understanding, was Isaiah's great pronouncement setting forth how Lucifer was "fallen from heaven," which ends with the statement that he shall not "be joined" with mortals "in burial," meaning he shall have no mortal body to go down in due course to the grave. (Isa. 14:12-20.)

Truly Lucifer fell with an everlasting fall, a fall from which there is no redemption. No ransom will ever be paid for his soul. He is damned, as are those also who are his, meaning those who, with him, rebelled in the Eternal Presence. And being himself miserable, he seeks a like misery for all mankind.

Adam Obeys and Falls

To "the first man of all men" (Moses 1:34), who is called Adam, and to "the first of all women," who is Eve, "the mother of all living" (Moses 4:26)—while they were yet immortal and thus incapable of providing mortal bodies for the spirit children of the Father—the command came: "Be fruitful, and multiply, and replenish the earth." (Moses 2:28.)

Be fruitful! Multiply! Have children! The whole plan of salvation, including both immortality and eternal life for all the spirit hosts of heaven, hung on their compliance with this command. If they obeyed, the Lord's purposes would prevail.

If they disobeyed, they would remain childless and innocent in their paradisiacal Eden, and the spirit hosts would remain in their celestial heaven—denied the experiences of mortality, denied a resurrection, denied a hope of eternal life, denied the privilege to advance and progress and become like their Eternal Father. That is to say, the whole plan of salvation would have been frustrated, and the purposes of

God in begetting spirit children and in creating this earth as their habitat would have come to naught.

"Be fruitful, and multiply." 'Provide bodies for my spirit progeny.' Thus saith thy God. Eternity hangs in the balance. The plans of Deity are at the crossroads. There is only one course to follow: the course of conformity and obedience. Adam, who is Michael—the spirit next in intelligence, power, dominion, and righteousness to the great Jehovah himself—Adam, our father, and Eve, our mother, must obey. They must fall. They must become mortal. Death must enter the world. There is no other way. They must fall that man may be.

Such is the reality. Such is the rationale. Such is the divine will. Fall thou must, O mighty Michael. Fall? Yes, plunge down from thy immortal state of peace, perfection, and glory to a lower existence; leave the presence of thy God in the garden and enter the lone and dreary world; step forth from the garden to the wilderness; leave the flowers and fruits that grow spontaneously and begin the battle with thorns, thistles, briars, and noxious weeds; subject thyself to famine and pestilence; suffer with disease; know pain and sorrow; face death on every hand—but with it all bear children; provide bodies for all those who served with thee when thou led the hosts of heaven in casting out Lucifer, our common enemy.

Yes, Adam, fall; fall for thine own good; fall for the good of all mankind; fall that man may be; bring death into the world; do that which will cause an atonement to be made, with all the infinite and eternal blessings which flow therefrom.

And so Adam fell as fall he must. But he fell by breaking a lesser law—an infinitely lesser law—so that he too, having thereby transgressed, would become subject to sin and need a Redeemer and be privileged to work out his own salvation, even as would be the case with all those upon whom the effects of his fall would come.

221

Adam and Eve Bear Children

Death and mortality go together; they are inseparably intertwined; one cannot exist without the other. Mortality is the state in which men are subject to death, and the existence of death is what makes man or any living creature mortal. And with mortality comes child bearing; mortal creatures father mortal children; mortality is the state where bodies are made of the dust of the earth to provide temporary residences for spirit creations.

And so, Adam and Eve partook of the forbidden fruit, were driven out of the Garden of Eden, "And they have brought forth children; yea, even the family of all the earth." (2 Ne. 2:20.) Every member of the human race is a descendant of the first man. Adam is our common progenitor. There are no exceptions.

Lehi, whose inspired words are so pointed and clear as to the heaven-directed fall of our first primeval parents, tells us that "if Adam had not transgressed he would not have fallen, but he would have remained in the garden of Eden." (2 Ne. 2:22.) Had this been the case, the billions of mortals who have dwelt on this lowly planet during the past six thousand years would still be spirit beings in the presence of the Lord; they would still be waiting for their mortal probation.

Having so taught with reference to the human race, Lehi expands the principle to cover every form of life, animals, plants, the fowls of the air, and the fish of the watery world; for all of them there is neither mortality nor death until the results of the fall were forthcoming. "All things which were created must have remained in the same state in which they were after they were created," Lehi says, "and they must have remained forever, and had no end." (2 Ne. 2:22.) That is, Edenic immortality would have reigned forever in every department of creation, among all created things, and there would have been no death for any form of life. It must be remembered that this earth and all forms of life were created in a paradisiacal state, that its present mortal state com-

222

menced with the fall, and that it will be renewed and receive again its paradisiacal state when the Lord comes to usher in the millennial era.

Of this Edenic or paradisiacal state of our first parents, Lehi says: "And they would have had no children; wherefore they would have remained in a state of innocence, having no joy, for they knew no misery; doing no good, for they knew no sin." (2 Ne. 2:23.) Eve spoke similarly when she gave forth this inspired utterance: "Were it not for our transgression we never should have had seed, and never should have known good and evil, and the joy of our redemption, and the eternal life which God giveth unto all the obedient." (Moses 5:11.)

This doctrine of the fall, of mortality and death beginning on earth, of the consequent peopling of the world, and of the redemption thereby required to save man, the earth, and all things thereon from the effects of the fall, has been known and taught by prophets in all dispensations. And all teachings connected therewith that occurred before the coming of Christ were Messianic in the very nature of things.

It was Enoch who said: "Because that Adam fell, we are; and by this fall came death; and we are made partakers of misery and woe. . . . [But] the Son of God hath atoned for original guilt, wherein the sins of the parents cannot be answered upon the heads of the children, for they are whole from the foundation of the world." (Moses 6:48-54.) And it was Father Lehi who phrased one of the most noted of all statements about the fall in these words: "Adam fell that men might be; and men are, that they might have joy. And the Messiah cometh in the fulness of time, that he may redeem the children of men from the fall." (2 Ne. 2:25-26.)

Christ Atones and Redeems

"Of every tree of the garden thou mayest freely eat" were the words of the Lord God to Adam, "But of the tree of the knowledge of good and evil, thou shalt not eat of it, nevertheless, thou mayest choose for thyself, for it is given unto thee; but, remember that I forbid it, for in the day thou eatest thereof thou shalt surely die." (Moses 3:16-17.) Adam ate, as eat he must; and Adam died, as die he must; and the death thereby brought into the world passed upon all mankind. Having transgressed and become mortal, Adam was cast out of the garden, lest he then partake of the fruit of the tree of life and, "having no space for repentance," live forever in his sins. Thus, "our first parents were cut off both temporally and spiritually from the presence of the Lord." (Alma 42:5-7.) Death reigned through Adam.

The first death, in point of time, was spiritual. Spiritual death is to die as pertaining to the things of the Spirit; it is to die as pertaining to the things of righteousness; it is to be cast out of the presence of the Lord, in which presence spirituality and righteousness abound. Adam died this death when he left Eden, and he remained dead until he was born again by the power of the Spirit following his baptism.

Temporal death is the natural death. It consists of the separation of the body and the spirit, the one going to the grave, the other to a world of waiting spirits to await the day of resurrection. Adam died temporally within a thousand years, which is a day unto the Lord.

Thus the *temporal fall* is to die and lose the house prepared as an habitation for the eternal spirit, and the *spiritual fall* is to be denied the presence of God and the righteousness which there abounds.

"To atone is to ransom, reconcile, expiate, redeem, reclaim, absolve, propitiate, make amends, pay the penalty." (*Mormon Doctrine*, 2nd ed., p. 62.) Our Lord's atoning sacrifice was one in which he conquered both temporal and spiritual death. Since by one man, Adam, death entered the world, so by one man, Christ, death is abolished. It ceases; it is no more. Life alone remains. "As in Adam all die, even so in Christ shall all be made alive." (1 Cor. 15:22.) All men come forth from the grave in immortality; all are resurrected. Adam's fall enables body and spirit to separate in the natural death; Christ's atonement causes body and spirit to reunite, inseparably, in immortality, never again to see that corruption which returns a mortal body to the dust whence its elements came. "O grave, where is thy victory?" (1 Cor. 15:55.) Truly, it is swallowed up by Him who holds the keys of death.

But immortality alone does not suffice. Those who inherit realms where the faces of God and Christ are never seen shall have immortality. The full glory of the atoning sacrifice of the Holy Messiah causes man to return to the presence of his God and to enjoy that kind and quality and state of life which is the possession of him who is the Father of us all. Those who, through faith and repentance and righteousness, are redeemed from the spiritual fall are raised not alone in immortality but unto eternal life. Whereas they were once dead as pertaining to the things of the Spirit, now they are alive in Christ and enjoy the fulness of the blessings of the Holy Spirit. Whereas they were dead as pertaining to the things of righteousness, now they are clean and pure and holy, and their immortal souls radiate righteousness. Whereas, being unclean and unworthy, they had been cast out of the presence of their Lord, now they are welcomed into his bosom, the light of his countenance shines upon them, and they dwell in the presence of the Father and Son forever. They are reconciled to God spiritually. They are redeemed in the full sense of the word. They have attained at-one-ment through the atonement.

It is clear; it is plain; it is perfect—the fall is father to the atonement. As Moroni expressed it, God "created Adam, and by Adam came the fall of man. And because of the fall of man came Jesus Christ, . . . and because of Jesus Christ came the redemption of man." (Morm. 9:12.)

Thus, if there had been no Adam, there would be no need for Christ. Those who are redeemed by him who is God's Son are the descendants of Adam. "His blood atoneth for the sins of those who have fallen by the transgression of Adam." (Mosiah 3:11.) "The atonement . . . was prepared from the foundation of the world for all mankind, which ever were since the fall of Adam, or who are, or who ever shall be even unto the end of the world. And this is the means whereby salvation cometh. And there is none other salvation save this." (Mosiah 4:7-8.)

Implicit in the doctrine of the fall and the consequent atonement is the bitter reality—if such it must be to those whose spiritual understanding has not yet been opened to the full truth—that there were no pre-Adamites, for mortality, death, and procreation began with Adam. And there is no salvation provided for any except Adam's seed, for it is they for whom Christ died.

Salvation Comes by Obedience

Redemption from the temporal fall, from the natural death, is a free gift; immortality comes to all men. But redemption from the spiritual fall comes by obedience to the laws and ordinances of the gospel. Its receipt is conditional. All mankind may be saved if they will believe and obey. "They that believe not," though they have been "raised in immortality," shall remain forever separated from the Lord and his righteousness, "for they cannot be redeemed from their spiritual fall, because they repent not; For they love darkness rather than light, and their deeds are evil, and they receive their wages of whom they list to obey." (D&C 29:43-45.) The atonement of Christ—coupled with conformance to his laws!—leads to a celestial inheritance.

"Redemption cometh in and through the Holy Messiah, . . . unto all those who have a broken heart and a contrite spirit; and unto none else." (2 Ne. 2:6-7.) So spake Lehi. "And he cometh into the world that he may save all men if they will hearken unto his voice." (2 Ne. 9:21.) So spake Jacob. "Speak of the atonement of Christ, and attain to a perfect knowledge of him"; through faith gain "a good hope of glory in him"; and "be reconciled" to God that ye may "be presented as the first-fruits of Christ" unto him. (Jacob 4:11-12.) So Jacob continues to speak.

From King Benjamin, as he quoted the words of an angel, we learn: Christ "cometh unto his own, that salvation might come unto the children of men, even through faith on his name. . . . For salvation cometh to none . . . except it be through repentance and faith on the Lord Jesus Christ. . . . For the natural man is an enemy to God, and has been from the fall of Adam, and will be, forever and ever, unless he yields to the enticings of the Holy Spirit, and putteth off the natural man and becometh a saint through the atonement of Christ the Lord, and becometh as a child, submissive, meek, humble, patient, full of love, willing to submit to all things which the Lord seeth fit to inflict upon him, even as a child doth submit to his father." (Mosiah 3:8-19.) Again from King Benjamin: "The atonement . . . has been prepared from the foundation of the world, that thereby salvation might come to him that should put his trust in the Lord, and should be diligent in keeping his commandments, and continue in the faith even unto the end of his life." (Mosiah 4:6.)

And so, if need be, we might continue until we fill volumes. Everywhere and always when inspired men speak or write of being redeemed from the spiritual fall, of gaining salvation in the presence of Gods and angels, their voice is one of faith, repentance, baptism, and of receiving the Holy Ghost, and of thereafter pressing forward with steadfastness and devotion conforming to every principle of eternal truth.

What If There Were No Atonement?

If there were no creation, we would not be, neither the earth, nor any life thereon. All things, in effect, would vanish away. And if there were no atonement, the purposes of creation would be frustrated; man would remain lost and fallen forever; there would be no resurrection nor eternal life;

227

Adam and all his posterity would be as Lucifer, cast out, damned, without hope, lost forever.

The Book of Mormon prophets have made these things exceedingly clear. In plain words, as they proclaimed the infinite glories of the atonement, they have affirmed such things as: "Were it not for the atonement, which God himself shall make for the sins and iniquities of his people, . . they must unavoidably perish. . . . For . . . there could not any man be saved except it were through the redemption of God." (Mosiah 13:28, 32; 15:19; 16:4; Jacob 7:12.) "There could be no redemption for mankind save it were through the death and sufferings of Christ, and the atonement of his blood." (Alma 21:9.)

Indeed, it is Nephi's brother Jacob to whom we turn for what is probably the clearest explanation found in any scripture now extant for the doctrinal explanation as to why all men would be lost if there were no atonement. "Our flesh must waste away and die," he says, which fact is one of the truisms of life. Then he puts death in its true perspective in the eternal plan with this explanation: "For as death hath passed upon all men, to fulfil the merciful plan of the great Creator, there must needs be a power of resurrection, and the resurrection must needs come unto man by reason of the fall; and the fall came by reason of transgression; and because man became fallen they were cut off from the presence of the Lord." (2 Ne. 9:4-6.) Thus, Adam accomplished his mission to fall and create the need for a Redeemer.

What then of redemption, of the promised deliverance, of the expiatory sacrifice of Him who did no sin, "who layeth down his life according to the flesh, and taketh it again by the power of the Spirit, that he may bring to pass the resurrection of the dead"? (2 Ne. 2:8.) Of his sinless sacrifice Jacob said: "It must needs be an infinite atonement—save it should be an infinite atonement this corruption could not put on incorruption." (2 Ne. 9:7.) Save for the infinite power of this, the most selfless act ever performed, Paul would never have been able to write of man's body: "It is sown in corruption; it is raised in incorruption: It is sown in dishonour; it is raised in glory: it is sown in weakness; it is raised in power: It is sown a natural body; it is raised a spiritual body." (1 Cor. 15:42-44.)

Save for this atonement, Jacob continues, "the first judgment which came upon man"—his banishment from the presence of the Lord because he transgressed the law and partook of the forbidden fruit, and also the natural death that attends his newly found mortal state—"must needs have remained to an endless duration. And if so, this flesh must have laid down to rot and to crumble to its mother earth, to rise no more." (2 Ne. 9:7.) There would have been no resurrection, no immortality, no reunion of body and spirit, no victory over the grave—nothing but endless death.

"But behold, all things have been done in the wisdom of him who knoweth all things." (2 Ne. 2:24.) The purposes of the Almighty neither have been nor can be frustrated. The fall was part of his plan; he designed and decreed it from the beginning. Its gloom is to turn into joy and gladness as both temporal and spiritual death are abolished in Gethsemane and on Calvary. And so Jacob exclaims: "O the wisdom of God, his mercy and grace! For behold, if the flesh should rise no more our spirits must become subject to that angel who fell from before the presence of the Eternal God, and became the devil, to rise no more." (2 Ne. 9:8.) Subject to whom? To Lucifer, the traitor and rebel who defied Deity and spread the woes of war in the heavenly courts. Christ is now our King and we worship him because we will it so. Had there been no atonement Lucifer would have been our eternal head and we would have worshiped him because he willed it so. Agency and freedom would have ceased for all those whom God had sired.

But this is not all. Jacob continues: "And our spirits must have become like unto him, and we become devils, angels to a devil, to be shut out from the presence of our God, and to remain with the father of lies, in misery, like unto himself." (2 Ne. 9:9.) Devils! Angels to a devil! Damned souls, denied a grave, denied a resurrection, purposeless creatures in whose souls the light we once had would become darkness!

"God himself shall come down among the children of men, and shall redeem his people." (Mosiah 15:1.) He shall redeem them from that (otherwise) everlasting death which is the grave, and that (otherwise) everlasting death which is eternal, abysmal darkness where none of the light of heaven is found, and where they would have no choice but to grovel before the Angel of Darkness. Ought we not, then, as did our friend Jacob, extol our Redeemer and Savior in such words of doctrine and beauty as these:

"O how great the goodness of our God, who prepareth a way for our escape from the grasp of this awful monster; yea, that monster, death and hell, which I call the death of the body, and also the death of the spirit.

"And because of the way of deliverance of our God, the Holy One of Israel, this death, of which I have spoken, which is the temporal, shall deliver up its dead; which death is the grave.

"And this death of which I have spoken, which is the spiritual death, shall deliver up its dead; which spiritual death is hell; wherefore, death and hell must deliver up their dead, and hell must deliver up its captive spirits, and the grave must deliver up its captive bodies, and the bodies and the spirits of men will be restored one to the other; and it is by the power of the resurrection of the Holy One of Israel.

"O how great the plan of our God! For on the other hand, the paradise of God must deliver up the spirits of the righteous, and the grave deliver up the body of the righteous; and the spirit and the body is restored to itself again, and all men become incorruptible, and immortal, and they are living souls, having a perfect knowledge like unto us in the flesh, save it be that our knowledge shall be perfect.

"O the greatness of the mercy of our God, the Holy One of Israel! For he delivereth his saints from that awful monster the devil, and death, and hell, and that lake of fire and brimstone, which is endless torment." (2 Ne. 9:10-13,19.)

Chapter 14

MESSIAH ATONES AND RANSOMS

Who Has Known of the Atonement?

How widespread has the knowledge been that salvation is in Christ because of his atoning sacrifice? Who has known that Adam our father—the great Michael, who led the hosts of heaven when Lucifer unwillingly left his heavenly home—that this noble personage who was "the first flesh upon the earth" (Moses 3:7) is he who laid the foundation for Messiah's ministry?

These are questions to which there are clear and positive answers; this is a field in which there need be no uncertainty, no misunderstanding, no speculation. All of the prophets, all of the saints, and all of the Lord's people in all dispensations have known of the fall, the atonement, and the salvation available to all men as a result thereof; for it is this very knowledge that makes a man a prophet, that sets a person apart as a saint, and that identifies an individual as one of the Lord's people.

This whole work—*The Promised Messiah: The First Coming of Christ*—contains one continuous recitation and analysis of how and under what circumstances and in what ways this knowledge was had and taught and foretold. For our present purposes let us sample some of the most explicit and plain of these prophetic utterances.

231

Lehi's Seed Testified of Atonement

Lehi, father of the Nephite and Lamanite nations, received from a heavenly visitant a book in which he read of the coming of a Messiah and the redemption of the world. (1 Ne. 1.) Later he taught plainly of the fall, with all its ills, and of the atonement, with all its blessings. (2 Ne. 2.) Nephi gloried in the redemption of his soul from hell (2 Ne. 1:15) and taught of the atonement, which is infinite for all mankind (2 Ne. 25:16). Jacob propounded some of the most fundamental concepts about the infinite and eternal atonement that are found in any scriptures. (2 Ne. 9.) An angel from heaven recited to King Benjamin what well may be the greatest sermon ever delivered on the atonement of Christ the Lord. (Mosiah 3.) Abinadi made it clear that God himself would redeem his people (Mosiah 13:32-33), that were it not for this redemption all mankind must have perished, and that the Lord redeemeth none of those who rebel against him and die in their sins (Mosiah 15).

Alma left us some of the most extensive utterances now known about the great plan of redemption. It is he who tells us, among other things, that "the time is not far distant [it was then about 83 B.C.] that the Redeemer liveth and cometh among his people," and that he would be the Son of God. (Alma 7:7-13.) "He cometh to redeem those who will be baptized unto repentance, through faith on his name," Alma says. (Alma 9:27.) Alma's explanations to Corianton about the fall and the great plan of redemption that it necessitated are superlative in every respect. (Alma 42.)

Amulek, who learned both from Alma and directly from the Spirit of the Lord, bore similar testimonies to those of his missionary companion. It was he who taught that the Son of God "shall come into the world to redeem his people; and he shall take upon him the transgressions of those who believe on his name; and these are they that shall have eternal life, and salvation cometh to none else." (Alma 11:37-45.) His explanations of the fall, the plan of redemp-

232

tion, and the atoning sacrifice of the Son of God, as these are recorded in the 12th and 34th chapters of Alma, show forth prophetic insight that is seldom equaled and never surpassed.

Nephi the son of Helaman spoke much of the atonement, including the fact that Abraham and the prophets who lived thousands of years before the coming of the Son of God in the flesh knew that their promised Redeemer would come and save them. (Hel. 8:14-23.) And Samuel the Lamanite was not one whit behind his Nephite brethren in proclaiming like eternal truths. (Hel. 14.)

Israel's Prophets Testified of Atonement

This partial summary of what the Hebrew prophets on the American continent knew about the fall of our first parents and about Him whose atoning and redeeming sacrifice brought to pass the purposes of the Father of us all—these plain and precious expositions of eternal truth found in the most correct of all books, the Book of Mormon, do not stand alone. Our Lehite brethren in America were one with their Israelitish kin in what men choose to call the Old World. The Biblical seers and revelators, inspired by the same spirit which spake peace to the hearts of their New World kindred, also knew and wrote of the same eternal truths.

As appears from the present Biblical accounts, Isaiah, the son of Amoz, commonly praised as the chief Messianic prophet, is the one who knew and taught more about redemption and atonement than any of Israel's seers. Let us now sample what his inspired pen has left us.

Abinadi preaches of "the coming of the Messiah"; states plainly "that God himself should come down among the children of men, and take upon him the form of a man, and go forth in mighty power upon the face of the earth"; and makes it clear that this doctrine, "that God himself should redeem his people," has been taught by "all the prophets

233

who have prophesied since the world began," and that all have "spoken more or less concerning these things." (Mosiah 13:33-34.)

I will make a more affirmative declaration than did Abinadi, which is, that not only have all the prophets "spoken more or less concerning these things," but that prophetic utterances about Christ and his atonement have been the most prominent part of the preachments of all the prophets, and that the testimony of Jesus consisted in knowing by revelation from the Holy Ghost that our Lord's redemption was and is the greatest work ever wrought.

But as to Abinadi's witness, having made the Spirit-guided utterance that was his, he then chose to quote as his chief illustration the entire 53rd chapter of Isaiah. To have the picture before us, let us quote a few phrases from that chapter, all of which are clear and plain when read in the light of the Nephite explanations to which we have already alluded. Of the atoning sacrifice of the future Messiah, Isaiah said:

Surely he has borne our griefs, and carried our sorrows.
He was wounded for our transgressions.
He was bruised for our iniquities.
The chastisement of our peace was laid upon him.
With his stripes we are healed.
The Lord has laid on him the iniquities of us all.
He is brought as a lamb to the slaughter.
He was cut off out of the land of the living.
For the transgression of my people was he stricken.
It pleased the Lord to bruise him; he hath put him to grief.
Thou shalt make his soul an offering for sin.
He shall see the travail of his soul.
By his knowledge shall my righteous servant justify many; for he shall bear their iniquities.
He hath poured out his soul unto death.
He bore the sins of many, and made intercession for the transgressors. (Mosiah 14; Isaiah 53.)

Chapter 15 of Mosiah contains Abinadi's prophetic interpretation of these and the other Messianic pronouncements of Isaiah 53. As our New Testament now stands, we find Matthew (Matt. 8:17), Philip (Acts 8:27-35), Paul (Rom. 4:25), and Peter (1 Pet. 2:24-25) all quoting, paraphrasing, enlarging upon, and applying to the Lord Jesus various of the verses in this great 53rd chapter of Isaiah. How many sermons have been preached, how many lessons have been taught, how many testimonies have been borne—both in ancient Israel and in the meridian of time—using the utterances of this chapter as the text, we can scarcely imagine.

Who Is the Redeemer?

The great question confronting all men of all ages of time is whether the word of salvation is in Christ or whether (if men are to be ransomed from their fallen state) we must look for another. Men are. They live and move and have a being. All are mortal; all are fallen; death reigns supreme over all the sons of Adam. The problem is one of finding a Redeemer, lest all mankind be lost eternally.

Lucifer, our common enemy, hearing the invitation of the Father which said in effect: 'Whom shall I send to be my Son, to redeem mankind, to work out the infinite and eternal atonement' (Abr. 3:27)—Lucifer who is Satan stepped forth and said: "Behold, here am I, send me, I will be thy son, and I will redeem all mankind, that one soul shall not be lost, and surely I will do it; wherefore give me thine honor." (Moses 4:1.) That his offer was declined with power all are aware; and then burst forth that war with unrighteousness which, starting in the very heavens themselves, continues now among us here on earth. (Rev. 12.)

That no man of himself, and no mass of men through any combined power that in them lies, can bring to pass a ransom, a redemption, a resurrection, is not open to question. "None of them can by any means redeem his brother, nor give to God a ransom for him: . . . That he should still

235

live for ever, and not see corruption." (Ps. 49:7-9.) "There is not any man that can sacrifice his own blood which will atone for the sins of another." (Alma 34:11.) No, never! Man can no more redeem himself than he can create himself. It takes a God to create and to redeem. And so Abinadi says: "God himself shall come down among the children of men, and shall redeem his people." (Mosiah 15:1.)

The issue then is: Who, if anyone, is the God who has or will redeem mankind? Where, if anywhere, is there a Savior of the world? Is salvation in Christ, or look we for another? Who is the Redeemer of men?

By opening the scriptures, almost at random we find the answers pleading to be believed. "I am the Only Begotten of the Father," came the word to Adam, and "as thou hast fallen thou mayest be redeemed, and all mankind, even as many as will." (Moses 5:9.) "I am he who was prepared from the foundation of the world to redeem my people" are the words of our Spirit Lord, spoken to Moriancumer millenniums before His mortal birth. And then He ties redemption in to Him who will be born in Bethlehem, saying simply: "Behold, I am Jesus Christ." (Ether 3:14.) "Redeem Israel, O God" (Ps. 25:22) was the pleading prayer of the prophets, and the echoing answer of the Spirit was, "The Lord redeemeth the soul of his servants: and none of them that trust in him shall be desolate" (Ps. 34:22).

Among the Lord's ancient people, no knowledge was more precious, no doctrine more cherished, than that "God was their rock, and the high God their redeemer." (Ps. 78:35.) Isaiah delighted to designate his Deity by the exalted name-titles Redeemer and Savior, doing so in a score of passages. He identified him specifically as the Lord Jehovah and "the Holy One of Israel" (Isa. 41:14; 43:14), as "the Lord of hosts" (Isa. 47:4), as "the Redeemer of Israel" (Isa. 49:7), as "thy Saviour and thy Redeemer, the mighty One of Jacob" (Isa. 49:26), and as "The God of the whole earth" (Isa. 54:5). How plain and precious are the words of the Great Jehovah, announcing to all who will hear: "I am the

Lord thy God, the Holy One of Israel, thy Saviour." (Isa. 43:3.)

Similar usage of these ransoming titles is found in the Book of Mormon. In more than forty passages her prophets speak of the Redeemer, and in a dozen he is called the Savior. Among others, the Book of Mormon speaks of the Messiah, who is the "Lord," the "Savior of the world," and the "Redeemer of the world" (1 Ne. 10:4-5, 14; 2 Ne. 1:10), and of "the gospel" of the Redeemer (1 Ne. 15:14). It promises that gathered Israel will come to know "that the Lord is their Savior and their Redeemer, the Mighty One of Israel." (1 Ne. 22:12; 2 Ne. 10:2.) It states plainly that "Jesus Christ" is the "Redeemer" (Alma 37:9), and says in so many words "that the Lamb of God is the Son of the Eternal Father, and the Savior of the world; and that all men must come unto him, or they cannot be saved" (1 Ne. 13:40).

But with it all—and the scriptures are not remiss in recording revelations relative to the redemption wrought by the Redeemer—what is more tender and true than the testimony of Job, spoken out of the depths of a perfect knowledge: "I know that my redeemer liveth, and that he shall stand at the latter day upon the earth: And though after my skin worms destroy this body, yet in my flesh shall I see God: Whom I shall see for myself, and mine eyes shall behold, and not another; though my reins be consumed within me." (Job 19:25-27.)

All this, known and believed of old, was revealed anew in the day that Jesus came to dwell in the flesh, even as it has been given yet again in our day. Of himself, while ministering among his fellowmen, Jesus said: "The Son of man came . . . to give his life a ransom for many" (Matt. 20:28)—that is, to ransom men from the effects of the fall, to pay the penalty for a broken law, to purchase those who otherwise were lost, to redeem his fellowmen.

After paying the price, after effecting the redeeming sacrifice, after he had himself come forth in immortality, he said: "By me redemption cometh. . . . And whoso cometh

237

unto me with a broken heart and a contrite spirit, him will I baptize with fire and with the Holy Ghost. . . . Behold, I have come unto the world to bring redemption unto the world, to save the world from sin." (3 Ne. 9:17-22; Morm. 7:7; 9:12-14.)

We might say more—ten or a hundred or a thousand times more—all of which would but echo and re-echo the rolling thunders of eternity as they forever acclaim and re-acclaim that Christ our Lord is the Redeemer and Savior of the world; that he paid the ransom; that redemption comes by him; and that we should therefore glorify and praise his name forever.

Christ Freeth the Prisoners

We have seen that if there were no atonement of Christ, all mankind would be lost eternally—none would be resurrected; the bodies of all would remain in their graves forever; the spirits of all would remain dead as to the things of righteousness; all would become devils, angels to a devil, subject to the father of lies forever; and the whole plan of salvation, and the very purposes of creation itself, would be frustrated and come to naught. We have also seen that through Christ none of this will happen, but men instead will be saved from death (which is the grave), from hell (which is spiritual death), from the devil (who is Lucifer the liar), and from endless torment (which is and would be the state of uncleansed souls).

Now let us review those Messianic prophecies which describe in a most graphic way how the Lord saves men from the direful fate that would be theirs if he had not atoned for their sins. It is known as freeing the hosts of men from prison—from the prison of death, of hell, of the devil, and of endless torment. And how apt and pointed the illustration is, for the prisons of ancient times were hell holes of death, disease, and despair. They were dungeons of filth, corruption, and creeping denizens. Sheol itself was known as the pit, the

238

dungeon of despair, the nether realms of torment, the Hades of hell. To be in prison was worse than a living hell, and to be freed therefrom was to arise from death to life. It is no wonder that the prophetic mind seized upon this illustration to teach what the Redeemer would do to ransom men from the fate that would be theirs if there were no atonement.

Thus it is that the Messianic witnesses proclaimed: "The Lord [who is Jehovah!] looseth the prisoners." (Ps. 146:7.) The Lord looketh down "from the height of his sanctuary, from heaven"; he heareth "the groaning of the prisoner" and looseth "those that are appointed to death." (Ps. 102:19-20.) Even those that "sit in darkness and in the shadow of death," who are "bound in affliction and iron; Because they rebelled against the words of God, and contemned the counsel of the most High"—even these, "He brought down their heart with labour; they fell down, and there was none to help. Then they cried unto the Lord in their trouble, and he saved them out of their distresses. He brought them out of darkness and the shadow of death, and brake their bands in sunder. Oh that men would praise the Lord for his goodness, and for his wonderful works to the children of men!" (Ps. 107:10-15.)

The prisoners even in hell cry out and the Lord hears! "Bring my soul out of prison," each repentant one pleads, "that I may praise thy name." (Ps. 142:7.) Of the wicked in general, and of those who perished in the flood of Noah in particular, Deity decrees: "I will shut them up; a prison have I prepared for them. And That which I have chosen [who is Christ] shall return unto me, and until that day they shall be in torment." (Moses 7:36-39.)

Isaiah's voice is also heard in the prophetic chorus that tells of prisoners being freed from their chains of darkness and hell. In one of his long Messianic prophecies that tells many things relative to our Lord's mortal ministry, Isaiah includes the promise that the Messiah will come "to open the blind eyes, to bring out the prisoners from the prison, and them that sit in darkness out of the prison house." (Isa.

42:7.) In contrast, Isaiah says that Lucifer, who sought redeeming power and was rejected, shall himself "be brought down to hell, to . . . the pit," and it shall be said of him, "Is this the man . . . that opened not the house of his prisoners." (Isa. 14:12-17.) In another passage Isaiah foretells that the Messiah, "in a day of salvation," shall "say to the prisoners, Go forth." He shall command "them that are in darkness, Shew yourselves, . . . for he . . . hath mercy on them." (Isa. 49:8-10.)

And in yet another passage, dealing also with several subjects, Isaiah records the voice of the Lord, speaking in the first person, relative to his coming ministry as the Messiah. These words are included: "The Spirit of the Lord God is upon me; because the Lord hath anointed me . . . to proclaim liberty to the captives, and the opening of the prison to them that are bound." (Isa. 61:1.) Of this and the longer passage of which it is a part, the Man Jesus, in Nazareth of Galilee, speaking in the synagogue on the sabbath day, bore record of his own divine Sonship by saying, "This day is this scripture fulfilled in your ears." (Luke 4:16-21.)

Messiah Visits Spirits in Prison

This doctrine that the Lord will free the prisoners from their prison, that he will deliver them from the depths of their dungeon, and that they will come forth from the pit and be free—free from the sorrow of sin, free from the chains of hell, free from that spiritual death which is to be dead as pertaining to the things of righteousness—all this is part of the glorious doctrine of salvation for the dead, and it includes the fact that our Lord ministered personally to the spirits in prison.

The doctrine of salvation for the dead is that all who die without a knowledge of the gospel, without a knowledge of Christ and his atoning sacrifice, without having the opportunity to believe and obey in this life and thereby qualify for celestial salvation—the doctrine of salvation for the dead is that all such, if they would have received the gospel with all of their hearts, had it been available to them, all such shall hear and believe and obey in the spirit world and thereby become heirs of the celestial kingdom of heaven. Gospel ordinances—baptisms, endowments, marriages, sealings—will be performed for them vicariously by those yet in mortality.

It was of these that Zechariah prophesied when as part of a longer Messianic utterance, he spoke of "prisoners of hope"; it was of these that he gave assurance that "the Lord their God shall save them." He gives the Messianic message in these words: "By the blood of thy covenant"—that is, because of the gospel covenant, which is efficacious because of the shedding of the blood of Christ—"I have sent forth thy prisoners out of the pit wherein is no water." (Zech. 9:11-16.) "Wherein is no water"—how aptly and succinctly this crystallizes the thought that the saving water, which is baptism, is an earthly ordinance and cannot be performed by spirit beings while they dwell in the spirit world. Did not Paul say in this same connection, "What shall they do which are baptized for the dead, if the dead rise not at all? why are they then baptized for the dead?" (1 Cor. 15:29.)

"It shall come to pass," intones Isaiah, "that the Lord shall punish the host of the high ones that are on high, and the kings of the earth upon the earth. And they shall be gathered together, as prisoners are gathered in the pit, and shall be shut up in the prison, and after many days shall they be visited." (Isa. 24:21-22.)

Visited? By whom? When and why? Jesus answers: "Verily, verily, I say unto you, The hour is coming, and now is, when the dead shall hear the voice of the Son of God: and they that hear shall live." (John 5:25.) He that hath "the keys of hell and of death" (Rev. 1:18); "he that openeth, and no man shutteth" (Rev. 3:7); he who seeks his own in the depths of hell, shall speak peace to the prisoners. They shall hear his voice. The voice of the Son of God shall be heard in the realms of the dead. His gospel shall be preached to all

241

men, either in the body or in the spirit, for he is no respecter of persons. Thus it is that Peter testified that Christ himself, as a spirit Being, while his body lay in Joseph's tomb, "went and preached unto the spirits in prison," including those who were swept into watery graves in the days of Noah. (1 Pet. 3:18-20.) Preached what? The same gospel which he and all the prophets had proclaimed to the living, all to the end that they "might be judged according to men in the flesh, but live according to God in the spirit." (1 Pet. 4:6.)

How is it that the prison doors swing open? What power unshackles the prisoners? Whence comes the newly found freedom that is theirs? Truly, it is with the dead as with the living. The spirit offspring of Deity, whether encased in clay or roaming free in the realms of the departed dead, are all subject to the same eternal laws. Our Lord's infinite and eternal atonement reaches out to all in every sphere of creation. Freedom from the bondage of sin, from the chains of hell, from the darkness of doubt and despair come to both the quick and the dead on the same terms and conditions, and these are made operative through his atoning sacrifice. All must repent to be free. All must obey to gain gospel blessings. All must keep the commandments to merit mercy. In the case of those who dwell in the realm "wherein is no water," we shall be baptized for them, and they with us will become heirs of salvation.

"Let your hearts rejoice, and be exceedingly glad," wrote the Prophet Joseph Smith as he pondered this glorious doctrine which opens the dungeons of death and lets the children of the Eternal Father flee from the pit. "Let the earth break forth into singing. Let the dead speak forth anthems of eternal praise to the King Immanuel, who hath ordained, before the world was, that which would enable us to redeem them out of their prison; for the prisoners shall go free. Let the mountains shout for joy, and all ye valleys cry aloud; and all ye seas and dry lands tell the wonders of your Eternal King! And ye rivers, and brooks, and rills, flow down with gladness. Let the woods and all the trees of the field praise the Lord; and ye solid rocks weep for joy! And let the sun, moon, and the morning stars sing together, and let all the sons of God shout for joy! And let the eternal creations declare his name forever and ever!" (D&C 128:22.)

"His Mercy Endureth Forever!"

Our revelations abound in prophetic utterances about the mercy of God, about his infinite goodness in claiming and saving that which is lost; about the hope that lost and fallen man will be reclaimed and saved because the Lord is merciful. There is scarcely a more compassionate and soul-satisfying doctrine than that crystallized in the oft-repeated declaration—"His mercy endureth forever!"

Unfortunately the professors of religion in an uninspired Christendom, along with masses of would-be Christians in general, including many in the true church itself, assume that somehow or other mercy will be poured out upon the generality of Christian mankind and that eventually they will be saved in the kingdom of heaven. How common it is to hear such things as: "Surely, if I confess the Lord Jesus with my lips and accept him as my personal Savior, a merciful God will save me in his kingdom." Or: "Surely a merciful God will not deny me my family in eternity just because I wasn't married in the temple in this mortal life." Or: "Surely, in the mercy of God, men will be able to progress from one kingdom of glory to another in the next life, so that if I don't gain the celestial kingdom in the first instance, eventually I will." Or: "Even if I don't keep the commandments and work out my salvation in this life, the Lord is merciful; he will give me another chance in the spirit world; and even those who reject it here will have a second chance there, and eventually they will be saved." Or any of a thousand other sophistries that Satan delights to whisper into the ears of the spiritually untutored.

But the doctrinal reality is that aside from the fact that a merciful and gracious Father created us and placed us here

243

on earth to undergo a mortal probation; aside from the fact that "he maketh his sun to rise on the evil and on the good, and sendeth rain on the just and on the unjust" (Matt. 5:45); aside from certain mortal blessings which come to the righteous and the wicked as a necessary part of mortality— aside from the fact that a merciful God provides immortality for all his children as a free gift—aside from such things as these, there is no such thing as mercy except for those who love the Lord and signify such by keeping his commandments. In other words, mercy is reserved for the faithful members of the Church and kingdom of God on earth, and for none else, except little children or others who have not arrived at the years of accountability.

As is so abundantly set forth in this work, with that emphasis and repetition which is essential to an analysis of all parts of the doctrine, we know that in the infinite wisdom of Him who knoweth all things, who created man in his own image and after his own likeness, who ordained and established the laws whereby his children could advance and progress and become like him—in the infinite wisdom of this holy being, Adam fell. We know that this fall came because of transgression, and that Adam broke the law of God, became mortal, and was thus subject to sin and disease and all the ills of mortality. We know that the effects of his fall passed upon all his posterity; all inherited a fallen state, a state of mortality, a state in which temporal and spiritual death prevail. In this state all men sin. All are lost. All are fallen. All are cut off from the presence of God. All have become carnal, sensual, and devilish by nature. Such a way of life is inherent in this mortal existence. Thus all are in the grasp of justice, and because God is just, all must pay the penalty for their sins.

This, Alma tells us, is the rationale "concerning the justice of God in the punishment of the sinner." Lost and fallen and sinful and carnal man has been in this state of opposition to God since the fall of Adam; such is his present state, and he will so remain forever, unless provision is made whereby he can escape from the grasp of justice. The provisions of the law of justice are so basic and so unvarying that if they ceased to operate, "God would cease to be God."

As justice is the child of the fall, so mercy is the offspring of the atonement. "Mercy cometh because of the atonement," Alma says, "and mercy claimeth the penitent." If there were no atoning sacrifice there would be no mercy—only justice. Thus all of the scriptures acclaiming the mercy of God presuppose that there will be or has been an atonement. Thus all of the Old Testament teachings about mercy are in fact Messianic declarations.

To his son Corianton, Alma said: "The plan of mercy could not be brought about except an atonement should be made; therefore God himself atoneth for the sins of the world, to bring about the plan of mercy, to appease the demands of justice, that God might be a perfect, just God, and a merciful God also. Now, repentance could not come unto men except there were a punishment, which also was eternal as the life of the soul should be, affixed opposite to the plan of happiness, which was as eternal also as the life of the soul. Now, how could a man repent except he should sin? How could he sin if there was no law? How could there be a law save there was a punishment? Now, there was a punishment affixed, and a just law given, which brought remorse of conscience unto man. . . .

"And if there was no law given, if men sinned what could justice do, or mercy either, for they would have no claim upon the creature? But there is a law given, and a punishment affixed, and a repentance granted; which repentance mercy claimeth; otherwise, justice claimeth the creature and executeth the law, and the law inflicteth the punishment; if not so, the works of justice would be destroyed, and God would cease to be God." The end conclusion of all this is then given in these words: "Justice exerciseth all his demands, and also mercy claimeth all which is her own; and thus, none but the truly penitent are saved." (Alma 42.)

Of these same principles, Abinadi says that the Son of

245

God "breaketh the bands of death" and maketh "intercession for the children of men," and that having so done, he "ascended into heaven, having the bowels of mercy; being filled with compassion towards the children of men; standing betwixt them and justice; having broken the bands of death, taken upon himself their iniquity and their transgressions, having redeemed them, and satisfied the demands of justice." (Mosiah 15:8-9.)

Amulek's words on the same matter are these: "God did call on men, in the name of his Son, (this being the plan of redemption which was laid) saying: If ye will repent, and harden not your hearts, then will I have mercy upon you, through mine Only Begotten Son; Therefore, whosoever repenteth, and hardeneth not his heart, he shall have claim on mercy through mine Only Begotten Son, unto a remission of his sins; and these shall enter into my rest. And whosoever will harden his heart and will do iniquity, behold, I swear in my wrath that he shall not enter into my rest." (Alma 12:33-35.)

These Book of Mormon statements (and they are but samples of much more that might be quoted) are plain and explicit. Mercy is for the merciful; mercy is reserved for the righteous; mercy comes to those who keep the commandments. And the Old Testament prophets had similar insight. Hosea said: "Sow to yourselves in righteousness, reap in mercy; break up your fallow ground: for it is time to seek the Lord, till he come and rain righteousness upon you." (Hosea 10:12.)

The great Sinaitic proclamation, issued through Moses, is built on the same foundation: "The Lord, The Lord God, merciful and gracious, longsuffering, and abundant in goodness and truth, Keeping mercy for thousands, forgiving iniquity and transgression and sin, and that will by no means clear the guilty." (Ex. 34:6-7.)

David, whose sins swept him from the hallowed blessings of mercy back into the awful grasp of justice, yet set forth the true Messianic principle, when he wrote: "The Lord is

246

merciful and gracious, slow to anger, and plenteous in mercy. . . . The mercy of the Lord is from everlasting to everlasting upon them that fear him, and his righteousness unto children's children; To such as keep his covenant, and to those that remember his commandments to do them." (Ps. 103:8, 17-18.)

What is this reconciling of the claims of justice and mercy, but a recitation of why men must suffer for their own sins unless they repent? Men are commanded to repent lest they be smitten by the Lord's wrath and their sufferings be both sore and exquisite. "I God, have suffered these things for all, that they might not suffer if they would repent; But if they would not repent they must suffer even as I." (D&C 19:16-17.) Truly, "mercy cometh because of the atonement" (Alma 42:23), and He "who was wounded for our transgressions" and who "bare the sins of many" (Isa. 53:5, 12) did so "on conditions of repentance" (D&C 18:12).

Chapter 15

MESSIAH'S BLOOD ATONES AND RECONCILES

Blood Atonement Brings Salvation

There is no more basic doctrine in the gospel than that of the atonement. This doctrine is that in and through the blood of Christ we have power, in our lost and fallen state, to be reconciled to God and to return to his presence and there inherit that eternal life which he himself enjoys. This doctrine is that "salvation was, and is, and is to come, in and through the atoning blood of Christ, the Lord Omnipotent." (Mosiah 3:18.) This doctrine is that "if we walk in the light, as he [God] is in the light, we have fellowship one with another, and the blood of Jesus Christ his Son cleanseth us from all sin." (1 Jn. 1:7.) This doctrine is that "the righteous shall sit down in his kingdom, to go no more out," because their garments are "made white through the blood of the Lamb." (Alma 34:36.)

Formulated in the wisdom of the Father, the doctrine of blood atonement was taught first in preexistence; was then revealed to all the ancient prophets who foretold the coming of our Lord; has been the burden of the preaching of inspired men from the day he shed his blood to ransom fallen man to the present moment; and will be the subject of praise and adoration forever, as saints and angels sing the song of the redeemed.

In the courts on high, while we all dwelt in the presence

of our Eternal Father, Christ was chosen and foreordained as the one whose blood should be shed to redeem mankind. It was known to us there that he would be born into mortality as the Son of God so that he would have power to live or to die, power to lay down his life and to take it up again, power to shed his blood that eternal life might come to all those who would believe in him. Having this in mind, Peter exhorts us, "Pass the time of your sojourning here in fear," because we have been "redeemed . . . with the precious blood of Christ, as of a lamb without blemish and without spot: Who verily was foreordained before the foundation of the world." (1 Pet. 1:17-19.)

The first proclamation on earth relative to the blood of Him who died on Calvary, and the redeeming power that is available because that blood would be shed by evil and conspiring men, is as old as mortal man. Some six thousand years ago, in giving Adam knowledge about "his Only Begotten . . . even Jesus Christ, a righteous Judge, who shall come in the meridian of time," the Lord said to all men: "By reason of transgression cometh the fall, which fall bringeth death"—truths of which we are so abundantly and acutely aware!—"and inasmuch as ye were born into the world by water, and blood, and the spirit, which I have made, and so became of dust a living soul, even so ye must be born again into the kingdom of heaven, of water, and of the Spirit, and be cleansed by blood, even the blood of mine Only Begotten; that ye might be sanctified from all sin, and enjoy the words of eternal life in this world, and eternal life in the world to come, even immortal glory." Then came from the mouth of Deity that ponderous proclamation: "By the water ye keep the commandment; by the Spirit ye are justified, and by the blood ye are sanctified," and it was followed by this conclusion, which put the whole matter in perfect perspective: "This is the plan of salvation unto all men, through the blood of mine Only Begotten, who shall come in the meridian of time." (Moses 6:57-62.)

Aware of these teachings, Enoch, the seventh from

Adam, whose life, however, began while the first man of all men was yet among mortals, "cried unto the Lord, saying: When shall the day of the Lord come? When shall the blood of the Righteous be shed, that all they that mourn may be sanctified and have eternal life? And the Lord said: It shall be in the meridian of time, in the days of wickedness and vengeance." Then Enoch, in vision, "saw the day of the coming of the Son of Man." (Moses 7:45-47.)

As we have seen, Zechariah foretold that the King of Israel would free the prisoners out of the pit by the blood of the covenant (Zech. 9:11), meaning that through the shedding of his blood even the spirits in hell have power, through faith and repentance, to escape their direful dungeon and come forth to honor and reward in the kingdoms of resurrection and glory.

As we have seen and shall see, other Old Testament prophets spoke of his death by violence—a death in which he would be smitten, wounded, and bruised; in which he would be brought "as a lamb to the slaughter"; and in which he would pour out his soul (Isa. 53), in all of which the shedding of his blood is an unspoken and assumed eventuality.

And as we shall set forth in detail in Chapters 21, 22, and 23, animal sacrifices were performed from Adam's day onward until the Lamb of God himself would be sacrificed for the sins of the world, all in "similitude of the sacrifice of the Only Begotten of the Father." (Moses 5:7.) That these sacrifices involved the deliberate shedding of blood and its subsequent use in specified rituals we shall hereafter note.

Nephites Teach Doctrine of Blood Atonement

As with almost all Messianic matters, it is to the Book of Mormon prophets that we turn for the clearest and plainest inspired assertions. In speaking, some six centuries before their day, of the twelve apostolic ministers who should direct the affairs of the Lord's earthly kingdom on the American continent, Nephi said: "They are righteous forever; for because of their faith in the Lamb of God their garments are made white in his blood" (1 Ne. 12:10), a statement that presupposes an extensive if not a complete understanding of how our Lord's blood was a symbol of his atonement and the redemption that comes thereby. Some five hundred years after Nephi's day, Alma, in propounding the doctrine of that priesthood which is "after the order of the Son, the Only Begotten of the Father," expands this sanctifying effect of the blood of the Lamb out far beyond the Nephite Twelve. "There were many who were ordained and became high priests of God; and it was on account of their exceeding faith and repentance, and their righteousness before God, they choosing to repent and work righteousness rather than to perish; Therefore they were called after this holy order, and were sanctified, and their garments were washed white through the blood of the Lamb. Now they, after being sanctified by the Holy Ghost, having their garments made white, being pure and spotless before God, could not look upon sin save it were with abhorrence; and there were many, exceeding great many, who were made pure and entered into the rest of the Lord their God." (Alma 13:9-12.)

We clean our garments by washing them in water. Filth, dirt, germs, odors, and whatever is unclean and offensive is thus removed; our wearing apparel becomes clean and spotless. A saved person is one whose soul is clean and spotless, one who is free from the filth and corruption of sin; and the prophetic way of describing such a person is to say that his garments are clean. Since the only way a human soul can be cleansed and perfected is through the atonement of Christ, it follows that the symbolic way of describing this process is to say that such a one has washed his garments in the blood of the Lamb, as we have here learned Nephi and Alma did.

In what is without question the greatest sermon of which we have knowledge on the subject of being "born of God," our friend Alma reasons on this matter of being saved through the blood of Christ. To members of the Church he says: "Can ye look up to God at that day with a pure heart and clean hands? . . . Can ye think of being saved when you have yielded yourselves to become subjects to the devil? I say unto you, ye will know at that day that ye cannot be saved; for there can no man be saved except his garments are washed white; yea, his garments must be purified until they are cleansed from all stain, through the blood of him of whom it has been spoken by our fathers, who should come to redeem his people from their sins. And now I ask of you, my brethren, how will any of you feel, if ye shall stand before the bar of God, having your garments stained with blood and all manner of filthiness? Behold, what will these things testify against you? Behold will they not testify that ye are murderers, yea, and also that ye are guilty of all manner of wickedness? Behold, my brethren, do ye suppose that such an one can have a place to sit down in the kingdom of God, with Abraham, with Isaac, and with Jacob, and also all the holy prophets, whose garments are cleansed and are spotless, pure and white? . . . Could ye say, if ye were called to die at this time, . . . That your garments have been cleansed and made white through the blood of Christ, who will come to redeem his people from their sins?" (Alma 5:19-27.)

Blood atonement makes salvation available to every living soul. "Through the atonement of Christ, all mankind may be saved, by obedience to the laws and ordinances of the Gospel." (A of F 3.) Little children and those who do not have opportunity to receive the gospel in this life reap special benefits from it. As to its universal application, Mosiah's son Aaron says, "There could be no redemption for mankind save it were through the death and sufferings of Christ, and the atonement of his blood." (Alma 21:9.) With reference to those who die without a knowledge of the truth, the angel said to King Benjamin: "His blood atoneth for the sins of those who have fallen by the transgression of Adam, who have died not knowing the will of God concerning them, or who have ignorantly sinned." And as to little children, that same angelic ministrant affirmed: "As in

Adam, or by nature, they fall, even so the blood of Christ atoneth for their sins." (Mosiah 3:11, 16.)

Blood Atonement Revealed in Our Lord's Day

When the time came to take upon himself the sins of all men on conditions of repentance, our Lord, dwelling in mortality, retired to Gethsemane to undergo the greatest suffering ever borne by man or God. While Peter, James, and John slept, he pled with his Father, "If thou be willing, remove this cup from me: nevertheless not my will, but thine, be done." Then there appeared an angel from heaven, who strengthened him as he bore the infinite burden that only he could carry. "And being in agony he prayed more earnestly: and his sweat was as it were great drops of blood falling down to the ground." (Luke 22:42-44.) It was of this agony beyond compare that he said to Joseph Smith: "Which suffering caused myself, even God, the greatest of all, to tremble because of pain, and to bleed at every pore, and to suffer both body and spirit—and would that I might not drink the bitter cup, and shrink—Nevertheless, glory be to the Father, and I partook and finished my preparations unto the children of men." (D&C 19:18-19.)

Later, on the cross, his life blood dripped from the cruel wounds in his tortured hands and feet, and finally, when the Roman spear pierced his side, "forthwith came there out blood and water" (John 19:34), after which he voluntarily gave up his life, that there might be three to "bear witness in earth, the spirit, and the water, and the blood" (1 Jn. 5:8).

After his demise, and the glorious resurrection that came thereby, his prophetic witnesses continued to teach that salvation was a living reality because he shed that blood which had given him mortal life. We have quoted the words of the Beloved John as to those who are cleansed from sin through "the blood of Jesus Christ." (1 Jn. 1:7.) We have also noted the testimony of Peter as to those who are redeemed "with the precious blood of Christ, as of a lamb without blemish

253

and without spot." (1 Pet. 1:18-19.) To these inspired declarations we now add the testimony of our beloved friend Paul.

As Paul journeyed to Jerusalem to face bonds and chains for the testimony of Jesus, he charged the Ephesian elders, whose faces he would not again see in mortality, "to feed the church of God, which he hath purchased with his own blood." (Acts 20:17-28.) To both the Colossians and the Ephesians he wrote that the saints have "redemption through his blood, even the forgiveness of sins." (Col. 1:14. See also Eph. 1:7.) To the Romans he testified that the law of justification itself is operative because of "his blood" (Rom. 5:9), and that we are thereby "justified freely by his grace through the redemption that is in Christ Jesus: Whom God hath set forth to be a propitiation through faith in his blood." That is to say, "remission of sins" comes to those who have "faith in his blood"; it is to them that the effects of his propitiatory sacrifice are given. (Rom. 3:24-25.) To the Hebrews, whose practice it then was to shed the blood of animals in blood sacrifices, Paul taught that all Mosaic sacrifices were in fact similitudes of the coming sacrifice of the Messiah. He showed them that under both the old and the new covenants sins are purged only "with blood," and that "without shedding of blood is no remission." His witness was that "the blood of Christ, who . . . offered himself without spot to God," was the only thing that would purge men from "dead works" and evil deeds and enable them "to serve the living God" and gain salvation in his kingdom. (Heb. 9.)

Also after our Lord's resurrection, we find John writing of him that he "loved us, and washed us from our sins in his own blood." (Rev. 1:5.) From John's writings we learn that the only way the saints can overcome the world and escape the wiles of Satan is "by the blood of the Lamb, and by the word of their testimony." (Rev. 12:11.) It was John also who saw the angelic hosts around the throne of God, worshiping

254

him and the Lamb, and heard the angelic elder ask: "What are these which are arrayed in white robes? and whence come they?" He it was who then heard the heavenly pronouncement: "These are they which came out of great tribulation, and have washed their robes, and made them white in the blood of the Lamb." (Rev. 7:9-14.) And it was John who saw our Lord coming in power and great glory in the last days, and, lo, "he was clothed with a vesture dipped in blood." (Rev. 19:13.)

But certainly one of the greatest of all proclamations on the atoning blood of Christ the Lord is his own words, given to the Nephites as he ministered among them in resurrected glory. Speaking of the law which the Father of us all has given to mankind, the Risen Lord said: "And no unclean thing can enter into his kingdom; therefore nothing entereth into his rest save it be those who have washed their garments in my blood, because of their faith, and the repentance of all their sins, and their faithfulness unto the end. Now this is the commandment: Repent, all ye ends of the earth, and come unto me and be baptized in my name, that ye may be sanctified by the reception of the Holy Ghost, that ye may stand spotless before me at the last day." (3 Ne. 27:19-20.)

Man Perverts Doctrine of Blood Atonement

This doctrine that blessings come through the shedding of the blood of the Sinless One—as with all pure and perfect principles and practices—has been subject to gross and evil and wicked perversions among degenerate and apostate peoples in all ages. To Abraham, for instance, the Lord said: "My people have gone astray from my precepts, and have not kept mine ordinances, which I gave unto their fathers; And they have not observed mine anointing, and the burial, or baptism wherewith I commanded them; But have turned from the commandment, and taken unto themselves the washing of children, and the blood of sprinkling; And have said that the blood of the righteous Abel was shed for sins; and have not known wherein they are accountable before me." (JST, Gen. 17:4-7.)

That these words of Deity, spoken to his friend Abraham and revealed anew in our day to Joseph Smith, were also known to Paul is apparent from the ancient apostle's statement about the saints coming "to Jesus the mediator of the new covenant, and to the blood of sprinkling, that speaketh better things than that of Abel." (Heb. 12:24.) It was, of course, the approved practice for the Levitical priests in Israel to sprinkle blood from their sacrifices in prescribed ways (Heb. 9:19-21), but as here used, "the blood of sprinkling" has clear reference to the blood of Jesus, which is symbolically sprinkled upon all the faithful.

This twisting of the divine intent in Abraham's day, where blood atonement is concerned, is only a fraction of what has prevailed among those who have gone astray in many nations and among many peoples. For the first four thousand years of man's mortal continuance on earth, sacrifices of all sorts were common among pagan peoples and even among such "enlightened" worshipers as the citizens of ancient Rome. Being a form of false worship, "that which is offered in sacrifice to idols," and "the things which the Gentiles sacrifice, they sacrifice to devils, and not to God." Having so said, Paul counsels: "And I would not that ye should have fellowship with devils." (1 Cor. 10:19-20.)

But the most horrifying and revolting perversion of the divine sacrificial system has been human sacrifice, the shedding of mortal blood by mortal man on one religious pretext or another. As Amulek said, "There is not any man that can sacrifice his own blood which will atone for the sins of another." (Alma 34:11.) Nor is God appeased, nor are the forces of nature controlled, by the most sincere slaying of the purest virgins or others. Such acts are the basest form of false worship. Performed by those whose religions ape portions of what once was had in perfection among their ancestors, they are almost inconceivable desecrations of the true and holy system of forgiveness through sacrifice. Mortal man is not authorized, except in imposing the requisite death penalties for crimes, to take the blood of his fellow beings under any circumstances. From the beginning, the Lord's law has been: "And whoso sheddeth man's blood, by man shall his blood be shed; for man shall not shed the blood of man. For a commandment I give, that every man's brother shall preserve the life of man, for in mine own image have I made man." (JST, Gen. 9:12-13.)

And yet Satan has such great hold on the hearts of men that he has prevailed upon them to sacrifice each other by the thousands in the name of religion. Unnumbered hosts were sacrificed—or should we say murdered?—on the altars of the Aztecs. In the days of Moses, and for centuries thereafter, sacrifices of children were made to Molech, the god of the Ammonites. The penalty for any in Israel who so dealt with their offspring was death. (Lev. 20:1-5.) And so it has been among many peoples in many places, the souls of men have poured out their blood in gory rituals on the altars of idols, all in the name of religion, all pursuant to Lucifer's will, which is to destroy the souls of men.

Why Blood Is the Symbol of Life and Death

When the Lord gave Israel their system of animal sacrifices, all to be performed in similitude of the future sacrifice of their Messiah, he singled out the blood as the sacrificial element to which special attention should be given. It was not the flesh of the sacrificial animal, not the sacred altar on which the Lord's fires burned, not the manner in which the Levites of Israel should perform their ministerial labors (though all these had a bearing and bore a relative share of importance), but it was the blood of the animals that concerned the Lord. He gave, as we have seen,

257

detailed instructions as to sprinkling the blood in the ransoming rituals, and the blood was singled out as the symbol of the whole atoning process.

Indeed, so sacred was the blood element in the sacrificial ordinance that Jehovah directed Moses to forbid the people to eat any blood at any time, lest they fail to reverence, as his law required, the particular blood chosen to make an atonement for them. The penalty for disobedience to what otherwise would have been an irrelevant and unreasonable dietary restriction was to be severed from one's inheritance in Israel. The penalty for any soul who ate blood was to be "cut off from among his people."

As to the sacrificial blood, the Lord said: "For the life of the flesh is in the blood," which is a truism that is both obvious and important to a proper understanding of the doctrine of blood atonement. Blood is the element and symbol of mortal life. When it courses in mortal veins, mortal life (meaning the temporary union of body and spirit) is present. When it is spilled or otherwise ceases to perform its life-giving function, death overtakes whatever form of mortal life is involved. Having so said, the Lord continues: "And I have given it to you upon the altar to make an atonement for your souls." That is, the element which assures mortal life will give eternal life. The blood by which men live on earth will be the blood which makes everlasting life available in heaven. "The life . . . is in the blood." The symbolism is perfect. And so the Lord concludes: "It is the blood that maketh an atonement for the soul." (Lev. 17:10-11.) From all of this it is apparent that those in Israel who were spiritually enlightened knew and understood that their sacrificial ordinances were in similitude of the coming death of Him whose name they used to worship the Father, and that it was not the blood on their altars that brought remission of sins, but the blood that would be shed in Gethsemane and on Calvary.

With all this in mind, no longer need men ask, "Why this emphasis on the shedding of blood? Why dwell with such emphasis, and so repetitively, on our Lord's death and the manner in which it came to pass?" The reasons are clear and compelling. Where salvation is concerned, we are dealing with life and death; we are born into mortality so that we may have the privilege of dying and coming forth in immortality. In our search for salvation, we are dealing with mortal life and the natural death; we are dealing with immortality and eternal life; we are seeking to learn how mortality becomes immortality, and how men, having bowed to the natural death, can yet come forth and gain eternal life. To crystallize in our minds and to dramatize before our eyes what is involved in all this, the Lord has chosen blood as the symbol of both life and death.

Death is ever before us. It is seen on every hand. All men must die, and all men are aware, daily or oftener, of the existence of death and the separations it entails. But it is not death, but life, upon which the mind of man should dwell. It is not the despair of the grave, but the joy of our redemption, that should fill our souls. How, then, can we make every death a reminder of life, every departure from this life a witness of an entrance into a better realm? How can we turn the sorrow of the grave into the joy of immortal glory? The shedding of man's blood brings death. The shedding of Christ's blood brings life. As death passes upon all men by Adam, so life comes to all by Christ. As in Adam, or by nature, all men fall and are subject to spiritual death, so in Christ and his atoning sacrifice all men have power to gain eternal life in the presence of their Creator. To every true believer every death becomes a reminder of life. That reminder is in the shedding of man's blood, which brings death, and the shedding of Christ's blood, which brings life. God be praised for the perfection of his similitudes!

"Be Ye Reconciled to God"

"The man Gabriel" came to Daniel and taught him that "Messiah the Prince" should come "to make reconciliation

259

for iniquity, and to bring in everlasting righteousness." (Dan. 9:24-25.) That is to say, the Messiah would come to make possible a reconciliation between God and man.

In his lost and fallen condition, man is in a state of sin and spiritual darkness and is himself subject to and guilty of sin. "All have sinned, and come short of the glory of God." (Rom. 3:23.) "There is not a just man upon the earth, that doeth good, and sinneth not." (Eccl. 7:20.) Christ only was sinless. All accountable men having sinned are thereby unclean and unable to dwell with or be in the presence of their God. Accordingly, "all men, everywhere, must repent, or they can in nowise inherit the kingdom of God, for no unclean thing can dwell there, or dwell in his presence; for, in the language of Adam, Man of Holiness is his name." (Moses 6:57.) As Amulek expressed it, "No unclean thing can inherit the kingdom of heaven; therefore, how can ye be saved, except ye inherit the kingdom of heaven? Therefore, ye cannot be saved in your sins." (Alma 11:37.)

Thus, to restore man to a state of harmony and unity with Deity, man must repent, receive a remission of his sins, become clean, and be thereby ransomed from his lost and fallen state. To be saved, man must be reconciled to God through the atonement of his Son. "Be reconciled unto him through the atonement of Christ, his Only Begotten Son," Jacob preached, "and ye may obtain a resurrection, according to the power of the resurrection which is in Christ, and be presented as the first-fruits of Christ unto God, having faith, and [having] obtained a good hope of glory in him." (Jacob 4:11.)

Can there be any more glorious concept than this, that lowly and fallen and mortal and sinful man—that all of us— can forsake our evil and wicked ways and find harmony and unity with our Eternal Father? Ought we not to shout praises to the Holy One of Israel forever for his goodness to us? "Cheer up your hearts," Jacob says to all of us, "and remember that ye are free to act for yourselves—to choose the way of everlasting death or the way of eternal life. . . . Reconcile yourselves to the will of God, and not to the will of the devil and the flesh; and remember, after ye are reconciled unto God, that it is only in and through the grace of God that ye are saved." (2 Ne. 10:23-24.) "Believe in Christ," Nephi adds, and "be reconciled to God; for we know that it is by grace that we are saved, after all we can do." (2 Ne. 25:23.) Also: "Be reconciled unto Christ, and enter into the narrow gate, and walk in the straight path which leads to life, and continue in the path until the end of the day of probation." (2 Ne. 33:9.)

Paul says that Christ came "to make reconciliation for the sins of the people." (Heb. 2:17.) "He is the propitiation for our sins." (1 Jn. 2:2.) If we repent, are baptized, receive the gift of the Holy Ghost, and keep the commandments, we are in fact reconciled to Deity. The great propitiation operates in our lives. We are then, as Paul expressed it, "in Christ." We have become new creatures. It is of such that the ancient apostle says: "God . . . hath reconciled us to himself by Jesus Christ, and hath given to us the ministry of reconciliation." That is, being reconciled we have also certain obligations. We have received not only the fact of reconciliation, and how glorious that is, but also "the ministry of reconciliation."

This ministry of reconciliation, in Paul's language, consists of two things: (1) "That God was in Christ, reconciling the world unto himself, not imputing their trespasses unto them," provided, of course, that they pursued a course of truth and righteousness; and (2) that he "hath committed unto us the word of reconciliation," that is, that he hath given to his legal administrators the message which must be preached and believed if any of us are to gain the blessings of reconciliation with that Man of Holiness, from whom we have been separated because we are unholy.

Having so taught, our apostolic friend of olden times gives this exhortation to all those who have yet to commit themselves in full to the cause of Christ: "Now then we are ambassadors for Christ, as though God did beseech you by

261

us: we pray you in Christ's stead, be ye reconciled to God." (2 Cor. 5:17-20.) That is to say: 'We represent the Lord Jesus Christ; he has commissioned us; we have his authority; and since we are legal administrators, when we speak it is as though the Father himself beseeched you to come and be reconciled to his Son, for the Son speaks the words of the Father, and we stand in the place and stead of Christ when we preach; we have his mind; we speak his words, and those words are: Be ye reconciled to God.'

Our mission is to preach "Jesus Christ, and him crucified." (1 Cor. 2:2.) Our mission is to proclaim the message of reconciliation to all men. Our mission also is to persuade men to forsake their sins, to "come unto Christ, and be perfected in him," and to deny themselves "of all ungodliness." (Moro. 10:32.)

"How great the importance to make these things known unto the inhabitants of the earth, that they may know that there is no flesh that can dwell in the presence of God, save it be through the merits, and mercy, and grace of the Holy Messiah," and then only when they believe and obey his laws. (2 Ne. 2:8.)

Chapter 16

MESSIAH BRINGETH THE RESURRECTION

Resurrection Proves Christ Is the Messiah

We shall now turn our attention to the resurrection—not the doctrine of resurrection in all its parts and phases; not to how the dead are raised up or with what body they shall come; not to the fact there is a resurrection of the just and of the unjust; not to the whole basic concept of immortality, which makes the trials of life bearable (though all these have some bearing upon the problem at hand), but rather to these two simple facts: (1) There is a resurrection; and (2) the Messiah bringeth it to pass.

If, as is clearly set forth in the poetry and prose of the prophets, the Promised Messiah was to be himself resurrected, being the first-fruits thereof, and if the effects of that resurrection were to pass upon all mankind, then any scriptures so teaching, plus any that merely mention or refer to the fact of being raised from death to life, are Messianic in nature. And if, as is also clearly set forth in the wondrous words of the New Testament and of latter-day revelation, the one who in fact burst the bands of death and thereby gave assurance that all men would come forth from the grave in due course, if such a one was the Man Jesus who is called Christ, then he is the Messiah; they are one and the same and are to be worshiped as such.

Further, if the Man Jesus was resurrected; if he came

forth from the Arimathean's tomb in glorious immortality; if he ate and drank with his disciples after he rose from the dead, and was by them handled and felt; if he was the first-fruits of them that slept, then he is the Son of God. And if he is God's Son, then all his words are true; his gospel has saving and damning power; and we, weak mortals that we are, must turn to him for a hope of eternal life.

We are witnesses that all of these things are true, that there neither is nor can be any question as to their verity, and that all those who accept them with full purpose of heart are on the course leading to that immortal glory which comes from God by way of his Son. Accordingly, as we pursue our Messianic studies, we shall now turn to the revealed records to see what they say as to our Lord's resurrection and the resurrection of all men.

Jehovah Shall Rise from Death

Our beginning point is the fact that the Lord Jehovah—after being brought as a lamb to the slaughter; after pouring out his soul unto death; after making his grave with the wicked, and being with the rich in his death, all as saith the prophet (Isa. 53)—was destined to come forth from the tomb and live forever in resurrected glory.

This concept of a God being resurrected, of a Redeemer and Savior coming to ransom his people, is neither novel nor mysterious. It was not a hidden nor unknown doctrine in days of old. It was not only inherent in, but was in fact the great cornerstone upon which the whole gospel plan rested. All those who had the gospel in ancient times knew of the future redemption and rejoiced in the One who should come to bring it to pass. This is perfectly clear and is not our present concern. What we are now desirous of doing is to show that it was the Lord Jehovah, so named and so identified, who would himself be resurrected and would make the resurrection possible for all others.

Isaiah, speaking for himself and for faithful Israel, addressed himself to their God, the God of Israel. As he spoke, the words which came forth in Hebrew were: "O Jehovah, thou art my God; I will exalt thee, I will praise thy name," and so forth. As these words now read in our King James Version of the Bible, the Hebrew for *Jehovah* has been anglicized to read *Lord,* and so Isaiah's cry of praise is preserved to us as "O Lord, thou art my God," and so forth.

After numerous expressions of praise for all that the Lord has done for his people, Isaiah called him "the Lord of hosts," and said of him: "He will swallow up death in victory; and the Lord God will wipe away tears from off all faces." Our incomparable theologian, Paul, writing and interpreting by the power of the Holy Ghost, as part of his greatest essay on the resurrection of Christ, picks up a part of Isaiah's prophecy and says: "For this corruptible must put on incorruption, and this mortal must put on immortality. So when this corruptible shall have put on incorruption, and this mortal shall have put on immortality, then shall be brought to pass the saying that is written, Death is swallowed up in victory." Having so stated, our apostolic interpreter gives the true meaning of Isaiah's prophecy. Paul asks: "O grave, where is thy victory?" His own inspired answer is: "Thanks be to God, which giveth us the victory through our Lord Jesus Christ." (1 Cor. 15:53-57.)

Let there be no misunderstanding here. Isaiah (who was inspired!) said that Jehovah would swallow up death in victory, meaning bring to pass the resurrection of all men; and Paul (who also was inspired!) said that the Lord Jesus Christ had in fact swallowed up death in victory, because Isaiah's words about Jehovah were Messianic and applied to Jesus our Lord. As to the promise that "God shall wipe away all tears from their eyes," we find John reciting that this will be fulfilled when Christ reigns among men during the millennial era. (Rev. 21:3-4; D&C 101:23-31.)

But now back to Isaiah. Having told of Jehovah's swallowing up of death in victory and of the millennial joy that shall prevail, Israel's great prophet continues: "And it

265

shall be said in that day, Lo, this is our God; we have waited for him, and he will save us: this is the Lord; we have waited for him, we will be glad and rejoice in his salvation." (Isa. 25:9.)

Then Isaiah records a song which shall be sung in the land of Judah, sung to Jehovah, in praise and thanksgiving and adoration for all that he has done for his people. Israel will say, among other things, "Trust ye in the Lord for ever: for in the Lord JEHOVAH is everlasting strength." Thereupon Jehovah will answer, "Thy dead men shall live, together with my dead body shall they arise." The Lord Jehovah will be resurrected! He that poured out his soul unto death shall live again! He that died upon the cross shall come forth from the grave! A God dies and a God lives! A mortal Messiah becomes an immortal being, like his Father, so that he may gain all power in heaven and on earth!

But it is not the great Jehovah only who shall live again. It is all men. "Thy dead men shall live," he says. "Awake and sing, ye that dwell in dust: for thy dew is as the dew of herbs, and the earth shall cast out the dead. . . . The earth also shall disclose her blood, and shall no more cover her slain." (Isa. 26.)

Perhaps one more prophetic passage as to Jehovah's resurrection will suffice for our present purposes. In a psalm of praise to Jehovah, David said: "Sing unto God, sing praises to his name: extol him that rideth upon the heavens by his name JAH, and rejoice before him." JAH is the familiar form of JEHOVAH. To this Jah, who is Jehovah, the song of praise extols: "Thou hast ascended on high, thou hast led captivity captive," and hast given gifts unto men. He is then identified as the God of our salvation, because "unto God the Lord belong the issues of death." (Ps. 68.) The issues of death? Our children are our issue; they come forth from us. The issues of death are those that come forth from the grave because Jah took captivity captive. That is, the captivity of the grave was swallowed up; it was overcome; it became the captive of Him who had power over death. Lest there be any doubt as to the identity of Jehovah who took captivity captive, we turn to Paul's writing. He says: It is Christ. (Eph. 4:7-10.)

Messiah Shall Rise from Death

What the prophets foretold of the resurrection of the Great Jehovah, they also said of him under his designation as the Messiah, as the Son of Man, as Jesus Christ, or whatever name they chose to apply to the Offspring of the Father. To list those prophets who so preannounced, and we do not have their full accounts, would be synonymous with listing those who were prophets. From the accounts that have come to us, we know, for instance:

Enoch saw that he was lifted up, meaning on the cross; that he was slain; that he arose from the dead and ascended to his Father; and that "the saints arose, and were crowned at the right hand of the Son of Man, with crowns of glory." (Moses 7:47-59.)

Abraham was told that though he should die, yet he should rise again to possess his Palestinian home as an "everlasting inheritance," and also that "the Son of Man" should live again in immortality. "But how can he live if he be not dead?" was the question put by Deity to the Father of the faithful. The heaven-sent answer was: "He must first be quickened." Then the record says: "And it came to pass, that Abram looked forth and saw the days of the Son of Man, and was glad, and his soul found rest, and he believed in the Lord; and the Lord counted it unto him for righteousness." (JST, Gen. 15:9-12.)

Lehi taught that after the Jews "had slain the Messiah, . . . he should rise from the dead, and should make himself manifest, by the Holy Ghost, unto the Gentiles." (1 Ne. 10:11.) Also: That "the Holy Messiah . . . layeth down his life according to the flesh, and taketh it again by the power of the Spirit, that he may bring to pass the resurrection of the dead, being the first that should rise." (2 Ne. 2:8.)

267

Nephi foretold that "they will crucify . . . the Messiah," who is "the Only Begotten of the Father, . . . and after he is laid in a sepulchre for the space of three days he shall rise from the dead, with healing in his wings; and all those who shall believe on his name shall be saved in the kingdom of God. Wherefore, my soul delighteth to prophesy concerning him, for I have seen his day, and my heart doth magnify his holy name." (2 Ne. 25:12-13; 26:3.)

King Benjamin said: "He shall be called Jesus Christ, the Son of God, . . . And he shall rise the third day from the dead." (Mosiah 3:8-10.)

Abinadi expressed it this way: "The bands of death shall be broken, and the Son reigneth, and hath power over the dead; therefore, he bringeth to pass the resurrection of the dead." Further: "All the prophets, and all those who have believed on their words, or all those that have kept the commandments of God, shall come forth in the first resurrection. . . . They are raised to dwell with God who has redeemed them; thus they have eternal life through Christ, who has broken the bands of death." (Mosiah 15:20-23.)

What need we say more? As to the prophetic word, particularly among the Nephite prophets, the record is clear and extensive. There is added testimony from Abinadi (Mosiah 16:7-15); the first Alma taught the doctrine of Abinadi at the waters of Mormon (Mosiah 18:1-9); the second Alma, who is the American Paul, as it were, was profound, prolific, and profuse in his prophetic utterances (Alma 4:14; 7:12-13; 16:19-20; 27:28; 33:22; 40:1-26; 41:1-15; 42:1-31). We have also the words of Amulek (Alma 11:37-45), of Aaron (Alma 22:14), and of Samuel the Lamanite (Hel. 14:15-17, 25; 3 Ne. 23:7-14). There was no want of inspired teaching, among the Americans of the house of Israel, relative to Christ and his coming, the redemption he alone would make, and the resurrection that would result therefrom, nor was there any among their Old World contemporaries and ancestors; but unfortunately the Old World accounts have not been preserved for us with the same clarity and perfection that appertains where Book of Mormon writings are concerned.

Old Testament Prophets Tell of Resurrection

Those prophecies about being raised from death to life which we have so far brought to the fore all speak of Christ, under one name-title or another, as the One through whom the resurrection is brought to pass. Their Messianic meaning is clear. Being thus fully indoctrinated with the eternal truth that he and he alone is the one by whom immortality comes, we are free—nay, we are bound and required—to read all revelations pertaining to the resurrection as being Messianic in nature, whether they mention our Lord by name, by necessary implication, or not at all. Since he brings to pass the resurrection, and without him there would be naught but dolorous death forever, it follows that the fact of resurrection is itself a witness of his wondrous works.

Let us be aware, then, of the true Messianic nature of what the Old Testament prophets were saying when they spoke of the resurrection, as they did, with greater force and factualness than some have supposed. What had the Psalmist in mind, for instance, but the resurrection when he sang to Jehovah, "I will behold thy face in righteousness: I shall be satisfied, when I wake, with thy likeness"? (Ps. 17:15.) Was it not the same assurance expressed by John when he wrote of Christ, "When he shall appear, we [meaning the faithful saints] shall be like him"? (1 Jn. 3:2.) And of what sang the Psalmist when he said to Jehovah, "My soul cleaveth unto dust: quicken thou me according to thy word"? (Ps. 119:25.) Was he not speaking of the same resurrection that Paul had in mind when he testified that all men would be quickened by the power of Christ when they were raised from mortality to immortality? (1 Cor. 15.)

"All the days of my appointed time will I wait, till my change come," are the words of Job. His Redeemer lived; he knew it; and therefore he knew he would be changed from

269

mortality to immortality, from corruption to incorruption, and that the grave would have no victory over him. So it has always been with the faithful. With Job, each of them says to the Lord: "Thou shalt call, and I will answer thee: thou wilt have a desire to the work of thine hands." (Job 14:14-15.) Truly, the work of the Lord's hands shall answer his call and the bands of death shall be broken for each individual.

Daniel spoke plainly of the resurrection at the end of the world in these words: "And many of them that sleep in the dust of the earth shall awake, some to everlasting life, and some to shame and everlasting contempt" (Dan. 12:2), which brings to mind our Lord's like-worded promise: "The hour is coming, in the which all that are in the graves shall hear" the voice of the Son of God, "and shall come forth; they that have done good, unto the resurrection of life; and they that have done evil, unto the resurrection of damnation." (John 5:28-29.)

To and of Israel, by the mouth of Hosea, the Lord God said: "There is no saviour beside me. . . . I will be thy king. . . . I will ransom them from the power of the grave; I will redeem them from death; O death, I will be thy plagues; O grave, I will be thy destruction." (Hosea 13:4-14.) That is: 'I Jehovah will do it,' all of which brings us to Paul's like-expressed witness that Christ shall ransom and redeem and resurrect, so that it may truly be said: "O death, where is thy sting? O grave, where is thy victory?" (1 Cor. 15:55.)

Nowhere in the scriptures do we have as explicit and as detailed a description of the resurrection as in the writings of Ezekiel. The Lord Jehovah, by the power of his Spirit, carried that ancient prophet to a valley that was full of dry bones, which were identified as the bones of the whole house of Israel. They were the bones of those who had been promised an inheritance in Palestine, which they had never received in the full sense of the word. "Can these bones live?" the Lord asked. By way of answer, Jehovah said to the bones: "I will cause breath to enter into you, and ye shall live: And I will lay sinews upon you, and will bring flesh

270

upon you, and cover you with skin, and put breath in you, and ye shall live."

There is nothing more real, more literal, more personal than the resurrection, as Ezekiel then beheld in vision. He saw the dead live again, live literally and personally, each one becoming in physical makeup as he had been in mortality. It was with each of them as it would be with their Lord, when he, having also come forth from his valley of dry bones, stood in the upper room with his disciples, ate before them, and permitted them to handle his physical body. To his people the Lord's voice came: "I will open your graves, and cause you to come up out of your graves, and bring you into the land of Israel." (Ezek. 37:1-14.) He who shall do all this, as we are now acutely aware, is the Lord Jesus Christ who is the God of Israel.

What Are the Sure Mercies of David?

King David's story is one of the saddest in all history. In his youth and in the forepart of his reign as king, he was faithful and true, a man after the Lord's own heart. (1 Sam. 13:13-14.) His throne and kingdom were established with power and became the symbol of the future throne and kingdom of the Son of David. But in the matter of Uriah and Bathsheba he fell; adultery stained his soul, and innocent blood dripped from his hands. In tears he sought forgiveness, which, because of Uriah's murder, was not forthcoming.

David knew he had forfeited his claim to eternal life and the continuation of the family unit in the realms ahead. Yet he importuned the Lord for such blessings as he still might receive. And though a just God could no longer confer upon his erring servant the fulness of that reward which might have been his, yet according to the great plan of mercy, which causes the resurrection to pass upon all men, he could bring him up eventually to a lesser inheritance. His soul need not be cast off eternally to dwell with Lucifer and those

271

who are in open and continuing rebellion against righteousness. True, because of his sins, he had cast his lot with the wicked "who suffer the vengeance of eternal fire," and "who are cast down to hell and suffer the wrath of Almighty God, until the fulness of times, when Christ shall have subdued all enemies under his feet, and shall have perfected his work." (D&C 76:105-6.) But in that day when death and hell deliver up the dead which are in them (Rev. 20:13), David and his fellow sufferers shall come forth from the grave. Because he was a member of the Church and had entered into the new and everlasting covenant of marriage and then had fallen into sin, the revelation says of him: "He hath fallen from his exaltation, and received his portion." (D&C 132:39.)

Implicit in this historical recitation of what David did to lose his salvation, and in the doctrinal laws which nonetheless guaranteed him a resurrection and a lesser degree of eternal reward, are two great truths: (1) That the Holy One of Israel, the Holy One of God, the Son of David, would die and then be resurrected; and (2) that because he burst the bands of death and became the first-fruits of them that slept, all men also would be resurrected, both the righteous and the wicked, including saints who became sinners, as was the case with David their king.

These two truths became known as and were called "the sure mercies of David," meaning that David in his life and death and resurrection was singled out as the symbol to dramatize before the people that their Holy One would be resurrected and that all men would also come forth from the grave. David knew and understood this and wrote about it. So also did Isaiah, which means the principle was known and taught in ancient Israel; and both Peter and Paul made it the basis of persuasive New Testament sermons, in which they identified the Holy One of Israel as that Jesus whom they preached.

Speaking of his own resurrection and that of his Lord, David wrote: "My flesh also shall rest in hope," meaning,

'My body shall come forth from the grave,' "For thou wilt not leave my soul in hell," meaning, 'My spirit shall not remain in hell forever, but shall be joined with my body when I am resurrected.' Death and hell shall thus deliver up dead David who is in them. Then David came forth with the great Messianic pronouncement, "Neither wilt thou suffer thine Holy One to see corruption." (Ps. 16:7-11.) That is, 'The Holy One of Israel shall come forth in his resurrection before his dead body is permitted to decay and become dust.'

With accusing words, Peter charged his fellow Jews with taking "Jesus of Nazareth, a man approved of God among you by miracles and wonders and signs," and causing him to be "crucified and slain" by wicked hands. But God hath raised him up, Peter testified, "having loosed the pains of death." Then Peter quotes the whole of that Messianic message with which we are now dealing, doing so with some improvement over the way it is recorded in the Old Testament. Peter says: "For David speaketh concerning him, I foresaw the Lord always before my face, for he is on my right hand, that I should not be moved: Therefore did my heart rejoice, and my tongue was glad; moreover also my flesh shall rest in hope: Because thou wilt not leave my soul in hell, neither wilt thou suffer thine Holy One to see corruption. Thou hast made known to me the ways of life; thou shalt make me full of joy with thy countenance."

This prophecy means, Peter says, that David "spake of the resurrection of Christ, that his soul was not left in hell, neither did his flesh see corruption." Then the Chief Apostle bears testimony of the fulfillment of the prophecy. "This Jesus hath God raised up," he says, "whereof we all are witnesses. . . . Therefore let all the house of Israel know assuredly, that God hath made that same Jesus, whom ye crucified, both Lord and Christ." He is the Lord who was ever before David's face. He is the Holy One who should come forth from the grave. Thus Peter has used David's words to prove the Holy One would be resurrected, and he has used his own testimony and that of his fellow apostles to prove that he was resurrected.

Lest his hearers be left in doubt, however, as to David's personal state, the Chief Apostle says, "Let me freely speak unto you of the patriarch David, that he is both dead and buried, and his sepulchre is with us unto this day. . . . For David is not ascended into the heaven." (Acts 2:22-36.) Further, David has not yet been resurrected, for he is numbered with "the spirits of men who are to be judged, and are found under condemnation; And these are the rest of the dead; and they live not again until the thousand years are ended, neither again, until the end of the earth." (D&C 88:100-101.)

Isaiah recorded the Lord's invitation that men should come unto him, believe his word, live his law, and be saved. Part of the invitation was couched in these words of Deity: "Incline your ear, and come unto me: hear, and your soul shall live; and I will make an everlasting covenant with you, even the sure mercies of David. Behold, I have given him for a witness to the people." (Isa. 55:1-4.) That is to say: To all who will believe in him, the Lord of heaven will make the same covenant that he made with David, in that they too will know of their Messiah's resurrection, and that the souls of all men are thereby raised from the grave. David had the promise that he would be saved from death and hell, through Christ, and all the faithful could have that same assurance, though, as here expressed, David is made the illustration, the "witness," the symbol of these great truths.

Paul preached that of David's seed "hath God according to his promise raised unto Israel a Saviour, Jesus." He said that those at Jerusalem, "and their rulers, because they knew him not, nor yet the voices of the prophets" who had prophesied of him, caused that he be put to death. After he was slain, Paul says, "they took him down from the tree, and laid him in a sepulchre. But God raised him from the dead: And he was seen many days of them which came up with him

274

from Galilee to Jerusalem, who are his witnesses unto the people."

Having so taught and testified, Paul followed the same course we have seen Peter pursue; he turned to David and his great Messianic utterance about the resurrection, but he wove in also Isaiah's statement about the sure mercies of David. "As concerning that he raised him up from the dead," Paul said, "now no more to return to corruption, he said on this wise, I will give you the sure mercies of David. Wherefore he said also in another psalm, Thou shalt not suffer thine Holy One to see corruption. For David, after he had served his own generation by the will of God, fell on sleep, and was laid unto his fathers, and saw corruption: But he, whom God raised again, saw no corruption." (Acts 13:22-37.)

"I Am the Resurrection and the Life"

Jesus our Lord, ministering as the mortal Messiah, on numerous occasions taught his apostolic witnesses, and his disciples generally, that he would die and rise again the third day. First he led them along the course of spiritual progression until they gained testimonies of his divine Sonship and were able to say, as Peter did, "Thou art the Christ, the Son of the living God." After they gained this witness, the record says: "From that time forth began Jesus to shew unto his disciples, how that he must go unto Jerusalem, and suffer many things of the elders and chief priests and scribes, and be killed, and be raised again the third day." (Matt. 16:13-21.) His enigmatic "Destroy this temple, and in three days I will raise it up," which "he spake of the temple of his body," had the same meaning. (John 2:19, 21.)

Though Jesus spoke often of his own resurrection and the resurrection of all men, in my judgment the most persuasive and convincing witness, both of his divine Sonship and of the reality of the resurrection, that ever came from mortal lips, his or any others, were the words he spoke at the tomb of Lazarus—Lazarus whom he loved; Lazarus the brother of Mary and Martha, whom also he loved. This blessed family lived in Bethany, on the outskirts of Jerusalem. Jesus and his disciples were in Perea. Lazarus was sick and the sisters sent word to Jesus. The Master deliberately remained away, letting Lazarus die and be buried. When our Lord finally chose to go to his friends, Martha said: "Lord, if thou hadst been here, my brother had not died. But I know, that even now, whatsoever thou wilt ask of God, God will give it thee." Where have we seen faith like unto this? 'Lord, if thou wilt, thou canst raise my brother from the grave; he will live again; once more we shall enjoy his association as a mortal man!'

"Jesus saith unto her, Thy brother shall rise again." 'Thy faith shall be rewarded; I will return the departed dead one to the intimacy of the family circle.'

Hearing but not understanding, "Martha saith unto him, I know that he shall rise again in the resurrection at the last day." Martha's faith was founded on knowledge, as true faith must always be. She knew the doctrine of the resurrection. She believed the gospel. The stage was now set for the momentous pronouncement that Jesus had come to make, a pronouncement Jesus would soon prove by doing that which never man has done before or since.

"Jesus saith unto her, I am the resurrection, and the life: he that believeth in me, though he were dead, yet shall he live: And whosoever liveth and believeth in me shall never die. Believest thou this?"

What wondrous words are these! The Carpenter of Galilee is making himself God. He is saying that he is the One who brings both immortality and eternal life; that he is the Messiah who has gained the power of immortality from his Immortal Father; that if men believe in him and obey his gospel laws, they shall be alive to the things of the Spirit in this life and gain eternal life in the realms ahead.

Does Martha believe? "Yea, Lord," she says, "I believe

that thou art the Christ, the Son of God, which should come into the world." Her faith is perfect.

Thereupon Mary is summoned. Jesus is taken to the cave where Lazarus is laid. At his direction the stone is rolled back so that he who has been dead four days—he who is rotting, decaying, stinking; he whose every vital organ has long since ceased to function; he whose spirit is in Abraham's bosom with the other Lazarus who ate the crumbs that fell from the rich man's table—at Jesus' direction the stone is rolled back, and the Son of God, in his own right and in his own name, says simply, "Lazarus, come forth." (John 11.) And it is so. The dead man rises. Life comes again. The corruption ceases; maggots no longer gnaw at his vital organs; the worms of death find other dust for their meal. Lazarus lives.

And so we ask: Is Jesus the Son of God or a blaspheming imposter? Can we deny or disbelieve the witness he bears of himself when he offers the living body of his friend Lazarus as living proof of his words?

To have before us the full import of the words "I am the resurrection, and the life," we should here note that in substance and thought content they are the same as the words spoken anciently by Deity: "This is my work and my glory—to bring to pass the immortality and eternal life of man." (Moses 1:39.) They have the same meaning as those written by Paul to Timothy: "Our Saviour Jesus Christ, . . . hath abolished death, and hath brought life and immortality to light through the gospel." (2 Tim. 1:10.) They contain the same message revealed to Joseph Smith that through the atonement of Christ, all men are "raised in immortality unto eternal life, even as many as would believe." (D&C 29:43.)

"Now Is Christ Risen"

Now is Christ risen! Or is he? How do we know? And whence comes our knowledge that the effects of his resurrection shall pass upon all mankind and that all shall gain the

277

victory over the grave? As Job said: "If a man die, shall he live again?" (Job 14:14.) And when we speak of resurrection, what do we mean? As Paul noted, "Some man will say, How are the dead raised up? and with what body do they come?" (1 Cor. 15:35.) Does the resurrection mean that our dry bones shall live? That the Lord will lay sinews upon us, and restore flesh, and cover us again with skin? And how shall we know these things?

There are answers to all these queries, or better, there is an answer to them all. The answer is: God must reveal to prophets and apostles what the eternal verities relative to resurrection are, and then the recipients of the divine word must bear testimony to the residue of men. There is no other way to gain sure knowledge in the realm that here concerns us. We may hope or reason or speculate that there is or might be a resurrection and that it consists of this or that, but until the voice of God is heard on the matter, no man can know with certainty.

After he came forth from his borrowed tomb, the risen Lord appeared to various of his saints, among them both men and women, so that they might become witnesses, first, that he was in fact raised from death to life, and second, as to the nature and kind of being he had then become. And as to the resurrection of others than our Lord, it is written: "And the graves were opened; and many bodies of the saints which slept arose, And came out of the graves after his resurrection, and went into the holy city, and appeared unto many." (Matt. 27:52-53.) Each person to whom such a resurrected saint ministered became a witness both of the resurrection and of such revealed knowledge relative to resurrected beings as he then received. (Hel. 14:25; 3 Ne. 23:7-13.)

As to the coming forth of Jesus as the first-fruits of the resurrection, as to the fact that the great Jehovah took up his body again, we know at least the following:

1. There was a great earthquake and two angels descended from heaven and rolled back the stone from the

door of the tomb and sat upon it. Those guarding the grave became as though they were dead men. (Matt 28:2-4; JST, Matt. 28:2-3.)

2. Mary Magdalene came to the sepulchre, early in the morning while it was yet dark, found the stone taken away and the tomb empty, and saw two angels sitting thereon. (JST, John 20:1.)

3. She told Peter and John, who then came hastily, entered the tomb, and found the burial clothes wrapped together as when they enshrouded the body of him who was dead, but the body of their Lord they found not. Peter and John then returned to their home. (John 20:1-10.)

4. Mary remained at the garden tomb weeping, where, taking precedence even over the apostles, she became the first mortal of whom we have record to see the risen Lord. He came. She saw. But she was restrained from embracing him. (John 20:11-18; Mark 16:9-11.)

5. Other women, also early in the morning, came to the sepulchre to anoint Jesus' body with sweet spices. Mary the mother of Joses, Salome, the mother of James and John, Joanna, and others who are not named were present. They all saw the stone rolled away, the angels sitting thereon, and they too entered the sepulchre and found not the body. It was to them that the angels said, "He is risen," and they were told to tell the disciples that Jesus would meet them in Galilee as he had promised. As they went to deliver the message, Jesus met these faithful sisters, and they were permitted to hold him by the feet as they worshiped him. (Matt. 28:1, 5-10; JST, Matt. 28:1, 4; Mark 16:1-8; JST, Mark 16:3-6; Luke 24:1-11; JST, Luke 24:1-4.)

6. Two disciples, Cleopas and another (possibly Luke, as it is he who records the event), walked from Jerusalem to Emmaus, some six or seven miles. As they discussed the reports of those who had seen the open tomb and heard the words of the angels, Jesus himself joined them in their travels. They walked and talked. He seemed in all respects like any wayfaring man. His speech, demeanor, dress,

physical appearance were all deemed by them to be that of a fellow mortal. They invited him to spend the night with them, and his true identity was made known only as he brake bread. How better could he have taught them the literal and personal nature of resurrected beings.

7. Jesus appeared to Peter. When and where we do not know, nor do we have any knowledge of what was experienced, felt, or taught, but it accords with the proprieties and the proper order in church administration to find Him whose church it is appearing to the one he had chosen to be the earthly head of his kingdom for the time and season then involved. (Luke 24:33-35; 1 Cor. 15:5.)

8. In an upper room in a dwelling in Jerusalem, where a group of believing disciples were assembled, among them ten of the Twelve, Jesus came to teach the nature of the resurrection as only he could. The group was eating and hearing the report of Cleopas and the other with whom the Lord had communed on the Emmaus road. Suddenly Jesus was there. He had come through the wall or roof. He spake. He said his body was one of flesh and bones. He permitted them to feel the nail marks in his hands and feet and to thrust their hands into his side. He ate fish and honeycomb before them. Why? Clearly it was to teach the fact of resurrection and the nature and kind of bodies possessed by resurrected beings. (Mark 16:14; Luke 24:36-44.)

9. Thomas was not present in the upper room, and he apparently questioned, not the fact of resurrection, but its literal nature. He had not yet envisioned that the nail marks and spear wound remained, and that resurrected personages ate food. Again to the disciples, through the opaque building, Jesus came. Thomas saw and felt and handled and became like his brethren a special witness. (John 20:24-29.)

10. Seven of the disciples, having fished all night without success, were invited by Jesus to cast their nets on the other side, which doing, they were immediately filled, almost to the breaking point. Then they recognized their Lord. Peter

swam ashore to greet him. Fish was eaten and instruction given. (John 21:1-14.)

11. Sometime along the line, Jesus apparently appeared to his brother James, but his great and glorious appearance was on a mountain in Galilee, and of it we know almost nothing. That it was a planned meeting, made by pre-arrangement, is clear. It may well have been the occasion when "he was seen of above five hundred brethren at once" (1 Cor. 15:6), and we may assume that it was in many respects comparable to his resurrected ministry among the Nephites (Matt. 28:16-20).

12. Thereafter, for forty days he ministered from time to time to his disciples, teaching them all things which it was expedient for them to know concerning the building up and rolling forth of his great work. (Acts 1:3.)

13. On the mount of Olives east of Jerusalem, in the presence of his disciples, while angels attended, a cloud receiving him out of their sight, Jesus our Lord ascended to his Father, there to reign with Almighty power forever. (Mark 16:19-20; Luke 24: 50-53.)

14. Later he came to Paul on the Damascus road (Acts 9:1-9); he was seen by John as he suffered banishment on Patmos, and no doubt by hosts of others of whom we have no record.

15. Sometime following his resurrection he appeared and ministered on successive days and at appreciable length among the Nephites, who also saw and felt and handled and knew. His resurrected ministry among the lost tribes of Israel is also noted in the Nephite record. (3 Ne. 11 through 26.)

16. In our day, he has appeared to Joseph Smith and others, not a few. Of some of these appearances we have record; others are sealed in secrecy in the hearts of the recipients.

17. All this is scarcely the beginning of his resurrected ministry among men. Every faithful member of his church—The Church of Jesus Christ of Latter-day Saints—has power,

through righteousness, to see his face and become a special witness of his holy name in this personal sense, while he or she yet dwells in mortality. (D&C 67:10-14; 93:1; 107:18-19.) And in a not distant day, when he shall reign personally among men, all of earth's inhabitants shall see and know for themselves.

How, then, can it be proved that Christ gained the victory over the grave and came forth with the same body he laid down? That all men—"every man in his own order" (1 Cor. 15:23)—shall come forth in like manner? The Lord's system is to prove his word by witnesses. "Ye are my witnesses, saith the Lord, that I am God." (Isa. 43:12.) To illustrate: When Peter was sent to the house of Cornelius the centurion, the Lord's chief apostolic witness proved to the complete satisfaction of all there assembled that Jesus rose from the dead. It was done by the simple expedient of bearing a personal, Spirit-filled witness of that fact. "Him God raised up the third day," Peter testified, "and shewed him openly; Not to all the people, but unto witnesses chosen before of God, even to us, who did eat and drink with him after he rose from the dead." (Acts 10:34-43.)

What more need Peter say? What is more conclusive and binding than personal testimony? Peter knew. What is there to argue about, and who can contend successfully against him who says: 'I was in an upper room; the doors and windows were closed; there was no opening into the room. The Lord Jesus appeared. He was the same Person with whom I traveled and ministered in Palestine, the same who dwelt in my home in Capernaum. He spoke; I recognized his voice. He ate and drank; I saw him consume food. He said his body was one of flesh and bones; I felt the nail marks in his hands and in his feet. I know. I saw and felt and handled and heard. He is the Son of God. He rose from the dead.'

Peter does not stand alone; others were with him in the upper room, and they heard and saw and felt and knew. Thomas gained the same witness eight days later, in the same upper room, the doors again being shut, Jesus again standing in their midst and saying: "Thomas, Reach hither thy finger, and behold my hands; and reach hither thy hand, and thrust it into my side," to which Thomas responded, "My Lord and my God." (John 20:27-28.)

And all of this is but the beginning. The ever-enlarging ocean of true believers will continue to increase until the knowledge of God shall cover the earth "as the waters cover the sea" (Isa. 11:9), until all men know, as this disciple knows, that Jesus is Lord of all, and that he rose from the dead, as all men shall. There is no fact of revealed religion more surely established than the fact of resurrection. And there is no Messianic utterance more certainly known than that the great Jehovah, Israel's Deliverer and Savior, is the Messiah who came and who has now risen from the grave.

Chapter 17

SALVATION IS IN CHRIST

How the Gospel Is Everlasting

We say, with justifiable pride and complete verity, that we have the everlasting gospel, God's eternal plan of salvation, the plan devised by the great Elohim to bring to pass the immortality and eternal life of all his spirit children, those on this little dot of a planet and those on all the infinite worlds that his hands have made. (Moses 1:29-39.) Our view and perspective and understanding of that which God hath wrought, both here among us and on the endless expanse of orbs and spheres which roll forth everlastingly at his word, our view of all this is as daylight compared to darkness, when we contrast it with what is known and believed in Christendom.

Those who have not yet had their souls illumined by the blazing light of the restored gospel assume that this earth only is inhabited and that only such portion of its inhabitants as have lived in the so-called Christian Era have had the gospel. By such persons it is naively imagined that Deity had some other system of salvation for all who lived before the coming of our Lord, some Mosaic law, or some patriarchal order that was less than and preparatory to the fulness that Christ brought. Let us now, however, open our hearts to that greater light and knowledge which a gracious God offers to all his children, and in doing so we shall

284

crystallize in our minds what is meant by the everlasting gospel.

While banished on Patmos for the word of truth and the testimony of our Lord, the Beloved Revelator saw an angel flying in the midst of the latter-day heavens, "having the everlasting gospel to preach unto them that dwell on the earth." (Rev. 14:1-7.) Now, that which is everlasting, whether it be the gospel or anything else, has neither beginning nor ending; it is from all eternity to all eternity; it did not commence and it will not cease. It is everlasting.

The everlasting gospel was with God in the beginning; it was taught in the councils of eternity before the foundations of this world were laid; we have it now; and it will continue forever, being enjoyed in its eternal fulness in those realms of light and joy where celestial beings abide. The Holy Book records: "In the beginning was the gospel preached through the Son." That is, the Son of God, before he was ever born into mortality, preached the gospel, preached it in the presence of the Father to all the spirit hosts of heaven. "And the gospel was the word," meaning the word of salvation, "and the word was with the Son, and the Son was with God," for he was yet in preexistence, "and the Son was of God. . . . In him was the gospel, and the gospel was the life, and the life was the light of men; And the light shineth in the world, and the world perceiveth it not." (JST, John 1:1-5.) And as John so wrote, two millenniums ago, so it is today: "the world perceiveth it not." The gospel is reserved for those who forsake the world, who come out of darkness into the marvelous light of Christ.

The gospel was in preexistence; the gospel is now on earth among mortals; the gospel is found in the paradise of God among the righteous spirits; and the gospel is perfected in the lives of all those who have so far come forth from the grave. Those who were with Christ in his resurrection included "all of the prophets, and all those that have believed in their words, or all those that have kept the commandments of God." (Mosiah 15:22.)

Further, the gospel is in operation in all the worlds created by the Father and the Son. Their work and their glory, in all the infinite creations that their hands have made, is to bring to pass immortality and eternal life for the children of the Father. Through the atonement of Christ, the inhabitants of all these worlds have power to become his sons and his daughters, to become joint-heirs with him of all the glory of his Father's kingdom, to be adopted into the family of the Father, which is to say that the inhabitants of all worlds "are [thus] begotten sons and daughters unto God." (D&C 76:24.)

The Gospel Is for All Men

Did the Lord save Adam and Abraham by one set of laws and requirements and use a different standard for Peter, James, and John? Will Moses and Elijah pass by the angels and the gods to their exaltation and glory in all things by obedience to a lesser law than that imposed upon Paul and Matthew? The questions answer themselves. Either God treats all men the same or he is not God. If he respects persons and shows partiality, he does not possess those attributes of perfection which make him the exalted being that he is.

Anyone who, with James, knows that the Almighty is a being "with whom is no variableness, neither shadow of turning" (James 1:17) thereby knows also that the gospel is everlasting and that all men are saved by conforming to the same eternal standards.

Anyone who, with Paul, believes the statement "Jesus Christ the same yesterday, and to day, and for ever" (Heb. 13:8), knows that Adam and Abraham, Moses and Elijah were saved by faith in the same person in whom the New Testament saints believed.

Anyone who, with Moroni, knows "that God is the same yesterday, today, and forever, and in him there is no variableness neither shadow of changing" (Morm. 9:9), also knows, automatically and instinctively, that Adam had the gospel of Jesus Christ in the same literal sense that the same plan of salvation was enjoyed by Paul. Modern religionists, with the light before them, choose darkness rather than light if they elect to believe that an eternal and unchangeable God saves one soul on one set of standards and another soul in some other way.

In Chapter 4 we defined the gospel. In Chapter 7 we set forth that this gospel was revealed to Abraham and Moses and others in a series of dispensations. Our purpose here is to make it plain that everyone, from the beginning, who has received the gospel has known of Christ and has worshiped the Father in his name. This means Adam, Enoch, Noah, Abraham, and Moses. It includes the Jaredites and the Nephites, through all their tumultuous years. It includes the house of Israel whenever there were prophets among them who held the Melchizedek Priesthood. It includes the lost tribes whom the Savior visited after his resurrection, to say nothing of peoples and nations of whose identity and existence we know next to nothing. We do not know how many dispensations there have been, and we do not know all the peoples and nations who have been favored with prophetic leadership and teachings, but we do know that whenever and wherever the Lord has revealed his truths to any people or nation, those favored mortals have known that salvation was in Christ.

Preparatory to the setting up of the formal church organization in this dispensation, the Prophet Joseph Smith, writing by the spirit of prophecy and revelation, summarized the great truths of revealed religion. He said: "We know that there is a God in heaven, who is infinite and eternal, from everlasting to everlasting the same unchangeable God"; that he created man in his own image; that man was commanded to worship the Lord, but that he fell and became sensual and devilish; that, accordingly, the Only Begotten came to ransom fallen man and atone for the sins of the world—all to the end "that as many as would believe and be baptized in his holy name, and endure in faith to the end, should be saved." The plan of salvation, designed by the Father, was thus made operative through the atonement of his Son.

Having so summarized, the Prophet, with Spirit-guided insight, threw back the shroud of sectarian darkness that had so long covered Christendom. In keeping with the principles taught in the Book of Mormon, he announced that the saving truths of the gospel had been had in all ages when prophets guided the people. He said that the revealed truths of salvation applied to all men—"Not only those who believed after he came in the meridian of time, in the flesh, but all those from the beginning, even as many as were before he came, who believed in the words of the holy prophets, who spake as they were inspired by the gift of the Holy Ghost, who truly testified of him in all things, should have eternal life, As well as those who should come after, who should believe in the gifts and callings of God by the Holy Ghost, which beareth record of the Father and of the Son." (D&C 20:17-27.)

Salvation Is Always in Christ

After the fall, the Lord revealed himself to Adam and his posterity and sent selected preachers forth to call upon all men everywhere, by the power of the Holy Ghost, to repent and believe the gospel. "And as many as believed in the Son, and repented of their sins, should be saved; and as many as believed not and repented not, should be damned. . . . And thus the Gospel began to be preached, from the beginning, being declared by holy angels sent forth from the presence of God, and by his own voice, and by the gift of the Holy Ghost. And thus all things were confirmed unto Adam, by an holy ordinance, and the Gospel preached, and a decree sent forth, that it should be in the world [in a series of dispensations], until the end thereof." (Moses 5:15, 58-59.)

The gospel which was thus preached from the beginning was, in the Lord's language, as follows: "If thou wilt turn

288

unto me, and hearken unto my voice, and believe, and repent of all thy transgressions, and be baptized, even in water, in the name of mine Only Begotten Son, who is full of grace and truth, which is Jesus Christ, the only name which shall be given under heaven, whereby salvation shall come unto the children of men, ye shall receive the gift of the Holy Ghost, asking all things in his name, and whatsoever ye shall ask, it shall be given you. . . . And now, behold, I say unto you: This is the plan of salvation unto all men, through the blood of mine Only Begotten, who shall come in the meridian of time." (Moses 6:52, 62.)

Man's course on earth is thus charted for him. An all-wise Father announces the provisions whereby mortals may return to his presence. Jesus Christ is the way. His gospel contains the laws which must be obeyed. In the beginning it was so; during all dispensations thereafter it was the same; it so remains to this hour; and it shall be so everlastingly. There is only one gospel, one plan of salvation, one Christ, one course back to our Father. God does not vary.

Let us sample the prophetic word which echoes and re-echoes the truths of which we now speak. Nephi says that "the Son of God was the Messiah who should come" and that the Holy Ghost "is the gift of God unto all those who diligently seek him, as well in times of old as in the time that he should manifest himself unto the children of men. For he is the same yesterday, to-day, and forever; and the way is prepared for all men from the foundation of the world, if it so be that they repent and come unto him. For he that diligently seeketh shall find; and the mysteries of God shall be unfolded unto them, by the power of the Holy Ghost, as well in these times as in times of old, and as well in times of old as in times to come; wherefore, the course of the Lord is one eternal round." (1 Ne. 10:17-19.)

Jacob says that "he cometh into the world that he may save all men if they will hearken unto his voice." (2 Ne. 9:21.) The plan of salvation is perfectly summarized in the 31st chapter of Second Nephi, at the conclusion of which is this assertion: "This is the way; and there is none other way nor name given under heaven whereby man can be saved in the kingdom of God. And now, behold, this is the doctrine of Christ, and the only and true doctrine of the Father, and of the Son, and of the Holy Ghost." (2 Ne. 31:21.)

To King Benjamin the angel said: "Salvation was, and is, and is to come"—which is past, present, and future—"in and through the atoning blood of Christ, the Lord Omnipotent." (Mosiah 3:18.) "Ought ye not to tremble and repent of your sins," Abinadi asked, "and remember that only in and through Christ ye can be saved?" (Mosiah 16:13.) Alma taught: "There is no other way or means whereby man can be saved, only in and through Christ. Behold, he is the life and the light of the world. Behold, he is the word of truth and righteousness." (Alma 38:9.)

Christ Bringeth Salvation

To a cult called Zoramites who had departed from the true faith, Amulek said: "The great question which is in your minds is whether the word be in the Son of God, or whether there shall be no Christ." By way of answer, he testified: "The word is in Christ unto salvation." (Alma 34:5-6.) To Zeezrom, burning with fever "caused by the great tribulations of his mind on account of his wickedness," and yet being repentant in his heart, Alma asked: "Believest thou in the power of Christ unto salvation?" Receiving an affirmative answer, Alma healed and baptized the zealot who had theretofore opposed the truth. (Alma 15:3-12.)

And so we now come to the basic premise that Christ came to bring salvation, a truth that is bountifully clear from all we have written in this work. We shall, at this point, simply note that the Messianic witnesses did so testify with clarity and emphasis. The Spirit Messiah said to Enoch: "Whoso cometh in at the gate and climbeth up by me shall never fall." (Moses 7:53.) The mortal Messiah said to his disciples: "I am the way, the truth, and the life: no man cometh unto the Father, but by me." (John 14:6.) Also: "All that ever came before me who testified not of me are thieves and robbers." (JST, John 10:8.)

To the first Alma, the Spirit Messiah said: "It is I that taketh upon me the sins of the world." (Mosiah 26:23.) Of him the second Alma said: "It is he that surely shall come to take away the sins of the world; yea, he cometh to declare glad tidings of salvation unto his people." (Alma 39:15.) "He bare the sin of many," said Isaiah. (Isa. 53:12.) Of the mortal Messiah, John the Baptist testified: "Behold the Lamb of God, which taketh away the sin of the world." (John 1:29.) Speaking as the resurrected Messiah, he himself said: "I have drunk out of that bitter cup which the Father hath given me, and have glorified the Father in taking upon me the sins of the world, in the which I have suffered the will of the Father in all things from the beginning." (3 Ne. 11:11.)

Amulek said: "He shall come into the world to redeem his people; and he shall take upon him the transgressions of those who believe on his name; and these are they that shall have eternal life, and salvation cometh to none else." (Alma 11:40.) Also: "He has all power to save every man that believeth on his name and bringeth forth fruit meet for repentance." (Alma 12:15.) Moroni called him "the author and the finisher" of our faith (Moro. 6:4), and Paul identified him as "the author [meaning *cause*] of eternal salvation unto all them that obey him" (Heb. 5:9).

Without Christ All Is Lost

Since Christ came to bring salvation, it follows that if he had not come, there would be no salvation. Since his atonement ransoms man from temporal and spiritual death, it follows that if there had been no atonement, there would be no ransom—all mankind would have been lost forever. "According to the great plan of the Eternal God there must be an atonement made, or else all mankind must unavoidably perish." (Alma 34:9; Mosiah 15:19.)

Since he came to save men from death, hell, the devil, and endless torment, it follows that if he had not come, the bodies of all men would have remained in the grave, their spirits would have stayed in hell, the devil would have been their ruler, and eternal torment would have been their way of life.

If Christ had not come, there would be no resurrection, no immortality, no hope of eternal glory, no eternal life, no exaltation in the kingdom of God. If he had not come, all men would be devils, angels to a devil, sons of perdition, suffering the torments of the damned forever. If Christ had not come, there would be no forgiveness of sins, no return to the presence of the Father, no spiritual rebirth, no continuation of the family unit in eternity—nothing of moment or merit. The purposes of creation would have vanished away, and all things would have come to naught. (2 Ne. 9.)

Is it any wonder that Nephi said: "My soul delighteth in proving unto my people that save Christ should come all men must perish." Indeed, the inexorable logic of the situation led that prophet to conclude and to testify: "If there be no Christ there be no God; and if there be no God we are not, for there could have been no creation. But there is a God, and he is Christ, and he cometh in the fulness of his own time." (2 Ne. 11:6-7.)

Believe in Christ

To gain salvation, men must believe in Christ. It matters not when or where they live. He is the Savior of all men, of all ages, and of all races. Let them dwell in darkest Africa or on the lost land of Atlantis; let them live four thousand years before his mortal birth or in our decadent day; let them be of Israel or Gentile lineage; let them be bond or free, black or white, pygmies or giants; let them be whosoever they are, live whensoever they do, dwell wheresoever they may, or be whatsoever it falls their lot to be—all must believe in Christ to be saved. Such is the law ordained by him and his Father before the world was.

Needless to say, the Lord wants men to be saved. Every soul who gains eternal life adds to Deity's kingdoms and glory. And so, in every dispensation, he reveals Christ and his laws. If men believe and obey, salvation will be their lot and eternal life their inheritance. In Adam's day the first proclamation of the gospel went forth in these words: "Believe on his Only Begotten Son, even him whom he declared should come in the meridian of time, who was prepared from before the foundation of the world." It is of this pronouncement that the record says: "And thus the Gospel began to be preached, from the beginning." (Moses 5:57-59.)

All the prophets taught this same doctrine. "To him give all the prophets witness," Peter said, "that through his name whosoever believeth in him shall receive remission of sins." (Acts 10:43.) One of the greatest Messianic utterances, relative to believing in Christ who should come, is contained in these words, spoken some five hundred and fifty years before his mortal birth: "The right way is to believe in Christ and deny him not; for by denying him ye also deny the prophets and the law. . . . The right way is to believe in Christ, and deny him not; and Christ is the Holy One of Israel; wherefore ye must bow down before him, and worship him with all your might, mind, and strength, and your whole soul; and if ye do this ye shall in nowise be cast out." (2 Ne. 25:28-29.)

After he came, the witness was the same. Always and everlastingly men are commanded to believe in him. "Whosoever believeth in him should not perish, but have everlasting life." (John 3:16.)

John the Baptist bore this witness: "He that believeth on the Son hath everlasting life: and he that believeth not the Son shall not see life; but the wrath of God abideth on him." (John 3:36.) And Jesus himself said: "Ye believe in God, believe also in me." (John 14:1.) "He that believeth on me hath everlasting life." (John 6:47.) "This is the work of God, that ye believe on him whom he hath sent." (John 6:29.)

How to Believe in Christ

We now have before us this basic verity: "He shall bring salvation to all those who shall believe on his name." (Alma 34:15.) So he shall. As an abstract principle, this concept presents no great problem. Our difficulties arise when we begin to define what is meant by believing in Christ and when we begin to segregate out the true believers from those whose ideas on the subject are false, but who nonetheless suppose that they believe in him.

What does it mean to believe in Christ? It means to accept him as the Son of God in the literal and full sense of the word. It means to believe that God is his Father in the same sense that all mortal men have fathers. It means to believe that the Spirit Jehovah was born as the Son of Mary; that the great Creator took upon himself a tabernacle of clay; that he came into the world to work out the infinite and eternal atonement. It presupposes that his Father is a personal being in whose image man is made. It presupposes that the Father is one person, the Son another. It presupposes a receptive, believing frame of mind, one that is willing and ready to hope for that which is not seen which is true.

It does not mean to believe that he is part of a spirit essence that fills the immensity of space, is everywhere and nowhere in particular present, and is in some indefinable and incomprehensible way three beings in one. It does not mean to believe that he is the same person as the Father, and that, as the Son, he is simply manifesting himself under a different name. It does not mean to believe that he finished his work in ages past and no longer works among men, in power, by revelation, performing signs and miracles by the hands of the faithful.

How do we identify true believers? Amid the cries "Lo, here is Christ; Lo, there," can we sift out those who truly believe from those who use gospel language without envisioning what the words really mean? It is one thing to believe Christ is the Son of God in some figurative way and another to believe that his Father has a body of flesh and bones as tangible as man's. Even in the Church itself, where the true doctrine is taught and should be known, there are those with limited and twisted ideas about their Lord, even as was the case in the meridian of time. "Some indeed preach Christ even of envy and strife," Paul said, "and some also of good will: The one preach Christ of contention," or of faction, "But the other of love." (Phil. 1:15-17.)

What are the signs by which true believers may be known? Do we believe in Christ if we reject revelation and signs and miracles? If we fail to accept the inspired utterances of living apostles and prophets? If we do not believe the Bible, or the Book of Mormon, or the Doctrine and Covenants? Belief is a serious and solemn thing. The issue is not sincerity of purpose, but one of fact and reality and truth. If we believe the truth, we can be saved; if we believe a lie, we shall surely be damned.

To identify true believers and to indicate how all may be numbered with that select and favored group, we should ponder and apply the following:

1. *Learn of Christ.*

Manifestly this is the beginning point. No man can believe in anything of which he is ignorant. Until we learn about our Lord we cannot exercise an intelligent judgment on the issue of belief or disbelief. A knowledge of Christ is found in the scriptures and is taught by his servants who are members of his church and who have already come to believe that he is Lord of all.

2. *Believe the words he has spoken.*

Some of our Lord's words are recorded in the Standard Works—that is, in the Bible, the Book of Mormon, the Doctrine and Covenants, and the Pearl of Great Price. Anyone who believes the words there written believes in Christ. Implicit in this statement is the fact that the words mean what they say. There are those who suppose they believe the Bible who do not believe in the true Christ because they choose to interpret the Biblical teachings to conform not to sense and reason, but to their preadopted and preconceived creeds. Words must be accepted according to their clear and obvious meaning and intent, and in the final analysis must be interpreted by the power of the Spirit.

Jesus said: "He that will not believe my words will not believe me—that I am," that is to say, that I exist, that I am the Christ, that I am he of whom the prophets testified, "and he that will not believe me will not believe the Father who sent me." He also said: "But he that believeth these things which I have spoken, him will I visit with the manifestations of my Spirit, and he shall know and bear record. For because of my Spirit he shall know that these things are true; for it persuadeth men to do good." (Ether 4:11-12.)

3. *Believe the testimonies of his disciples.*

Some of these are in the scriptures; others are found in various publications; many are never written down, except that they ofttimes sink into the hearts of receptive persons with such fixity that it is as though they were written in the souls of men. And our Lord's system for presenting truth to the world is to do it by the mouth of witnesses. He gives the Holy Ghost to his servants, and the words which they then speak are his own. They are his voice, his mind, and his will. They are scripture. (D&C 68:1-4.) They reveal Christ. Hence, to believe in him we must believe in his words as they fall from the lips of those who speak by the power of the Holy Ghost.

"He that receiveth whomsoever I send receiveth me," Jesus said, "and he that receiveth me receiveth him that sent me." (John 13:20.) Also: "And he that believeth not my words believeth not my disciples." (Ether 4:10.) And, of course, the reverse of that is also true, that he that believeth the words of the disciples believeth in him. "For whoso receiveth not the words of Jesus and the words of those whom he hath sent receiveth not him; and therefore he will not receive them at the last day." (3 Ne. 28:34.) We know of Christ today because he has been manifest through the teachings of his disciple Joseph Smith, to whom the Lord said: "This generation shall have my word through you." (D&C 5:10.) And, we might add, if they do not get it through Joseph Smith, they will not get it.

4. *Believe the Book of Mormon.*

This volume of holy scripture is sent forth "to the convincing of the Jew and Gentile that Jesus is the Christ, the Eternal God, manifesting himself unto all nations." (Title Page, Book of Mormon.) The book itself is a new witness for Christ. From first to last it bears record that he is the Son of God and teaches in plainness and perfection the truths of his everlasting gospel. Anyone who believes the Book of Mormon believes in Christ. And conversely, anyone who believes in Christ believes in the Book of Mormon.

"Believe in Christ," Nephi said, "And if ye shall believe in Christ ye will believe in these words [those written in the Book of Mormon], for they are the words of Christ, and he hath given them unto me." (2 Ne. 33:10.) In this connection, it is worthy of note that anyone who believes the Bible will also believe the Book of Mormon. (Morm. 7:8-9.) The great problem in the sectarian world is that people have the Bible but neither understand nor believe it, except in a casual and superficial way; and they know about Christ but neither accept nor believe in him in the full sense required to attain salvation with him and his Father.

5. *Receive the Holy Ghost.*

This is the perfect and conclusive way to know of the divine Sonship of our Lord. The Holy Ghost is a revelator; that is his commission as a member of the Godhead. He bears witness of the Father and the Son. (2 Ne. 31:18.) Anyone who receives the Holy Ghost thereby knows that Jesus is the Christ. Moroni said: "Ye may know that he is, by the power of the Holy Ghost." (Moro. 10:7.) The thing which the Lord requires of men is that they obey the law which entitles them to receive the Holy Ghost so they can

297

thereby believe in Christ and chart for themselves a course leading to eternal life.

6. *Keep the commandments.*

Jesus said: "My doctrine is not mine, but his that sent me. If any man will do his will, he shall know of the doctrine, whether it be of God, or whether I speak of myself." (John 7:16-17.) It follows, unfailingly and absolutely, that any person who keeps the commandments of God, as he would have him do, shall gain the knowledge that Christ is the Lord. Among the commandments are these:

"Search the scriptures." (John 5:39.)

Treasure up "my word." (JS-H 37.)

Repent, be baptized, receive the Holy Ghost, and endure in righteousness to the end. (3 Ne. 27:20-21.)

Seek that salvation prepared for the faithful, for "he cometh into the world that he may save all men if they will hearken unto his voice." (2 Ne. 9:21.)

7. *Work miracles.*

If there is one thing that always attends and identifies those who believe in Christ it is this: they work miracles. Signs and gifts always attend their ministry. However much it may run counter to the course of Christendom, however severe the indictment may seem, speaking of the gifts of the Spirit, the word of the Lord is: "These signs shall follow them that believe." (Mark 16:17.) "And if it so be that the church is built upon my gospel then will the Father show forth his own works in it." (3 Ne. 27:10.)

Anyone who believes what the apostles believed will receive the same gifts they enjoyed, will perform the same miracles, and will do the same works. "He that believeth on me, the works that I do shall he do also." (John 14:12.)

8. *See his face.*

We repeat again what so few know in the full and true sense of the word, that those who believe and obey the whole law shall see the face of their Lord while they yet dwell as mortals on earth. He is no respecter of persons. If the brother of Jared, because of his perfect knowledge,

298

"could not be kept from beholding within the veil," so shall it be with any of like spiritual perfection. (Ether 3:19-26.)

"Hallowed Be Thy Name"

As with the Father, so with the Son: "Hallowed be thy name." (Matt. 6:9.) To the Son hath God the Father given a name and a power that are above all names and powers whether in heaven or on earth. Only the Father is above him. Because the Son ransoms and redeems and saves, the hopes and the destinies of all men center in him. His name is above all names. His character and honorable reputation, his illustrious fame, his rank and position, all are above those of men and angels.

Of him it is written: He "made himself of no reputation, and took upon him the form of a servant, and was made in the likeness of men: And being found in fashion as a man, he humbled himself, and became obedient unto death, even the death of the cross." Such was the mortal life of the Eternal One. Hence, also, it is written: "Wherefore God also hath highly exalted him, and given him a name which is above every name: That at the name of Jesus every knee should bow, of things in heaven, and things in earth, and things under the earth; And that every tongue should confess that Jesus Christ is Lord, to the glory of God the Father." (Phil. 2:7-11.)

There is no language available to men or angels that can record with deserved emphasis the reality that salvation is in Christ and that his holy name is exalted above all others. Nephi said: "All those who believe on his name shall be saved in the kingdom of God. . . . And as the Lord God liveth, there is none other name given under heaven save it be this Jesus Christ, of which I have spoken, whereby man can be saved." (2 Ne. 25:13, 20.) The angel said to King Benjamin: "There shall be no other name given nor any other way nor means whereby salvation can come unto the children of men, only in and through the name of Christ, the

299

Lord Omnipotent." (Mosiah 3:17.) Peter echoed the same thought in his day in these words: "There is none other name under heaven given among men, whereby we must be saved." (Acts 4:12.) And now, for myself and all others who have like knowledge and feelings, I say:

The name of Jesus—wondrous name—the name in which the truths of salvation are taught; the name in which the ordinances of salvation are performed; the name in which miracles are wrought, in which the dead are raised and mountains moved;

The name of Jesus—wondrous name—the name by which worlds come rolling into existence; the name by which redemption comes; the name which brings victory over the grave and raises the faithful to eternal life;

The name of Jesus—wondrous name—the name by which revelation comes and angels minister; the name of him by whom all things are and into whose hands the Father hath committed all things; the name of him to whom every knee shall bow and every tongue confess in that great day when the God of Heaven makes this planet his celestial home.

Is it any wonder, then, that we preach that all men everywhere should live a Christ-centered life, and that those who have knowledge of these things, who are the Latter-day Saints, above all others, should let their thoughts dwell upon him unceasingly!

We are counseled: "Feast upon the words of Christ; for behold the words of Christ will tell you all things what ye should do." (2 Ne. 32:3.)

We are promised: "If ye shall press forward, feasting upon the word of Christ, and endure to the end, behold, thus saith the Father: Ye shall have eternal life." (2 Ne. 31:20.)

O that it might be said of us, as it was of them of old, "We talk of Christ, we rejoice in Christ, we preach of Christ, we prophesy of Christ, and we write according to our prophecies, that our children may know to what source they may look for a remission of their sins." (2 Ne. 25:26.)

300

"Come unto Christ"

We are approaching the day—it has not yet arrived, but soon shall—"when the knowledge of a Savior shall spread throughout every nation, kindred, tongue, and people." Even in this age of enlightenment, there are many yet upon the earth who know nothing of Christ and his laws or who have only a casual awareness that there is such a thing as Christianity. They do not know enough, as yet, to form an intelligent opinion that they should come unto Christ, live his laws, and prepare for a continuing life with him hereafter.

But when the knowledge of a Savior is taken to them— and I take it that such knowledge has already gone to all who have the Bible—then "none shall be found blameless before God, except it be little children, only through repentance and faith on the name of the Lord God Omnipotent." (Mosiah 3:20-21.) That is, all who know of Christ and all who should know because the opportunity is available have the responsibility to seek him out. Men have an obligation to seek the truth. The Spirit of Christ is given to every soul born into the world; its function is to guide them to that light and truth which saves, and all who follow its enticings and promptings come unto Christ and salvation. Those who die without this knowledge because it was not available to them shall have opportunity to believe and obey in the spirit world, and if they do so with all their hearts, they shall be heirs with the living of salvation in our Father's kingdom.

It is true that we have an obligation to preach the gospel to the world and invite them to receive that further light and knowledge that a gracious Father offers to all his children. But this does not diminish or abrogate their responsibility to follow the light they already have, to seek truth, and to come to the place and people where salvation is found. This applies to pagan and Christian alike—all are to come unto Him of whom we here teach and testify.

What we here say applies only to those who are accountable, meaning those who have arrived at the age of accountability, which is eight years, and those who have normal faculties and mentality. Little children are saved through the atonement of Christ without any act on their part. He does not bear their sins, for they have none. "Little children are redeemed from the foundation of the world through mine Only Begotten," the Lord says, "Wherefore, they cannot sin, for power is not given unto Satan to tempt little children, until they begin to become accountable before me." (D&C 29:46-47.) "Little children," Abinadi said, "have eternal life." (Mosiah 15:25.) "Little children are alive in Christ, even from the foundation of the world." (Moro. 8:12.)

As to those whose mental circumstances preclude them from getting a knowledge of Christ, those who do not therefore know right from wrong, the revelation says: "Whoso having knowledge, have I not commanded to repent? And he that hath no understanding, it remaineth in me to do according as it is written." (D&c 29:49-50.) All such, being as little children, are saved through the atonement of their Lord.

But as to accountable persons, the eternal decree is: Come unto Christ; come unto him with full purpose of heart and be saved. Hear the prophetic voices:

King Benjamin tells us who can be saved, in these thoughtful and Spirit-filled words: "If ye have come to a knowledge of the goodness of God, and his matchless power, and his wisdom, and his patience, and his long-suffering towards the children of men; and also, the atonement which has been prepared from the foundation of the world, that thereby salvation might come to him that should put his trust in the Lord, and should be diligent in keeping his commandments, and continue in the faith even unto the end of his life, I mean the life of the mortal body—I say, that this is the man who receiveth salvation, through the atonement which was prepared from the foundation of the world for all mankind, which ever were since the fall of Adam, or who are, or who ever shall be, even unto the end of the world. And this is the means whereby salvation cometh. And there is none other salvation save this which hath been spoken of; neither are there any conditions whereby man can be saved except the conditions which I have told you." (Mosiah 4:6-8.)

Amaleki, who kept the Nephite records in his day, issued this proclamation: "Come unto Christ, who is the Holy One of Israel, and partake of his salvation, and the power of his redemption. Yea, come unto him, and offer your whole souls as an offering unto him, and continue in fasting and praying, and endure to the end; and as the Lord liveth ye will be saved." (Omni 26.)

Moroni climaxed his writings with this plea: "Come unto Christ, and be perfected in him, and deny yourselves of all ungodliness; and if ye shall deny yourselves of all ungodliness and love God with all your might, mind and strength, then is his grace sufficient for you, that by his grace ye may be perfect in Christ." (Moro. 10:32.)

And the Lord Jesus, he who rose from the dead and who liveth still, issues this invitation to all his brethren, spirit children of the same Father: "I have come unto the world to bring redemption unto the world, to save the world from sin. Therefore, whoso repenteth and cometh unto me as a little child, him will I receive, for of such is the kingdom of God. Behold, for such I have laid down my life, and have taken it up again; therefore repent, and come unto me ye ends of the earth, and be saved." (3 Ne. 9:21-22.)

Who can question this call? What more need we say? Christ is God. Salvation is in him. Those who believe and obey shall gain peace in this life and eternal life in the world to come. So be it.

Chapter 18

SALVATION IS IN JEHOVAH

Christ Has Many Names

Since salvation is in Christ and him only in all ages of the world; since his is the only name given under heaven whereby men can be saved, whether they lived before, during, or after his mortal ministry—why do we not find his name in the Old Testament? Several facts and circumstances should be noted in seeking an answer to this vital question:

1. His name was in the Old Testament when the books comprising that holy volume were first written. At least his name, as there recorded in Hebrew, should have been translated into the Greek as Christ. We know this because of the way the Prophet Joseph Smith has given us the Book of Moses in the Pearl of Great Price. It is there specified that all of the prophets and saints, from Adam to Noah and his sons, called him Jesus Christ, and we may rest assured that they taught their children after them the same nomenclature.

2. He was known by the name of Jesus Christ among the Jaredites, whose historical time span covered about two millenniums, commencing in the day of the tower of Babel (Ether 1:4-5) and going down to the day of Coriantumr and the city of Zarahemla (Omni 21).

3. Approximately 87 percent of the Book of Mormon deals with history and doctrine that preceded the personal ministry of our Lord among the Nephites. Through all of the

more than 450 pages of Holy Writ covering that ancient period, our Lord was known among the people as Jesus Christ. All of this is of course Old Testament times; Nephi and Jeremiah, for instance, were contemporaries.

4. By joining the foregoing with the practice of the Christian Era, it is clear that we can trace the usage of our Lord's most prevalent name during the entire six thousand years of time that has elapsed since Adam was cast out of Eden.

5. We should note here that many plain and precious parts of the Old Testament were torn from between its sacred covers by evil and designing men in days long past. (1 Ne. 13.) It is perfectly clear that their intent was to destroy the knowledge of Christ and of the plan of salvation, because many of the things restored by Joseph Smith, by the spirit of inspiration, deal specifically with these things. We have seen that the Book of Moses restores to the Old Testament the knowledge about the Son of God under his New Testament names. This restoration is made in the Book of Genesis down to the 13th verse of the 6th chapter; Genesis, chapter 14, in the Joseph Smith Translation contains additions that name our Lord as the Son of God.

6. Careless scribes and poor translators, not knowing that our Lord had revealed himself by the name of Christ from the beginning, failed to translate references to him by that designation. An example of making a translation conform to a prevailing doctrinal concept is found in the 8th Psalm where the original account says that God made man a little lower than Elohim. Not knowing that man is of the same race as Deity, that he dwelt with his Father in preexistence, and that his potential is to become as Elohim is, the translators made the passage read that God had made man a little lower than the angels.

7. "All the holy prophets which were before us," said the Nephite Jacob, "believed in Christ and worshiped the Father in his name, and also we worship the Father in his name." (Jacob 4:4-5.) This blanket assertion includes the

305

worship performed by Abraham, Isaac, and Jacob, by Moses, Elijah, and Samuel, by Isaiah, Hosea, and Micah, and by all the inspired saints from Adam's day on down. And what was said of those who went before applies also to all who came after. God does not change.

8. In our present Old Testament, Christ is called the Lord, which is the anglicized rendition of Jehovah. Thus, Christ is Jehovah. Our Messianic studies would fall far short of the mark if we were not keenly aware that these two great name-titles apply to one and the same person. Such is shown repetitiously throughout this work.

9. Names applied to our Lord are numerous. Each has a differing shade of meaning and teaches some special thing relative to him and his work. But each refers to the same individual. Old Testament prophets refer to him as the Savior, Redeemer, Deliverer, Messiah, God of Israel, Jehovah, and so forth, all being names that identify the Only Begotten of the Father. It follows that a prayer to the Father in any of these names is a prayer in the name of Christ. Indeed, the great command to Adam was, "Thou shalt do all that thou doest in the name of the Son, and thou shalt repent and call upon God in the name of the Son forevermore." (Moses 5:8.) Sometimes today we hear prayers in the name of the Son, or in the name of Israel's God, or in whatever title the sincere supplicant chooses to use, all of which is valid and proper and approved.

Salvation Is the Burden of the Scriptures

In Chapter 8 we set forth that, in the true and complete sense of the word, salvation is eternal life. It is exaltation in the highest heaven of the celestial kingdom. It is to be as God is. Chapter 17 is devoted to the thesis that salvation is in Christ, that it comes in and through his holy name and in no other way. Our present concern is to make it clear beyond controversy or question that salvation is in Jehovah and comes in and through and because of him, and therefore that Jehovah is Christ.

To gain salvation is and should be the chief concern of all men. Those who are spiritually inclined and enlightened make it the chief goal of their very existence. "If thou wilt do good, yea, and hold out faithful to the end," the Lord says, "thou shalt be saved in the kingdom of God, which is the greatest of all the gifts of God; for there is no gift greater than the gift of salvation." (D&C 6:13.) That the Lord wants men to be saved is axiomatic. Making immortality and eternal life available is his work, his business, the active enterprise to which he devotes all of his strength and power. And in those holy scriptures which come from him, he sets forth the terms and conditions whereby this greatest of all gifts may be won.

Salvation is mentioned by name 62 times in the Psalms, 28 times in Isaiah, and another 26 times in the balance of the Old Testament, for a total of 116 times in that ancient scripture. All of these references, plus two in the Book of Abraham, talk about salvation as it relates to, comes from, and is effected by the Lord Jehovah. All of them are in that sense Messianic, and many of them apply expressly and pointedly to the mortal ministry of that member of the Godhead.

By way of comparison, there are 44 references to salvation by name in the New Testament, 88 in the Book of Mormon, 50 in the Doctrine and Covenants, and four (besides the two in Abraham) in the Pearl of Great Price. All of these associate salvation with Christ. In all of the scriptures, but especially in those received by us during the so-called Christian Era, there are many passages dealing with salvation which do not use the word itself.

To catch the vision of how the ancient scriptures associate salvation with Jehovah, let us, in addition to the numerous illustrations quoted elsewhere in this work, note the following:

307

"My name is Jehovah," the Lord said to Abraham, "And I will make of thee a great nation, . . . for as many as receive this Gospel shall be called after thy name, . . . and in thy seed after thee . . . shall all the families of the earth be blessed, even with the blessings of the Gospel, which are the blessings of salvation, even of life eternal." (Abr. 2:8-11.) That is to say: The gospel of the Lord Jesus Christ—the everlasting gospel!—is the gospel of the Lord Jehovah.

After his resurrection, the Savior appeared to his disciples in an upper room, permitted them to touch and handle his glorified body, ate before them, and then said: "These are the words which I spake unto you, while I was yet with you, that all things must be fulfilled, which were written in the law of Moses, and in the prophets, and in the psalms, concerning me." (Luke 24:44.) They then received from him power to understand the scriptures.

The law of Moses, the prophets, and the psalms—these were the sources to which those in time's meridian could turn for Messianic knowledge. And now that our Lord had been raised from the dead, now that his mortal ministry and atoning sacrifice were accomplished fact, the disciples could look back to these sources and see wherein they foretold all that had happened in the life of him whom they accepted as Lord and Christ.

As to the Psalms, truly do they abound in declarations that Jehovah is the Savior. "Save me, O my God. . . . Salvation belongeth unto the Lord." (Ps. 3:7-8.) "We will rejoice in thy salvation, and in the name of our God." (Ps. 20:5.) "He only is my rock and my salvation. . . . In God is my salvation and my glory." (Ps. 62:6-7.) "Shew us thy mercy, O Lord, and grant us thy salvation." (Ps. 85:7.) "The Lord taketh pleasure in his people: he will beautify the meek with salvation." (Ps. 149:4.) And so the pleas for grace and the songs of praise continue through more than three score passages. In each of them the Lord mentioned is Jehovah. He will save. Salvation is in him.

As illustrations from Isaiah, let us quote these passages,

all having reference to Jehovah: "Behold, God is my salvation; I will trust, and not be afraid: for the Lord JEHOVAH is my strength and my song; he also is become my salvation." (Isa. 12:2.) After reciting how Jehovah will "swallow up death in victory" and "wipe away tears from off all faces," Isaiah says: "And it shall be said in that day, Lo, this is our God; we have waited for him, and he will save us: this is the Lord; we have waited for him, we will be glad and rejoice in his salvation." (Isa. 25:8-9.) One of the most noted of all Isaiah's utterances says: "The Lord is our judge, the Lord is our lawgiver, the Lord is our King; he will save us." (Isa. 33:22.) Truly, O Israel, "thy salvation cometh," and "his [Jehovah's] reward is with him, and his work before him." (Isa. 62:11.) There are, of course, many other such passages in the prophetic writings of Israel's Messianic seer.

Truly, "Salvation is of the Lord." (Jonah 2:9.) Such is the burden of the scriptures and the message of the Old Testament prophets. And our message is that all of their sayings tie into Christ through whose atoning power salvation has now come. Those who are his saints have put on "the breastplate of faith and love; and for an helmet, the hope of salvation." As Paul says: "God hath not appointed us to wrath, but to obtain salvation by our Lord Jesus Christ, Who died for us, that . . . we should live together with him." (1 Thes. 5:8-10.)

And so the heavenly choirs sing of Christ. "Alleluia [meaning, praise Jehovah]; Salvation, and glory, and honour, and power, unto the Lord our God. . . . Alleluia: for the Lord God omnipotent reigneth." (Rev. 19:1, 6.)

Jehovah Is the Savior

All believing Christians accept Jesus as the Savior of the world. This concept is set forth clearly in the New Testament, the Book of Mormon, and the Doctrine and Covenants. It is one of the plainest and most widely received truths of revealed religion. From the day the angelic ministrant hailed his birth by saying, "Unto you is born this day in the city of David a Saviour, which is Christ the Lord" (Luke 2:11), the apostles and prophets of the New Testament acclaimed and accepted him as their Savior. Beginning with Nephi, who spoke of "a Messiah, or, in other words, a Savior of the world" (1 Ne. 10:4), the inspired preachers on the American continent bore the same witness. Among many passages, the Doctrine and Covenants speaks of him as "the Savior of the world, even of as many as believe" on his name. (D&C 66:1.)

It is hoped that all those who accept Jesus as Lord and Savior know also that the Old Testament prophets and seers knew him as Jehovah, which is to say, Jehovah is the Savior of the world. The writings of Moses, as originally recorded by the great lawgiver, contained these words: "Mine Only Begotten is and shall be the Savior, for he is full of grace and truth." (Moses 1:6.) Isaiah and various of the prophets recorded the words of the Eternal Jehovah in such ways as: "I am the Lord thy God, the Holy One of Israel, thy Saviour. . . . I, even I, am the Lord; and beside me there is no saviour." (Isa. 43:3, 11.) "I am the Lord thy God. . . . There is no saviour beside me." (Hosea 13:4.) And there are many other such statements.

To show that the New Testament authors knew that Christ their Savior was Jehovah, the Savior of Israel, let us examine these words spoken by Jehovah to Isaiah. That holy being identifies himself as the "God of Israel, the Saviour"; announces that "Israel shall be saved in the Lord with an everlasting salvation"; says to "the seed of Jacob: . . . There is no God else beside me; a just God and a Saviour; there is none beside me." Having so spoken to Israel, his chosen, he then affirms: "Look unto me, and be ye saved, all the ends of the earth: for I am God, and there is none else." (Isa. 45:15-22.)

That is to say, Jehovah is the Savior; come unto him, all ye ends of the earth; he "is the Saviour of all men, specially of those that believe." (1 Tim. 4:10.) "The Lord is God and

310

beside him there is no Savior." (D&C 76:1.) Let all men come to him.

Having so stated, having issued the great invitation to come to him, the Lord Jehovah then says: "I have sworn by myself, the word is gone out of my mouth in righteousness, and shall not return, That unto me every knee shall bow, every tongue shall swear." (Isa. 45:23.) Before Jehovah, Judge of all, shall all things bow in humble reverence; to him every tongue that speaks shall swear an allegiance that shall never end! Well and gloriously spoke the great God by the mouth of Isaiah.

Now, what says our friend Paul of this same day of coming judgment? With the same Spirit resting upon him that gave utterance to Isaiah, the theologically gifted apostle wrote: "Christ both died, and rose, and revived, that he might be Lord both of the dead and living, . . . for we shall all stand before the judgment seat of Christ. For it is written, As I live, saith the Lord, every knee shall bow to me, and every tongue shall confess to God." (Rom. 14:9-11.) It is thus from Christ's bar that judgment shall be rendered; it is he who is judge of all; it is to him that every knee shall bow; and it is to him that every tongue shall swear eternal allegiance. Blessed be his holy name!

Jehovah Is the Redeemer

Who is the Redeemer? That it is Christ, all sound theologians agree. But, surprisingly, the Lord Jesus is not so named in our present New Testament. What the New Testament does is teach that salvation comes "through the redemption that is in Christ Jesus" (Rom. 3:24), and that "we have redemption through his blood, the forgiveness of sins, according to the riches of his grace." (Eph. 1:7.) Such being the case, it is easy, in propriety and in truth, for Christians to pick up the name itself from Job's testimony—"I know that my redeemer liveth" (Job 19:25)—and from other Old Testament passages.

311

That it is Christ, we also know from numerous latter-day revelations and from a multitude of Messianic pronouncements found in the Book of Mormon. Nephi, for instance, speaks of Israel coming "to the knowledge of the true Messiah, their Lord and their Redeemer." (1 Ne. 10:14.) In about 83 B.C., Alma prophesied that "the time is not far distant that the Redeemer liveth and cometh among his people." (Alma 7:7.) Some ten years later that same prophet taught that "the Lord their God" was "Jesus Christ their Redeemer." (Alma 37:9.)

But our present purpose is to point out that the Old Testament prophets identified Jehovah as the Redeemer, and that the New Testament authors taught that the Holy One so identified was Christ. The Psalmist said, "God was their rock, and the high God their redeemer." (Ps. 78:35.) Jeremiah said of Israel: "Their Redeemer is strong; the Lord of hosts is his name." (Jer. 50:34.) And Isaiah recorded many statements from Jehovah himself to this effect: "Thy Maker is thine husband," he said to Israel; "the Lord of hosts is his name; and thy Redeemer the Holy One of Israel; The God of the whole earth shall he be called. . . . With everlasting kindness will I have mercy on thee, saith the Lord thy Redeemer." (Isa. 54:5-8.) "And the Redeemer shall come to Zion, and unto them that turn from transgression in Jacob, saith the Lord." (Isa. 59:20.)

An Old Testament passage that was spoken by Jehovah of himself, and which has clear and plain fulfillment in Christ, is preserved for us in these words: "Thus saith the Lord the King of Israel, and his redeemer the Lord of hosts; I am the first, and I am the last; and beside me there is no God. . . . For the Lord hath redeemed Jacob, and glorified himself in Israel." (Isa. 44:6, 23.) We are, of course, fully aware that Christ is the one who redeemed both Israel and all who would join with the chosen people in doing the deeds of true devotion. But it is more than mere chance to hear the voice of the risen and embodied Lord say to John the same thing the yet-unborn and unembodied Lord had

312

said to Isaiah. "I am the first and the last," came the Voice, "I am he that liveth, and was dead; and, behold, I am alive for evermore." (Rev. 1:17-18.)

We need have no hesitancy, in view of all that is known and written, in both general and specific terms, to testify that Jehovah the Redeemer is he who was born of Mary and who is known in all Christendom as Christ the Redeemer.

Have Faith in the Lord Jesus Christ

Most Christians believe their salvation is based upon accepting Christ as their Savior; some feel it is also necessary to receive certain ordinances or sacraments or both; and a limited few even envision the eternal verity that it is necessary to keep the commandments and live godly and upright lives. What Christians in general do not know is that the same beliefs, the same ordinances, the same obedience and personal righteousness which now lead to salvation were also required of all men from the beginning. That is to say, salvation comes through faith in the Lord Jesus Christ no matter what age of the earth is involved. It was so with Adam and Enoch; it was so with Noah and Abraham; it was so with Moses and Elijah; it was so with Peter and Paul; and it is so today. Faith in the Lord Jesus Christ is the first principle of the gospel, the beginning of all righteousness, the open door to the path leading to eternal life in our Father's kingdom.

Mormon, whose name is forever enshrined in the hearts of true believers because he abridged the Nephite records, spoke plainly and powerfully of faith in Christ with words to this effect: "God knowing all things, being from everlasting to everlasting," he said, "sent angels to minister unto the children of men, to make manifest concerning the coming of Christ. . . . And God also declared unto prophets, by his own mouth, that Christ should come. . . . Wherefore, by the ministering of angels, and by every word which proceeded forth out of the mouth of God, men began to exercise faith in

Christ; . . . and thus it was until the coming of Christ."
(Moro. 7:22-25.)

From the day of the first prophet, whose name was
Adam, to the day of the messenger, whose name was John
and who prepared the way before and introduced the Savior
to his Israelitish kinsmen—during those four long millenniums of mortal existence, every prophet, every seer, every
saint, all true believers, without exception and without de-
viation from the divine pattern, all had faith in the Lord
Jesus Christ! He is eternal. His laws are eternal. The gospel
is eternal. Truth never varies. Salvation always comes in the
same way. And so our friend Mormon says: "And after that
he came men also were saved by faith in his name." (Moro.
7:26.) We today but follow the pattern of the past. God does
not vary.

With this concept in our minds, let us sample the sayings
of our brethren of old who believed as we believe, and who
rejoiced in Christ as we rejoice in him. In the days of Helaman the second, the Church among the Nephites pros-
pered exceedingly. Tens of thousands of souls were
converted and baptized. In abridging the events of that period, Mormon wrote: "Thus we see that the gate of heaven is
open unto all, even to those who will believe on the name of
Jesus Christ, who is the Son of God. Yea, we see that
whosoever will may lay hold upon the word of God, which is
quick and powerful, which shall divide asunder all the cun-
ning and the snares and the wiles of the devil, and lead the
man of Christ in a straight and narrow course across that
everlasting gulf of misery which is prepared to engulf the
wicked—And land their souls, yea, their immortal souls, at
the right hand of God in the kingdom of heaven, to sit down
with Abraham, and Isaac, and with Jacob, and with all our
holy fathers, to go no more out." (Hel. 3:28-30.)

Be it known that Abraham, Isaac, and Jacob, and "all
our holy fathers," were men of Christ, men who believed
and obeyed, men who wrought righteousness, men who
perfected their faith in that Lord for whose coming they

looked and whose law they loved. They in their day were as the faithful in Helaman's day, of whom the record says: "They did fast and pray oft, and did wax stronger and stronger in their humility, and firmer and firmer in the faith of Christ, unto the filling their souls with joy and consolation, yea, even to the purifying and the sanctification of their hearts, which sanctification cometh because of their yielding their hearts unto God." (Hel. 3:35.)

We need not pursue this issue further. Any truth seeker, with the Book of Mormon in hand, can discover scores of passages from many prophets, all written in the so-called pre-Christian Era, which state plainly that faith in that Christ who shall come is essential to salvation. Manifestly this same truth is interwoven into all that the New Testament teaches about him whose name we so much revere and on whose arm we everlastingly rely.

Have Faith in the Lord Jehovah

It is by faith that miracles are wrought—not faith as an abstract, unembodied, vaporous nothingness, floating like a fog in the universe, but faith in the living Lord, faith centered in Christ our Head. The eternal law is: "Whoso believeth in Christ, doubting nothing, whatsoever he shall ask the Father in the name of Christ it shall be granted him; and this promise is unto all, even unto the ends of the earth." (Morm. 9:21.) Accordingly, any person who has ever performed a miracle, in any age, has done it by faith in Christ. For the past, at the present, and in the future, all miracles are wrought by faith in that Lord who is Christ.

Jesus our Lord said to his apostles: "These signs"— meaning gifts and miracles—"shall follow them that believe." (Mark 16:17.) The signs involved were the same as those which had followed true believers from the beginning. Faith is power. Where the Lord's power is poured out upon his people, there is faith, and where the power of God is not found, there is no faith. "When faith comes," the Prophet

315

said, "it brings its train of attendants with it—apostles, prophets, evangelists, pastors, teachers, gifts, wisdom, knowledge, miracles, healings, tongues, interpretation of tongues, etc. All these appear when faith appears on the earth, and disappear when it disappears from the earth; for these are the effects of faith, and always have, and always will, attend it. For where faith is, there will the knowledge of God be also, with all things which pertain thereto—revelations, visions, and dreams, as well as every necessary thing, in order that the possessors of faith may be perfected, and obtain salvation; for God must change, otherwise faith will prevail with him. And he who possesses it will, through it, obtain all necessary knowledge and wisdom, until he shall know God, and the Lord Jesus Christ, whom he has sent— whom to know is eternal life." (*Lectures on Faith,* p. 69.)

With these principles before us, we come to a consideration of those Old Testament miracles performed by faith in Jehovah, and once again we hear the apostolic witness testify that Jehovah is Christ. In his great sermon on faith, Paul tells us it was by faith (power!) that the world was made. He says Abel, Enoch, Noah, Abraham, Isaac, Jacob, and Joseph wrought their mighty deeds by faith, meaning faith in that Jehovah whom they all served. Then he comes to Moses to whom the great I AM revealed himself, saying, "I appeared unto Abraham, unto Isaac, and unto Jacob. I am the Lord God Almighty; the Lord JEHOVAH. And was not my name known unto them?" (JST, Ex. 6:3.)

Who appeared to Moses, in whose ministry did he serve, and at whose behest did he labor? The Lord JEHOVAH! But what says Paul? Hear these words: "By faith Moses, when he was come to years, refused to be called the son of Pharaoh's daughter; Choosing rather to suffer affliction with the people of God, than to enjoy the pleasures of sin for a season; Esteeming the reproach of Christ greater riches than the treasures in Egypt: for he had respect unto the recompence of the reward." Having named Christ as the center of Moses' faith, our apostolic author recites various deeds done by Moses through faith. Faith in whom? Jehovah? Yes. Faith in Christ? Yes.

"And what shall I say more?" Paul asks, as he proceeds to name the Old Testament worthies, "Who through faith subdued kingdoms, wrought righteousness, obtained promises, stopped the mouths of lions, Quenched the violence of fire, escaped the edge of the sword, out of weakness were made strong, waxed valiant in fight, turned to flight the armies of the aliens." (Heb. 11.) The miracles of the Old Testament, performed as our Christian brethren suppose by faith in Jehovah, were in fact performed by faith in the Lord Jesus Christ, which makes every miracle, of itself, a Messianic performance.

Enter into the Rest of the Lord

One of the sweet and gracious doctrines of the gospel, a doctrine that brings comfort and serenity to the saints, is that those who are true and faithful in all things enter into the rest of the Lord their God.

Mortality is the state in which men are tried and tested; in which they are subject to temptation, disease, sorrow, and death; in which there is violent opposition to every true principle; in which the generality of mankind is wafted hither and yon by every wind of doctrine; in which Satan has great hold upon the hearts of most of mankind. It is not a state of peace and rest; in it there is work and turmoil and dissension. It is a probationary estate where choices must be made; where all men, the saints included, are being tried and tested, to see if they will choose liberty and eternal life through the atonement of Christ the Lord, or whether they will walk in subjection to that angel who fell from before the presence of the Eternal God and became the devil to rise no more.

Peace and rest, in the full and true sense, come only

317

through the gospel and are reserved for those who place themselves in harmony with those Holy Beings who are the embodiment of these godly attributes.

What does it mean to enter into the rest of the Lord? To this question there is a three-pronged answer: one aspect deals with the rest of the Lord here and now in mortality; the next is concerned with a more perfected rest that comes to those who, departing this sphere, find themselves in the paradise of God; and the final one applies to the saved saints who have risen in immortal glory ever to be with their Lord.

Mormon had some counsel for the saints, for those who believe the gospel and are seeking to live its laws. He addressed them in this way: "I would speak unto you that are of the church, that are the peaceable followers of Christ, and that have obtained a sufficient hope by which ye can enter into the rest of the Lord, from this time henceforth until ye shall rest with him in heaven." (Moro. 7:3.) To enter into the rest of the Lord in this life is to gain a sure knowledge of the truth and divinity of the Lord's work on earth. It is to have the testimony of Jesus and to know by personal revelation that The Church of Jesus Christ of Latter-day Saints is the kingdom of God on earth. It is to have such fixity of purpose that the calls, Lo, here is Christ, and Lo, there, seem like idle chatter. Those who have entered into the rest of the Lord here and now are not driven about by every wind of doctrine. They are not trying to find the truth. The Holy Spirit of God has already manifest to their souls where the truth is. They have charted a course leading to that eternal rest which is eternal life. They have received that peace which passeth all understanding and is known and felt only by the power of the Holy Ghost.

As to the rest of the Lord enjoyed by faithful saints when they depart this life, Alma says: "The spirits of those who are righteous are received into a state of happiness, which is called paradise, a state of rest, a state of peace, where they shall rest from all their troubles and from all care, and sorrow." (Alma 40:12.)

As to that rest which is enjoyed by those who dwell in immortal glory, Amulek says: "God did call on men, in the name of his Son, (this being the plan of redemption which was laid) saying: If ye will repent, and harden not your hearts, then will I have mercy upon you, through mine Only Begotten Son; Therefore, whosoever repenteth, and hardeneth not his heart, he shall have claim on mercy through mine Only Begotten Son, unto a remission of his sins; and these shall enter into my rest." (Alma 12:33-35.)

There are a number of other Book of Mormon exhortations that men should so live as to enter into the rest of the Lord. Christ, who is Jehovah, is of course the Lord who is meant, as he himself testified in this comforting invitation: "Come unto me, all ye that labour and are heavy laden, and I will give you rest. Take my yoke upon you, and learn of me; for I am meek and lowly in heart: and ye shall find rest unto your souls. For my yoke is easy, and my burden is light." (Matt. 11:28-30.)

Now let us see how the God of the Old Testament invites people to enter his rest and how the New Testament specifies that the God so speaking is Christ. Jehovah speaks, let earth give ear, "For the Lord is a great God, and a King above all gods. . . . For he is our God; and we are the people of his pasture, and the sheep of his hand. To day if ye will hear his voice, Harden not your heart, as in the provocation, and as in the day of temptation in the wilderness: When your fathers tempted me, proved me, and saw my work. Forty years long was I grieved with this generation, and said, It is a people that do err in their heart, and they have not known my ways: Unto whom I sware in my wrath that they should not enter into my rest." (Ps. 95:3-11.) It is of this same period of Israelitish rebellion and unbelief that our latter-day revelation says: "The Lord in his wrath, for his anger was kindled against them, swore that they should not enter into his rest while in the wilderness, which rest is the fulness of his glory." (D&C 84:24.)

We now turn to the use Paul made of these words from

the 95th Psalm, which he says were given to David by the Holy Ghost. Addressing himself to those who hold the holy priesthood, Paul says: "Brethren, . . . consider the Apostle and High Priest of our profession, Christ Jesus," who "was counted worthy of more glory than Moses." Why? Because he as God built the house in which Moses served. Moses was a faithful servant who bare testimony of Christ who should come, which Christ, Paul says, is the one who sware in his wrath that ancient Israel should not enter his rest because of unbelief. With this example of what happens to those who reject their Lord, as many in ancient Israel did, Paul exhorts the Hebrew saints of his day to be faithful lest they too fail, as did some of their fathers, to gain the promised blessings. "Let us therefore fear, lest, a promise being left us of entering into his rest, any of you should seem to come short of it. For unto us [the saints in Paul's day] was the gospel preached, as well as unto them [those in ancient Israel]: but the word preached did not profit them, not being mixed with faith in them that heard it. . . . There remaineth therefore a rest to the people of God." (Heb. 3 and 4.)

O that all men might come unto Christ and gain that rest and peace, both now and forever, that comes from him and him only!

Beware of False Gods

The worship of false gods and the following of false Christs lie at the root of all the ills and all the evils of all the world. There is no salvation in worshiping a false god, and a false Christ will never lift the burden of sin from fallen man nor lead him into realms of joy and light. Man was not created by idols of stone; he was not redeemed by the forces of nature; he will not come forth from the grave at the call of Baal; and an incomprehensible nothingness did not make ready a place for him in the mansions that are prepared. False gods have no power to create or redeem or enlighten or save or do any of the things which further the interests of

320

men either in this world or in the world to come. And men must either worship the true God and follow the true Christ, or they shall with the wicked lift up their eyes in hell, being in torment.

That almost all men have and do worship false gods and follow false Christs is the saddest fact of all history. The divine decree is: "Thou shalt worship the Lord thy God, and him only shalt thou serve." (Luke 4:8.) But to name nations and peoples, with isolated exceptions, is to list those who have not had the true order and system of worship while in this life.

Few things are more offensive to the modern mind than to view the worship of past peoples. We have a justified feeling of revulsion toward Molech of the Ammonites and Chemosh of the Moabites, both hideous idols in whose worship children were sacrificed by fire; and yet Solomon himself, in his declining and apostate years, built places of worship for these and other gods of abomination on the Mount of Olives beside the Holy City. We shudder and stare in unbelief at the lascivious practices and child sacrifice, all in the name of religion, that were involved in the worship of Baal of the Canaanites; and yet this abomination of the heathens was the god of Ahab and Jezebel, and it took a confrontation on Mount Carmel, in which fire came down from heaven, for Elijah to dramatize before Israel that Jehovah and not Baal was the God of power. We find it difficult to believe that the Babylonians worshiped Bel, and yet their sincerity and devotion was such that they cast Shadrach, Meshach, and Abednego into the fiery furnace when these devout Hebrews refused to bow before his image. Nor can we look with any favor on the intellect that would worship Diana; and yet her temple at Ephesus was one of the seven wonders of the world. Athena, whose image was in the Greek Parthenon on the acropolis at Athens, and to whom Paul referred when he said, "God that made the world and all things therein, seeing that he is Lord of heaven and earth, dwelleth not in temples made with hands" (Acts 17:24), is in a like category.

Nor has the picture of false worship changed among the seemingly and supposedly more civilized peoples of the world. Rome accepted and honored all the gods of all the nations conquered by her sword, and for that matter deified some of her emperors. Buddha, symbolized by an obese idol, is worshiped in central and eastern Asia. Allah is the Supreme Being of the Mohammedans, and their scripture, the Koran, in its most meaningful and pointed passages denies the divinity of Christ and ridicules the concept that God had need of a Son. There are those today who suppose that the forces of nature or the laws of the universe, however they came to be, are the only god or gods.

There are others whose political and social philosophies supplant religious feelings. Communism is a way of life that becomes a religion in the hearts of those who espouse it to the full. If the creeds of Christendom may be believed—and they cannot be by anyone whose mind has been touched by sense and logic—the Christian God is incomprehensible, unknowable, and uncreated; he is a spirit essence that fills immensity and is everywhere and nowhere in particular present; he is incorporeal and has neither body, parts, nor passions; and in some mystical way he is three gods and yet one god.

Knowing the proclivity of wayward men to forsake the living God and go after gods of wood and stone and gold; knowing their tendency to revere the forces of nature, to worship mystical spirits and powers, to center their hearts on false philosophies; and knowing also that blessings here and hereafter flow from true worship only—is it any wonder that the Eternal Jehovah commanded his people Israel: "I am the Lord thy God. . . . Thou shalt have no other gods before me. Thou shalt not make unto thee any graven image, or any likeness of any thing that is in heaven above, or that is in the earth beneath, or that is in the water under the earth: Thou shalt not bow down thyself to them, nor serve them." (Ex. 20:2-5.) Is it any wonder that he forewarned them of false teachers who would come among them, saying, "Let us go after other gods, which thou hast not known, and let us serve them." In all such eventualities the decree of Jehovah was: "Thou shalt not hearken" unto any such, "for the Lord your God proveth you, to know whether ye love the Lord your God with all your heart and with all your soul. Ye shall walk after the Lord your God, and fear him, and keep his commandments, and obey his voice, and ye shall serve him, and cleave unto him." (Deut. 13:1-4.)

Beware of False Christs

Just as men have and do worship false gods, so they have and do follow false Christs. As Jesus and his disciples sat upon the Mount of Olives, our Lord told them that false prophets and false Christs would come in their day and again in the last days before his Second Coming. As to the day then involved, he said: "Many shall come in my name, saying—I am Christ—and shall deceive many. . . . And many false prophets shall arise, and shall deceive many." As to our day, the latter days, our Lord said: "In those days there shall also arise false Christs, and false prophets, and shall show great signs and wonders, insomuch, that, if possible, they shall deceive the very elect, who are the elect according to the covenant." (JS-H 1-22.)

In practical effect it is the same whether we are dealing with false gods (and their priests) who may lead ancient Israel away from the worship of the true Jehovah, or false Christs (and false teachers) who may lead us away from true religion. Since the Nephites used the name Christ with reference to Jehovah, we find Book of Mormon prophets inveighing against false Christs and false prophets. (W. of M. 15-16.) Korihor, for one, to whom the devil appeared as an angel of light, was anti-Christ. (Alma 30.) In one period of Nephite history, the record says: "There was another church which denied the Christ; and they did persecute the true church of Christ." (4 Ne. 29.) The saints in New Testament times faced the same problem. "Many false prophets are gone out into the world," John wrote, for "every spirit that confesseth not that Jesus Christ is come in the flesh is not of God: and this is that spirit of antichrist, whereof ye have heard that it should come; and even now already is it in the world." (1 Jn. 4:1-3.) "He is antichrist, that denieth the Father and the Son." (1 Jn. 2:22.)

It is not difficult to envision that there will be false prophets and false teachers in the last days. But what of the promise that there will be false Christs? In our age of enlightenment and sophistication, as we suppose, is it to be assumed that there will be those come who will profess to be Christ? As a prelude to finding answer to these questions, let us note these words of Jesus, spoken along with the others on the Mount of Olives: "If they shall say unto you: Behold, he is in the desert; go not forth; Behold, he is in the secret chambers; believe it not; For as the light of the morning cometh out of the east, and shineth even unto the west, and covereth the whole earth, so shall also the coming of the Son of Man be." (JS-H 25-26.)

There are, of course, those deluded souls who announce, from time to time, that they are Christ or God or the Holy Ghost, or one mighty and strong, or whatever Satan or the workings of a deranged mind places in their thoughts. But in a larger and more realistic sense, false Christs are false systems of religion that use his name and profess to present his teachings to the world. The cries, "Lo, here," and "Lo, there," which went forth in Joseph Smith's day, when "some were contending for the Methodist faith, some for the Presbyterian, and some for the Baptist" (JS-H 5), meant that each group of gospel expounders was saying, "Lo, here is Christ; we have his system of salvation; ours is the true church; we know the way; come, join with us."

Beware of false gods. The Lord is God and beside him there is no other. He alone is Creator, Redeemer, and Savior. Gods of wood and stone, or of spirit nothingness, or whatever, have no saving power.

Beware also of false Christs. There is one Christ, and he

is God and has but one true system of salvation. He is not found in a desert retreat of a monastic order. His doctrine is not hidden in secret chambers to be withheld from all those who are without. The great restoration of all things has begun, and like the light of the rising sun, it shall spread over all the earth until the darkness of Babylon shall be no more, and the Son of Man shall come to be seen and admired by those who wait for him.

"Salvation Is Free"

Come unto Christ; come unto Jehovah; salvation is free! The way is prepared from the foundation of the world, and all who will may walk therein and be saved. "Ho, every one that thirsteth, come ye to the waters," saith Jehovah, "and he that hath no money; come ye, buy, and eat; yea, come ye, buy wine and milk without money and without price. . . . Hearken diligently unto me, and eat ye that which is good, and let your soul delight itself in fatness." (Isa. 55:1-2.)

"The Spirit is the same yesterday, today, and forever"— in the day of Jehovah, in the day of Christ, in all days, both now and forever. "And the way is prepared from the fall of man, and salvation is free." (2 Ne. 2:4.)

"Hath he commanded any that they should not partake of his salvation?" Nephi asks. "Behold I say unto you, Nay," he replies, "but he hath given it free for all men; and he hath commanded his people that they should persuade all men to repentance. Behold, hath the Lord commanded any that they should not partake of his goodness? Behold I say unto you, Nay; but all men are privileged the one like unto the other, and none are forbidden. . . . And he inviteth them all to come unto him and partake of his goodness; and he denieth none that come unto him, black and white, bond and free, male and female; and he remembereth the heathen; and all are alike unto God, both Jew and Gentile." (2 Ne. 26:27-28, 33.)

325

Chapter 19

MESSIAH—OUR ADVOCATE, INTERCESSOR, AND MEDIATOR

What Is the Law of Intercession?

We have heretofore seen that the Almighty God sent his Only Begotten Son into the world to work out the infinite and eternal atonement; that through this supreme sacrifice all men are ransomed from their temporal fall in that they shall be resurrected; and that those who believe and obey are ransomed from their spiritual fall in that they shall come forth, not only in immortality, but shall be raised unto eternal life. We have seen that mercy comes because of the atonement and is the gift of God to the penitent; that mercy is the gracious inheritance of those whose sins are borne by their loving Lord; and that it is through repentance and righteousness that men are freed from the grasp of that justice which otherwise would impose upon them the full penalty for their sins. (Chapter 14.) We are aware that intercession is made for the saints by their Friend and Advocate, the Lord Jesus. Now it is our purpose to inquire more particularly into the nature of that intercession and to catch the vision of the great Messianic utterances which have taken it as their theme.

As we take up this portion of our inquiry into the Messianic status of him who was both Jehovah and Jesus, we must first ask: What are the laws of intercession, of advocacy, and of mediation? Why must someone intercede on our behalf? What need is there for a Mediator? How do the divine laws operate with respect to these matters?

By way of answer we might raise such queries as these: Did man create himself? Did he cause to come into being the earth and all that thereon is? Is he the author of the plan of salvation? Can he choose to live or die at will? Is annihilation of the soul within his power? Can he resurrect himself? Or crown himself with eternal glory?

Whether we like it or not, whether we are pleased or displeased with the eternal realities involved, the fact is we are not creatures of our own creating. We are not masters of our fate. Within the limits assigned to us, we can live and move and have our being. We can eat and drink and breathe and sleep and think. We can use our agency within the sphere of our assignment. But we cannot waft ourselves from orb to orb or choose the planet upon which to plant our feet. We are subject to law, law ordained by Him who created us and to whom we are and were and everlastingly shall be in subjection.

And the eternal realities—which can be known only by revelation—are these: There is a God who is our Father. He is a glorified, perfected Man of Holiness with a body of flesh and bones as tangible as man's. He begat us as spirits, and we were born in his courts. He ordained the laws, and he prepared the plan whereby we might advance and progress and become like him.

To become like him, we needed tangible bodies, bodies which were first mortal and then immortal. To become like him, we needed the probationary experiences of earth life, experiences we could gain in no other way. To become like him, we needed to taste the bitter that we might know the sweet; we needed to be subject to sin and death and to gain the victory over them both. Such was his plan.

Accordingly, he placed the spirit Michael and his chosen consort in the Garden of Eden and gave them immortal bodies made from the dust of the earth. Known then as Adam and Eve, our first parents then dwelt in a state of innocence, "having no joy, for they knew no misery; doing no good, for they knew no sin." (2 Ne. 2:23.) Agreeable to the divine will, these first members of the human family chose to fall from their paradisiacal state and to bring mortality, disease, death, sin, and sorrow into the world. They chose to estrange themselves from God; they elected to depart from the divine presence; they sought the toils and trials and tests of mortality—all with a purpose—all to see if they could overcome the world and prove worthy of eternal blessings. They were cast out of the presence of God; they died spiritually; they lost the light which had guided them in Eden—all to enable them to be tried and tested to the full. Such was the divine plan.

The divine plan also called for a Savior, a Chosen Vessel: One endowed by the Father with the power of immortality; One who could thereby gain the victory over the grave and restore fallen mortals to their immortal state; One who could restore them to their sinless state, if they would cleanse themselves in the way he provided. That way was to be in and through his atoning sacrifice and by obedience to the laws and ordinances of his gospel.

All of this is the foundation for the doctrine of advocacy, of intercession, and of mediation. To be saved man must be reconciled with God. He must rise above the natural man and become a saint. He must be freed from the chains of sin. He must return again in harmony, love, and peace to the eternal family circle. The blessings of Eden—and more, yea, infinitely more—must be his again.

But how can it be? Who will ransom and atone? Who will pay the penalty for man's sins? Who will satisfy the demands of divine justice? Who will intercede for fallen man before the Father's throne? Who will advocate his cause in the courts above? Who will mediate the differences between him and his Maker, so that once again he can have peace and harmony with his God? Verily, it is Christ. He is our Advocate, Intercessor, Mediator. Such is the rationale underlying the laws of intercession, of advocacy, and of mediation. Such is the divine plan.

Messiah Maketh Intercession

Addressing himself to the Father, Zenos said: "Thou hast turned away thy judgments because of thy Son." Zenock prayed similarly: "Thou art angry, O Lord, with this people, because they will not understand thy mercies which thou hast bestowed upon them because of thy Son." (Alma 33:13, 16.) Why is it that judgments are withheld and mercies are poured out—because of the Son? The answer is clear: He intercedes on man's behalf, advocating his cause in the courts above. "He . . . made intercession for the transgressors." (Isa. 53:12.) In the atonement that he wrought, he paid the penalty for the sins of men, on conditions of repentance, so that all might escape the judgments decreed for disobedience. In the same way and for the same reason, mercy replaces the justice that otherwise would impose the decreed judgments. Such is the law of intercession, a law that is valid and operative because of the atonement.

As taught by Lehi, this law is that "the Holy Messiah . . . shall make intercession for all the children of men; and they that believe in him shall be saved. And because of the intercession for all, all men come unto God" (2 Ne. 2:8-10), meaning they come unto God and are reconciled to their Maker if they believe and obey.

As taught by Abinadi this law is that God gave "the Son power to make intercession for the children of men," and that he thereby "redeemed them, and satisfied the demands of justice." (Mosiah 15:8-9.) Those, on the other hand, for whom no intercession is made are said by Abinadi to be damned—"Having gone according to their own carnal wills and desires; having never called upon the Lord while the arms of mercy were extended towards them; for the arms of mercy were extended towards them, and they would not;

they being warned of their iniquities and yet they would not depart from them; and they were commanded to repent and yet they would not repent." (Mosiah 16:12.)

As taught by Paul, the pleasing reality is that Christ "is able to save them to the uttermost that come unto God by him, seeing he ever liveth to make intercession for them." (Heb. 7:25.) Mormon expressed it this way: "He advocateth the cause of the children of men; and he dwelleth eternally in the heavens." (Moro. 7:28.)

But the most perfect summary of this law found anywhere in Holy Writ is given to us in these words of latter-day revelation: "Listen to him who is the advocate with the Father, who is pleading your cause before him—Saying: Father, behold the sufferings and death of him who did no sin, in whom thou wast well pleased; behold the blood of thy Son which was shed, the blood of him whom thou gavest that thyself might be glorified; Wherefore, Father, spare these my brethren that believe on my name, that they may come unto me and have everlasting life." (D&C 45:3-5; 110:4.)

Jehovah Maketh Intercession

It is Jehovah—the promised Messiah!—who makes intercession for his people. From the foundations of the world, in anticipation of the atonement he would make in Gethsemane's gloomy garden, the Great Jehovah pled the cause of righteous men before the fiery throne of his Father.

Men in Noah's day rebelled, rejected the Lord and his gospel, and were buried in a watery grave. Their spirits then found themselves in that prison prepared for those who walk in darkness when light is before them. Are they lost forever? Who will plead their cause?

To Enoch, concerning them, came these words of the Father: "And That which I have chosen hath plead before my face. Wherefore, he suffereth for their sins; inasmuch as they will repent in the day that my Chosen shall return unto me, and until that day they shall be in torment." (Moses 7:39.)

Ancient Israel rebelled, rejected the Lord and his prophets, and were scattered to the ends of the earth. From then until now, they and their seed have been far removed from the wonders and miracles and truth that blessed their fathers. But are they lost forever, and who will plead their cause?

Through Isaiah, in a marvelous and moving passage, Jehovah calls to the scattered remnants of his ancient people. "Look unto the rock from whence ye are hewn," he pleads. Return unto me, "For the Lord shall comfort Zion. . . . He will make her wilderness like Eden, and her desert like the garden of the Lord. . . . Hearken unto me, my people; and give ear unto me, O my nation: for a law shall proceed from me, and I will make my judgment to rest for a light of the people." That is to say, 'The fulness of my everlasting gospel shall be restored, and it shall be as it was in days of old.' Those who believe and obey shall be blessed. And then "the redeemed of the Lord shall return, and come with singing unto Zion; and everlasting joy shall be upon their head." And how shall all this be? The answer: "Thus saith thy Lord the Lord, and thy God"—Jehovah!—"that pleadeth the cause of his people, Behold, I have taken out of thine hand the cup of trembling, even the dregs of the cup of my fury; thou shalt no more drink it." (Isa. 51.)

This same offer of forgiveness, of joy and comfort, and of salvation for gathered Israel is held out to them in the great Messianic prophecy which includes the declaration: "Comfort ye, comfort ye my people, saith your God. Speak ye comfortably to Jerusalem, and cry unto her, that her warfare is accomplished, that her iniquity is pardoned." (Isa. 40:1-2.) In another wondrous and scarcely known passage, Jehovah tells of his power to save, of Israel's apostasy, of the need for an intercessor, and of how he put on the breastplate of righteousness and the helmet of salvation in the warfare that finally turned transgression from Jacob and brought

331

them again into his everlasting covenant. (Isa. 59.) Truly, when his people repent and return unto him, the importunings of the Great Jehovah are heeded by his Father and our Father and by his God and our God.

Christ-Jehovah Forgives Sins

Both Jehovah and Jesus forgive sins; or rather, Jehovah who is Jesus forgives sins; or even more particularly, sins are forgiven by the Lord, who is Jehovah, at all times, and they were forgiven by that same Lord, who is Jesus, during his mortal ministry, and at such times and among such peoples as he, Jehovah, was known and revered by the more familiar name, Jesus.

Anciently, in Palestine, Israel had failed to perform the sacrificial ordinances to Jehovah, by which forgiveness of sins came to them. "Thou has not . . . honoured me with thy sacrifices," the Lord said, "but thou hast made me to serve with thy sins, thou hast wearied me with thine iniquities." Israel had not made use of the saving processes whereby the Lord's people become clean and spotless before him. And so he issued anew the great proclamation: "I, even I, am he that blotteth out thy transgressions for mine own sake, and will not remember thy sins." 'I, Jehovah, am he who doeth it.' Therefore, "Put me in rememberance." 'Return to me; keep my law; forgiveness and salvation are available to you through me; I am your Intercessor with the Father.' "Let us plead together." That is, 'I, Jehovah, will join with you in a plea for forgiveness from our Father, if you will keep my commandments.' (Isa. 43:22-28.)

Glorious doctrine this—Jehovah pleads for his people. He is their Intercessor. He it is who forgives sins through his atoning sacrifice. "I have blotted out, as a thick cloud, thy transgressions, and, as a cloud, thy sins: return unto me; for I have redeemed thee. Sing, O ye heavens; for the Lord hath done it: shout, ye lower parts of the earth: break forth into singing, ye mountains, O forest, and every tree therein: for the Lord hath redeemed Jacob, and glorified himself in Israel." (Isa. 44:22-23.)

This matter of turning to Jehovah so that sins might be blotted out, so that the Lord's people might become spotless and clean before him, was in full operation on the American continent also, except that the name of Jehovah in common usage was Christ. "Concerning the coming of Christ," Alma said, "it is he that surely shall come to take away the sins of the world." (Alma 39:15.) His own proclamation, made to the Nephites after his resurrection, confirmed the prophetic promises. "I . . . have glorified the Father in taking upon me the sins of the world, in the which I have suffered the will of the Father in all things from the beginning," he said. (3 Ne. 11:11.)

One of the sweetest and most refreshing stories of repentance and conversion, of forgiveness and salvation, of turning to that Jesus who blots out sins, is that of Alma the younger. The time was about one hundred years before our Lord's birth among mortals. This American Paul, along with the equally rebellious sons of Mosiah, had been going about destroying the Church of God. An angelic visitant, exhibiting the power of God so that the earth shook, called him to repentance. For the space of three days and three nights, the future witness of the name of Christ lay unconscious to his mortal surroundings, while he suffered the agonies of the damned and was then blessed with marvelous spiritual manifestations. Here are his words, written in sweet sublimity and with convincing power:

"I was racked with eternal torment, for my soul was harrowed up to the greatest degree and racked with all my sins. Yea, I did remember all my sins and iniquities, for which I was tormented with the pains of hell; yea, I saw that I had rebelled against my God, and that I had not kept his holy commandments. Yea, and I had murdered many of his children, or rather led them away into destruction; yea, and in fine so great had been my iniquities, that the very thought of coming into the presence of my God did rack my soul

333

with inexpressible horror. Oh, thought I, that I could be banished and become extinct both soul and body, that I might not be brought to stand in the presence of my God, to be judged of my deeds.

"And now, for three days and for three nights was I racked, even with the pains of a damned soul. And it came to pass that as I was thus racked with torment, while I was harrowed up by the memory of my many sins, behold, I remembered also to have heard my father prophesy unto the people concerning the coming of one Jesus Christ, a Son of God, to atone for the sins of the world. Now, as my mind caught hold upon this thought, I cried within my heart: O Jesus, thou Son of God, have mercy on me, who am in the gall of bitterness, and am encircled about by the everlasting chains of death. And now, behold, when I thought this, I could remember my pains no more; yea, I was harrowed up by the memory of my sins no more.

"And oh, what joy, and what marvelous light I did behold; yea, my soul was filled with joy as exceeding as was my pain! Yea, I say unto you, my son, that there could be nothing so exquisite and so bitter as were my pains. Yea, and again I say unto you, my son, that on the other hand, there can be nothing so exquisite and sweet as was my joy. Yea, methought I saw, even as our father Lehi saw, God sitting upon his throne, surrounded with numberless concourses of angels, in the attitude of singing and praising their God; yea, and my soul did long to be there. But behold, my limbs did receive their strength again, and I stood upon my feet, and did manifest unto the people that I had been born of God." (Alma 36:12-23; 38:8.)

This same power, vested in Jehovah and seen by Alma to reside in the yet unborn Jesus, was also exercised by our Lord as he dwelt among men. For instance, in Capernaum, his own city, probably in the home of Peter, our Lord taught a multitude through whom it was not possible to make a path because of their number and the crowded circumstances. Four men came bearing on a couch one sick of the palsy—a paralytic—whom they lowered down through the roof. Jesus said: "Son, be of good cheer; thy sins be forgiven thee." The scribes and Pharisees reasoned on the point, saying, "Who can forgive sins, but God alone?" Jesus, perceiving their reaction to his assumption of divine powers and with the clear intent of proving that he was that Jehovah who forgave sins, said: "Whether is easier, to say, Thy sins be forgiven thee; or to say, Rise up and walk? But that ye may know that the Son of man hath power upon earth to forgive sins, (he said unto the sick of the palsy,) I say unto thee, Arise, and take up thy couch, and go into thine house. And immediately he rose up before them, and took up that whereon he lay, and departed to his own house, glorifying God." (Matt. 9:1-8; Mark 2:1-12; Luke 5:18-26.)

Sing Praises to Jehovah

As is clear from the whole body of revealed writ, the eternal decree of the Eternal God is that men should worship the Father, in the name of the Son, by the power of the Holy Ghost. As it is written: "All the holy prophets . . . believed in Christ and worshiped the Father in his name." (Jacob 4:4-5.)

There is nothing clearer or plainer than this. We pray to the Father, not the Son; but according to the laws of intercession, advocacy, and mediation, our answers come from the Son. Reference to nearly every section in the Doctrine and Covenants bears this out. None, therefore, need to suppose, as is found in the prayer books of sectarianism, that it is proper to pray to either Christ or the Holy Ghost.

However, righteous persons do have a close, personal relationship with their Savior. It is through him that forgiveness comes. Because of his atonement we may be free from sin. Salvation is in Christ. He pleads our cause. He is our Mediator and Intercessor. And we do and should sing praises to his holy name, as do the angels of God in heaven also. Among their hymns of praise are such wondrous words as these: "Worthy is the Lamb that was slain to receive power, and riches, and wisdom, and strength, and honour, and glory, and blessing. . . . Blessing, and honour, and glory, and power, be unto him that sitteth upon the throne, and unto the Lamb for ever and ever." (Rev. 5:9-13.)

There is no language of worship and adoration that surpasses the language of prayer. What is more natural than to use the noblest and most perfect expressions utterable by mortal tongues in addressing Him who sits upon the great white throne? It is no wonder, then, that in praising the Lord Jehovah we often do so as though we were addressing him in prayer, even as though we were pleading with him for eternal blessings.

We have already seen that Alma, in wonder and amazement at the forgiving grace poured out upon him, addressed Jesus in words of praise and thanksgiving. The Old Testament prophets followed a similar course. Having the same understanding prevalent among the Nephites, they sought to extol and magnify that name by which these incalculably great blessings come. The words of the Psalmists, because they were writing hymns of praise, show forth the most numerous examples of this type of divine salutation. One Psalmic utterance says of "the Holy One of Israel," who of course is Jehovah, that "he, being full of compassion, forgave their iniquity, and destroyed them not" (Ps. 78:38-41), which by itself is simply a doctrinal and historical statement. But another Psalmic declaration, dwelling on the same concept, could be interpreted, if we did not know better, as a prayer to Jehovah in these words: "O remember not against us former iniquities: let thy tender mercies speedily prevent us: for we are brought very low. Help us, O God of our salvation, for the glory of thy name: and deliver us, and purge away our sins, for thy name's sake." (Ps. 79:8-9.) The 86th Psalm, though in the language of prayer, is in reality a hymn of praise: "I will praise thee, O Lord my God, with all my heart: and I will glorify thy name for evermore." (Verse 12.) Psalms of praise, in language akin to that of prayer, and

336

dealing with the mercy of the Great Jehovah, are also found in such references as Psalm 89:1-2, 14; 103:11-22; 136:1-26; and 145:8-9.

For that matter, we even have in the Doctrine and Covenants, in a revealed prayer addressed to the "Father, in the name of Jesus Christ," such expressions as, "O Jehovah, have mercy upon this people, and as all men sin forgive the transgressions of thy people, and let them be blotted out forever" (D&C 109:4, 34)—all of which simply means that we pray to the Father, and because our answers come from Jehovah, we sometimes give forth accolades of praise to him, in the language of prayer, which those untutored in the things of the Spirit might mistakenly interpret to be prayers to the Son and not the Father.

How to Gain Forgiveness

The Messiah came to "bare the sin of many" (Isa 53:12); to suffer "the pain of all men . . . on conditions of repentance" (D&C 18:11-12); to redeem those who believe and obey; to give mercy to the repentant and justice to the unrepentant. The great problem facing all of us is how to gain a forgiveness of sins; it is how to be numbered with those whose sins are born by the Lord; it is how to become clean and spotless so we can go where God and Christ are and enjoy the fulness of light and glory in their presence.

Forgiveness is available because of the atoning sacrifice of the Great Jehovah. Forgiveness is available because Christ the Lord sweat great drops of blood in Gethsemane as he bore the incalculable weight of the sins of all who ever had or ever would repent. Forgiveness is available because "God suffereth according to the flesh that he might take upon him the sins of his people, that he might blot out their transgressions according to the power of his deliverance." (Alma 7:13.) Forgiveness comes because of the effectual and fervent pleadings of Him who is our Intercessor and Advocate. Forgiveness precedes salvation, and salvation comes after men are freed from their sins. Thus forgiveness is in Christ, even as salvation is in Christ. But he has done his work. The atonement is an accomplished fact. It is inscribed forever in the eternal records; it is written for all to read in the wracked body and the spilt blood of the one perfect man who bowed in agony, alone, in a garden outside Jerusalem's walls. The issue now is, What must each of us do to come within the pale of saving grace and thus gain forgiveness of our sins?

The divine formula is an easy one; the way and the path provided is clearly marked; none need stumble or be diverted onto bye and forbidden paths. The way to gain forgiveness is as follows:

1. *Come to a knowledge of the truth.*

In plain, simple language, as pertaining to all men now living, this means to accept the gospel as restored by Joseph Smith and to join The Church of Jesus Christ of Latter-day Saints. As it was in Paul's day, so it is today, there is "one Lord, one faith, one baptism, One God and Father of all." (Eph. 4:5-6.) Truth is not a conflicting mass of confusion; it is not divergent views that are diametrically opposed to each other; it is not the vagaries and nonsense of sectarianism. Truth is the everlasting gospel restored anew in our day. It is things as they are, and as they were, and as they shall be.

There is neither forgiveness nor salvation in worshiping false gods or following false systems of religion. However much some people may think that cows or crocodiles are god, neither the four-legged bovine nor the big lizard in the dismal swamp has power to forgive, or to resurrect, or to save. And as with cows and crocodiles, so with the spirit nothingness to which professors of religion ascribe the attributes of Deity. As Alma said, Ye must "worship the true and the living God," and through that worship "look forward for the remission of your sins, with an everlasting faith." (Alma 7:6.)

2. *Believe in the Lord Jesus Christ.*

Forgiveness of sins comes only to those who believe in

338

Christ. It never has, does not now, and never will come to anyone else. It is Christ "that cometh to take away the sins of the world, yea, the sins of every man who steadfastly believeth on his name." (Alma 5:48.) "Believe on the Lord Jesus Christ, and thou shalt be saved." (Acts 16:31.) That is, 'Believe on him and thou shalt be forgiven of thy sins, and being thus free from sin, salvation shall be thy natural inheritance.' To believe in Christ is to accept his gospel; it is to accept the prophets and apostles whom he has sent to reveal him to the world; in our day it is to accept without reservation the divine mission of the Prophet Joseph Smith and those who have since worn his prophetic mantle. To believe in Christ is to accept him as the promised Messiah, to worship him as the Great Jehovah, to know that he is the Son of God. Jesus said: "If ye believe not that I am he"—the Messiah, the Son of God—"ye shall die in your sins." (John 8:24.)

3. *Keep the commandments.*

Having chosen to worship the true and living God, him by whom all things are and who is our Eternal Father; having elected to believe in his Son, through whose atoning sacrifice salvation comes, there remains but one requisite to gain forgiveness, and it is: *to keep the commandments.*

What commandments? They are many, and they may be stated in many ways. In one manner of speaking they are all embraced within the divine decrees: (1) "Thou shalt love the Lord thy God with all thy heart, with all thy might, mind, and strength; and in the name of Jesus Christ thou shalt serve him," and (2) "Thou shalt love thy neighbor as thyself." (D&C 59:5-6.) "On these two commandments hang all the law and the prophets." (Matt. 22:40.)

But embraced within the plan of worship and service thus decreed are many things. All men everywhere are commanded to repent and believe the gospel and to be baptized in the name of Jesus Christ for the remission of their sins. (D&C 33:9-11.) "Now this is the commandment," so the risen Lord announced to the Nephites; "Repent, all ye ends

339

of the earth, and come unto me and be baptized in my name, that ye may be sanctified by the reception of the Holy Ghost, that ye may stand spotless before me at the last day." (3 Ne. 27:20.) "Yea, blessed are they who shall believe in your words," that same Lord said to his Nephite apostles, "and come down into the depths of humility and be baptized, for they shall be visited with fire and with the Holy Ghost, and shall receive a remission of their sins." (3 Ne. 12:2.) Baptism for the remission of sins is a commandment! Those who do not repent and are not baptized thereby break the commandment of God, and for this disobedience they shall be damned. (3 Ne. 11:34.)

But baptism alone, baptism without more, baptism without subsequent obedience to all of the laws and ordinances of the gospel—that is, the mere rite of being authoritatively immersed in water—does not of itself save a soul. From the lips of the Lord Jesus we quote: "And no unclean thing can enter into his kingdom; therefore nothing entereth into his rest save it be those who have washed their garments in my blood, because of their faith, and the repentance of all their sins, and their faithfulness unto the end." (3 Ne. 27:19.) Obedience follows baptism. For those who have entered in at the gate of repentance and baptism, the command is: "Ye must press forward with a steadfastness in Christ, having a perfect brightness of hope, and a love of God and of all men. Wherefore, if ye shall press forward, feasting upon the word of Christ, and endure to the end, behold, thus saith the Father: Ye shall have eternal life." (2 Ne. 31:20.)

All of the saints are tried and tested after baptism. All commit sins. All must renew the covenant of obedience made in the waters of baptism. (Mosiah 18:8-14.) All must gain anew, time and time again, the assurance "that they may always have his Spirit to be with them." (D&C 20:77.) This occurs when the faithful partake worthily of the sacrament.

The first Alma, the one who baptized at the waters of Mormon, received a revelation that perfectly sets forth the law of forgiveness as it pertains both to those in and out of the Church. The occasion was one in which many Nephites were rebelling and refusing to believe in Christ and become members of the true church. These unbelievers persuaded many members of the Church to walk in the ways of wickedness and to commit grievous sins. Alma was the president of the Church, and he pleaded with the Lord for guidance as to what action should be taken against the erring saints. In answer the Lord set forth his law of forgiveness as it applies to member and nonmember alike.

"Whoso is baptized shall be baptized unto repentance," came the voice from heaven. "And whomsoever ye receive shall believe in my name; and him will I freely forgive. For it is I that taketh upon me the sins of the world." Such is the law as pertaining to nonmembers, with the added proviso, "that he that will not hear my voice, the same shall ye not receive into my church, for him I will not receive at the last day."

As to erring members of the Church, the Lord Jesus, more than a hundred years before his mortal birth, gave this direction: "Whosoever transgresseth against me, him shall ye judge according to the sins which he has committed; and if he confess his sins before thee and me, and repenteth in the sincerity of his heart, him shall ye forgive, and I will forgive him also. Yea, and as often as my people repent will I forgive them their trespasses against me. . . . And whosoever will not repent of his sins the same shall not be numbered among my people." (Mosiah 26:1-32.)

David, a member of the Church, sets forth in the 25th Psalm a classical plea for personal forgiveness. Daniel, also a member of the Church, speaking for all Israel, whose hosts constituted the Church in that day, preserves for us in the ninth chapter of his writings the classical pleas to the Lord for forgiveness for a whole people. These two Old Testament passages speak of mercy, of pardoning iniquity, of prayer, supplication, fasting, repenting in sackcloth and ashes, and of keeping the commandments. I have collated and analyzed the details of the law of forgiveness for members of the Church in *Mormon Doctrine,* 2nd ed., pages 292-98. For our purposes here, as part of this Messianic study, it suffices for us to know that belief in Christ is the sure foundation upon which the house of salvation is built; that those who believe—who believe in Spirit and in truth!—immediately, automatically, in the very nature of things, begin to build the walls, the roof, and all the parts of the house of their salvation.

"I do know that Christ shall come among the children of men," Amulek said, "to take upon him the transgressions of his people, and that he shall atone for the sins of the world." It is our Lord's divine Sonship, his status as God's Son; it is his atoning sacrifice; it is the burden he bore in Gethsemane; it is his death upon the cross; it is the fact that he voluntarily laid down his life that he might take it again—these are the things that enabled him to take upon himself the transgressions of his people. These are the things that enabled him to bear the sins of repentant persons. These are the things that enable men to gain a forgiveness of sins. Without the atonement, "all mankind must unavoidably perish."

"Thus"—that is, in the light of all these things—as Amulek taught, "he shall bring salvation to all those who shall believe on his name." Through his atonement, mercy overpowers justice so that men "may have faith unto repentance." That is to say, forgiveness comes to those who forsake their sins. Forgiveness and consequent salvation are for those only who have faith unto repentance. They alone gain mercy rather than justice. "And thus mercy can satisfy the demands of justice, and encircles them in the arms of safety, while he that exercises no faith unto repentance is exposed to the whole law of the demands of justice; therefore only unto him that has faith unto repentance is brought about the great and eternal plan of redemption." (Alma 34:8-16.)

To those who have made covenant in the waters of baptism to forsake the world and serve the Lord, and who have fallen short of the mark, his call is: "Seek ye the Lord while he may be found, call ye upon him while he is near: Let the wicked forsake his way, and the unrighteous man his thoughts: and let him return unto the Lord, and he will have mercy upon him; and to our God, for he will abundantly pardon." (Isa. 55:6-7.)

Christ Justifies the Righteous

Mediation is akin to and not divisible from intercession and advocacy. Christ the Lord is our Mediator, even as he is our Advocate and our Intercessor. In prophesying that the Messiah would come, Lehi said to his sons: "I would that ye should look to the great Mediator, and hearken unto his great commandments; and be faithful unto his words, and choose eternal life, according to the will of his Holy Spirit." (2 Ne. 2:28.) We shall hereafter consider, in Chapter 24, our Lord's status as the great Mediator, the Mediator of the new covenant, when we set forth how Moses, the mediator of the old covenant, was a prototype of that Lord whose witness he was.

With reference to our present analysis, that forgiveness of sins comes because of the advocacy, intercession, and mediation of the Messiah, we shall add to what we have here written only the concepts that remission of sins is reserved for those who are justified and that justification and salvation are free.

In the constitutional document of the restored Church we read: "And we know that justification through the grace of our Lord and Savior Jesus Christ is just and true." (D&C 20:30.) In summarizing the plan of salvation for Adam, the Lord said: "By the water ye keep the commandment; by the Spirit ye are justified, and by the blood ye are sanctified." (Moses 6:60.) Both Paul and James write extensively about how men are justified—by faith, by works, by the blood of Christ, by the power of the Spirit, and so forth. A large part of Paul's Epistle to the Romans deals with this subject.

What, then, is the doctrine of justification, and what are the Messianic implications? To be justified is to be made righteous and therefore to be saved. Men are justified in what they do when their deeds conform to divine standards. Righteous acts are approved of the Lord; they are ratified by the Holy Ghost; they are sealed by the Holy Spirit of Promise; or, in other words, they are justified by the Spirit. Such divine approval must be given to "all covenants, contracts, bonds, obligations, oaths, vows, performances, connections, associations, or expectations"—that is, to all things—if they are to have "efficacy, virtue, or force in and after the resurrection from the dead." (D&C 132:7.) Such a requirement is part of the terms and conditions of the gospel covenant.

It comes as no surprise, then, to read that the Messiah, as the Prototype of salvation, would be and was justified in all that he did, and that all those who believe in him must be justified, in like manner, if they are to go where he is and be like him. David speaks of Jehovah being justified (Ps. 51:4), and Paul quotes this truism with approval (Rom. 3:4). In one of Isaiah's most pointed Messianic prophecies—the one in which he has the Messiah say: "I gave my back to the smiters, and my cheeks to them that plucked off the hair: I hid not my face from shame and spitting"—he also has the Messiah say: "The Lord God will help me. . . . He is near that justifieth me." (Isa. 50:5-8.) And Paul, speaking of Jehovah, meaning Christ, says: "God was manifest in the flesh, justified in the Spirit, seen of angels, preached unto the Gentiles, believed on in the world, received up into glory." (1 Tim. 3:16.) It is thus perfectly clear that the Lord Jehovah, the Promised Messiah, and Jesus who is called Christ—all being one and the same Person—was justified, saved, and exalted, as a pattern for all those to whom he says: Follow thou me.

As Christ is not alone in baptism, nor in good works, nor in righteous deeds, nor in pursuing the course back to the presence of the Eternal Father, so he is not alone in the need to be justified. It is Jehovah who shall justify his people, as Isaiah says. "Look unto me, and be ye saved" is Jehovah's invitation to "all the ends of the earth," for he it is unto whom "every knee shall bow, every tongue shall swear." The faithful shall have "righteousness and strength" in him, "and all that are incensed against him shall be ashamed." Having thus set forth that salvation is in Christ, Isaiah proclaims: "In the Lord"—that is, in Jehovah who is the Messiah—"shall all the seed of Israel be justified, and shall glory." (Isa. 45:22-25.) Israel—the faithful!—shall be justified, which is to say, "All Israel shall be saved." (Rom. 11:26.)

All Israel shall be justified; all Israel shall be saved—meaning, all those who keep the commandments shall be saved and justified, and those so doing shall be called by the name *Israel.* As Paul expressed it: "They are not all Israel, which are of Israel: Neither, because they are the seed of Abraham, are they all children: . . . That is, They which are the children of the flesh, these are not children of God." (Rom. 9:6-8.) In the eternal sense, Israel consists of the members of the Church who keep the commandments and are thereby justified in this life and saved in the life to come. The wicked, of course, are not justified. (Alma 41:13-15.)

With the concept thus before us that Jehovah justifies the faithful, let us note this Messianic prophecy: "By his knowledge shall my righteous servant justify many; for he shall bear their iniquities." (Isa. 53:11.) Then let us note these words of Paul: "Be it known unto you therefore, men and brethren, that through this man is preached unto you the forgiveness of sins." What man? The Lord Jesus Christ. "And by him all that believe are justified from all things, from which ye could not be justified by the law of Moses." (Acts 13:38-39.) As to this matter of the law, Lehi said: "The law is given unto men. And by the law no flesh is justified; or, by the law men are cut off. Yea, by the temporal law they were cut off; and also, by the spiritual law they perish from that which is good, and become miserable forever. Wherefore, redemption cometh in and through the Holy

Messiah; for he is full of grace and truth." (2 Ne. 2:5-6.) And as to the matter of who it is that justifies the faithful, we have this revealed answer: Jehovah justifies; Messiah justifies; Christ justifies—all of which brings us again up against the stark reality that these three are one and the same Person.

Salvation and Justification Come by Grace

All that we have said about advocacy, intercession, and mediation; about the forgiveness of sins and the justification of the righteous; about the fact that it is Jehovah-Messiah-Christ who is our Advocate, Intercessor, and Mediator, the One by whose power we are forgiven, justified, and saved— all of this comes to us by the grace of God.

"Salvation is free." (2 Ne. 2:4.) Justification is free. Neither of them can be purchased; neither can be earned; neither comes by the law of Moses, or by good works, or by any power or ability that man has. Rather, the invitation of the Lord Jehovah is: "Ho, every one that thirsteth, come ye to the waters, and he that hath no money; come ye, buy, and eat; yea, come, buy wine and milk without money and without price." (Isa. 55:1.) Come and partake freely of the goodness and grace of the Lord. Come to him through whose goodness and grace all men are raised in immortality. Come to him through whose goodness and grace eternal salvation is available for all those who believe and obey. Salvation is free, freely available, freely to be found. It comes because of his goodness and grace, because of his love, mercy, and condescension toward the children of men.

When the prophets who were before Christ preached that salvation is free, they were announcing the same doctrine that would thereafter fall from apostolic lips in the pronouncement that we are saved by grace. Free salvation is salvation by grace. The questions then are: What salvation is free? What salvation comes by the grace of God? With all the emphasis of the rolling thunders of Sinai, we answer: All salvation is free; all comes by the merits and mercy and

346

grace of the Holy Messiah; there is no salvation of any kind, nature, or degree that is not bound to Christ and his atonement. Specifically, our Lord's atoning sacrifice brings all men forth in the resurrection with immortal bodies, thus freeing them from death, hell, the devil, and endless torment; and our Lord's atoning grace raises those who believe and obey, not only in immortality, but unto eternal life; it raises them to sit down with Abraham, Isaac, and Jacob in God's everlasting kingdom forever.

"How great the importance to make these things known unto the inhabitants of the earth," Lehi says, "that they may know that there is no flesh that can dwell in the presence of God, save it be through the merits, and mercy, and grace of the Holy Messiah." That is to say, 'All men must partake of that salvation which is freely available, if they are to go to the celestial kingdom; all who gain eternal life do so because of the grace of God.' Then Lehi says that by this same power Christ shall "bring to pass the resurrection of the dead," meaning that all shall come forth from the grave because of his grace, but, Lehi adds, only "they that believe in him shall be saved." (2 Ne. 2:8-9.)

"O the wisdom of God, his mercy and grace!" Jacob exults. Why? Because if there were no atonement, there would be no resurrection; and if there were no resurrection, "our spirits must become subject to that angel who fell from before the presence of Eternal God, and became the devil, to rise no more. And our spirits must have become like unto him, and we become devils, angels to a devil, to be shut out from the presence of our God, and to remain with the Father of lies, in misery, like unto himself." (2 Ne. 9:8-9.) That is to say, if there were no resurrection, which comes by the grace of God, all men would be sons of perdition, the most horrible and awful punishment in all the eternities.

As to that salvation which consists of both immortality and eternal life, Jacob says that after men are reconciled to God by obedience to the laws of his gospel, it is still "only in and through the grace of God" that they are saved. We shall

347

be raised "from death by the power of the resurrection," he says, and also, we "may be received into the eternal kingdom of God" because of that same atonement, all to the end that we "may praise him through grace divine." (2 Ne. 10:24-25.) "My soul delighteth in his grace," Jacob continues, "and in his justice, and power, and mercy in the great and eternal plan of deliverance from death. And my soul delighteth in proving unto my people that save Christ should come all men must perish." (2 Ne. 11:5-6.)

Jacob's brother Nephi preaches the same doctrine. "Believe in Christ, and . . . be reconciled to God," he says, "for we know that it is by grace that we are saved, after all we can do." (2 Ne. 25:23; 33:9.) And as he climaxes his writings on the plates of Mormon, the great Moroni relates the grace of God to an inheritance of eternal life in these pleading words: "Come unto Christ, and be perfected in him, and deny yourselves of all ungodliness; and if ye shall deny yourselves of all ungodliness and love God with all your might, mind and strength, then is his grace sufficient for you, that by his grace ye may be perfect in Christ." (Moro. 10:32.)

What more need we say than to praise God for his goodness and grace? What more need we do than to keep the commandments of Him who hath done all things for us?

Chapter 20

CHRIST IS "THE EVERLASTING FATHER"

The Lord's People Are Born Again

We set forth in Chapter 4 how the blessed Christ, in his role as Creator, is the Father of heaven and earth. In Chapter 8 we considered how Christ is the Father by divine investiture of authority, in that the Father has placed his name upon the Son so that the words and acts of the Offspring become and are the sayings and deeds of the Parent. It is now our purpose to show how Christ, in and through and because of his atoning sacrifice, becomes the Father of all those who believe and obey his laws. To envision what is involved in this concept, we must first consider the matter of being born again.

We are the spirit children of the Eternal Elohim with whom we lived and dwelt in the premortal eternities. We entered mortality by birth. Each of us was sired by a mortal father, conceived in the womb of a mortal mother, and came forth by the birth processes to breathe the breath of mortal life. In this way the eternal spirit takes upon itself a tabernacle of clay, is born into mortality, and launches forth into the probationary experiences of this sphere of existence. This passing from preexistence to mortality is called birth; for our purposes now it is considered to be the first birth.

Death entered the world by means of Adam's fall—death of two kinds, temporal and spiritual. Temporal death passes

349

upon all men when they depart this mortal life. It is then that the eternal spirit steps out of its earthly tenement, to take up an abode in a realm where spirits are assigned, to await the day of their resurrection. Spiritual death passes upon all men when they become accountable for their sins. Being thus subject to sin they die spiritually; they die as pertaining to the things of the Spirit; they die as pertaining to the things of righteousness; they are cast out of the presence of God. It is of such men that the scriptures speak when they say that the natural man is an enemy to God and has become carnal, sensual, and devilish by nature.

If a man "yields to the enticings of the Holy Spirit, and putteth off the natural man and becometh a saint through the atonement of Christ the Lord" (Mosiah 3:19), then he is born again. His spiritual death ceases. He becomes alive to the things of the Spirit; he returns to the presence of God because he receives the gift of the Holy Ghost; and he is alive to the things of righteousness. He crucifies the old man of sin, becomes a new creature of the Holy Ghost, and walks in a newness of life. This is what is meant by being born again.

We have no better scriptural account of what happens in the life of a repentant sinner when he is born again than the record of what Alma came to know and feel and be. Of the marvelous spiritual rebirth that came to him, he said: "I have repented of my sins, and have been redeemed of the Lord; behold I am born of the Spirit. And the Lord said unto me: Marvel not that all mankind, yea, men and women, all nations, kindreds, tongues and people, must be born again; yea, born of God, changed from their carnal and fallen state, to a state of righteousness, being redeemed of God, becoming his sons and daughters; And thus they become new creatures; and unless they do this, they can in nowise inherit the kingdom of God. I say unto you, unless this be the case, they must be cast off; and this I know, because I was like to be cast off. Nevertheless, after wandering through much tribulation, repenting nigh unto death, the Lord in mercy hath seen fit to snatch me out of an everlasting burning, and I am born of God. My soul hath been redeemed from the gall of bitterness and bonds of iniquity. I was in the darkest abyss; but now I behold the marvelous light of God. My soul was racked with eternal torment; but I am snatched, and my soul is pained no more." (Mosiah 27:24-29.)

As to the way in which men are born again, Jesus said they must "be born of water and of the Spirit" (John 3:5), meaning by baptism and by the laying on of hands for the gift of the Holy Ghost. The symbolism here involved is more fully set forth, in the Lord's language, as he commanded Adam to teach his children—"That by reason of transgression cometh the fall, which fall bringeth death, and inasmuch as ye were born into the world by water, and blood, and the spirit, which I have made, and so became of dust a living soul, even so ye must be born again into the kingdom of heaven, of water, and of the Spirit, and be cleansed by blood, even the blood of mine Only Begotten; that ye might be sanctified from all sin, and enjoy the words of eternal life in this world, and eternal life in the world to come, even immortal glory; For by the water ye keep the commandment; by the Spirit ye are justified; and by the blood ye are sanctified." (Moses 6:59-60.)

Sometimes men are born again miraculously and suddenly, as was Alma. They become alive to the things of the Spirit and completely reverse the whole course of their life almost in an instant. But for most members of the Church the spiritual rebirth is a process that goes on gradually. The faithful are sanctified degree by degree as they add to their faith and good works. The tests which set forth the extent to which the saints have been born again are set forth in the 5th chapter of Alma.

Saints Are the Children of Christ

Few doctrines are better known by members of the true church than the doctrine of preexistence. We are well aware

351

that all men are the children of God, the offspring of the Father, his sons and his daughters. We know that we were all born in his courts as spirit beings, long before the foundations of this earth were laid, and that the Lord Jehovah was in fact the Firstborn Son. What is not so well known is that nearly all the passages of scripture, both ancient and modern, which speak of God as our Father and of men on earth being the sons of God, have no reference to our birth in preexistence as the children of Elohim, but teach rather that Jehovah is our Father and we are his children.

In setting forth that all men must be born again to gain salvation, we have seen that this means they must be "born of God, changed from their carnal and fallen state, to a state of righteousness, being redeemed of God, becoming his sons and daughters." (Mosiah 27:25.) Whose sons and whose daughters do we become when we are born again? Who is our new Father? The answer is, Christ is our Father; we become his children by adoption; he makes us members of his family. Nowhere is this set forth better than in the words of King Benjamin to his Nephite subjects. "Because of the covenant ye have made," he said (and it is the same covenant all of us make in the waters of baptism), "ye shall be called the children of Christ, his sons, and his daughters; for behold, this day he hath spiritually begotten you; for ye say that your hearts are changed through faith on his name; therefore, ye are born of him and have become his sons and his daughters." (Mosiah 5:7.) Something akin to this appears to have occurred in ancient Israel when "Jehoiada made a covenant between the Lord and the king and the people, that they should be the Lord's people." (2 Kgs. 11:17.)

Among the first words recorded by the Beloved John in the Gospel account that bears his name is the affirmation that "the Word" who "was made flesh, and dwelt among" men "came unto his own, and his own received him not. But as many as received him, to them gave he power to become the sons of God, even to them that believe on his name." (John 1:11-14.) When this same Lord came to the Nephites, resurrected and glorified as he then was, he confirmed the words of his Beloved Disciple. "I came unto my own, and my own received me not," he said, "And as many as have received me, to them have I given to become the sons of God; and even so will I to as many as shall believe on my name." (3 Ne. 9:16-17.) And he has reaffirmed these same truths again and again in our day (D&C 11:30; 34:2-3; 39:1-4; 42:52; 45:8), with this added exposition: "He that receiveth my gospel receiveth me; and he that receiveth not my gospel receiveth not me" (D&C 39:5).

What we are here saying is that "by faith" we may "become the sons of God." (Moro. 7:26.) First we must believe and be baptized. This puts us in a position to exercise the "power" referred to in the foregoing passages. As Mormon said, "If ye will lay hold upon every good thing, and condemn it not, ye certainly will be a child of Christ." (Moro. 7:19.) After Alma baptized at the waters of Mormon, he organized the people and taught them their duties—to dwell together in unity and love, to honor the sabbath day, to impart of their substance to the poor, to walk uprightly before the Lord—"and thus they became the children of God." (Mosiah 18.) That is to say, these Nephites, following baptism, exercised the power to become the sons of God and did in fact attain that blessed state.

Those who become the sons of God in this life gain exaltation in the life to come. They are sons of God here; they are Gods in eternity—because they are like Christ and are one in him as he is one in the Father. Thus we read: "I am Jesus Christ, the Son of God, who was crucified for the sins of the world, even as many as will believe on my name, that they may become the sons of God, even one in me as I am one in the Father, as the Father is one in me, that we may be one." (D&C 35:2.) Also: "Ye shall be even as I am, and I am even as the Father; and the Father and I are one." (3 Ne. 28:10.)

Addressing himself to the saints, and speaking of the high status reserved for those who become members of the family of their Lord, the apostle John wrote: "Behold, what manner of love the Father hath bestowed upon us, that we should be called the sons of God." It is with wonder and amazement that we even dare to think of such a thing. Sons of God! Members of the family of Christ, who shall see his face and abide in his presence! "Beloved," John continues, "now are we the sons of God"—that is, here and now, while yet weak, faltering mortals, we have been adopted—"and it doth not yet appear what we shall be: but we know that, when he shall appear, we shall be like him; for we shall see him as he is." Like Christ! One with him as he is one with the Father! Because Christ was "like unto God" (Abr. 3:24), he became the Creator of all things from the beginning. If we become like unto him, what shall we be? Is it any wonder that John concludes: "And every man that hath this hope in him purifieth himself, even as he is pure." (1 Jn. 3:1-3.) Or is it any wonder that Mormon acclaimed: "My beloved brethren, pray unto the Father with all the energy of heart, that ye may be filled with this love"—the same love of which John wrote—"which he hath bestowed upon all who are true followers of his Son, Jesus Christ; that ye may become the sons of God; that when he shall appear we shall be like him, for we shall see him as he is; that we may have this hope; that we may be purified even as he is pure." (Moro. 7:48.)

Saints Become the Sons of Elohim

It is perfectly clear that faithful saints become the sons and daughters of Jesus Christ by adoption. But there is more than this to the doctrine of becoming sons of God. Those who so obtain are adopted also into the family of Elohim. They become his adopted sons so that they can receive, inherit, and possess along with his natural Son.

To envision what is meant by being sons of God, meaning the Father, let us follow Paul's reasoning in two passages of superlative insight and inspiration. To the Romans our apostolic friend of old wrote: "For as many as are led by the

Spirit of God, they are the sons of God." Standing alone, this could be taken to mean that by faith the saints become the sons of the Lord Jesus. But the perspective begins to change when our apostolic colleague says: "Ye have received the Spirit of adoption, whereby we cry, Abba, Father." That is, we call upon our Eternal Father in a familiar and friendly way, as children here call to their fathers with whom they maintain a familiar intimacy. Having attained this state of friendship with the Eternal One, "The Spirit itself beareth witness with our spirit," Paul continues, "that we are the children of God." He has now laid the groundwork. A pronouncement of deep and wondrous import is immediately forthcoming. "And if children"—note it well—"then heirs; heirs of God, and joint-heirs with Christ." (Rom. 8:14-17.)

Now here is a wondrous presumption, one that neither Paul nor any sane man would dare make, unless its verity burst upon him by the spirit of revelation. It is a case of a man making himself a God. It is a plain statement that mortal man shall inherit equally with Christ. It is the promise: "All that my Father hath shall be given unto him." (D&C 84:38.) The reasoning is perfect. The Father had a Son, a natural Son, his own literal Seed, the Offspring of his body. This Son is his heir. As an heir he inherits all things from his Father—all power, all might, all dominion, the world, the universe, kingship, eternal exaltation, all things. But our revelations speak of men being exalted also and of their ascending the throne of eternal power. How is it done? Paul has explained it perfectly. They are adopted into the family of the Father. They become joint-heirs with his natural Son, "For it became him, for whom are all things, and by whom are all things, in bringing many sons unto glory, to make the captain of their salvation perfect." (Heb. 2:10.)

Analyzing the problem in a similar way for the saints in Galatia, and through them for all of us, the ancient apostle said: "Ye are all the children of God by faith in Christ Jesus.

355

For as many of you as have been baptized into Christ have put on Christ." Here again we have the concept of adoption for those who make the gospel live in their lives. "And if ye be Christ's, then are ye Abraham's seed, and heirs according to the promise." Heirs according to the promise? What promise? Heirs according to the promise which God gave to Abraham: the promise of exaltation, the promise that in him and in his seed all generations should be blessed. "Abraham received promises concerning his seed, and of the fruit of his loins . . . which were to continue so long as they were in the world; and as touching Abraham and his seed, out of the world should they continue; both in the world and out of the world should they continue as innumerable as the stars; or, if ye were to count the sand upon the seashore ye could not number them. This promise is yours also, because ye are of Abraham, and the promise was made unto Abraham." (D&C 132:30-31.) That is to say, the seed of Abraham, who through faith become the "children of God," shall inherit the same blessings of exaltation promised to their faithful father.

"Now I say," Paul continues, "That the heir, as long as he is a child, differeth nothing from a servant, though he be lord of all; But is under tutors and governors until the time appointed of the father." Thus, men are schooled, tested, trained, prepared, made ready for the day of adoption, the day in which they step out of their role as servants and receive the homage of sons. That this might come to pass, "God sent forth his Son, . . . that we might receive the adoption of sons. And because we are sons, God hath sent forth the Spirit of his Son into your hearts, crying, Abba, Father. Wherefore thou art no more a servant, but a son; and if a son, then an heir of God through Christ." (Gal. 3:26-29; 4:1-7.)

This time Paul calls us heirs rather than joint-heirs, but the meaning is the same. We are adopted into the family of the Father; we are adopted sons, appointed to inherit along with his natural Son.

356

The laws whereby faithful men may enter into their exaltation and become "gods, even the sons of God" (D&C 76:58) are infinite and eternal. They govern in all worlds and from one eternity to the next without end. They constitute the sole and only way the eternal increase of an Eternal Father can become like their great Progenitor. As pertaining to this earth, they were revealed first to father Adam. He was baptized, born again, received the priesthood, and kept the commandments. As a result thereof, "a voice out of heaven" proclaimed: "Thou art one in me, a son of God; and thus may all become my sons." (Moses 6:65-68.) "Our father Adam taught these things," the scripture says, "and many have believed and become the sons of God, and many have believed not, and have perished in their sins." (Moses 7:1.)

As to the infinite scope of the laws of adoption and sonship, the voice from heaven spoke also to Joseph Smith and Sidney Rigdon, bearing testimony that the Lamb of God is the Only Begotten of the Father, and saying: "That by him, and through him, and of him, the worlds are and were created, and the inhabitants thereof are begotten sons and daughters unto God." (D&C 76:21-24.) This means that through the infinite and eternal atonement, those who are true and faithful on all the endless creations of Christ are adopted into the family of the Father as heirs, as joint-heirs, who will with him receive, inherit, and possess all that the Father hath.

Saints Are the Children of Jehovah

Aware, as we are, that faithful mortals become the sons and daughters of Christ; knowing, as we do, that this system of adoption has been in force from the beginning; and realizing, as is the case, that the Lord Jesus and the Lord Jehovah are one and the same person—we would expect to find Old Testament passages that refer to Jehovah as the Father and to the saints as his sons and daughters. And this is precisely what we do find. As we now refer to some of

357

these, we should do so with the realization that each one is a Messianic prophecy; each attributes to Jehovah what we have seen from the New Testament and latter-day revelation is in fact referring to the Lord Jesus.

"Ye are the children of the Lord your God," that is, of Jehovah your God, Moses proclaimed to Israel. Even if it were falsely supposed that Jehovah was the Father and not the Son, as some sectarian Christians do believe, still it would be apparent that this statement could not be a reference to the preexistence of spirits, which the sectarians do not believe in anyway, because it is not speaking of all men but of a chosen few. The context says: "For thou art an holy people unto the Lord thy God, and the Lord hath chosen thee to be a peculiar people unto himself, above all the nations that are upon the earth." Peculiar indeed! They had been adopted into the family of their God; they were his children, heirs of the promises made to Abraham their father.

Speaking of Jehovah, their "Rock," who had "spiritually begotten" (Mosiah 5:7) his people, Moses asked: "Is not he thy father that hath bought thee?" Then referring to Israel's oft-repeated acts of rebellion and wickedness, Moses said: "Of the Rock that begat thee thou art unmindful, and hast forgotten God that formed thee." (Deut. 32:4, 6, 18.) Speaking of Jehovah, the Psalmist in similar vein intoned: "Thou art my father, my God, and the rock of my salvation." (Ps. 89:26.) One of Isaiah's Messianic prophecies says: "He shall be a father to the inhabitants of Jerusalem, and to the house of Judah." (Isa. 22:21.) "Thou, O Lord, art our father," Isaiah also said, "our redeemer; thy name is from everlasting. . . . Our adversaries have trodden down thy sanctuary. We are thine: thou never barest rule over them; they were not called by thy name." (Isa. 63:16-19.) "But now, O Lord, thou art our father." (Isa. 64:8.)

Some of our best Old Testament pronouncements on the Fatherhood of Jehovah and the sonship of his people are found in prophecies telling of the gathering of scattered Israel in the day of restoration. "It shall come to pass," Hosea prophesied, "that in the place where it was said unto them, Ye are not my people, there it shall be said unto them, Ye are the sons of the living God. Then shall the children of Judah and the children of Israel be gathered together." (Hosea 1:10-11; Rom. 9:25-26.) During the darkness of their long dispersion, Israel shall not be known as the Lord's people, but when they accept the restored gospel, they shall once again be adopted into the same family in which their ancient forebears found peace and salvation.

"I have redeemed thee," Jehovah says to Israel, ". . . thou art mine. . . . I am the Lord thy God, the Holy One of Israel, thy Savior. . . . I will bring thy seed from the east, and gather thee from the west; I will say to the north, Give up; and to the south, Keep not back: bring my sons from far, and my daughters from the ends of the earth; Even every one that is called by my name." (Isa. 43:1-7.) Truly this is what has been and is transpiring in this day. The scattered remnants of Israel, hearing again the voice of their Shepherd, are believing his gospel, accepting baptism at the hands of his servants, coming into his sheepfold, taking upon themselves his name, and once again becoming his sons and his daughters.

Messiah Shall See His Seed

Of the Messiah who shall come, Isaiah says: "When thou shalt make his soul an offering for sin, he shall see his seed, he shall prolong his days, and the pleasure of the Lord shall prosper in his hand." (Isa. 53:10.)

He shall see his seed! How aptly, in poetic and prophetic language, this reminds all who believe that they are the children of their Messiah. Seed is the progeny of the species. Among us men it is our children. The children of the Lord Jesus Christ are those who believe in him and obey his gospel, those who exercise the power given them to become his sons and his daughters, and who as a consequence are adopted into his family.

It is to Abinadi that we turn for the inspired interpretation of Isaiah's prophecy about Christ's seed. Our Nephite friend has just quoted all of the 53rd chapter of Isaiah. He is now expounding on verse 10. "Behold, I say unto you," he says, "that when his soul has been made an offering for sin he shall see his seed. And now what say ye? And who shall be his seed?"

By way of definition and in language that cannot be misunderstood, Abinadi now identifies Messiah's seed. "Behold I say unto you," he continues, "that whosoever has heard the words of the prophets, yea, all the holy prophets who have prophesied concerning the coming of the Lord—I say unto you, that all those who have hearkened unto their words, and believed that the Lord would redeem his people, and have looked forward to that day for a remission of their sins, I say unto you, that these are his seed, or they are the heirs of the kingdom of God. For these are they whose sins he has borne; these are they for whom he has died, to redeem them from their transgressions. And now, are they not his seed? Yea, and are not the prophets, every one that has opened his mouth to prophesy, that has not fallen into transgression, I mean all the holy prophets ever since the world began? I say unto you that they are his seed. And these are they who have published peace, who have brought good tidings of good, who have published salvation; and said unto Zion: Thy God reigneth!" (Mosiah 15:10-14.)

Included in this group of whom Abinadi speaks are all those who have been faithful from the day of father Adam to that moment; all are members of their Messiah's family. They are his spiritual progeny, his seed, his children. In principle the same thing will apply to all the faithful yet to come, all who shall be spiritually born of him. But Isaiah's prophecy and Abinadi's interpretation speak only of those who have been and not of those who shall yet believe and who shall gain the adoption of sonship in a future day. A clear awareness of this fact is essential to a full understanding of what Isaiah and Abinadi really mean.

With our Lord's seed thus clearly identified, let us note the time and circumstances under which he will see them. Abinadi's rendition of Isaiah's inspired utterance says: "When his soul has been made an offering for sin he shall see his seed." In other words, he shall see his seed after he has worked out the infinite and eternal atonement. He shall see his seed after he has sweat great drops of blood in Gethsemane; after he has been crucified by wicked men; after he has said, "It is finished"; after he has voluntarily let his spirit leave its mortal tenement.

What was it that then occurred which enabled him to see his seed? His own declaration, made while on the cross itself, was that he would go that very day to paradise. (Luke 23:40-43.) Peter affirmed that he did in fact go to a world of waiting spirits, to those who were awaiting the day of their resurrection, to those who felt themselves imprisoned because of the long absence of their spirits from their bodies, and that there he preached the gospel. (1 Pet. 3:18-20; 4:6.) In his glorious vision of the redemption of the dead, President Joseph F. Smith saw what transpired when the Messiah visited the departed dead. "The eyes of my understanding were opened, and the Spirit of the Lord rested upon me," he said, "and I saw the hosts of the dead, both small and great. And there were gathered together in one place an innumerable company of the spirits of the just, who had been faithful in the testimony of Jesus while they lived in mortality. . . . All these had departed the mortal life, firm in the hope of a glorious resurrection, through the grace of God the Father and his Only Begotten Son, Jesus Christ." (JFS-V 11-14.) The promise was that when his soul should be made an offering for sin, then he would see his seed, which seed consisted of all the righteous persons who had departed this life up to that time. How wondrously this prophecy was fulfilled reminds us anew of the depth and glory of the Messianic utterances which deal with Him who has adopted us into his family.

This vision of what Isaiah meant by the Messiah seeing his seed gives sense and meaning to the balance of the prophetic statement: "When thou shalt make his soul an offering for sin, he shall see his seed, he shall prolong his days, and the pleasure of the Lord shall prosper in his hand." (Isa. 53:10.) If this prophecy was meant to be fulfilled during his mortal sojourn on earth, we would list it as having failed. He did not prolong his days; a voluntary death overtook him in the prime of life. Nor did the pleasure of the Lord find full fruition while he dwelt in a state where death lies in wait for the weary pilgrim. It is only in the resurrection that the pleasure of the Lord is perfected, for it is only when "spirit and element" are "inseparably connected" that either God or man can "receive a fulness of joy." (D&C 93:33.) Thus, having made his soul an offering for sin; having seen his seed—all the righteous dead from the days of Adam to that moment—as they assembled to greet and worship him in the paradise of their Lord; and having thereafter risen in glorious immortality to live and reign forever, our Messiah truly fulfilled the prophetic utterance, for then his days were prolonged forever and the pleasure in his hand was infinite.

There is one other Old Testament passage that speaks of Christ's seed, this time with a different emphasis. It is not a prophecy in which our Lord sees and rejoices in his righteous family members, but one in which they pledge allegiance to him as he is loved, served, and worshiped by them. As part of a great Messianic Psalm, David looks forward from the sorrow and seeming defeat of the cross to the millennial triumph of truth and righteousness. He speaks of the praise the Crucified One shall receive when "all the ends of the world shall remember and turn unto the Lord: and all the kindreds of the nations shall worship before" him; when "the kingdom is the Lord's: and he is the governor among the nations." In that day—"A seed shall serve him. . . . They shall come, and shall declare his righteousness." (Ps. 22.)

362

Needless to say, those who are now his seed look forward with rejoicing and fervently pray that his kingdom may come and that there will soon be ushered in that day in which all shall love and serve him without molestation or hindrance of any sort.

Saints Bear Their Lord's Name

Family members bear the family name; by it they are known and called and identified; it sets them apart from all those of a different lineage and ancestry. Adopted children take upon themselves the name of their newfound parents and become in all respects as though they had been born in the family. And so it is that the children of Christ, those who are born again, those who are spiritually begotten by their new Father, take upon themselves the name of Christ. By it they are known; in it they are called; it identifies and sets them apart from all others. They are now family members, Christians in the real and true sense of the word.

Do they themselves become Christs? Not in the sense that they are called upon to atone for the sins of others and make immortality and eternal life available for themselves or their fellowmen on this or any world. But they do carry his name and are obligated to bear it in decency and dignity. No taint of shame or disgrace, no sliver of dishonor must ever be permitted to attach itself to that name "which is above every name," for "at the name of Jesus every knee should bow" (Phil. 2:9-10) and pay homage to him who is above all save the Father only. The saints of God must remember who they are and act accordingly.

Thus, when King Benjamin desired to set his people apart from the world and plant their feet in that course leading to peace and joy here in mortality and to everlasting renown in the realms ahead, he said: "I shall give this people a name, that thereby they may be distinguished above all the people which the Lord God hath brought out of the land of Jerusalem; and this I do because they have been a diligent

363

people in keeping the commandments of the Lord. And I give unto them a name that never shall be blotted out, except it be through transgression." (Mosiah 1:11-12.)

Later, in a tender and moving passage, addressing himself to those who had been born again, thereby becoming "the children of Christ, his sons, and his daughters," the beloved and upright King of the Nephites counseled his people: "Take upon you the name of Christ. . . . And it shall come to pass that whosoever doeth this shall be found at the right hand of God, for he shall know the name by which he is called; for he shall be called by the name of Christ. And now it shall come to pass, that whosoever shall not take upon him the name of Christ must be called by some other name; therefore, he findeth himself on the left hand of God. And I would that ye should remember also, that this is the name that I said I should give unto you that never should be blotted out, except it be through transgression; therefore, take heed that ye do not transgress, that the name be not blotted out of your hearts. I say unto you, I would that ye should remember to retain the name written always in your hearts, that ye are not found on the left hand of God, but that ye hear and know the voice by which ye shall be called, and also, the name by which he shall call you. For how knoweth a man the master whom he has not served, and who is a stranger unto him, and is far from the thoughts and intents of his heart?" (Mosiah 5:7-13.)

When the first Alma was struggling with the administrative burdens of the Church in his day, he pled with the Lord for direction relative to church members who transgressed the laws of their Sovereign. Included in the answer from the Lord were these words: "Blessed is this people who are willing to bear my name; for in my name shall they be called; and they are mine. . . . For it is I that taketh upon me the sins of the world; for it is I that hath created them; and it is I that granteth unto him that believeth unto the end a place at my right hand. For behold, in my name are they called; and if they know me they shall come forth, and shall have a place eternally at my right hand." (Mosiah 26:18, 23-24.)

Thus we learn that those who take upon themselves the name of Christ, who thereafter hearken and hear when he continues to call them in the name which is both his and theirs, and who keep the standards of the Christian family, having enjoyed the fellowship of hosts of brothers and sisters in the Church, go on to eternal joy and felicity as members of the family of God in the celestial kingdom! What a pleasing concept this is! (Alma 34:38; D&C 18:21-25.)

In the same sense in which faithful people become the sons and daughters of their Lord, thus inheriting from him the joys of salvation, so rebellious and unbelieving people become the sons and daughters of Satan, thus inheriting from him the sorrows of damnation. So we find the second Alma, as part of his great sermon on being born again, addressing himself to "workers of iniquity" in this way: "The good shepherd doth call you; yea, and in his own name he doth call you, which is the name of Christ; and if ye will not hearken unto the voice of the good shepherd, to the name by which ye are called, behold, ye are not the sheep of the good shepherd.

"And now if ye are not the sheep of the good shepherd, of what fold are ye? Behold, I say unto you, that the devil is your shepherd, and ye are of his fold; and now, who can deny this? Behold, I say unto you, whosoever denieth this is a liar and a child of the devil. For I say unto you that whatsoever is good cometh from God, and whatsoever is evil cometh from the devil. Therefore, if a man bringeth forth good works he hearkeneth unto the voice of the good shepherd, and he doth follow him; but whosoever bringeth forth evil works, the same becometh a child of the devil, for he hearkeneth unto his voice, and doth follow him. And whosoever doeth this must receive his wages of him; therefore, for his wages he receiveth death, as to things pertaining unto righteousness, being dead unto all good works." (Alma 5:38-42.)

These views of the American Paul accord perfectly with

365

those of the Lord Jesus, spoken to rebellious Jews, in these words: "Ye are of your father the devil, and the lusts of your father ye will do." (John 8:44.)

The way in which the name Christian is bestowed upon those who take upon themselves the name of Christ is set forth in that episode of Nephite history when General Moroni set up the title of liberty. On that occasion, the record says, "he prayed mightily unto his God for the blessings of liberty to rest upon his brethren, so long as there should a band of Christians remain to possess the land—For thus were all the true believers of Christ, who belonged to the church of God, called by those who did not belong to the church. And those who did belong to the church were faithful; yea, all those who were true believers in Christ took upon them, gladly, the name of Christ, or Christians as they were called, because of their belief in Christ who should come. And therefore, at this time, Moroni prayed that the cause of the Christians, and the freedom of the land might be favored." (Alma 46:13-16.)

This doctrine whereunder the true saints take upon themselves the name of their Lord so that ever thereafter they are called by the sacred name of Christ, or Christians, is also the basis for the proper choice of the name of the Church. "Lord, we will that thou wouldst tell us the name whereby we shall call this church; for there are disputations among the people concerning this matter," was the petition of the Nephite Twelve to the risen Lord Jesus. "Why is it that the people should murmur and dispute because of this thing?" he replied. "Have they not read the scriptures, which say ye must take upon you the name of Christ, which is my name? For by this name shall ye be called at the last day; And whoso taketh upon him my name, and endureth to the end, the same shall be saved at the last day.

"Therefore, whatsoever ye shall do, ye shall do it in my name; therefore ye shall call the church in my name; and ye shall call upon the Father in my name that he will bless the church for my sake. And how be it my church save it be

366

called in my name? For if a church be called in Moses' name then it be Moses' church; or if it be called in the name of a man then it be the church of a man; but if it be called in my name then it is my church, if it so be that they are built upon my gospel." (3 Ne. 27:3-8.)

Saints Bear Jehovah's Name

As we are aware, the chief designation of Christ that has been preserved for us in the Old Testament, as that ancient work is now published, is the exalted name-title Jehovah. Since the saints must take upon themselves the name of Christ to gain salvation, it follows that they took upon themselves the name of Jehovah when that was the designation being applied to the Messiah. Accordingly, all Old Testament passages that show that the Lord's people either knew or had taken upon themselves or were called by the name of Jehovah are Messianic in nature. The whole system of Old Testament worship was one in which the Lord's people were to "fear this glorious and fearful name, THE LORD THY GOD" (Deut. 28:58), the Lord Jehovah. It will profit us to note some of the passages that apply the name itself to the Lord's people.

Our clearest recitation of the fact that the ancients took upon themselves Jehovah's name is found in the newly revealed writings of Old Testament Abraham. To the father of the faithful, the Lord appeared saying: "Abraham, Abraham, behold, my name is Jehovah. . . . Behold, I will lead thee by my hand, and I will take thee, to put upon thee my name. . . . As it was with Noah so shall it be with thee; but through thy ministry my name shall be known in the earth forever, for I am thy God." (Abr. 1:16-19.) Again: "I have purposed . . . to make of thee a minister to bear my name. . . . My name is Jehovah." (Abr. 2:6, 8.)

In the Old Testament record itself, Jehovah says: "Put my name upon the children of Israel; and I will bless them." (Num. 6:27.) Why put his name upon them? Because, as he said, "Thou art an holy people unto the Lord thy God: the Lord thy God hath chosen thee to be a special people unto himself, above all people that are upon the face of the earth." (Deut. 7:6.) With what result? "All people of the earth shall see that thou art called by the name of the Lord; and they shall be afraid of thee." (Deut. 28:10.)

Would it be amiss here to note that when the Lord places his name upon a people they become Christians? True, we are dealing with the so-called pre-Christian Era, but so were we also when we quoted the account about General Moroni. (Alma 46.) And for that matter, did not true Christianity begin with Adam, who had faith, repented of his sins, was baptized by immersion, received the gift of the Holy Ghost, and worked righteousness all his days?

These words were spoken by the Lord to one of his ancient servants: "If my people, which are called by my name, shall humble themselves, and pray, and seek my face, and turn from their wicked ways; then will I hear from heaven, and will forgive their sin, and will heal their land." To whom did this message come? Was it Alma or Moroni or Samuel the Lamanite? It sounds as though it came right out of the Book of Mormon and that the Lord Jesus was calling his people, those who had taken upon themselves his name, to repentance. And well might these words have come to these or others of the Hebrew prophets who dwelt on the American continent, but in fact they are the words of Jehovah to Solomon as recorded in Second Chronicles, chapter 7, verse 14. But what does it matter to whom the message came? Or by what name the Speaker was known? The words spoken are true. The name placed upon the Lord's people has the same saving power be it Jehovah or Jesus.

As we have already seen, in the day of Israel's gathering Jehovah promised to bring his sons from afar and his daughters from the ends of the earth. Now, however, let us note that those being thus gathered again into the sheepfold of the good Shepherd are identified as "Even every one that is called by my name" (Isa. 43:7), that is, by the name of Jehovah.

Speaking of this day when Israel shall be gathered in from her long dispersion, when Jerusalem shall become again a holy city, when the redeemed of the Lord shall once again know the God of their fathers, Jehovah says: "Therefore my people shall know my name: therefore they shall know in that day that I am he that doth speak: behold, it is I." (Isa. 52.) The risen Christ, ministering among the Nephites, quotes, paraphrases, and amplifies Isaiah's writings about the glorious latter-day work of restoration and gathering and then takes these words of Jehovah and specifically and expressly applies them to himself, saying: "Verily, verily, I say unto you, that my people shall know my name; yea, in that day they shall know that I am he that doth speak." (3 Ne. 20.) Jehovah who spoke to Isaiah of the day when Israel would receive again her ancient glory was this same Jesus who taught the same truths to the Nephites.

From all of the foregoing it is apparent that whenever Jehovah says, "Thou art my people" (Isa. 51:16); or whenever the people say of Jehovah, "We are his people, and the sheep of his pasture" (Ps. 100:3); or when they say, "Thou, O Lord, art in the midst of us, and we are called by thy name; leave us not" (Jer. 14:9); or "Our adversaries have trodden down thy sanctuary. We are thine: thou never barest rule over them; they were not called by thy name" (Isa. 63:18-19); or when Jehovah promises (of gathered Israel), "They shall know that my name is The Lord" (Jer. 16:21)—whenever these or any equivalent utterances are made, they mean that the name of the Lord Jehovah (who is Christ) has been placed upon his people, and they, knowing the name by which they are called, are heirs of salvation.

Christ Is the Father and the Son

As we are now aware, there are three senses in which Christ is the Father. He is the Father of heaven and earth, by

369

which we mean he is the Creator. He is the Father by divine investiture of authority, meaning that the Father has placed his name and power upon the Son, so that the words and acts of the Son are and become those of the Father. He is the Father of all those who believe on his name, who are born again, who are adopted into his family.

Our clearest Messianic prophecy, equating the Fatherhood of Christ with his status as the newfound Father of every true believer, is contained in the conversations he had with Moriancumer when that seer ascended the summits of Shelem with the sixteen small stones which were soon to give light in the Jareditish barges. When the Lord withdrew the veil from the eyes and mind of Jared's brother, the eternal words then uttered by Deity were: "Ye are redeemed from the fall; therefore ye are brought back into my presence; therefore I show myself unto you." These words are being spoken more than two millenniums before what men choose to call the Christian Era. They continue: "Behold, I am he who was prepared from the foundation of the world to redeem my people. Behold, I am Jesus Christ. I am the Father and the Son. In me shall all mankind have light, and that eternally, even they who shall believe on my name; and they shall become my sons and my daughters." (Ether 3:13-14.)

"I am Jesus Christ. I am the Father and the Son." How so? 'I am the Only Begotten Son, the One chosen and foreordained from the beginning, the One destined to be born into mortality as the offspring of the Father. But I am also the Father, the Father of all who shall believe on my name, for they shall become my sons and my daughters, members of my family, chosen vessels to bear my name.' There was never any ambiguity or uncertainty about this pleasing doctrine so far as the saints of old were concerned. Nor was there any difficulty in the minds of the ancients where his Fatherhood as Creator or his Fatherhood as the voice and agent of the Father were concerned. The confusion and delusion relative to the status and relationship of the Father and the Son that now prevails is an outgrowth from the false creeds of an apostate Christendom.

Some passages that specify that Christ is the Father do not spell out the sense in which the designation is being used. In these cases there is no impropriety in interpreting the prophetic statements as applying to any or all of the senses in which our Lord carries his Father's name. In one of the most famous of all Messianic statements, Isaiah exults: "Unto us a child is born, unto us a son is given: and the government shall be upon his shoulder: and his name shall be called Wonderful, Counseller, The mighty God, The everlasting Father, The Prince of Peace." (Isa. 9:6.) The everlasting Father! In what sense? Perhaps in all of them, in every way and sense in which the Son carries that exalted name-title.

In the course of an exposition relative to the creation, the fall, and the redemption, Moroni says: God "created Adam, and by Adam came the fall of man. And because of the fall of man came Jesus Christ, even the Father and the Son; and because of Jesus Christ came the redemption of man." (Morm. 9:12.) How is our Lord the Father? It is because of the atonement, because he received power from his Father to do that which is infinite and eternal. This is a matter of his Eternal Parent investing him with power from on high so that he becomes the Father because he exercises the power of that Eternal Being.

Nephi the son of Nephi, on the night before our Lord's birth into mortality, received this message from that holy being: "Behold, I come unto my own, to fulfil all things which I have made known unto the children of men from the foundation of the world, and to do the will, both of the Father and of the Son—of the Father because of me, and of the Son because of my flesh." (3 Ne. 1:14.) It is clear that he is the Son because of the flesh, meaning that he was born into the world as other mortals are. He had a body that was conceived and nurtured in the womb of a mortal woman. It is more difficult to envision how he was the Father because of himself. This can only be taken to mean that he was the Father because he had the power of the Father; that his will was swallowed up in the will of the Father; that he could do all things because of his inheritance from that Supreme Being. The same thought is put forth in latter-day revelation in these words: "I am in the Father, and the Father in me, and the Father and I are one—The Father because he gave me of his fulness, and the Son because I was in the world and made flesh my tabernacle, and dwelt among the sons of men." (D&C 93:3-4.)

After Moroni, in abridging the writings of Ether, sets forth that Christ is the Father because those who believe in him become his sons and his daughters, he receives a revelation of his own which is identified as coming from "Jesus Christ, the Son of God, the Father of the heavens and of the earth, and all things that are in them." In this revelation the Son continues to speak and in due course gives forth this declaration: "He that will not believe my words will not believe me—that I am; and he that will not believe me will not believe the Father who sent me. For behold, I am the Father, I am the light, and the life, and the truth of the world." (Ether 4:7-12.) When he says "I am the Father," in what sense does he mean it? Perhaps this is another case where the name-title is of general and not specific application.

Abinadi's exposition relative to the Father and the Son and the great atoning sacrifice to be wrought by him in his capacity as the Son, as he acted in the power of the Father, is one of the deepest and most thought-filled Messianic passages we have. "God himself shall come down among the children of men, and shall redeem his people," Abinadi says. This is clear: Christ is God; he is the Lord Omnipotent; he is like unto the Father. "And because he dwelleth in flesh he shall be called the Son of God, and having subjected the flesh to the will of the Father, being the Father and the Son—The Father, because he was conceived by the power of God; and the Son, because of the flesh; thus becoming the

372

Father and Son—And they are one God, yea, the very Eternal Father of heaven and of earth. And thus the flesh becoming subject to the Spirit, or the Son to the Father, being one God, suffereth temptation, and yieldeth not to the temptation, but suffereth himself to be mocked, and scourged, and cast out, and disowned by his people." He shall be slain, Abinadi says, "the will of the Son being swallowed up in the will of the Father. And thus God breaketh the bands of death, having gained the victory over death; giving the son power to make intercession for the children of men." (Mosiah 15:1-9.)

In this powerful passage we have a wondrous summary of divine truth. Christ is God and he comes to redeem his people. He is the Son because he is born into mortality. He is the Father because he inherits from his Father all the might of omnipotence, and what he says and what he does become and are the words and works of him whose name he bears.

Chapter 21

ALL THINGS BEAR RECORD OF CHRIST

"All Things Denote There Is a God"

An all-wise Creator has structured all the creations of his hands in such a way, not only to call attention to himself as the Maker, Preserver, and Upholder of all things, but to bear record of the nature and kind of Being he is. The mere fact that all things are, that fact standing alone, establishes that there is a Supreme Being; and the orderliness and system which prevails in the universe is a sufficient witness that the Creator is almighty, knows all things, and has made man, his crowning creature, as the natural heir of all his goodness.

Thus David acclaims, "The heavens declare the glory of God; and the firmament sheweth his handywork." In the sidereal heavens, in the broad expanse of the universe, in all the orbs that roll in their assigned spheres, in the heavens above and the earth beneath, is seen the hand of God. The sun rises in the morning; lilies bloom in the fields; wheat whitens for the harvest; birds soar in the firmament above and fish swim in the waters beneath—all nature operating in harmony with the laws of Nature's God—all things denote (nay, prove!) there is a God.

"Day unto day uttereth speech, and night unto night sheweth knowledge." Whose speech? Whose knowledge? Though the voice of the Creator be stilled, yet the voice of his creations declare his divinity. The heavens and the earth

374

declare his glory. His voice is heard in the rolling thunder; his words are read in the vivid lightning; his speech is recorded in the lilac's bloom. "There is no speech nor language, where their voice"—the voice of all created things—"is not heard. Their line is gone out through all the earth, and their words to the ends of the world." (Ps. 19:1-4.) None but fools say, "We have not heard the voice of Deity," for that voice is everywhere. If men fail to live that law which enables them to see the divine face and converse with their Creator in plain words, at least they are obligated to hear the voice of Nature, which is also the voice of God.

This concept was taught to Joseph Smith by "him who sitteth upon the throne and governeth and executeth all things." Speaking of himself, the Divine Teacher averred: "He comprehendeth all things, and all things are before him, and all things are round about him; and he is above all things, and in all things, and is through all things, and is round about all things; and all things are by him, and of him, even God, forever and ever."

Continuing to speak of himself, Christ the Creator says: "He hath given a law unto all things, by which they move in their times and their seasons; And their courses are fixed, even the courses of the heavens and the earth, which comprehended the earth and all the planets. And they give light to each other in their times and in their seasons, in their minutes, in their hours, in their days, in their weeks, in their months, in their years—all these are one year with God, but not with man. The earth rolls upon her wings, and the sun giveth his light by day, and the moon giveth her light by night, and the stars also give their light, as they roll upon their wings in their glory, in the midst of the power of God."

Then comes the question: "Unto what shall I liken these kingdoms, that ye may understand?" There follows a parable which teaches that he will visit "every kingdom"—and the inhabitants thereof—"in its hour, and in its time, and in its season." But our immediate concern is the divine announcement: "All these are kingdoms, and any man who hath seen any or the least of these hath seen God moving in his majesty and power. I say unto you, he hath seen him; nevertheless, he who came unto his own was not comprehended." It is then said that in a future day the faithful shall "comprehend even God," as pertaining to which time it is written: "Then shall ye know that ye have seen me." (D&C 88:40-62.)

In these sayings we find reinforcement of two great verities: (1) All men have seen God, in preexistence, for they lived and dwelt with him before ever the foundations of this earth were laid, a fact which all will remember at a future time; and (2) God is seen in the heavens above and the earth beneath, whose voices combine to declare his glory and goodness.

In a dramatic confrontation, Korihor (an intellectual without faith!) defied Alma and derided what he called "the foolish ordinances and performances" of the gospel. He accused the church leaders of keeping the saints in bondage, "that ye may glut yourselves with the labors of their hands." His thesis was that no man could know there was a God, or a fall of man, or that Christ would come to redeem his people. In reply, Alma testified, "there is a God, and . . . Christ shall come." There is, of course, no way to argue with a testimony. Then Alma said: "And now what evidence have ye that there is no God, or that Christ cometh not? I say unto you that ye have none, save it be your word only. But, behold, I have all things as a testimony that these things are true; and ye also have all things as a testimony unto you that they are true. . . . The scriptures are laid before thee, yea, and all things denote there is a God; yea, even the earth, and all things that are upon the face of it, yea, and its motion, yea, and also all the planets which move in their regular form do witness that there is a Supreme Creator." Thereafter, because he demanded a sign, Korihor was struck dumb, confessed he had been deceived by the devil, and suffered an ignominious death. (Alma 30:23-60.)

Gospel Taught with Similitudes

To crystallize in our minds the eternal verities which we must accept and believe to be saved, to dramatize their true meaning and import with an impact never to be forgotten, to center our attention on these saving truths, again and again and again, the Lord uses similitudes. Abstract principles may easily be forgotten or their deep meaning overlooked, but visual performances and actual experiences are registered on the mind in such a way as never to be lost. It is one thing to talk of faith as an abstract principle, another to see the Red Sea parted by its power. It is one thing to talk of the word of God coming down from heaven, another to actually gather and taste the angelic manna. It is one thing to teach that God is our Father in an abstract and impersonal way, thus expecting all Christendom to envision that he is a personal being in whose image man is created. It is another thing to say: Here is his Son; he is in the express image of his Father's person; he is in the similitude of the Father; observe what he does and see how he acts and you will know what the Father is like, for God is in Christ manifesting himself to men.

"I . . . am the Lord thy God," is the introduction of Jehovah to his people. Such is the voice of him who knows all things, reveals what he will, and chooses what his children shall be taught. How, then, does he present his message? "I have also spoken by the prophets," he says, "and I have multiplied visions, and used similitudes, by the ministry of the prophets." (Hosea 12:9-10.) He uses ordinances, rites, acts, and performances; he uses similarities, resemblances, and similitudes so that whatever is done will remind all who are aware of it of a greater and more important reality. He uses similes; he uses parables; he uses allegories. If two things have the same semblance or form, if they are like each other in appearance, if they correspond in qualities, it may suit his purposes to compare them. To liken one thing to another is one of the best teaching procedures.

After setting forth that as men were born into the world of water, and blood, and the spirit, and so became of dust living souls, so they must be born again of water, and of the Spirit, and be cleansed by the blood of Christ to enter the kingdom of heaven—itself a perfect similitude—the Lord says: "Behold, all things have their likeness, and all things are created and made to bear record of me, both things which are temporal, and things which are spiritual; things which are in the heavens above, and things which are on the earth, and things which are in the earth, and things which are under the earth, both above and beneath: all things bear record of me." (Moses 6:59-63.) "All things" includes the heavens and the earth, as also all of the ordinances and performances of the gospel.

"My soul delighteth in proving unto my people the truth of the coming of Christ," says Jacob, the Nephite, "for, for this end hath the law of Moses been given; and all things which have been given of God from the beginning of the world, unto man, are the typifying of him." (2 Ne. 11:4.) It follows that if we had sufficient insight, we would see in every gospel ordinance, in every rite that is part of revealed religion, in every performance commanded of God, in all things Deity gives his people, something that typifies the eternal ministry of the Eternal Christ. The performance of all such ordinances or acts, from Adam to Christ, falls thereby into the category of Messianic acts and performances. We shall now consider samples of these matters and note some of their Messianic implications.

"Why Dost Thou Offer Sacrifices?"

In point of time one of the first great symbolic ordinances was that of sacrifice, animal sacrifice, the shedding of the blood of chosen beasts in similitude of that which was to be in time's meridian. After Adam and Eve were cast out of Eden to till the dust whence they came and to gain the experiences available only in a mortal probation, the Lord "gave unto them commandments, that they should worship the Lord their God, and should offer the firstlings of their flocks, for an offering unto the Lord. And Adam was obedient unto the commandments of the Lord." He complied with the heavenly commandments and worshiped the Lord, in manner and form, as that holy being had directed, including the offering of sacrifices.

We do not know the details and specifics of his worship, except that the gospel plan was given to him, line upon line and precept upon precept, until he was the possessor of its everlasting fulness. He must have been told how and in what manner to offer sacrifices; at least what he did gained the approval of his Lord. And so it was that "after many days," how long we can only surmise, but certainly long enough for him to prove his devotion and integrity, "an angel of the Lord appeared unto Adam, saying: Why dost thou offer sacrifices unto the Lord? And Adam said unto him: I know not, save the Lord commanded me."

Blind obedience? Perhaps, although probably not more so than is the case with much that the Lord directs us to do. Adam knew he was obligated to keep the commandments and that blessings would flow therefrom, just as we do, although we cannot see, nor could he, the treasures being laid up on earth and in heaven by obedience to the laws of the Lord. In any event, "the angel spake, saying: This thing is a similitude of the sacrifice of the Only Begotten of the Father, which is full of grace and truth. Wherefore, thou shalt do all that thou doest in the name of the Son, and thou shalt repent and call upon God in the name of the Son forevermore." (Moses 5:4-8.)

There we have it. Sacrifice is a similitude. It is performed to typify the coming sacrifice of the Son of God. For four thousand long years, from Adam to that bleak day when our Lord was lifted up by sinful men, all of his righteous followers sought remission of their sins through sacrifice. It was an ordinance of the Melchizedek Priesthood; it antedated the law of Moses by two and a half millenniums, although that lesser law did give rise to many sacrificial requirements not theretofore practiced. We shall consider the details of sacrifical symbolism in Chapter 23 as part of our consideration of the law of Moses. For our purposes now it suffices to know that there neither was nor could have been any ordinance or system devised that would have dramatized more perfectly the coming eternal sacrifice that was and is the heart and core of revealed religion. For our purposes now it suffices to say that such Messianic utterances as that of Isaiah, that the Messiah should "make his soul an offering for sin" (Isa. 53:10), or that of Lehi, that "he offereth himself a sacrifice for sin" (2 Ne. 2:7), were well and perfectly understood by all Israel and all others in whose hearts the light of truth dwelt, and that the righteous of all ages looked forward with hope to the day when the Lamb of God should be slain for the sins of the world.

After the final great sacrifice on the cross, the use for the similitude that looked forward to our Lord's death ceased. Blood sacrifices became a thing of the past. New symbolisms, found in the sacrament of the Lord's supper, were adopted so that the saints might look back with reverence and worship upon his atoning ordeal. "Ye shall offer up unto me no more the shedding of blood," the risen Lord said to the Nephites, "yea, your sacrifices and your burnt offerings shall be done away, for I will accept none of your sacrifices and your burnt offerings. And ye shall offer for a sacrifice unto me a broken heart and a contrite spirit." (3 Ne. 9:19-20; Ps. 51:17.)

"Behold the Lamb of God"

As the prophets sought for similitudes to use in teaching the great and eternal truths of salvation to the people, how natural it was for them to designate him who should sacrifice himself for the sins of the world as the Lamb of God. He was to be God's Son. He would "bare the sin of many." (Isa. 53:12.) He would lay down his life for his people. Through

380

his atoning sacrifice the way would be open to gain a remission of sins. Sacrifices were performed in similitude of his infinite and eternal sacrifice. In large measure the firstlings of the flocks slain on the altars of sacrifice were lambs, lambs without spot or blemish. What could be more appropriate than to name Him who would make the supreme sacrifice, whose own shed blood would give efficacy and force to four thousand years of sacrificial ordinances, to designate him who came from God to sacrifice his soul as the Lamb of God.

And so it was. In point of time, the first Messianic designation of Christ as the Lamb of which we have record came from the lips of Enoch, who "saw the day of the coming of the Son of Man, even in the flesh; and his soul rejoiced, saying: The Righteous is lifted up, and the Lamb is slain from the foundation of the world." (Moses 7:47.) Our Nephite brethren, having the fulness of the gospel as Enoch had it, and also being Israelites and living in the Mosaic dispensation, offered sacrifices according to the order of heaven. It was, therefore, perfectly natural for them to use this same terminology. Thus when Lehi saw in vision the ministry of John, as the forerunner of the Lord and as the one who should immerse him in the murky waters of Jordan, we find the Nephite record saying of John: "And after he had baptized the Messiah with water, he should behold and bear record that he had baptized the Lamb of God, who should take away the sins of the world." (1 Ne. 10:10; 11:27.) Thus when Nephi saw in vision the Virgin of Nazareth who was to be "the mother of the Son of God, after the manner of the flesh," and when he saw her "bearing a child in her arms," he was also privileged to hear the angelic proclamation: "Behold the Lamb of God, yea, even the Son of the Eternal Father!" (1 Ne. 11:13-21.)

Knowing and rejoicing in this title of his Lord, Nephi called the church which should be set up by restoration in the last days "the church of the Lamb." (1 Ne. 14:12.) Thus also the Nephite Alma invited those of his nation to "come

381

and be baptized unto repentance, that ye may be washed from your sins, that ye may have faith on the Lamb of God, who taketh away the sins of the world, who is mighty to save and to cleanse from all unrighteousness." (Alma 7:14.) Alma also spoke of the faithful having "their garments . . . washed white through the blood of the Lamb." (Alma 13:11; 34:36.) If we had the full and complete accounts of all the sayings of all the prophets, and especially those who lived when the law of Moses was imposed upon the Lord's people, we would undoubtedly find many references to the Messiah as the Lamb. Isaiah, for one, who also prophesied of the virgin birth, would have known in substance and thought content the same things that his fellow prophets Lehi and Nephi were privileged to know.

Our New Testament accounts pick up the same manner of identifying Him who laid down his life in sacrifice for the sins of the world. As Lehi had foreseen, John the Baptist testified: "Behold the Lamb of God, which taketh away the sin of the world." (John 1:29.) With the sacrificial system of his ancestors in mind, Peter, the chief apostle, said the saints were "redeemed . . . with the precious blood of Christ, as of a lamb without blemish and without spot." (1 Pet. 1:18-19.) And John, the beloved apostle, had much to record that adds perspective and luster to the proper use of the Lamb's name. As did Enoch, John spoke of "the Lamb slain from the foundation of the world." (Rev. 13:8.) He saw in vision "a Lamb as it had been slain"; he saw heavenly creatures fall "down before the Lamb" in worship; and he heard heavenly choirs, composed of one hundred million voices, sing praises to his holy name. "Thou wast slain, and hast redeemed us to God by thy blood out of every kindred, and tongue, and people, and nation," they sang. Also: "Worthy is the Lamb that was slain to receive power, and riches, and wisdom, and strength, and honour, and glory, and blessing." At this point the vision expanded, the numbers in the choirs increased, and the ancient apostle heard every living creature join in the grand amen, saying: "Blessing, and honour, and glory, and power, be unto him that sitteth upon the throne, and unto the Lamb for ever and ever." (Rev. 5:6-13.) Of the Lamb, John also says: "He is Lord of lords, and King of kings" (Rev. 17:14), to whose marriage supper the faithful shall be invited, on which occasion they will sing: "Alleluia"—praise Jehovah! (for Jehovah is the Lamb)—"for the Lord God omnipotent reigneth." (Rev. 19:5-7.)

"This Do in Remembrance of Me"

A long, wearisome road runs from Eden to Gethsemane, from the garden in which the promise of a Redeemer was first given to the garden in which the promised redemption was wrought. Long, wearisome centuries—forty periods of one hundred years each—separated the promise of a Redeemer from his destined crucifixion. During all these slow-passing years millions upon millions of faithful souls looked forward, with an eye of faith, to that day when Messiah's infinite and eternal atoning sacrifice would free them from their sins. Lest they forget, the Lord gave them the ordinance of sacrifice, an ordinance perfectly designed to keep them in remembrance of that which was to be. "This thing," the angelic voice proclaimed, "is a similitude of the sacrifice of the Only Begotten of the Father." (Moses 5:7.)

A long, wearisome road also runs from Calvary and the cross to us mortals who now seek the same blessings sought by the ancients—a forgiveness of sins through our Lord's atoning sacrifice. Two millenniums—twenty centuries—now separate us from the death of a God at Golgotha. Lest we forget, the Lord has given us a sacramental ordinance that points our attention back to his spilt blood and broken flesh. It is as though we heard the angelic voice proclaim: 'This thing also is a similitude; it is an ordinance designed to keep thee in remembrance of that which Messiah-God has done for thee.' As four thousand years of sacrifices kept the Lord's people in remembrance of what their Messiah would do for them in a garden and on a cross, so two thousand years of sacramental administrations have kept them in re-membrance of what he did for them in time's meridian.

The sacrament of the Lord's supper is an ordinance of salvation in which all the faithful must participate if they are to live and reign with him. It may well have been prefigured, some two thousand years before its formal institution among men, when "Melchizedek, king of Salem, brought forth bread and wine; and he brake bread and blest it, and he blest the wine, he being the priest of the most high God. And he gave to Abram." (JST, Gen. 14:17-18.) It will be administered after the Lord comes again, to all the faithful of all ages, as they in resurrected glory assemble before him. (D&C 27.) It had its beginning as an authorized ordinance and as a required rite when Jesus and his apostolic witnesses celebrated the feast of the Passover during the week of our Lord's passion. In *Doctrinal New Testament Commentary*, volume 1, pages 716-25, I have set forth in detail how the blessing and eating and drinking of the bread and the wine grew naturally out of similar requisites that were then part of that Jewish feast. As to the symbolism of that which Jesus then instituted we read: "That the Lord Jesus the same night in which he was betrayed took bread: And when he had given thanks, he brake it, and said, Take, eat: this is my body, which is broken for you: this do in remembrance of me. After the same manner also he took the cup, when he had supped, saying, This cup is the new testament in my blood: this do ye, as oft as ye drink it, in remembrance of me. For as often as ye eat this bread, and drink this cup, ye do shew the Lord's death till he come." (1 Cor. 11:23-26.)

This sacred ordinance in which bread is eaten, in simil-itude and remembrance of our Lord's broken flesh, and in which water or wine is drunk, in similitude and remem-brance of his spilt blood, will be found among the Lord's people so long as the earth shall stand. It was had, of course, among the Nephites, and it is from their sacred writings that we gain the most perfect recitation of its meaning and pur-pose. Jesus had his Nephite disciples bring bread and wine, which he brake and blessed and gave to them to eat. He then commanded that this should thereafter be done "unto the people of my church, unto all those who shall believe and be baptized in my name. . . . And this shall ye do in remembrance of my body, which I have shown unto you. And it shall be a testimony unto the Father that ye do always remember me. And if ye do always remember me ye shall have my Spirit to be with you." Then he caused them to drink of the wine, after which he gave this counsel and commandment: "Blessed are ye for this thing which ye have done, for this is fulfilling my commandments, and this doth witness unto the Father that ye are willing to do that which I have commanded you. And this shall ye always do to those who repent and are baptized in my name; and ye shall do it in remembrance of my blood, which I have shed for you, that ye may witness unto the Father that ye do always remember me. And if ye do always remember me ye shall have my Spirit to be with you." (3 Ne. 18:1-14.)

In the waters of baptism faithful people covenant to take upon themselves the name of Christ, to love and serve him all their days, and to keep his commandments. He in turn promises them that if they so do, he will "pour out his Spirit more abundantly" upon them, and they shall "be redeemed of God, and be numbered with those of the first resurrection," and "have eternal life." (Mosiah 18:8-10.) Having in mind this same conformity to his eternal law and speaking in beautiful symbolism, our Lord said to the Jews: "Whoso eateth my flesh, and drinketh my blood, hath eternal life; and I will raise him up at the last day." (John 6:54.)

From Paul's instruction to the Corinthians (1 Cor. 11:24-30), from the Nephites' account of the introduction of the sacrament among them (3 Ne. 18), and from the sacramental prayers as revealed both to the Nephites and to us (Moro. 4 and 5; D&C 20:75-79), it is clear that when we partake worthily of the sacramental ordinance we renew the covenant made in the waters of baptism. Once again we covenant to remember and rely upon the atoning sacrifice of

Christ, to take his name upon us, and to keep his commandments. He in turn promises us that we shall always have his Spirit to be with us and that we shall have eternal life in his Father's kingdom.

Baptism is for the remission of sins. Those who are baptized worthily have their sins remitted because of the shedding of the blood of Christ. Their garments are washed in the blood of the Lamb. When they thereafter partake worthily of the sacrament, they renew the covenant made in the waters of baptism. The two covenants are the same. In each the promise is given that the Lord's Spirit will be poured out upon the contrite soul, and since the Spirit will not dwell in an unclean tabernacle, this means, of necessity and in the very nature of things, that the recipient of this glorious indwelling power becomes free from sin. In Chapter 23 we shall analyze the Mosaic sacrificial system, with specific reference to the fact that sacrifices were performed to free the people from their sins—all of which leads to the inescapable conclusion that those who were participants in sacrifices anciently were in fact making covenants with the Lord to always remember him, to take his name upon them, and to keep his commandments, all in return for his promise to let his Spirit be with them and to give them the eventual inheritance of eternal life. Symbolisms change but the principles are always the same.

Baptism Bears Record of Christ

Every baptism—properly performed by a legal administrator!—from Adam to Christ was itself a Messianic prophecy. It bore record of Christ, who was to come, and was so understood by the saints of old. Similarly, every baptism—properly performed by a legal administrator!—from our Lord's day to the present moment (and it shall so continue forever) has been an act of testimony, an ordinance that bears record of Jesus the Messiah. It matters not what uninspired Christendom may think relative to the need for or the mode of performance of this sacred ordinance. In the hearts of all those to whom the Spirit has borne witness that Jesus is the Lord is found the desire to be immersed in water after the manner of his burial and to come forth out of the water in a newness of life after the manner of his resurrection. Baptism in all ages bears witness of Christ.

Baptism began with Adam. "He was caught away by the Spirit of the Lord, and was carried down into the water, and was laid under the water, and was brought forth out of the water." He was given to know, by revelation, that he was thus "born again into the kingdom of heaven." He was expressly told that this new birth—symbolic of mortal birth, which comes "by water, and blood, and the spirit"—was also one in which men must be born "of water, and of the Spirit, and be cleansed by blood, even the blood of mine Only Begotten." He was then taught that "by the blood ye are sanctified," meaning that the cleansing power of baptism rests upon and grows out of the atoning sacrifice of the Only Begotten. (Moses 6:59-68.) That is to say, without the atonement and without the shedding of the blood of God's Son, neither baptism nor any ordinance would have any efficacy, virtue, or force in and after the resurrection of the dead.

These three elements—water, blood, and spirit—are associated not only with birth into mortality and with birth into the kingdom of heaven, which second birth comes because of the blood of Christ, but they are also the three elements present in the death of Christ, thus pointing our attention to the fact that it is his atoning sacrifice that makes the blessing of salvation available through baptism.

Speaking of Jesus as the Son of God, John says: "This is he that came"—came to make his soul a ransom for sin; came as the Savior and Redeemer—"This is he that came by water and blood, even Jesus Christ; not by water only, but by water and blood. And it is the Spirit that beareth witness, because the Spirit is truth." (1 Jn. 5:5-6.) That is to say, water, blood, and spirit were all present and played their part in his atoning sacrifice. As to the presence of blood, the

387

meaning is clear. Our Lord sweat great drops of blood from every pore as he bowed in agony in Gethsemane; then again, on the cross, his blood was shed as Roman steel pierced his flesh. As to the presence of spirit, the meaning also is clear. He voluntarily gave up his mortal life; he chose to let the eternal spirit, the Spirit which was the Great Jehovah, leave the tenement of clay and enter the paradise of peace. But what of the element of water? How was this present in his atoning sacrifice? The answer is given to us in the words of the same John who set forth that water, blood, and spirit were all present on that transcendent occasion. Of the last moments of our Lord's mortal life, the Beloved Apostle wrote: "One of the soldiers with a spear pierced his side, and forthwith came there out blood and water. And he that saw it bare record, and his record is true: and he knoweth that he saith true, that ye might believe." (John 19:34-35.)

With the vision of that cruel event still shining in his mind, John later wrote, "There are three that bear record in heaven, the Father, the Word, and the Holy Ghost: and these three are one." He is speaking of those that bear record that "Jesus is the Son of God," and having first identified those who bear this witness in heaven, he turns to a symbolical witness that is borne on earth. "And there are three that bear witness in earth," he says, "the spirit, and the water, and the blood: and these three agree in one." That is to say, the presence of these three elements in the death of Christ unite in testifying of his divine Sonship. "If we receive the witness of men, the witness of God is greater: for this is the witness of God which he hath testified of his Son"— meaning: 'We believe the testimony of men when they certify to what they know to be true; should we not more readily accept the testimony which God himself bears of his Son, whom he sent by water, and blood, and the spirit to atone for the sins of the world.' "He that believeth on the Son of God hath the witness in himself." (1 Jn. 5:5-10.) In other words, those with faith and understanding not only know of the Lord's divine mission by the power of the Spirit, but their minds are also riveted on the blessings which come from the cross of crucifixion as symbolized in the water, blood, and spirit, which were the elements of his death. How aptly the Lord uses similitudes to teach his everlasting truths.

It is common among us to say that baptisms are performed in similitude of the death, burial, and resurrection of Christ, and that they should therefore be performed by immersion. This is true, but it is an oversimplification and tells only part of the story. Baptism is a new birth; it is symbolical of our new life in the kingdom of God, which new birth is a living reality because of the shedding of the blood of Christ, or in other words because of his death, burial, and resurrection. The new birth grows out of the atonement wrought by our Lord; the newness of life comes to the repentant sinner because he has bowed to the will of the Lord and has been immersed in water by a legal administrator. Paul states it this way: "Know ye not, that so many of us as were baptized into Jesus Christ were baptized into his death?" That is, even as Christ died on the cross, so we die in baptism. "Therefore we are buried with him by baptism into death." Dead people are buried, Christ in the Arimathean's tomb, every baptized person in a watery grave. But death is not eternal, and "like as Christ was raised up from the dead by the glory of the Father, even so we also should walk in newness of life." That is to say: 'Glory be to the Father by whose almighty power our Lord rose from the dead; he took up his body again in glorious immortality; the resurrection became a reality; he lived again. And even so, every baptized person, coming forth from the water, lives again in a newness of life.' "For if we have been planted together in the likeness of his death, we shall be also in the likeness of his resurrection: Knowing this, that our old man is crucified with him, that the body of sin might be destroyed, that henceforth we should not serve sin." Sometimes the spiritual struggle to slay sin, that the new convert may be free therefrom, is as savage a warfare as death by crucifixion. But when sin is destroyed in our lives, it is no longer our master.

We are "dead indeed unto sin, but alive unto God through Jesus Christ our Lord." (Rom. 6:3-11.)

Why, then, must baptisms be performed by immersion? (3 Ne. 11:26; D&C 20:74; 128:12.) For the same reason that sacrifices required the shedding of blood, and the sacrament requires the eating of bread and the drinking of water or wine. All these things are performed in similitude of and center attention in the atoning sacrifice of the Messiah. We might as well perform sacrifices by chopping down trees or digging holes in the ground, or we might as well partake of the sacrament by eating a wafer while an officiator sips wine, as to baptize by pouring or sprinkling. Baptism is either in similitude of the death, burial, and resurrection of Christ or it is not. It either serves to dramatize the crucifixion of the old man of sin and the resurrection, as it were, of the man of God to a newness of life—all through the atonement of Him whose we are—or it does not. Any so-called baptisms, or for that matter any gospel ordinances of any kind or form, which do not center the attention of those for whom they are performed in the atoning sacrifice of Him whose blood makes all ordinances efficacious, any such ordinances fail to meet the requirements of the law of similitudes and therefore do not have divine approval.

The Sabbath Bears Witness of Christ

Sabbath worship, that system which singles out one day in seven to be used exclusively for spiritual things, is a sign which identifies the Lord's people. Whatever the world may do, day in and day out, without cessation, in the way of toil and revelry, the saints of God rest from their labors and pay their devotions to the Most High on his holy Sabbath. True religion always has and always will call for a Sabbath on which men rest from their temporal labors and work exclusively on spiritual matters. True religion requires—it is not optional; it is mandatory—that one day in seven be devoted exclusively to worshiping the Father in Spirit and in truth.

Without a Sabbath of rest and worship, men's hearts will never be centered on the things of the Spirit sufficiently to assure them of salvation.

The law of the Sabbath is so basic, so fundamental, that the Lord Jehovah named it as number four in the Ten Commandments themselves. The first three commandments call upon men to worship the Lord and reverence his great and holy name. The fourth gives us the Sabbath day as the weekly occasion on which we perfect our worship and put ourselves in tune to the full with Him by whom all things are. It is in no sense an exaggeration nor does it overstate the fact one whit to say that any person who keeps the Sabbath, according to the revealed pattern, will be saved in the celestial kingdom. The Sabbath is a day of worship; the requirement to rest from our labors, to do no servile work therein, is simply an incident to the real purpose of the day. Vital as it is to refrain from toil and to turn away from temporalities, these requirements are for the purpose of putting men in a position to do what should be done on the Sabbath, that is, to worship the Father in the name of the Son, to worship him in Spirit and in truth. True worship includes keeping the commandments, and those who devote their Sabbaths to true and proper worship obtain the encouragement that leads to full obedience.

From all this it follows that there are few things which bear a more pointed witness of the Holy Messiah and his mission than, first, the fact that there is a Sabbath, and secondly, the nature and kind of worship carried out on this holy day. The great thing about the Sabbath is that it is the day appointed for men to learn to know those Holy Beings whom it is life eternal to know. (John 17:3.) "I am the Lord your God," came the voice of Jehovah to Ezekiel as he spoke by way of commandment to all Israel; "walk in my statutes, and keep my judgments, and do them; And hallow my sabbaths; and they shall be a sign between me and you." Why were they to keep the commandments, why should they hallow the Lord's Sabbaths? The answer: "That ye may know that I am the Lord your God." (Ezek. 20:19-20; Ex. 31:12-17.) God is known by revelation; revelation comes to those who worship the Lord; and worship is perfected on the Sabbath day. It was neither chance nor happenstance that the Beloved Revelator wrote, "I was in the Spirit on the Lord's day," when he heard the voice of one saying, "I am Alpha and Omega, the first and the last," and when he saw "the Son of man" in power and glory, and heard him say, "I am the first and the last: I am he that liveth, and was dead; and, behold, I am alive for evermore." (Rev. 1:10-18.) This is Sabbath worship perfected to the point that mortal man not only knows of the reality of his Maker by the power of the Holy Ghost, but is also privileged to hear his voice and see his face.

Sabbath worship requires attendance at those meetings which are appointed as the times and places where the knowledge of God and his laws are taught. It is as much a law in our day as it was three thousand years ago. "The children of Israel shall keep the sabbath, to observe the sabbath throughout their generations, for a perpetual covenant." (Ex. 31:16.) Keeping the Sabbath includes worshiping in the congregation of the saints. "Six days shall work be done," saith the Lord, "but the seventh day is the sabbath of rest, an holy convocation; ye shall do no work therein: it is the sabbath of the Lord in all your dwellings. . . . In the seventh day it is an holy convocation: ye shall do no servile work therein." (Lev. 23:3, 8.) A holy convocation? A gathering together of the people for holy purposes, a sacrament meeting, as it were; an occasion when the saints gather to worship the Lord and partake of his Spirit; or, as he has said to us in our day: "That thou mayest more fully keep thyself unspotted from the world, thou shalt go to the house of prayer and offer up thy sacraments upon my holy day; For verily this is a day appointed unto you to rest from your labors, and to pay thy devotions unto the Most High; Nevertheless thy vows shall be offered up in righteousness on all days and at all times; But remember that on this, the Lord's day, thou shalt offer thine oblations and thy sacraments unto the Most High, confessing thy sins unto thy brethren, and before the Lord. And on this day thou shalt do none other thing, only let thy food be prepared with singleness of heart that thy fasting may be perfect, or, in other words, that thy joy may be full. Verily, this is fasting and prayer, or in other words, rejoicing and prayer." (D&C 59:9-14.)

When we begin to envision the true meaning of the Sabbath and the part it plays in preparing men to gain that salvation which is in Christ, we can see the eternal wisdom in such scriptural accounts as the following:

1. Rest from temporal pursuits is to be total and complete on the Sabbath. (Ex. 20:10; D&C 59:13.) Israel is to do no work, neither in the time of ploughing nor of harvest. (Ex. 34:21.) No fires are to be lit (Ex. 35:3), nor purchases to be made (Neh. 10:31).

2. Wrath and desolation come upon the Lord's people for "profaning the sabbath." (Neh. 13:18; Jer. 17:27.)

3. The penalties for Sabbath violation anciently are listed as both excommunication and death, probably depending on the severity of the offense. (Ex. 31:14; 35:2; Num. 15:32-36.)

4. There was even a Sabbath for the land itself, a year in which crops were not to be planted nor harvested. (Ex. 23:10-12.)

5. Temporal prosperity is promised those who keep the Sabbath. (D&C 59:16-17.)

6. Eunuchs and foreigners and strangers—those who according to ancient law were cut off from the blessing of Israel—should yet be saved if they would accept the Lord's covenant and keep his Sabbath. (Isa. 56:4-8.)

7. Israel was promised that if she kept the Sabbath she would remain a glorious and triumphant nation forever. "Hallow the sabbath day," the Lord said, giving this promise if such should eventuate: "Then shall there enter into the gates of this city kings and princes sitting upon the throne of David, riding in chariots and on horses, they, and their

princes, the men of Judah, and the inhabitants of Jerusalem: and this city shall remain for ever." (Jer. 17:25.)

In addition to all that is here written, as to how the Sabbath day is used as an occasion to learn of Christ and his laws and as a day on which to bear witness of him and his goodness, we shall now note how the day itself stands as a witness of our Lord's divinity. In this connection there are three related, yet differing, situations:

1. Christ is the Creator. "By him, and through him, and of him, the worlds are and were created." (D&C 76:24.) Specifically, at the direction of his Father, he created this earth in six days; and on the seventh day, as he viewed the finished work and saw that it was good, he rested from all his creative labors. "And I, God, blessed the seventh day, and sanctified it; because that in it I had rested from all my work which I, God, had created and made." (Moses 3:1-3.) Accordingly, he appointed the seventh day as a Sabbath in which man was commanded to commemorate and rejoice in the creative enterprises by which this earth came into being as a place where the spirit offspring of the Father might undergo their mortal probations. The Sabbath day thus bears witness that Christ is the Creator; it is a weekly reminder that he rested from his creative labors on the seventh day; it keeps us in remembrance of his grace and goodness in providing an earth whereon we might dwell for a time and a season. Thus when the Ten Commandments were first given to Moses, the reason for Sabbath observance was listed as being: "For in six days the Lord made heaven and earth, the sea, and all that in them is, and rested the seventh day: wherefore"—that is, for this very reason, to commemorate the creation—"the Lord blessed the sabbath day, and hallowed it." (Ex. 20:11.) This is the reason men kept the Sabbath day from Adam to Moses.

2. Christ is the God of Israel who delivered the children of Israel from Egyptian bondage. It was his voice that spoke to Moses in the burning bush: "Come now therefore, and I will send thee unto Pharaoh, that thou mayest bring forth

my people the children of Israel out of Egypt." (Ex. 3:10.) It was his mighty and outstretched arm that poured out the plagues on Pharaoh and his people. It was his power that parted the Red Sea so that the "waters were divided," forming "a wall unto them on their right hand, and on their left." (Ex. 14:21-22.) He brought the quails, sent the manna, gave the revelations, drove out the inhabitants of the land before them, and settled his people in a garden spot. How important it was for Israel to have in continuous remembrance all these and ten thousand other wonders that attended their deliverance from the merciless taskmasters of a wicked king! What better way to do this than to commemorate, each week, the day of this mighty and miraculous deliverance. What day was it? It was the day the Lord designated as their Sabbath.

Thus when Moses received the Ten Commandments the second time, as part of the Mosaic law rather than as part of the fulness of the gospel, the reason for keeping the Sabbath was changed. No longer was it to commemorate the creation (at least not that alone), but now it was to keep the children of Israel in remembrance of the glory of their deliverance from Egypt. Hence the Lord said, as part of the commandment itself, "And remember that thou wast a servant in the land of Egypt, and that the Lord thy God"—who is Christ—"brought thee out thence through a mighty hand and by a stretched out arm: therefore the Lord thy God commanded thee to keep the sabbath day." (Deut. 5:15.) Manifestly a Sabbath of this sort no longer falls on the seventh day, but is in fact on a different day each year. Samuel Walter Gamble, in his book *Sunday, the True Sabbath of God,* has analyzed this and a host of related and difficult Old Testament passages, all of which show that from Moses to Christ the Jewish Sabbath changed days of the week each year. And during all that period, for nearly fifteen hundred of the four thousand years that passed between Adam and Christ, the purpose of the Sabbath was to commemorate, not the creation (except incidentally), but those events of deliverance from Egyptian bondage that so exulted the feelings of all Israel.

3. Christ is also the resurrection and the life. He is the firstfruits of them that sleep. He burst the bands of death, and in a way incomprehensible to us the effects of his resurrection pass upon all men so that all are raised from the grave. His atonement is the crowning event of all history, and the resurrection is the triumphant climax of the atonement. How those of all ages should rejoice in the fact of our Lord's coming forth in glorious immortality to live and reign forever with his Father. How important it is for all men, if they are to follow in his footsteps, so that they also shall live and reign in celestial glory, how important it is for them to have always in remembrance the atonement and resurrection that makes this possible. How shall this be done? Again it is through Sabbath worship. And so the Lord appointed the day of the resurrection, the first day of the week, to be the new Sabbath, the day of remembrance and worship. It is still called the Sabbath, which means day of rest, but it is also now called the Lord's day, meaning the day on which he rose from the dead. This is the day on which the saints worshiped in the meridian of time. (Acts 20:7.) And it is the day on which the Lord has commanded us to pay our devotions to him in an especial manner, although we are to remember him on all days. (D&C 59:9-17.)

Our present needs call for us to mention but one other thing pertaining to the great system of Sabbath worship which the Lord our God has given us. It is that the millennial era of this earth, the period of one thousand years that is just ahead, is destined to be the earth's Sabbath, the day when the earth shall rest and peace and righteousness shall abide on its face. In that day the Lord himself will dwell personally among his brethren on earth and the worship of all who are privileged to live in such a glorious era will be perfect.

All Ordinances Bear Witness of Christ

We shall speak of the symbolisms commemorated in the Feast of the Passover when we consider the law of Moses and the great host of similitudes found therein. We shall not endeavor to point out the likenesses and figures found in temple ordinances, priesthood ordinations, the blessing of children, administrations for the sick, celestial marriage, and other matters. Suffice it to say that in "the ordinances" of the holy priesthood "the power of godliness is manifest" unto men (D&C 84:20), and that those whose interests lead them in that direction can find true and proper symbolisms in all things. For our present purposes we desire only to mention three special symbolical situations that existed anciently for limited periods only. That the Lord may give us special symbols and similitudes in the future is evident, but here are the three of special interest in this present study:

1. *Manna—the bread from heaven.*

For forty long, tiring years as Israel trudged wearily from one desert camp to another, awaiting the death of the rebels among them who must pass away before their promised inheritance could be gained, during all these years they sowed no crops, reaped no harvests, and built no granaries. Instead they ate manna from heaven. Six days each week this bread from heaven was spread before them as the morning dew; each day they gathered for that day only; any left over until the next day crawled with worms and stank with decay, except that on the sixth day they gathered for two days and the angelic food was preserved in purity for Sabbath use. This heaven-sent food was ground in mills, beaten in mortars, baked in pans, and eaten as cakes. It had the taste of fresh oil. Because of it, Israel lived; without it starvation and death would have been inevitable. There was no other food and no other way to gain food for all those years of desert wandering. (Ex. 16; Num. 11:6-9.) The manna ceased the first day after Israel ate of the dry corn of their promised land. (Josh. 5:12.)

Why did the Lord choose to feed his people in this way? Why not send them rains so they could plant crops? Why not lead them to a land where they could grow their own food? Certainly the supplying of manna, without which they could not have survived, taught them to depend upon the Lord for their temporal sustenance. As Moses said to them with reference to this bread from heaven, "The Lord thy God led thee forty years in the wilderness, to humble thee, and to prove thee, to know what was in thine heart, whether thou wouldest keep his commandments, or no. And he humbled thee, and suffered thee to hunger, and fed thee with manna, which thou knewest not, neither did thy fathers know." Having so said, with Israel reminded of their need to rely daily on the Lord even for the food to maintain life, Moses gave this as the reason the Lord had chosen that particular way to feed his people: "That he might make thee know that man doth not live by bread only, but by every word that proceedeth out of the mouth of the Lord doth man live." (Deut. 8:2-3.) Thus, the fact of receiving daily manna to keep them alive temporally was a repeated witness that if they were to live spiritually and have that eternal life reserved for the faithful, they must live each day in harmony with the word of Jehovah their Savior. The symbolism is perfect. What better daily reminder could there be of their need for spiritual food?

Our Jewish brethren, even in Christ's day, understood what was involved in the manna showered upon their fathers. They knew it symbolized their need to rely continually upon Jehovah and to live by every word that proceeded forth from his mouth—all of which laid the foundation for some of the most powerful testimony born by Jesus during his mortal ministry. After he had fed the five thousand with loaves and fishes provided miraculously by his creative power, our Lord spoke of the manna that Jehovah had given their fathers and said that he himself was the living bread, the word of God by which they must live to gain salvation. It was the will of the Father, he said, that all men "believe on him whom he hath sent," who had come down from heaven, "and giveth life unto the world." That none might misunderstand he said: "I am the bread of life: he that cometh to me shall never hunger; and he that believeth on me shall never thirst. . . . He that believeth on me hath everlasting life. I am the bread of life. Your fathers did eat manna in the wilderness, and are dead. This is the bread which cometh down from heaven, that a man may eat thereof, and not die. I am the living bread which came down from heaven: if any man eat of this bread, he shall live for ever. . . . As the living Father hath sent me, and I live by the Father: so he that eateth me, even he shall live by me. This is the bread which came down from heaven: not as your fathers did eat manna, and are dead: he that eateth of this bread shall live for ever." (John 6:1-58.)

For their whole sojourn in the wilderness, nearly fifteen thousand consecutive days, their fathers had eaten manna, to preserve them temporally, in similitude of the fact that all men forever, both they and their fathers and all others, must eat of the Bread of Life if they are to gain eternal life. That their fathers understood this, even if it was hidden from some of them, is seen from these words of Paul: "Our fathers," he said, "did all eat the same spiritual meat; And did all drink the same spiritual drink: for they drank of that spiritual Rock that followed them: and that Rock was Christ." (1 Cor. 10:1-3.)

2. *The brazen serpent—a likeness of Christ.*

During one of the Israelites' more rebellious periods, as they dwelt in the wilderness awaiting the day when their feet should be planted on Canaan's sod, "the Lord sent fiery serpents among the people" to punish them, and the serpents "bit the people; and much people of Israel died." Thereupon "Moses prayed for the people. And the Lord said unto Moses, Make thee a fiery serpent, and set it upon a pole: and it shall come to pass, that every one that is bitten, when he looketh upon it, shall live." Moses did as he was bidden, made a serpent of brass, and placed it upon a pole. Then, "if a serpent had bitten any man, when he beheld the serpent of brass, he lived." (Num. 21:4-9.)

Knowing, as we do, that by faith all things are possible, we may conclude that the brazen serpent became a means of helping the people center their faith in the Lord so as to gain his healing power. One of the gifts of the Spirit that Christ promised his saints is that "they shall take up serpents" and yet be free from their poisonous bites. (Mark 16:18.) In any event, those anciently who were bitten had but to look, in the approved manner, and they lived, while those failing so to do died.

Our Old Testament simply preserves the story of the serpents and how life or death hung in the balance for those who were bitten. It makes no explanation of what the Lord was really doing for his people and why he chose this unique way to bring to pass his purposes. But from the New Testament and the Book of Mormon we learn why and in what manner the Lord was testing his people. Nephi confirms and amplifies the Old Testament account by saying the Lord "sent fiery flying serpents among them." We have no idea what kind of poisonous creatures were here used, but we do know that after men were bitten, the Lord "prepared a way that they might be healed; and the labor which they had to perform was to look; and because of the simpleness of the way, or the easiness of it, there were many who perished." (1 Ne. 17:41; 2 Ne. 25:20.)

Alma speaks of the brazen serpent as a type of something else. "A type was raised up in the wilderness," he says, "that whosoever would look upon it might live. And many did look and live. But few understood the meaning of those things, and this because of the hardness of their hearts." (Alma 33:19.) As to the full meaning of the type, we turn to the writings of Nephi the son of Helaman. "Moses . . . hath spoken concerning the coming of the Messiah," he writes. "Yea, did he not bear record that the Son of God should come? And as he lifted up the brazen serpent in the wilderness, even so shall he be lifted up who should come." The brazen serpent was lifted up upon the pole in similitude of the fact that the Redeemer of the world would be lifted up upon the cross. And as to the lesson thus taught, Nephi continues: "And as many as should look upon that serpent should live, even so as many as should look upon the Son of God with faith, having a contrite spirit, might live, even unto that life which is eternal." (Hel. 8:13-15.)

Now back to the words of Alma. "But there were many who were so hardened that they would not look" upon the serpent, "therefore they perished," he continues. "Now the reason they would not look is because they did not believe that it would heal them." And we might interject: 'And there are many whose hearts are so hardened that they will not look to Christ, and they shall perish.' And is it too much to add that the reason they do not look to Christ is because they do not believe that he will save them if they keep his commandments. "O my brethren, if ye could be healed by merely casting about your eyes that ye might be healed," Alma pleads, "would ye not behold quickly, or would ye rather harden your hearts in unbelief, and be slothful, that ye would not cast about your eyes, that ye might perish?" And our echoing cry is: 'If we can be saved by accepting Christ; if we can gain eternal life by living his laws, why should we harden our hearts and perish in unbelief? If there is joy and peace in this life and eternal reward in the life to come for all those who keep the commandments, why should we be slothful? Why should we hesitate to walk in paths of truth and righteousness?' (Alma 33:20-21.)

We have from the lips of the Lord Jesus his own witness of the doctrines here expounded. Said he: "As Moses lifted up the serpent in the wilderness, even so must the Son of man be lifted up: That whosoever believeth in him should not perish, but have eternal life." (John 3:14-15.) The New Testament does not amplify the teaching, but from this statement of our Lord it is clear that it was known and understood and taught by and among the true believers in Palestine in the meridian of time. Their teachings and their exhortations would have been no different from those of their Book of Mormon counterparts, which brings us again back to the words of Alma. The conclusion he draws from the fact that those who cast their eyes upon the brazen serpent were healed is that men should cast their eyes upon Christ and thereby be saved. "Cast about your eyes and begin to believe in the Son of God," he says, "that he will come to redeem his people, and that he shall suffer and die to atone for their sins; and that he shall rise again from the dead, which shall bring to pass the resurrection, that all men shall stand before him, to be judged at the last and judgment day, according to their works." (Alma 33:22.)

3. *The Liahona—a likeness of Christ.*

Our Nephite brethren were given a special type and shadow of Christ that was akin to the brazen serpent of Moses, but that was suited to the particular needs and circumstances in which Lehi and his family found themselves. Called the Liahona, it was a compass, "a round ball of curious workmanship." Like Moses' serpent, it was made of fine brass. "Within the ball were two spindles," which pointed out the course they should travel. Nephi says these pointers worked "according to the faith and diligence and heed which we did give unto them." From time to time messages of divine origin were written upon the Liahona, also "according to the heed and diligence which we gave unto it." (1 Ne. 16:10, 28-29.) This divine compass ceased to work whenever its Nephite owners acted in unrighteousness. (1 Ne. 18:12.)

Alma explained the use and purpose of the Liahona to his son Helaman in these words: "It did work for them according to their faith in God; therefore, if they had faith to believe that God could cause that those spindles should point the way they should go, behold, it was done." That this same requisite was present when people were healed by looking at the brazen serpent there can be no doubt. But it was with the Nephites as it had been with their Israelite ancestors; they were not always faithful. Alma says: "They were slothful, and forgot to exercise their faith and diligence and then those marvelous works ceased, and they did not progress in their journey; Therefore, they tarried in the wilderness, or did not travel a direct course, and were afflicted with hunger and thirst, because of their transgressions."

Of itself the Liahona was a great blessing. Food was found, courses were charted through perilous areas, and messages of incomparable worth were written on its face. But as with the brazen serpent, its greatest function was the witness of Christ that came because of its proper usage. "These things are not without a shadow," Alma said, "for as our fathers were slothful to give heed to this compass (now these things were temporal) they did not prosper; even so it is with things which are spiritual. For behold, it is as easy to give heed to the word of Christ, which will point to you a straight course to eternal bliss, as it was for our fathers to give heed to this compass, which would point unto them a straight course to the promised land. And now I say, is there not a type in this thing? For just as surely as this director did bring our fathers, by following its course, to the promised land, shall the words of Christ, if we follow their course, carry us beyond this vale of sorrow into a far better land of promise." (Alma 37:38-45.)

Chapter 22

LAW OF MOSES BEARS WITNESS OF CHRIST

The Gospel of Christ and the Gospel of Moses

There are two gospels—the preparatory gospel and the fulness of the everlasting gospel. There are two proclamations, two pronouncements of glad tidings, two messages of light and truth and power, which God has given to his people at one time or another. What the people receive at any given moment in time depends upon them. The Lord gives them all of his word, or only a portion, depending on "the heed and diligence which they give unto him." If all men had open hearts and receptive minds; if they desired righteousness and sought truth in preference to all else; if they conformed to every true principle they received—all would accept the fulness of his gospel and join that church and kingdom which is always administered for the benefit and blessing of mankind. As it is written: "He that will harden his heart, the same receiveth the lesser portion of the word; and he that will not harden his heart, to him is given the greater portion of the word, until it is given unto him to know the mysteries of God until he know them in full." (Alma 12:9-10.)

As is evident from the pure meaning of the words themselves, the fulness of the everlasting gospel has always existed and will continue to endure forever; the preparatory gospel, on the other hand, is not eternal in nature, but is something that goes before and makes people ready for the receipt of the fulness of saving truth. The everlasting gospel existed before the world was; it is "the gospel of God . . . Concerning his Son Jesus Christ our Lord" (Rom. 1:1-3), and it now bears the name of the Son and is called the gospel of Christ. In contrast, the preparatory gospel is as an Elias who goes before to prepare the way for something greater; it is reserved for those who are not yet able to bear the eternal fulness. Our revelations speak of "the gospel of Abraham," meaning the divine commission given to the father of the faithful to bless himself and his seed after him. (D&C 110:12.) Since the preparatory gospel was a divine commission given to Israel through Moses, to bless and train them through all the generations when they were a distinct and separate people, it is with propriety that we call it the gospel of Moses, though in fact it came from the Lord Jehovah, as also did the divine commission or gospel given to Abraham.

Since salvation is in Christ, and not in Moses or any other man, the Lord always seeks to dispense from heaven his everlasting gospel to his children on earth. If they will receive the fulness of the message of salvation, it is theirs to enjoy, theirs for the taking, without money and without price. Adam, Enoch, Noah, Abraham, and many of the ancients had dispensations of the gospel and enjoyed its saving powers in their eternal fulness. The fulness of the everlasting gospel consists of all the truths, powers, priesthoods, keys, ordinances, laws, and covenants by conformity to which mortal men can obtain a fulness of eternal glory in the highest heaven of the celestial world.

In keeping with the pattern followed for twenty-five hundred years in his dealings with men, the Lord revealed the fulness of the everlasting gospel to Moses, and this mighty man of faith sought diligently to persuade his Israelitish brethren to believe its truths and live its laws. They refused. They hardened their hearts and chose to walk in carnal paths. The eternal fulness was more than they could

405

bear. As a consequence, God in his mercy—lest they be damned for rejecting that which they could not live, and as a means of preparing them and their seed for the higher standards which all saved beings must eventually live—the Lord in his mercy gave them the law of Moses. It did not replace the gospel, which had been offered to them in the first instance; rather, it was added to the more perfect system, for as we shall see, there were times when the ancient and chosen seed had both the fulness of the gospel and the preparatory gospel, when they had all of the saving truths and yet kept the terms and conditions of the law of Moses.

Among our sectarian brethren it is falsely assumed that Deity dealt in one way with the patriarchs, in another with the Israel of Moses, and in yet another with mankind after he sent his Son to open the so-called Christian Era. Knowing, however, that the gospel is everlasting; that God is the same yesterday, today, and forever; and that all flesh, no matter when it is found in mortal guise, will be saved on the same principles—we are in a position to comprehend the true relationship between the gospel and the law of Moses and to understand Paul's statements with reference to them. To the Galatians he said plainly, "God . . . preached before the gospel unto Abraham." Then he spoke of the law of Moses and said, "No man is justified by the law," meaning that salvation does not come by the law alone. It is, rather, "Christ [that] hath redeemed us," so that "the blessing[s] of Abraham . . . through Jesus Christ" are still in effect. That is to say, the blessings of Abraham, which are the blessings of the gospel, because Abraham had the gospel, were in effect for him, and are in effect for us, because of Christ and his atonement. Then came this inspired utterance: "The covenant, that was confirmed before of God in Christ, the law, which was four hundred and thirty years after, cannot disannul, that it should make the promise of none effect." In other words, 'God gave the gospel of Jesus Christ to Abraham, and the law of Moses which came 430 years later cannot disannul or replace the gospel promises.' "Wherefore then serveth the law?" Paul asks, meaning, 'Why did the Lord give the law of Moses since the gospel itself had been given to the ancestors of Moses?' He answers: "It was added because of transgressions," but, he repeats, righteousness and salvation do not come by the law, but through faith in Christ and obedience to his gospel law. Hence: "The law was our schoolmaster to bring us unto Christ, that we might be justified by faith." We are thus saved because of faith in Christ, and "after that faith is come, we are no longer under a schoolmaster." (Gal. 3.)

"How long shall I bear with this evil congregation, which murmur against me?" So spake the Lord of his chosen yet rebelling people. "Your carcases shall fall in this wilderness," he said. All who were twenty years of age and older, except Joshua and Caleb, should die in the wilderness; only the younger generation should have an inheritance in their promised land. And so it was. (Num. 14:27-38.) And such was the historical situation Paul had in mind when he said that many, but not all, who came out of Egypt hardened their hearts and provoked the Lord. "With whom was he grieved forty years?" Paul asks. "Was it not with them that had sinned, whose carcases fell in the wilderness?" It is in that context that Paul explains to the Hebrews, in effect, how the law of Moses was "added because of transgressions." "For unto us was the gospel preached, as well as unto them: but the word preached did not profit them, not being mixed with faith in them that heard it." (Heb. 3:15-19; 4:1-2.) The saints in Paul's day had the gospel, the same gospel that had been offered in the Mosaic era. The meridian saints accepted its saving truths; ancient Israel, lacking faith, ended up with a schoolmaster to lead them until they could abide the higher law.

There were, of course, those in Israel, in the day of Moses and during the long years during which they awaited the advent of their Messiah, who had faith and were blessed with the fulness of the gospel, as we shall hereafter point out. Moses was one of these, in consequence of which the New

Testament testimony of him is that he chose "to suffer affliction with the people of God" because he esteemed "the reproach of Christ greater riches than the treasures of Egypt."
(Heb. 11:25-26.)

The Law of Christ and the Law of Moses

There are two laws—the law of Christ and the law of
Moses. The one is the gospel, the other is the preparatory
gospel. There are two sets of commandments—the commandments which assure a celestial inheritance, and the law
of carnal commandments, which, standing alone, carry no
such assurance of eternal reward. The one is for those who
are "anxiously engaged in a good cause," who "do many
things of their own free will," who use their agency to "bring
to pass much righteousness"; the other is for those who are
slothful and rebellious by nature, who need to be commanded in all things, who neglect good works unless they
are compelled to perform them. (D&C 58:26-27.) Of these
two laws, John wrote: "The law was given through Moses,
but life and truth came through Jesus Christ. For the law
was after a carnal commandment, to the administration of
death; but the gospel was after the power of an endless life,
through Jesus Christ, the Only Begotten Son, who is in the
bosom of the Father." (JST, John 1:17-18.)

Christ's law is his gospel. By obedience to its laws and by
conformity to its ordinances, all mankind may gain a celestial inheritance. It is, in fact, the law of a celestial
kingdom and has been given to us mortals to qualify us to go
where God and Christ and holy beings are. "And they who
are not sanctified through the law which I have give unto
you," the Lord says, "even the law of Christ, must inherit
another kingdom, even that of a terrestrial kingdom, or that
of a telestial kingdom. For he who is not able to abide the
law of a celestial kingdom cannot abide a celestial glory."
(D&C 88:21-22.)

Moses' law is the law of carnal commandments, or in

other words the law which is concerned, in detail and specifically, with carnal and evil acts—warning, exhorting, encouraging, commanding, all to the end that men will be left without excuse and, hopefully, will avoid the snares of the evil one. Paul uses the name "the law of a carnal commandment" (Heb. 7:16) to describe it, and also calls it "the law of commandments contained in ordinances" (Eph. 2:15). Abinadi speaks of it as "a law of performances and of ordinances, a law which they were to observe strictly from day to day, to keep them in remembrance of God and their duty towards him." (Mosiah 13:30.) Our revelation, speaking of the preparatory gospel, says: "Which gospel is the gospel of repentance and of baptism, and the remission of sins, and the law of carnal commandments, which the Lord in his wrath caused to continue with the house of Aaron among the children of Israel until John." (D&C 84:27.)

Historically, this law first came into being when Israel rejected the gospel and failed to live as Jehovah, their Lord, commanded them to do. Moses, having destroyed the tablets of stone on which the law as first revealed was written, received this commandment from the Lord: "Hew thee two other tables of stone, like unto the first, and I will write upon them also, the words of the law, according as they were written at the first on the tables which thou brakest; but it shall not be according to the first, for I will take away the priesthood out of their midst; therefore my holy order, and the ordinances thereof, shall not go before them; for my presence shall not go up in their midst, lest I destroy them. But I will give unto them the law as at the first, but it shall be after the law of a carnal commandment; for I have sworn in my wrath, that they shall not enter into my presence, into my rest, in the days of their pilgrimage." (JST, Ex. 34:1-2.)

The Priesthood of Christ and the Priesthood of Israel

There are two priesthoods—the priesthood of Melchizedek and the priesthood of Aaron. The one is the highest and holiest order on earth or in heaven; it is "The Holy Priesthood, after the Order of the Son of God"; it has power, dominion, and authority over all things; "all other authorities or offices in the church are appendages" to it; and it holds "the keys of all the spiritual blessings of the church." The other—"the Aaronic or Levitical Priesthood"—is the lesser; "it was conferred upon Aaron and his seed, throughout all their generations"; it holds "the keys of the ministering of angels"; and it is empowered "to administer in outward ordinances, the letter of the gospel." (D&C 107:1-20.) Beginning in the meridian of time, since Israel was no longer to exist as a separate nation and the offering of Levitical sacrifices was discontinued, the Lord authorized others who were not of the tribe of Levi or the lineage of Aaron to hold this lesser priesthood.

For our purposes here, the great distinction between the Melchizedek Priesthood and the Aaronic or Levitical Priesthood is this: The Melchizedek Priesthood administers the gospel in its everlasting fulness, but the Aaronic Priesthood administers the preparatory gospel only, which preparatory gospel is the law of Moses and includes the law of carnal commandments.

All of the prophets from Adam to Moses held the higher or Melchizedek Priesthood. There was no Aaronic Priesthood during the two and a half millenniums there involved. The higher priesthood "continueth in the church of God in all generations, and is without beginning of days or end of years." It is an eternal priesthood and has existed with God from all eternity. "This greater priesthood administereth the gospel and holdeth the key of the mysteries of the kingdom, even the key of the knowledge of God." (D&C 84:17-19.) Those who hold it and are true and faithful in all things "have the privilege of receiving the mysteries of the kingdom of heaven, to have the heavens opened unto them, to commune with the general assembly and church of the Firstborn, and to enjoy the communion and presence of God the Father, and Jesus the mediator of the new covenant."

(D&C 107:19.) Worthy holders "can see the face of God, even the Father." Such were its powers anciently, such are they today, with reference to which our scriptures say: "Now this Moses plainly taught to the children of Israel in the wilderness, and sought diligently to sanctify his people that they might behold the face of God; But they hardened their hearts and could not endure his presence; therefore, the Lord in his wrath, for his anger was kindled against them, swore that they should not enter into his rest while in the wilderness, which rest is the fulness of his glory. Therefore, he took Moses out of their midst, and the Holy Priesthood also." (D&C 84:22-25.)

When the Lord took Moses and the holy priesthood from Israel, he thereby took from them the fulness of his everlasting gospel, because it takes the Melchizedek Priesthood to administer the gospel. For one thing it is only this higher priesthood that can lay on hands for the gift of the Holy Ghost. The Holy Ghost is a sanctifier, and unless men are sanctified they cannot see the face of God; as we have seen, it was their failure to use this power whereby sanctification comes that caused the Lord to withdraw it from them. But when the Lord left the Aaronic Priesthood in Israel he thereby left the power and authority to administer the law of Moses in all its parts and ramifications.

We should here observe that the Aaronic Priesthood was added to the Melchizedek. This is true even though the power of the lesser priesthood is automatically embraced within the greater power of the higher priesthood. The historical fact is that Aaron and his sons already held the Melchizedek Priesthood and were numbered with the elders of Israel when the Lord first conferred the lesser authority upon them. This is precisely what we do today when we take a holder of the Melchizedek Priesthood and ordain him a bishop in the Aaronic Priesthood. But our point is that in the day of the origin of the lesser order, it was with the lesser priesthood as it was with the law of Moses, both were "added because of transgressions." (Gal. 3:19.) A lesser law was

411

added to a higher law, and a lesser priesthood was added to a greater priesthood.

We should here observe also that when the scripture says the Lord took Moses and the holy priesthood out of the midst of Israel, it means that he took from them the prophet who held the keys and who could authorize the priesthood to be conferred upon others. Any who thereafter held either the keys or the Melchizedek Priesthood gained them by special dispensation. The Aaronic Priesthood thus became the priesthood of administration; it was in effect the priesthood of Israel; it handled the affairs of the Church and officiated in the offering of sacrifices. However, there were at many times and may have been at all times prophets and worthy men who held the Melchizedek Priesthood. Joseph Smith said, "All the prophets had the Melchizedek Priesthood and were ordained by God himself." (*Teachings,* p. 181.) Elijah was the last prophet in Israel to hold the keys of the sealing power, and the Melchizedek Priesthood was the only priesthood held by the Nephites for the first 634 years of their separate existence. There were, of course, none of the tribe of Levi among them, and the Levites were the only ones anciently who held the lesser priesthood.

A New Priesthood Brings a New Law

Priesthood, without which the true church cannot exist, and without which the gospel cannot be administered, is always found among the Lord's people. Whenever men possess the fulness of the priesthood they have also the fulness of the gospel. The higher priesthood administers the whole gospel system; the lesser priesthood can go no further than to operate the performances and ordinances of the law of Moses. When Jesus came among the Jews they had Levitical power only. Zacharias was a priest of that order, and the priests and Levites, as legal administrators whose acts were recognized by Jehovah, were offering sacrifices, receiving tithes, and giving guidance to the people. Theirs was the power to baptize, but not to confer the Holy Ghost. Priestly administrations were limited to outward ordinances; the people were not blessed with the higher authority which deals with inward ordinances, as it were, that is, with spiritual things. John the Baptist was the last recognized legal administrator who held the keys and powers of the Aaronic Priesthood. As the Elias who prepared the way before the Lord, he said: "I indeed baptize you with water unto repentance: but he that cometh after me is mightier than I, whose shoes I am not worthy to bear: he shall baptize you with the Holy Ghost, and with fire." (Matt. 3:11.) John held the Aaronic Priesthood, Christ the Melchizedek. Ordinances and blessings denied the people by John were freely offered to them by Jesus.

Most of the Jews of that day, being darkened in their mind and apostate in their feelings, rejected their Messiah and chose to believe that their Levitical powers sufficed for salvation. What need had they, so they thought, for new revelation, new powers, a new priesthood, a new gospel. It was as though they said, 'We have Aaron and his sons who serve as priests; we have all these Levites to minister to our needs; we walk where Moses walked; what else could such a blessed people want?' But, so that the whole matter might be set at rest, once and for all, and that they might know that the Mosaic system laid the foundation for and introduced the new law of the Lord, Paul wrote his Epistle to the Hebrews. In it he reasoned thus:

'You Jews—meaning those who had gone before, for the kingdom had been taken from those then living—you Jews have the law of Moses with all its powers and prerogatives. Your priests are called of God to offer sacrifices and to direct all the performances of that divine system. They hold the Aaronic Priesthood. Aaron is their father, and they act in his name and use his priesthood. But come now, let us "consider the Apostle and High Priest of our profession, Christ Jesus." (Heb. 3:1.) He is "Jesus the Son of God," "a great high priest," who has "passed into the heavens." (Heb. 4:14.)

413

Your own scriptures testify of him, saying, "Thou art my Son, to day have I begotten thee," and also, "Thou art a priest for ever after the order of Melchisedec." (Heb. 5:5-6.) Even as your priests, who served after the order of Aaron, offered "sacrifices for sins" (Heb. 5:1), so did this "Jesus" whom God "made an high priest for ever after the order of Melchisedec" (Heb. 6:20), for he truly offered up himself as a sacrifice for sin. The sacrifices of your priests are made daily, "But this man, because he continueth ever, hath an unchangeable priesthood. Wherefore he is able also to save them to the uttermost that come unto God by him, seeing he ever liveth to make intercession for them. For such an high priest became us, who is holy, harmless, undefiled, separate from sinners, and made higher than the heavens; Who needeth not daily, as those high priests, to offer up sacrifice, first for his own sins, and then for the people's: for this he did once, when he offered up himself." (Heb. 7:24-27.) And that he was to come and change your law you know because David, your father, who was subject to the law of Moses as then administered by the priests of the Aaronic order, in prophesying of a day future to his own, said that a priest would arise after the order of Melchizedek, and this priest, who is Christ, would bring a new and higher law so that salvation might come to his people. "If therefore perfection were by the Levitical priesthood, (for under it the people received the law), what further need was there that another priest should arise after the order of Melchisedec, and not be called after the order of Aaron? For the priesthood being changed, there is made of necessity a change also of the law. For he of whom these things are spoken pertaineth to another tribe, of which no man gave attendance at the altar. For it is evident that our Lord sprang out of Juda; of which tribe Moses spake nothing concerning priesthood. And it is yet far more evident: for that after the similitude of Melchisedec there ariseth another priest, Who is made, not after the law of a carnal commandment, but after the power of an endless life. For he testifieth, Thou art a priest for ever after the order of Melchisedec." ' (Heb. 7:11-17.)

Why There Was a Law of Moses

Why was there a law of Moses? Two reasons are apparent:

1. It was a divine and uplifting system of goodness and right. Those who obeyed its precepts and kept its ordinances bettered themselves temporally and spiritually. They were in the line of their duty, received revelations, and came to know their God. While the world around them was in darkness, the morning rays of divine truth were opening their vision to the wonders and glories mortal man might obtain. It was not that eternal fulness which earth's pilgrims must receive if they are to return to that Presence whence they came, but it was an open door, an invitation to step forward and receive the fulness of the word. It was a preparatory gospel. And it is better to walk in godly paths for fear of the penalties of disobedience than not to walk in them at all. It is better to maintain marital fidelity for fear of the death penalty imposed on adulterers by the law of Moses than to walk in unclean paths and go to hell when earth's probation is over. We must not belittle or downgrade the law of Moses. It was the most perfect system of worship known to man, excepting only the fulness of the gospel. Out of it have come nearly all the principles of ethics and decency that have been incorporated into our whole system of modern jurisprudence. And lest there be any doubt in anyone's mind as to the excellence and beauty of the Mosaic system, let us ponder this conclusion: Even now, after two thousand years of exposure to the new covenant, there are but few of earth's inhabitants who conform to the standards of decency, excellence, and righteousness that even approach those which God imposed upon his ancient covenant people by the mouth of Moses the great lawgiver.

2. Just as our conformity to gospel standards, while dwelling as lowly mortals apart from our Maker, prepares us to return to his presence with an inheritance of immortal glory, so the Mosaic standards prepared the chosen of Israel to believe and obey that gospel by conformity to which eternal life is won. The law of Moses was an Elias; it prepared the way for something far greater. "Ye have heard that it was said by them of old time, Thou shalt not commit adultery," Jesus said of the Mosaic proscription, saying it as a prelude to giving them the gospel standard in these words: "But I say unto you, That whosoever looketh on a woman to lust after her hath committed adultery with her already in his heart." (Matt. 5:27-28.) The law of Moses urged, almost compelled, obedience; at least it put great pressures on Israel to keep ever before them the goodness of their Lord and to seek his face. The gospel says instead: 'Here is the way; walk ye in it; choose of your own free will to do good and work righteousness; and the Lord will bless you accordingly,' all of which makes for much greater development of character; it is, in fact, a greater test of personal integrity than were the provisions of the old covenant. Hence, everything connected with the lesser law pointed to the higher law, or in other words it pointed to Christ and his gospel. Each Mosaic performance was so arranged and so set up that it was a type and a shadow of what was to be. Their sacrifices were performed in similitude of the coming sacrifice of their Messiah; the rituals out of which they gained forgiveness of sins were tokens of what was to be in the life of Him whose atonement made forgiveness possible; their every act, every ordinance, every performance—all that they did—pointed the hearts and minds of believing worshipers forward to Jesus Christ and him crucified. All this was understood by those among them who were faithful and true; the rebellious and slothful were like their modern counterparts, unbelieving, nonconforming, unsaved.

It is the will of the Lord, and has been from the beginning, that all men everywhere should believe in Christ, accept the fulness of his everlasting gospel, and rely on the merits of his atoning sacrifice for salvation. Accordingly, as affirmed by an angel to King Benjamin, "the Lord God hath sent his holy prophets among all the children of men, to declare these things to every kindred, nation, and tongue, that thereby whosoever should believe that Christ should come, the same might receive remission of their sins, and rejoice with exceeding great joy, even as though he had already come among them. Yet the Lord God saw that his people were a stiffnecked people, and he appointed unto them a law, even the law of Moses. And many signs, and wonders, and types, and shadows showed he unto them, concerning his coming; and also holy prophets spake unto them concerning his coming; and yet they hardened their hearts, and understood not that the law of Moses availeth nothing except it were through the atonement of his blood." (Mosiah 3:13-15.)

With this same theme in mind, Abinadi said: "It was expedient that there should be a law given to the children of Israel, yea, even a very strict law; for they were a stiffnecked people, quick to do iniquity, and slow to remember the Lord their God; Therefore there was a law given them, yea, a law of performances and of ordinances, a law which they were to observe strictly from day to day, to keep them in remembrance of God and their duty towards him. But behold, I say unto you, that all these things were types of things to come." (Mosiah 13:29-31.)

Paul named various of the Mosaic ordinances and performances and said they were a "shadow of heavenly things." (Heb. 8:4-5.) The "meats and drinks, and divers washings, and carnal ordinances, imposed on them until the time of reformation," he said, were designed as "a figure for the time then present." He spoke of the various formalities involved in sprinkling blood as "patterns" of things of a much higher nature. "The law," he said, was "a shadow of good things to come." (Heb. 9:1-10, 19-23; 10:1.) But perhaps Amulek's statement is the clearest and best of them all. He said: "This is the whole meaning of the law, every whit pointing to that great and last sacrifice; and that great and last sacrifice will be the Son of God, yea, infinite and eternal." (Alma 34:14.)

Salvation Cannot Come by the Law of Moses

Israel had many wicked kings who led the chosen seed astray. Some adopted false religions and imposed false ordinances upon the people; others gave lip service to the law of Moses, but chose to walk in carnal paths and be guided by apostate priests who drew near to the Lord with their lips but whose hearts were far from him. To such kings and false priests the Lord sent his prophets, crying repentance, warning, exhorting, condemning, as the needs required. One such king was the American Hebrew, Noah, to whom Abinadi was sent, who, being so commanded, prophesied ill against the people and the kingdom. In a confrontation with the false priests who upheld King Noah's wicked course, Abinadi asked: "What teach ye this people?" They answered, "We teach the law of Moses." Abinadi's prophetic condemnation then fell upon them in these words: "If ye teach the law of Moses why do ye not keep it? Why do ye set your hearts upon riches? Why do ye commit whoredoms and spend your strength with harlots, yea, and cause this people to commit sin, that the Lord has cause to send me to prophesy against this people, yea, even a great evil against this people?"

Change the names and move to another day and location and we can see Samuel rejecting Saul, or Nathan condemning David, or Elijah cursing Ahab. Wickedness is the same in every day and at all times. Only the people and the historical settings change. And so Abinadi, reacting to the needs of his hour and giving the word of the Lord to those before whom he stood, said these prophetic words: "It shall come to pass that ye shall be smitten for your iniquities, for ye have said that ye teach the law of Moses. And what know

418

ye concerning the law of Moses? Doth salvation come by the law of Moses? What say ye?" The question might have been asked by a long line of prophets of a long line of false priests who also had lost the meaning and import of the divine pronouncements made by mighty Moses. And so, sadly for their sake and that of their people, the record says that Noah's priests answered "that salvation did come by the law of Moses." (Mosiah 12.)

After some further doctrinal exposition, Abinadi said: "I say unto you that it is expedient that ye should keep the law of Moses as yet; but I say unto you, that the time shall come when it shall no more be expedient to keep the law of Moses. And moreover, I say unto you, that salvation doth not come by the law alone; and were it not for the atonement, which God himself shall make for the sins and iniquities of his people, that they must unavoidably perish, notwithstanding the law of Moses." Following this he spoke of the strict and straitened nature of the restrictions and performances imposed in the law, and of how others, in addition to these false priests of Noah, had not understood the law; he told how all the prophets had spoken of the coming of a Messiah; and with reference to their testimony, he asked: "Have they not said that God himself should come down among the children of men, and take upon him the form of a man, and go forth in mighty power upon the face of the earth? Yea, and have they not said also that he should bring to pass the resurrection of the dead, and that he, himself, should be oppressed and afflicted?" At this point he quoted the incomparable Messianic prophecies of Isaiah 53, expounded their meaning at some length, and concluded with these warning words: "And now, ought ye not to tremble and repent of your sins, and remember that only in and through Christ ye can be saved? Therefore, if ye teach the law of Moses, also teach that it is a shadow of those things which are to come— Teach them that redemption cometh through Christ the Lord, who is the very Eternal Father." (Mosiah 13, 14, 15, and 16.)

In his writings to the Hebrews, Paul bears a similar testimony. As we have already seen, he taught that "perfection" did not come "by the Levitical priesthood," but through "the order of Melchisedec," which Christ should restore. One obvious reason for this is that it is by the power of the Melchizedek Priesthood that men receive the gift of the Holy Ghost, and without the Holy Ghost they cannot be sanctified. Hence, says Paul, "the law made nothing perfect, but the bringing in of a better hope did; by the which we draw nigh unto God." (Heb. 7:11-19.) There are a number of other like assertions in Hebrews, and a good portion of Romans was written to show that salvation is not in the law of Moses but in Christ. I have written on this at some length on pages 221 to 248 of *Doctrinal New Testament Commentary*, volume 2. But to put the whole matter to rest forever, the Lord has said in our day: "All old covenants have I caused to be done away, . . . for you cannot enter in at the strait gate by the law of Moses, neither by your dead works." (D&C 22.)

Nephites Followed Both Moses and Christ

Those Israelites known as Nephites, though separated from their forebears and kindred by oceans of water, yet kept the law of Moses. (2 Ne. 5:10; Jarom 1:5; Hel. 15:5.) But they did so with a proper understanding, knowing that salvation was in Christ who should come and that "the law of Moses was a type of his coming." Accordingly, "They did not suppose that salvation came by the law of Moses; but the law of Moses did serve to strengthen their faith in Christ; and thus they did retain a hope through faith, unto eternal salvation, relying upon the spirit of prophecy, which spake of those things to come." (Alma 25:15-16.) The souls of their prophets delighted in proving unto the people "the truth of the coming of Christ; for, for this end hath the law of Moses been given." (2 Ne. 11:4.) Of the Nephite worship, Jacob says: "We knew of Christ, and we had a hope of his glory many hundred years before his coming; and not only we ourselves had a hope of his glory, but also all the holy prophets which were before us. Behold, they believed in Christ and worshiped the Father in his name, and also we worship the Father in his name. And for this intent we keep the law of Moses, it pointing our souls to him." (Jacob 4:4-5; Jarom 1:11.) To them the law was not an end in itself, but a means to an end. The blindness of their Jewish relatives in the Old World came "by looking beyond the mark" (Jacob 4:14), meaning they did not have a proper perspective of the law and know how it was designed to lead them to Christ and his gospel.

These Nephites, who were faithful and true in keeping the law of Moses, had the Melchizedek Priesthood, which means they had also the fulness of the gospel. In many respects, for instance, the greatest sermon we have on baptism and the receipt of the Holy Ghost is 2 Nephi 31; our best passages on being born again are in Mosiah 27 and Alma 5; our most explicit teachings on the atonement of Christ are in 2 Nephi 2 and 9 and Alma 34; and some of our best information about the Melchizedek Priesthood is found in Alma 13—all of which doctrines were set forth during what men falsely call the pre-Christian Era.

Of this remarkable situation, in which men lived under both the law and the gospel at one and the same time, Nephi says: "We labor diligently to write, to persuade our children, and also our brethren, to believe in Christ, and to be reconciled to God; for we know that it is by grace that we are saved, after all we can do. And, notwithstanding we believe in Christ, we keep the law of Moses, and look forward with steadfastness unto Christ, until the law shall be fulfilled. For, for this end was the law given; wherefore the law hath become dead unto us, and we are made alive in Christ because of our faith; yet we keep the law because of the commandments. And we talk of Christ, we rejoice in Christ, we preach of Christ, we prophesy of Christ, and we write according to our prophecies, that our children may know to what source they may look for a remission of their sins. Wherefore, we speak concerning the law that our children may know the deadness of the law; and they, by knowing the deadness of the law, may look forward unto that life which is in Christ, and know for what end the law was given. And after the law is fulfilled in Christ, that they need not harden their hearts against him when the law ought to be done away." (2 Ne. 25:23-27.)

That there were selected portions of Old World Israel to whom the law became dead and who rejoiced in their perfect knowledge of Christ and his gospel laws is perfectly clear. Such would have been the case with all of the prophets, for they all held the Melchizedek Priesthood. Elijah, for instance, had the fulness of the gospel—meaning all that was necessary to save and exalt him with a fulness of glory in the highest heaven—for he was the very one chosen of the Lord to restore this power and authority in modern times.

Law of Moses Fulfilled in Christ

If Jesus Christ was the promised Messiah, then the law of Moses was fulfilled in his coming. If he was not the Son of God, then the law of Moses is still in force, and we and all who seek religious truth should be engaged in a diligent performance of all its rites and ordinances. The fact is that Mary's Child was God's Son and that he did in fact work out the infinite and eternal atoning sacrifice. And since the whole purpose of the law is to prepare men to receive him and his gospel, it automatically follows that when he came and established that gospel, the purpose of the law was fulfilled. Since all the sacrifices and performances of the law looked forward to and were in similitude of his atoning sacrifice, it follows that once he had shed his blood for the sins of repentant men, sacrifices should cease. Since the preparatory priesthood of Aaron was to train and qualify men to take the covenant appertaining to the Melchizedek

Priesthood, it is instinctive to know that when that higher priesthood comes it swallows up the lesser order, and men are no longer governed by the system that the lesser order was authorized to administer.

True, our Lord's coming was in a day when Jewish Israel was blinded in mind and spirit. Like so many of their fathers, they had made the law of Moses an end in itself; its real purpose and import was lost to them; and they, looking beyond the mark, failed to recognize Him of whom the law testified. Hence we find repeated and emphatic declarations in Holy Writ that teach that the old order no longer prevailed because He of whose coming it testified had in fact made flesh his tabernacle and had performed all the works assigned him of his Father. For instance, Paul said that Christ "obtained a more excellent ministry" than Moses, and came to be "the mediator of a better covenant, which was established upon better promises" than was the case with the old covenant of Mosaic vintage. "For if that first covenant had been faultless," the apostle wrote, "then should no place have been sought for the second. But finding fault with them," the Lord promised to "make a new covenant with the house of Israel." With reference to this, Paul reaches this conclusion: "In that he [the Lord] saith, A new covenant, he hath made the first old. Now that which decayeth and waxeth old is ready to vanish." (Heb. 8:6-13.) Paul then launches forth into a detailed comparison of many of the features of the two covenants. (Heb. 9 and 10.) Amulek expresses the same principle in this way: "It is expedient that there should be a great and last sacrifice; and then shall there be, or it is expedient there should be, a stop to the shedding of blood; then shall the law of Moses be fulfilled; yea, it shall be all fulfilled, every jot and tittle, and none shall have passed away." (Alma 34:13.)

Our Lord, ministering among his beloved Nephites, explained when and how and why the law was fulfilled. "Believe on my name," he said, "for behold, by me redemption cometh, and in me is the law of Moses fulfilled. I am the

423

light and the life of the world." (3 Ne. 9:17-18.) From that day forth men were to turn to him and his law; he was the light; no longer were they to perform Mosaic ordinances; redemption had now come unto all those who would believe.

Shortly thereafter, as part of what we have come to call the Nephite version of the Sermon on the Mount, he said: "Think not that I am come to destroy the law or the prophets. I am not come to destroy but to fulfil; For verily I say unto you, one jot nor one tittle hath not passed away from the law, but in me it hath all been fulfilled. And behold, I have given you the law and the commandments of my Father, that ye shall believe in me, and that ye shall repent of your sins, and come unto me with a broken heart and a contrite spirit. Behold, ye have the commandments before you, and the law is fulfilled. Therefore come unto me and be ye saved." (3 Ne. 12:17-20.) Again his people are commanded to look to him—not to Moses of old, but to him and the new covenant; he it is in whom salvation is found. "Those things which were of old time, which were under the law, in me are all fulfilled. Old things are done away, and all things have become new." (3 Ne. 12:46-47.)

In spite of these plain declarations, there were yet some among them who marveled and wondered concerning the law, and so our Lord climaxed his teachings to them by saying: "Marvel not that I said unto you that old things had passed away, and that all things had become new. Behold, I say unto you that the law is fulfilled that was given unto Moses. Behold, I am he that gave the law, and I am he who covenanted with my people Israel; therefore, the law in me is fulfilled, for I have come to fulfill the law; therefore it hath an end. Behold, I do not destroy the prophets, for as many as have not been fulfilled in me, verily I say unto you, shall all be fulfilled. And because I said unto you that old things have passed away, I do not destroy that which hath been spoken concerning things which are to come. For behold, the covenant which I have made with my people is not all fulfilled; but the law which was given unto Moses hath an end in me. Behold, I am the law, and the light. Look unto me, and endure to the end, and ye shall live; for unto him that endureth to the end will I give eternal life. Behold, I have given unto you the commandments; therefore keep my commandments. And this is the law and the prophets, for they truly testified of me." (3 Ne. 15:2-10.)

From all of this, can we do other than to conclude that if the law of Moses was divine, then Jesus Christ is the Messiah?

Chapter 23

MOSAIC FEASTS AND SACRIFICES TESTIFY OF CHRIST

Sacrifice—A Form of Worship

Sacrifice was a way of worship in Israel. The divine decree, given to Adam, that men should repent and call upon God in the name of the Son forevermore, was still in force among them. Compliance with that decree still required them to "offer the firstlings of their flocks" as sacrifices in "similitude of the sacrifice of the Only Begotten of the Father." (Moses 5:5-8.) In addition, through Moses they had received an intricate, extensive, and detailed sacrificial system, a system of performances and ordinances that called upon them to pledge new allegiance to the Lord each day of their lives. They did not inherit their sacrificial rites from their pagan neighbors, nor did they perform them in imitation of what other peoples were doing in that day and age. What others did was, in fact, a degenerate imitation and perversion of what had come down by descent from the pure and perfect system revealed to Adam. But what Israel did, she did by direct revelation, just as what the Latter-day Saints do is performed by the command of Deity and is not patterned after the fallen forms of Christianity that surround them.

We need not weigh and evaluate all the performances and ordinances of the law of Moses, and for that matter, from the fragmentary recitations preserved in the Old Testament, it is not possible so to do. We cannot always tell, for instance, whether specific sacrificial rites performed in Israel were part of the Mosaic system or whether they were the same ordinances performed by Adam and Abraham as part of the gospel law itself. Further, it appears that some of the ritualistic performances varied from time to time, according to the special needs of the people and the changing circumstances in which they found themselves. Even the Book of Mormon does not help us in these respects. We know the Nephites offered sacrifices and kept the law of Moses. Since they held the Melchizedek Priesthood and there were no Levites among them, we suppose their sacrifices were those that antedated the ministry of Moses and that, since they had the fulness of the gospel itself, they kept the law of Moses in the sense that they conformed to its myriad moral principles and its endless ethical restrictions. We suppose this would be one of the reasons Nephi was able to say, "The law hath become dead unto us." (2 Ne. 25:25.) There is, at least, no intimation in the Book of Mormon that the Nephites offered the daily sacrifices required by the law or that they held the various feasts that were part of the religious life of their Old World kinsmen. For our purposes it will suffice to give an overview of the "law of performances and of ordinances" (Mosiah 13:30), and to select enough of the detailed procedures to show that all that was done was a figure, a type, a shadow, a similitude of Him of whom the rituals and performances bore record.

To have the proper understanding and perspective, however, of what went on ordinance-wise in Israel, we must keep in remembrance that their sacrifices were a mode and form of worship. This is our key to a proper understanding, whether we are speaking of the public sacrifices made for the whole nation or of the private sacrifices made for families or individuals or small groups of people having special needs at the time involved. Without launching forth on a treatise on sacrifices, suffice it to say that the Old Testament preserves for us accounts of sacrifices that were performed—as pure acts of worship and veneration, as covenant renewal ceremonies, as acts of atonement, on occasions of thanksgiving, when seeking forgiveness, in fulfillment of vows, in confirmation of a treaty, as acts of dedication and rededication to the Lord's work, as acts of consecration, in expiation for sins, to extend hospitality to a guest, at the cleansing of a leper, for purification after childbirth, at the consecration of a priest or Levite, upon the release of a Nazarite from his vows, at sanctuary dedications, at royal coronations, on days of national penitence, in preparation for battle, and no doubt on other occasions. A classical example of worship through sacrifice is found in the account of Father Lehi's family. So gratified were they when Nephi and his brethren returned with the plates of brass, which had been in the custody of Laban, that the whole family "did rejoice exceedingly, and did offer sacrifice and burnt offerings unto the Lord; and they gave thanks unto the God of Israel." (1 Ne. 5:9.)

Feast of the Passover—A Type of Christ

Three times each year all male Israelites were commanded to appear before the Lord, at a place appointed, to worship him and renew their covenants. The first of these was the Feast of the Passover (including the Feast of Unleavened Bread); the Passover portion of the feast lasted one day, with the Feast of Unleavened Bread continuing for an additional seven. It was to celebrate the Passover that Joseph and Mary took the boy Jesus when he, having attained the age of twelve, was considered to be "a son of the law," one upon whom its obligations then rested. It was there that he confounded the learned doctors of the law with his heaven-sent wisdom; it was there that he bore the first testimony, of which we have record, of his own divine Sonship. (Luke 2:41-50.) The other two feasts to which attendance was mandatory were the Feast of Weeks (also called the Feast of the Harvest, or the Feast of the Firstfruits, or—to us today—

simply, the day of Pentecost), and the Feast of Tabernacles, which was called also the Feast of Ingathering. Sacrifices were offered at all three of these great feasts, and the instructions to all who attended were: "They shall not appear before the Lord empty: Every man shall give as he is able." (Deut. 16:16-17.)

At the time appointed for their deliverance from Egyptian bondage, the Lord commanded each family in Israel to sacrifice a lamb, to sprinkle its blood on their doorposts, and then to eat unleavened bread for seven more days—all to symbolize the fact that the destroying angel would pass over the Israelites as he went forth slaying the firstborn in the families of all the Egyptians; and also to show that, in haste, Israel should go forth from slavery to freedom. As a pattern for all the Mosaic instructions yet to come, the details of the performances here involved were so arranged as to bear testimony both of Israel's deliverance and of her Deliverer. Among other procedures, the Lord commanded, as found in Exodus 12:

1. "Your lamb shall be without blemish, a male of the first year," signifying that the Lamb of God, pure and perfect, without spot or blemish, in the prime of his life, as the Paschal Lamb, would be slain for the sins of the world.

2. They were to take of the blood of the lamb and sprinkle it upon the doorposts of their houses, having this promise as a result: "And the blood shall be to you for a token upon the houses where ye are: and when I see the blood, I will pass over you, and the plague shall not be upon you to destroy you," signifying that the blood of Christ, which should fall as drops in Gethsemane and flow in a stream from a pierced side as he hung on the cross, would cleanse and save the faithful; and that, as those in Israel were saved temporally because the blood of a sacrificial lamb was sprinkled on the doorposts of their houses, so the faithful of all ages would wash their garments in the blood of the Eternal Lamb and from him receive an eternal salvation. And may we say that as the angel of death passed by the

families of Israel because of their faith—as Paul said of Moses, "through faith he kept the passover, and the sprinkling of blood, lest he that destroyed the firstborn should touch them" (Heb. 11:28)—even so shall the Angel of Life give eternal life to all those who rely on the blood of the Lamb.

3. As to the sacrifice of the lamb, the decree was, "Neither shall ye break a bone thereof," signifying that when the Lamb of God was sacrificed on the cross, though they broke the legs of the two thieves to induce death, yet they brake not the bones of the Crucified One "that the scripture should be fulfilled, A bone of him shall not be broken." (John 19:31-36.)

4. As to eating the flesh of the sacrificial lamb, the divine word was, "No uncircumcised person shall eat thereof," signifying that the blessings of the gospel are reserved for those who come into the fold of Israel, who join the Church, who carry their part of the burden in bearing off the kingdom; signifying also that those who eat his flesh and drink his blood, as he said, shall have eternal life and he will raise them up at the last day. (John 6:54.)

5. As "the Lord smote all the firstborn in the land of Egypt" because they believed not the word of the Lord delivered to them by Moses and Aaron, even so should the Firstborn of the Father, who brings life to all who believe in his holy name, destroy worldly people at the last day, destroy all those who are in the Egypt of darkness, whose hearts are hardened as were those of Pharaoh and his minions.

6. On the first and seventh days of the Feast of Unleavened Bread, the Israelites were commanded to hold holy convocations in which no work might be done except the preparation of their food. These were occasions for preaching and explaining and exhorting and testifying. We go to sacrament meetings to be built up in faith and in testimony. Ancient Israel attended holy convocations for the same purposes. Knowing that all things operate by faith, would it be

amiss to draw the conclusion that it is as easy for us to look to Christ and his spilt blood for eternal salvation as it was for them of old to look to the blood of a sacrificed lamb, sprinkled on doorposts, to give temporal salvation, when the angel of death swept through the land of Egypt?

It was, of course, while Jesus and the Twelve were keeping the Feast of the Passover that our Lord instituted the ordinance of the sacrament, to serve essentially the same purposes served by the sacrifices of the preceding four millenniums. After that final Passover day and its attendant lifting up upon the cross of the true Paschal Lamb, the day for the proper celebration of the ancient feast ceased. After that Paul was able to say: "Christ our passover is sacrificed for us," and to give the natural exhortation that flowed therefrom: "Therefore let us keep the feast, not with old leaven, neither with the leaven of malice and wickedness; but with the unleavened bread of sincerity and truth." (1 Cor. 5:7-8.)

Feast of Pentecost—A Type of Christ

One of the three great feasts to which all the males of Israel must go each year was the Feast of Weeks, the Feast of Firstfruits, the Feast of the Harvest, or, as we are wont to say, the Feast of Pentecost. It came fifty days after the beginning of the Feast of the Passover. The burnt offerings of Pentecost included a sin-offering and a peace-offering, indicating that the great purpose of the feast was to gain a remission of sins and obtain a reconciliation with God. The procedures also called for a holy convocation in which the truths of heaven would be taught and instruction given to the people. (Lev. 23:15-22.)

With the closing of the Old and the opening of the New Dispensation, the Feast of Pentecost ceased as an authorized time of religious worship. And it is not without significance that the Lord chose the Pentecost, which grew out of the final Passover, as the occasion to dramatize forever the fulfillment of all that was involved in the sacrificial fires of

431

the past. Fire is a cleansing agent. Filth and disease die in its flames. The baptism of fire, which John promised Christ would bring, means that when men receive the actual companionship of the Holy Spirit, then evil and iniquity are burned out of their souls as though by fire. The sanctifying power of that member of the Godhead makes them clean. In similar imagery, all the fires on all the altars of the past, as they burned the flesh of animals, were signifying that spiritual purification would come by the Holy Ghost, whom the Father would send because of the Son. On that first Pentecost of the so-called Christian Era such fires would have performed their purifying symbolism if the old order had still prevailed. How fitting it was instead for the Lord to choose that very day to send living fire from heaven, as it were, fire that would dwell in the hearts of men and replace forever all the fires on all the altars of the past. And so it was that "when the day of Pentecost was fully come, they were all with one accord in one place. And suddenly there came a sound from heaven as of a rushing mighty wind, and it filled all the house where they were sitting. And there appeared unto them cloven tongues like as of fire, and it sat upon each of them. And they were all filled with the Holy Ghost." (Acts 2:1-4.)

Feast of Tabernacles—A Type of Christ

One of the three great feasts at which the attendance of all male Israelites was compulsory, the Feast of Tabernacles, was by all odds Israel's greatest feast. Coming five days after the Day of Atonement, it was thus celebrated when the sins of the chosen people had been removed and when their special covenant relation to Jehovah had been renewed and restored. Above all other occasions it was one for rejoicing, bearing testimony, and praising the Lord. In the full sense, it is the Feast of Jehovah, the one Mosaic celebration which, as part of the restitution of all things, shall be restored when Jehovah comes to reign personally upon the earth for a thousand years. Even now we perform one of its chief rituals in our solemn assemblies, the giving of the Hosanna Shout, and the worshipers of Jehovah shall yet be privileged to exult in other of its sacred rituals.

Also known as the Feast of Booths, because Israel dwelt in booths while in the wilderness, and as the Feast of Ingathering, because it came after the completion of the full harvest, it was a time of gladsome rejoicing and the extensive offering of sacrifices. More sacrifices were offered during the Feast of the Passover than at any other time because a lamb was slain for and eaten by each family or group, but at the Feast of Tabernacles more sacrifices of bullocks, rams, lambs, and goats were offered by the priests for the nation as a whole than at all the other Israelite feasts combined. The fact that it celebrated the completion of the full harvest symbolizes the gospel reality that it is the mission of the house of Israel to gather all nations to Jehovah, a process that is now going forward, but will not be completed until that millennial day when "the Lord shall be king over all the earth," and shall reign personally thereon. Then shall be fulfilled that which is written: "And it shall come to pass, that every one that is left of all the nations . . . shall even go up from year to year to worship the King, the Lord of hosts, and to keep the feast of tabernacles. And it shall be, that whoso will not come up of all the families of the earth unto Jerusalem to worship the King, the Lord of hosts, even upon them shall be no rain." (Zech. 14:9-21.) That will be the day when the law shall go forth from Zion and the word of the Lord from Jerusalem. Manifestly when the Feast of Tabernacles is kept in that day, its ritualistic performances will conform to the new gospel order and not include the Mosaic order of the past.

Included in the Feast of Tabernacles was a holy convocation, which in this instance was called also a solemn assembly. In our modern solemn assemblies we give the Hosanna Shout, which also was associated with the Feast of Tabernacles anciently, except that ancient Israel waved palm branches instead of white handkerchiefs as they exulted in such declarations as "Hosanna, Hosanna, Hosanna, to God and the Lamb." By the time of Jesus some added rituals were part of the feast, including the fact that a priest went to the Pool of Siloam, drew water in a golden pitcher, brought it to the temple, and poured it into a basin at the base of the altar. As this was done the choir sang the Hallel, consisting of Psalms 113 to 118. "When the choir came to these words, 'O give thanks to the Lord,' and again when they sang, 'O work then now salvation, Jehovah;' and once more at the close, 'O give thanks unto the Lord,' all the worshippers shook their lulavs [palm branches] towards the altar," which is closely akin to what we do in giving the Hosanna Shout to-day. "When, therefore, the multitudes from Jerusalem, on meeting Jesus, 'cut down branches from the trees, and strewed them in the way, and . . . cried, saying, O then, work now salvation to the Son of David!' they applied, in reference to Christ, what was regarded as one of the chief ceremonies of the Feast of Tabernacles, praying that God would now from 'the highest' heavens manifest and send that salvation in connection with the Son of David, which was symbolised by the pouring out of water." (Alfred Edersheim, *The Temple,* p. 279.)

Jesus and his disciples celebrated this and other Jewish feasts during the period of our Lord's active ministry. It was on "the last day, that great day of the feast," called in the Rabbinical writings the "Day of the Great Hosannah," as the priest was pouring out the water from the Pool of Siloam and the multitudes were waving their palm branches toward the altar, that "Jesus stood and cried, saying, If any man thirst, let him come unto me, and drink. He that believeth on me, as the scripture hath said, out of his belly shall flow rivers of living water." (John 7:37-38.) It was as though he said: 'This feast is designed to point your attention to me and the salvation which I bring. Now I have come; if ye will believe in me, ye shall be saved; and then from you, by the power of the Spirit, shall also go forth living water.'

There were also other feasts in Israel: the Feast of Trumpets, which came on the new moon of the seventh month; the Feast of Purim, which was instituted in the days of Esther; and the Feast of Dedication, a post-Old Testament feast, which, however, was kept in the days of Jesus and his disciples. It goes without saying that all of these feasts involved ordinances and worship that should have centered the hearts of the people on their Promised Messiah.

The Day of Atonement—A Type of Christ

Now we come to the heart and core and center of the whole Mosaic structure, namely, the atonement of the Lord Jesus Christ. This is what the law of Moses is all about. The law itself was given so that men might believe in Christ and know that salvation comes in and through his atoning sacrifice and in no other way. Every principle, every precept, every doctrinal teaching, every rite, ordinance, and performance, every word and act—all that appertained to, was revealed in, and grew out of the ministry of Moses, and all the prophets who followed him—all of it was designed and prepared to enable men to believe in Christ, to submit to his laws, and to gain the full blessings of that atonement which he alone could accomplish. And the chief symbolisms, the most perfect similitudes, the types and shadows without peer, were displayed before all the people once each year, on the Day of Atonement.

On one day each year—the tenth day of the seventh month—Israel's high priest of the Levitical order, the one who sat in Aaron's seat, was privileged to enter the Holy of Holies in the house of the Lord, to enter as it were the presence of Jehovah, and there make an atonement for the sins of the people. In the course of much sacrificial symbolism, he cleansed himself, the sanctuary itself, the priesthood bearers as a whole, and all of the people. Sacrificial animals were slain and their blood sprinkled on the mercy seat and before the altar; incense was burned, and all of the

435

imagery and symbolism of the ransoming ordinances was carried out. One thing, applicable to this day only, is of great moment. Two goats were selected, lots were cast, and the name of Jehovah was placed upon one goat; the other was called Azazel, the scapegoat. The Lord's goat was then sacrificed as the Great Jehovah would be in due course, but upon the scapegoat were placed all of the sins of the people, which burden the scapegoat then carried away into the wilderness. The high priest, as the law required, "lay both his hands upon the head of the live goat" and confessed "over him all the iniquities of the children of Israel, and all their transgressions in all their sins, putting them upon the head of the goat." The goat then bore upon him "all their iniquities unto a land not inhabited," even as the Promised Messiah should bear the sins of many. "For on that day shall the priest make an atonement for you, to cleanse you," Moses said, "that ye may be clean from all your sins before the Lord." (Lev. 16.)

Knowing, as we do, that sins are remitted in the waters of baptism; that baptisms were the order of the day in Israel; and that provision must be made for repentant persons to free themselves from sins committed after baptism—we see in the annual performances of the Day of Atonement one of the Lord's provisions for renewing the covenant made in the waters of baptism and receiving anew the blessed purity that comes from full obedience to the law involved. In our day we gain a similar state of purity by partaking worthily of the sacrament of the Lord's supper.

The symbolism and meaning of the ordinances and ceremonies performed on the Day of Atonement are set forth by Paul in his Epistle to the Hebrews. He calls the tabernacle-temple "a worldly sanctuary," wherein sacrificial ordinances were performed each year by Levitical priests to atone for the sins of men and prepare them to enter the Holy of Holies. These ordinances were to remain "until the time of reformation," when Christ should come as a high priest of "a greater and more perfect tabernacle," to prepare himself and

436

all men, by the shedding of his own blood, to obtain "eternal redemption" in the heavenly tabernacle. The old covenant was but "a shadow of good things to come, . . . For it is not possible that the blood of bulls and of goats should take away sins. . . . But this man, after he had offered one sacrifice for sins for ever, sat down on the right hand of God." (Heb. 9 and 10.) How perfectly the Mosaic ordinances testify of Him by whom salvation comes and in whose holy name all men are commanded to worship the Eternal Father forevermore!

Chapter 24

PROPHETIC TYPES
OF CHRIST

Moses—Mediator of the Old Covenant

It has pleased God to make covenants with his people, from time to time, according to the heed and diligence that they give unto him. Those who devote themselves to righteousness receive more of his word and inherit greater rewards; those who harden their hearts and stiffen their necks are denied what otherwise would be theirs.

Covenants are contracts. Gospel covenants are made between God in heaven and men on earth. These covenants are the solemn promises of Deity to pour out specified blessings upon all those who keep the terms and conditions upon which their receipt is predicated. The new and everlasting covenant is the fulness of the gospel; it is new in every age and to every people to whom it comes; it is everlasting in that from eternity to eternity it is the same, and its laws and conditions never change. From Adam to Moses, righteous men received and rejoiced in the everlasting covenant. It was offered to and rejected by Israel as a nation, and in its stead came a lesser law, a law of ordinances and performances designed to prepare them for the eventual receipt of the fulness of the gospel. Thus when the original covenant of salvation was revealed anew by Christ in his day, it was called the new covenant or new testament, in contrast to the old covenant or old testament to which the people had been subject for the preceding fifteen hundred years.

For each covenant—the old covenant and the new—there is both a revelator and a mediator. The revelator makes known the mind and will of the Lord, which the people are then privileged to accept or reject. The mediator stands between the Giver of the covenant and the people to mediate their differences; he interposes himself between the two parties of the covenant when they are at variance; he seeks to reconcile them to each other, to bring them into agreement. Moses was the mediator of the old covenant; Jesus is the mediator of the new covenant.

Moses' struggles and sorrows as a revelator and a mediator are seen in the sad story of the golden calf. Because he was so long gone from them into the holy mountain, where he received the Ten Commandments and the law of the gospel, backsliding Israel prevailed upon Aaron to make a calf of gold, like unto the gods of Egypt. "These be thy gods, O Israel, which brought thee up out of the land of Egypt," they then said, and—unbelievably—they worshiped and offered sacrifices to this molten idol. While Moses was yet on the mount, the Lord told him of the idolatrous worship and revelry going on in the camp. "I have seen this people, and, behold, it is a stiffnecked people," the Lord said. "Now therefore let me alone, that my wrath may wax hot against them, and that I may consume them: and I will make of thee a great nation." (Ex. 32:1-10.)

Thereupon Moses pled for the people. Among other things he said to the Lord: "Wherefore should the Egyptians speak, and say, For mischief did he bring them out, to slay them in the mountains, and to consume them from the face of the earth? Turn from thy fierce wrath. Thy people will repent of this evil; therefore come thou not out against them." Then Moses reminded the Lord of the promises made to Abraham, Isaac, and Jacob concerning their seed, and the Lord, relenting, said to Moses: "If they will repent of the evil which they have done, I will spare them, and turn away my fierce wrath; but, behold, thou shalt execute my judgment upon all that will not repent of this evil this day.

Therefore, see thou do this thing that I have commanded thee, or I will execute all that which I had thought to do unto my people." (JST, Ex. 32:12-14.)

Returning to the camp, Moses in righteous anger brake the two tablets of stone on which the law was written; destroyed the calf; sent forth the cry, "Who is on the Lord's side"; accepted the offer of the Levites, and sent them forth to slay three thousand of the wicked in Israel. On the morrow, Moses said to Israel: "Ye have sinned a great sin: and now I will go up unto the Lord; peradventure I shall make an atonement for your sin. And Moses returned unto the Lord, and said, Oh, this people have sinned a great sin, and have made them gods of gold. Yet now, if thou wilt forgive their sins—; and if not, blot me, I pray thee, out of thy book which thou hast written. And the Lord said unto Moses, Whosoever hath sinned against me, him will I blot out of my book." (Ex. 32:15-35; 33:13; 34:9; Deut. 5:5; 9:24-29; 10:10; Ps. 106:23.)

Jesus—Mediator of the New Covenant

Knowing that Moses was the mediator of the old covenant gives meaning to the scriptural passages which speak of Jesus as the mediator of the new covenant. If Moses had not been the mediator of the old covenant, the inspired writers would have spoken of our Lord's mediatorial role as such, without the repeated scriptural stress on the fact that his mediation pertained to the new covenant. But it is in fact the contrast between the role of Moses and the infinitely greater role of Christ that enables us to comprehend what Jesus actually does in the way of intercession and mediation. Moses' status as a mediator thus becomes—as all things in the law of Moses were—a type and shadow of a greater mediatory labor that was to be when the Messiah of whom Moses testified came to work out the infinite and eternal atonement. Thus we find Paul writing, "The law was added because of transgressions, till the seed should come to whom the promise was made in the law given to Moses, who was ordained by the hand of angels to be a mediator of this first covenant, (the law). Now this mediator was not a mediator of the new covenant; but there is one mediator of the new covenant, who is Christ, as it is written in the law concerning the promises made to Abraham and his seed. Now Christ is the mediator of life; for this is the promise which God made unto Abraham." (JST, Gal. 3:19-20.) Also: "For this is good and acceptable in the sight of God our Saviour; Who is willing to have all men to be saved, and to come unto the knowledge of the truth which is in Christ Jesus, who is the Only Begotten Son of God, and ordained to be a Mediator between God and man; who is one God, and hath power over all men. For there is one God, and one mediator between God and men, the man Christ Jesus; Who gave himself a ransom for all, to be testified in due time." (JST, 1 Tim. 2:3-6.)

Salvation is in Christ, not in Moses. Israel's ancient law-giver mediated the cause of his people to prepare them for the gospel. Israel's later Lawgiver mediated their cause to prepare them for eternal life. "It was by faith that they of old were called after the holy order of God," Moroni said. "Wherefore, by faith was the law of Moses given. But in the gift of his Son hath God prepared a more excellent way." (Ether 12:10-11.) Hence, as Lehi said: "Look to the great Mediator, and hearken unto his great commandments; and be faithful unto his words, and choose eternal life, according to the will of his Holy Spirit." (2 Ne. 2:28.)

We respect and reverence Moses, but we worship Christ. We admire and appreciate the lesser law, but we enjoy and rejoice in the higher. Moses went before to prepare the way; Christ came after to fulfill and to save. "Consider the Apostle and High Priest of our profession," Paul says, "Christ Jesus; Who was faithful to him that appointed him, as also Moses was faithful in all his house. For this man was counted worthy of more glory than Moses, inasmuch as he who hath builded the house hath more honour than the house. For every house is builded by some man; but he that built all things is God. And Moses verily was faithful in all his house, as a servant, for a testimony of those things which were to be spoken after; But Christ as a son over his own house; whose house are we, if we hold fast the confidence and the rejoicing of the hope firm unto the end." (Heb. 3:1-6.) Christ, thus, hath "obtained a more excellent ministry, by how much also he is the mediator of a better covenant, which was established upon better promises." (Heb. 8:6.)

And all those who receive this new covenant and conform to its terms and conditions shall be saved. They are the ones for whom Christ intercedes; they are reconciled to God because of his mediation. "These are they who are just men made perfect through Jesus the mediator of the new covenant, who wrought out this perfect atonement through the shedding of his own blood." (D&C 76:69; 107:19; Heb. 12:22-24.)

Moses—Like unto Christ

Moses was in the similitude of Christ, and Christ was like unto Moses. Of all the hosts of our Father's children, these two are singled out as being like each other. All men are created in the image of God, both spiritually and temporally. "In the day that God created man, in the likeness of God made he him; In the image of his own body, male and female, created he them, and blessed them, and called their name Adam." (Moses 6:8-9.) And all men are endowed with the characteristics and attributes which, in their eternal fulness, dwell in Deity. But it appears there is a special image, a special similitude, a special likeness where the man Moses and the man Jesus are concerned. It is reasonable to suppose that this similarity, this resemblance, is both physical and spiritual; it is a likeness where both qualities and appearance are concerned. Nor should this seem unreasonable or outside the realm of the probabilities. Christ stands preeminent

442

among all the spirit children of the Father. While yet in preexistence he became "like unto God." (Abr. 3:24.) But surely some of the other spirit sons approached him in goodness and obedience, and hence in might, power, and dominion. It is clear that Michael (Adam) stood next to the Firstborn, and that Gabriel (Noah) ranks next to our first father. Where the priorities then fall we do not know, but surely the great dispensation heads are next, including Enoch, Abraham, and Moses. Specific orders of priority do not especially concern us, but on principle it is clear that Moses was one of the six or eight or ten or twenty, or at least one of a small and select group, of the greatest of all the spirit hosts. Is it unreasonable, then, that he should be in the similitude of the Only Begotten, who should in turn be like unto him? For that matter, all who gain exaltation—not just Adam, Enoch, Noah, Abraham, Moses and the mighty ones—shall become like Christ, joint-heirs with him, inheriting, receiving, and possessing as he does in glorious immortality in due course.

And so we find the Father, speaking by the mouth of the Son, upon whom he has placed his name, saying: "I have a work for thee, Moses, my son; and thou art in the similitude of mine Only Begotten; and mine Only Begotten is and shall be the Savior, for he is full of grace and truth." Thereafter, when Satan came to Moses and said "Worship me," that mighty prophet had the courage and confidence to reply: "Who art thou? For behold, I am a son of God, in the similitude of his Only Begotten. . . . For God said unto me: Thou art after the similitude of mine Only Begotten." (Moses 1:1-16.) That is to say, Moses bore the resemblance of his Lord. In appearance, guise, and semblance, they were the same. The qualities of the one were the qualities of the other. Any differences were in degree only.

As Moses summarized the law he had given to Israel, and left that counsel and direction which the Almighty desired them to receive, the great lawgiver gave forth this Messianic prophecy: "The Lord thy God will raise up unto thee a

Prophet from the midst of thee, of thy brethren, like unto me; unto him ye shall hearken." Then Moses said: "And the Lord said unto me, . . . I will raise them up a Prophet from among their brethren, like unto thee, and will put my words in his mouth; and he shall speak unto them all that I shall command him. And it shall come to pass, that whosoever will not hearken unto my words which he shall speak in my name, I will require it of him." (Deut. 18:15-19.)

This Mosaic-Messianic prophecy is quoted twice in the Book of Mormon, twice in the New Testament, and once in the Pearl of Great Price. In each of these five places, the latter part of the prophecy is quoted differently than it is now found in Deuteronomy. The words "I will require it of him" are quoted as meaning "Shall be cut off from among the people," which more accurately describes the fate of those who reject the Messiah. Thus the Risen Lord, appearing to the Nephites, says: "Behold, I am he of whom Moses spake, saying: A prophet shall the Lord your God raise up unto you of your brethren, like unto me; him shall ye hear in all things whatsoever he shall say unto you. And it shall come to pass that every soul who will not hear that prophet shall be cut off from among the people." (3 Ne. 20:23.) When Nephi quoted Moses' words, he did so substantially the same way that Jesus did, and then added, "This prophet of whom Moses spake was the Holy One of Israel; wherefore, he shall execute judgment in righteousness." (1 Ne. 22:20-21.) Peter and Stephen both quoted Moses' words and applied them to Christ. (Acts 3:22-23; 7:37.) And Moroni recited them to the Prophet Joseph Smith as he told him about the coming forth of the Book of Mormon and other great latter-day events. He said the prophet foretold was Christ and that the time would soon come when "they who would not hear his voice should be cut off from among the people," meaning that such would occur at his Second Coming. (JS-H 40.)

How Christ Was Like unto Moses

To set forth in full how our Lord's life and ministry was patterned after and like unto that of Moses is beyond the scope of this work. It would involve, among other things, a more extended analysis of the law of Moses than is of general value and interest now that the law itself has been fulfilled and replaced. The following partial outline will show sufficient of what is involved for our purposes and perhaps serve as an open door for further analysis by those whose interests fall in this field. Christ was like unto Moses in at least the following particulars:

1. Both were among the noble and great in the premortal life; both kept the commandments, followed the Father, and acquired the attributes of godliness before ever they were born into mortality; both participated in the creation of this earth and looked forward with rejoicing to that day when each should gain a mortal body, undergo earth's probationary experiences, and qualify for immortality and eternal life in the full and unlimited sense of the word.

2. Both were foreordained to perform the mortal labors chosen for them, and both were called by name, generations before their mortal births, with their specified labors being set forth in advance by the spirit of prophecy—the work of Christ being to redeem his people, that of Moses to "deliver my people out of Egypt in the days of thy bondage, . . . for a seer will I raise up to deliver my people out of the land of Egypt; and he shall be called Moses. And by his name he shall know that he is of thy house [the house of Joseph who was sold into Egypt]; for he shall be nursed by the king's daughter, and shall be called her son." (JST, Gen. 50:24-29.)

3. Moses delivered Israel from Egypt, from bondage, from the lash, from abject and hopeless slavery, from a state in which they were physically oppressed and spiritually sick;

and then for forty years he led them through a wasted wilderness, schooling and training the while, that they might finally be prepared for their promised land. Christ, the Great Deliverer, offers freedom to all who are under the bondage of sin and leads them through the wilderness of life to an Eternal Promised Land, where they will be free forever from the slavery of sin and the oppression of unrighteousness.

4. Moses was the lawgiver of Israel, the one who revealed to that favored nation the laws, in detail and with prolixity, that served them well for generations; Christ was the great Lawgiver who set forth for all peoples of all ages the system of heavenly rule by which they can qualify for a celestial inheritance.

5. As we have seen, Moses was the mediator of the old covenant, Christ of the new—Moses in his day pleading, interceding, reconciling, standing between the Lord and his people; Christ in all days and at all times intervening between God and man so that all who believe and obey may be reconciled to the Father.

6. Jesus and Moses were both born in perilous times, the One when the nation whence they both sprang was subject to the yoke of Rome, the other when Pharaoh's rule was imposed upon the people. Both were preserved in birth and childhood by divine providence. Jesus was born in a stable and was soon thereafter preserved from Herod's sword, at the time the other innocents were slain, because an angel warned Joseph to flee with the young child into Egypt. Moses was preserved in birth because the Hebrew midwives defied the king of Egypt and slew not the male children of their race, and soon thereafter he was preserved in an ark hidden in the bulrushes, lest he be found and slain by Pharaoh's executioners.

7. Moses performed many signs and wonders and miracles before Pharaoh and his court and in the presence of all Israel. Our Lord acted in like manner throughout his whole ministry as he opened blind eyes, loosed dumb tongues, strengthened lame legs, and raised dead bodies.

8. Both Moses and Jesus had control over mighty waters. The one stretched forth his hand over the Red Sea, the waters divided, and Israel went through on dry ground, with walls of water congealed on the right hand and on the left. The Other walked on the waters of the Galilean Sea and also commanded the wind and the waves to cease their tempestuous raging. Moses turned the water at Marah from bitter to sweet and smote the rock at the waters of Meribah, in both instances providing drink for thirsting Israel. Our Lord smites the rocks of unbelief and rebellion in the hearts of sinful men, so that all who will may drink living water and thirst no more forever.

9. Under Moses' ministry manna fell from heaven, that Israel, for forty years, perished not for want of food. Jesus came to bring that bread from heaven which if men eat they shall never hunger more.

10. Moses sat on the judgment seat, from morning to night, hearing the causes of the people and dispensing judgment, even as the great Judge shall dispense justice and judgment forever.

11. "Now the man Moses was very meek, above all the men which were upon the face of the earth." (Num. 12:3.) Jesus said: "I am meek and lowly in heart." (Matt. 11:29.) The meek are the godfearing and the righteous.

12. Moses and Christ were prophets, mighty prophets, the one foreshadowing the Other, but both acclaiming the divine Sonship of Him of whom all the prophets testify. "And there arose not a prophet since in Israel like unto Moses, whom the Lord knew face to face." (Deut. 34:10.) Nor has there been, nor shall there be, a greater prophet than Jesus, not in Israel only, but in all the world and among all peoples of all ages.

13. Those who defied Moses and rebelled against his law were destroyed, like Korah and his band, concerning whom it is written that the earth opened and they and their houses and all that appertained to them were swallowed up. At our Lord's Second Coming all those who are in rebellion against

Christ and his laws shall be cut off from among the people, for they that come shall burn them up, leaving neither root nor branch.

14. There are no doubt many other ways in which Christ was like unto Moses; and certainly there are other ways of summarizing the numerous realities involved. But whatever approach is made to the matter, all proper presentations lead to this one conclusion, here stated in the words of the Lord Jesus: "Do not think that I will accuse you to the Father: there is one that accuseth you, even Moses, in whom ye trust. For had ye believed Moses, ye would have believed me: for he wrote of me. But if ye believe not his writings, how shall ye believe my words?" (John 5:45-47.) Christ and Moses go together. If one was a prophet, sent of God, so was the other. If the words of one are true, so are those of the other. They are one, and their united voice is that Jesus Christ is the Son of the living God—the Promised Messiah.

All Prophets Are Types of Christ

With the foundation securely built that Christ was like unto Moses, we are prepared to build thereon and show that all the ancient prophets and all righteous men who preceded our Lord in birth were, in one sense or another, patterns for him. That is, to the degree they were true and faithful and acquired for themselves the attributes of godliness, their Elder Brother, the Lord Jesus, is like unto them. All the prophets testified of him, for it was the very fact of knowing and proclaiming his divinity that caused them to be prophets. A prophet is one who has the testimony of Jesus, who knows by the revelations of the Holy Ghost to his soul that Jesus Christ is the Son of God. In addition to this divine knowledge, many of them lived in special situations or did particular things that singled them out as types and patterns and shadows of that which was to be in the life of him who is our Lord. Let us illustrate this principle by naming some of those who are listed in the scriptures as types of Christ:

448

1. Paul names one of these as Adam. "Death reigned from Adam to Moses," he says, "even over them that had not sinned after the similitude of Adam's transgression, who is the figure of him that was to come." That is, Adam is a similitude of Christ. How and in what way? It is because Adam brought death and sin into the world, as the natural inheritance of all men, as a prelude to our Lord's bringing life and righteousness to all who will believe and obey. Death passes upon all through Adam; life comes to all through Christ. One man brought death for all; one man brought life for all. "Therefore as by the offence of one judgment came upon all men to condemnation; even so by the righteousness of one the free gift came upon all men unto justification of life. For as by one man's disobedience many were made sinners, so by the obedience of one shall many be made righteous." (Rom. 5:14-21.)

Writing of this personal relationship between Adam and Christ, a relationship in which one is a type of the other, Paul also said: "The first man Adam was made a living soul; the last Adam was made a quickening spirit." That is, the first Adam, the one who dwelt in Eden, was the first flesh upon the earth, the first mortal man; and the last Adam, who is Christ, was the first person resurrected, the first immortal man. Adam's mortality reaches perfection in Christ's immortality. "The first man is of the earth, earthy: the second man is the Lord from heaven." Adam was made of the dust of the earth, for mortality goes with this sphere of existence, but the Second Adam came down from heaven with the power of immortality so that death could be swallowed up in life through his atonement. "As is the earthy, such are they also that are earthy: and as is the heavenly, such are they also that are heavenly. And as we have borne the image of the earthy, we shall also bear the image of the heavenly." (1 Cor. 15:45-49.)

2. Melchizedek is named as a type of Christ. Our revelations tell us he was known as the Prince of Peace, the King of Peace, the King of Heaven, and the King of Righteous-

ness, all of which are the very name-titles that apply to our Lord. Further, the priesthood held by Melchizedek is the very priesthood promised the Son of God during his mortal sojourn, which is to say that Christ was to be like unto Melchizedek.

Our revelations say that "Melchizedek was a man of faith, who wrought righteousness," that he was "approved of God" and "ordained an high priest after the order of the covenant which God made with Enoch, It being after the order of the Son of God; which order came, not by man, nor the will of man; neither by father nor mother; neither by beginning of days nor end of years; but of God; And it was delivered unto men by the calling of his own voice, according to his own will, unto as many as believed on his name. . . . And now, Melchizedek was a priest of this order; therefore he obtained peace in Salem, and was called the Prince of peace. . . . And this Melchizedek, having thus established righteousness, was called the king of heaven by his people, or, in other words, the King of peace." (JST, Gen. 14:26-36.) In referring to these things, Paul adds to Melchizedek the title King of Righteousness. (JST, Heb. 7:1-3.)

One of the great Messianic prophecies, spoken by the mouth of David, says: "The Lord hath sworn, and will not repent, Thou art a priest for ever after the order of Melchizedek." (Ps. 110:4.) Paul names Christ as the "High Priest of our profession" (Heb. 3:1), who came in fulfillment of David's prophecy; shows that his coming involved the receipt of a different priesthood than that held by the Levites; and says that Christ came "after the similitude of Melchisedec" (Heb. 7:15). It appears that Paul's statement— "Who in the days of his flesh, when he had offered up prayers and supplications with strong crying and tears unto him that was able to save him from death, and was heard in that he feared; Though he were a Son, yet learned he obedience by the things which he suffered" (Heb. 5:7-8)— has reference both to Melchizedek and to Christ, which

450

harmonizes with the concept that Christ was like unto Melchizedek.

3. Every holder of the Melchizedek Priesthood is or should be a type of Christ. Those who lived before he came were types and shadows and witnesses of his coming. Those who have lived since he came are witnesses of such coming and are types and shadows of what he was. Thus Paul says that Melchizedek was "King of righteousness, and after that also King of Salem, which is, King of peace; For this Melchizedek was ordained a priest after the order of the Son of God, which order was without father, without mother, without descent, having neither beginning of days, nor end of life. And all those who are ordained unto this priesthood are made like unto the Son of God, abiding a priest continually." (JST, Heb. 7:1-3.)

Alma, in about 82 B.C., discoursed at length on the Melchizedek Priesthood and on those who held it from the beginning. "Those priests," he said, meaning high priests of the Melchizedek Priesthood, "were ordained after the order of his Son, in a manner that thereby the people might know in what manner to look forward to his Son for redemption." That is to say, they were types and shadows of our Lord's coming; they were living, walking, breathing Messianic prophecies, even as we should be living witnesses that he has come.

They were "called with a holy calling, yea, with that holy calling which was prepared with, and according to a preparatory redemption." They could preach redemption; they could foretell its coming; but their work was preparatory only. Redemption itself would come through the ministry of Him of whom they were but types and shadows. Then, after setting forth many things connected with this priesthood, Alma says: "Now these ordinances were given after this manner, that thereby the people might look forward on the Son of God, it being a type of his order, or it being his order, and this that they might look forward to him

451

for a remission of their sins, that they might enter into the rest of the Lord." (Alma 13:1-13.)

4. "Take now thy son, thine only son Isaac, whom thou lovest, and get thee into the land of Moriah; and offer him there for a burnt offering upon one of the mountains which I will tell thee of." (Gen. 22:2.) Of this Paul says: "By faith Abraham, when he was tried, offered up Isaac: and he that had received the promises offered up his only begotten son, Of whom it is said, That in Isaac shall thy seed be called: Accounting that God was able to raise him up, even from the dead; from whence also he received him in a figure." (Heb. 11:17-19.) What is the figure of which Paul speaks? Jacob answers in these plain words: "Abraham," he explains, was "obedient unto the commands of God in offering up his son Isaac, which is a similitude of God and his Only Begotten Son." (Jacob 4:5.) How many thousands of sermons have been preached since that day, preached among those with faith and understanding, all using this dramatic episode from the life of the father of the faithful!

5. King David was a type of Christ in two respects: First, his Seed, who is Christ, should reign on his throne forever, as we have heretofore set forth; and, second, through Christ would come the resurrection which, in spite of David's sins, would eventually redeem his soul from hell. "I will make an everlasting covenant with you," the Lord says to his people, "even the sure mercies of David," which mercies are that the resurrection will pass even upon the wicked. "Behold, I have given him for a witness to the people" is the promise. (Isa. 55:3-4.) In other words, if David, who committed adultery and on whose hands was found the blood of Uriah, will be resurrected, then all men should rest in the hope that they shall rise from the grave.

6. We must not overlook Jonah as one whose life and conduct became a type of Christ. His experiences with the great fish have ever since been known as "the sign of the prophet Jonas." It was Jesus who left us this symbolic meaning of the acts of Jonah: "For as Jonas was three days and

three nights in the whale's belly," he said, "so shall the Son of man be three days and three nights in the heart of the earth." (Matt. 12:39-40.)

7. No doubt there are many events in the lives of many prophets that set those righteous persons apart as types and shadows of their Messiah. It is wholesome and proper to look for similitudes of Christ everywhere and to use them repeatedly in keeping him and his laws uppermost in our minds. But let us conclude this part of our inquiry by noting that the whole house of Israel was a type and a shadow of their Messiah. An illustration of this is the use Matthew makes of one of Hosea's statements. "When Israel was a child, then I loved him, and called my son out of Egypt" (Hos. 11:1), Hosea said with apparent reference to the deliverance of Israel from Egyptian bondage. But Matthew, guided by the Holy Ghost, saw in this statement a prophetic foretelling that Joseph and Mary and the child Jesus would flee to Egypt to escape the sword of Herod and would there remain until the Lord called them forth to continue their habitation in Palestine. (Matt. 2:12-15.) In other words, the passage has a dual meaning and was intended as a type and a shadow of one of the important occurrences in the life of a Child who was God's Son.

Chapter 25

JEHOVAH BECOMES THE MORTAL MESSIAH

Why Messiah Became Mortal

Two views and perspectives face us as we consider the gospel verity that God himself should be born among mortals, should grow to maturity, and should, himself a mortal, partake of the normal experiences incident to that state of existence. They are:

1. How almost unthinkable it is that a God should become a man; that the Creator of all things from the beginning should come down and be himself created from the dust of the earth; that he being infinite forever should become finite for a season; that the Maker of men should become subject to them; that he who has ascended above all things should now descend below them all; that he who knows all things and has all might, power, and dominion should begin anew, as it were, and go himself from grace to grace until the eternal fulness was his once again.

2. And yet how normal and right such a process is! How could it be otherwise? If the spirit Michael needed a body and the experiences of mortality to gain all power in heaven and on earth, why not the spirit Jehovah also? If the second-born son of the Father, whoever he may have been, needed the probationary experiences of earth life, why not the Firstborn also? If the plan of salvation, ordained by the

454

Father, was to enable all of his spirit children to advance and progress and become like him, then Jehovah also was subject to its terms and conditions. And how better could he be favored above all others than to be born, not of mortality only but of Immortality, not of man only but of God, not of the earth only but of Heaven?

With these two perspectives before us—one, that it is wondrous beyond belief that a God becomes mortal; the other, that it is the most normal, natural, and needful course that could be devised—we are prepared to suggest why the Messiah became mortal. Let us, then, suggest three reasons why, in the wisdom of Him who knoweth all things, the Eternal One should take upon himself a mortal state; why the Lord Jehovah should become the Lord Jesus; why he was born among men as the Son of God. These are:

1. *Our Lord's mortality was a preparation for and a condition precedent to his atonement.*

The great plan of redemption, prepared from before the foundations of the world, contemplated that one should fall and Another redeem; that the first Adam should bring temporal and spiritual death into the world, with the Second Adam ransoming men from the otherwise eternal effects of these two deaths; and that as Adam, who was immortal, became mortal so that mortality would pass upon all men, even so Christ, who as the Seed of Adam had taken upon himself mortality, should become immortal so that immortality should become the unquestioned inheritance of all his brethren.

It must needs be, for so it was ordained of the Father, that One subject to death gain the victory over the grave; and One who was in all points tempted like his brethren should so live that he, being sinless, gained eternal life, thus showing that man could be ransomed from both the temporal and the spiritual fall. The atonement must needs come by power, not alone the power of the Father which opened the grave, but the power of the mortal Son that overcame the world. The plan called for a mortal Man, endowed with

God's power, to ransom men from the dual effects of Adam's fall.

2. *Our Lord's mortality was essential to his own salvation.*

The eternal exaltation of Christ himself—though he was a God and had power and intelligence like unto his Father— was dependent upon gaining a mortal body, overcoming the world by obedience, passing through the portals of death, and then coming forth in glorious immortality with a perfected celestial body. Christ came into the world to work out his own salvation with fear and trembling before the Father. There neither was, nor is, nor shall be any other way for anyone. To house a spirit body, even that of a God, in an eternal tabernacle like that of the Father, requires a mortal birth and a mortal death. Christ wrought his atonement, first for himself and his own salvation, then for the salvation of all those who believe on his name, and finally and in a lesser degree for all the sons of Adam.

3. *Our Lord's mortality shows man can be saved by obedience to the laws and ordinances of his everlasting gospel.*

While in mortality He, by whom all things are, lived a perfect life. He kept the whole law of the whole gospel. He was and is the Sinless One. He rose above temptation, overcame the world, and rebuked the devourer. His life set the perfect pattern in all things, and it is his voice we hear, saying: "What manner of men ought ye to be? Verily I say unto you, even as I am." (3 Ne. 27:27.) And also: "Follow thou me." (2 Ne. 31:10.)

Our Lord's perfect life shines as a beacon beckoning all those from Adam on down to choose to live as he lived and to merit the rewards he himself gained. Most of earth's total inhabitants shall dwell as mortals in the so-called Christian Era. All of these are invited to look back at his life, to see how he lived, and to go forth themselves and do likewise. Those who lived before his day, who were righteous, knew by the spirit of inspiration that his would be the perfect life, and they, therefore, buoyed up by this knowledge, sought beforehand to be even as he would be in the day of his mortal probation.

When Messiah Shall Come

In our day we look forward with hope and joy to the Second Coming of the Son of Man, and to the setting up of the millennial kingdom of peace and righteousness, over which he shall assume personal rule for the space of a thousand years. We do not know and shall not learn either the day or the hour of that dreadful yet blessed day. We are expected to read the signs of the times and know thereby the approximate time of our Lord's return and to be in constant readiness therefor.

There was an element of this same uncertainty associated with his first coming, although such appears to have arisen because of lack of faith on the part of the people and not from the deliberate design of the Lord to withhold such knowledge from them. The Nephites, whose faith was greater, did know the precise year in which he should be born. It was identified as six hundred years from the time Lehi left Jerusalem. (1 Ne. 10:4; 19:8; 2 Ne. 25:19.) As the time drew near, mention of this fact was made by various of the American prophets. (Alma 7:7; 9:26-27; 13:25-26.)

In a wondrous outburst of spiritual insight, Samuel the Lamanite was privileged to name the time and set forth the attendant signs to be shown forth incident to our Lord's mortal birth. "Behold, I give unto you a sign," he said, "for five years more cometh, and behold, then cometh the Son of God to redeem all those who shall believe on his name. And behold, this will I give unto you for a sign at the time of his coming; for behold, there shall be great lights in heaven, insomuch that in the night before he cometh there shall be no darkness, insomuch that it shall appear unto man as if it was day. Therefore, there shall be one day and a night and a day, as if it were one day and there were no night; and this shall be unto you for a sign; for ye shall know of the rising of the sun and also of its setting; therefore they shall know of a surety that there shall be two days and a night; nevertheless the night shall not be darkened; and it shall be the night before he is born. And behold, there shall a new star arise, such an one as ye never have beheld; and this also shall be a sign unto you. And behold this is not all, there shall be many signs and wonders in heaven. And it shall come to pass that ye shall all be amazed, and wonder, insomuch that ye shall fall to the earth. And it shall come to pass that whosoever shall believe on the Son of God, the same shall have everlasting life." (Hel. 14:2-8.) It does not appear that the Lord had any design or purpose for keeping secret the time of his mortal birth.

We do not know what revelations were extant among the Jews in Jerusalem that would lead them to know to some extent what the Nephites knew. Perhaps the Lord gave the American Hebrews more signs and wonders to identify the time because they were far removed from the scene of action. But it does appear that the Jews had some knowledge on the subject of which we are not aware.

We do know that all of the ancient prophets had looked forward with great anticipation to Messiah's mortal ministry and that some of them had sought to learn when it would be. Enoch asked: "When shall the day of the Lord come? When shall the blood of the Righteous be shed, that all they that mourn may be sanctified and have eternal life?" He was answered: "It shall be in the meridian of time, in the days of wickedness and vengeance." (Moses 7:45-46.) Father Jacob had prophesied: "The sceptre shall not depart from Judah, nor a lawgiver from between his feet, until Shiloh come; and unto him shall the gathering of the people be." (Gen. 49:10.) From the Joseph Smith Translation we learn that "the Messiah . . . is called Shilo." (JST, Gen. 50:24.) And from historical sources we know that Jewish kings still reigned and the Jewish Sanhedrin still functioned until the destruction of

Jerusalem in A.D. 70, when the temple was destroyed, the sacrificial system discontinued, and the Jews as a nation and as a people scattered among all nations.

Isaiah spoke of the Messiah coming "in an acceptable time" (Isa. 49:8), and Daniel named the very time, but he used imagery and figurative language that can only be understood by the spirit of revelation. He said that "from the going forth of the commandment to restore and to build Jerusalem unto the Messiah the Prince shall be seven weeks, and threescore and two weeks." He said that after that period "shall Messiah be cut off." Then he described the post-New Testament destruction of Jerusalem by the Roman legions. (Dan. 9:24-26.) And it was Jesus who said to some of his disciples: "Blessed are your eyes, for they see: and your ears, for they hear. For verily I say unto you, That many prophets and righteous men have desired to see those things which ye see, and have not seen them; and to hear those things which ye hear, and have not heard them." (Matt. 13:16-17.)

But none of this lets us know why the Jews were so anxiously expecting their Messiah in the very day in which he came. As is well known, their whole social structure was alive with the ferment of Messianic hope. False messiahs found followers; true prophets were queried to ascertain their claims, if any, to Messiahship. When John the Baptist cried repentance and immersed worthy souls in Jordan for the remission of their sins, it was an automatic thing for the Jews to send "priests and Levites from Jerusalem to ask him, Who art thou? . . . What sayest thou of thyself?" As to the main point at issue, his witness was: "I am not the Christ." (John 1:19-25.) And it did not seem to strike anyone as strange, neither Herod nor the masses of the people, that wise men should come from the east, asking: "Where is he that is born King of the Jews? for we have seen his star in the east, and are come to worship him." The account says "all Jerusalem" was troubled as to where he might be, out of which fearful anxiety, coupled with the evil jealousy of a wicked king, came the slaughter of the innocent children in Bethlehem. (Matt. 2.)

But however much the people knew or did not know, whatever their state of spirituality, it was the six-hundredth year since Lehi left the locale in which Messiah should come, and so come he did as come he must. Among the Nephites the unbelievers had appointed a day on which all who looked forward to his coming should be put to death unless the promised sign was seen. Nephi the son of Helaman cried mightily unto the Lord for the preservation of the faithful, and the answering voice acclaimed: "Lift up your head and be of good cheer; for behold, the time is at hand, and on this night shall the sign be given, and on the morrow come I into the world." (3 Ne. 1:13.)

In Jewry, as most of the people walked in their own willful ways, a few righteous souls came to know the purposes and acts of the Lord. To Zacharias, Elisabeth, Mary, and Joseph, each in turn, an angelic ministrant made known the conception and coming forth of the Lord and his forerunner. Sheltered in a stable, Mary brought forth that which had been conceived by the power of the Holy Ghost; a heavenly herald announced to the shepherds: "I bring you good tidings of great joy, which shall be to all people. For unto you is born this day in the city of David a Saviour, which is Christ the Lord"; and the celestial choirs sang: "Glory to God in the highest, and on earth peace, good will toward men." (Luke 2:1-14.)

Truly, a God now dwelt in mortality!

Where Messiah Became Mortal

Planet earth is of immense proportion from the standpoint of the people who tread its paths. In what corner of its great expanse would the Heavenly King be born? Would it be in the Holy City, in the palace of the king, perhaps even in the Temple of the Most High itself? How can you find a place good enough for a God to choose as his natal home? No doubt many of the prophets wondered and inquired about the place where the Messiah would begin his mortal life. Nephi was told by an angel that "Christ . . . should come among the Jews" (2 Ne. 10:3), and he saw in vision that Mary would dwell in Nazareth (1 Ne. 11:13). Alma said that our Lord would "be born of Mary, at Jerusalem which is the land of our forefathers" (Alma 7:10), meaning that he would be born in the land of Jerusalem. Bethlehem, being some six miles from Jerusalem's walls, is in effect in the metropolitan area of that great city.

But it was to Micah, as far as our present scriptures reveal, that the actual site of our Lord's birth was given. "Thou, Bethlehem Ephratah, though thou be little among the thousands of Judah, yet out of thee shall he come forth unto me that is to be ruler in Israel; whose goings forth have been from of old, from everlasting." The everlasting God shall be born in Bethlehem! "She which travaileth hath brought forth," Micah says of our Lord's mother. Then of her Son, he speaks these Messianic words: "And he shall stand and feed in the strength of the Lord, in the majesty of the name of the Lord his God; and they shall abide: for now shall he be great unto the ends of the earth." (Micah 5:2-4.) That this prophecy, spoken by Micah some seven hundred years before the promised event, was understood by the Jews of Jesus' day is seen from the fact that when Herod demanded of "the chief priests and scribes . . . where Christ should be born," they responded: "In Bethlehem of Judea: for thus it is written by the prophet, And thou Bethlehem, in the land of Juda, art not the least among the princes of Juda: for out of thee shall come a Governor, that shall rule my people Israel." This reply was the basis for the search and slaughter in Bethlehem and its environs. (Matt. 2.)

Accordingly, that our Lord might enter mortality at the proper place, Joseph and Mary left Nazareth, as part of the taxation requirements of their day, and went "unto the city of David, which is called Bethlehem." There, not in a palace,

461

not in a temple, but in a stable, "because there was no room for them in the inn," Mary "brought forth her firstborn son, and wrapped him in swaddling clothes, and laid him in a manger." (Luke 2:1-7.)

No room in the inn—not an inn as we know such places today, but probably a caravansary, a kind of inn known among eastern peoples where caravans rest for the night; a covered place where travelers slept and prepared their food, while their animals, after being unharnessed, were tethered nearby. If such was the inn in Bethlehem, as seems probable, then the Jewish Messiah was symbolically rejected by his people even in birth, as they relegated his travailing mother to a bed of straw with the beasts of burden rather than make room for her among the camping members of the human race.

How Messiah Became Mortal

Messiah is the firstborn Spirit Son of Elohim. How came he into mortality that he then might be raised in immortality and become like his Father in the full and eternal sense? What was the process by which he traveled from his primeval spirit home to that state of resurrected glory which he now possesses, and in which he has received "all power . . . in heaven and in earth"? (Matt. 28:18.)

In most respects his coming was comparable to that of all mortals; in one respect—and oh, how vital this is!—his coming was singled out and set apart and different from that of any other person who ever has or ever will dwell on earth. That the true account of his coming might be had among the faithful, Matthew begins his recitation of how the Messiah became mortal; how he took upon himself flesh and blood; how he made clay his tabernacle; how our Elder Brother in the spirit took upon himself that mortality which we all undergo—that all this might be known, Matthew commences his account by saying: "Now the birth of Jesus Christ was on this wise," and then follows a recitation of what took place.

Thus, the Messiah was born! On the one hand, his birth was like that of all men; on the other it was unique, unlike that of any of the infinite hosts of our Father's children. And so Matthew says: "When as his mother Mary was espoused to Joseph, before they came together, she was found with child of the Holy Ghost." The marriage discipline of the day called, in effect, for two ceremonies. The participating parties were considered to be husband and wife after the first ceremony, comparable to a formal engagement in our culture, but they did not commence their association as husband and wife until the final marriage ceremony, which often was performed an appreciable period later. It was during this period that Mary "was found with child," a situation that would cause great embarrassment and sorrow among those who believed in and followed the divine laws of chastity and virtue.

Thus the record says: "Then Joseph her husband, being a just man, and not willing to make her a publick example, was minded to put her away privily"—a reaction that dramatizes the compassion and spiritual stature of the one destined to be the foster father of our Lord—"But while he thought on these things, behold, the angel of the Lord appeared unto him in a dream, saying, Joseph, thou son of David, fear not to take unto thee Mary thy wife: for that which is conceived in her is of the Holy Ghost. And she shall bring forth a son, and thou shalt call his name JESUS: for he shall save his people from their sins. . . . Then Joseph being raised from sleep did as the angel of the Lord had bidden him, and took unto him his wife: And knew her not till she had brought forth her firstborn son: and he called his name JESUS." (Matt. 1:18-25.)

Jesus was thus conceived in the womb of Mary. He took upon himself the nature of man in the same way that all men do. And yet the account is particular to say Mary "was found with child of the Holy Ghost," and "that which is conceived in her is of the Holy Ghost." If this is interpreted to mean that the Holy Ghost is the Father of our Lord, we can only

463

say the record has come down to us in a corrupted form, for the Holy Spirit and the Father are two separate personages. But providentially there are parallel passages that clarify and expand upon the paternity of Him whom Mary bare.

The Messianic language of Abinadi, speaking of things to come as though they had already happened, says: "He was conceived by the power of God." (Mosiah 15:3.)

Gabriel's great proclamation to Mary was: "Behold, thou shalt conceive in thy womb, and bring forth a son, and shalt call his name JESUS. He shall be great, and shall be called the Son of the Highest: and the Lord God shall give unto him the throne of his father David: And he shall reign over the house of Jacob for ever; and of his kingdom there shall be no end." Mary asked how this could be, "seeing I know not a man?" Gabriel replied: "The Holy Ghost shall come upon thee, and the power of the Highest shall overshadow thee: therefore also that holy thing which shall be born of thee shall be called the Son of God." (Luke 1:31-35.)

All ambiguity and uncertainty of meaning, if there is any, is removed by Alma, whose Messianic utterance announced: "The Son of God cometh upon the face of the earth. And behold, he shall be born of Mary, . . . she being a virgin, a precious and chosen vessel, who shall be overshadowed and conceive by the power of the Holy Ghost, and bring forth a son, yea, even the Son of God." (Alma 7:9-10.) Jesus, thus, is the Son of God, not of the Holy Ghost, and properly speaking Mary was with child "by the power of the Holy Ghost," rather than "of the Holy Ghost," and she was, of course, "overshadowed" by the Holy Spirit, in a way incomprehensible to us, when the miraculous conception took place.

"A Virgin Shall Conceive"

An easy heresy to grow into would be that since the Messiah is a God; since he is the Eternal One, the Lord Jehovah, who created all things; since he has all power, all might, and all dominion—and yet must be born among men—surely he must have more than a mortal woman as a mother. High prelates and persons of note and influence in the Catholic fold have argued that Mary should be proclaimed co-redemptrix with Christ, making her bear equally with him the sins of the world. But lest there be any misconceptions in the minds of men, the Messianic messages are pointed and clear as to the person and status of the one chosen to be the mother of God's Son.

In extolling his maternal source, a certain woman said to Jesus, "Blessed is the womb that bare thee, and the paps which thou hast sucked." Our Lord's response admitted the blessed status of her to whom Gabriel had truly said, "Blessed art thou among women" (Luke 1:28), but adroitly turned the thinking of the conversationalist away from undue adoration and toward that which all men must do to be saved. He said: "Yea rather, blessed are they that hear the word of God, and keep it." (Luke 11:27-28.)

Mary's name and appointment to be the chief mother in Israel were known and discussed by them of old. Ammon testified: "I have seen my Redeemer; and he shall come forth, and be born of a woman, and he shall redeem all mankind who believe on his name." (Alma 19:13.) Jeremiah proclaimed: "The Lord hath created a new thing in the earth, A woman shall compass a man." (Jer. 31:22.) The angelic preacher who taught the doctrine of the atonement to King Benjamin said: "He shall be called Jesus Christ, the Son of God, . . . and his mother shall be called Mary." (Mosiah 3:8.) As we have already seen, Alma called her Mary and spoke of her as "a virgin, a precious and chosen vessel" (Alma 7:10); she herself told Gabriel she had never known a man (Luke 1:34), and Matthew left us the witness that she was with child before she and Joseph had associated together as man and wife (Matt. 1:18-25). The great Biblical pronouncement as to the virgin birth comes, of course, from Isaiah, who foretold: "A virgin shall conceive, and bear a son, and shall call his name Immanuel." (Isa. 7:14.) Matthew tells us this prophecy was fulfilled in the birth of Jesus. (Matt. 1:22-23.) And Nephi bears a like testimony, as we shall now see in discussing the condescension of God. (1 Ne. 11:13-19.) For our present purposes, suffice it to say that our Lord was born of a virgin, which is fitting and proper, and also natural, since the Father of the Child was an Immortal Being.

"Knowest Thou the Condescension of God?"

Nearly six hundred years before Mary was with child of God, by the power of the Holy Ghost, Nephi saw in vision what would transpire in time's meridian. "I beheld the city of Nazareth," he says, "and in the city of Nazareth I beheld a virgin, and she was exceedingly fair and white." Clearly the vision was intended to show the high and holy place of Mary. She was foreordained. There is only one Mary, even as there is only one Christ. We may suppose that she was more highly endowed spiritually than any of her mortal sisters, but with it all, she was a mortal, not a God. Her mission was to bring the Son of God into the world, not to redeem mankind, not to intercede for them. She was destined to be a mother, not a mediator; hers was the blessed privilege, being mortal, to bring into the world Him by whom immortality should come. And blessed is she forever!

Asked by an angel what he saw, Nephi said: "A virgin, most beautiful and fair above all other virgins." Then, from the lips of the heavenly being came this question of eternal import: "Knowest thou the condescension of God?" And since even the greatest of prophets do not know all things—their knowledge, as with the rest of us, coming line upon line and precept upon precept—Nephi responded: "I know that he loveth his children; nevertheless, I do not know the meaning of all things." Thereupon the angel answered his own question by saying: "Behold, the virgin whom thou seest is the mother of the Son of God, after the manner of the flesh."

The angelic answer is perfect. The great God, the Eternal Elohim, the Father of us all, the Supreme Being, the Maker and Upholder and Preserver of all things, the Creator of the sidereal heavens, the One whose might and omnipotence we can scarcely glimpse and cannot begin to comprehend, this Holy Being to whom we, by comparison, are as the dust of the earth, this Almighty Personage, in his love, mercy, and grace, condescended to step down from his Almighty throne, to step down to a lesser and benighted state, as it were, and become the Father of a Son "after the manner of the flesh."

"And it came to pass that I beheld," Nephi writes, "that she was carried away in the Spirit; and after she had been carried away in the Spirit for the space of a time the angel spake unto me, saying: Look! And I looked and beheld the virgin again, bearing a child in her arms. And the angel said unto me: Behold the Lamb of God, yea, even the Son of the Eternal Father!" This then is the condescension of God— that a God should beget a man; that an Immortal Parent should father a mortal Son; that the Creator of all things from the beginning should step down from his high state of exaltation and be, for a moment, like one of the creatures of his creating.

Later the angelic ministrant bade Nephi to look and behold the condescension of God, meaning this time that of the Son, and Nephi did so, seeing the persecutions and trials of the Redeemer of the world as he, in condescension, ministered among his fellow mortals. (1 Ne. 11:13-36.)

Messiah Is the Only Begotten

We have spoken plainly of our Lord's conception in the womb of Mary; in reality the plain assertions are found in the revealed word, and we have but certified that the words mean what they say and cannot be spiritualized away. And as it is with reference to our Lord's mother, so it is as pertaining to his Father. The scriptures say that Jesus Christ is the Only Begotten Son. The problem is that the intellectually led ministry and laity of the day assume, as Satan leads them to do, that a name-title of this sort is simply figurative and does not have the same literal meaning as when the words are spoken in ordinary conversation. Perhaps again the best service we can render, on the issue here involved, is somehow to get the message across that words mean what they say, and that if Christ is the Only Begotten of the Father, it means just that.

Some words scarcely need definition. They are on every tongue and are spoken by every voice. The very existence of intelligent beings presupposes and requires their constant use. Two such words are *father* and *son*. Their meaning is known to all, and to define them is but to repeat them. Thus: A son is a son is a son, and a father is a father is a father. I am the son of my father and the father of my sons. They are my sons because they were begotten by me, were conceived by their mother, and came forth from her womb to breathe the breath of mortal life, to dwell for a time and a season among other mortal men.

And so it is with the Eternal Father and the mortal birth of the Eternal Son. The Father is a Father is a Father; he is not a spirit essence or nothingness to which the name Father is figuratively applied. And the Son is a Son is a Son; he is not some transient emanation from a divine essence, but a literal, living offspring of an actual Father. God is the Father; Christ is the Son. The one begat the other. Mary provided the womb from which the Spirit Jehovah came forth, tabernacled in clay, as all men are, to dwell among his fellow spirits whose births were brought to pass in like manner. There is no need to spiritualize away the plain meaning of the scriptures. There is nothing figurative or hidden or beyond comprehension in our Lord's coming into mortality. He is the Son of God in the same sense and way that we are the sons of mortal fathers. It is just that simple. Christ was born of Mary. He is the Son of God—the Only Begotten of the Father.

These are points upon which we need not elaborate. The concordances to the Standard Works list the numerous references involved. Let us quote but one Messianic prophecy from the Old Testament and one from the Book of Mormon. We suppose this declaration in one of the Messianic Psalms is plain enough: "Thou art my Son," is the voice of the Father to the Messiah; "this day have I begotten thee." (Ps. 2:7.) And certainly there can be no gainsaying these words of Nephi: "When the day cometh that the Only Begotten of the Father, yea, even the Father of heaven and of earth, shall manifest himself unto them in the flesh, behold, they will reject him, because of their iniquities, and the hardness of their hearts, and the stiffness of their necks. Behold, they will crucify him; and after he is laid in a sepulchre for the space of three days he shall rise from the dead, with healing in his wings; and all those who shall believe on his name shall be saved in the kingdom of God." (2 Ne. 25:12-13.)

What Is the Doctrine of Divine Sonship?

When, on the mount, "the veil was taken from off the eyes of the brother of Jared," that worthy "saw the finger of the Lord; and it was as the finger of a man, like unto flesh and blood." In fear and wonder he exclaimed, "I knew not that the Lord had flesh and blood." In response Jehovah said, "I shall take upon me flesh and blood. . . . This body, which ye now behold, is the body of my spirit; . . . and even as I appear unto thee to be in the spirit will I appear unto my people in the flesh." To this account Moroni appends this comment: "Jesus showed himself unto this man in the spirit, even after the manner and in the likeness of the same body even as he showed himself unto the Nephites." (Ether 3:16-17.) That is to say, as a spirit being, as a mortal being, and as a resurrected being, our Lord appeared to be and was

469

the same except for the putting on and taking off of the house provided for his spirit.

When this Jesus, seen thus by Moriancumer, came in the flesh, he was born as God's Son. His birth was the birth of a God. He came as the Offspring of the Father. The Messianic promise was: "God should come down among the children of men, and take upon him flesh and blood, and go forth upon the face of the earth." (Mosiah 7:27.) The fulfillment is recorded in these words: "And the Word was made flesh, and dwelt among us, (and we beheld his glory, the glory as of the only begotten of the Father,) full of grace and truth." (John 1:14.) Isaiah's prophecies that identify the Messiah as both God and the Son of God include these two: "For unto us a child is born, unto us a son is given: and the government shall be upon his shoulder: and his name shall be called Wonderful, Counseller, The Mighty God, The everlasting Father, The Prince of Peace. Of the increase of his government and peace there shall be no end, upon the throne of David, and upon his kingdom to order it, and to establish it with judgment and with justice from henceforth and for ever." (Isa. 9:6-7.) Also, Isaiah said that the name of the Child born to the virgin should be "Emmanuel," which means "God with us." (Matt. 1:23.)

"Thou, being a man, makest thyself God," was the charge hurled at Jesus by certain Jews who "took up stones again to stone him." The basis of this charge was our Lord's sermon, which included these assertions: "I am the good shepherd: the good shepherd giveth his life for the sheep. . . . As the Father knoweth me, even so know I the Father: and I lay down my life for the sheep. . . . Therefore doth my Father love me, because I lay down my life, that I might take it again. No man taketh it from me, but I lay it down of myself. I have power to lay it down, and I have power to take it again. This commandment have I received of my Father. . . . I and my Father are one." (John 10.)

What, then, is the doctrine of the divine Sonship? It is:

1. That God was his Father, from which Immortal Per-

sonage (who has a body of flesh and bones as tangible as man's) he inherited the power of immortality, which is the power to live forever; or, having chosen to die, it is the power to rise again in immortality, thereafter to live forever without again seeing corruption; and

2. That Mary was his mother, from which mortal woman (who was like all other women as pertaining to her mortality) he inherited the power of mortality, which is the power to die, the power to separate body and spirit, the one going back to the dust whence it came and the other going to a world of waiting spirits, there to remain until the trump of God calls both body and spirit forth.

It was because of this doctrinal reality, this intermixture of the divine and the mortal in one person, that our Lord was able to work out the infinite and eternal atonement. Because God was his Father and Mary was his mother, he had power to live or to die, as he chose, and having laid down his life, he had power to take it again, and then, in a way incomprehensible to us, to pass on the effects of that resurrection to all men so that all shall rise from the tomb.

"Who Shall Declare His Generation? "

Who shall give the genealogy of the Messiah? Who shall tell the Source whence he sprang? Who can name his ancestors and tell the progenitors who preceded him? What of his Father and mother, his grandparents? Who shall declare his beginning, his genesis, his generation?

Matthew begins his gospel by saying, "The book of the generation of Jesus Christ, the son of David." Thereupon he names an apparent genealogical line from Abraham to "Joseph the husband of Mary, of whom was born Jesus, who is called Christ." (Matt. 1:1-17.) Luke starts with Joseph and travels genealogically back to Adam without conforming to Matthew's account. (Luke 3:23-28.) Scholars are unable to unravel or bring into harmony the accounts here involved, and we have not been told by revelation the specifics of our Lord's ancestry. There is no way from a historical standpoint to search out the generation of Christ. One of the Biblical accounts may be the genealogy of Mary, the other of Joseph; one may assay to set forth kingly descent, the other give the lineal ancestry. We do not know. The only point upon which there is surety is the fact that Mary was his mother and God was his Father; other than that, his generation, his genesis, his beginnings are lost in antiquity except for a few obvious facts, as we shall now note.

"Blessed is he [Noah] through whose seed Messiah shall come," the Lord said to Enoch. We know in general terms and within a broad framework who some of his ancestors were. Manifestly he is a descendant of Adam, the first man. Indeed, the first Messianic prophecy of which we have record was spoken to Eve, "the mother of all living" (Gen. 3:20), while she and Adam were yet in Eden's garden. "I will put enmity between thee and the woman," the Lord said to Lucifer, "between thy seed and her seed; and he shall bruise thy head, and thou shalt bruise his heel." (Moses 4:21.) Ever since, the seed of Satan, those who follow him, have thwarted and plagued the Lord's work, as far as in them lay, with the ultimate triumph and success in the great warfare of life being reserved for Him as he crushes Satan and his followers under his heel.

Manifestly our Lord's descent, going downward, is Adam, Seth, Enos, Cainan, Mahalaleel, Jared, Enoch, Methuselah, Lamech, and Noah. It was to Noah that the Lord said, "With thee will I establish my covenant, even as I have sworn unto thy father Enoch, that of thy posterity shall come all nations." (JST, Gen. 8:23.) After Noah we go down through Shem to Abraham, Isaac, Jacob, and Judah. In that tribe we center in David, and then the problem of tracing descent is beyond our ability to solve.

But perhaps Isaiah's query "Who shall declare his generation?" has a greater Messianic meaning than is found in a mere attempt to trace genealogical ancestry. It is a true

472

principle that "no man can say [or, rather, know] that Jesus is the Lord, but by the Holy Ghost." (1 Cor. 12:3.) The testimony of Jesus, which is also the spirit of prophecy, is to know by personal revelation that Jesus Christ is the Son of the living God. In the full and complete sense of the word no one ever knows that Jesus is Lord of all except by personal revelation; and all persons to whom that testimony or revelation comes are then able to declare His generation, to assert from a standpoint of personal knowledge that they know that Mary is his mother and God is his Father. And so, in the final analysis it is the faithful saints, those who have testimonies of the truth and divinity of this great latter-day work, who declare our Lord's generation to the world. Their testimony is that Mary's son is God's Son; that he was conceived and begotten in the normal way; that he took upon himself mortality by the natural birth processes; that he inherited the power of mortality from his mother and the power of immortality from his Father—in consequence of all of which he was able to work out the infinite and eternal atonement. This is their testimony as to his generation and mission.

Chapter 26

MESSIAH MINISTERS AS A MORTAL

Why Messiah Ministered Among Mortals

To minister is to act in the name and place and stead of another in teaching those truths and performing those acts which are necessary for the salvation of those on whose behalf the ministerial service is rendered. We are the Lord's agents and represent him in administering salvation by teaching his truths and performing his ordinances. We stand in his place and stead, and act in his name, in doing for others what they cannot do for themselves. He in like manner came to earth to minister in his Father's name, power, and authority for and on behalf of all mankind, all of whom are our Father's children. He came as the Father's agent and representative to do for all men one thing that no other man, and no group of men, could do for themselves, and to do many things that no one else could do as well as he did them. His earthly ministerial service may be summarized under these heads:

1. *He came to atone for the sins of the world.*

This is the chief and crowning purpose of his earthly sojourn, the one thing none other could do. It required a mortal man who possessed the power of immortality because God was his Father. No other person or power could take captivity captive, could raise all men in immortality, with those who believe and obey ascending to heights of glory and exaltation. The concepts here involved are spread throughout this whole work and are considered particularly in Chapters 13 and 25.

2. *He came to reveal his Father.*

To gain salvation, men must worship and serve the true God and him only. He is the Father, and he was in Christ manifesting himself to the world. Matthew, Mark, Luke, and John, the four New Testament Gospels, contain more revealed truth about the nature and kind of being that God is than all the rest of the scriptures combined, simply because they reveal the personality, powers, and perfections of the Son of God, who is in the express image and likeness of the Father. The mere fact of knowing the Son and those things which unto him do appertain is of itself sufficient to reveal and identify the Father, because they are like each other in personality and appearance and in character, perfections, and attributes. Hence, the saying of Jesus, "He that hath seen me hath seen the Father." (John 14:9.)

3. *He came to testify of himself.*

Faith in the Lord Jesus Christ, founded as it is on the fact that God is his Father, is the first principle of the gospel. It is the beginning point on the path to salvation. Salvation is in Christ and no other. He alone made it available according to the terms and conditions of the Father's plan. Hence, he came to testify of his own divine Sonship, as set forth, among other places, in Chapter 9 herein.

4. *He came to set a perfect example for all men.*

This we have set forth in Chapter 12. Christ is our Pattern, our Exemplar, the One we must imitate if we are to become one in him as he is one in his Father.

5. *He came to teach the gospel, set up the kingdom, bless those among whom he ministered, and perform the ordinances of salvation.*

It is now our purpose, as we shall set forth in this and the next two chapters, to inquire into those things in his teaching and ministry which were known to and foretold by those who testified of his coming. The foreknown details of his

475

mortal ministry are more than a miracle. Their recitation in ancient Messianic writ makes us wonder if some of the ancient prophets did not then know as much about his future mortal life as we now know with the records of the past open before us. In any event, that Power which knows the end from the beginning and is pleased to let faithful men know in advance all things pertaining to their salvation which they are prepared to receive, that Omnipotent Power revealed to his prophets a great reservoir of detail about the daily life of the only perfect life ever lived. We shall now sample the sayings of the seers relative to the life of our Savior.

What Manner of Man Was the Messiah?

We know very little about the personality, form, visage, and general appearance of the Lord Jesus. Whether he had long or short hair, was tall or short of stature, and a thousand other personal details, are all a matter of speculation and uncertainty. We suppose he was similar in appearance to other Abrahamic Orientals of his day, and that he was recognized by those who knew him and went unheeded in the crowds by those unacquainted with him. A Judas was needed to identify him to the arresting officers; people spoke of him as though he were the carpenter's son; and he seemingly appeared as other men do. Perhaps the New Testament is silent on these points because it is more important to center attention on the principles poured forth than on the physical appearance of the Person who pronounced them. Perhaps also it makes it easier for us to dwell on his moral stature rather than any bodily perfection he may have had, and it certainly is a deterrent to the making of those graven images which apostate peoples so anxiously desire to venerate.

We suppose that a knowledge of these personal matters—his appearance, demeanor, and familial relationships—was also withheld from the ancients. Their

Messianic prophecies, at least, also draw a reverent veil of silence over many things in the realm of human interest. There are, however, two passages that do have a general bearing on his physical and human nature: one is in Isaiah, the other in the Psalms. These we should note, leaving in part at least to each person the problem of application and interpretation, for we too are bound to maintain the same curtain of dimness over those things upon which our ancient counterparts have not seen fit to dwell.

Of the Promised Messiah, Isaiah said: "He shall grow up before him as a tender plant, and as a root out of dry ground: he hath no form nor comeliness; and when we shall see him, there is no beauty that we should desire him." (Isa. 53:2.) Would it be amiss to interpret these words of our Messianic friend somewhat along these lines:

"He," the Messiah, "shall grow up before him," his Father; that is the growing, maturing, aging processes shall follow their normal course. We know he was born; we know he suckled at Mary's breasts; the record speaks of him as a "young child." (Matt. 2:11.) We know he "grew up with his brethren" (JST, Matt. 3:24), and that when he was about thirty years of age he began a strenuous full-time mission that would tax the strength of the most physically powerful of men. During that ministry we read of him eating and drinking; of his being hungry, tired, and thirsty; of his walking long distances, climbing high mountains, and sleeping soundly amid storms and terrors. We know he was smitten, scourged, and crucified, and that nails pierced his hands and feet and a spear was thrust into his side. There can be no doubt that he grew up and lived as other men live, subject to the ills and troubles of mortality.

"He shall grow up . . . as a tender plant, and as a root out of a dry ground"—"not like a stately tree, but like a lowly plant, struggling in arid soil. So the human life of the Messiah was one of obscurity and humility." (*Dummelow,* p. 446.) Or: "Messiah grew silently and insensibly, as a sucker from an ancient stock, seemingly dead (*viz.,* the house of

477

David, then in a decayed state)." (*Jamieson,* p. 490.) Or: Perhaps better still, he grew up as a choice and favored plant whose strength and achievement did not come because of the arid social culture in which he dwelt; it was not poured into him by the erudition of Rabbinical teachers; but it came from the divine Source whence he sprang, for as the Inspired Version has it, "He spake not as other men, neither could he be taught; for he needed not that any man should teach him." (JST, Matt. 3:25.)

"He hath no form nor comeliness; and when we shall see him, there is no beauty that we should desire him." There is no mystique, no dynamic appearance, no halo around his head, thunders do not roll and lightnings do not flash at his appearance. He is the Son of the Highest, but he walks and appears as the offspring of the lowest. He is a man among men, appearing, speaking, dressing, seeming in all outward respects as they are.

When he was a young child, not yet three years of age, Joseph being warned in a dream so to do, the Offspring of the Most High was taken into Egypt to escape Herod's executioners. Egypt was chosen as the place of temporary exile, so that upon his return, while he was still in his youth, the Messianic utterance might be fulfilled which says, "Out of Egypt have I called my son." (Hosea 11:1.) The slaughter of the innocent children of Bethlehem fulfilled Jeremiah's prophecy that Rachel should weep for her children and not be comforted (Jer. 31:15), and the fact that he was taken to Nazareth to live and grow and mature fulfilled the words of an unknown prophet, "He shall be called a Nazarene" (Matt. 2).

From one of the great Messianic Psalms we extract these references, spoken of the mortal life of the Messiah. "Thou art fairer than the children of men." This language, in the light of Isaiah's comments about our Lord's lack of comeliness, is not to be interpreted as meaning that Jesus was overly beautiful or handsome in appearance. Dictionary definitions of *fair* include the following: "Clean; pure; spot-

478

less; as, a fair name." Also: "Characterized by frankness, honesty impartiality, or candor; just." Any such usage has obvious meaning as applied to the Lord Jesus.

"Grace is poured into thy lips," the Psalmist continues, meaning the Messiah would have great powers of speech, and "therefore God hath blessed thee for ever." The kingship, "truth and meekness and righteousness," of the Messiah are then extolled, followed by these two verses: "Thy throne, O God, is for ever and ever: the sceptre of thy kingdom is a right sceptre. Thou lovest righteousness, and hatest wickedness: therefore God, thy God, hath anointed thee with the oil of gladness above thy fellows," which verses are quoted by Paul in Hebrews 1:8-9 and applied to Christ. The oil of gladness is a token of gladness, as used anciently in feast times or other times of solemn joy. The Psalm then continues in Messianic vein. (Ps. 45.)

"Prepare Ye the Way of the Lord"

Messiah's mortal ministry among men did not come unannounced. His was to be no secret mission; his message was not to be limited to a chosen few. His coming was no surprise to those who read the prophets and who rejoiced in the library of inspired literature in which the Messianic teachings were recorded.

For four thousand years all the holy prophets had foreseen, foreknown, and foretold what was to be in time's meridian. Each inspired witness of a coming Lord had told what people in his day and in all days should do to prepare for the divine advent. Alma, for instance, though a continent and a century removed from the Personal Presence who would dwell in the land of Canaan, said to his Nephite brethren such things as: "Repent ye, and prepare the way of the Lord, and walk in his paths, which are straight; for behold, the kingdom of heaven is at hand, and the Son of God cometh upon the face of the earth." (Alma 7:9) Also: "Not many days hence the Son of God shall come in his glory;

479

and his glory shall be the glory of the Only Begotten of the Father, full of grace, equity, and truth, full of patience, mercy, and long-suffering, quick to hear the cries of his people and to answer their prayers. And behold, he cometh to redeem those who will be baptized unto repentance, through faith on his name. Therefore, prepare ye the way of the Lord, for the time is at hand that all men shall reap a reward of their works, according to that which they have been, . . . and ye ought to bring forth works which are meet for repentance." (Alma 9:26-30.) That is to say, the way for men to prepare for the advent of their coming Lord, regardless of the day in which they lived, was to believe his gospel, repent of all their sins, be baptized for their remission, and then keep his commandments! And as it was with his first coming, so it is among us today as we prepare for his return: the voice of preparation has again been heard, and it is a voice of repentance and baptism and righteousness.

It is common, however, to speak of one prophet in particular as the forerunner of our Lord, because he is the one who proclaimed the message of preparation at the very hour when the Son of God came forth to commence his ministry. That prophet is John, John the Baptist—so named, not alone because he baptized repentant souls in great numbers, for many there were and many there are who have performed such sacred ordinances in great numbers, but because he alone baptized the Messiah himself.

Isaiah, speaking in measured tones of both the first and the second advents of our Lord, and with greater emphasis on the final glorious appearing, proclaimed a message of comfort and peace to the remnants of Israel. Among other things, he spoke of "the voice of him that crieth in the wilderness, Prepare ye the way of the Lord, make straight in the desert a highway for our God." (Isa. 40:1-11.) Malachi, speaking also of both comings but more particularly of the great and dreadful day yet ahead, gave forth the Lord's promise in these words: "Behold, I will send my messenger, and he shall prepare the way before me." (Mal. 3:1-6.)

Our Lord himself applied Malachi's prophecy to John by saying: "This is he, of whom it is written, Behold, I send my messenger before thy face, which shall prepare thy way before thee," to which pronouncement he added this testimony relative to his cousin and forerunner: "Among them that are born of women there hath not risen a greater than John the Baptist: notwithstanding, he that is [considered] least in the kingdom of heaven [that is, I myself] is greater than he." (Matt. 11:9-11.)

Matthew, writing of John's preparatory preaching and of the baptism of Jesus, said: "In those days came John the Baptist, preaching in the wilderness of Judea, And saying, Repent ye: for the kingdom of heaven is at hand. For this is he that was spoken of by the prophet Esaias, saying, The voice of one crying in the wilderness, Prepare ye the way of the Lord, make his paths straight." (Matt. 3:1-3.)

Hearing John's message, the people asked, "What shall we do then?" His answers were specific. Already they had been told to repent. Now the word came, "He that hath two coats, let him impart to him that hath none; and he that hath meat, let him do likewise." To the publicans he added, "Exact no more than that which is appointed you," and to the soldiers, "Do violence to no man, neither accuse any falsely; and be content with your wages"—that is to say, having repented and been baptized, now work the works of righteousness that you may be prepared for the fellowship of Him who is to follow. Thus Luke says, "And as the people were in expectation, and all men mused in their hearts of John, whether he were the Christ, or not; John answered, saying unto them all, I indeed baptize you with water; but one mightier than I cometh, the latchet of whose shoes I am not worthy to unloose: he shall baptize you with the Holy Ghost and with fire." (Luke 3:10-16.)

That these prophetic words of Isaiah and Malachi apply with force and vigor to John and his mission (though in their contexts they are oriented primarily toward the latter appearing of our Lord) is also borne out by Nephi, who recorded that his father Lehi "spake also concerning a prophet who should come before the Messiah, to prepare the way of the Lord—Yea, even he should go forth and cry in the wilderness: Prepare ye the way of the Lord, and make his paths straight; for there standeth one among you whom ye know not; and he is mightier than I, whose shoe's latchet I am not worthy to unloose." (1 Ne. 10:7-8.)

Why Jesus Was Baptized

Since baptism always has been and always will be singled out as the symbol and token of conversion to the gospel; since those who believe and are baptized shall be saved, while those who do not believe and are not baptized shall be damned; since baptism is the way earth's inhabitants receive the sanctifying power of the Holy Ghost and gain the constant companionship of that Holy Spirit; and since the Messiah came to earth to work out his own salvation, as well as to make salvation available to all men—we are justified in concluding that he himself needed baptism, and that the ancient prophets foreknew such would be the case. Indeed, the fact that baptism would apply to him as well as to all others is inherent in the whole scheme of things.

If we had the teachings of all the prophets, there is no question we would find our Lord's mortal baptism referred to by many of them. The Book of Mormon gives us our direction in this regard. In recording his father's teaching that a prophet should prepare the way before the Messiah, Nephi included these words: "My father said he [our Lord's forerunner] should baptize in Bethabara, beyond Jordan; and he also said he should baptize with water; even that he should baptize the Messiah with water. And after he had baptized the Messiah with water, he should behold and bear record that he had baptized the Lamb of God, who should take away the sins of the world." (1 Ne. 10:9-10.) Since Isaiah foreknew and wrote of this same prophetic preparation for the mortal labors of the Messiah, we may suppose that he also knew that Jesus would be baptized by the one sent to prepare the way before him.

Indeed, baptism is the very thing that prepares men for ministerial service, and why should anyone think that the Chief Minister of all other ministers would forgo the blessings which attend the performance of such a sacred and holy ordinance?

As we have seen, baptism, with its purifying power, prepared men for the coming of their Lord in the meridian of time. As we are also aware, this same ordinance purifies and prepares men for the Second Coming of the Son of Man. And as we also know, baptism has prepared and does prepare all of the Lord's agents for their ministerial service. Does it come then as a surprise to find Jesus undergoing that same ordinance to prepare him for his formal ministry?

When the time for his ministry had arrived, Jesus came "from Galilee to Jordan"—"in Bethabara beyond Jordan," John says (John 1:28)—"unto John, to be baptized of him. But John forbad him, saying, I have need to be baptized of thee, and comest thou to me? And Jesus answering said unto him, Suffer it to be so now: for thus it becometh us to fulfil all righteousness. Then he suffered him. And Jesus, when he was baptized, went up straightway out of the water: and, lo, the heavens were opened to him, and he [John the Baptist] saw the Spirit of God descending like a dove, and lighting upon him: And lo a voice from heaven, saying, This is my beloved Son, in whom I am well pleased." (Matt. 3:13-17.)

So speaks the sacred script. Our Lord is baptized! In a miraculous manner the forerunner who performed the ordinance sees the heavens open and the personage of the Holy Ghost come down: "I saw the Spirit descending from heaven like a dove, and it abode upon him." (John 1:32.) How closely these solemn occurrences conform to what Lehi and Nephi had seen in vision more than six centuries before! "And I looked and beheld the Redeemer of the world, of whom my father had spoken," Nephi said, "and I also beheld the prophet who should prepare the way before him. And the Lamb of God went forth and was baptized of him; and after he was baptized, I beheld the heavens open, and the Holy Ghost come down out of heaven and abide upon him in the form of a dove." (1 Ne. 11:27.)

In a passage of surpassing literary and doctrinal excellence, Nephi sets forth the rationale underlying the baptism of a sinless and perfect Being, one who had no need to be baptized for the remission of sins, for he had none. "If the Lamb of God, he being holy, should have need to be baptized by water, to fulfil all righteousness, O then, how much more need have we, being unholy, to be baptized, yea, even by water!" he reasons.

Then comes the query: "And now, I would ask of you, my beloved brethren, wherein the Lamb of God did fulfil all righteousness in being baptized by water?" That is, why be baptized for the remission of sins that do not exist? What divine providence is fulfilled, what righteous purpose is served under such circumstances? "Know ye not that he was holy?" Nephi continues. "But notwithstanding he being holy, he showeth unto the children of men that, according to the flesh he humbleth himself before the Father, and witnesseth unto the Father that he would be obedient unto him in keeping his commandments."

Our Lord was baptized as a token of humility. Can the proud and the mighty of the earth expect to do less in subjecting themselves to the divine will? By baptism Jesus entered into a covenant to keep the commandments; he bore record that he would conform to the will of the Father. Who among us can do less?

"Wherefore, after he was baptized with water the Holy Ghost descended upon him in the form of a dove." Such is the way and the means provided of the Father for mortals to receive the constant companionship of his Holy Spirit, and the law applies to his Only Begotten Son and to all his other children.

"And again, it showeth unto the children of men the

484

straightness of the path, and the narrowness of the gate, by which they should enter, he having set the example before them." The Great I Am, the Almighty Jehovah, the Messiah, the very Son of God, the King of the kingdom, he who presides supreme in his own celestial realm, even he cannot return from mortality to his state of eternal glory without entering in at the gate, the gate of baptism. "Except a man be born of water and of the Spirit, he cannot enter into the kingdom of God." (John 3:5.) The Lord Jesus, being a man, required baptism, even as other men. There is no other way.

"And he said unto the children of men: Follow thou me. Wherefore, my beloved brethren, can we follow Jesus save we shall be willing to keep the commandments of the Father? And the Father said: Repent ye, repent ye, and be baptized in the name of my Beloved Son. And also, the voice of the Son came unto me, saying: He that is baptized in my name, to him will the Father give the Holy Ghost, like unto me; wherefore, follow me, and do the things which ye have seen me do." (2 Ne. 31:5-12.) The great Exemplar has acted; he has marked the way. Let all men follow in his footsteps. The Holy Ghost descended upon him, and so shall it come upon all those who do as he did.

Elias Both Precedes and Attends Messiah

As I have written elsewhere (*Mormon Doctrine*, 2nd ed., pp. 219-22; *Doctrinal New Testament Commentary*, 1:128-30) the designation *Elias* is, among other things, the name of a number of different persons, a title conferred upon any prophet who performs a specified preparatory work, and a spirit and calling that attended John the Baptist. This whole matter, though complex and confusing to those who are not fully advised in the premises, is nonetheless one of considerable import to us and one that was of great concern among the Jews of Jesus' day. It is evident that they knew of some Messianic utterances that are lost to us, but which associated the ministries of Elias and Messiah. They knew that Elias would come and prepare the way before the Messiah, and also that Elias would come to restore all the might and glory and doctrine and power that their fathers in days past had possessed.

From inspired statements now available to us, we can piece together this much of the Elias picture. Gabriel came to Zacharias with the word that Elisabeth should bear a son, John the Baptist, whose ministry and work would be great in the sight of the Lord. "Many of the children of Israel shall he turn to the Lord their God," Gabriel said. "And he shall go before him"—that is, before the Lord—"in the spirit and power of Elias, to turn the hearts of the fathers to the children, and the disobedient to the wisdom of the just; to make ready a people prepared for the Lord." (Luke 1:13-17.)

This is perfectly clear. John was foreordained to go before his Lord and prepare the way. He was to prepare a people, by baptism, for their King. This he did, and it was the same thing that had been done by others before him as they sought also to prepare their people to see the face of that same Lord. "The spirit of Elias is to prepare the way for a greater revelation of God," Joseph Smith said. It "is the Priesthood of Elias, or the Priesthood that Aaron was ordained unto. And when God sends a man into the world to prepare for a greater work, holding the keys of the power of Elias, it was called the doctrine of Elias, even from the early ages of the world." (*Teachings*, pp. 335-41.)

Jewish knowledge of Messianic prophecies dealing with Elias as a forerunner and with Elias as a restorer is shown in the account of the conversation of John the Baptist with the priests and Levites who asked, "Who art thou?" The record says: "And he confessed, and denied not that he was Elias; but confessed, saying; I am not the Christ. And they asked him, saying; How then art thou Elias? And he said, I am not that Elias who was to restore all things. And they asked him, saying, Art thou that prophet? And he answered, No. Then said they unto him, Who art thou? that we may give an answer to them that sent us. What sayest thou of thyself? He said, I am the voice of one crying in the wilderness, Make straight the way of the Lord, as saith the prophet Esaias. And they who were sent were the Pharisees. And they asked him, and said unto him; Why baptizest thou then, if thou be not the Christ, nor Elias who was to restore all things, neither that prophet? John answered them, saying; I baptize with water, but there standeth one among you, whom ye know not; He it is of whom I bear record. He is that prophet, even Elias, who, coming after me, is preferred before me, whose shoe's latchet I am not worthy to unloose, or whose place I am not able to fill; for he shall baptize, not only with water, but with fire, and with the Holy Ghost." (JST, John 1:21-28.) Thus, for that day and dispensation, John is the Elias who was to prepare the way, and Jesus is the Elias who was to restore those things which had been had aforetimes.

Peter, James, and John were with Jesus in the holy mount when our Lord was transfigured before them and when Moses and Elijah, Israelite prophets who were taken into heaven without tasting death, ministered to him and to them. It was then that the Lord's apostles received from him and from Moses and Elijah (Elias) the keys of the priesthood. (*Teachings,* p. 158.) As they came down from the mountain, the three disciples asked Jesus: "Why say the scribes that Elias must first come?" That is, why do the scribes teach that Elias will precede the coming of the Lord, when in fact the Lord came first and then Elias (Elijah) came and gave the keys on this very mountain? "And Jesus answered and said unto them, Elias truly shall first come, and restore all things, as the prophets have written." This is a clear reference to some ancient prophetic utterance, known to the scribes, known to Jesus, and known to his disciples, but unknown to us. "And again I say unto you," Jesus continued, "that Elias has come already, concerning whom it is written, Behold, I will send my messenger, and he shall prepare the way before me; and they knew him not, and have done unto him, whatsoever they listed. Likewise shall also the Son of Man suffer of them. But I say unto you, Who is Elias? Behold, this is Elias, whom I sent to prepare the way before me. Then the disciples understood that he spake unto them of John the Baptist, and also of another who should come and restore all things, as it is written by the prophets." (JST, Matt. 17:1-14.)

Chapter 27

MESSIAH MINISTERS AS A MAN OF SORROWS

Messiah Wrought Miracles

Jesus wrought miracles, as the Messiah was destined to do. If there is any one thing all Christendom knows about him, it is that he healed the sick, caused the lame to leap, unstopped deaf ears, gave sight to blind eyes, and raised the dead. The trademark of his ministry is that he made the sick and the decrepit, the lame and the palsied, the diseased and the leper to be new again. Health and sight and hearing and life returned to those whom he blessed and who in faith sought his goodness and grace. Miracles were a way of life with him. And the perfecting of the diseased, the disabled, and the decrepit was but a type of that greater healing—the making whole of sin-sick souls, the destroying of diseases of the mind, and the spiritual rebirth of those who were dead to the things of righteousness.

We need not quote or cite the inspired record to remind ourselves of such things as a certain beggar, blind from his mother's womb, who saw again because he had faith to go at Jesus' behest and wash in the pool of Siloam; or of ten lepers who shed their leprous plague because he spoke; or of Lazarus, dead four days, his body rotting and stinking in a sealed tomb, coming forth because the divine Son so decreed; or of any of the almost endless stream of health-creating acts that attended his way of life. Everyone knows that health and healings, sight and hearing, life and vigor, were everywhere because he willed it so.

Let us instead alert ourselves to the fact that the prophets of old foretold that their Messiah would perform a ministry of healing and of health-giving such as had never before been known. Healing and miracles have been common among the Lord's people from the beginning. Jehovah himself is in fact the Great Healer. "I am the Lord that healeth thee," he said to his people Israel as he promised to remove from them the diseases of Egypt. (Ex. 15:26.)

It is but natural that the prophets, feeling and knowing their Lord's healing powers, would speak of his using them when he came to earth as a mortal. Thus, in speaking of our Lord's humiliation and suffering, Isaiah says, "Surely he hath borne our griefs, and carried our sorrows." (Isa. 53:4.) Alma and Matthew both paraphrase Isaiah's words and apply them to Christ's mortal labors. Alma says, as he also speaks Messianically, "He shall go forth, suffering pains and afflictions and temptations of every kind; and this is that the word might be fulfilled which saith he will take upon him the pains and sicknesses of his people. . . . And he will take upon him their infirmities, that his bowels may be filled with mercy, according to the flesh, that he may know according to the flesh how to succor his people according to their infirmities." (Alma 7:11-12.) Matthew speaks of the fulfillment of these Messianic utterances when he says, "They brought unto him many that were possessed with devils: and he cast out the spirits with his word, and healed all that were sick: That it might be fulfilled which was spoken by Esaias the prophet, saying, Himself took our infirmities, and bare our sicknesses." (Matt. 8:16-17.)

Nephi saw in vision what Isaiah and others must also have seen. "I beheld the Lamb of God going forth among the children of men," he said. "And I beheld multitudes of people who were sick, and who were afflicted with all manner of diseases, and with devils and unclean spirits. . . . And they were healed by the power of the Lamb of God; and the devils and the unclean spirits were cast out." (1 Ne. 11:31.) The angelic ministrant who came to King Benjamin foretold that the Lord "shall come down from heaven among the children of men, and shall dwell in a tabernacle of clay, and shall go forth amongst men, working mighty miracles, such as healing the sick, raising the dead, causing the lame to walk, the blind to receive their sight, and the deaf to hear, and curing all manner of diseases. And he shall cast out devils, or the evil spirits that dwell in the hearts of the children of men." (Mosiah 3:5-6.)

What he had done as the Lord Jehovah for ancient Israel, what he did among the Jews as their mortal Messiah, he continued to do among the Nephites after he rose from the dead. "Have ye any that are sick among you?" he asked. "Bring them hither. Have ye any that are lame, or blind, or halt, or maimed, or leprous, or that are withered, or that are deaf, or that are afflicted in any manner? Bring them hither and I will heal them, for I have compassion upon you; my bowels are filled with mercy. . . . And it came to pass that when he had thus spoken, all the multitude, with one accord, did go forth with their sick and their afflicted, and their lame, and with their blind, and with their dumb, and with all them that were afflicted in any manner; and he did heal them every one as they were brought unto him." (3 Ne. 17:7-9.)

And again we say that all of our Lord's healings—dramatic and wondrous as they were—are but similitudes and types that point to the even greater reality, that through him the spiritually sick, the spiritually diseased, the sin crippled of the world, may come forth in a newness of life if they have faith in his holy name. He it is, according to the promises made to his people, who "healeth the broken heart, and bindeth up their wounds." (Ps. 147:3.) And he it is who has arisen "with healing in his wings" (Mal. 4:2; 2 Ne. 26:9), with the spiritual healing that qualifies his brethren for an inheritance with him and his Father. "The Lord openeth the eyes of the blind"—temporally and spiritually. (Ps.146:8.)

491

Messiah Rejected by the Jews

"I am become a stranger unto my brethren, and an alien unto my mother's children." (Ps. 69:8.) Such was the Messianic prophecy. "He came unto his own, and his own received him not." (John 1:11.) Such was the Messianic fulfillment.

What an indictment! God himself ministers among men and they reject him! His own people, his own kindred, his own house, his own nation—the very people who knew the Messianic prophecies, who read the scriptures in their synagogues each Sabbath, who offered sacrifices in similitude of his infinite sacrifice—these are the ones who closed their minds and sealed their hearts, and whose voices acclaimed: Him we will not receive, away with him, crucify him. And this, in spite of all that he did among them. He healed the sick, blind eyes saw, deaf ears heard, lame men leaped, dead men breathed anew the breath of life, stinking corpses partook again of the sweet smell of life—and yet he was rejected! A God was rejected! The one perfect man, the only member of Adam's race who did all things well, whose every act and thought was for the benefit and blessing of his fellowmen—he it was who was rejected by the bigots, the fanatics, the insanely jealous, the mad religionists, and (note it well!) the generality of those among whom he ministered.

We need not refer to the New Testament account nor to the historical recitations of uncounted authors to remind ourselves that the Jews rejected their Messiah. As with the miracles he wrought, so with the fact of his rejection—it is an established and universally known verity. It is something of which the court of world opinion takes judicial knowledge, and therefore no evidence is required to prove it. Let us, then, simply follow our established pattern of pointing out that the prophets who went before knew by the spirit of revelation that their promised Messiah would be rejected, reviled, cursed, and (as we shall note more particularly hereafter) persecuted, scourged, and finally crucified.

Let us start with our friend Isaiah, a noble soul whose preserved Messianic teachings exceed those of any of the Old Testament seers, at least when we speak of direct teachings in words and do not take into account the Messianic performances revealed through Moses. Thus saith Isaiah, or better, thus saith the Lord by the mouth of Isaiah: The Promised Messiah shall—and these words we extract from the midst of more extended Messianic pronouncements—the Promised Messiah shall be one "whom man despiseth, . . . whom the nation abhoreth, . . . a servant of rulers." (Isa. 49:7.) Also: "When I came, was there no man? when I called, was there none to answer? Is my hand shortened at all, that it cannot redeem?" (Isa. 50:2.) And further (and we are but sampling): "He is despised and rejected of men; a man of sorrows, and acquainted with grief: and we hid as it were our faces from him; he was despised, and we esteemed him not." (Isa. 53:3.)

The second Psalm is Messianic. The first two verses speak of the rejection of Jesus by the Jews in these words: "Why do the heathen rage, and the people imagine a vain thing? The kings of the earth set themselves, and the rulers take counsel together, against the Lord, and against his anointed." Habakkuk, in a passage having no immediately apparent Messianic association, records, "Behold ye among the heathen, and regard, and wonder marvellously: for I will work a work in your days, which ye will not believe, though it be told you." (Hab. 1:5.) That these words are Messianic is certified by Paul, who, in speaking of Christ, says that "through this man is preached unto you the forgiveness of sins: And by him all that believe are justified from all things, from which ye could not be justified by the law of Moses. Beware therefore, lest that come upon you, which is spoken of in the prophets; Behold, ye despisers, and wonder, and perish: for I work a work in your days, a work which ye shall in no wise believe, though a man declare it unto you." (Acts 13:38-41.) It was in this same sermon that the ancient apostle said: "They that dwell at Jerusalem, and their rulers, be-

493

cause they knew him not, nor yet the voices of the prophets which are read every sabbath day, they have fulfilled them in condemning him." (Acts 13:27.)

Our Nephite brethren had similar views as to how their Jewish kinsmen in Jerusalem would treat the Lord of Life who would come among them. That they expressed themselves more pointedly and clearly than did those Old Testament prophets whose words have come down to us goes almost without saying. Nephi tells us: "Even the very God of Israel do men trample under their feet; I say, trample under their feet but I would speak in other words— they set him at naught, and hearken not to the voice of his counsels. . . . And the world, because of their iniquity, shall judge him to be a thing of naught." (1 Ne. 19:7-9; 2 Ne. 25:12.) His brother Jacob said "that Christ . . . should come among the Jews, among those who are the more wicked part of the world; and they shall crucify him, . . . and there is none other nation on earth that would crucify their God. For should the mighty miracles be wrought among other nations they would repent, and know that he be their God." (2 Ne. 10:3-4; Jacob 4:15.)

How Men Reject the Messiah

We speak with wonder and horror, and properly we should, of the fact that the Jews, with the scriptures, the miracles, and the mighty works before them, yet rejected their God, and did it so violently and with such a fixed determination that they brought about his death by Roman hands. To enable us to keep our perspective, however, we need to view with fairness and dispassion how and in what manner he was rejected and ask whether he would be so treated today. As Jacob said, only the Jews, among all the then existing nations, seeing the miracles he did and being aware of the wonders he performed, would have crucified him. (1 Ne. 19:7-9.) But would others among men have rejected him, and how and in what manner do men reject so great a thing as the ministry of a God among them?

In our day, that Lord who of old was rejected by his own, in speaking of that very rejection, said: "He that receiveth my gospel receiveth me; and he that receiveth not my gospel receiveth not me." (D&C 39:1-6.) Therein is the key. When men reject a man they reject a message; when they reject a message they reject the bearer thereof. To reject Christ is to reject his gospel, and to reject his gospel is to turn one's back on him and, if the animus attending the rejection is of sufficient proportion, to trample him underfoot and cause him to be crucified.

Speaking Messianically, Isaiah asked: "Who hath believed our report? and to whom is the arm of the Lord revealed?" (Isa. 53:1.) That is to say: Who among mortals has accepted the Messiah and his message? That it was not those among whom he ministered, we read in the words of John, who said: "Though he had done so many miracles before them, yet they believed not on him: That the saying of Esaias the prophet might be fulfilled, which he spake, Lord, who hath believed our report? and to whom hath the arm of the Lord been revealed? Therefore they could not believe, because that Esaias said again"—and this itself is another Messianic utterance (Isa. 6:10)—"He hath blinded their eyes, and hardened their heart; that they should not see with their eyes, nor understand with their heart, and be converted, and I should heal them. These things said Esaias, when he saw his glory, and spake of him." (John 12:37-41.)

Paul also made the acceptance of the gospel the deciding factor in whether men accepted their Lord. Inviting men to confess the Lord Jesus with their lips and believe in their hearts that God had raised him from the dead, he said: "But they have not all obeyed the gospel. For Esaias saith, Lord, who hath believed our report?" (Rom. 10:9-17.)

It was, of course, of both the message and the Man that the Lord spoke (through Isaiah) when he said: "This people draw near me with their mouth, and with their lips do

495

honour me, but have removed their heart far from me, and their fear toward me is taught by the precept of men." (Isa. 29:13.) Or, as the latter portion might better be translated, "And their fear toward me is a commandment of men which hath been taught them." Having in mind the many rituals, traditions, and formalities followed by the Jews in their form of worship, which imitated but did not conform to the Mosaic standard, they asked our Lord: "Why walk not thy disciples according to the tradition of the elders, but eat bread with unwashen hands?" His excoriating reply contains the perfect rendition of Isaiah's prophetic words. Jesus said: "Well hath Esaias prophesied of you hypocrites, as it is written, This people honoureth me with their lips, but their heart is far from me. Howbeit in vain do they worship me, teaching for doctrines the commandments of men." (Mark 7:1-9.)

In vain do we worship him, unless we accept him and his gospel!

We would be remiss if we did not at this point bear record that the Lord Jesus has in these last days revealed himself anew from heaven and given again the fulness of his everlasting gospel, which, if men accept, they accept him, and which, if they reject, they reject him. And the reason for rejection is the same today as it was then: "Men loved darkness rather than light, because their deeds were evil." (John 3:19.)

Messiah Oppressed, Persecuted, Mocked, Scourged

Arrested, bound, on trial for his life, our Lord was questioned by the high priest about his disciples and his doctrine. Jesus responded that his teachings had been in public, and therefore his interrogator should ask those who heard him. "When he had thus spoken, one of the officers which stood by struck Jesus with the palm of his hand, saying, Answerest thou the high priest so? Jesus answered him, If I have spoken evil, bear witness of the evil: but if well, why smitest thou me?" (John 18:12-14, 19-23.)

Later, before Caiaphas, having been mistreated and accused of blasphemy, it was said, "He is guilty of death. Then did they spit in his face, and buffeted him; and others smote him with the palms of their hands, Saying, Prophesy unto us, thou Christ, Who is he that smote thee?" (Matt. 26:57-68.)

Before Pilate for the second time, he, "willing to content the people, released Barabbas unto them, and delivered Jesus, when he had scourged him, to be crucified." (Mark 15:15-19.) "This brutal practice [of scourging], a preliminary to crucifixion, consisted of stripping the victim of clothes, strapping him to a pillar or frame, and beating him with a scourge made of leather straps weighted with sharp pieces of lead and bone. It left the tortured sufferer bleeding, weak, and sometimes dead." (*Doctrinal New Testament Commentary,* 1:807.) After the scourging, "they clothed him with purple, and platted a crown of thorns, and put it about his head, And began to salute him, Hail, King of the Jews! And they smote him on the head with a reed, and did spit on him, and bowing their knees worshipped him." (Mark 15:17-19.)

Decent men in all ages shudder at the vile and demeaning indignities heaped upon the Sinless Soul who came to save and redeem even the most degenerate of men on conditions of repentance. It shocks the souls of refined persons everywhere simply to think of the Satanic mockery, of the foul and blasphemous language, of the filthy spittle spewed in his face, of the pain wrought by piercing thorns and bloody scourge. And yet it was all part of the plan; it was all foreknown and foretold. The advance account is found in the Messianic prophecies.

"They shall smite the judge of Israel with a rod upon the cheek," Micah prophesies. (Micah 5:1.) "They gather themselves together against the soul of the righteous, and condemn the innocent blood," intones the Psalmist. (Ps. 94:21.) "We did esteem him stricken, smitten of God, and afflicted. . . . He was oppressed, and he was afflicted," Isaiah says. (Isa. 53:4, 7.) He "suffereth himself to be mocked, and scourged, and cast out, and disowned by his people," Abinadi testifies. (Mosiah 15:5.) And Nephi gives these details: "They scourge him, and he suffereth it; and they smite him, and he suffereth it. Yea, they spit upon him, and he suffereth it, because of his loving kindness and his long-suffering towards the children of men." (1 Ne. 19:9.) Through David, the Lord speaks in the first person, saying, "All that hate me whisper together against me: against me do they devise my hurt." (Ps. 41:7.) Through Isaiah, also given in the first person, the Messianic promise is: "I was not rebellious, neither turned away back. I gave my back to the smiters, and my cheeks to them that plucked off the hair: I hid not my face from shame and spitting." (Isa. 50:5-6.) And Jesus himself, speaking before the events, said to the Twelve: "Behold, we go up to Jerusalem; and the Son of Man shall be betrayed unto the chief priests and unto the scribes, and they shall condemn him to death, And shall deliver him to the Gentiles to mock, and to scourge, and to crucify him: and the third day he shall rise again." (Matt. 20:17-19.)

Messiah Suffers and Is Tempted

We take up now the philosophical question of whether a God can suffer and be tempted. We shall speak of suffering as undergoing pain of body and mind, and of being tempted as being enticed and induced to do that which is wrong with an accompanying promise of pleasure or gain. And we shall approach our problem with a full awareness that the scripture says: "God cannot be tempted with evil." (James 1:13.)

But we are not now dealing with God in his glorified and exalted state, a state in which he has overcome all things and become like all the Gods who so attained before him. We are speaking of the Lord our God as he dwelt among men; as he ate and drank and slept; as he was thirsty, hungry, and tired; as he dwelt as an earthbound mortal—not as he wafts himself in immortal glory from universe to universe.

As a mortal, Jesus our Lord was like all other mortals. He too was here to gain the experiences of earth life, to choose good rather than evil, to overcome the world, that he might rise in immortal glory and be like his Father. Pain, suffering, and temptation are an essential part of every adult probation. Without opposition we cannot overcome; and unless we overcome we cannot progress; and unless we advance and progress we cannot become like Him whose we are. Only little children who die before they arrive at the years of accountability are relieved from facing the temptations of this evil, wicked world.

It follows that the Mortal Messiah was destined to suffer pain and anguish and sorrow—"a man of sorrows, and acquainted with grief," Isaiah says (Isa. 53:3)—and that he would be tempted as all men are. That he did so is fully attested in the inspired records.

As to our Lord being tempted, Matthew tells us that Jesus was "led up of the spirit into the wilderness to be tempted of the devil." There, after a forty-day fast, weakened physically but strengthened spiritually, he met Lucifer the arch-tempter and was invited to turn stones into bread that he might feed his hunger and prove his divine Sonship. Passing this test, he was enticed to prove his divine status by casting himself from a high pinnacle and letting the angels save him from death. Then came the enticement to worship Satan in return for all the kingdoms and glory of the world. (Matt. 4:1-11.) That these temptations were real, poignant, actual tests, given to prove his devotion to the Father, we cannot doubt. Our latter-day revelation says simply: "He suffered temptations but gave no heed unto them." (D&C 20:22.)

As to our Lord suffering pain and sorrow and anguish, this is inherent in the whole account of his mortal life. He wept over doomed Jerusalem (Luke 19:41-44), the Holy City, "which spiritually is called Sodom and Egypt" (Rev. 11:8). We are aware of his physical and mental sufferings in many situations, climaxed in the agonies of Gethsemane and the cruelties of the cross—"Which suffering caused myself, even God, the greatest of all, to tremble because of pain, and to bleed at every pore, and to suffer both body and spirit," he says. (D&C 19:18.) Indeed, so much was he subject to suffering that even after his resurrection he prayed: "Father, I am troubled because of the wickedness of the people of the house of Israel" (3 Ne. 17:14), and he also said to the Nephites, "It sorroweth me because of the fourth generation from this generation, for they are led away captive" by sin and lust (3 Ne. 27:32).

Paul's Spirit-guided reasoning on the matter of the temptations and sufferings to which our Lord was subject brought forth these gospel conclusions: "Jesus," he said, came to suffer "death," and to "taste death for every man." Accordingly, Paul continues, "It became him, for whom are all things, and by whom are all things, in bringing many sons unto glory, to make the captain [leader] of their salvation perfect through sufferings." Jesus attained perfection, eternal perfection, through sufferings! And all others who so obtain must do likewise. "Wherefore in all things it behoved him [Christ] to be made like unto his brethren, that he might be a merciful and faithful high priest in things pertaining to God, to make reconciliation for the sins of the people. For in that he himself hath suffered being tempted, he is able to succour them that are tempted." (Heb. 2:10, 17-18.) "Jesus the Son of God," Paul says, is "touched with the feeling of our infirmities," because he "was in all points tempted like as we are, yet without sin." (Heb. 4:14-15.)

Peter held up our Lord's incomparably great sufferings and the manner in which he bore them as a standard for all the saints. In effect the Chief Apostle says: 'Be thou as he was, suffering all things for righteousness' sake.' "Christ also suffered for us, leaving us an example, that ye should follow his steps." It was Christ our Lord, he said, "who did no sin, neither was guile found in his mouth." It was he "who, when he was reviled, reviled not again; when he suffered, he threatened not; but committed himself to him that judgeth righteously." It was he "who his own self bare our sins in his own body on the tree, that we, being dead to sins, should live unto righteousness: by whose stripes ye were healed." (1 Pet. 2:21-24.) "Forasmuch then as Christ hath suffered for us in the flesh," Peter continues with the voice of exhortation, "arm yourselves likewise with the same mind: for he that hath suffered in the flesh hath ceased from sin; That he no longer should live the rest of his time in the flesh to the lusts of men, but to the will of God." (1 Pet. 4:1-2.) Peter concludes this part of his sayings with these words of prayer: "The God of all grace, who hath called us unto his eternal glory by Christ Jesus, after that ye have suffered a while, make you perfect, stablish, strengthen, settle you." (1 Pet. 5:10.)

It was in this same spirit that James wrote that the Immortal and Eternal God cannot be tempted. The context of his words is: "Blessed is the man that endureth temptation: for when he is tried, he shall receive the crown of life, which the Lord hath promised to them that love him. Let no man say when he is tempted, I am tempted of God: for God cannot be tempted with evil, neither tempteth he any man: But every man is tempted, when he is drawn away of his own lust, and enticed." (James 1:12-14.)

Having set forth the fact of our Lord's temptations and sufferings, and having seen the inspired doctrinal teachings based on these realities, let us now sample the Messianic utterances which spoke of them in advance. We have already used in various contexts Isaiah's pronouncements that he was a man of sorrows and acquainted with grief; that he hath borne our griefs, and carried our sorrows; that he was stricken, smitten of God, and afflicted; that he was wounded for our transgressions, and bruised for our iniquities; that with his stripes we are healed; that the Lord hath laid upon him the iniquity of us all; that he was oppressed and afflicted; that he was cut off out of the land of the living; that he was stricken for the transgression of his people; that he made his soul an offering for sin; that he bare the iniquities of many; that he poured out his soul unto death; and that he bare the sins of many—implicit in all of which is the fact of temptation, of anguish, of sorrow, of suffering. (Isa. 53.)

To these Biblical prophecies let us add the agreeing and concurring witness of the Nephite prophets. King Benjamin, quoting the angelic sermon, gives us this Messianic word: "And lo, he shall suffer temptations, and pain of body, hunger, thirst, and fatigue, even more than man can suffer, except it be unto death; for behold, blood cometh from every pore, so great shall be his anguish for the wickedness and the abominations of his people." (Mosiah 3:7.) Abinadi says, "He suffereth temptation, and yieldeth not to the temptation." (Mosiah 15:5.) Alma says, "He shall go forth, suffering pains and afflictions and temptations of every kind; and this that the word [spoken by Isaiah] might be fulfilled which saith he will take upon him the pains and the sicknesses of his people." (Alma 7:11; 16:19; 22:14.) And Samuel the Lamanite said that He "shall suffer many things and shall be slain for his people." (Hel. 13:6.)

Shall Messiah Save the Gentiles?

Those of Israel who, by the time Jesus began his ministry, had not been scattered among all people and on the isles of the sea; those who then dwelt in their promised Canaan and in Jerusalem, the city of the Great King; those who then looked for the coming of a Messiah, to save and deliver and redeem; those who considered themselves to be the chosen people and who looked upon all others as outside the pale of saving grace; those to whom the Messiah did in fact come and by whom he was summarily rejected—this race and assemblage of people believed, with a fixity and determination that could not be shaken, that their Messiah would come to save them, and them alone, and that for the Gentiles there was no hope. In their darkened state they failed utterly to understand the Messianic utterances relative to salvation going to the Gentiles, and of the Messiah being the God of the whole earth and not of them only. It is to this concept and to these scriptures that we will now give attention.

To read Isaiah (with understanding!) is to know that the Messianic gospel was for all men; that none were to be denied its blessings; that this included the Gentiles, however hated and opposed they had been theretofore; and that King-Messiah would surely say to his loyal followers: "Go ye into all the world, and preach the gospel to every creature." (Mark 16:15.) The God of the whole earth would offer salvation to the inhabitants of the whole earth. None were excepted.

The Stem of Jesse, that is, the Branch growing out of the root of David's father, is Christ. (D&C 113:1-2.) After naming him, Isaiah delineates the manner in which he will minister among men at both his first and second comings. With particular reference to the Second Coming, Israel's Messianic prophet says that an ensign shall be raised around which the outcasts of Israel shall rally. Part of the promise is: "To it shall the Gentiles seek." (Isa. 11.) Paul takes this whole passage, destined to have complete fulfillment only in our day, and uses it to justify his course of taking the gospel to Gentiles in his day. "Esaias saith," he records, in his paraphrasing quotation of the great prophet's words, "There shall be a root of Jesse, and he that shall rise to reign over the Gentiles; in him shall the Gentiles trust." (Rom. 15:12.) For Paul's immediate purpose, the quotation he selected established, at least, that the gospel was to go to the Gentiles, and that it was an ensign to which "the nations," who are the Gentiles, should look. He might, however, have chosen other Isaiah passages better suited to his purposes, some of which passages we shall now note.

Included in a long Messianic prophecy, other parts of which are quoted Messianically in the New Testament, we find these promises: "He shall bring forth judgment to the Gentiles," and the Lord calls him "for a light of the Gentiles." (Isa. 42:1-7.) In another passage, which Paul says specifically has reference to "Christ" (Rom. 14:10-11), Isaiah has "Christ" say: "Look unto me, and be ye saved, all the ends of the earth: for I am God, and there is none else." (Isa. 45:22-23.) That is to say, that salvation which is in Israel's Messiah is for all men, for all the ends of the earth. A parallel passage in the Psalms says: "All the ends of the earth have seen the salvation of our God." (Ps. 98:3.)

When Paul and Barnabas ceased to give Israel preferential treatment in hearing the gospel message and turned their attention to the Gentiles, Paul quoted Isaiah's Messianic words: "I have set thee to be a light of the Gentiles, that thou shouldest be for salvation unto the ends of the earth." (Acts 13:44-52.) This inspired interpretation is one of several reasons we know that this particular chapter of Isaiah's writings is Messianic. In it, in addition to the words quoted by Paul, we find the Messianic assurances that "Kings shall see and arise, princes also shall worship, because of the Lord that is faithful, and the Holy One of Israel." He it is that shall say "to the prisoners, Go forth." Of the way in which these kings and princes, these who are not of the house of Israel, shall help that chosen people, Isaiah says: "Thus saith the Lord God, Behold, I will lift up mine hand to the Gentiles, and set up my standard to the people: and they shall bring thy sons in their arms, and thy daughters shall be carried upon their shoulders. And kings shall be thy nursing fathers, and their queens thy nursing mothers. . . . And all flesh shall know that I the Lord am thy Saviour and thy Redeemer, the mighty One of Jacob." (Isa. 49.)

It is also Isaiah who preserves for us this promise: "Behold, my servant [the Messiah] shall deal prudently, he shall be exalted and extolled, and be very high. . . . So shall he sprinkle [startle] many nations; the kings shall shut their mouths at him: for that which had not been told them shall they see; and that which they had not heard shall they consider." (Isa. 52:13-15.) These, incidentally, are the words which introduce the great Messianic message of Isaiah 53, and the things which shall be startling and new are summarized in the Messianic message there recorded.

Lest their thinking remain forever provincial and limited, Isaiah tells Israel, "Thy Redeemer the Holy One of Israel," whom we have long since shown to be the Lord Jesus Christ, is "The God of the whole earth." So "shall he be called," says the prophet. (Isa. 54:5.) Further, the promise is that the Lord will gather strangers, the sons of strangers, eunuchs, and "others," along with Israel, and they shall all be saved together. (Isa. 56:1-8.)

As to the glory of Zion and of Israel, the record says: "Arise, shine; for thy light is come, and the glory of the Lord is risen upon thee." What wondrous blessings await faithful Israel! But then the record adds: "And the Gentiles shall come to thy light, and kings to the brightness of thy rising. . . . Thou shalt also suck the milk of the Gentiles, and shalt suck the breast of kings: and thou shalt know that I the Lord am thy Saviour and thy Redeemer, the mighty One of Jacob." (Isa. 60.) Further: "They shall declare my glory among the Gentiles." (Isa. 66:19.)

Other prophets add their testimony to that of Isaiah. Through Malachi the Lord said: "From the rising of the sun even unto the going down of the same my name shall be great among the Gentiles; . . . for my name shall be great among the heathen, saith the Lord of hosts." (Mal. 1:11.) Even Moses said, "Rejoice, O ye nations, with his people" (Deut. 32:43), which Paul interpreted to mean "Rejoice, ye Gentiles, with his people" (Rom. 15:10). The Psalmist wrote: "O praise the Lord, all ye nations: praise him, all ye people" (Ps. 117:1), which Paul recorded as "Praise the Lord, all ye Gentiles; and laud him, all ye people" (Rom. 15:11).

From all this, and there is more that could be presented, it should be perfectly clear that there is no justification whatever for the provincial views found in Jerusalem and her environs, and in all of Canaan, that there was no hope or salvation for the Gentiles; and it is also clear beyond question that Paul knew what he was about when he said: "Lo, we turn to the Gentiles." (Acts 13:46.)

How the Gospel Is for Both Jew and Gentile

If the Messiah meant to bring salvation and honor and truth to the Gentiles as well as the Jews; if his name was to be adored among them as well as in the house of Israel; if the heathen were to be blessed along with the chosen and royal seed; if the God of Israel was also the God of the whole earth—what of the doctrine of a chosen people? How is it that the great Redeemer had dealt only with Abraham's seed for some two thousand years? If for two millenniums all other nations had been cursed by the Lord of hosts, as his armies smote and drove and destroyed all who opposed his chosen Israel, why should things change with the personal coming of the Messiah?

Based on the revealed word, and as a matter of sense and reason, we know that a just and impartial Deity has offered and will offer his blessings to all of his children, whether Jew or Gentile, on the same terms and conditions. The issue is not whether the Messiah and his gospel will bless all mankind; that assurance is given in the scriptures and is itself so just and right that we would be bound, in sense and wisdom, to assume it to be so even if it had not been revealed. The sole issue is, When will the Messiah come; when will he minister to Israel; when will his truth go to the Gentiles; and why does it not go to all men at the same time?

To set forth how and when the gospel goes to Jew and Gentile is simply to specify the system of priorities prepared and provided by Him who made salvation possible. As a result of preexistent faithfulness, certain of the Father's children earned the right to receive preferential treatment during their mortal sojourn. Some who were noble and great were foreordained, as the Messiah himself was to his mission, to minister as apostles and prophets on earth. Others merited birth into the house of Jacob, so they would be in a position to hear the word of truth and begin the processes of repentance, and of working out their salvation, before that same gift was given to others.

Abraham's mortal seed, because of long ages of preparation and devotion, while they yet dwelt as spirits in the presence of their Eternal Father earned the "right" to the gospel and the priesthood and an eventual inheritance of eternal life. (Abr. 2:10-12.) That is, they were foreordained to be the children of the father of the faithful and to work the works of righteousness as did faithful Abraham. Though the gospel is for all men, in due course—"For verily the voice of the Lord is unto all men, and there is none to escape; and there is no eye that shall not see, neither ear that shall not hear, neither heart that shall not be penetrated" (D&C 1:2)—yet some are entitled to receive it before it is presented to others. The Lord sends forth his word on a priority basis. It goes to all men eventually, but some are entitled to hear the voice before others.

When the Messiah ministered among men, he said, "I am not sent but unto the lost sheep of the house of Israel." (Matt. 15:24.) When he sent the Twelve forth, while he was yet among them, he commanded: "Go not into the way of the Gentiles. . . . But go rather to the lost sheep of the house of Israel." (Matt. 10:5-6.) For the time and season that then was, the gospel was for the Jews and not for the Gentiles. But after the Messiah rose from the dead, the apostolic commission to proclaim the word of truth was expanded to include all men. "Go ye into all the world, and preach the gospel to every creature," our Lord then said. (Mark 16:15.) That the import of this new commandment did not register fully in the minds of his apostolic witnesses is shown by the fact that Peter thereafter was given a vision and a renewed command to take the gospel to others than those of the chosen seed. (Acts 10.) And much of Paul's preaching and writing was designed to show that at long last the day of the Gentile had fully come.

For our present purposes it suffices to say that in the meridian of time the gospel went first to the Jews and then to the Gentiles, but that in our day it goes first to the Gentiles (meaning those who are not Jews, but who are in fact a remnant of scattered Israel) and then to the Jews. Thus Nephi wrote: "There is one God and one Shepherd over all the earth. And the time cometh that he shall manifest himself unto all nations, both unto the Jews and also unto the Gentiles; and after he has manifested himself unto the Jews and also unto the Gentiles, then he shall manifest himself unto the Gentiles and also unto the Jews, and the last shall be first, and the first shall be last." (1 Ne. 13:41-42.)

As to how and by what means the gospel should go to Israel and to the Gentiles, the arrangement was that during his earthly ministry—including his mortal labors among the Jews in Jerusalem and his immortal labors among the Jews on the American continent, for the Nephites also were Jews (2 Ne. 33:8)—the Messiah would present his message in person, with the Holy Ghost bearing record that he spoke the truth. But for the Gentiles to whom the word of salvation would come after the resurrection, there was to be no personal manifestation of the Son of God. Rather, the gospel would be preached by the Lord's ministers, with the Holy Ghost attesting to the truth and verity of their inspired utterances. Lehi spoke of "the gospel which should be preached among the Jews, and also concerning the dwindling of the Jews in unbelief." He told also that "after they had slain the Messiah, who should come, and after he should rise from the dead," then he "should make himself manifest, by the Holy Ghost, unto the Gentiles." (1 Ne. 10:11.) Continuing his personal ministry in time's meridian, our Lord said to the Nephites: "Ye are they of whom I said: Other sheep I have which are not of this fold; them also I must bring, and they shall hear my voice; and there shall be one fold, and one shepherd. . . . And they [the disciples in Jerusalem] understood me not that I said they shall hear my voice; and they understood me not that the Gentiles should not at any time hear my voice—that I should not manifest myself unto them save it were by the Holy Ghost." (3 Ne. 15:21-23.)

Chapter 28

MESSIAH CAME TO PREACH AND TEACH

Why the Messiah Came as a Teacher

Gospel teaching is one of the most desirable of all talents, and gospel preaching the most needed of all gifts. The world needs now, as it needed in Jesus' day, teachers and preachers to present the word of truth and righteousness so that salvation will be available to the children of men. "It pleased God by the foolishness of preaching," the holy record says, "to save them that believe." (1 Cor. 1:21.) Men are saved if they believe, damned if they do not. Salvation comes to those who believe in the Lord, who call upon his holy name, who receive by revelation his laws and ordinances, and who keep the commandments. "How then shall they call on him in whom they have not believed? and how shall they believe in him of whom they have not heard? and how shall they hear without a preacher?" True it is that "faith cometh by hearing" the word of God taught by a legal administrator who has power and authority from his Maker to present the words of eternal life to his fellow beings. (Rom. 10:12-17.) What more important thing can any man do than present the message of salvation to his fellowmen so that they, if they believe and obey, can merit eternal life in the eternal kingdom of the Eternal God?

In the eternal perspective, and where the Lord's work among men is concerned, teachers stand next in importance

509

to apostles and prophets, who themselves also are teachers and who could not perform their apostolic and prophetic labors unless they were. In listing the gifts given of God to those who believe and obey, Paul places them in this order: "God hath set some in the church," he said, "first apostles, secondarily prophets, thirdly teachers." After these three come "miracles, then gifts of healings, helps, governments, [and] diversities of tongues." (1 Cor. 12:28.)

From Adam down, whenever the Lord has had a people on earth who would receive his word and hearken to his voice, he has had among them "preachers of righteousness" who have spoken, prophesied, taught faith, and called upon men to repent. (Moses 6:23.) These preachers, these teachers, these personal representatives of the Lord in heaven have made known to the residue of men the things which must be done to return to the Eternal Presence. That the Son of God, ministering as a mortal, should be the preeminent Preacher of Righteousness, the greatest Teacher ever to grace the earth, is an obvious and self-evident reality. As the Chief Prophet and the Presiding Apostle, as the Pattern and Exemplar in all things, it follows that he was destined to be the Master Teacher whose message and methods would set the perfect standard for all apostles, all prophets, all preachers of righteousness, all teachers, of all ages. And so, as we would expect, we find prophetic pronouncements in profuse abundance telling of the teaching ministry of the Messiah, and we find in the life of our Lord a flow of spoken words and performed deeds that woven together comprise the greatest teaching labor ever performed among men on this or any of the endless creations of Him whose we are.

Messiah Shall Come to Teach

Messiah came to save man. No one can be saved in ignorance of God, of Christ, and of the truths of that everlasting gospel which comes from them. It follows that the Messiah came to teach the gospel, the Father's gospel and his gospel, the Father's plan of salvation and his plan of salvation. He came to chart the course and mark the way, the way to perfection. He came to teach, preach, exhort, command, and plead with fallen man to be reconciled with the Father.

When the time came to choose and foreordain a Savior and Redeemer, who would be born as the Son of God and who would make operative the Father's eternal plan, this call went forth from the Father: "Whom shall I send?" (Abr. 3:27.) Christ volunteered, and he was chosen and foreordained to work out the infinite and eternal atonement on planet earth in time's meridian. When the time came to designate and foreordain the One, above all others, who would take the Father's message of salvation to the earth, a similar call was made: "Whom shall I send, and who will go for us?" The answer came from the same preeminent Spirit Son: "Here am I; send me." Then came this instruction to the One so chosen: "Go, and tell this people, Hear ye indeed, but understand not; and see ye indeed, but perceive not. Make the heart of this people fat, and make their ears heavy, and shut their eyes; lest they see with their eyes, and hear with their ears, and understand with their heart, and convert, and be healed." (Isa. 6:8-10.) That these words, preserved for us by Isaiah, are Messianic, and that they applied to the ministry of the Lord Jesus among men, is amply attested in the New Testament record. Jesus quotes them as applying to himself (Matt. 13:14-15; Mark 4:12; Luke 8:10), and both John and Paul use them to describe our Lord's teachings (John 12:39-41; Acts 28:23-31; Rom. 11:8). They have obvious reference to the fact that the Messiah's message would be rejected by the generality of those who heard it.

Many passages recite that the Lord Jehovah will teach his people. "He will teach us of his ways," Isaiah records. (Isa. 2:3.) Also: "I am the Lord thy God which teacheth thee, . . . which leadeth thee by the way that thou shouldst go." (Isa. 48:17.) Such scriptures have immediate reference to the Lord's teachings before and after he dwelt as a mortal, but since he is eternal and unvarying, they apply also to the stream of sayings that fell from his lips while he dwelt in his tabernacle of clay.

Many other passages speak with specific reference to the teachings he would give as the Mortal Messiah. Speaking Messianically, Isaiah gives him the very name "Counseller" (Isa. 9:6), thereby dramatizing the directions that he would give. "The spirit of the Lord shall rest upon him," Isaiah foretold, "the spirit of wisdom and understanding, the spirit of counsel and might, the spirit of knowledge and of the fear of the Lord." (Isa. 11:2.) Also: "I have raised up one, . . . and he shall come: from the rising of the sun shall he call upon my name. . . . He is righteous. . . . I will give to Jerusalem one that bringeth good tidings." (Isa. 41:25-29.) Of this One, Isaiah continues: "Behold my servant, whom I uphold; mine elect, in whom my soul delighteth; I have put my spirit upon him: he shall bring forth judgment to the Gentiles." Then come these words, which apply to those occasions when he spoke only to his disciples and did not proclaim his message, for one reason or another, to the people generally: "He shall not cry, nor lift up, nor cause his voice to be heard in the street."

Despite all that happened to him, and in the face of the almost total rejection of his teachings, we find Isaiah giving forth these remarkable words: "He shall not fail nor be discouraged, till he have set judgment in the earth: and the isles shall wait for his law." Part of his ministry was "to open the blind eyes, to bring out the prisoners from the prison, and them that sit in darkness out of the prison house. . . . I will bring the blind by a way that they knew not; I will lead them in paths that they have not known: I will make darkness light before them, and crooked things straight." (Isa. 42:1-16.) All of this, the promised Messiah would do in and through the teachings he gave.

Nor is this all. Isaiah records these words spoken by the Messiah: "The Lord God hath given me the tongue of the learned, that I should know how to speak a word in season; . . . he wakeneth mine ear to hear as the learned. . . . For the Lord God will help me; therefore shall I not be confounded; . . . I know that I shall not be ashamed." (Isa. 50:4-7.) But among all the sayings of the seers relative to our Lord's teaching ministry, perhaps nothing is so sweet and expressive, to a pastoral people, as the declaration: "The Lord God will come. . . . He shall feed his flock like a shepherd: he shall gather the lambs with his arm, and carry them in his bosom, and shall gently lead those that are with young." (Isa. 40:10-11.)

There are various passages in the Psalms that bear agreeing witness with the words of Isaiah. (Ps. 25:8-10; 32:8-9; 45:2; 119:12, 26, 29, 33; 143:10.) One of these deserves particular note: "Lo, I come: in the volume of the book it is written of me, I delight to do thy will, O my God: yea, thy law is within my heart. I have preached righteousness. . . . I have declared thy faithfulness and thy salvation. I have not concealed thy lovingkindness and thy truth from the great congregation." (Ps. 40:7-10.)

Our Nephite friends had similar foreknowledge of what the Master Teacher would do among his brethren. Lehi said he would preach "the gospel . . . among the Jews" (1 Ne. 10:11), and Nephi saw in vision that he would go "forth ministering unto the people, in power and great glory; and the multitudes were gathered together to hear him" (1 Ne. 11:28). Alma said simply: "He cometh to declare glad tidings of salvation unto his people." (Alma 39:15.)

The fulfillment of the many Messianic prophecies relative to our Lord's teaching ministry is found in the New Testament. Mark records, for instance, that "Jesus came into Galilee, preaching the gospel of the kingdom of God, And saying, The time is fulfilled, and the kingdom of God is at hand: repent ye, and believe the gospel." (Mark 1:14-15.) To his account of the Sermon on the Mount, Matthew appends these words: "When Jesus had ended these sayings, the people were astonished at his doctrine: For he taught them as one having authority, and not as the scribes." (Matt. 7:28-29.) Even his enemies testified: "Never man spake like this man." (John 7:46.)

How the Gospel Should Be Taught

Teaching the gospel is a unique and peculiar process, unlike any other teaching, distinct and different from any other forms of pedagogy. Special powers are available to those so engaged, and they are also subject to some very limiting restrictions. We have what may be termed "The Teacher's Divine Commission," which is the only approved way to present those truths which come from God in heaven and are sent to man on earth for his benefit and blessing and salvation.

Those who are properly authorized to teach the gospel are agents and representatives of the Lord. He authorizes them to present his truths in the way he wants them presented and in no other way. The Lord is the Author of the plan of salvation, and it is his right and prerogative to say what portion of his truth shall be taught at any given time and to prescribe the manner and way in which it goes from the heart and lips of the teacher to the ears and souls of the hearers. Jesus our Lord taught in strict conformity to this divine commission, he being the agent and representative of his Father. Indeed, the pattern he set perfectly shows how all others should teach. The provisions of the teacher's divine commission are:

1. *Teach the gospel.*

This means teach the plan of salvation. Stay with gospel truths. Personal views and speculation are unwelcome. The Lord's agents are authorized to tell others what they must do to be saved. Men are entitled to hear the word of God taught so that faith will dwell in their hearts. It is gospel truths and gospel truths only which beget faith. "Teach the principles of my gospel," the Lord says. (D&C 42:12.) "The law of the Lord is perfect, converting the soul: the testimony of the

Lord is sure, making wise the simple. The statutes of the Lord are right, rejoicing the heart: the commandment of the Lord is pure, enlightening the eyes." (Ps. 19:7-8.)

2. *Teach from the scriptures.*

Use the Standard Works of the Church as the basic source of gospel knowledge. Therein is found the approved summary of the plan of salvation. Search the scriptures is the unvarying counsel of Him whose Spirit inspired those who wrote the holy records. It is the scriptures which testify of Christ. In them is found the basic and approved foundation upon which the Lord's house of doctrine is built. In our day the scriptures mean the Bible, the Book of Mormon, the Doctrine and Covenants, and the Pearl of Great Price.

3. *Teach by the power of the Holy Ghost.*

This is the great overriding consideration, the chief and greatest requisite for all gospel teachers. Gospel teachers have the gift of the Holy Ghost, meaning they have the right to the constant companionship of that member of the Godhead based on faithfulness. The Holy Ghost is a Revelator. He is the agent the Lord uses to reveal to his earthly representatives those things they should say and do at any given moment. So basic is this concept that the revelation decrees: "The Spirit shall be given unto you by the prayer of faith; and if ye receive not the Spirit ye shall not teach." When an earthly agent teaches without the Spirit, he is on his own. Only when he is moved upon by the Holy Ghost do his words become the mind and voice and word of the Lord. "As ye shall lift up your voices by the Comforter," the Lord promises, "ye shall speak and prophesy as seemeth me good; For, behold, the Comforter knoweth all things, and beareth record of the Father and of the Son." (D&C 42:14-17.)

Those who preach by the power of the Holy Ghost use the scriptures as their basic source of knowledge and doctrine. They begin with what the Lord has before revealed to other inspired men. But it is the practice of the Lord to give added knowledge to those upon whose hearts the true meanings and intents of the scriptures have been impressed. Many

515

great doctrinal revelations come to those who preach from the scriptures. When they are in tune with the Infinite, the Lord lets them know, first, the full and complete meaning of the scriptures they are expounding, and then he ofttimes expands their views so that new truths flood in upon them, and they learn added things that those who do not follow such a course can never know. Hence, as to "preaching the word," the Lord commands his servants to go forth "saying none other things than that which the prophets and apostles have written, and that which is taught them by the Comforter through the prayer of faith." (D&C 52:9.) In a living, growing, divine church, new truths will come from time to time and old truths will be applied with new vigor to new situations, all under the guidance of the Holy Spirit of God.

4. *Apply the principles taught to the needs of the hearers.*

It does not suffice to present gospel truths in an abstract and impersonal way. True principles benefit mankind only when they live in the souls of men. Testimony as an abstract principle has no saving power, but a testimony in the heart of a living person opens the door to a course leading to eternal life. Gospel principles are always the same; they never vary. But the circumstances in which men find themselves are as varied as the number of living persons. The inspired teacher always applies the eternal truths to the circumstances of his hearers. Thus Nephi, in quoting the truths taught by Isaiah, says: "Hear ye the words of the prophet, which were written unto all the house of Israel, and liken them unto yourselves." (1 Ne. 19:24.) That is, Isaiah wrote concerning the whole house of Israel, and Nephi is now applying his words to the Nephites and the peculiar situation in which they found themselves.

5. *Teach with the seal of personal testimony.*

The crowning, convincing, converting power of gospel teaching is manifest when an inspired teacher says, "I know by the power of the Holy Ghost, by the revelations of the Holy Spirit to my soul, that the doctrines I have taught are true." This divine seal of approval makes the spoken word binding upon the hearers. Alma preached a powerful sermon about the spiritual rebirth that should come into the life of every true saint. He quoted the sayings of the fathers and expounded his doctrinal views with clarity and certainty. Then he said: "And this is not all. Do ye not suppose that I know of these things myself? Behold, I testify unto you that I do know that these things whereof I have spoken are true." It should be noted that Alma is not bearing testimony that the work in which he is engaged is true; he is certifying that the doctrinal principles he is expounding are themselves the mind and will of the Lord. "And how do ye suppose that I know of their surety?" he asks. "Behold, I say unto you they are made known unto me by the Holy Spirit of God," he replies. "Behold, I have fasted and prayed many days that I might know these things of myself," he continues. "And now I do know of myself that they are true; for the Lord God hath made them manifest unto me by his Holy Spirit; and this is the spirit of revelation which is in me." (Alma 5:45-46.) It should be added that when the Lord's servants preach in power, by the promptings of the Holy Spirit, the Lord adds his own witness to the truth of their words. That witness comes in the form of signs and gifts and miracles. Such are always found when the preached word, given in power, is believed by hearers with open hearts. And we shall now take particular note of how the Lord Jesus interwove his spoken words and his healing powers to leave a witness of his own divine calling that could not have been given in any other way. We shall see, by way of sample only, how and in what manner he taught gospel truths.

How Jesus Taught the Greatest Truths

Let us name the greatest truths known to Gods, angels, or men; known in time or in eternity; known on this or any earth; known either here among us or among any intelligent beings in all the wide expanse of immensity. Then let us note how Jesus our Lord, the Master Teacher, chose to teach and reveal these truths to his fellowmen.

We believe it to be self-evident that the greatest truth in all eternity is: That there is a God in heaven who created all things—the universe, man, and all forms of life; that there is existence, creation, and being—all controlled and governed by an intelligent Head; that God is, and we are, and all things exist. As to the facts of existence and creation, such need no proof. As to the wisdom and omnipotence of the Creator, such is shown by the extent, complexity, and organized nature of created things.

But as to the fact that the Most High God is a Holy Man, an Eternal Father, an Exalted Personage in whose image man is created, this is something that must be revealed. It is something that men must learn from sources other than reason. And the greatest revelation ever given of the Father is the revelation of the Son. It is that the Father had a Son who in the very nature of things was a manifestation of his Parent. As set forth in Chapter 2, God was in Christ manifesting himself to the world. Christ is the revelation of the Father; by learning about the Son we automatically know what kind of Being his Father is. Thus the accounts about our Lord, as recorded by Matthew, Mark, Luke, and John, become the most extended and perfect recitations about the Father himself. Jesus taught the greatest of all truths—the facts about his Father—by the life he lived, the deeds he did, and the words he spoke.

We also believe it to be self-evident that the second greatest truth in all eternity is that Christ our Lord is the Son of God who came into the world to manifest his Father and to bring to pass the immortality and eternal life of man. In Chapter 9 we gave three illustrations of how he both taught and proved that he was the Son of God. One was the instance in which he forgave the sins of a paralytic, which none but God can do, and then when the Jews murmured at his seeming blasphemy, in order to show that he himself was

God, he commanded the sick of palsy to arise, take up his bed, and walk. Another case was that of healing the man born blind. This he did in order to gain a congregation of hearers so that he could declare unto them in plain words that he was the Good Shepherd and that he and his Father were one. And the third instance was that of raising Lazarus from his four-day sleep of death, after he first declared to Martha and Mary and the Jewish mourners that he himself was in fact the resurrection and the life. The reasoning in each of these case studies is that when he said "I am the Son of God" (John 10:36), either in plain words or by necessary implication, his teaching must be true because he was also causing the lame to walk, the blind to see, and the dead to rise. To these three illustrations might be added such other instances as his feeding of the five thousand, on which occasion he taught that he was the Bread of Life who came down from heaven. (John 6.)

It may well be that the third greatest truth in the eternal scheme of things is that man can commune with his Maker and gain a knowledge of the plan of salvation by the power of the Holy Ghost. Such an order of priorities centers the greatest of all truths in the Father, the next greatest in the Son, and the third in the Holy Ghost. In any event, there is little in life as important to man as coming to a knowledge of those things he must believe and do to gain eternal life.

This matter of gaining knowledge from the Holy Spirit was taught by the Master Teacher primarily in plain words. "Ask, and it shall be given you," he said. (Matt. 7:7.) Also: "Blessed are all they that do hunger and thirst after righteousness; for they shall be filled with the Holy Ghost." (JST, Matt. 5:8.) And: "When he, the Spirit of truth, is come, he will guide you into all truth: for he shall not speak of himself; but whatsoever he shall hear, that shall he speak: and he will shew you things to come." (John 16:13.)

It may not be amiss to insert at this point what so many of those who become bewitched with teaching methodology so often overlook, which is that one of the best ways to teach a doctrine is just to state it in plain and simple and persuasive language. Teaching aids and symbolisms play their part in proper situations and for special reasons, but nothing can overshadow the simple pedagogical approach of saying what is involved in a pleasing and compelling way. Such was the course pursued in large measure by the resurrected Lord when he taught the Nephites, and such also was the course pursued by the Nephite prophets in general as they preached the various doctrines of peace and salvation.

How Jesus Taught the Doctrine of Resurrection

May we suggest that the fourth greatest truth centers around that immortality and eternal life which our Lord came to bring. In this connection, what teaching on the matter of the resurrection equals that given by Jesus on the Emmaus road and in the upper room? Jesus, being resurrected, walked for perhaps eight miles along a dusty Judean lane with Cleopas and another disciple, probably Luke. He talked and appeared as any mortal would. He took special occasion to expound the scriptures concerning Christ as they are found in Moses and in the Psalms. In dress, demeanor, and physical appearance, he was like any wayfaring teacher of the day. And the disciples knew him not until he chose to make his identity known when at eventide he brake bread with them. How better could he have taught that immortality is but a continuation of mortality, and that when men rise from the dead, they go on living in tangible bodies like those they had before death and the resurrection?

Cleopas and his fellow disciple immediately returned to Jerusalem, found the apostles and a congregation of saints who were eating in a closed upper room, and recited what had transpired. As they recounted their experiences with a Resurrected Being, that same Jesus, whose body was tangible and real, came through the wall of the room. He spoke, teaching doctrine, reciting that he had a body of flesh and bones which those present were invited to handle and feel.

He was recognized; the congregation knew him. He asked for food, which he ate before them. The apostles felt the nail marks in his hands and feet and thrust their hands into the spear wound in his side, all to the end that this congregation of saints, this group of living witnesses, might know that a resurrected person has power over physical objects and yet is a personal being, having a body of flesh and bones which can eat and digest food as though mortal. Surely the Master Teacher here crowns his and all other teaching about the nature of resurrected bodies! (Luke 24.)

And what teaching about eternal life compares with the doctrine of John 17:3: "And this is life eternal, that they might know thee, the only true God, and Jesus Christ, whom thou hast sent," which means that to gain eternal life we must become like the Gods of heaven, knowing and experiencing as they do, and living in the family unit as does our own Eternal Father. Could a teacher couch an eternal truth in words more graphically than Jesus did here in his great Intercessory Prayer?

Jesus' Teachings Fulfill Messianic Promises

Volumes have been written about the methods and approaches and techniques of the Master Teacher. Authors generally have been more concerned with his use of parables and of the common things of Jewish culture and geography to drive home his points than they have been with the infinitely important truths he taught. They analyze his use of illustrations involving flowers and birds and animals, his references to seed time and harvest, and the like; they speak primarily of the how and the manner of his teaching, rather than the nature and import of the message. These procedures and techniques are simply the garments used to clothe the eternal truths set forth. Important as they are, the great glory and beauty and perfection of the teaching of the Mortal Messiah are found in the doctrine he taught, the truths he expounded, as he set an example of how all other teachers should operate within the terms and conditions of the teacher's divine commission.

It is not our purpose to dwell upon the excellence and transcendent nature of his manner of teaching. We are simply showing that as a teacher he excelled all others, and that his teaching ministry was foreknown to the ancients and foretold by them in their Messianic utterances. We need not here evaluate our Lord's Sermon on the Mount, which presented gospel truths for the benefit of all men, nor his discourse on the Second Coming, which presented doctrines that only his spiritually enlightened disciples could understand. It is not our purpose to show how the parable of Lazarus and the rich man reveals great truths relative to salvation for the dead, and how the parable of the wheat and the tares hides from all but the enlightened saints the doctrine our Lord was then teaching. (D&C 86.)

For our purposes, it suffices to gain an acute awareness that when Jesus taught, he was fulfilling his foreordained destiny. When he dwelt and taught in Capernaum, for instance, he was doing so "in the borders of Zabulon and Nephthalim: That it might be fulfilled which was spoken by Esaias the prophet, saying, The land of Zabulon, and the land of Nephthalim, by the way of the sea, beyond Jordan, Galilee of the Gentiles; The people which sat in darkness saw great light; and to them which sat in the region and shadow of death light is sprung up." (Matt. 4:12-16; Isa. 9:1-2.) When he blessed little children, he was but carrying the lambs of his flock in his arms as Isaiah foretold. (Isa. 40:11.) When he chose Twelve to carry his message, he was but fulfilling the Nephite prophecies. (1 Ne. 1:9-11; 11:29-36; 12:7-10; 13:26.)

Truly, as spake the Psalmist of him: "Grace is poured into thy lips: therefore God hath blessed thee for ever." (Ps. 45:2.)

Chapter 29

MESSIAH CRUCIFIED AND SLAIN

A God Dies!

Interwoven into every concept presented throughout this whole work is the great reality that God himself must die for man; that the Almighty Jehovah, the Creator of all things from the beginning, the Mighty Messiah, Israel's Deliverer, must lay down his life; that the Lord Jesus Christ, the very Son of God, came into the world—above all other reasons—to die, to die upon the cross, to die as he suffered more than man can suffer.

The death of a God! The great Creator dies! Not only does he die—he is slain, crucified, pierced. Nails are driven through his hands and feet. A Roman spear is hurled into his side. He hangs in agony upon a cross, feeling again the weight of the sorrow he bore in Gethsemane.

A God dies and the rocks rend; a God dies and all creation shudders; a God dies and all the hosts of heaven both sorrow and rejoice. A God dies that he may live again; that he may come forth from the tomb as the firstfruits of them that sleep; that he may bring immortality to all and eternal life to those who believe and obey. A God dies that all the terms and conditions of the Father's plan may be fulfilled. A God descends below all things that he may rise to heights above the stars; he lives again, as all men shall; and the infinite and eternal atonement is complete. The will of the

Son is swallowed up in the will of the Father. The will of the Father in all things from the beginning is done!

All these things have been known in greater or lesser degree by prophets and saints in all dispensations. The nature of this work is such that we have referred to many things concerning the Lord Messiah's death as we have dealt with the various Messianic concepts. It is now, however, our privilege to collate and comment upon the Messianic utterances relative to his death as such, so that we may have before us the wondrous things known by the ancients about Him who is our Deliverer.

Jehovah, Israel's God, Shall Die

We are aware that the ancient prophets and saints knew that their Messiah must die. He is spoken of as "the Lamb slain from the foundation of the world" (Rev. 13:8), meaning his sacrificial death was planned and foreordained from the beginning as part of the Father's plan. And the revelatory processes making the fact and reasons for his death known to mortal man commenced in the day of the first man. Each time the Lord revealed his atoning truths, the death of the Atoner was set forth, either in plain words or by necessary implication. The angelic pronouncement to Adam that his sacrificial performances were in "similitude of the sacrifice of the Only Begotten of the Father" (Moses 5:7) carries with it the verity that the Only Begotten will lay down his life in sacrifice. Throughout this work we have considered those passages and doctrines which presuppose and assume Messiah's death. Now we shall show some of the revelations which deal specifically with matters connected with his passing from mortality.

First, let us make it clear that the ancient prophets had in mind that it was the Lord Jehovah, their Creator, the Lord God of Israel, who should die. Nephi says that "even the very God of Israel do men trample under their feet," and that "the God of Abraham, and of Isaac, and the God of Jacob, yieldeth himself" into the hands of men to be slain. (1 Ne. 19:7, 10.) Jacob says, "It behooveth the great Creator that he suffereth himself to become subject unto man in the flesh, and to die for all men." (2 Ne. 9:5.) Also, "The Lord God . . . loveth the world, even that he layeth down his own life that he may draw all men unto him." (2 Ne. 26:23-24.) And our angelic co-laborer told King Benjamin that it was "the Lord Omnipotent who reigneth, who was, and is, from all eternity to all eternity" who should suffer death for his people. (Mosiah 3:5-7.) These passages illustrate the plainness with which Book of Mormon prophets spoke in identifying the Person who should come to redeem mankind.

The numerous statements in Isaiah to the effect that Jehovah is the Redeemer and Savior have the same meaning. One particularly expressive Old Testament passage counsels: "Trust ye in the Lord for ever: for in the Lord JEHOVAH is everlasting strength." In that setting the voice of Jehovah then says to his people: "Thy dead men shall live, together with my dead body shall they arise. Awake and sing, ye that dwell in the dust: . . . and the earth shall cast out the dead." (Isa. 26:4, 19.) Jehovah, having first died, shall rise in immortality and thereby bring to pass the resurrection of all men.

Messiah Shall Be Slain

Most of what the prophets foretold relative to the death of the Infinite One speaks of him under the name-title of *Messiah*, which is the Hebrew designation, or of *Christ*, which is the Greek rendition of the same word. By way of illustration, the Messiah passages say that the Jews shall slay "the Messiah, who should come," and that "the Son of God was the Messiah who should come." (1 Ne. 10:11, 17.) They say that "the Holy Messiah . . . layeth down his life according to the flesh, and taketh it again by the power of the

Spirit" (2 Ne. 2:8), and that "after the Messiah shall come there shall be signs given unto my people [the Nephites] of his birth, and also of his death and resurrection" (2 Ne. 26:3). Daniel speaks of the fact that the "Messiah shall be cut off." (Dan. 9:26.) And we shall note other Messianic passages when we speak of the mode and manner of his death, that of crucifixion.

Also by way of illustration, the even more numerous passages using the name *Christ* say such things as: "We would to God that we could persuade all men not to rebel against God, to provoke him to anger, but that all men would believe in Christ, and view his death, and suffer his cross and bear the shame of the world." (Jacob 1:8.) "The resurrection of the dead, and the redemption of the people . . . was to be brought to pass through the power, and sufferings, and death of Christ, and his resurrection and ascension into heaven." (Mosiah 18:2.) "Now Aaron began to open the scriptures unto them concerning the coming of Christ, and also concerning the resurrection of the dead, and that there could be no redemption for mankind save it were through the death and sufferings of Christ, and the atonement of his blood." (Alma 21:9.) "Nothing can save this people save it be repentance and faith on the Lord Jesus Christ, who surely shall come into the world, and shall suffer many things and shall be slain for his people." (Hel. 13:6.) "Jesus Christ, the Son of God, . . . the Creator of all things from the beginning, . . . surely must die that salvation may come; yea, it behooveth him and becometh expedient that he dieth, to bring to pass the resurrection of the dead, that thereby men may be brought into the presence of the Lord." (Hel. 14:12, 15.) Indeed, so profuse are these prophecies and so commonly were they taught among the saints that Nephi the son of Helaman said, "Almost all of our fathers, even down to this time . . . have testified of the coming of Christ, and have rejoiced in his day which is to come. And behold, he is God, and he is with them, and he did manifest himself unto them, that they were redeemed by him; and they gave unto him glory, because of that which is to come." (Hel. 8:22-23.)

These prophetic declarations of the appointed slaying of earth's Chief Citizen continued right up to the hour of our Lord's betrayal and crucifixion. Even he kept the concept alive in the hearts of his disciples by saying such things as: "The Son of man shall be betrayed into the hands of men: And they shall kill him, and the third day he shall be raised again." (Matt. 17:22-23.) Of his statements along this line, Matthew says: "From that time forth began Jesus to shew unto his disciples, how that he must go unto Jerusalem, and suffer many things of the elders and chief priests and scribes, and be killed, and be raised again the third day." (Matt. 16:21.)

Messiah Shall Be Crucified

It did not suffice for the Messianic prophecies to set forth that Christ should die to redeem his people. It pleased God to show beforehand the way and manner of his death, a death on a cross, a death by cruel crucifixion. The very manner in which his redeeming blood was shed was itself a means of teaching great truths connected with the atonement. For instance, it enabled him, after the event, to say: "My Father sent me that I might be lifted up upon the cross; and after that I had been lifted up upon the cross, that I might draw all men unto me, that as I have been lifted up by men even so should men be lifted up by the Father, to stand before me, to be judged of their works, whether they be good or whether they be evil—And for this cause have I been lifted up; therefore, according to the power of the Father I will draw all men unto me, that they may be judged according to their works." (3 Ne. 27:14-15.)

And so we now turn to the Messianic prophecies that tell the fact of crucifixion and that go into remarkable detail as to the words and acts that become part of that humiliating and agonizing indignity. "Enoch saw the day of the coming of the Son of Man," which caused him to give forth this exulting statement: "The Righteous is lifted up, and the Lamb is slain from the foundation of the world. . . . And the Lord said unto Enoch: Look, and he looked and beheld the Son of Man lifted up on the cross, after the manner of men." (Moses 7:47, 55.) Obviously this doctrine that Christ would be crucified was taught among all the ancient saints.

From the Nephite record we learn that Nephi "saw that he was lifted up upon the cross and slain for the sins of the world." (1 Ne. 11:33.) An angel also told Nephi that Christ would yield himself "into the hands of wicked men, to be lifted up, according to the words of Zenock, and to be crucified, according to the words of Neum. . . . And as for those who are at Jerusalem," Nephi said, "they shall be scourged by all people, because they crucify the God of Israel." (1 Ne. 19:10, 13.) Nephi's brother Jacob left the witness that "the Lord God, the Holy One of Israel, should manifest himself unto them in the flesh [who were at Jerusalem]; and after he should manifest himself they should scourge him and crucify him." (2 Ne. 6:9.) Nephi said of the Jews that "there is none other nation on earth that would crucify their God." (2 Ne. 10:3; 25:12-13.) After all the marvels of his ministry, in the angelic language received by King Benjamin, "they shall consider him a man, and say that he hath a devil, and shall scourge him, and shall crucify him." (Mosiah 3:9.) "Yea, even so he shall be led, crucified, and slain," Abinadi prophesied, "the flesh becoming subject even unto death, the will of the Son being swallowed up in the will of the Father." (Mosiah 15:7.)

Jesus' own Messianic declarations concerning his coming demise, and the manner in which it would be accomplished, are thus recorded: "And Jesus going up to Jerusalem took the twelve disciples apart in the way, and said unto them, Behold, we go up to Jerusalem; and the Son of man shall be betrayed unto the chief priests and unto the scribes, and they shall condemn him to death, And shall deliver him to the Gentiles to mock, and to scourge, and to crucify him: and the third day he shall rise again." (Matt. 20:17-19.) And also: "Ye know that after two days is the feast of the passover, and the Son of man is betrayed to be crucified." (Matt. 26:2.)

Old World Prophets Tell of the Crucifixion

Old Testament prophecies about the crucifixion, as that volume of Holy Writ now stands, do not use the word crucify, but notwithstanding this, in some respects they are even more pointed and express than their Book of Mormon counterparts. Isaiah says the Messianic Servant, who came to do his Father's will, would suffer intense pain and disfigurement. "His visage"—his aspect and appearance, his countenance and the way he looked—"was so marred more than any man"—this because of the anguish and pain which writhed through his soul both in Gethsemane and on the cross—"and his form more than the sons of men"—having reference among other things to the gashing holes made by the nails and the gaping wound left by the spear. (Isa. 52:14-15.) Ezra even speaks of "a nail in his holy place" (Ezra 9:8), and Isaiah of "the nail that is fastened in the sure place." having reference to the nails driven in the Crucified One. "And I will fasten him as a nail in a sure place; and he shall be for a glorious throne to his father's house. And they shall hang upon him all the glory of his father's house." (Isa. 22:21-25.) As to these prophecies, whoso readeth let him understand.

Isaiah says further that he was despised, rejected, stricken, smitten, afflicted, wounded, bruised, beaten with stripes, and oppressed, and that he went as a lamb to the slaughter. He opened not his mouth, meaning he did not defend himself when hailed before wicked earthly tyrants. He was cut off out of the land of the living, made his soul an offering for sin, and poured out his soul unto death (Isa. 53), meaning that he was slain, that he was sacrificed by Satanic priests as it were, and that even so he voluntarily gave up his life. "No man taketh it from me," he said, "but I lay it down of myself. I have power to lay it down, and I have power to take it again. This commandment have I received of my Father." (John 10:18.)

"All things must be fulfilled, which were written in the law of Moses, and in the prophets, and in the psalms, concerning me," the risen Lord said to the assembled saints in the upper room. (Luke 24:44.) To Cleopas and another disciple, on the Emmaus road, the resurrected Jesus said: "O fools, and slow of heart to believe all that the prophets have spoken: Ought not Christ to have suffered these things, and to enter into his glory? And beginning at Moses and all the prophets, he expounded unto them in all the scriptures the things concerning himself." (Luke 24:25-27.) Surely those things we shall now quote from the Psalms—pointed, express, detailed utterances about his sufferings, death, and atoning sacrifice—were included in those things which he expounded unto them.

The Holy Ghost, through David, said: "My God, my God, why hast thou forsaken me?" (Ps. 22:1)—thus revealing aforetime the very words Jesus would speak on the cross in that moment when, left alone that he might drink the dregs of the bitter cup to the full, the Father would entirely withdraw his sustaining power. And so Matthew records: "And about the ninth hour Jesus cried with a loud voice, saying, Eli, Eli, la ma sabach tha ni? that is to say, My God, my God, why hast thou forsaken me?" (Matt. 27:46.)

The same Psalm says: "All they that see me laugh me to scorn: they shoot out the lip, they shake the head, saying, He trusted on the Lord that he would deliver him: let him deliver him, seeing he delighted in him." (Ps. 22:7-8.) The fulfillment, as Jesus hung on the cross, is found in these words: "The chief priests mocking him, with the scribes and elders, said, He saved others; himself he cannot save. If he be the King of Israel, let him now come down from the cross, and we will believe him. He trusted in God; let him deliver him now, if he will have him: for he said, I am the

Son of God. The thieves also, which were crucified with him, cast the same in his teeth." (Matt. 27:41-44.)

Next the Psalmist speaks of our Lord's birth, of his reliance on God, of his troubles, and then coming back to the mob at the foot of the cross, he says: "They gaped upon me with their mouths, as a ravening and a roaring lion." Then the record says: "I am poured out like water" (Ps. 22:9-14), an expression akin to Isaiah's that "he hath poured out his soul unto death" (Isa. 53:12).

"Thou hast brought me into the dust of death," the Psalmist continues, "For dogs have compassed me, the assembly of the wicked have inclosed me: they pierced my hands and my feet," which is exactly what transpired on the gloomy day of crucifixion. Then this: "They part my garments among them, and cast lots upon my vesture" (Ps. 22:15-18), of which prediction Matthew says, "And they crucified him, and parted his garments, casting lots: that it might be fulfilled which was spoken by the prophet, They parted my garments among them, and upon my vesture did they cast lots" (Matt. 27:35). John gives this more extended account of the fulfillment of this promise: "Then the soldiers, when they had crucified Jesus, took his garments, and made four parts, to every soldier a part; and also his coat: now the coat was without seam, woven from the top throughout. They said therefore among themselves, Let us not rend it, but cast lots for it, whose it shall be: that the scripture might be fulfilled, which saith, They parted my raiment among them, and for my vesture they did cast lots. These things therefore the soldiers did." (John 19:23-24.)

After this the Psalmist has the Messiah say, in words applicable to his Father, "I will declare thy name unto my brethren: in the midst of the congregation will I praise thee," a course that our Lord pursued with diligence during his whole ministry. And then this counsel: "Ye that fear the Lord, praise him; all ye the seed of Jacob, glorify him; and fear him, all ye the seed of Israel." Following this is the promise that the Lord shall be praised "in the great congregation," and that "all the ends of the world shall remember and turn unto the Lord: and all the kindreds of the nations shall worship before thee. For the kingdom is the Lord's: and he is the governor of the nations." Clearly this has reference to the final millennial triumph of truth, a triumph that is to be when the gospel brought by the Messiah is restored again and carried according to his will to all men. Finally, in this Psalm, it is of the Messiah that the account speaks in these words: "A seed shall serve him; it shall be accounted to the Lord for a generation"; that is, the Seed of David, generated by the Father, shall serve in righteousness, with this result: "They shall come, and shall declare his righteousness unto a people that shall be born, that he hath done this." (Ps. 22:22-31.) And in harmony with this prophetic assurance, we now declare unto all people born after Messiah's day, the righteousness of the Father in sending his Son and the righteousness of the Son in doing all things for men that needed to be done to bring to them both immortality and eternal life.

Other Psalms also revealed, before the events, additional specifics that would attend or be associated with the cross of Christ and the agonizing death he would suffer thereon. With reference to the conniving and conspiring plots incident to our Lord's arrest and judicial trials the prophecy was: "They took counsel together against me, they devised to take away my life." (Ps. 31:13.) As to the role of Judas in those conspiracies, the Psalmist says: "Mine own familiar friend, in whom I trusted, which did eat of my bread, hath lifted up his heel against me." (Ps. 41:9.) On that occasion when he washed their feet, Jesus spoke in laudatory terms of the twelve, but, said he, "I speak not of you all," for a moment later he was to say, "one of you shall betray me." "I know whom I have chosen," he continued, "but that the scripture may be fulfilled, He that eateth bread with me hath lifted up his heel against me. Now I tell you before it come, that, when it is come to pass, ye may believe that I am he." After a few more words, he dipped the sop and gave it to

Judas, thus identifying the traitor in their midst. (John 13:18-30.)

"The zeal of thine house hath eaten me up," is the Messianic word which foretold the driving of the money changers from the temple and caused Jesus to say, "Make not my Father's house an house of merchandise," and which caused his disciples to remember the words of the Psalm. (John 2:13-17.) But the full Messianic statement, which forecasts more than the cleansing of the then-polluted temple, says: "The zeal of thine house hath eaten me up; and the reproaches of them that reproached thee are fallen upon me. . . . Reproach hath broken my heart; and I am full of heaviness: and I looked for some to take pity, and there was none; and for comforters, but I found none." (Ps. 69:9, 20.) Who can fail to see in these words our Lord's piteous state as, hailed before the rulers of this world, he found none to comfort him, but instead was reproached for testifying of that Father whom his Jewish persecutors had rejected?

After these words comes the Psalmic declaration: "They gave me also gall for my meat; and in my thirst they gave me vinegar to drink." (Ps. 69:21.) Their fulfillment is noted by Matthew in these words: "They gave him vinegar to drink mingled with gall: and when he had tasted thereof, he would not drink. And they crucified him." Also: After Jesus had, as they supposed, called for Elias, the account says: "And straightway one of them ran, and took a spunge, and filled it with vinegar, and put it on a reed, and gave him to drink." (Matt. 27:34-35, 47-48.) John's account of this same occurrence ties the act at the crucifixion in with David's prediction by recounting: "Jesus knowing that all things were now accomplished, that the scripture might be fulfilled, saith, I thirst." It is as though advisedly and with deliberation, though he was in agony beyond compare, yet he consciously continued to the last moment of mortal life, with the avowed purpose of fulfilling all of the Messianic utterances concerning his mortal Messiahship. "Now there was set a vessel full of vinegar," John's account continues, "and they filled a spunge with vinegar, and put it upon hyssop, and put it to his mouth. When Jesus therefore had received the vinegar, he said, It is finished: and he bowed his head, and gave up the ghost." (John 19:28-30.)

Viewing in advance, as it were, this last awesome moment of the Messiah's mortal life, David wrote: "Into thine hand I commit my spirit." (Ps. 31:5.) Recording after the fact what took place as the last breath of mortal air filled the lungs of the Man on the cross, Luke said: "And when Jesus had cried with a loud voice, he said, Father, into thy hands I commend my spirit: and having said thus, he gave up the ghost." (Luke 23:46.)

With our Lord's last breath, all things were fulfilled which pertained to that period when the breath of life sustained his life and being. But other predicted acts were to occur while his body yet hung on the cross, and still others pertaining to his burial and resurrection, after that body was taken down. Of the events on the cross, John says: "The Jews therefore, because it was the preparation, that the bodies should not remain upon the cross on the sabbath day, (for that sabbath day was an high day,) besought Pilate that their legs might be broken, and that they might be taken away. Then came the soldiers, and brake the legs of the first, and of the other which was crucified with him. But when they came to Jesus, and saw that he was dead already, they brake not his legs: But one of the soldiers with a spear pierced his side, and forthwith came there out blood and water. And he that saw it bare record, and his record is true: and he knoweth that he saith true, that ye might believe. For these things were done, that the scripture should be fulfilled, A bone of him shall not be broken. And again another scripture saith, They shall look on him whom they pierced." (John 19:31-37.)

Three scriptures were thus fulfilled. In the account of the original passover, it was expressly provided with reference to the lamb slain in similitude of the coming sacrificial offering of the Lamb of God, "neither shall ye break a bone thereof."

534

(Ex. 12:46.) These words are the actual source of John's quotation, but their thought content and meaning were restated by David in this way: "He keepeth all his bones; not one of them is broken." (Ps. 34:20.) The scripture "They shall look upon me whom they have pierced" (Zech. 12:10) is part of a long passage in Zechariah that deals with the Second Coming of Christ and the conversion of the Jewish people at that time. Manifestly those around the cross did look upon the Pierced One, for the wound was then gashed into his unprotected side. But the great fulfillment of Zechariah's prophecy is yet ahead. As a people, those Jews who remain after the destructions incident to our Lord's return shall look on him whom they pierced and shall be converted. It is then, as Zechariah also records, that they shall say: "What are these wounds in thine hands? Then he shall answer, Those with which I was wounded in the house of my friends." (Zech. 13:6.) These conversationally expressed statements, uttered by Zechariah, preserved to us in the Old Testament and confirmed as part of the divine plan by the New Testament reference to them, these words in their more complete and perfect rendition are: "Then shall the Jews look upon me and say: What are these wounds in thine hands and in thy feet? Then shall they know that I am the Lord; for I will say unto them: These wounds are the wounds with which I was wounded in the house of my friends. I am he who was lifted up. I am Jesus that was crucified. I am the Son of God." (D&C 45:51-52.)

It was also Zechariah who said in the course of this same Messianic recitation: "Smite the shepherd, and the sheep shall be scattered: and I will turn mine hand upon the little ones." (Zech. 13:7.) After instituting the sacrament and as he turned his face to Gethsemane, Jesus said to the Twelve: "All ye shall be offended because of me this night: for it is written, I will smite the shepherd, and the sheep of the flock shall be scattered abroad." (Matt. 26:31.)

Then Jesus went to Gethsemane for his atoning ordeal. Returning therefrom he met the traitor to whom the chief priests had given thirty pieces of silver to betray his Master. "What will ye give me, and I will deliver him unto you?" he asked. "And they covenanted with him for thirty pieces of silver. And from that time he sought opportunity to betray him." (Matt. 26:14-16.) And this was to fulfill that which Zechariah had said: "If ye think good, give me my price; and if not, forbear. So they weighed for my price thirty pieces of silver. And the Lord said unto me, Cast it unto the potter: a goodly price that I was prised at of them. And I took the thirty pieces of silver, and cast them to the potter in the house of the Lord." (Zech. 11:12-13.) "Then Judas, which had betrayed him, when he saw that he was condemned, repented himself, and brought again the thirty pieces of silver to the chief priests and elders, Saying, I have sinned in that I have betrayed the innocent blood. And they said, What is that to us? see thou to that. And he cast down the pieces of silver in the temple, and departed, and went and hanged himself. And the chief priests took the silver pieces, and said, It is not lawful for to put them into the treasury, because it is the price of blood. And they took counsel, and bought with them the potter's field, to bury strangers in. Wherefore that field was called, The field of blood, unto this day. Then was fulfilled that which was spoken by Jeremy the prophet, saying, And they took the thirty pieces of silver, the price of him that was valued, whom they of the children of Israel did value; And gave them for the potter's field, as the Lord appointed me." (Matt. 27:3-10.)

Prophets Reveal Signs of Messiah's Death

Matthew alone of the Gospel authors tells of the physical upheaval in Jerusalem that came as Jesus died. "Jesus, when he had cried again with a loud voice, yielded up the ghost," the account says. "And, behold, the veil of the temple was rent in twain from the top to the bottom; and the earth did quake, and the rocks rent. . . . Now when the centurion, and they that were with him, watching Jesus, saw the earthquake, and those things that were done, they feared greatly, saying, Truly this was the Son of God." (Matt. 27:50-54.)

That the very elements themselves were revolted at the death of a God we cannot doubt. Certainly the earthquake, of such magnitude that it rent the rocks, was felt throughout the whole area where the evil crucifixion was wrought. But compared to the other events there and then crying for the attention of those who recorded the events connected with the life and death of their Lord, the physical changes in the earth were of lesser importance. Earthquakes of the sort there shown forth had occurred in great numbers, in many places, and at many times. But only at this one time and place had a God been lifted up upon a cross under circumstances that fulfilled the ancient prophecies in detail. For those in the Old World who were privy to all the circumstances surrounding the crucifixion, or who might learn them from witnesses who saw and heard and knew for themselves, these circumstances were a sufficient witness that the Messiah had been slain. The earthquake was only incidental to other and more important matters. Hence, neither Mark, Luke, nor John thought it of sufficient import to include in their recitation of the transcendent events of that gloomy day.

For that matter, our Old Testament, as it now stands, does not preserve for us any pointed prophecies foretelling the destructions and physical upheavals destined to attend the death of the One by whom life would come. The Messianic prophecies in that volume of ancient scripture were for the especial guidance of those in the Old World and dealt with things that would identify as the Messiah the One who ministered personally among them. We do have one prophecy recorded in Moses that would have been had among the Jews if the ancient record had been preserved in its perfection. In that passage Enoch, seeing the crucifixion in vision, also "heard a loud voice; and the heavens were veiled; and all the creations of God mourned; and the earth groaned; and the rocks were rent; and the saints arose, and

537

were crowned at the right hand of the Son of Man, with crowns of glory." (Moses 7:56.)

One of Israel's prophets, Zenos, whose writings have been lost to us, but which were on the brass plates of Laban and were thus preserved for Nephite usage, did speak of the destructions that would attend our Lord's death. "He spake concerning the three days of darkness," we are told, "which should be a sign given of his death unto those who should inhabit the isles of the sea," and which should be "more especially given unto those who are of the house of Israel." That is to say, the portions of Israel far removed from Jerusalem and Canaan and who would not see the Messiah personally, or hear the testimony of those who did, were destined to receive special signs of his death and the atoning ransom that came thereby.

"The Lord God surely shall visit all the house of Israel at that day," Zenos prophesied, "some with his voice, because of their righteousness, unto their great joy and salvation," and this would include those Nephites who were righteous and were not slain in the destructions; "and others [would be visited] with the thunderings and lightnings of his power, by tempest, by fire, and by smoke, and vapor of darkness, and by the opening of the earth, and by mountains which shall be carried up"; these would include all those among the Nephites who were slain because they were the more wicked part of the people. "And all these things must surely come, saith the prophet Zenos. And the rocks of the earth must rend; and because of the groanings of the earth, many of the kings of the isles of the sea shall be wrought upon by the Spirit of God, to exclaim: The God of nature suffers."

Then come these words pertaining to those in Canaan: "And as for those who are at Jerusalem, saith the prophet, they shall be scourged by all people, because they crucify the God of Israel, and turn their hearts aside, rejecting signs and wonders, and the power and glory of the God of Israel. And because they turn their hearts aside, saith the prophet, and have despised the Holy One of Israel, they shall wander in the flesh, and perish, and become a hiss and a byword, and be hated among all nations." (1 Ne. 19:10-14.) That is to say, the scattering and treatment of the Jews as a people during the past two thousand years is itself a sign and a witness that they crucified their God.

Because the Nephites were on the opposite side of the world from where the actual events would occur, and would have no way except by prophetic pronouncement to know what there transpired, the Lord set up signs to signify when their Deliverer's death had occurred. Nephi saw that very meridian day in vision and described what he saw in these words: "And it came to pass that I saw a mist of darkness on the face of the land of promise; and I saw lightnings, and I heard thunderings, and earthquakes, and all manner of tumultuous noises; and I saw the earth and the rocks, that they rent; and I saw mountains tumbling into pieces; and I saw the plains of the earth, that they were broken up; and I saw many cities that they were sunk; and I saw many that they were burned with fire; and I saw many that did tumble to the earth, because of the quaking thereof. And it came to pass after I saw these things, I saw the vapor of darkness, that it passed from off the face of the earth; and behold, I saw multitudes who had fallen because of the great and terrible judgments of the Lord. And I saw the heavens open, and the Lamb of God descending out of heaven; and he came down and showed himself unto them." (1 Ne. 12:4-6.)

Also: "And after the Messiah shall come there shall be signs given unto my people of his birth, and also of his death and resurrection; and great and terrible shall that day be unto the wicked, for they shall perish; and they perish because they cast out the prophets, and the saints, and stone them, and slay them; wherefore the cry of the blood of the saints shall ascend up to God from the ground against them. Wherefore, all those who are proud, and that do wickedly, the day that cometh shall burn them up, saith the Lord of Hosts, for they shall be as stubble. And they that kill the prophets, and the saints, the depths of the earth shall swallow them up, saith the Lord of Hosts; and mountains shall cover them, and whirlwinds shall carry them away, and buildings shall fall upon them and crush them to pieces and grind them to powder. And they shall be visited with thunderings, and lightnings, and earthquakes, and all manner of destructions, for the fire of the anger of the Lord shall be kindled against them, and they shall be as stubble, and the day that cometh shall consume them, saith the Lord of Hosts. O the pain, and the anguish of my soul for the loss of the slain of my people! For I, Nephi, have seen it, and it well nigh consumeth me before the presence of the Lord; but I must cry unto my God: Thy ways are just. But behold, the righteous that hearken unto the words of the prophets, and destroy them not, but look forward unto Christ with steadfastness for the signs which are given, notwithstanding all persecution—behold, they are they which shall not perish. But the Son of righteousness shall appear unto them; and he shall heal them, and they shall have peace with him, until three generations shall have passed away, and many of the fourth generation shall have passed away in righteousness." (2 Ne. 26:3-9.)

Samuel the Lamanite, centuries later and a bare forty years before the crucifixion, rehearsed in detail to the Nephites the destructions and desolations that would attend that event. "In that day that he shall suffer death," the Lamanite prophet said, "the sun shall be darkened and refuse to give his light unto you; and also the moon and the stars; and there shall be no light upon the face of this land, even from the time that he shall suffer death, for the space of three days, to the time that he shall rise again from the dead." While our Lord's body lay in the tomb, while his eternal Spirit preached among the righteous dead, darkness enshrouded the Americas. Far removed though they were from the criminal events, no Nephite and no Lamanite would be unaware that their prophets had foretold the death of their Messiah and said that it would be known by three days of dooming darkness. Where else in all the history of the earth have continents been enveloped in darkness for three days? How could such an event do aught but witness the truth of the promised event?

"Yea, at the time that he shall yield up the ghost," Samuel continued, "there shall be thunderings and lightnings for the space of many hours, and the earth shall shake and tremble; and the rocks which are upon the face of this earth, which are both above the earth and beneath, which ye know at this time are solid, or the more part of it is one solid mass, shall be broken up; Yea, they shall be rent in twain, and shall ever after be found in seams and in cracks, and in broken fragments upon the face of the whole earth, yea, both above the earth and beneath. And behold, there shall be great tempests, and there shall be many mountains laid low, like unto a valley, and there shall be many places which are now called valleys which shall become mountains, whose height is great. And many highways shall be broken up, and many cities shall become desolate. And many graves shall be opened, and shall yield up many of their dead; and many saints shall appear unto many. And behold, thus hath the angel spoken unto me; for he said unto me that there should be thunderings and lightnings for the space of many hours. And he said unto me that while the thunder and the lightning lasted, and the tempest, that these things should be, and that darkness should cover the face of the whole earth for the space of three days."

It is perfectly clear that these destructions came as a just judgment upon the wicked, and that they are in similitude of the outpourings of wrath that shall come upon the whole world at the Second Coming, but they also came as a sign and a witness to the righteous who remained and who were not destroyed. "And the angel said unto me," Samuel went on to say, "that many shall see greater things than these, to the intent that they might believe that these signs and these wonders should come to pass upon all the face of this land, to the intent that there should be no cause for unbelief among the children of men—And this to the intent that

541

whosoever will believe might be saved, and that whosoever will not believe, a righteous judgment might come upon them; and also if they are condemned they bring upon themselves their own condemnation." (Hel. 14:20-29.)

No single historical event in the whole Book of Mormon account is recorded in so great detail or at such extended length as the fulfillment of the signs signifying that Jesus had been lifted up upon the cross and had voluntarily laid down his life for the world. Here is part of the account: "And the people began to look with great earnestness for the sign which had been given by the prophet Samuel, the Lamanite, yea, for the time that there should be darkness for the space of three days over the face of the land. And there began to be great doubtings and disputations among the people, notwithstanding so many signs had been given. And it came to pass in the thirty and fourth year, in the first month, on the fourth day of the month, there arose a great storm, such an one as never had been known in all the land. And there was also a great and terrible tempest; and there was terrible thunder, insomuch that it did shake the whole earth as if it was about to divide asunder. And there were exceeding sharp lightnings, such as never had been known in all the land. And the city of Zarahemla did take fire. And the city of Moroni did sink into the depths of the sea, and the inhabitants thereof were drowned. And the earth was carried up upon the city of Moronihah that in the place of the city there became a great mountain. And there was a great and terrible destruction in the land southward.

"But behold, there was a more great and terrible destruction in the land northward; for behold, the whole face of the land was changed, because of the tempest and the whirlwinds and the thunderings and the lightnings, and the exceeding great quaking of the whole earth; And the highways were broken up, and the level roads were spoiled, and many smooth places became rough. And many great and notable cities were sunk, and many were burned, and many were shaken till the buildings thereof had fallen to the earth, and the inhabitants thereof were slain, and the places were left desolate. And there were some cities which remained; but the damage thereof was exceeding great, and there were many of them who were slain. And there were some who were carried away in the whirlwind; and whither they went no man knoweth, save they know that they were carried away. And thus the face of the whole earth became deformed, because of the tempests, and the thunderings, and the lightnings, and the quaking of the earth. And behold, the rocks were rent in twain; they were broken up upon the face of the whole earth, insomuch that they were found in broken fragments, and in seams and in cracks, upon all the face of the land. And it came to pass that when the thunderings, and the lightnings, and the storm, and the tempest, and the quakings of the earth did cease—for behold, they did last for about the space of three hours; and it was said by some that the time was greater; nevertheless, all these great and terrible things were done in about the space of three hours—and then behold, there was darkness upon the face of the land. And it came to pass that there was thick darkness upon all the face of the land, insomuch that the inhabitants thereof who had not fallen could feel the vapor of darkness; And there could be no light, because of the darkness, neither candles, neither torches; neither could there be fire kindled with their fine and exceedingly dry wood, so that there could not be any light at all; And there was not any light seen, neither fire, nor glimmer, neither the sun, nor the moon, nor the stars, for so great were the mists of darkness which were upon the face of the land.

"And it came to pass that it did last for the space of three days that there was no light seen; and there was great mourning and howling and weeping among all the people continually; yea, great were the groanings of the people, because of the darkness and the great destruction which had come upon them. And in one place they were heard to cry, saying: O that we had repented before this great and terrible day, and then would our brethren have been spared, and they would not have been burned in that great city Zarahemla. And in another place they were heard to cry and mourn, saying: O that we had repented before this great and terrible day, and had not killed and stoned the prophets, and cast them out; then would our mothers and our fair daughters, and our children have been spared, and not have been buried up in that great city Moronihah. And thus were the howlings of the people great and terrible." (3 Ne. 8:3-25.)

Then it was that the people who were yet alive heard the voice of the Lord as he spoke in the first person and announced that he had wrought all these destructions, adding more details to the account. (3 Ne. 9; 10:1-8.) "And now it came to pass that after the people had heard these words, behold, they began to weep and howl again because of the loss of their kindred and friends. And it came to pass that thus did the three days pass away. And it was in the morning, and the darkness dispersed from off the face of the land, and the earth did cease to tremble, and the rocks did cease to rend, and the dreadful groanings did cease, and all the tumultuous noises did pass away. And the earth did cleave together again, that it stood; and the mourning, and the weeping, and the wailing of the people who were spared alive did cease; and their mourning was turned into joy, and their lamentations into the praise and thanksgiving unto the Lord Jesus Christ, their Redeemer. And thus far were the scriptures fulfilled which had been spoken by the prophets.

"And it was the more righteous part of the people who were saved, and it was they who received the prophets and stoned them not; and it was they who had not shed the blood of the saints, who were spared—And they were spared and were not sunk and buried up in the earth; and they were not drowned in the depths of the sea; and they were not burned by fire, neither were they fallen upon and crushed to death; and they were not carried away in the whirlwind; neither were they overpowered by the vapor of smoke and of darkness.

"And now, whoso readeth, let him understand; he that hath the scriptures, let him search them, and see and behold if all these deaths and destructions by fire, and by smoke, and by tempests, and by whirlwinds, and by the opening of the earth to receive them, and all these things are not unto the fulfilling of the prophecies of many of the holy prophets. Behold, I say unto you, Yea, many have testified of these things at the coming of Christ, and were slain because they testified of these things. Yea, the prophet Zenos did testify of these things, and also Zenock spake concerning these things, because they testified particularly concerning us, who are the remnant of their seed." (3 Ne. 10:8-16.)

Messiah Shall Be Buried in a Sepulchre

Crucified criminals and other victims of Roman vengeance were often left on their crosses to rot away as signs and warnings to others. Blasphemers and others who were stoned to death among the Jews often had their bodies dumped unceremoniously in the Valley of Hinnom outside Jerusalem where the fires of Gehenna burned everlastingly. Decent burial was a mark of honor and respect. Reverence for those who passed on was unbounded. Abraham purchased the cave of Machpelah from the sons of Heth as a resting place for his beloved Sarah. Joseph required Israel to covenant that they would take his bones out of Egypt when they returned to their promised Canaan so that he could be buried with his fathers. It would have been the most natural and expected thing for the ingrates and rebels who instigated the death of their King to expect to add the ignominy and disgrace of a tombless disposal of his remains. And yet things were not intended to and did not eventuate in this way.

Joseph of Arimathea, a rich man who had an expensive tomb hewn from the rock, a tomb in which no man had lain, entreated Pilate that he might have the body of the deceased

Christ. Pilate, after receiving the assurance of the centurion that Jesus was in fact dead, and because it was contrary to the Jewish custom for one of their people to hang on the cross on the Sabbath, granted the Arimathean's request. Nicodemus, another rich and influential Jew, brought myrrh and aloes in large amounts for the embalming. The faithful women embalmed and clothed the body that soon was to rise from death, wrapping it carefully in linen clothes as was the custom among the Jews. Then it was placed in the tomb, which was sealed with a large stone, and a guard was placed, lest Jesus' followers steal the body and claim he had risen on the third day as he had promised to do. But on resurrection morn, angelic power rolled back the stone; he arose, went forth from the tomb, and began a series of appearances to faithful followers. Peter and John, entering the tomb, found the linen wrappings placed in such a manner as to show that they had not been unwrapped, but rather that the immortal body of their Lord had risen through the mortal cloth as a resurrected body would naturally do.

Why all this detail where his death and burial and coming forth were concerned? Would it not have sufficed, he having been slain, for him simply to rise from the dead no matter where his body was and without regard to the manner in which it had been cared for after his demise? Perhaps; but how much more persuasive it was for a cloud of witnesses to know the intimate details of his burial and coming forth and to be able to certify from personal knowledge to the reality of all the events incident thereto. Obviously it was so intended because the prophets of old had made special mention of the burial and the sepulchre and the wealth of those who would lay the body away, and so in this as in all things it was needful that the scriptures be fulfilled.

Isaiah said, "He made his grave with the wicked, and with the rich in his death" (Isa. 53:9), both of which promises were fulfilled. Zenos said he would "be buried in a sepulchre." (1 Ne. 19:10.) Nephi gave this promise: "They will crucify him; and after he is laid in a sepulchre for the space of three days he shall rise from the dead." (2 Ne. 25:13.) The prophet Jonah's unparalleled experience in being swallowed and then vomited up by a great fish was all done in similitude of and to teach the fact of our Lord's burial and resurrection. When the Jews sought from Jesus a sign, he condemned them as "an evil and adulterous generation," and said, "There shall no sign be given to it, but the sign of the prophet Jonas: For as Jonas was three days and three nights in the whale's belly; so shall the Son of man be three days and three nights in the heart of the earth." (Matt. 12:38-40.)

Truly, "though they found no cause of death in him," yet they caused "that he should be slain. And when they had fulfilled all that was written of him, they took him down from the tree, and laid him in a sepulchre. But God raised him from the dead: And he was seen many days of them which came up with him from Galilee to Jerusalem, who are his witnesses unto the people. And we declare unto you glad tidings, how that the promise which was made unto the fathers, God hath fulfilled the same unto us their children, in that he hath raised up Jesus again." (Acts 13:28-33.)

Truly, "He was crucified, died, and rose again the third day." (D&C 20:23.)

Chapter 30

BLESSED BE THE LORD

What Think Ye of Christ?

The Promised Messiah—what think ye of him? Who is he, and has he come? What is his work, and what has he done for that innumerable host of spirits, all children of the Eternal Father?

We shall set forth in Chapter 31 the crowning mortal blessing bestowed upon all those who turn to their Messiah with full purpose of heart and who gain a perfect knowledge of him and his mission. That blessing is to see his face, to stand in his presence, and to have intimate and personal communion with him as did many of those of old.

Before taking up the holy and sacred matters there summarized, however, we must be sure the house of faith and knowledge has been built with no part missing. And so we ask: What think ye of Christ, of his Father, of their plan of salvation, of the infinite and eternal atonement wrought by the Son of God, of the holy gospel through which life and immortality come? What think ye of the Promised Messiah?

We need not restate our conclusions in extenso, nor quote again the inspired word upon which they are based, but we should at least summarize the great and eternal truths concerning Christ and his ministry that have come to us from him who is the Author of our being and who is the Maker, Upholder, and Preserver of all things. This we now do both by way of doctrine and of testimony.

There is a God in heaven who is infinite and eternal. He has all power, all might, and all dominion. He knows all things, and there is nothing which he takes into his heart to do that he cannot accomplish. He is the Creator of all things—this earth and all forms of life and the very universe itself. He is omnipotent, omniscient, and omnipresent.

This Eternal God is a Holy Man in whose image mortal men are made. He has a body of flesh and bones as tangible as man's. He is a resurrected, glorified, exalted Personage of tabernacle. And he lives in the family unit.

We are the spirit children of God the Eternal Father, as also are all those yet unborn and all those who have and do and will dwell on any of the infinite number of earths he has created, in an ever-expanding universe, already composed of worlds without number. All of us lived in his presence, saw his face, heard his voice, knew him as our Father, and were taught eternal truths by him. He endowed us with agency and ordained and established those laws, by obedience to which we could advance and progress and become like him, those laws whereby we could gain eternal life, which is the name of the kind of life he lives. The plan of salvation which he established and offered to all his spirit offspring is named *The Gospel of God.*

The Lord Jesus Christ was the Firstborn Spirit Son of the Father. He was born as a spirit man, as were all his spirit brethren; he was the Offspring of the Almighty, as all of us were. In that spirit state he was true and faithful, obedient to every trust. His advancement was such that he became like the Father in power and intelligence. He became, under the Father, the Creator of worlds without number. His name was Jehovah, the Great I AM, the Eternal One. He was the Lord Omnipotent who was and is from all eternity to all eternity.

After The Gospel of God had been taught to all the hosts of heaven; after it was known that the course of progression leading to eternal life required a mortal probation; after we all knew that to become like our Father we must gain mortal bodies, pass through death, and rise again in immortality; after we knew that mortality was to be a probationary estate, a time of testing, a period when we would walk by faith and not by sight; after it was known that Adam must fall and bring temporal and spiritual death into the world; after the need for a Redeemer had been explained; after we knew that the Father would beget a mortal Son, an Only Begotten in the flesh, who would have power to work out the infinite and eternal atonement—after all this and much more, the Father asked for volunteers to be the Redeemer. 'Whom shall I send? Who will be my Son? To whom shall I give the power of immortality so that he can come forth in the resurrection himself and also bring to pass the resurrection of all men? Who will ransom men from the effects of Adam's fall?'

Then it was that the One, the Lord's Beloved and Chosen from the beginning, said, 'Father, here am I, send me; I will be thy Son and do thy will; thy gospel shall be my gospel; and the glory be thine forever.'

Then it was that the Father said: 'Thou art the man; thou shalt be my Son; thou shalt go down, the noblest of great Michael's race. A virgin shall thy mother be, and thou shalt redeem all mankind, even as many as will. My gospel shall be thy gospel.'

Then it was that the Promised Messiah was foreordained, became the Lamb slain from the foundation of the world, became the Word of God, the Messenger of Salvation for all men. His message was The Gospel of God, now named after the Son and known as *The Gospel of Jesus Christ.*

Thus it is that salvation is in Christ. He abolished death and brought life and immortality to light through the gospel. Through his atoning sacrifice all men are raised in immortality, while those who believe and obey inherit also the glories of eternal life and become as he and his Father are.

If there had been no atonement of Christ, there would be no salvation, no immortality, no eternal life, and the whole purpose and plan of the Father would have been frustrated. The very purposes of creation itself would have come to naught. All men would have mouldered forever in the grave, their bodies being sleeping dust forever and their spirits becoming devils, angels to a devil. If there had been no atonement of Christ, all men would be sons of perdition, cast out and cast off, doomed to suffer the wrath of God to all eternity.

From the beginning, from the day of the first mortal man, who is Adam our father, salvation became available because of the shedding of the blood of Christ. It was won by those who had faith in him, repented of all their sins, received the sanctifying power of the Holy Ghost in their lives, and then continued, all their mortal days, to do the works of righteousness.

Our Lord thus became the Mediator and Intercessor between fallen man and his Maker. His mission was one of reconciliation, of bringing his mortal brethren into full fellowship with the Infinite.

That all men might know of the great plan of redemption, our Lord revealed himself and his laws to Adam and to those among his posterity who obeyed the laws which permitted that revelation to come. By definition a prophet is one to whom the Lord gives revelation relative to some phase of his divine Sonship. All of the prophets from Adam to Christ foretold one thing or another about that redeeming day. All of the prophets and apostles who have lived since he came have testified by the power of the Holy Ghost of those same eternal gospel truths.

In ancient Israel, the Promised Messiah was known as the God of Abraham, Isaac, and Jacob, the God of Israel, the Holy One of Israel. He revealed himself as their Redeemer and Savior, their friend Jah, the Great Jehovah. He was the Shepherd of Israel, the Stone of Israel, the Branch, the Stem of Jesse, the Son of David, and a host of other things. Each name taught some special thing concerning his mission and ministry.

All of the ancient prophets and saints worshiped and served the Father in his holy name. Upon those in all ages who had faith, he poured out the gifts of the Spirit. Miracles abounded among them. Their sick were healed, their dead raised, seas parted, rivers turned out of their course, the sun stopped in the firmament, and the armies of opposing nations were destroyed.

All things given the saints in all ages were so ordained as to bear record of the Messiah. Sacrifices were performed in similitude of the future sacrifice of the Only Begotten. Baptisms were in similitude of his death, burial, and resurrection. The Sabbath day testified of his creative powers. All the ordinances and feasts and performances of the Mosaic law centered the attention of the people in their Messiah.

At the appointed time he came, born of Mary, in Bethlehem of Judea. He worked out his own salvation, revealed his Father, preached the gospel, wrought miracles, organized anew the earthly kingdom, was rejected by his own, and died a voluntary death on a cross at Calvary.

In a garden called Gethsemane, outside Jerusalem's walls, in agony beyond compare, he took upon himself the sins of all men on conditions of repentance. Then he yielded himself into the hands of traitors and wicked men to have his flesh gashed and pierced and his body hung on a tree. He came into the world to die, and die he did, die as only a God could.

Then on a Sunday morning, on the Lord's day, angelic power rolled back the stone from the Arimathean's tomb, and the only Perfect Man who ever lived arose from the dead in both physical and spiritual perfection. For forty days his ministry continued among selected mortals, and finally on Olivet, not far from Gethsemane, while his disciples looked on and angels attended, he ascended to his Father.

These are some of the things which we think of Christ, and they are but a small part of his doings. "There are also many other things which Jesus did, the which, if they should be written every one," the Beloved Disciple says, "even the world itself could not contain the books that should be written." (John 21:25.) But what we have written suffices for our purposes because it enables us to know that salvation is in Christ, and that all blessings flow to us because of him. Into his hands the Father hath committed all things. He has become the Author and Finisher of our faith, and in him do we trust and glory.

Sing unto the Lord

Music is part of the language of the Gods. It has been given to man so he can sing praises to the Lord. It is a means of expressing, with poetic words and in melodious tunes, the deep feelings of rejoicing and thanksgiving found in the hearts of those who have testimonies of the divine Sonship and who know of the wonders and glories wrought for them by the Father, Son, and Holy Spirit. Music is both in the voice and in the heart. Every true saint finds his heart full of songs of praise to his Maker. Those whose voices can sing forth the praises found in their hearts are twice blest. "Be filled with the Spirit," Paul counseled, "Speaking to yourselves in psalms and hymns and spiritual songs, singing and making melody in your heart to the Lord." (Eph. 5:18-19.) Also: "Let the word of Christ dwell in you richly in all wisdom; teaching and admonishing one another in psalms and hymns and spiritual songs, singing with grace in your hearts to the Lord." (Col. 3:16.)

Unfortunately not all music is good and edifying. Lucifer uses much that goes by the name of music to lead people to that which does not edify and is not of God. Just as language can be used to bless or curse, so music is a means of singing praises to the Lord or of planting evil thoughts and desires in the minds of men. Of that music which meets the divine standard and has the Lord's approval, he says: "My soul delighteth in the song of the heart; yea, the song of the righteous is a prayer unto me, and it shall be answered with a blessing upon their heads." (D&C 25:12.)

In view of all that the Lord Jesus Christ has done for us,

ought we not to sing praises to his holy name forever? "I will sing unto the Lord; I will sing praise to the Lord God of Israel," said Deborah and Barak. (Judg. 5:3.) King Benjamin so lived that he would go down to the grave in peace, so that his "immortal spirit may join the choirs above in singing the praises of a just God." (Mosiah 2:28.) Mormon preached that men should "believe in Jesus Christ" and all that he has done for them; that "he hath brought to pass the redemption of the world, whereby he that is found guiltless before him at the judgment day hath it given unto him to dwell in the presence of God in his kingdom, to sing ceaseless praises with the choirs above, unto the Father, and unto the Son, and unto the Holy Ghost, which are one God, in a state of happiness which hath no end." (Morm. 7:5-7.)

The Lord's inspired counsel on singing praises to his name is found in such passages as: "I will be glad and rejoice in thee: I will sing praise to thy name, O thou most High. . . . Sing praises to the Lord, which dwelleth in Zion: declare among the people his doings." (Ps. 9:2, 11.) "Sing unto the Lord, O ye saints of his, and give thanks at the remembrance of his holiness." (Ps. 30:4.) "Make a joyful noise unto God, all ye lands: Sing forth the honour of his name: make his praise glorious." (Ps. 66:1-2.) "Sing unto God, sing praises to his name: extol him that rideth upon the heavens by his name JAH, and rejoice before him." (Ps. 68:4.) "O sing unto the Lord a new song: for he hath done marvellous things: . . . the Lord hath made known his salvation. . . . All the ends of the earth shall see the salvation of our God. Make a joyful noise unto the Lord, all the earth: make a loud noise, and rejoice, and sing praise. Sing unto the Lord with the harp; with the harp, and the voice of a psalm. With trumpets and sound of cornet make a joyful noise before the Lord, the King." (Ps. 98:1-6; 96:1-7.) There is of course much more; and from all of it we learn that the true saints praise the Lord in song, both here and hereafter, both now and forever, for all that he has done for them and for all men.

"Praise Ye the Lord"

Among the true saints, cries of praise and blessing and thanksgiving to the Lord Jehovah are spoken from every lip. So great is their gratitude to him for his redeeming power that, from the rising of the sun to its going down, in every heart is found one grand Hallelujah, one great cry, praise ye the Lord, praise Jah, praise Jehovah. There are three obvious ways in which the saints praise their Messiah:

1. They sing the songs of Zion and the great Christian anthems, which musical presentations teach and testify of our Lord's wondrous works. Cries of "We thank thee, O God, for a prophet" are heard in every congregation. Great choirs acclaim: "We'll sing and we'll shout with the armies of heaven, Hosanna, hosanna to God and the Lamb! Let glory to them in the highest be given, Henceforth and forever; Amen and amen!" And the sound of worshipful voices sings: "Jesus, our Lord and God, Bore sin's tremendous load; Praise ye his name! Tell what his arm has done, What spoils from death he won; Sing his great name alone, Worthy the Lamb!"

2. They preach mighty sermons, pray in faith to the Father in the name of the Son, shout praises, speak forth the thoughts, intents, and desires of their hearts—all as guided by the Comforter, who "knoweth all things, and beareth record of the Father and of the Son." (D&C 42:17.)

3. They live as their Lord lived, keep his commandments, do as he did, and thus become living witnesses of the truth and divinity of his work. They become living epistles in whose hearts and lives the gospel is seen and is available to be "known and read of all men." (2 Cor. 3:2.) Others, seeing their good works, are thus led to glorify Those whose work it is. "Be holy, for I am holy" (Lev. 11:45) was Jehovah's word to Israel. There neither is nor can be any greater or more perfect way to praise the Lord than to keep his commandments, to become like him, and to let him thereby live in and through his obedient follower.

555

It is the divine will that the saints praise their God. Hence such scriptural injunctions as these: Be baptized and receive the Holy Ghost, and "then cometh the baptism of fire and of the Holy Ghost; and then can ye speak with the tongue of angels, and shout praises unto the Holy One of Israel." (2 Ne. 31:13.) "Fear this glorious and fearful name, THE LORD THY GOD," spake Moses to Israel. (Deut. 28:58.) "Bless ye the Lord," said Deborah and Barak. (Judg. 5:9.) "Let the Lord be glorified," as it is written in Isaiah. (Isa. 66:5.) Speaking Messianically, Isaiah said: "He shall be exalted and extolled, and be very high" (Isa. 52:13), and, "I will divide him a portion with the great, and he shall divide the spoil with the strong" (Isa. 53:12).

In the course of a longer Messianic recitation, the Psalmist says: "Blessed be he that cometh in the name of the Lord." (Ps. 118:26.) The believing multitude, on the occasion of our Lord's triumphal entry into Jerusalem, gave their witness on this point by acclaiming: "Hosanna to the son of David: Blessed is he that cometh in the name of the Lord; Hosanna in the highest." (Matt. 21:9.) And Jesus himself certified that the rebellious of Jerusalem "shall not see me henceforth, till ye shall say [at my Second Coming], Blessed is he that cometh in the name of the Lord." (Matt. 23:39.)

From the Psalms we extract these samples of the divine counsel that men should praise Jehovah: "I will praise the Lord according to his righteousness: and will sing praise to the name of the Lord most high." (Ps. 7:17.) "O Lord our Lord, how excellent is thy name in all the earth!" (Ps. 8:1.) "Let my mouth be filled with thy praise and with thy honour all the day. . . . My mouth shall shew forth thy righteousness and thy salvation all the day." (Ps. 71:8, 15.) "Bless the Lord, O my soul: and all that is within me, bless his holy name. Bless the Lord, O my soul, and forget not all his benefits. . . . Bless the Lord, ye his angels, that excel in strength, that do his commandments, hearkening unto the voice of his word. Bless ye the Lord, all ye his hosts; ye ministers of his, that do his pleasure. Bless the Lord, all his works in all places of his dominion: bless the Lord, O my soul." (Ps. 103:1-2, 20-22.) "Bless the Lord, O my soul. O Lord my God, thou art very great; thou art clothed with honour and majesty." (Ps. 104:1.) "Oh that men would praise the Lord for his goodness, and for his wonderful works to the children of men!" (Ps. 107:8.) Psalms 148, 149, and 150 recite who should praise the Lord and tell why. They end with these exulting words: "Let every thing that hath breath praise the Lord. Praise ye the Lord."

Pray unto the Lord

Brief reference was made in Chapter 19 to the fact that prayers are always made to the Father, but that the language and form of prayer are also used in praising and extolling the Son, and also, that when we pray to the Father, because of the laws of mediation and intercession, answers come from the Son. These concepts are basic to our whole system of worship and must be understood by those who come to know the only true God and Jesus Christ whom he hath sent, both of whom must be known if we are to gain eternal life. (John 17:3.) Accordingly, let us now set forth with some particularity the true form of prayer and show how and in what manner both the Father and the Son are involved.

Proper prayers are made to the Father, in the name of the Son, by the power of the Holy Ghost. The Father answers prayers, but he does it through the Son, into whose hands he has committed all things. For instance, Joseph Smith prayed to the Father in the name of Christ—seeking guidance, direction, doctrine—and the answers included such language as: "Thus saith the Lord your God, even Jesus Christ, the Great I AM, Alpha and Omega, the beginning and the end." (D&C 38:1.)

The Nephite Twelve "were united in mighty prayer and fasting. . . . They were praying unto the Father in the name of Jesus." This is the perfect pattern for gaining revelation or whatever is needed. In this setting, the record says: "And Jesus came and stood in the midst of them, and said unto them: What will ye that I shall give unto you?" (3 Ne. 27:1-2.) The prayer was addressed to the Father; the answer came by way of the Son.

As we are also aware, whenever the Son speaks, he assumes the prerogative of speaking in the first person as though he were the Father. "Listen to the voice of Jesus Christ, your Redeemer, the Great I AM, whose arm of mercy hath atoned for your sins; . . . Behold, I say unto you, that little children are redeemed from the foundation of the world through mine Only Begotten." (D&C 29:1, 46.) Christ speaks, but when occasion requires, he speaks by divine investiture of authority as though he were the Father.

The patterns of prayer were set in the earliest days of man's mortal probation. In revealing to Adam that sacrifices were offered in "similitude of the [future] sacrifice of the Only Begotten of the Father," an angelic ministrant said: "Wherefore"—that is, because the Only Begotten will sacrifice himself for mankind, and because he "is full of grace and truth"—"thou shalt do all that thou doest in the name of the Son, and thou shalt repent and call upon God in the name of the Son forevermore." (Moses 5:7-8.)

Proper prayers are not addressed to the Blessed Virgin, though we may suppose she was the greatest mortal of her sex. They are not addressed to Eve, the mother of all living, nor to Sarah, who with Abraham has entered into her exaltation and sits at her husband's side on the throne of eternal power. They are not made to any of the saints of either sex, whether they became such by Catholic fiat, as they suppose, or whether they gained that blessed state by faith and righteousness. They are not made to Moses, the mediator of the Old Covenant, nor to Jesus, the Mediator of the New Covenant, nor to the Holy Spirit of God, who knows all things and has all power. Proper prayers are offered to the Father, and to him only, but they are always offered in the name of his Only Begotten Son, or any of its synonyms. If this truth were known and believed, men would stand at the starting point and be in a position to get in tune with the Infinite and receive personal revelation from him.

All of the ancient prophets and all of the ancient saints followed the pattern given to Adam by the angel. They prayed to the Father in the name of his Only Begotten. Enoch prayed: "I ask thee, O Lord, in the name of thine Only Begotten, even Jesus Christ, that thou wilt have mercy upon Noah and his seed, that the earth might never more be covered by the floods." (Moses 7:50.) To Moses the Lord said: "Call upon God in the name of mine Only Begotten." (Moses 1:17.) "We knew of Christ, and we had a hope of his glory many hundred years before his coming," wrote the Nephite Jacob, "and not only we ourselves had a hope of his glory, but also all the holy prophets which were before us. Behold, they believed in Christ and worshiped the Father in his name, and also we worship the Father in his name." (Jacob 4:4-5.) All of the holy prophets worshiped the Father in the name of the Son! There is no other way. The first and great commandment, revealed anew in our day but given to the Lord's people in all dispensations, is: "Thou shalt love the Lord thy God with all thy heart, with all thy might, mind, and strength; and in the name of Jesus Christ thou shalt serve him." (D&C 59:5.)

Prayer and faith are perfectly united in the instructions of Jesus to the Nephites. "Ye must always pray unto the Father in my name," he told them, "And whatsoever ye shall ask the Father in my name, which is right, believing that ye shall receive, behold it shall be given unto you. Pray in your families unto the Father, always in my name, that your wives and your children may be blessed." (3 Ne. 18:20-21.) Explicit instruction to this effect abounds in the Nephite record. (2 Ne. 32:8-9; 33:12; 3 Ne. 18:30; Moro. 2:2; 3:2; 4:2; 7:48; 8:3.) Indeed, Jesus himself, as a mortal among the Jews (John 17) and as an immortal among the Nephites (3 Ne. 17), prayed in persuasive power to his Father. And for that matter the angels of God in heaven both speak and pray by the power of the Holy Ghost and in the name of that same Savior who is also our Savior.

There is one other great and eternal truth about prayer that cannot be emphasized too strongly. It is that if there had been no atonement of Christ; if the Son of God, in whose name we pray, had not ransomed man from the fall; if he had not put the great plan of redemption into operation by the shedding of his blood—except for these things, prayer in his name or any name, offered to the Father or any other person or thing, would be of no avail. Prayer is efficacious because of the atonement. As we have repeatedly pointed out in other connections, if there had been no atonement, the Father's plan would have been frustrated and all his purposes, including the reason for creation itself, would have become void. Thus, with reference to prayer, Amulek is able to say: "May God grant unto you, my brethren, that ye may begin to exercise your faith unto repentance, that ye begin to call upon his holy name, that he would have mercy upon you." (Alma 34:17.) That is to say, exercise faith, repent, and call upon God in the name of the Son for that mercy which comes because of the atonement to those who believe and obey. Truly, the atonement is the rock foundation of revealed religion.

We are being very express and pointed in setting forth the one and only true doctrine of prayer and worship in order to avoid any uncertainty or misapprehension in now noting that there are three exceptions, or seeming exceptions, to the order that prayers are to be offered to the Father in the name of the Son and in no other way. These are:

1. On that Pentecostal occasion when the Nephites received the gift of the Holy Ghost, they offered approved prayers directly to Jesus and not to the Father. But there was a special reason why this was done in this instance and on a onetime basis. Jesus had already taught them to pray in his name to the Father, which they first did. "They knelt again and prayed to the Father in the name of Jesus," the record says. "And they did pray for that which they most desired;

and they desired that the Holy Ghost should be given unto them." Thereupon the heavens opened, they were circled about with fire, angels ministered unto them, and Jesus commanded them to pray again. They did so. But this time "they did pray unto Jesus, calling him their Lord and their God." Jesus was present before them as the symbol of the Father. Seeing him, it was as though they saw the Father; praying to him, it was as though they prayed to the Father. It was a special and unique situation that as far as we know has taken place only once on earth during all the long ages of the Lord's hand-dealings with his children. It is analogous to the fact that the true believers in Jerusalem did not receive and enjoy the gift of the Holy Ghost as long as Christ personally ministered among them, although the receipt of that member of the Godhead as a gift, and the enjoyment of the companionship of the Holy Spirit, is essential to salvation.

At this point in the Nephite experience, Jesus prayed to the Father, thanking him for all that was then transpiring, and saying: "Thou seest that they believe in me because thou hearest them, and they pray unto me; and they pray unto me because I am with them." (3 Ne. 19:8-22.) When the special circumstances here involved no longer prevailed; when the circling flames of fire no longer blazed around them; and when the angels had returned to their heavenly abodes, the Nephites reverted to the established order and prayed again to the Father in the name of the Son. (3 Ne. 27:2.)

2. It is part of the divine program to use the form and language of prayer in crying Hallelujah, which means praise Jehovah, or praise the Lord, or praise Christ who is Jehovah. These ejaculations of joy are uttered in the spirit of prayer and of thanksgiving. They arise from every believing heart because of all that Christ the Lord has done in bringing to pass the immortality and eternal life of man. Such cries or shouts or expressions of praise to Jehovah, and also a formal prayer to the Father, given in the true and proper sense of the word, are perfectly linked together in the revealed dedi-

catory prayer of the Kirtland Temple. With joy and in the spirit of exultation the revelation begins: "Thanks be to thy name, O Lord God of Israel, who keepest covenant and showest mercy unto thy servants who walk uprightly before thee, with all their hearts"—that is, thanks be to Christ whose arm of mercy is over his saints—"Thou who hast commanded thy servants to build a house to thy name in this place [Kirtland]. And now thou beholdest, O Lord, that thy servants have done according to thy commandment." The command to build the house came from the Lord Jesus. He conveyed the Father's will and gave the direction. It was his voice that spoke to Joseph Smith.

"And now we ask thee, Holy Father, in the name of Jesus Christ, the Son of thy bosom, in whose name alone salvation can be administered to the children of men, we ask thee, O Lord, to accept of this house, the workmanship of the hands of us, thy servants, which thou didst command us to build." (D&C 109:1-4.) The dedicatory prayer is addressed to the Father, as all prayers should be; it is addressed to the One whose original command it was that the house be built, which direction had been revealed to the builders by the Son through whom all revelation comes. The only occasions when the Father gives personal direction and revelation are when he introduces and bears testimony of the Son, as in the case of Joseph's First Vision. Having made the introduction and given the testimony, the instruction then is, "Hear Him!" (JS-H 17.) Man then receives his instruction from the Son.

3. We also worship Christ in the true and proper sense of the word, which concept we shall now set forth.

Worship the Lord Jesus Christ

Nephi sets the stage for an understanding of the doctrine that true believers worship Christ, as well as the Father, in these words: "We talk of Christ, we rejoice in Christ, we preach of Christ, we prophesy of Christ, and we write according to our prophecies, that our children may know to what source they may look for a remission of their sins." (2 Ne. 25:26.) Remission of sins and consequent salvation come because of Christ! Hence, our worship of him: "Worthy is the Lamb that was slain to receive power, and riches, and wisdom, and strength, and honour, and glory, and blessing." (Rev. 5:13.) And worship! "[My words] are sufficient to teach any man the right way," Nephi continues, "for the right way is to believe in Christ and deny him not. . . . And Christ is the Holy One of Israel; wherefore ye must bow down before him, and worship him with all your might, mind, and strength, and your whole soul; and if ye do this ye shall in nowise be cast out." (2 Ne. 25:28-29.)

Perhaps the most dramatic and detailed account of perfect worship being given to Jesus is in connection with his immortal ministry among the Nephites. He appeared and testified of himself. He invited the multitude, all twenty-five hundred of them, to come forth one by one and thrust their hands into his side and to feel the prints of the nails in his hands and in his feet. They did so. "And when they had all gone forth and had witnessed for themselves, they did cry out with one accord, saying: Hosanna! Blessed be the name of the Most High God! And they did fall down at the feet of Jesus, and did worship him. . . . And Nephi . . . went forth, and bowed himself before the Lord and did kiss his feet." (3 Ne. 11:1-19.) Later, after Jesus taught them and healed their sick, "they did all, both they who had been healed and they who were whole, bow down at his feet, and did worship him; and as many as could come for the multitude did kiss his feet, insomuch that they did bathe his feet with their tears." (3 Ne. 17:10.)

In small part and to a lesser degree some of these same feelings of gratitude, adoration, and worship had welled up in the hearts of Jewish believers in Jerusalem, when "a very great multitude spread their garments in the way" and strewed branches before him as they acclaimed: "Hosanna to the son of David: Blessed is he that cometh in the name of the Lord; Hosanna in the highest." (Matt. 21:8-9.) And it was Jesus, quoting the Messianic message of Jehovah and applying it to himself, who said: "In vain they do worship me, teaching for doctrines the commandments of men." (Matt. 15:9.)

Throughout our Lord's mortal ministry there were in fact numerous instances when certain believers worshiped him. The wise men from the east, guided by the star and finding "the young child with Mary his mother, . . . fell down, and worshipped him." (Matt. 2:11.) As he came down from the mountain, having just preached that incomparable sermon, the Sermon on the Mount, "there came a leper and worshipped him, saying, Lord, if thou wilt, thou canst make me clean. And Jesus put forth his hand, and touched him, saying, I will; be thou clean. And immediately his leprosy was cleansed." (Matt. 8:1-3.)

Jesus raised the daughter of Jairus from the dead because that ruler "came . . . and worshipped him, saying, My daughter is even now dead: but come and lay thy hand upon her, and she shall live." (Matt. 9:18-25.) After Jesus walked on the water, bade Peter so to do, and calmed the boisterous waves with his word, the record says: "Then they that were in the ship came and worshipped him, saying, Of a truth thou art the Son of God." (Matt. 14:22-33.) A Gentile woman of Canaan, whose daughter was "grievously vexed with a devil," besought Jesus for help, which he declined to give, saying, "I am not sent but unto the lost sheep of the house of Israel." But the earnest supplicant was not to be denied. She yet came "and worshipped him, saying, Lord, help me." After further importuning, because of her faith and worship, Jesus commended her for her faith and healed her daughter. (Matt. 15:21-28.)

Jesus cast a legion of unclean spirits out of a man, fettered and bound in the tombs, when "he ran and worshipped him," and when one of the spirits by the mouth of the man called out, "thou Son of the most high God." These were the evil spirits which our Lord permitted to enter the herd of swine, causing their consequent destruction. (Mark 5:1-20.) The man born blind, whose eyes were opened as a prelude to Jesus' great sermon on the Good Shepherd, testified to the Great Healer: "Lord, I believe. And he worshipped him." (John 9 and 10.) At the open tomb, the seal of death having been broken, the angelic word was given to certain women, commanding them to tell the disciples that Jesus had risen. "And as they went to tell his disciples, behold, Jesus met them, saying, All hail. And they came and held him by the feet, and worshipped him." Later when the disciples "saw him," they also "worshipped him." (Matt. 28:1-17.)

With both the Nephite and the Jewish accounts before us, each of them showing that Jesus our Lord accepted the reverential worship of his fellow beings, and indeed expected it of them, we are led to ask: What kind of a Man was he? That he considered himself to be and was in fact the Son of God, who can doubt? But our present inquiry, dealing as it does with Messianic utterances, should lead us also to answer that all of the worship here and everywhere bestowed upon God's Almighty Son came in direct fulfillment of the Messianic promises. Some of these we shall now note. Quoting a passage from the Septuagint, which is not in our King James Bible, Paul preserves for us a Messianic utterance relative to bringing "the firstbegotten into the world," which says: "And let all the angels of God worship him." (Heb. 1:6.) Christ is worshiped by men and angels! In their great vision of the degrees of glory, Joseph Smith and Sidney Rigdon "saw the holy angels, and them who are sanctified before his throne, worshiping God, and the Lamb, who worship him forever and ever." (D&C 76:21.)

From the Psalms—those wondrous poetical recitations which so abundantly speak of our Lord's great ministries: that is, of his work in preexistence, of his mortal deeds, and of his eternal continuance in glorious exaltation—we take these sample statements: "Kiss the Son. . . . Blessed are all

565

they that put their trust in him." (Ps. 2:12.) "Give unto the Lord the glory due unto his name; worship the Lord in the beauty of holiness." (Ps. 29:2; 96:1-13.) "He is thy Lord; and worship thou him." (Ps. 45:11.) "All the earth shall worship thee, and shall sing unto thee; they shall sing to thy name." (Ps. 66:4.) "Worship him, all ye gods." (Ps. 97:7.)

How to Worship the Father and the Son

Jesus said: "It is written, Thou shalt worship the Lord thy God, and him only shalt thou serve." (Luke 4:8.) The great Creator gave unto Adam and Eve, and through them to all of their posterity, "commandments that they should love and serve him, the only living and true God, and that he should be the only being whom they should worship." (D&C 20:19.) The plan of salvation for all men, the plan of worship for all men, is that they should worship the Father in the name of the Son. This is our whole approach to true and revealed religion. It is the pattern that has been followed in all dispensations. To the Samaritan woman with whom he conversed at Jacob's well, Jesus said: "The hour cometh, and now is, when the true worshippers shall worship the Father in spirit and in truth; for the Father seeketh such to worship him. For unto such hath God promised his Spirit. And they who worship him, must worship in spirit and in truth." (JST, John 4:25-26.)

We have also learned that in addition to worshiping the Father, our great and eternal Head, by whose word men are, there is a sense in which we worship the Son. We pay divine honor, reverence, and homage to him because of his atoning sacrifice, because immortality and eternal life come through him. He does not replace the Father in receiving reverence, honor, and respect, but he is worthy to receive all the praise and glory that our whole souls have power to possess.

It is our purpose now to ask how we worship the Lord, be he the Father or the Son or both. The forms of worship are many. Prayers, sermons, testimonies, gospel ordinances, attendance at church meetings, doing missionary service, visiting the fatherless and the widows in their afflictions, and a great many other things are all part of pure religion and true worship. But there is a way of worship that includes all these and yet is more than any one of them alone or all of them together. That way is made known to us in one of our deepest and most profound revelations.

We have in the first chapter of the Gospel of John an account of our Lord's status as the Word of God, as the Creator of all things, and as the life of the world. This account leads into the ministry and experience of John the Baptist in preparing the way before the Lord. In section 93 in the Doctrine and Covenants, we have a partial revelation of what is called "John's record," which deals with and adds to this same account and which includes what the Baptist saw after he immersed the Lord Jesus in Jordan. Clearly the original account of these doings was written by John the Baptist, portions of it were quoted by John the Beloved in his gospel, and added portions (with more yet to come) were revealed to Joseph Smith in modern times. Our present chief interest is in some of the things revealed anew in our day.

Our revelation says: "And I, John," meaning John the Baptist, "bear record that I beheld his glory, as the glory of the Only Begotten of the Father, full of grace and truth, even the Spirit of truth, which came and dwelt in the flesh, and dwelt among us." To our Lord's cousin and kinsman the heavens had been opened. He had seen and knew of the glory and greatness of the One whose forerunner he was and of whom he testified: "Behold the Lamb of God, which taketh away the sin of the world." (John 1:29.) "And I, John, saw that he received not of the fulness at the first, but received grace for grace," the newly revealed data continues, "And he received not of the fulness at first, but continued from grace to grace, until he received a fulness; And thus he was called the Son of God, because he received not of the fulness at the first." At this point John tells of seeing the heavens opened and the Holy Ghost descending upon Jesus, and tells of hearing the voice out of heaven say: "This is my beloved Son."

Then comes the climax of John's account, a climax that is in large measure the reason why the whole recitation was revealed. It says: "And I, John, bear record that he received a fulness of the glory of the Father. And he received all power, both in heaven and on earth, and the glory of the Father was with him, for he dwelt in him." This ends the renewed setting forth of what was known anciently.

Then the Lord says to Joseph Smith: "I give unto you these sayings that you may understand and know how to worship, and know what you worship, that you may come unto the Father in my name, and in due time receive of his fulness." Receive of his fulness, the fulness of the glory of the Father! Receive all power in heaven and on earth! Of those who so obtain it is written: "They shall pass by the angels, and the gods, which are set there, to their exaltation and glory in all things, . . . which glory shall be a fulness and a continuation of the seeds forever and ever. Then shall they be gods. . . . Then shall they be above all, because all things are subject unto them." (D&C 132:19-20.) Eternal life is to receive the fulness of the Father; it is to be like him; it is to live as he lives; it is the greatest of all the gifts of God; it is the object and end of our existence. Then the revelation sets forth this promise: "For if you keep my commandments you shall receive of his fulness, and be glorified in me as I am in the Father; therefore, I say unto you, you shall receive grace for grace." (D&C 93:6-20.)

Come worship the Lord! How is it done? Perfect worship is emulation. We honor those whom we imitate. The most perfect way of worship is to be holy as Jehovah is holy. It is to be pure as Christ is pure. It is to do the things that enable us to become like the Father. The course is one of obedience, of living by every word that proceedeth forth from the mouth of God, of keeping the commandments.

How do we worship the Lord? We do it by going from grace to grace, until we receive the fulness of the Father and are glorified in light and truth as is the case with our Pattern and Prototype, the Promised Messiah.

Chapter 31

"SEEK THE FACE OF THE LORD ALWAYS"

Seek the Spirit

Our divine commission—the teacher's divine commission, whose terms and conditions are binding upon all legal administrators, upon all who are authorized to teach the Lord's gospel—our divine commission calls for us:

To teach the principles of the everlasting gospel, to teach them unmixed with personal opinions and the philosophies of the world;

To teach them out of the scriptures, and as they are revealed by the Comforter;

To do it by the power of the Holy Ghost;

To apply the teachings to our present needs; and

To do it all with the seal of personal testimony.

We have followed this pattern, and conformed to the best of our ability to this divine commission, in our consideration of all things relative to *The Promised Messiah— The First Coming of Christ.* We have dealt with the life and mission and ministry of the Lord Jesus Christ, showing that all the holy prophets since the world began have prophesied of him and his wondrous works; showing that they and all the saints of all ages have known and do now know that salvation is in Christ; and showing that his atoning sacrifice is the rock foundation upon which revealed religion rests.

Our source material has come almost exclusively from

the Standard Works; we have searched the scriptures diligently to learn all that the prophets have said about Him in whom our faith centers. We have sought to interpret the prophetic utterances by the spirit of inspiration, knowing that "no prophecy of the scripture is of any private interpretation" and that if "holy men of God spake as they were moved by the Holy Ghost" (2 Pet. 1:20-21), we must be moved upon by that same Spirit if we are to catch the full vision and meaning of the prophecies. In the very nature of things we have shown, and it also has been stated in plain words over and over again, that if the truths presented are believed and lived, they will assure us of peace in this life and eternal life in the world to come. The seal of personal testimony has been interwoven throughout the whole work as occasion has required and propriety has permitted. The work itself is what it is, and stands or falls on its own merits.

There are, however, two additional applications to be made of these great and eternal truths concerning the Promised Messiah. As believing saints it is our privilege:

1. To enjoy the gift of the Holy Ghost; to receive personal revelation; to possess the signs that always follow true believers; to work miracles; and to have the gifts of the Spirit; and

2. To see the Lord face to face; to talk with him as a man speaketh with his friend; to have his Person attend us from time to time; and to have him manifest to us the Father.

Members of the true church receive the gift of the Holy Ghost by the laying on of hands. This gift is the right to the constant companionship of this member of the Godhead based on faithfulness. It is well known among us that the Holy Ghost is a Revelator and a Sanctifier; that if we ask of God in faith, we shall receive revelation upon revelation, until the mysteries of the kingdom are unfolded in full; that faith precedes the miracle; and that signs always follow those who believe. Our obligation is to seek and obtain the Spirit so that all of these things will flow to us as they did to the ancients.

As to the possession of signs and the working of miracles, we have this assurance from the Lord Jesus: "Whatsoever ye shall ask the Father in my name, which is right, believing that ye shall receive, behold it shall be given unto you." (3 Ne. 18:20.) Four centuries later, the prophet Mormon rendered Jesus' promise in these words: "Whatsoever thing ye shall ask the Father in my name, which is good, in faith believing that ye shall receive, behold, it shall be done unto you." (Moro. 7:26.) If it be right, if it be good, faith will bring it to pass. Moroni affirmed the same truth by saying: "Whoso believeth in Christ, doubting nothing, whatsoever he shall ask the Father in the name of Christ it shall be granted him; and this promise is unto all, even unto the ends of the earth." (Morm. 9:21.) Moroni then quotes Jesus' promise that miracles and signs shall follow them that believe.

With specific reference to the fact that miracles are always found among faithful people, our Book of Mormon prophets leave us these testimonies: "Who shall say that Jesus Christ did not many mighty miracles? And there were many mighty miracles wrought by the hands of the apostles. And if there were miracles wrought then, why has God ceased to be a God of miracles and yet be an unchangeable Being? And behold, I say unto you he changeth not; if so he would cease to be God; and he ceaseth not to be God, and is a God of miracles. And the reason why he ceaseth to do miracles among the children of men is because that they dwindle in unbelief, and depart from the right way, and know not the God in whom they should trust." (Morm. 9:18-20.) "Have miracles ceased?" Mormon asked. "I say unto you, Nay," he answers, "for it is by faith that miracles are wrought; and it is by faith that angels appear and minister unto men; wherefore, if these things have ceased wo be unto the children of men, for it is because of unbelief, and all is vain. For no man can be saved, according to the words of Christ, save they shall have faith in his name; wherefore, if these things have ceased, then has faith ceased also; and aw-

572

ful is the state of man, for they are as though there had been no redemption made." (Moro. 7:27, 37-38.)

As to personal revelation—not revelation to apostles and prophets for the guidance and direction of the Lord's earthly affairs, but personal revelation for the perfecting of each individual saint—we have some wondrous words of counsel and direction that the Lord gave to Joseph Smith. They are appropriately prefaced with these expressions of praise and glory to Him from whom revelation comes: "Hear, O ye heavens, and give ear, O earth, and rejoice ye inhabitants thereof, for the Lord is God, and beside him there is no Savior. Great is his wisdom, marvelous are his ways, and the extent of his doings none can find out. His purposes fail not, neither are there any who can stay his hand. From eternity to eternity he is the same, and his years never fail." In this setting the inspired record continues: "For thus saith the Lord—I, the Lord, am merciful and gracious unto those who fear me, and delight to honor those who serve me in righteousness and in truth unto the end. Great shall be their reward and eternal shall be their glory. And to them will I reveal all mysteries, yea, all the hidden mysteries of my kingdom from days of old, and for ages to come, will I make known unto them the good pleasure of my will concerning all things pertaining to my kingdom. Yea, even the wonders of eternity shall they know, and things to come will I show them, even the things of many generations. And their wisdom shall be great, and their understanding reach to heaven; and before them the wisdom of the wise shall perish, and the understanding of the prudent shall come to naught. For by my Spirit will I enlighten them, and by my power will I make known unto them the secrets of my will—yea, even those things which eye has not seen, nor ear heard, nor yet entered into the heart of man." (D&C 76:1-10.)

God is no respecter of persons. His invitation to all men is: "If any of you lack wisdom, let him ask of God, that giveth to all men liberally, and upbraideth not; and it shall be given him." (James 1:5.) All who ask in faith receive an

573

answer, and the greater the faith the more wondrous are the forthcoming revelations. After receiving and recording the Vision of the Degrees of Glory, Joseph Smith, still writing by way of revelation, said: "This is the end of the vision which we saw, which we were commanded to write while we were yet in the Spirit. But great and marvelous are the works of the Lord, and the mysteries of his kingdom which he showed unto us, which surpass all understanding in glory, and in might, and in dominion; Which he commanded us we should not write while we were yet in the Spirit, and are not lawful for man to utter; Neither is man capable to make them known, for they are only to be seen and understood by the power of the Holy Spirit, which God bestows on those who love him, and purify themselves before him; To whom he grants this privilege of seeing and knowing for themselves; That through the power and manifestation of the Spirit, while in the flesh, they may be able to bear his presence in the world of glory. And to God and the Lamb be glory, and honor, and dominion forever and ever." (D&C 76:113-19.)

A great congregation of Nephites had one of the experiences here described on that sacred occasion when Jesus prayed to the Father for them. "The eye hath never seen, neither hath the ear heard, before, so great and marvelous things as we saw and heard Jesus speak unto the Father," the account says. "And no tongue can speak, neither can there be written by any man, neither can the hearts of men conceive so great and marvelous things as we both saw and heard Jesus speak; and no one can conceive of the joy which filled our souls at the time we heard him pray for us unto the Father." (3 Ne. 17:16-17.)

We need not pursue further the concept that all saints, all true believers, all who have faith in the Lord Jesus Christ, all who love and serve him with all their hearts, receive revelations and spiritual gifts, enjoy signs, and work miracles. Suffice it to say that true greatness, from an eternal standpoint, is measured not in worldly station nor in ecclesiastical office, but in the possession of the gifts of the Spirit and in the enjoyment of the things of God. If an application is needed for all the Messianic messages with which we are dealing, it is surely found in the fact that those with true Messianic insight will be led to seek and obtain the Holy Spirit of God and all the consequent gifts that attend the receipt of this incomparable gift.

The Pure in Heart Shall See God

After the true saints receive and enjoy the gift of the Holy Ghost; after they know how to attune themselves to the voice of the Spirit; after they mature spiritually so that they see visions, work miracles, and entertain angels; after they make their calling and election sure and prove themselves worthy of every trust—after all this and more—it becomes their right and privilege to see the Lord and commune with him face to face. Revelations, visions, angelic visitations, the rending of the heavens, and appearances among men of the Lord himself—all these things are for all of the faithful. They are not reserved for apostles and prophets only. God is no respecter of persons. They are not reserved for one age only, or for a select lineage or people. We are all our Father's children. All men are welcome. "And he inviteth them all to come unto him and partake of his goodness; and he denieth none that come unto him, black and white, bond and free, male and female; and he remembereth the heathen; and all are alike unto God, both Jew and Gentile." (2 Ne. 26:33.)

Seeing the Lord is not a matter of lineage or rank or position or place of precedence. Joseph Smith said: "God hath not revealed anything to Joseph, but what he will make known unto the Twelve, and even the least saint may know all things as fast as he is able to bear them, for the day must come when no man need say to his neighbor, Know ye the Lord; for all shall know him . . . from the least to the greatest." (*Teachings*, p. 149.) The fact is that the day of personal visitations from the Lord to faithful men on earth has no more ceased than has the day of miracles. God is an unchangeable Being; otherwise he would not be God. The sole issue is finding people who have faith and who work righteousness. "For if there be no faith among the children of men God can do no miracle among them; wherefore, he showeth not himself until after their faith." (Ether 12:12.)

In the Sermon on the Mount, Jesus said: "Blessed are the pure in heart: for they shall see God." (Matt. 5:8.) The Book of Mormon rendition is even more express. It says: "And blessed are all the pure in heart, for they shall see God." (3 Ne. 12:8.) Ten days after the laying of the cornerstones for the Kirtland Temple, the Lord said to his little flock: "Inasmuch as my people build a house unto me in the name of the Lord, and do not suffer any unclean thing to come into it, that it be not defiled, my glory shall rest upon it; Yea, and my presence shall be there, for I will come into it, and all the pure in heart that shall come into it shall see God. But if it be defiled I will not come into it, and my glory shall not be there; for I will not come into unholy temples." (D&C 97:15-17.)

When the Lord has a house on earth, it is the natural and normal place for him to use in visiting his earthly friends. In the spring of 1820 the Father and the Son came to a grove of trees in western New York, because there was no temple on earth dedicated to serve as their abode. In May of 1829 John the Baptist came to Joseph Smith and Oliver Cowdery on the banks of the Susquehanna River; shortly thereafter Peter, James, and John came to them in a wilderness area. But once the saints had built a holy house for the Lord to use, he and his messengers visited that house to give instruction and confer keys. It was to the Kirtland Temple, the first holy temple of this dispensation, that Jehovah came on April 3, 1836, to be followed by Elias, Elijah, and Moses, each of which angelic ministrants conferred keys and powers upon their earthly fellow laborers. And so we turn to the Kirtland

Temple to see the literal nature of these promises that the pure in heart shall see God, and what happened in the Kirtland Temple is but illustrative of what can be in any of the Lord's houses whenever his worshiping saints generate the faith to pull down from heaven these same heavenly manifestations.

By January of 1836 the saints were getting ready to dedicate the Kirtland Temple. Because of their faith and as an expression of the divine approval that attended their labors, the Lord poured out upon them great Pentecostal manifestations. On January 21, the Prophet Joseph Smith; his father, Joseph Smith, Sr.; Oliver Cowdery; and the two counselors in the First Presidency, Sidney Rigdon and Frederick G. Williams, were participating in sacred ordinances in an upper room in the Kirtland Temple. "The heavens were opened upon us," the Prophet said, "and I beheld the celestial kingdom of God, and the glory thereof, whether in the body or out I cannot tell. I saw the transcendent beauty of the gate through which the heirs of that kingdom will enter, which was like unto circling flames of fire; Also the blazing throne of God, whereon was seated the Father and the Son." (JS-V 1-3.)

That same day, and on others that followed, the Prophet and many others saw vision upon vision. Included among them were these: "The visions of heaven were open to them also," the Prophet said with reference to the First Presidency and the members of bishoprics and high councils from both Zion and Kirtland. "Some of them saw the face of the Savior, and others were ministered unto by holy angels, and the spirit of prophecy and revelation was poured out in mighty power; and loud hosannas, and glory to God in the highest, saluted the heavens, for we all communed with the heavenly host." (*History of the Church*, 2:382.)

On January 28, 1836, "president Zebedee Coltrin, one of the seven presidents of the Seventy, saw the Savior extended before him, as upon the cross, and a little after, crowned with glory upon his head above the brightness of the sun."

577

(*Ibid.,* p. 387.) Of a meeting attended by about three hundred members, on March 30, 1836, in the Kirtland Temple, the Prophet wrote: "The brethren continued exhorting, prophesying, and speaking in tongues until five o'clock in the morning. The Savior made his appearance to some, while angels ministered to others, and it was a Pentecost and an endowment indeed, long to be remembered." (*Ibid.,* pp. 432-33.) The crowning appearance of the Lord during that special period of grace occurred, of course, on April 3, when the Great Jehovah appeared in his glory and majesty to Joseph Smith and Oliver Cowdery. (D&C 110.) These appearances of the Lord to his saints are but samples taken from a fragmentary account and covering a brief period of spiritual rejoicing, but they suffice for our purposes. There is no question but that the pure in heart do see God.

Associated with the promise that the pure in heart shall see God is the decree that those who are not pure in heart shall not see their Lord. Even Moses, with whom it was the practice of God to converse on a face-to-face basis, was denied that privilege on one occasion, as these words of scripture attest: "And he said unto Moses, Thou canst not see my face at this time, lest mine anger is kindled against thee also, and I destroy thee and thy people; for there shall no man among them see me at this time, and live, for they are exceeding sinful. And no sinful man hath at any time, neither shall there be any sinful man at any time, that shall see my face and live." (JST, Ex. 33:20.)

How to Seek and See the Lord

If we keep the commandments and are true and faithful in all things, we shall inherit eternal life in our Father's kingdom. Those who attain this high state of glory and exaltation shall dwell in the presence of God. They shall see his face and converse with him mouth to mouth. They shall know him in the full sense of the word because they have become like him. And all who are now living those laws to the full which will enable them to go where God and Christ are, and there enjoy eternal association with them—that is, all those who are now living in its entirety the law of the celestial kingdom—are already qualified to see the Lord. The attainment of such a state of righteousness and perfection is the object and end toward which all of the Lord's people are striving. We seek to see the face of the Lord while we yet dwell in mortality, and we seek to dwell with him everlastingly in the eternal kingdoms that are prepared.

Our scriptures contain such counsel as: "Seek ye the Lord while he may be found, call ye upon him while he is near: Let the wicked forsake his way, and the unrighteous man his thoughts: and let him return unto the Lord, and he will have mercy upon him; and to our God, for he will abundantly pardon." (Isa. 55:6-7.) "Seek the Lord, and ye shall live. . . . Seek him that maketh the seven stars and Orion. . . . The Lord is his name." (Amos 5:6, 8.) "Seek ye the Lord, all ye meek of the earth, which have wrought his judgment; seek righteousness, seek meekness." (Zeph. 2:3.) "Seek the face of the Lord always, that in patience ye may possess your souls, and ye shall have eternal life." (D&C 101:38.)

We know that all things are governed by law, and that "when we obtain any blessing from God, it is by obedience to that law upon which it is predicated." (D&C 130:20-21.) "For all who will have a blessing at my hands shall abide the law which was appointed for that blessing," the Lord says, "and the conditions thereof, as were instituted from before the foundation of the world." (D&C 132:5.) This means that if we obey the law that enables us to see the Lord, so shall it be, but if we do not meet the divine standard, our eyes shall not behold him. There is no secret as to what laws are involved. They are everywhere recited in the scriptures. That which must be done is described in various ways in different passages. But the general meaning is the same. It all comes down to one basic conclusion—that of keeping the commandments. Let us now consider some of the specific things

579

the scriptures say we must do if we are to see the face of God while we yet dwell as mortals.

The pure in heart shall see God. This we have already seen, but we restate it again because the process of becoming pure in heart is the process that prepares us to see the face of Deity. In an early revelation, the Lord spoke of the members of his newly set up earthly kingdom as "mine own elect." Of them he said: "They will hear my voice, and shall see me, and shall not be asleep, and shall abide the day of my coming; for they shall be purified, even as I am pure." (D&C 35:21.) John spoke similarly when he described what is now our Lord's imminent appearance: "When he shall appear, we shall be like him," he said, "for we shall see him as he is. And every man that hath this hope in him purified himself, even as he is pure." (1 Jn. 3:2-3.) Knowing that Christ is pure, and that if we are to see him now, or be with him hereafter, we must be pure as he is pure, this becomes a great incentive to the purifying of our lives.

A perfectly stated and marvelously comprehensive formula that shows us what we must do to see the Lord is given us in these words: "Verily, thus saith the Lord: It shall come to pass that every soul who forsaketh his sins and cometh unto me, and calleth on my name, and obeyeth my voice, and keepeth my commandments, shall see my face and know that I am." (D&C 93:1.) Who made the promise? The Lord Jesus Christ. To whom is it given? To every living soul. What must we do to see his face? Five specifics are named: (1) Forsake our sins, for no unclean or impure person, no sinful man, can abide in his presence. (2) Come unto him; accept him as our Savior; receive his gospel, as it has been restored in our day. (3) Call on his name in mighty prayer as did the brother of Jared. (4) Obey his voice; do what he directs; put first in our lives the things of his kingdom; close our ears to the evil voices of the world. (5) Keep the commandments; endure in righteousness; be true to the faith. Those who do these things, being pure in heart, shall see God.

Faith and knowledge unite together to pave the way for the appearance of the Lord to an individual or to a whole people. The brother of Jared saw the Lord because he had a perfect knowledge that the Lord could and would show himself. His faith on the point of seeing within the veil was perfect; it had become knowledge. Because he knew, nothing doubting, he saw. Moroni, who had the plates of Ether and who summarized the account of Moriancumer's great vision, tells us why that prophet saw his God: "Because of the knowledge of this man he could not be kept from beholding within the veil," Moroni says, "and he saw the finger of Jesus, which, when he saw, he fell with fear; for he knew that it was the finger of the Lord; and he had faith no longer, for he knew, nothing doubting. Wherefore, having this perfect knowledge of God, he could not be kept from within the veil; therefore he saw Jesus; and he did minister unto him." (Ether 3:19-20.)

It was on this same basis that Jared's brother saw all the inhabitants of the earth and many other things that he wrote, but that "shall not go forth unto the Gentiles until the day that they shall repent of their iniquity, and become clean before the Lord. And in that day that they shall exercise faith in me, saith the Lord, even as the brother of Jared did, that they may become sanctified in me, then will I manifest unto them the things which the brother of Jared saw, even to the unfolding unto them all my revelations, saith Jesus Christ, the Son of God, the Father of the heavens and of the earth, and all things that in them are. And he that will contend against the word of the Lord, let him be accursed; and he that shall deny these things, let him be accursed; for unto them will I show no greater things, saith Jesus Christ; for I am he who speaketh." (Ether 4:6-8.) The message here is so clear that it cannot be clarified by commentary. The brother of Jared saw the Lord because of his faith and knowledge and because he sanctified himself before the Lord. Other men do not receive the same blessings because they have not built the same foundation of righteousness. If and when we obtain the spiritual stature of this man Moriancumer, then we shall see what he saw and know what he knew.

Commenting upon the appearance of Christ to the thousands of Nephites in the land Bountiful, Moroni says: "Faith is things which are hoped for and not seen; wherefore, dispute not because ye see not, for ye receive no witness until after the trial of your faith. For it was by faith that Christ showed himself unto our fathers, after he had risen from the dead; and he showed not himself unto them until after they had faith in him; wherefore, it must needs be that some had faith in him, for he showed himself not unto the world." (Ether 12:6-8.)

In a revelation addressed to those among the saints whom he considered to be his "friends," the Lord gave this commandment: "Call upon me while I am near—Draw near unto me and I will draw near unto you; seek me diligently and ye shall find me; ask, and ye shall receive; knock, and it shall be opened unto you." Surely, this is what we must do if we ever expect to see his face. He is there waiting our call, anxious to have us seek his face, awaiting our importuning pleas to rend the veil so that we can see the things of the Spirit.

"Whatsoever ye ask the Father in my name," he continues, "it shall be given unto you, that is expedient for you." Would it be expedient for us to see and know what the brother of Jared saw and knew? Are there blessings others have received that should be withheld from us? "And if your eye be single to my glory, your whole bodies shall be filled with light, and there shall be no darkness in you; and that body which is filled with light comprehendeth all things." Clearly this is the state attained by Moriancumer when he saw and understood all things and when the Lord could not withhold anything from him.

"Therefore, sanctify yourselves that your minds become single to God"—and now we come to the crowning promise of the gospel—"and the days will come that you shall see him; for he will unveil his face unto you, and it shall be in his own time, and in his own way, and according to his own will." That is the Lord's promise, his great promise, his crowning promise, his last promise. What is there that can excel in importance the obtaining of that spiritual stature which enables one to see the Lord? And so the next words spoken by the Lord to his friends were: "Remember the great and last promise which I have made unto you."

Then follows some counsel relative to right living, which is climaxed with these words, the full import of which is known only by those who are endowed with power from on high in holy places: "Sanctify yourselves; yea, purify your hearts, and cleanse your hands and your feet before me, that I may make you clean; That I may testify unto your Father, and your God, and my God, that you are clean from the blood of this wicked generation." Why? "That I may fulfil this promise, this great and last promise," this promise that you shall see me and that I will unveil my face, that I may fulfill this promise "which I have made unto you, when I will." (D&C 88:62-75.) To those of understanding we say: The purpose of the endowment in the house of the Lord is to prepare and sanctify his saints so they will be able to see his face, here and now, as well as to bear the glory of his presence in the eternal worlds.

In a poetic passage, which can only be understood, as is the case with most of the book of Isaiah, by those with a background knowledge of the gospel, Isaiah says of the righteous in Israel: "Thine eyes shall see the king in his beauty." That is: You shall see the face of the Lord. Any who so obtain are identified with this language: "He that walketh righteously, and speaketh uprightly; he that despiseth the gain of oppressions, that shaketh his hands from holding of bribes, that stoppeth his ears from hearing of blood, and shutteth his eyes from seeing evil." (Isa. 33:15.) These are the ones who shall see the Lord in this life and dwell with him in the life to come.

"How do men obtain a knowledge of the glory of God,

583

his perfections and attributes?" asked the Prophet Joseph Smith. His answer: "By devoting themselves to his service, through prayer and supplication incessantly strengthening their faith in him, until, like Enoch, the Brother of Jared, and Moses, they obtain a manifestation of God to themselves." (*Lectures on Faith,* p. 32.)

Those Whose Calling and Election Is Sure May See the Lord

It is the privilege of all those who have made their calling and election sure to see God; to talk with him face to face; to commune with him on a personal basis from time to time. These are the ones upon whom the Lord sends the Second Comforter. Their inheritance of exaltation and eternal life is assured, and so it becomes with them here and now in this life as it will be with all exalted beings in the life to come. They become the friends of God and converse with him on a friendly basis as one man speaks to another.

It is not our present purpose to discuss what it means to have one's calling and election made sure nor to recite the things that must be done so to obtain. A full discussion of these matters is found in my *Doctrinal New Testament Commentary,* volume 3, pages 323 to 355. For our present needs we shall simply quote this one sentence found on pages 330 and 331: "To have one's calling and election made sure is to be sealed up unto eternal life; it is to have the unconditional guarantee of exaltation in the highest heaven of the celestial world; it is to receive the assurance of godhood; it is, in effect, to have the day of judgment advanced, so that an inheritance of all the glory and honor of the Father's kingdom is assured prior to the day when the faithful actually enter into the divine presence to sit with Christ in his throne, even as he is 'set down' with his 'Father in his throne.' (Rev. 3:21.)"

In one of his greatest doctrinal expositions, the Prophet Joseph Smith equated the making of one's calling and election sure, spoken of by Peter, with "the sealing power spoken of by Paul." He said that those who were sealed up unto eternal life were the ones of whom Jeremiah spoke when he said that the Lord "will make a new covenant with the house of Israel, and with the house of Judah." In the day of this new covenant the Lord promised: "I will put my law in their inward parts, and write it in their hearts; and will be their God, and they shall be my people." Then comes the glorious promise that those who receive the covenant and keep its terms and conditions shall see the Lord. "And they shall teach no more every man his neighbour, and every man his brother, saying, Know the Lord: for they shall all know me, from the least of them unto the greatest of them, saith the Lord: for I will forgive their iniquity, and I will remember their sin no more." (Jer. 31:31-34.)

Having referred to this promise, the Prophet Joseph Smith asked: "How is this to be done?" How will it come to pass that every man shall know the Lord? Why will it not be necessary for men to continue to teach one another the doctrines of the kingdom? The Prophet answers: "It is to be done by this sealing power, and the other Comforter spoken of, which will be manifest by revelation."

Building on that foundation, he then proceeds to give forth his discourse on the Two Comforters. He tells how converted persons receive the Holy Ghost, are born again, become new creatures, and, if they are of Gentile lineage, how they are adopted into the house of Israel. "The other Comforter spoken of is a subject of great interest, and perhaps understood by few of this generation. After a person has faith in Christ, repents of his sins, and is baptized for the remission of his sins and receives the Holy Ghost, (by the laying on of hands), which is the first Comforter, then let him continue to humble himself before God, hungering and thirsting after righteousness, and living by every word of God, and the Lord will soon say unto him, Son, thou shalt be exalted. When the Lord has thoroughly proved him, and finds that the man is determined to serve Him at all hazards,

585

then the man will find his calling and his election made sure, then it will be his privilege to receive the other Comforter, which the Lord hath promised the saints. . . .

"Now what is this other Comforter? It is no more nor less than the Lord Jesus Christ Himself; and this is the sum and substance of the whole matter; that when any man obtains this last Comforter, he will have the personage of Jesus Christ to attend him, or appear unto him from time to time, and even he will manifest the Father unto him, and they will take up their abode with him, and the visions of the heavens will be opened unto him, and the Lord will teach him face to face, and he may have a perfect knowledge of the mysteries of the Kingdom of God; and this is the state and place the ancient saints arrived at when they had such glorious visions—Isaiah, Ezekiel, John upon the Isle of Patmos, St. Paul in the three heavens, and all the saints who held communion with the general assembly and Church of the Firstborn." (*Teachings*, pp. 149-51.)

There are, of course, those whose callings and election have been made sure who have never exercised the faith nor exhibited the righteousness which would enable them to commune with the Lord on the promised basis. There are even those who neither believe nor know that it is possible to see the Lord in this day, and they therefore are without the personal incentive that would urge them onward in the pursuit of this consummation so devoutly desired by those with spiritual insight.

Priesthood Prepares Men to See God

When we speak of seeing the Lord and of talking to him face to face, we have reference to the Lord Jesus Christ, to our Messiah, to the Son of the Father who comes to represent his Father, to minister for and on his behalf and to act in his place and stead. But as we are aware, those who receive the Second Comforter not only have the personage of Jesus Christ to attend them from time to time, but the Son manifests the Father unto them, and the two of them take up their abode, as it were, with mortal men, men who also hold "communion with the general assembly and Church of the Firstborn." (*Teachings,* p. 151.)

It follows that both the Father and the Son may be and often are involved in the appearances of Deity to man. In his own discourse on the Second Comforter, and after having said that he himself would come to his disciples, the Lord Jesus said: "If a man love me, he will keep my words: and my Father will love him, and we will come unto him, and make our abode with him." (John 14:23.) With reference to this, speaking by the spirit of revelation, the Prophet Joseph Smith said: "John 14:23—The appearing of the Father and the Son, in that verse, is a personal appearance; and the idea that the Father and the Son dwell in a man's heart is an old sectarian notion, and is false." (D&C 130:3.) In point of practical reality, it is fair to say that there have been, as we shall note shortly, "many, exceeding great many" appearances of the Lord, meaning Christ, and a more limited number of appearances of the Lord, meaning the Father. And we shall also hereafter note the limitations that the Father imposes upon himself with reference to his own personal appearances.

Brethren whose calling and election is made sure always hold the holy Melchizedek Priesthood. Without this delegation of power and authority they cannot be sealed up unto eternal life. Our revelation itself says: "The more sure word of prophecy means a man's knowing that he is sealed up unto eternal life, by revelation and the spirit of prophecy, through the power of the Holy Priesthood." (D&C 131:5.)

It follows that the priesthood is the power, authority, and means that prepares men to see their Lord; also, that in the priesthood is found everything that is needed to bring this consummation to pass. Accordingly, it is written: "The power and authority of the higher, or Melchizedek Priesthood, is to hold the keys of all the spiritual blessings of the church—To have the privilege of receiving the mysteries of the kingdom of heaven, to have the heavens opened unto them, to commune with the general assembly and church of the Firstborn, and to enjoy the communion and presence of God the Father, and Jesus the mediator of the new covenant." (D&C 107:18-19.)

"The keys of all the spiritual blessings of the church"! Clearly no spiritual blessing is available to mortal man on earth that can compare with personal communion and converse with the Gods of heaven. Such attainments on the part of the prophets of old are the very things that set them apart above all their fellows. Keys open doors; keys are the directing and controlling power where priestly things are concerned. Thus, through the priesthood the door may be opened and the way provided for men to see the Father and the Son. From all of this it follows, automatically and axiomatically, that if and when the holy priesthood operates to the full in the life of any man, he will receive its great and full blessings, which are that rending of the heavens and that parting of the veil of which we now speak.

Truly, as Paul said of holders of the Melchizedek Priesthood who magnified their callings, thus qualifying to receive all of the blessings held in store for such faithful persons: "Ye are come unto mount Sion, and unto the city of the living God, the heavenly Jerusalem, and to an innumerable company of angels"; that is, the heavens are opened unto you, and as with Enoch and Moses and the brother of Jared, nothing is withheld from your view and understanding. "Ye are come . . . To the general assembly and church of the firstborn, which are written in heaven, and to God the Judge of all, and to the spirits of just men made perfect"; that is, you are in communion with the faithful of all ages past who now mingle together in a state of exaltation, you see God who is the Judge of all, and you commune with the departed spirits of the just. "Ye are come . . . To Jesus the mediator of the new covenant, and to the blood of sprinkling, that speaketh better things than that of Abel"; that is, you see Jesus, by the sprinkling of whose blood, as it were, salvation comes. Having so taught, Paul issues this warning: "See that ye refuse not him [the Lord] that speaketh." (Heb. 12:22-25.) Rather, accept the priesthood and let it operate in your life to the full until all these blessings flow to you as they flowed to those of old who magnified their callings.

All of the holy prophets and righteous men of old held the holy Melchizedek Priesthood. This "priesthood continueth in the church of God in all generations, and is without beginning of days or end of years. . . . And this greater priesthood administereth the gospel and holdeth the key of the mysteries of the kingdom, even the key of the knowledge of God." God is known in and through and because of the priesthood; without it he would remain unknown. Through the priesthood the Holy Ghost is given to men, which Comforter is sent forth to bear record of the Father and the Son; also, through the priesthood men are able to progress in spiritual things until they gain personal communion with Deity. "Therefore, in the ordinances thereof," the revelation continues, "the power of godliness is manifest. And without the ordinances thereof, and the authority of the priesthood, the power of godliness is not manifest unto men in the flesh; For without this no man can see the face of God, even the Father, and live." That is to say, in and through the holy priesthood, including all the laws and rites that go with it, the power of godliness, or in other words the power of righteousness, is brought to pass in the lives of men. Without these priesthood laws and powers, God's power and glory would not be revealed to man on earth. Without them they would not see the face of God, for if they did, his glory would destroy them. Sinful men cannot see the face of God and live. (JST, Ex. 33:20.)

"Now this Moses plainly taught to the children of Israel in the wilderness, and sought diligently to sanctify his people that they might behold the face of God; But they hardened their hearts and could not endure his presence; therefore, the Lord in his wrath, for his anger was kindled against them, swore that they should not enter into his rest while in the wilderness, which rest is the fulness of his glory. Therefore, he took Moses out of their midst, and the Holy Priesthood also." (D&C 84:17-26.) What a calamity! Because they did not use the priesthood for the purpose for which it was given—and it was given that they might sanctify themselves so as to "behold the face of God"—the Lord withdrew the very priesthood itself. Israel, as a people, was left with the preparatory gospel only, with the law of Moses. Her people were denied what they might have had because they did not magnify their callings in the priesthood. A little thoughtful reflection will cause us to conclude that there are those in latter-day Israel who are not striving to use the Melchizedek Priesthood for the purpose for which it was given any more than did our ancient ancestors. Again—what a calamity!

However sad it is that Israel (except for isolated groups and occasional instances) failed to use the holy priesthood to sanctify themselves so as to be able to see the face of God and live, it is refreshing to know that there were other peoples in other places who did take advantage of these blessings when they were offered to them. From Alma's great discourse on the higher priesthood we learn: "There were many who were ordained and became high priests of God; and it was on account of their exceeding faith and repentance, and their righteousness before God, they choosing to repent and work righteousness rather than to perish; Therefore they were called after this holy order, and were sanctified, and their garments were washed white through the blood of the Lamb. Now they, after being sanctified by the Holy Ghost, having their garments made white, being pure and spotless before God, could not look upon sin save it were with abhorrence; and there were many, exceeding great many, who were made pure and entered into the rest of the Lord their God." Though Israel failed to sanctify themselves and enter into the rest of the Lord, others did; others by faith and righteousness attained the fulness of the glory of God. And note how many were so involved: "There were many, exceeding great many."

After having recited what others had obtained through righteousness, Alma exhorted his own people in these words: "My brethren, I would that ye should humble yourselves before God, and bring forth fruit meet for repentance, that ye may also enter into that rest." (Alma 13:10-13.) Along this same line, the Prophet Joseph Smith said to his brethren, the elders of latter-day Israel: "It is the privilege of every elder to speak of the things of God; and could we all come together with one heart and one mind in perfect faith the veil might as well be rent today as next week, or any other time, and if we will but cleanse ourselves and covenant before God, to serve him, it is our privilege to have an assurance that God will protect us." (*Teachings*, p. 9.)

In November 1831, the Lord said to the little flock of elders so far ordained in his newly established latter-day kingdom: "It is your privilege, and a promise I give unto you that have been ordained unto this ministry, that inasmuch as you strip yourselves from jealousies and fears, and humble yourselves before me, for ye are not sufficiently humble, the veil shall be rent and you shall see me and know that I am—not with the carnal neither natural mind, but with the spiritual. For no man has seen God at any time in the flesh, except quickened by the Spirit of God. Neither can any natural man abide the presence of God, neither after the carnal mind. Ye are not able to abide the presence of God now, neither the ministering of angels; wherefore, continue in patience until ye are perfected. Let not your minds turn back; and when ye are worthy in mine own due time, ye shall see and know that which is conferred upon you by the hands of my servant Joseph Smith, Jun." (D&C 67:10-14.) That which had been conferred upon them by the Prophet was the power to see the Lord. The name of that power is the Melchizedek Priesthood. Many of these first elders in the kingdom did qualify in due course, while they yet dwelt in the flesh, to see the face of their King. How much spiritual progress we have made in the Church since the day of this revelation may be measured in terms of the number of the elders of Israel for whom the veil has been rent and who have seen the face of Him whose we are.

Apostles and Elders Should See God

All Christendom knows, or should know, that the ancient apostles were special witnesses of the Lord's name; that they saw him after he rose from the dead; that he spent forty days with them as a resurrected being, teaching them all things that it was expedient for them to know pertaining to his kingdom. Those who believe the Book of Mormon are aware that, as with the Twelve in Jerusalem, so with the Twelve on the American continent: they were all witnesses of the Lord—they all felt the nail marks in his hands and feet; they all thrust their hands into his side. There is general awareness in the Church that the latter-day Twelve hold the same office, possess the same priesthood and keys, and bear the same witness of the divine Sonship of him who redeemed us as did their predecessors in days of old. It is true that the witness of the Holy Ghost is sure and absolute and that a man can know with a perfect knowledge, by the power of the Holy Ghost, that Jesus Christ is the Son of the living God who was crucified for the sins of the world. This unshakeable certainty can rest in his soul even though he has not seen the face of his Lord. But it is also true that those who have this witness of the Spirit are expected, like their counterparts of old, to see and hear and touch and converse with the Heavenly Person, as did those of old.

Oliver Cowdery, the Associate President of the Church, who held the keys of the kingdom jointly with the Prophet Joseph Smith, having received them from holy angels sent to earth for that very purpose, was appointed to give the apostolic charge to the first quorum of apostles called in this dispensation. Speaking by the spirit of inspiration and by virtue of visions he had received, Elder Cowdery set forth, in the spirit of pure inspiration, the nature of the apostolic office and what is expected of those who hold it. We shall quote those portions of his charge which deal with the obligation that rests upon all members of the Council of the Twelve to see the face of Him whose witnesses they are.

In a special charge to Elder Parley P. Pratt, we find these words: "The ancients . . . had this testimony—that they had seen the Savior after he rose from the dead. You must bear the same testimony; or your mission, your labor, your toil, will be in vain. You must bear the same testimony, that there is but one God, one Mediator; he that hath seen him, will know him, and testify of him."

In the general charge to all of the Twelve, Elder Cowdery said: "It is necessary that you receive a testimony from heaven to yourselves; so that you can bear testimony to the truth of the Book of Mormon, and that you have seen the face of God. That is more than the testimony of an angel. When the proper time arrives, you shall be able to bear this testimony to the world. When you bear testimony that you have seen God, this testimony God will never suffer to fall, but will bear you out; although many will not give heed, yet others will. You will therefore see the necessity of getting this testimony from heaven.

"Never cease striving until you have seen God face to face. Strengthen your faith; cast off your doubts, your sins, and all your unbelief; and nothing can prevent you from coming to God. Your ordination is not full and complete till God has laid his hand upon you. We require as much to qualify us as did those who have gone before us; God is the same. If the Savior in former days laid his hands upon his disciples, why not in latter days? . . .

"The time is coming when you will be perfectly familiar with the things of God. . . . You have our best wishes, you have our most fervent prayers, that you may be able to bear this testimony, that you have seen the face of God. Therefore call upon him in faith in mighty prayer till you prevail, for it is your duty and your privilege to bear such a testimony for yourselves." (*History of the Church* 2:192-98.)

Few faithful people will stumble or feel disbelief at the doctrine here presented that the Lord's apostolic witnesses are entitled and expected to see his face, and that each one individually is obligated to "call upon him in faith in mighty prayer" until he prevails. But the Twelve are only a dozen in number. There are seldom more than fifteen men on earth at a time who have been ordained to the holy apostleship, which brings us to another statement made by Elder Cowdery in his apostolic charge: "God does not love you better or more than others." That is, apostles and prophets do not gain precedence with the Lord unless they earn it by personal righteousness. The Lord loves people, not office holders. Every elder is entitled to the same blessings and privileges offered the apostles. Indeed, an apostle is an elder; such is the title by which he is proud to be addressed. The priesthood is greater than any of its offices. No office adds any power, dignity, or authority to the priesthood. All offices derive their rights, virtues, authorities, and prerogatives from the priesthood. It is greater to hold the Melchizedek Priesthood than it is to hold the office of an elder or of an apostle in that priesthood. The Lord loves his priesthood holders, all of whom are given the same opportunity to do good and work righteousness and keep the commandments. All of the elders in the kingdom are expected to live the law as strictly as do the members of the Council of the Twelve, and if they do so live, the same blessings will come to them that flow to apostles and prophets.

Apostles and prophets are named as examples and patterns of what others should be. The Quorum of the Twelve should be a model quorum after which every elders quorum in the Church might pattern its course. For instance, before long there will be a great sacrament meeting at which the Lord Jesus himself will partake of the sacrament. Others who will be in attendance and who will partake of the sacrament also will be Moroni, Elias, John the Baptist, Elijah,

Abraham, Isaac, and Jacob, Joseph the son of Jacob, Peter, James, and John, and Michael the archangel who is Adam. These are the ones who are listed by name in the revelation. They shall all be there. The immediate impression arises— what a marvelous meeting this will be, to have the Lord Jesus and all these holy prophets in attendance. Such an impression is of course proper.

But those named are listed merely to illustrate and dramatize what is to be. After naming them as the ones with whom the Lord will partake of the sacrament, the revelation says, "And also with all those whom my Father hath given me out of the world." (D&C 27:5-14.) In other words, every faithful person in the whole history of the world, every person who has so lived as to merit eternal life in the kingdom of the Father will be in attendance and will partake, with the Lord, of the sacrament.

I repeat: apostles and prophets simply serve as patterns and examples to show all men what they may receive if they are true and faithful. There is nothing an apostle can receive that is not available to every elder in the kingdom. As we have heretofore quoted, from the Prophet's sermon on the Second Comforter: "God hath not revealed anything to Joseph, but what he will make known unto the Twelve, and even the least saint may know all things as fast as he is able to bear them." (*Teachings*, p. 149.) It follows that everything stated by Elder Oliver Cowdery in his charge to the apostles could also be given as a charge to all elders. Every elder is entitled and expected to seek and obtain all the spiritual blessings of the gospel, including the crowning blessing of seeing the Lord face to face.

Chapter 32

WHO HAS SEEN THE LORD?

Many Prophets See the Lord

We have in Holy Writ numerous accounts of prophets and holy men who have seen the Lord—some face to face, others in dreams and visions; some in his glory, others when that glory was withheld from mortal view. These accounts have been preserved for us as examples and patterns of what has been, what is, and what yet shall be. They let us know the manner in which the Lord works, and they show us that other men, with passions and faults like ours, have yet overcome the world and gained surpassing outpourings of spiritual enlightenment.

When we speak of seeing the Lord, we have the Lord Jesus Christ in mind, although there are instances when the Father appears. Those who receive the Second Comforter have not only the personage of Jesus Christ to appear to them from time to time, but he also manifests unto them the Father. But the Father's appearances are for the purpose of introducing and bearing testimony of the Son.

Our King James Bible says: "For the law was given by Moses, but grace and truth came by Jesus Christ. No man hath seen God at any time; the only Begotten Son, which is in the bosom of the Father, he hath declared him." (John 1:17-18.) This passage should read: "For the law was given through Moses, but life and truth came through Jesus Christ.

For the law was after a carnal commandment, to the administration of death; but the gospel was after the power of an endless life, through Jesus Christ, the only Begotten Son, who is in the bosom of the Father. And no man hath seen God at any time, except he hath borne record of the Son; for except it is through him no man can be saved." (JST, John 1:17-19.) That is to say, the Father appears for the sole purpose of attesting the divine Sonship of him through whom the word of truth and salvation does and must come to the children of men. This is what is involved in the law of intercession and of mediation. Christ is the Mediator between God and man, and he reveals the Father; and unless men accept the Son, they cannot receive the Father. "No man cometh unto the Father, but by me," Jesus said. (John 14:6.) The Father dealt directly with Adam before the fall, and he apparently (as we shall note shortly) dealt directly with Enoch after that prophet was translated. Otherwise, all the dealings of Deity with men on earth have been through the Son.

We shall now collate and comment upon some of the more important manifestations of Deity to man so as to have before us what we may expect if we have faith like the ancients.

1. *Adam sees the Lord.*

Adam, our father, the first man, was the first of earth's inhabitants to see the Lord. He and his wife, Eve, had intimate and extended association with both the Father and the Son before the fall and while they dwelt in Eden's hallowed vales. (Moses 3 and 4.) They then knew, before mortality entered the world, that they were the offspring of Exalted Parents in whose image they were made. It was as automatic and instinctive for them to know their ancestry, their family relationship, and the exalted destiny they might obtain, as it is for mortal children to grow and assume they will be like their parents.

Then came the fall. Adam and Eve, his wife, were cast out of the Garden. Theirs was no longer a life of peace and serenity in Eden. Thorns and thistles, briars and noxious weeds sprang up unwanted in their earthly dwelling place. Deserts and drouths, disease and death now entered their lives. They and their posterity were shut out from the presence of God. We know that after the fall Adam was visited by angels, that he heard the voice of God, received revelations, and was in tune with the spiritual realm. How often he saw the Lord personally we do not know. It has been revealed to us, however, that after mortal life had gone on for nearly a thousand years, the ancient saints held a great conference to which the Lord came personally. "Three years previous to the death of Adam," the scripture says, "he called Seth, Enos, Cainan, Mahalaleel, Jared, Enoch, and Methuselah, who were all high priests, with the residue of his posterity who were righteous, into the valley of Adam-ondi-Ahman, and there bestowed upon them his last blessing. And the Lord appeared unto them, and they rose up and blessed Adam, and called him Michael, the prince, the archangel. And the Lord administered comfort unto Adam, and said unto him: I have set thee to be at the head; a multitude of nations shall come of thee, and thou art a prince over them forever. And Adam stood up in the midst of the congregation; and, notwithstanding he was bowed down with age, being full of the Holy Ghost, predicted whatsoever should befall his posterity unto the latest generation." (D&C 107:53-56.)

2. *Enoch sees the Lord.*

Those who saw the Lord, and who understood his gospel, taught the saving truths to their fellow mortals so that others might believe and gain spiritual experiences of their own. Enoch, who was present in the great Adam-ondi-Ahman congregation when the Lord appeared, also had continual personal communion with him. "He saw the Lord, and he walked with him, and was before his face continually; and he walked with God three hundred and sixty-five years," before he was translated. (D&C 107:49; Moses 6:39.)

It may well be that more people saw the Lord in Enoch's

day than at any other time in the entire history of the earth, or that more people saw him than at all other times combined. "I beheld the heavens open, and I was clothed upon with glory," Enoch said, "And I saw the Lord; and he stood before my face, and he talked with me, even as a man talketh one with another, face to face; and he said unto me: Look, and I will show unto thee the world for the space of many generations." Enoch was commanded to preach and baptize, and the resultant faith among his converts was so great that the record says: "The Lord came and dwelt with his people, and they dwelt in righteousness." The Lord called his people Zion; they built the City of Holiness, even Zion, which in process of time was taken up into heaven. Then Enoch "was high and lifted up, even in the bosom of the Father, and of the Son of Man," which is to say that he saw both the Father and the Son and conversed with them. There are then recorded some three and a half pages of these conversations, some statements being made by the Father, others by the Son. (Moses 7.)

3. *The brother of Jared sees the Lord.*

Moriancumer, Jared's brother, took sixteen small stones, which were "white and clear, even as transparent glass," to the top of a mountain where he asked the Lord to touch them that they might give light in the seagoing vessels that the Jaredites had built. "And the veil was taken from off the eyes of the brother of Jared, and he saw the finger of the Lord; and it was as the finger of a man, like unto flesh and blood." He said: "I knew not that the Lord had flesh and blood." The Lord responded: "I shall take upon me flesh and blood; and never has man come before me with such exceeding faith as thou hast."

Then the Lord said: "I am he who was prepared from the foundation of the world to redeem my people. Behold, I am Jesus Christ. . . . And never have I showed myself unto man whom I have created, for never has man believed in me as thou hast." That is to say: 'Never have I showed myself in the manner and form now involved; never has there been such a complete revelation of the nature and kind of being I am; never before has the veil been lifted completely so that a mortal man has been able to see my spirit body in the full and complete sense of the word.'

As the brother of Jared beheld the spirit body of the Firstborn of the Father, he was told: "Behold, this body which ye now behold, is the body of my spirit; . . . and even as I appear unto thee to be in the spirit will I appear unto my people in the flesh." In commenting upon this Moroni said, "Jesus showed himself unto this man in the spirit, even after the manner and in the likeness of the same body even as he showed himself unto the Nephites. And he ministered unto him even as he ministered unto the Nephites." (Ether 3:1-18.)

4. *Abraham sees the Lord.*

Abraham saw the Lord many times; and he saw him because he sought him in faith. When Pharaoh's priests tried to sacrifice Abraham upon an altar, the father of the faithful lifted up his voice unto the Lord his God and pleaded for deliverance. In answer he was "filled with the vision of the Almighty. . . . And his voice was unto me: Abraham, Abraham, behold, my name is Jehovah, and I have heard thee, and have come down to deliver thee." (Abr. 1:15-16.) After Abraham left Ur, of the Chaldees, and went to Haran to dwell, his account says: "The Lord appeared unto me, and said unto me: . . . I am the Lord thy God. . . . My name is Jehovah, and I know the end from the beginning; therefore my hand shall be over thee. And I will make of thee a great nation." (Abr. 2:6-9.) Again upon the plains of Moreh, Abraham says, "The Lord appeared unto me in answer to my prayers, and said unto me: Unto thy seed will I give this land." (Abr. 2:18-19.)

Of another appearance the record says: "I, Abraham, talked with the Lord, face to face, as one man talketh with another; and he told me of the works which his hands had made; And he said unto me: My son, my son (and his hand was stretched out), behold I will show you all these. And he

600

put his hand upon mine eyes, and I saw those things which his hands had made, which were many; and they multiplied before mine eyes, and I could not see the end thereof." (Abr. 3:11-12.) Genesis also preserves for us accounts of some of the appearances of Deity to his friend Abraham. (Gen. 12:1-7; 13:14-18; 15:1-21; 17:1-21; 18:1-33; 22:15-18.)

5. *Moses sees the Lord.*

Moses stands preeminent above all Israel's prophets. "With him will I speak mouth to mouth, even apparently, and not in dark speeches," the Lord said, "and the similitude of the Lord shall he behold." (Num. 12:8.) Hence we read: "And the Lord spake unto Moses face to face, as a man speaketh unto his friend." (Ex. 33:11.) And: "Moses stood in the presence of God, and talked with him face to face." (Moses 1:31.) After he was taken from the midst of Israel, the account attests: "And there arose not a prophet since in Israel like unto Moses, whom the Lord knew face to face." (Deut. 34:10.)

Two of the Lord's appearances to Moses deserve special mention. In one of them the record says: "Then went up Moses, and Aaron, Nadab, and Abihu, and seventy of the elders of Israel: And they saw the God of Israel: and there was under his feet as it were a paved work of sapphire stone, and as it were the body of heaven in his clearness. . . . They saw God, and did eat and drink." (Ex. 24:9-11.) It was following this that Moses went up into the mount to receive the tables of stone and the commandments.

In the other account "Moses was caught up into an exceedingly high mountain, And he saw God face to face, and he talked with him, and the glory of God was upon Moses; therefore Moses could endure his presence." The God here involved was the Lord Jehovah, though his words were those of the Father; he was, of course, speaking by divine investiture of authority. After Moses had seen "the world and the ends thereof," and had come to know many things, he said: "Now mine own eyes have beheld God; but not my natural, but my spiritual eyes, for my natural eyes could not

601

have beheld; for I should have withered and died in his presence; but his glory was upon me; and I beheld his face, for I was transfigured before him." (Moses 1:1-11.) Moses' experience accords with the reality revealed to Joseph Smith that "no man has seen God at any time in the flesh, except quickened by the Spirit of God," and that "neither can any natural man abide the presence of God, neither after the carnal mind." (D&C 67:11-12.)

6. *Joseph Smith sees the Lord.*

Joseph Smith saw the Father and the Son, as we assume was also the case with all dispensation heads. "I saw two Personages," he testified, "whose brightness and glory defy all description, standing above me in the air. One of them spake unto me, calling me by name, and said, pointing to the other —*This is My Beloved Son. Hear Him!*" (JS-H 17.) The Son, who is the Mediator, then delivered the message. The Father's part was to introduce the One into whose hands he had committed all things.

Jehovah came to Joseph Smith and Oliver Cowdery on the third day of April in 1836 in the Kirtland Temple. "The veil was taken from our minds, and the eyes of our understanding were opened," the scripture says. "We saw the Lord standing upon the breastwork of the pulpit, before us; and under his feet was a paved work of pure gold, in color like amber. His eyes were as a flame of fire; the hair of his head was white like the pure snow; his countenance shone above the brightness of the sun; and his voice was as the sound of the rushing of great waters, even the voice of Jehovah, saying: I am the first and the last; I am he who liveth, I am he who was slain; I am your advocate with the Father." (D&C 110:1-4.)

7. *Many other prophets have seen the Lord.*

We have singled out Adam, Enoch, the brother of Jared, Abraham, Moses, and Joseph Smith because the various accounts of what they saw, taken together, are sufficiently detailed to give us a general concept of what is involved. Great hosts of other prophets have also seen and heard and felt and known. Some of their writings have been preserved for our study and use, and here and there in these prophetic writings we find language which means that the authors had seen within the veil.

We have every reason to believe that the Father himself was present on the mount of transfiguration and that his Son communed with him face to face. Peter, James, and John, however, were only aware that a bright cloud overshadowed the transfigured persons and that a voice from the cloud said, "This is my beloved Son, in whom I am well pleased; hear ye him." (Matt. 17:1-9.) Isaac and Jacob, each in turn, saw and learned what had previously been manifest to their father Abraham. (Gen. 26:1-25; 28:10-22; 32:24-30; 35:9-15.) "And God revealed himself unto Seth." (Moses 6:3.) Emer "saw the Son of Righteousness, and did rejoice and glory in his day." (Ether 9:22.) Nephi, Isaiah, and Jacob all saw their Redeemer. (2 Ne. 11:2-3.)

"In the year that king Uzziah died I saw also the Lord sitting upon a throne, high and lifted up, and his train filled the temple. Above it stood the seraphims," Isaiah said, "And one cried unto another, and said, Holy, holy, holy, is the Lord of hosts: the whole earth is full of his glory." Then Isaiah testified: "Mine eyes have seen the King, the Lord of hosts." (Isa. 6:1-5.)

Joshua (Josh. 5:12-15), Manoah and his wife (Judg. 13:22), Ezekiel (Ezek. 1:1; 10:1), and Daniel (Dan. 10:5-6) were all similarly visited. Solomon saw him twice in a vision. (1 Kgs. 3:5-14; 9:2-9.) Joseph Smith and Sidney Rigdon also saw him in vision in the eternal worlds. (D&C 76:11-24.) Lehi and Nephi both saw him born of Mary and growing up in Nazareth. (1 Ne. 11.) Lehi, being "overcome with the Spirit, . . . was carried away in a vision, even that he saw the heavens open, and he thought he saw God sitting upon his throne, surrounded with numberless concourses of angels in the attitude of singing and praising their God." Thereafter "he saw one descending out of the midst of heaven, and he beheld that his luster was above that of the sun at noon-day.

603

And he also saw twelve others following him." (1 Ne. 1:7-12.) Alma was privileged to see what his father Lehi had seen. (Alma 36:22.) Stephen saw the heavens open "and Jesus standing on the right hand of God." (Acts 7:51-60.) The beloved John saw our Lord in his transcendent glory, even as he was seen by our modern prophet in the Kirtland Temple. (Rev. 1:13-18.)

One of the sweetest and most appealing accounts of all is that of Moroni, who said: "And now I, Moroni, bid farewell unto the Gentiles, yea, and also unto my brethren whom I love, until we shall meet before the judgment-seat of Christ, where all men shall know that my garments are not spotted with your blood. And then shall ye know that I have seen Jesus, and that he hath talked with me face to face, and that he told me in plain humility, even as a man telleth another in mine own language, concerning these things; And only a few have I written, because of my weakness in writing. And now, I would commend you to seek this Jesus of whom the prophets and apostles have written, that the grace of God the Father, and also the Lord Jesus Christ, and the Holy Ghost, which beareth record of them, may be and abide in you forever." (Ether 12:38-41.)

How Many People Have Seen or Will See the Lord?

We all saw the Lord (meaning the Father) in pre-existence. Every living soul, every spirit offspring of the Eternal Father saw him and dwelt in his presence. We saw his face, heard his voice, felt his power and influence, and knew he was our God. Even the very devils now in hell enjoyed an intimate familiarity with him in that day. They were acquainted with his person and his teachings; indeed, the very reason they became devils was that they rebelled against him and his laws with the full and perfect knowledge that he was their Omnipotent Father and had himself established the rules of conduct for his spirit offspring.

We all saw the Lord (meaning the Son) in preexistence.

We lived in the Father's presence for millions of years and knew that his Firstborn Son was next to him in power and might and dominion. We were present in the Grand Council when Christ was chosen and foreordained to be the Savior and Redeemer. We knew him; he was our brother. We associated with him in the family unit. We saw his face, heard his voice, and felt his power and influence. Our knowledge of him was like our knowledge of the Father.

Speaking of the planets and orbs that spin in the sidereal heavens, the Lord says: "Any man who hath seen any or the least of these hath seen God moving in his majesty and power." That is, the heavens themselves declare the glory of God. The existence of the sun, moon, and stars, and of all things, is a witness that he lives and has all power. But the Lord says this simply to introduce a much greater truth, which is, that all of us who see these things have also seen him personally. "I say unto you, he hath seen him," the Lord continues, "nevertheless, he who came unto his own was not comprehended. The light shineth in darkness, and the darkness comprehendeth it not." All this has reference to the coming of our Lord into mortality and his rejection by his own, they preferring darkness rather than light because their deeds were evil. "Nevertheless, the day shall come when you shall comprehend even God, being quickened in him and by him. Then shall ye know that ye have seen me, that I am, and that I am the true light that is in you, and that you are in me; otherwise ye could not abound." (D&C 88:47-50.) We have seen God; true, it was in that day when we walked by sight; and now, walking by faith, we no longer remember our association with him; nonetheless, we have in fact seen him.

We have no way of knowing how many mortal persons have seen the Lord. Individual saints and prophets have seen him in all dispensations, and sometimes he has appeared to large congregations. We know that "many, exceeding great many" (Alma 13:12), as Alma expressed it, have enjoyed this privilege. We are left to assume that there are far more occasions—thousands or tens of thousands of times over—that we do not know of than those of which we do have knowledge. Let us look at the rays of light that have come through to us and reason a little as to how many people were of necessity involved.

We know categorically that from the fall of Adam to the Second Coming of Christ is a period of some six thousand years, and that the millennial era will then continue for another thousand years. Such is the chronology recited in the Bible, which has been confirmed by revelation to the Prophet Joseph Smith. Our revelation speaks of "this earth during the seven thousand years of its continuance, or its temporal existence," and also specifies that Christ will come "in the beginning of the seventh thousand years." (D&C 77.) This in no way names the day nor the hour of our Lord's return, and it does not put a stamp of divine approval upon our calendars as they now exist. It simply lets us know that the Biblical account of the chronology relative to Adam and his posterity is either correct or substantially so. The number of years there recited is either accurate or so nearly so that it does not make any real difference for our purposes.

According to the Biblical chronology, Adam fell in 4004 B.C. and died 930 years later, in 3074 B.C.. By latter-day revelation we know that the meeting at Adam-ondi-Ahman, which was attended by all of his righteous posterity and to which the Lord himself came, was three years previous to Adam's death, that is, in 3077 B.C. (D&C 107:53-56.) Also according to Biblical chronology, Enoch was translated in 3017 B.C., his city having existed for the preceding 365 years, which means that it was founded in 3382 B.C. "And all the days of Zion, in the days of Enoch, were three hundred and sixty-five years. And Enoch and all his people walked with God, and he dwelt in the midst of Zion; and it came to pass that Zion was not, for God received it up into his own bosom; and from thence went forth the saying, ZION IS FLED." (Moses 7:68-69.)

The chronology with which we are dealing is thus as follows:

4004 B.C.—Adam and Eve fall and become mortal.

3382 B.C.—Enoch founds "the city of Holiness, even Zion."

3077 B.C.—The Lord appears at the meeting in Adam-ondi-Ahman.

3074 B.C.—Adam dies.

3017 B.C.—Enoch and his city are translated and taken up into heaven.

3382 B.C. to 3017 B.C.—A duration of 365 years, a period of one year for each day of our years, during which the Lord Jesus Christ personally dwelt on earth and was seen by his people. We assume, of course, that he came and went during this period, as he will during that millennial age when he is destined, again, to dwell personally upon the earth.

Our present interest in this chronology is to call attention to the great number of people who, in the very nature of things, saw their Lord in the early days of this earth's temporal existence. We do not know how many there were, and we do not say how many there were. But it is perfectly obvious there were "many, exceeding great many." (Alma 13:12.) We do not know the population of the earth in the days before the flood. We do know that the childbearing years of women continued to great ages and that sufficient time was involved for great populations to arise. If the population of the earth had doubled every thirty-three years, from the day of Adam to the appearing of the Lord at Adam-ondi-Ahman, there would have been four and a half billion people on earth. We do not suppose for a moment that such was the case, but we cannot escape the conclusion that many people were then alive, and we do know that all the righteous among them saw the Lord.

If Enoch founded his city with a mere one thousand people, and they doubled in population every third of a century, there would have been more than a million saints resident therein when the Lord took them to his abodes. Our sole point in drawing these numbers out of the ethereal blue, as it were, is to show that great hosts of people saw the Lord in days gone by even as great hosts will see him in the coming millennial day.

As to the millennial era itself, once again we have no way of knowing how many people will dwell on earth, but whatever their number, all will see the Lord. Certainly the totals will be billions upon billions. We cannot escape the conclusion that more people will dwell on the earth, many times over, when it becomes again an Edenic garden, than have dwelt thereon during the long years of its fallen state.

As to the number of people assembled in paradise to wait upon the Lord, while his body lay in the tomb, again we can only speculate. We know that all the righteous dead from Adam to that time, plus those who had dwelt in Enoch's Zion, were there to hear him proclaim the glad tidings of redemption. And we also know that he did not go among the wicked and ungodly who were then in their spirit prison. (Joseph F. Smith—Vision.)

We do have some reasonable judgments to make relative to various of his other appearances. During his mortal ministry, those who believed in him saw the divinity that set him apart from all men. "The Word was made flesh, and dwelt among us, (and we beheld his glory, the glory as of the only begotten of the Father,) full of grace and truth," John says. (John 1:14.) Though his glory was clothed in mortal flesh, those with true spiritual insight recognized him for what he was. And for that matter, it is only those with great spiritual insight who see him as God's Son whether on this or the other side of the veil. Comparatively, those who saw, in his Mortal Person, the divinity that was his were few in number, and yet in their aggregate they totaled many souls.

Before his birth he appeared to Moses, Aaron, Nadab, Abihu, and seventy of the elders of Israel, seventy-four souls at once. (Ex. 24:9-11.) After his resurrection he walked on the Emmaus road with two disciples and then appeared in the upper room to ten of the Twelve, "and them that were with them," possibly a small congregation. (Luke 24.) He made a series of visits to various disciples, including one on a mountain in Galilee, which probably was the time when "he was seen of above five hundred brethren at once." (1 Cor. 15:6.) He of course continued with the apostles for forty days after his resurrection, "speaking of the things pertaining to the kingdom of God." (Acts 1:2-3.)

Our most detailed account of his resurrected appearances is of those appearances he made to the Nephites. What then transpired is recounted in chapters 11 to 26 inclusive in Third Nephi. Those who first heard his words in the land Bountiful "were in number about two thousand and five hundred souls; and they did consist of men, women, and children." (3 Ne. 17:25.) This, however, was only the beginning of what was to be. After Jesus ascended into heaven that first day, "it was noised abroad among the people immediately, before it was yet dark, that the multitude had seen Jesus, and he had ministered unto them, and that he would also show himself on the morrow unto the multitude." On the next day, among the increased throngs, the record says of the Twelve: "They went forth and stood in the midst of the multitude. And behold, the multitude was so great that they did cause that they should be separated into twelve bodies." Soon thereafter, "Jesus came and stood in the midst and ministered unto them." (3 Ne. 19:1-15.)

How many Nephites were then and there assembled to hear the teachings of the risen Lord? The inference is that there were twelve times as many as on the first day. That would be a total of thirty thousand, which is not unreasonable to suppose. In any event great numbers of righteous persons were involved. And it was not just a happenstance of coming to a group who chanced to be there at the moment. Those involved were qualified by personal righteousness to see the face of their God. As Moroni says, "it was by faith that Christ showed himself unto our fathers, after he had risen from the dead; and he showed not himself unto them until after they had faith in him." (Ether 12:7.)

Leaving his Nephite kinsmen, our Lord, risen and glorified, went to minister unto the lost tribes of Israel. (3 Ne. 16:1-5; 17:4.) Where he went and what he did we do not know. Did he visit one group or many? Did twenty-five hundred or thirty thousand more Israelites see his face? Someday we shall know. As of now we know in principle that these other Israelites were prepared and worthy, as all men must be who stand in the divine presence.

The tribes of Israel also have the promise that they shall again see their God in the days of redemption and gathering. "I will plead with you face to face. Like as I pleaded with your fathers in the wilderness of the land of Egypt, so will I plead with you, saith the Lord God. And I will cause you to pass under the rod, and I will bring you into the bond of the covenant. . . . And ye shall know that I am the Lord." (Ezek. 20:33-38.) To some extent this has already been fulfilled through the restoration of the gospel covenant and the appearance of the Lord to certain of his prophets. A yet more glorious fulfillment lies ahead and will be found when Israel's God appears personally to each worthy member of that chosen race.

Some appearances of the Lord, glorious and awesome ones, shall yet be made to infinitely large numbers of people. "Wo unto all those who die in their sins," Jacob says, "for they shall return to God, and behold his face, and remain in their sins." (2 Ne. 9:38.) On the other hand, it is said of the righteous, "When he shall appear, we shall be like him; for we shall see him as he is." (1 Jn. 3:2.) And finally, in celestial exaltation, all who gain eternal life shall forever behold the face of him who redeemed them. John saw a group of these singing praises to the Lamb and said that they numbered one hundred million, plus thousands of thousands. (Rev. 5:9-13.)

There will be another great gathering of saints at Adam-ondi-Ahman. Once again the Lord will be there, this time to receive from Adam, the Ancient of days, an accounting of his stewardship. This gathering, at which the Lord will be given "dominion, and glory, and a kingdom, that all people, nations, and languages, should serve him," will usher in the millennial reign. Those in attendance will be the righteous of all ages, each of whom in turn will give an accounting of his own stewardship. We suppose it will be those of all ages who shall partake of the sacrament with their risen Lord. (D&C 27:4-14.) As to their number, Daniel's account speaks of ten thousand times ten thousand and of thousands of thousands, which is to say an innumerable host. All these, being present, shall see and worship the Lord. (Dan. 7:9-14.)

Now this Lord, whose face has been seen by hosts of the righteous and whose face will yet be seen by multitudes that cannot be numbered, is in our midst from time to time, and we as a people do not see him nearly as often as we should. We are not speaking of him being in our midst in the spiritual sense that he is here by the power of his Spirit. We are speaking of his personal literal presence. "Lift up your hearts and be glad, for I am in your midst, and am your advocate with the Father; and it is his good will to give you the kingdom." (D&C 29:5.) "Verily, verily, I say unto you that mine eyes are upon you. I am in your midst and ye cannot see me; But the day soon cometh that ye shall see me, and know that I am; for the veil of darkness shall soon be rent, and he that is not purified shall not abide the day." (D&C 38:7-8.)

In this connection let us note one of the visions shown forth to the Prophet Joseph Smith during that Pentecostal period which preceded and attended the dedication of the Kirtland Temple. "I saw the Twelve Apostles of the Lamb, who are now upon the earth," he said, "who hold the keys of this last ministry, in foreign lands, standing together in a circle, much fatigued, with their clothes tattered and feet swollen, with their eyes downward, and Jesus standing in their midst, and they did not behold him. The Savior looked upon them and wept." (*History of the Church*, 2:381.) "I am

611

in your midst, and I am the good shepherd, and the stone of Israel. He that buildeth upon this rock shall never fall. And the day cometh that you shall hear my voice and see me, and know that I am." (D&C 50:44-45.) It is worthy of note that the Lord uses the same kind of language to describe his personal presence on earth during the millennial era as he uses with reference to his unseen visits from time to time among the Latter-day Saints. "For the Lord shall be in their midst," he says of his coming millennial sojourn on earth, "and his glory shall be upon them, and he will be their king and their lawgiver." (D&C 45:59.)

The Promised Messiah Is the Lord

We have now made our presentation. We have searched the scriptures diligently, choosing the most important Messianic prophecies for our study and exposition. We have set forth in simple language how and in what manner the prophetic word has found fulfillment in Christ. Through it all we have interwoven our personal witness of the divinity of Him of whom all the prophets testify.

From the first Alpha on the first page to the last Omega on the last page, the message of this work is:

God is our Father, by whom all things are;

Jesus Christ is the Son of the living God, by whom redemption cometh;

Salvation is in Christ, whose atoning blood ransoms men from the temporal and spiritual death brought into the world by the fall of Adam; and

All the prophets, from first to last—from father Adam, who dwelt in Eden's vale, to John the Baptist, who abode in the deserts of Judea; from the first man, who partook of the forbidden fruit that man might be, and who was given a coat of skins to cover his nakedness, to the man John, our Lord's forerunner, who ate locusts and honey and wore raiment made of camel's hair; from Moses, who worshiped in the holy mount, and with whom God spake face to face and not

612

in dark similitudes, to Peter, James, and John, who, also on a holy mount, saw Christ transfigured before them and heard the voice of the Father attest our Lord's divinity—from the beginning to the end, be they whosoever they were, all of the prophets were witnesses of Christ. All proclaimed him as the Son of God. All taught the principles of eternal truth by conformity to which the faithful have power to ascend the throne of eternal power and sit with God on his throne.

And as we bring our own Messianic writings to a close we rejoice in spirit with all the prophets of the past. Their words sink deep into our hearts. Our bosoms burn within us. We feel in our souls the truth and divinity of the testimonies they have borne and the doctrines they have preached.

As with Lehi and Alma—both of whom, being enlightened by the power of the Spirit, thought they "saw God sitting upon his throne, surrounded by numberless concourses of angels in the attitude of singing and praising their God" (1 Ne. 1:8; Alma 36:22)—so we seem to hear and seem to see again what our fellowservants heard and saw in times past.

We seem to hear their voices anew as they acclaim, by the power of the Holy Ghost, that Jesus, who is called Christ, is Lord of all. We seem to see anew the vision of "the Lord sitting upon a throne, high and lifted up," and hear the cries: "Holy, holy, holy, is the Lord of hosts: the whole earth is full of his glory." (Isa. 6:1, 3.)

We hear a modern voice, addressed to all men, to the living and the dead, saying: "Hear, O ye heavens, and give ear, O earth, and rejoice ye inhabitants thereof, for the Lord is God, and beside him there is no Savior. Great is his wisdom, marvelous are his ways, and the extent of his doings none can find out. His purposes fail not, neither are there any who can stay his hand. From eternity to eternity he is the same, and his years never fail." (D&C 76:1-4.)

We see an angel before an open tomb. "I know that ye seek Jesus, which was crucified," he says. Then comes the portentous proclamation from angelic lips: "He is not here:

for he is risen, as he said. . . . He is risen from the dead." (Matt. 28:5-7.) Christ, the Lord, is risen! "Death is swallowed up in victory. . . . O grave, where is thy victory?" (1 Cor. 15:54-55.)

We hear a great choir—"ten thousand times ten thousand, and thousands of thousands" in number—saying: "Worthy is the Lamb that was slain to receive power, and riches, and wisdom, and strength, and honour, and glory, and blessing."

An echoing chorus fills heaven's dome as all created things acclaim: "Blessing, and honour, and glory, and power, be unto him that sitteth upon the throne, and unto the Lamb for ever and ever." (Rev. 5:9-13.)

"Great voices" from out the wide expanse of eternity add their testimony: "The kingdoms of this world are become the kingdoms of our Lord, and of his Christ; and he shall reign for ever and ever." (Rev. 11:15.)

From others comes the cry: "Alleluia; Salvation, and glory, and honour, and power, unto the Lord our God: . . . [He is] KING OF KINGS, AND LORD OF LORDS." (Rev. 19:1, 16.)

To the voices of the past is added one of latter days. "Let the mountains shout for joy," cries Joseph Smith, the American witness of Christ, "and all ye valleys cry aloud; and all ye seas and dry lands tell the wonders of your Eternal King! And ye rivers, and brooks, and rills, flow down with gladness. Let the woods and all the trees of the field praise the Lord; and ye solid rocks weep for joy! And let the sun, moon, and the morning stars sing together, and let all the sons of God shout for joy! And let the eternal creations declare his name forever and ever! And again I say, how glorious is the voice we hear from heaven, proclaiming in our ears, glory, and salvation, and honor, and immortality, and eternal life; kingdoms, principalities, and powers!" (D&C 128:23.)

How fitting is the oft-repeated Psalmic word: "Praise ye the Lord . . . Let everything that hath breath praise the Lord. Praise ye the Lord." (Ps. 150:1-6.) Hallelujah!

614

"And now, after the many testimonies which have been given of him, this is the testimony, last of all, which we give of him: That he lives! For we saw him, even on the right hand of God; and we heard the voice bearing record that he is the Only Begotten of the Father—That by him, and through him, and of him, the worlds are and were created, and the inhabitants thereof are begotten sons and daughters unto God." (D&C 76:22-24.)

And now it but remains for this disciple, in plain words, to testify that he also, independent of all others, does, by the power of the Holy Ghost, know of the truth and verity of that which is written concerning God's Son.

Jesus Christ is the Son of the living God; he was crucified for the sins of the world; he is our Lord, our King, our God—the Promised Messiah!

He came in the meridian of time to work out the infinite and eternal atonement.

He has set up his kingdom again on earth in these last days to prepare a people for his Second Coming.

He shall soon come again to live and reign on earth with faithful men for the space of a thousand years.

Blessed be his holy name both now and forever.

"Praise ye the Lord."

INDEX

Aaron: teachings of, to Lamanites, 83; on atonement, 146
Aaronic or Levitical Priesthood: administers preparatory gospel only, 410; ordaining a bishop in, 411; power of, is limited to performing outward ordinances, 412-13
Abel, slaying of, 32
Abinadi: prophesied of Christ, 26-27, 61; explanation of, about Christ as Father and Son, 61, 372-73; on prophets, 78; on Christ's Godhood, 99; knew of atonement, 232, 233-34; quotes Isaiah, 234; on atonement, 245-46; on resurrection, 268; on salvation, 290; on the wicked who receive not mercy, 329-30; identifies seed of Messiah, 360; on law of Moses, 409, 417, 419; preaching of, to King Noah, 418-19
Abraham: capture of, 32, 104, 600; saw the hosts of heaven, 53; Christ is God of, 103, 163-64, 551; Jehovah's covenant with, 106, 110, 164, 308; belief in, is belief in Christ, 109-10; saw the days of the "Son of Man," 141; look unto, 163; on resurrection, 267; men become heirs of God according to promise made to, 356; was called by Jehovah's

name, 367; was to sacrifice Isaac in similitude of God's offering of Christ, 452; seed of, were foreordained, 507; saw the Lord many times, 600-601
Accountability, age of, 302
Adam, 79, 328; fall of, 66-67, 217, 244; was commanded to perform works in Christ's name, 69, 138, 306, 558; was commanded to be fruitful, 220; was commanded to fall, 221; and Eve brought forth children, 222; knew doctrine of blood atonement, 249; preaching of gospel in time of, 288, 293; offered up sacrifices, 379; is a similitude of Christ, 449; dwelt with God, 597; bestows his last blessing, 598. *See also* Fall
Adam-ondi-Ahman: Lord visits Adam at, 598; latter-day gathering at, 610-11
Adoption: into Christ's family, 352, 354; into Elohim's family, 354, 356-67
Agency: men possess, 219; atonement preserves, 229
Ahman and Son Ahman, 140
Allah, 322
Alleluia: translation of, 111-12; heavenly choirs sing, 309
Alma the elder, teachings of, on law of forgiveness, 340-41
Alma the younger: speaks to

617

men knew, in preexistence, 604-5; many mortals have seen, 605, 607-12. *See also* Jehovah; Messiah

——atonement of: salvation comes through, 1, 4, 26, 105, 290; in Gethsemane, 2, 253, 552; was part of God's plan of salvation, 49, 52, 137; saves man from death, 67, 224, 230; is the core of the gospel, 218; Adam's fall is foundation of, 218; is dependent on Christ's divine Sonship, 218, 471; causes body and spirit to reunite, 225; was foreordained, 225-26, 249; absence of, would frustrate purposes of creation, 227-30, 238, 292, 550-51; must be infinite, 228; mercy cometh because of, 245; on Calvary, 253; made possible reconciliation between God and man, 260; mankind would be lost but for, 291; makes valid the law of intercession, 329; forgiveness of sins is available because of, 337, 343; Messiah shall see his seed after, 361; water, blood, and spirit were part of, 387-88; Sabbath observance keeps us in memory of, 396; required him to be mortal, 455; was the chief purpose of Christ's life, 474; prayer becomes effective because of, 560. *See also* Atonement

——First Coming of: purpose for, 2; prophets looked forward to, 2, 31, 458-59; knowledge of, is important to understanding of Second Coming, 31-32; is a prophetic type of Second Coming, 32; Nephites knew precise year of, 457-58; Jews looked anxiously forward to, 459-60

——mortality of: man's difficulty in comprehending, 454; need for, 454-55; was preparation for and condition of his atonement, 455-56; was essential to his own salvation, 456, 552; gave man an example to follow, 456-57, 475;

began in Bethlehem, 461-62; coming about of, 462-64; came by the power of God, 464; chief purpose for, was to atone for man's sins, 474; prophetic foreknowledge of details of, 475-76; Christ's physical appearance during, little is known about, 476-77; made him subject to ills and troubles of all men, 477; Christ's disciples recognized his glory during, 608

——prophecies concerning. *See* Messianic prophecies

——relationship of, to God, 13; unity in, 9, 18, 119-20; eternal nature of, 46; as his Son, 53-54, 118, 468-69, 549; in creating man, 62; oneness of words and acts in, 64, 121-22; similarities in, 198; allowed Christ to inherit immortality, 471; as his minister and agent, 474

——role of: in plan of salvation, 1-2, 49-52, 550-51, 612; in revealing the Father, 4, 17, 475, 518; mysteries concerning, 6-8; in creation, 7, 55-65, 199; as last Comforter, 15, 584, 585-86; was foreordained, 49, 161; as Father of heaven and earth, 57, 369; as Savior from temporal and spiritual death, 67, 309-10; as God, 98, 122; in judgment, 111, 213, 311; explained by Christ, 154; in forgiving sins, 160, 332-35; in working miracles, 160-61, 489; as foundation upon which men must build, 169; in sitting upon David's throne, 192-95; in offering living water, 205-7; in redemption, 236-38; in reconciliation, 259-62; in answering prayers, 335, 557-58; in justifying mankind, 345-46; as Father of the righteous, 352, 370; as the Father and the Son, 370; in fulfilling the law of Moses, 422-25, 441-42; as Mediator of the new covenant, 440-42, 551; as Elias, 486, 487; in healing the

627

Christ's sufferings, 497-98, 501-2;
of Christ's teaching ministry, 522.
See also Prophets
Micah prophesies of Christ's birth in
Bethlehem, 461
Michael: Adam is, 221; led the hosts
of heaven against Lucifer, 231
Millennium: is the earth's Sabbath,
396; many will see the Lord
during, 608. *See also* Jesus Christ,
Second Coming of
Miracles: gospel of Christ is, 52;
bear witness of Christ, 159-61;
identify true believers in Christ,
298, 315, 552, 572; are wrought by
faith, 315; trademark of Christ's
ministry is, 489; cease only when
faith ceases, 572-73
Mission of saints is to preach of
Christ, 262
Molech, sacrifices to, 257
Mormon: on oneness of God, 115;
testifies to Lamanites of Christ,
152; on how men began to
exercise faith, 313-14; on
salvation through faith, 314; on
entering into the rest of the Lord,
318; on becoming sons of God,
354; on ceasing of miracles,
572-73
Moroni: on seeking Christ, 45; on
judgment, 110-11; admonishes
men to come unto Christ, 303; on
grace, 348; on Christ as Father
and Son, 371, 372; on faith, 582;
hath seen Christ, 604
Moroni, General, prayed for
Christians, 366
Mortality: is a probationary state, 84,
217, 317; definition of, 222. *See
also* Jesus Christ, mortality of
Moses: prophesied of Christ, 26;
esteemed the "reproach of
Christ," 32, 107, 316, 408; on
prophets, 80; on Christ's
Godhood, 99; God appeared to,
in burning bush, 164; on Christ as
Rock, 170-71; smote the rock for
water, 205; on mercy, 246; was
told to forbid people to eat blood,
258; gospel of, 405; received a

lower set of commandments for
Israel, 409; was mediator of the
old covenant, 439, 446; mediation
of, was a type of Christ's
mediation, 440; hath not Christ's
glory, 441-42; was in the
similitude of Christ, 442-44;
similarities between Christ and,
445-48; premortal works of, 445;
foreordination of, 445; spoke
with the Lord face to face, 601-2
Mount of transfiguration, 603
Mulekites, corruption of language
among, 90
Multiply and replenish the earth,
Adam and Eve were commanded
to, 220-21
Music: edifying, is a divine means of
expressing praise to God, 553;
can be corrupt, 553
Mystery of Godliness: uncovering
of, 5; examples of, 6-8; great is,
113; understanding of, 124
Name of Christ: taking of, upon
ourselves, 7, 364; is above all
others, 299; bringeth salvation,
299-300; Christ's children are
called by, 363
Nathaneal, 149
Nation: God speaks to every, 94-96;
kindred, tongue, and people,
knowledge of God will spread to
every, 301
Natural man, putting off of, 350
Nazarene, Christ is called a, 184, 478
Nephi: intent of, to bring men to
God, 29; couched prophecies in
plain language, 44; heard God's
voice, 72; prophesied of Christ,
82, 147, 469; on obtaining the
records, 88; on Christ's Godhood,
99; on oneness of God, 114-15;
on righteous Nephites at time of
Christ, 142; on God of Israel,
165; on Christ's First and Second
Comings, 194; taught of fall and
atonement, 232; on the twelve
apostles, 250-51; on being
reconciled to God, 261; on
resurrection, 268; on salvation
through Christ's name, 299; on

Promise: Holy Spirit of, 344; the
Lord's last and great, 583. *See
also* Covenant
Prophecies. *See* Messianic
prophecies
Prophecy: gift of, 23-24; among
Nephites, 24; spirit of, 44, 113;
testimony of Christ is, 123
Prophets: looked forward to both
comings of Christ, 2, 31;
definition of, 23; spheres of
authority of, 25; all who bear
testimony are, 25, 72; have always
taught the same doctrines, 29, 77,
293, 551, 613; reasons for
persecution of, 32-40; Lucifer
hates, 34; false, 37; rewards of,
40-41; Christ's Godhood affirmed
by, 99-100; bore record of Christ's
coming birth, 147; are witnesses
of the Lord, 148; have taught of
the fall of Adam, 223, 231; have
all known of the atonement, 231,
233-34; Nephite, all taught of
resurrection, 268; all worshiped
God in Christ's name, 305-6, 335,
559; all had faith in Christ, 314;
all held the Melchizedek
Priesthood, 410, 412, 589; knew
their Messiah must die, 524;
many, have seen the Lord, 602-4.
See also Apostles; Messianic
prophecies; Twelve apostles
Propitiation, Christ is, 201
Psalms: on Christ as rock of
salvation, 170; on the Lord as
King, 185-86; on salvation
through Jehovah, 308; praising
God, 336-37, 554, 614; on the
fairness of Christ, 478-79; on
Christ's role as teacher, 513; on
the events surrounding Christ's
death, 530-35; contain fulfillment
of prophecies on Christ's death,
530-35; on worshiping Christ,
565-66. *See also* David
Punishment, 245
Pure: sons of God become, 354; in
heart shall see God, 576, 580

Realities, eternal, 327

Reason, insufficiency of, in knowing
God, 113
Rebirth: of water, blood, and spirit,
249, 351; spiritual, 350
Reconciliation: between God and
man, made possible by Christ,
260; through the atonement, 260;
ministry of, 261
Redeemer: Christ is, 237-38, 311-12;
Jehovah is, 312
Redemption: comes through Christ,
226-27, 237-38, 311-12; from
spiritual fall, 226; Jehovah
bringeth, 312
Rejection of Christ: by Jews, 94, 99,
173-75, 492-94; through rejection
of his message, 495
Repentance: mercy claimeth, 245,
247, 319; is prerequisite to
reconciliation, 260; is
commanded of God, 339-40
Rest of the Lord: the faithful enter
into, 317; three stages of, 318;
definitions of, 318-19; Israel was
denied, 319-20, 407, 411, 589-90
Resurrection: Christ's ministry after
his, 150-52, 278-81, 552; proves
Christ's divinity, 263-64; of
Jehovah foretold, 264-66; all will
have part in, 266; all prophets
taught of, 267; questions
concerning, 277-78; of Christ,
events following, 278; Messiah
saw his seed after his, 362; Christ
teaches of, 520-21
Revelation: God is known only by,
14, 101; through visions, 14-15;
by the power of the Holy Ghost,
16, 75; through testimony of
others, 16-17; through accepting
Christ, 17-18; through obedience,
18-19; comes as quickly as men
prepare themselves, 145, 575; is
necessary to understand
resurrection, 278; personal, 573
Rigdon, Sidney, testifies of Christ,
152
Right hand of God, Christ sits on,
102-3, 152
Righteousness: God is called, 141;
Son of, 141-42; of Christ, 202; is

ratified by the Holy Ghost, 344
Rock: of Israel, Christ is, 108; build
upon the Lord's, 169-71; many
prophets speak of Christ as their,
169, 170-72; Jehovah is, 358
Rome, false worship in, 322

Sabbath observance: identifies the
Lord's people, 390; is a
commandment, 391; puts man in
tune with God, 391, 392; bears
witness of Christ, 391; requires
attendance at meetings, 392; rules
and penalties governing, 393;
symbolizes the day Christ rose
from the dead, 393; witnesses of
Christ as Creator, 394; reason for,
394; to keep Israel in
remembrance of her God, 394-95
Sacrament: worthy partaking of,
127-28, 340; replaced sacrifice,
380; is a similitude, 383; was
officially instituted at Feast of the
Passover, 384, 431; Christ
introduced ordinance of, to
Nephites, 384-85; partaking of,
renews baptismal covenants,
385-86; Christ will partake of,
with saints, 594-95, 611
Sacrifices: of animals, in similitude
of Christ's sacrifice, 250, 257, 379;
Mosaic, were similitudes, 254,
258, 427; to idols and devils, 256,
321; human, 256-57; blood was
the vital element in, 257; failure
of Israel to perform, 332; ceased
with the crucifixion, 380; lambs
offered as, 381; were a form of
worship in Israel, 426, 427-28;
occasions for, 428; ritual for,
during Passover, 429-30
Salvation: is in Christ, 1, 26, 290,
612; is available to all, 93, 325; is
of the Spirit, 113; universal vs.
individual, 129; definition of, 130,
depends on unity, 131-32;
depends on obedience, 226; for
the dead, 240-42; men must
believe in Christ to gain, 292; is in
Jehovah, 306; should be man's
chief concern, 307; number of

references to, in Holy Writ, 307;
has always come through faith in
Christ, 313, 551; is free, 325,
346-47; forgiveness of sins
precedes, 337-38; house of, 342
Samaritan woman at Jacob's well,
153-54, 206, 566
Samuel the Lamanite: on
persecution of prophets, 37; on
false prophets, 37; Christ
commands Nephites to write of,
87-88; knew of atonement, 233;
on the sign of Christ's birth,
457-58; on signs of Christ's death,
540-41
Sanctification comes through blood
of Christ, 249
Sanhedrin, Christ before the, 155
Satan: whisperings of, about God's
nature, 132-33; fall of, as
lightning, 219; incites men to
sacrifice each other, 256; children
of, 365. See also Lucifer
Savior: Christ as, 67, 309; man's
need for, 76; Jehovah is, 310
Scapegoat, purpose for, in Israel, 436
Scourging, 497
Scripture: modern application of, 3;
definition of, 24-25; canonization
of, 25; importance of studying,
45; is Messianic utterance, 72;
necessity of, to salvation, 86,
88-90; withholding of, 91-92;
points to Christ as Redeemer,
236; belief in, implies belief in
Christ, 295; mention of salvation
in, 307; teachers should utilize,
515
Sealing: of the wicked unto
judgment, 173; of the righteous
unto eternal life, 174
Second Comforter, 15, 584, 585-86
Second Coming. See Jesus Christ,
Second Coming of
Seed: of Abraham, promises
concerning, 106, 110, 164, 308,
356; definition of, 359; Messiah
shall see his, 359; of Messiah
identified, 360; of Abraham were
foreordained, 507
Seeing the Lord: all pure men may

gospel truths, 514-15; should teach from the scriptures, 515; should teach by power of the Holy Ghost, 515-16; should apply principles to needs of hearers, 516; should bear testimony of truths taught, 516-17; can most effectively use plain and simple language, 520

Temples: the Lord will not come into unholy, 576; God will visit men in his, 576. *See also* Kirtland Temple

Temptations: are an important part of mortality, 498-99; of Christ in wilderness, 499

Test, earth life is a, 84

Testimony: of others, belief in, 16-17, 296; of author, 17, 615; of Jesus is spirit of prophecy, 23, 71-72; Messianic, 26, 71; of Christ was borne by his associates, 148-50; pure, borne by Christ of his divine Sonship, 153-56; teachers should teach with the seal of personal, 516-17; Oliver Cowdery admonishes Twelve to gain, 593

Thomas saw the resurrected Christ, 151, 280, 282-83

Throne of David, Christ will sit upon, 192-95

Tomb of Christ, 546; stone rolled back from, 278-79, 552; women came to, 279

Translation of Bible left out many truths, 305

Trinity: Church of England's conception of, 115; Catholics' conception of, 116-17

Truth: men are obligated to seek, 301; definition of, 338; naming of greatest, 517-18; second greatest, 518-19; third greatest, 519; fourth greatest, 520

Twelve apostles, ancient and Nephite: to sit in judgment, 216; were special witnesses of the Lord, 592; of latter day bear the same witness as, 592. *See also* Apostles; Prophets

Types, prophetic: of Second Coming, 31; reasons for using, 43-44; David, 189, 452; manna, 398-99; brazen serpent, 400-401; the Liahona, 402-3; law of Moses, 416; Feast of the Passover, 429-30; Feast of Pentecost, 431-32; Feast of Tabernacles, 432-35; Day of Atonement, 435-37; Moses, 442-48; Adam, 449; Melchizedek, 449-51; Melchizedek Priesthood holders, 451; Abraham's sacrifice of Isaac, 442; Jonah, 452-53; house of Israel, 453. *See also* Imagery; Similitude

Unity: mortal attainment of, 120-21, 260, 353; of saints with Christ, 123-24; salvation is, 130-32

Uriah, murder of, 271

Variableness, there is none in God, 286

Vinegar, Christ was given, 533-34

Virgin birth, 464, 465-66

Visions, God reveals himself in, 14-15

Water: need for, 204; imagery of, 204-5; living, Christ offers, 205-7, 434

Water, blood, and spirit: birth of, 249, 351, 387; were all a part of the atonement, 387-88; bear witness on earth, 388

War in heaven, 51, 231, 235

Weeks, Feast of, 428-29, 431-32

Whitney, Orson F., poem by, 50-51

Wicked, curses to fall upon, 173-77

Wickedness, prophets reveal, 38

Will of the Son swallowed up in the Father's, 524

Wisdom, God is not known by, 100-101, 114

Wise men: came in search of the King, 186; worshiped Christ, 564

Witnesses: law of, 84; salvation made available through, 85; of the resurrection, 278; Christ works through, 282, 296; three, in

635